Vegetable Crops

McGRAW-HILL PUBLICATIONS IN THE AGRICULTURAL SCIENCES

ADRIANCE AND BRISON · Propagation of Horticultural Plants
AHLGREN · Forage Crops
ANDERSON · Diseases of Fruit Crops
BROWN AND WARE · Cotton
CARROLL, KRIDER AND ANDREWS · Swine Production
CHRISTOPHER · Introductory Horticulture
CRAFTS AND ROBBINS · Weed Control
CRUESS · Commercial Fruit and Vegetable Products
DICKSON · Diseases of Field Crops
ECKLES, COMBS, AND MACY · Milk and Milk Products
ELLIOTT · Plant Breeding and Cytogenetics
FERNALD AND SHEPARD · Applied Entomology
GARDNER, BRADFORD, AND HOOKER · The Fundamentals of Fruit Production
GUSTAFSON · Conservation of the Soil
GUSTAFSON · Soils and Soil Management
HAYES, IMMER, AND SMITH · Methods of Plant Breeding
HERRINGTON · Milk and Milk Processing
JENNY · Factors of Soil Formation
JULL · Poultry Husbandry
KOHNKE AND BERTRAND · Soil Conservation
LAURIE AND RIES · Floriculture
LEACH · Insect Transmission of Plant Diseases
MAYNARD AND LOOSLI · Animal Nutrition
METCALF, FLINT, AND METCALF · Destructive and Useful Insects
NEVENS · Principles of Milk Production
PATERSON · Statistical Technique in Agricultural Research
PETERS AND GRUMMER · Livestock Production
RATHER AND HARRISON · Field Crops
RICE, ANDREWS, WARWICK, AND LEGATES · Breeding and Improvement of Farm Animals
ROADHOUSE AND HENDERSON · The Market-milk Industry
STEINHAUS · Principles of Insect Pathology
THOMPSON · Soils and Soil Fertility
THOMPSON AND KELLY · Vegetable Crops
THORNE · Principles of Nematology
TRACY, ARMERDING, AND HANNAH · Dairy Plant Management
WALKER · Diseases of Vegetable Crops
WALKER · Plant Pathology
WILSON · Grain Crops
WOLFE AND KIPPS · Production of Field Crops

Professor R. A. Brink was Consulting Editor of this series from 1948 until January 1, 1961.
The late Leon J. Cole was Consulting Editor of this series from 1937 to 1948.
There are also the related series of McGraw-Hill Publications in the Botanical Sciences, of which Edmund W. Sinnott is Consulting Editor, and in the Zoological Sciences, of which Edgar J. Boell is Consulting Editor. Titles in the Agricultural Sciences were published in these series in the period 1917 to 1937.

VEGETABLE CROPS

Homer C. Thompson, Ph.D.

PROFESSOR EMERITUS OF VEGETABLE CROPS
CORNELL UNIVERSITY

William C. Kelly, Ph.D.

PROFESSOR OF VEGETABLE CROPS
CORNELL UNIVERSITY

FIFTH EDITION

McGRAW-HILL BOOK COMPANY

New York   Toronto   London

1957

Preface

The four previous editions were written by H. C. Thompson, but this edition has a joint authorship.

The main purpose of this book has been and still is to acquaint the student with the facts and principles on which successful production and handling of vegetables are based. While the authors have not deemed it necessary to present many of the experimental data, the discussion and conclusions are based largely on their interpretation of the experimental evidence. In the preparation of this edition the authors have attempted to bring the discussion up to date by incorporating the results of studies that have been made since publication of the previous edition.

Since the publication of the fourth edition in 1949, greater advances have been made in the methods of producing and handling vegetables than in any similar period of the past. These advances have been made largely as a result of research conducted by specialists in many different fields. The great amount of new knowledge developed since 1949 has made it necessary to make essentially a complete revision of the text. Some of these new developments are: improvements in machinery and equipment allowing increased mechanization in all phases of growing and handling; new and improved insecticides, fungicides, and herbicides; the use of growth-regulating compounds other than herbicides; consumer packaging; improved handling of vegetables after harvest, such as vacuum cooling and hydrocooling; and the development and use of new containers for marketing vegetables.

Extensive use has been made of material presented in the publications of the U.S. Department of Agriculture and the various state experiment stations and in technical and semitechnical journals. Credit is given for the material used, and the citations are given under Literature Cited.

The authors are indebted to a large number of teachers, research workers, and others for suggestions and criticism and for many of the illustrations. They wish to express their appreciation to all of them, and especially to Drs. Paul Work, Robert D. Sweet, and F. M. R. Isenberg; to Mrs. Mayrene Slack and Miss Helen Cole for typing and checking the manuscript; to Mrs. H. C. Thompson and Mrs. W. C. Kelly for their assistance in reading the proof and preparing the index, and for their encouragement.

HOMER C. THOMPSON
WILLIAM C. KELLY

Contents

Preface . . . . *v*

CHAPTER 1. VEGETABLES AND VEGETABLE GROWING 1

    Importance of vegetables. Types of vegetable growing. Climate as a factor
in vegetable growing. Soil as a factor in vegetable growing. Food value of
vegetables. Per capita consumption of vegetables.

CHAPTER 2. CLASSIFICATION OF VEGETABLES 17

CHAPTER 3. SOILS AND SOIL PREPARATION 24

    Classification of mineral soils. Soil preparation. Control of soil erosion.

CHAPTER 4. MANURES AND SOIL-IMPROVING CROPS 37

CHAPTER 5. COMMERCIAL FERTILIZERS AND LIME 52

CHAPTER 6. SEEDS AND SEED GROWING 75

    Buying Seed. Variety and strain testing. Seed growing. Longevity of
vegetable seeds.

CHAPTER 7. PLANT GROWING AND PLANT-GROWING STRUCTURES 86

    Greenhouses. Hotbeds. Cold frames. Plant growing.

CHAPTER 8. PLANTING VEGETABLE CROPS IN THE OPEN 107

CHAPTER 9. CULTIVATION, MULCHES, AND CHEMICAL METHODS OF WEED
    CONTROL 117

CHAPTER 10. IRRIGATION 136

CHAPTER 11. ROTATION, SUCCESSION, AND INTERCROPPING 145

CHAPTER 12. CONTROL OF DISEASES AND INSECTS 153

CHAPTER 13. MARKETING 167

CHAPTER 14. STORAGE OF VEGETABLES 179

CHAPTER 15. PERENNIAL CROPS 186

    Asparagus. Rhubarb. Artichoke. Jerusalem artichoke. Sea kale.

CHAPTER 16. POTHERBS, OR GREENS 214

    Spinach. New Zealand spinach. Orach. Chard. Kale. Mustard. Collards.
Dandelion.

vii

CHAPTER 17. SALAD CROPS 230

    Celery. Lettuce. Endive. Chicory. Parsley. Chervil. Cress. Water cress.

CHAPTER 18. COLE CROPS 275

    Cabbage. Cauliflower. Sprouting broccoli. Brussels sprouts. Kohlrabi. Chinese cabbage.

CHAPTER 19. ROOT CROPS 318

    Beet. Carrot. Parsnip. Salsify. Scorzonera, or black salsify. Scolymus, or Spanish salsify. Turnip. Rutabaga. Radish. Horse-radish. Turnip-rooted chervil. Skirret. Celeriac.

CHAPTER 20. BULB CROPS 347

    Onion. Leek. Cibol (ciboule), or Welsh onion. Garlic. Shallot. Chive.

CHAPTER 21. THE POTATO 372

CHAPTER 22. THE SWEET POTATO 405

CHAPTER 23. BEANS AND PEAS 431

    Beans. Broad bean. Soybean. Mung bean. Tepary bean. Southern pea. Scarlet runner, or multiflora, bean. Common, or kidney, bean. Lima bean. Peas.

CHAPTER 24. SOLANACEOUS FRUITS 471

    Tomato. Eggplant. Pepper. Husk tomato.

CHAPTER 25. THE CUCURBITS, OR VINE CROPS 513

    Cucumber. Muskmelon. Watermelon. Pumpkin and squash.

CHAPTER 26. SWEET CORN, OKRA, MARTYNIA 544

CHAPTER 27. CHAYOTE, YAM, DASHEEN, MANIOC 565

List of Agricultural Experiment Stations 577

Literature Cited 579

Index 601

CHAPTER 1

Vegetables and Vegetable Growing

IMPORTANCE OF VEGETABLES

Vegetable growing is one of the major branches of horticulture, and from the point of view of value of the products, it is the most important branch. The term *vegetable gardening,* formerly used, no longer defines commercial vegetable growing since a large part of the production of the major crops is conducted on a large scale as a specialized type of farming rather than as gardening.

In many parts of the world vegetables constitute a larger part of the diet than they do in the United States. For example, the consumption of potatoes is much greater in Germany and other western European countries than in the United States. Sweet potatoes, true yams, dasheen (taro), manioc (cassava, yuca), and other plants, grown for their underground parts, make up a large part of the diet of millions of persons in tropical and subtropical regions of the world. Dry beans supply a large part of the protein food of the population of the Latin American countries.

Value of Vegetables Grown in the United States. Vegetable growing in the United States is an important agricultural industry and has been increasing in importance for many years. According to estimates of the U.S. Department of Agriculture,[1] the value of vegetables produced on farms, exclusive of those grown in the farm home garden, was $612,579,-000 in 1939, $2,034,100,000 in 1952, and $1,545,700,000 in 1953, as shown in Table 1.1. The figures given do not include the value of vegetables produced in farm gardens for home use. The U.S. Department of Agriculture estimates the value of the vegetables from farm gardens at farm prices as about 400 million dollars. No account is taken of the vegetables grown in millions of nonfarm gardens.

The very great difference in value of the various crops between 1939 and the later years, shown in Table 1.1, is due in large part to difference in value of the dollar.

[1] *Agricultural Statistics,* 1954.

Table 1.1. Farm Value of Vegetable Crops Produced on Farms in the United
States in 1939, 1952, and 1953, with Three Other Important
Crops for Comparison
(*Agricultural Statistics,* 1954)
(000 omitted)

Crop	1939	1952	1953
Truck crops*.....................	$ 284,135	$1,122,000	$1,027,000
Potatoes.......................	236,839	685,500	295,000
Dry beans.....................	46,265	130,100	138,700
Sweet potatoes.................	45,340	96,500	85,000
Total vegetables..............	612,579	2,034,100	1,545,700
Wheat........................	512,427	2,714,404	2,348,852
Corn..........................	1,465,117	5,019,313	4,730,679
Cotton........................	537,010	2,617,644	2,651,675

* Includes crops for fresh market and for processing. Market crops included are
artichoke, asparagus, Lima beans, snap beans, beets, broccoli, Brussels sprouts,
cabbage, cantaloupes, carrots, cauliflower, celery, sweet corn, cucumbers, eggplants,
escarole, garlic, Honey Ball melons, Honey Dew melons, kale, lettuce, onions, green
peas, green peppers, shallots, spinach, tomatoes, and watermelons. Broccoli was
included for only 3 states prior to 1949, 10 states since 1949. Sweet corn was
included for 3 states prior to 1948, 4 states in 1948, and 16 states since 1949. Crops
for processing include asparagus, Lima beans, snap beans, beets, cabbage (sauer-
kraut), sweet corn, cucumbers (pickles), green peas, pimientos, spinach, and
tomatoes. Production of other vegetables processed are included in fresh-market
series of estimates.

The relative importance of 15 of the principal vegetable crops grown
commercially in the United States is shown in Table 1.2. It will be
noticed that there are marked differences in value from year to year.
With most of the crops a relatively low total production will result in
greater money returns than a relatively high total production. For example, 349 million bushels of potatoes in 1952 had a farm value of 685.5
million dollars, whereas 373.7 million bushels in 1953 had a value of
294.5 million dollars. In other words, an increase in production of 24.7
million bushels of potatoes in 1953 over 1952 resulted in a decrease in
farm value of about 391 million dollars. Similar results of large crops
are shown with onions and cabbage. In 1952 about 40 million sacks of
onions had a farm value of nearly 92 million dollars, whereas slightly
over 49 million sacks in 1953 had a value of 36.6 million dollars. With
cabbage a total crop of slightly over a million tons had a value of a
little over 61 million dollars in 1952, whereas 1,228,400 tons in 1953 had
a value of $34,944,000. Large production of other crops has a similiar
effect on returns, although not so striking as with potatoes, onions, and
cabbage.

Table 1.2. Farm Value of 15 of the Most Important Vegetable Crops of 1939, 1945, 1952, and 1953 in Order of Value for 1953
(000 omitted)

Vegetable crop	1939	1945	1952	1953
Potatoes...............	$236,839	$588,325	$685,500	$294,538
Tomatoes:				
Market.............	38,983	112,906	138,774	127,624
Processing...........	24,545	70,359	102,595	89,261
Lettuce...............	30,126	88,777	125,203	121,329
Sweet potatoes.........	45,340	124,306	96,488	85,236
Snap beans:				
Market.............	17,439	45,934	46,234	46,912
Processing...........	4,051	22,358	28,624	36,664
Sweet corn:				
Market.............	2,777*	11,925*	42,708	46,422
Processing...........	5,619*	21,983	36,537	35,082
Cantaloupes...........	12,909	34,618	49,604	57,129
Celery...............	19,624	62,908	57,842	52,799
Carrots...............	11,831	43,578	47,238	51,658
Peas:				
Market.............	10,805	14,087	3,780	3,271
Processing...........	9,217	41,380	39,137	43,473
Watermelons...........	9,056	37,517	43,883	43,308
Cucumbers:				
Market.............	4,999	13,578	19,725	20,762
Pickles.............	6,790	7,966	11,167	12,775
Cabbage:				
Market.............	16,178	40,722	61,317	34,944
Kraut...............	1,113	3,096	3,526	2,860
Onions...............	16,209	63,254	91,979	36,611
Asparagus:				
Market.............	8,080	16,359	15,374	14,816
Processing...........	5,125	17,285	20,269	18,988

* Prior to 1948 estimates for only three states.

Important Regions of Commercial Production in the United States.
Although some vegetables are grown for sale in all of the states, six states produced over half of the commercial truck crops produced in the important states in 1953, as shown in Table 1.3. These figures include only those crops listed in the notes under Table 1.1. They do not include potatoes, sweet potatoes, and field beans. If these three crops were included, the order would be changed in a few instances and Idaho, Maine, and North Carolina would be included in the first 15 states. Other important states in vegetable production, including potatoes and sweet potatoes, are Colorado, Virginia, Minnesota, Louisiana, South Carolina, and Indiana.

Vegetable growing for local markets is important in the vicinity of nearly all of the large cities of the United States. It is of some importance also in areas around most of the smaller cities. The production of crops for processing is distributed over a large part of the United States but is of relatively small importance in the South Central states. California was far in the lead in value of processing crops produced in 1953, followed by Wisconsin, New York, New Jersey, Oregon, Illinois, Washington, Maryland, Michigan, and Pennsylvania (Table 1.3).

Table 1.3. Estimated Acreage and Farm Value of Principal Truck Crops Grown for Fresh Market and for Processing by Geographical Division and 15 Leading States, 1953
(*Agricultural Statistics*, 1954)
(000 omitted)

Division or state	For market		For processing		Total	
	Acres	Value	Acres	Value	Acres	Value
North Atlantic....	269	$102,748	273	$ 53,809	542	$ 156,577
North Central....	165	54,378	804	87,903	969	142,281
South Atlantic....	603	173,583	238	31,349	841	204,932
South Central....	531	77,556	79	8,360	610	85,916
Western..........	563	344,180	404	92,926	968	437,106
United States.....	2,131	752,445	1,798	274,347	3,929	1,026,792
California........	403	270,731	175	53,239	579	323,870
Florida...........	297	116,026	26	5,052	323	121,078
Texas............	404	58,606	28	2,130	432	60,736
New York........	103	40,326	116	20,274	219	60,600
New Jersey.......	77	30,911	71	19,303	148	50,214
Arizona..........	81	41,685	....	54	81	41,739
Michigan.........	57	20,598	73	11,309	129	31,907
Wisconsin........	10	2,881	303	27,425	313	30,306
Pennsylvania.....	48	12,503	62	10,919	110	23,422
Ohio.............	30	14,013	41	9,233	71	23,246
Washington......	20	9,288	92	13,493	112	22,781
Oregon...........	16	6,972	75	15,681	91	22,653
Illinois...........	27	6,308	121	14,407	148	20,715
Maryland........	23	6,341	88+	11,666	112	18,007
Georgia..........	92	14,517	29	3,284	121	17,801

TYPES OF VEGETABLE GROWING

Vegetable growing may be grouped into five divisions, based on the objects sought and the methods employed in producing and in disposing of the crops. These divisions are: (1) home gardening, (2) market gardening, (3) truck growing or truck gardening, (4) production of crops for processing, and (5) vegetable forcing. These types of vegetable growing have developed as the population has changed step by step from a rural toward an urban population and may be considered as an evolution.

Home Gardening. In the colonial days in America the family was mainly self-supporting and the vegetables that were consumed were grown in the family garden. This is still an important part of vegetable production. It is estimated that the farm value of the vegetables produced for home use on the farms where grown was about 400 million dollars in 1953. This estimate is based on farm value, not on what farm families would have had to pay at retail. In addition to farm home gardens, there are millions of home gardens in villages, suburban areas, and cities.

Some farmers say they cannot afford to grow their own vegetables because they can buy them cheaper than they can produce them. Farmers making such statements are thinking of the price at which vegetable growers sell their produce at wholesale, not what the consumer has to pay in retail stores. It is the latter price that should be used in estimating the value of home-grown produce.

LOCATION OF THE HOME GARDEN. As most of the work in caring for the garden is done in spare time, the location selected should be as close to the house as is practicable. Nearness to the house is also of importance in the gathering of vegetables, since this is usually done by the women of the family. In dry regions it is desirable to locate the garden where it can be irrigated easily and conveniently, and in cold, exposed sections of the country location with reference to protection from the winds is important. In most sections of the North a southern or southeastern exposure is desirable since the soils on these exposures get warm earlier in the spring.

CROPS FOR THE HOME GARDEN. The crops that one should grow in the home garden depend on the region, the size of the area available, and the preferences of the family. Only those crops should be grown that are adapted to the region and will produce satisfactory yields. Where the available area is large enough, it is desirable to produce all the kinds of vegetables that the family likes, provided they can be grown satisfactorily in the region. If space is limited, it is wise to grow those crops that produce a large yield per unit of area, considering the time they occupy the space. Tomatoes, snap beans, cabbage, broccoli, lettuce, spinach, chard and other greens, beets, carrots, and other root crops are desirable crops for the small garden. Spinach does not produce a large yield per square foot, but it occupies the land only a short time. When a choice has to be made between crops that meet the other requirements, one should choose those in which freshness is of great importance from the standpoint of edibility and food value.

PLAN AND ARRANGEMENT OF THE GARDEN. The plan and arrangement of the garden should be determined by the size of the area to be used, the slope of the land, and the kind of cultivation to be given. In a small garden cultivated by hand the rows may be closer together than for horse cultivation. The farm garden should usually be planned for horse or tractor cultivation, and the area should be long and narrow rather than square. The rows should run the long way of the garden, and it is desirable to have turning spaces at the ends (Fig. 1.1).

FIG. 1.1. A well-planned home garden.

The size of the garden depends on the number of persons to be supplied, but it is better to have a small well-kept garden than a large one poorly cared for. By close attention to succession cropping and inter-cropping, ¼ acre of land may be made to supply a family of six. Where land is plentiful, it is often desirable to set aside enough land to allow a part of the garden to be planted to a soil-improving crop each year, but this is not essential where plenty of manure is available.

The location of perennial crops such as asparagus, rhubarb, and small fruits should be given careful consideration. These should be placed at one side or at one end of the garden where they will not be in the way when the garden is plowed. Long-season crops or those occupying the land throughout the growing season should be planted together. Quick-maturing crops should be planted in contiguous rows so that the area may be planted to a single late crop. It is desirable to plant tall-growing crops together and locate them so they will not shade the lower-growing crops.

An inexperienced person should make a plan on paper before undertaking the planting of a garden. This plan should show the location of all the crops, the space devoted to each, the crops that are to follow the early ones, and the distance between the rows. It should be possible to calculate from the plan the quantity of seed required for each vegetable.

The principles of production of vegetables for home use are essentially the same as for production for market. In the selection of varieties for home use, edible quality should be given first consideration.

Market Gardening. Market gardening may be defined as that branch of vegetable growing which has for its object the production of vegetables for a local market.

In the early days when the population was scattered and there were no cities and towns, each family produced its own vegetables. As towns and cities sprang up, market gardening developed to meet the needs of those members of the population who had no land. For a long time this industry was confined to the immediate vicinity of the cities, but as the population increased and the demand for vegetables grew the area was greatly enlarged. However, until comparatively recent times (since 1900) most market gardens were within 10 to 15 miles of the cities, but with the building of good roads and the development of the motor truck the market-gardening area has been greatly extended.

Prior to 1860 market gardeners supplied a large part of the vegetables consumed in cities, for truck growing was almost unknown at that time, except to a very limited extent along the railroad and steamship lines leading out 50 miles or so from a few of the larger cities. The market-garden areas around many of the large cities are decreasing in size.

Owing to the increasing production of vegetables in regions especially suited to their production, market gardeners are facing keen competition. This is leading to more specialization in production and to more attention to the grade and appearance of the products. Markets are no longer local. Consumers in villages and cities are able to obtain fresh produce from all parts of the United States and during most of the year. These changes, which were made possible by the development of good transportation and good refrigeration, have removed many of the advantages the market gardener had in the early days of the industry. On the other hand, the development of good roads and of the motor truck has so extended the market-gardening area that the market gardener is no longer forced to confine his operations to the immediate environs of the market. These developments have so changed the situation that the old distinction between market gardening and truck growing no longer holds. In the main the market gardener is producing those crops for which the climate and soil are best suited.

Truck Growing. Truck growing may be defined as the producing of special crops in relatively large quantities for distant markets. In general, truck growing is more extensive and less intensive than market gardening, but there are exceptions. Some crops grown by truck growers are produced intensively.

The early development of truck growing was along the railroad lines and water courses of the Eastern seaboard, especially in New Jersey, Delaware, Maryland, and Virginia. According to the census report for 1900 the steamer *Roanoke* in 1854 carried the first shipment of 200 barrels of vegetables from Norfolk, Va., to New York. Prior to the development of refrigeration and the refrigerator car, production of perishables for market was limited to regions relatively near the market. The first experiments in the use of ice for refrigeration in transit were made in the fifties, but it was not until after 1880 that the carrying of vegetables in refrigerator cars began. The first all-rail shipment of vegetables to New York City from Norfolk, Va., was in 1885, from North Carolina in 1887, and from Charleston, S.C., in 1888. Since about 1900 there has been a rapid development of vegetable growing in the various parts of the United States, especially in the South and West. The Southern states and parts of California have become important in vegetable production largely because vegetables can be produced in those regions at times of the year when they cannot be produced in other regions.

Production of Vegetables for Processing. The growing of crops for processing is an important industry in many parts of the United States and has increased more rapidly than production for market in the fresh condition. In 1939 the acreage of 11 vegetable crops grown for processing was 1,155,000 acres, 1,919,000 in 1945, and 1,798,000 in 1953. The corresponding values were $56,020,000, $201,362,000, and $274,347,-000. The leading crops grown for processing in 1952 and 1953 were tomatoes, sweet corn, peas, snap beans, and asparagus.

The total acreage and value are greater than the figures indicate since they do not include some products that are processed on a relatively small scale. Vegetables for processing are produced on contract in many regions and on a low-cost basis. In many areas the crops are grown by general farmers in rotation with grains and other general farm crops. Many such growers produce only one crop for processing, and relatively few farmers produce any considerable number of processing crops. Market gardeners and truck growers, in some regions, grow crops for processing along with their other vegetable production. In some cases, where no contract is entered into, the grower does not know at the time of planting a crop whether it will be sold on the fresh market or to a processor. He may sell part on the market and the remainder to the processor.

The regions that have the most favorable growing conditions tend to become leaders in the production of certain vegetables for processing. Other factors, however, have an effect on the development of the vegetable-processing industry even where the growing conditions are not especially favorable. In some instances processing plants are located at certain points because of the supply of fruits available; vegetables are processed also, even though the growing conditions are not very favorable for their production.

Since large yields and low cost of production are more important in the growing of crops for processing than earliness, heavier soils are selected for processing crops in the North than for the same crops grown for market. The cost of production per acre and per ton is usually less for processing crops than for the same crops grown for market, because of the generally lower land value, less hand labor, and lower cost of handling. The lower cost of handling is due to the fact that processing crops are not packed as for shipment, and where containers are used, they are returned and used over and over.

CANNING. Preservation by canning is by far the most important method from the standpoint of quantity packed. The total pack of 12 of the principal vegetables canned was 123,251,000 cases in 1939, 217,180,000 in 1945, 236,777,000 in 1952, and 234,516,000 in 1953. The figures are based on 24 No. 2 cans per case. In number of cases of canned vegetables packed the leading ones in 1953 were tomatoes, peas, sweet corn, and snap beans. One of the striking developments in vegetable canning since 1929 is the increase in tomato-juice manufacture. In 1929 it was estimated that there were only 231,000 cases of commercially manufactured tomato juice packed in the United States; by 1939 the quantity had reached 13,659,000 cases; in 1945 the pack was 28,237,000, and in 1953 it was 37,754,000 cases. Another important development is the canning of baby foods, including vegetables.

QUICK FREEZING. The quick-freezing method of preservation of vegetables began in a small way about 1928 and has grown rapidly since 1937. It is estimated that approximately 70 million pounds of vegetables was preserved by freezing in 1937. The estimated frozen pack in 1945 was about 308 million pounds and in 1953 slightly over 1 billion pounds. These figures represent commercially frozen vegetables. Home freezing has developed rapidly also. The leading vegetables frozen commercially in 1953 were peas with slightly over one-fifth of the total, followed by Lima beans, sweet corn, snap beans, broccoli, and spinach. These five crops made up slightly over 60 per cent of the commercial pack of those crops on which estimates are available.

The most important area of production for freezing is the Northwestern states and California. Eight states of this area produced about 60 per cent of the pack of frozen vegetables in the United States in 1953. The Eastern and Southern states, including Missouri (19 states) produced about 33 per cent, and 8 Middle-Western States produced the remainder (largely sweet corn and peas).

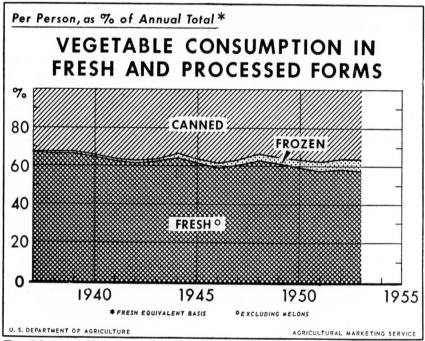

Fig. 1.2. Vegetable consumption in fresh and processed forms per person in per cent of annual total. (*Courtesy of U.S. Department of Agriculture.*)

Frozen vegetables compete with both fresh and canned products, and it is probable that the competition will increase. Consumers prefer the frozen product of some crops to the fresh, especially of those vegetables that deteriorate rapidly in transit and on the market. This preference is in evidence in the case of green peas, Lima beans, and broccoli. While frozen vegetables constitute only a very small part of the total consumed, the frozen product is increasing rapidly. In 1943 the average per capita consumption was 0.7 pound (as purchased). In 1949 it had increased to 3.0 and to 5.3 pounds in 1950 (Fig. 1.2).

Results of studies by several workers indicate that there are marked varietal differences (in many crops) in adaptability to quick freezing.

Some varieties of snap beans, Lima beans, peas, sweet corn, and other crops are superior to others, and this fact is taken into consideration in the development of new varieties and strains. Persons interested in growing vegetables for freezing should consult the processor and specialists of the experiment stations and extension services before deciding which varieties to grow. New processors should do likewise.

Frozen foods should be kept in a frozen condition until they are to be prepared for the table. This requires low-temperature storage, usually from —5 to +5°F., depending on the kind of vegetable; transportation at 10°F. or lower; and display in the retail store in refrigerator cases at 10°F. or lower. Storage in the home for any considerable period should be the same as for storage elsewhere.

DEHYDRATION. Dehydration expanded rapidly during the Second World War owing to the need for large shipments of foods overseas and the necessity for conserving shipping space. The quantity of dehydrated vegetables increased from about 5 million pounds before the war to about 190 million pounds in the year ending June 30, 1944. About 95 per cent of the total was made up of seven vegetables. Irish potatoes represented about 70 per cent of the total, carrots 11, onions 7, sweet potatoes 6, cabbage 4, beets 3, and rutabagas 1 per cent. Since the large increase was related to demands of the Armed Forces for shipment out of the United States, vegetable dehydration was sharply curtailed soon after hostilities ceased.

Dehydrated vegetables will continue to be consumed in areas where it is too cold to keep the canned product and impossible to provide quick-frozen food.

Vegetable Forcing. Vegetable forcing is the growing of vegetables out of their normal season of outdoor production and is accomplished by use of artificial heat, or in some cases by protection from cold. Greenhouses are the common structures used for forcing vegetables, especially in regions of very cold winters. Hotbeds and cold frames are used to some extent as forcing structures in milder regions and for growing cool-season crops in fall or spring in some areas. Cellars, caves, and specially built houses are employed in growing mushrooms and in forcing rhubarb and asparagus. Since these are grown in the dark, glass is not necessary.

Vegetable forcing developed because of the demand for fresh vegetables out of the normal season of production. In some regions it developed where the summer season is too short or too cold for growing warm-season crops in the open. In the United States it grew up mainly as an adjunct to market gardening but has changed to a specialized forcing industry in some cases. The great expansion in vegetable production in the open during the winter in the United States since the

First World War has resulted in serious competition between greenhouse-grown and outdoor-grown products. The cost of production of vegetables under glass is so high that they cannot compete on a price basis with the same kinds grown in the open. To be successful, greenhouse vegetable growers must produce the crops when the outdoor supply is limited, or they must produce quality products that will command premium prices. Most of them aim to meet both of the conditions mentioned. The quantity of greenhouse-grown vegetables that can be sold at a price to pay cost of production and a profit is very limited, for most consumers cannot afford the price demanded.

Since vegetable forcing is a very specialized industry, it is not considered further in this book.

CLIMATE AS A FACTOR IN VEGETABLE GROWING

Climate is the most important factor in determining the regions of production of vegetables. Of course, transportation facilities must be available, but since all important agricultural regions of the United States are provided with good transportation facilities the present regions of production have no monopoly on these facilities. Nearly all the important vegetable-growing regions of the South and of parts of California and the Southwest are important because the climate of those regions permits production during winter and spring when other regions cannot produce vegetables. In fact, these regions have become important in spite of transportation handicaps in the form of long hauls and high cost of transportation. While good refrigerator car service and good railroads make it possible for the Imperial Valley of California to be an important lettuce and muskmelon center, no one would produce these crops there because of these factors alone, for regions nearer the important markets have as good transportation facilities with shorter hauls and lower costs. All vegetable regions located at long distances from market are important primarily because of suitable climatic conditions for the production of the crop or crops at the time they are grown. For example, the Imperial Valley produces lettuce during the winter when the climate is satisfactory for the crop, and muskmelons in the spring and summer when the hot, dry weather is favorable for the growth and ripening of this crop. The area around Salinas, Calif., is the most important summer lettuce–producing region of the United States primarily because of the relatively low summer temperatures. In spite of high transportation costs, these regions and a few others in the West now control the lettuce market in the large cities of the Middle West and East.

In growing for local markets the market gardener no longer grows all the kinds of vegetables that it is possible for him to produce. He confines his efforts largely to those for which his climatic and other conditions are favorable, for he has found that he cannot compete successfully with other growers who produce under the most favorable conditions.

The climatic factors that are important are temperature, rainfall, and atmospheric humidity. Of these, temperature is most important in determining the broad localization of vegetable growing. Rainfall is of great importance where irrigation is not practiced, and atmospheric humidity is important with many crops. Low humidity along with high temperature make the Imperial Valley and some sections of Arizona and Colorado important in muskmelon production. In the production of many kinds of vegetable seeds, absence of rain, or relatively light rainfall, and low humidity during ripening, harvesting, and curing of the seed are very important. Parts of California and of some of the Northwestern states are important in the production of some kinds of seeds largely because of these favorable climatic factors.

SOIL AS A FACTOR IN VEGETABLE GROWING

The character of the soil usually is an important factor in localizing vegetable growing within a region having suitable climate for the crop or crops to be grown. The soil, however, does not determine the broad general region of production, because soils of similar characteristics are found in nearly all regions of the United States. Within a region having suitable climatic conditions, the location of areas of desirable soil determines to a large extent the localization of vegetable production. For example, deposits of good muck soil determine the important areas of production of celery, lettuce, onions, and some of the root crops in many areas where climatic conditions are suitable.

While vegetables for nearby markets are often produced on soils not well suited to their growth, the soils selected are usually the best available. In this case, nearness to market may offset the disadvantages of ill-adapted soils, provided other conditions are favorable. Growers located near a good market can afford to go to considerable expense to improve the soil, since they have relatively low transportation costs and the advantage of getting the products to market in a fresh condition.

The characteristics of desirable soils for vegetable production are discussed in Chap. 3.

FOOD VALUE OF VEGETABLES

Vegetables play a very important role in the human diet, supplying some of the things in which other food materials are deficient. They are important in neutralizing the acid substances produced in the course of digestion of meats, cheese, and other foods; they are of value as roughage, which promotes digestion and helps to prevent constipation; they are important sources of the mineral elements needed by the body, being especially rich in calcium and iron; they are valuable sources of vitamins. Although vegetables, in general, are not considered of great importance in furnishing proteins, carbohydrates, and fats, some of them, such as dried seeds of beans, peas, and lentils, are rich in proteins. Others, such as potatoes, sweet potatoes, parsnips, carrots, and rutabagas, are important sources of carbohydrates.

Vegetables as a Source of Minerals. At least 10 mineral elements are needed for the proper growth and development of the body. Extensive investigations have shown that calcium, phosphorus, and iron, except in rare instances, are the only mineral elements that are not present in foods in quantities sufficient for the needs of the body. The green vegetables are good sources of the important mineral elements, as shown in Table 1.4. Potatoes, sweet potatoes, and mature onions contain appreciable quantities of phosphorus.

Vegetable Foods as Sources of Roughage. A certain quantity of bulky food is necessary for good health; vegetables are the main source of "roughage." Most vegetables, particularly the leafy ones, as celery, cabbage, spinach, and lettuce, are characterized by high water content and relatively high percentage of cellulose or fiber. Because of their succulence and relatively large bulk, the leafy vegetables and most of the root crops probably aid in the digestion of the more concentrated foods.

Vegetables as a Source of Vitamins. The name *vitamin* has been given to a group of food substances other than fats, proteins, carbohydrates, and salts that occur in small quantities in natural food materials. They are essential for growth, for reproduction, and for the maintenance of health.

Green and yellow vegetables are important sources of vitamin A. These leafy, green and yellow vegetables contribute about 33 per cent of the vitamin A supplied by the major food groups. They supply also about 25 per cent of the ascorbic acid and appreciable quantities of thiamine, niacin, and folic acid. Potatoes and sweet potatoes supply about 16 per cent of ascorbic acid, while citrus fruits and tomatoes furnish about 34 per cent. The vegetables ranking highest in vitamin A are carrots, turnip greens, spinach, sweet potatoes, beet greens, mustard greens, winter squash, chard, and broccoli. It should be borne in mind, however, that the number of milligrams, or International Units, of a vitamin to the pound of food does not tell the whole story. A vegetable may be rich in vitamins, but if only a small quantity of that vegetable is eaten, the consumer will need other sources of supply. A pound of green peppers contains about seven times as many milligrams

Table 1.4. Nutritive Value of 1 Pound of Selected Vegetable Foods, as Purchased, with a Few Others for Comparison
(U.S. Dept. Agr., Misc. Pub. 572)

Kind of product	Refuse, per cent	Food energy, calories	Protein, grams	Fat, grams	Carbohydrates, grams	Calcium, milligrams	Phosphorus, milligrams	Iron, milligrams	Vitamin A, value Int. Units	Thiamine, milligrams	Riboflavin, milligrams	Niacin, milligrams	Ascorbic acid, milligrams
Asparagus	25	90	7.5	0.7	13.3	71	211	3.1	3,430	0.54	0.59	3.9	113
Beans, Lima, green	60	239	13.6	1.5	42.8	115	288	4.2	520	0.45	0.26	1.7	58
Beans, snap	10	172	9.8	0.8	31.5	266	180	4.5	2,560	0.32	0.41	2.5	79
Beet greens	25	112	6.8	1.0	19.0	401*	153	10.9	22,700	0.18	0.57	1.1	115
Beets	25	155	5.4	0.3	32.6	92	146	3.4	80	0.11	0.17	1.4	34
Broccoli	39	103	9.1	0.6	15.2	360	211	3.6	9,700	0.26	0.59	2.5	327
Brussels sprouts	23	203	15.4	1.8	31.2	119	273	4.6	1,390	0.40	(0.22)	(0.9)	328
Cabbage	27	95	4.4	0.7	17.5	152	103	1.7	270	0.23	0.21	0.9	173
Carrots	12	179	4.8	1.2	37.2	156	148	3.2	48,000	0.27	0.26	2.0	24
Cauliflower	55	63	4.9	0.4	10.0	45	147	2.2	200	0.21	0.22	1.2	141
Celery	37	63	3.7	0.4	10.6	143	114	1.4	0	0.09	0.12	0.9	20
Chard	14	98	5.5	0.8	17.2	410*	140	15.5	10,920	0.22	0.51	0.9	148
Corn, sweet	62	186	6.4	2.1	35.5	16	208	0.9	680†	0.27	0.24	2.4	20
Cucumbers	30	46	2.2	0.3	8.6	32	67	1.0	0	0.12	0.28	0.5	27
Kale	36	144	11.3	1.7	21.0	655	180	6.4	21,950	0.35	1.01	(2.4)	335
Lettuce, head	31	57	3.8	0.6	9.1	69	78	1.6	1,710	0.20	0.21	0.5	24
Lettuce, all other	31	57	3.8	0.6	9.1	194	63	3.4	5,060	0.20	0.21	0.5	57
Mustard greens	27	92	7.6	1.0	13.2	728	126	9.6	21,370	0.31	0.68	2.8	338
Onions, mature	6	208	6.0	0.8	44.0	137	188	2.1	210	0.15	0.10	0.7	38
Parsnips	22	295	6.5	1.8	64.4	202	283	2.5	0	0.40	0.32	0.7	63
Peas, green	55	206	13.7	0.8	36.1	45	249	3.3	1,390	0.72	0.37	4.2	54
Peppers, green	16	112	4.6	0.8	21.7	42	95	1.5	2,410	0.27	0.17	1.4	457
Potatoes	16	325	7.6	0.4	72.8	42	213	2.7	70	0.40	0.15	4.4	64
Spinach	3	92	8.6	1.1	11.9	301*	205	11.2	35,040	0.44	0.90	2.6	219
Squash, summer	8	83	2.6	0.4	17.2	66	66	1.8	1,140	0.18	0.23	5.0	75
Squash, winter	26	147	5.0	1.1	29.6	64	94	2.0	16,640	0.16	0.26	2.8	28
Sweet Potatoes	14	488	7.0	2.7	108.8	117	191	2.7	30,030‡	0.37	0.23	2.5	86
Tomatoes	12	91	4.0	1.2	16.0	44	108	2.4	4,380	0.24	0.16	2.5	93
Turnip green	16	140	11.0	1.5	20.6	987	190	9.1	36,370	0.37	2.15	2.9	518
Turnips	13	136	4.3	0.8	28.0	158	134	2.0	20	0.26	0.24	1.8	113
For comparison:													
Whole-wheat bread	0	1,187	43.1	15.9	217.9	(272)	1,680	11.8	(0)	1.28	0.70	16.1	0
Milk, whole	0	312	15.9	17.7	22.2	536	422	0.3	(720)	0.16	0.78	0.5	6
Eggs	11	636	51.7	46.5	2.8	218	848	10.9	4,590	0.47	1.35	0.3	(0)
Round steak	11	789	78.0	53.0	0.0	44	840	11.7	(0)	0.48	0.61	21.0	0
Apples	12	258	1.2	3.6	59.6	24	40	1.2	360	0.15	0.08	1.0	18
Oranges	28	164	2.9	0.7	36.6	108	75	1.3	(620)	0.25	0.08	0.8	162

* May not be available because of the presence of oxalic acid.
† Based on yellow corn.
‡ If pale varieties only were used, the value would be lower.

15

of ascorbic acid as a pound of Irish potatoes, but the average consumer obtains more of his requirements from potatoes than from peppers because of a much higher consumption of potatoes.

PER CAPITA CONSUMPTION OF VEGETABLES

The per capita consumption of vegetables, excluding potatoes and sweet potatoes, has increased markedly since about 1910, as shown in Fig. 1.3. The greatest increase has been in tomatoes and in the leafy,

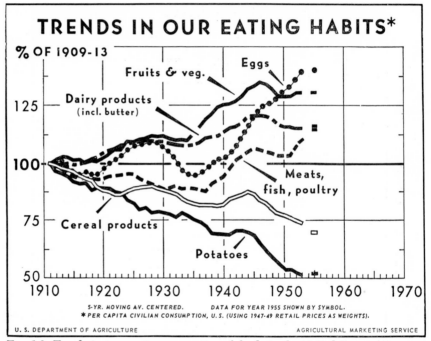

Fig. 1.3. Trends in per capita consumption of foods in the United States. (*Courtesy of U.S. Department of Agriculture.*)

green and yellow vegetables. Per capita consumption of Irish potatoes in 1954 was only slightly more than half of the average for the period 1909–1913. The sweet-potato consumption per capita has shown a decline similar to that of the Irish potato.

While there has been a marked increase in the per capita consumption of tomatoes and the leafy, green and yellow vegetables since about 1910, nutrition authorities believe that there should be a further increase. The continued increase in per capita consumption together with increase in population should provide a market for more vegetables than has ever been produced in the United States.

CHAPTER 2

Classification of Vegetables

Before an attempt is made to give an analysis of the methods of growing vegetables it seems desirable to classify the crops. Any method of classification systematizes to some extent the preparation and presentation of the material and eliminates unnecessary repetition of some of the principles of culture. While an alphabetical arrangement of crops is the best for reference, it does not contribute to an understanding of relationship or similarity of cultural requirements. There are four general methods of classification as follows: (1) a botanical classification, (2) a classification based on hardiness, (3) a classification based on parts used, (4) a classification based on essential methods of culture. A fifth method combining parts of the four mentioned may be used to advantage in grouping crops for discussion.

Botanical Classification. A classification based entirely on relationship is the most exact system, but in many cases this is of little value in giving principles of culture since crops within a family may vary widely in their requirements. Potatoes and eggplant belong to the same family, but their requirements are very different. However, other crops in this family, as tomatoes, eggplant, and peppers, have similar requirements. Most of the vegetables belonging to the family Cucurbitaceae have similar cultural requirements as well as the same disease and insect pests. This is also true of plants in many other families.

The botanical system of classification is of value in showing relationship and is given to show the families represented, as well as the important vegetable crops belonging to each.

Plants are divided into four great groups, or as Bailey calls them, "subcommunities." These are as follows:

    I. Thallophyta. The thallophytes
   II. Brophyta. Mosses and liverworts
  III. Pteridophyta. Ferns and their allies
   IV. Spermatophyta. The spermatophytes, or seed plants

17

We are concerned here with the Spermatophyta only, and this group or subcommunity is grouped into two divisions, with subdivisions as follows:

Division I. Gymnospermae: ovules naked, not enclosed in an ovary
Division II. Angiospermae: ovules in a carpel or ovary
  Class I. Monocotyledoneae: one seed leaf
  Class II. Dicotyledoneae: two seed leaves
    Series I. Choripetalae: petals (or sepals) distinct or separate
    Series II. Gamopetalae: petals (or sepals) united

No vegetables belong in the division Gymnospermae, so we are concerned only with the second division, Angiospermae.

Taxonomists are not in complete agreement as to the correct scientific names of many kinds of vegetable-crop plants. As might be expected, the groups of plants that have been studied the most are the ones in which there is the greatest difference of opinion as to the correct names. While most changes have been in the names of the species, many generic names have been changed and, in one case, a genus has been placed in a different family. The genus Allium was listed as a member of the family Liliaceae by early taxonomists but is now placed in the family Amaryllidaceae. The generic and specific names selected are those the authors believe are the most authentic or, in some cases, those most widely recognized.

The class, family, genus, species, subspecies, or botanical variety to which vegetable-crop plants belong and the common names are as follows:

Monocotyledoneae
  Gramineae—grass family
    Zea Mays.................. var. *rugosa*   Sweet corn
    Zea Mays.................. var. *everta*   Popcorn
  Liliaceae—lily family
    Asparagus officinalis..........   Asparagus
  Araceae—arum family
    Colocasia esculenta...........   Taro, dasheen
  Amaryllidaceae—amaryllis family
    Allium cepa.......... ....   Onion
    Allium cepa................ var. *aggregatum*   Multiplier onion
    Allium cepa................ var. *viviparum*   Top onion, or tree onion
    Allium porrum..............   Leek
    Allium sativum..............   Garlic
    Allium fistulosum..........   Welsh onion
    Allium ascalonicum...........   Shallot
    Allium schoenoprasum.........   Chive
  Dioscoreaceae—yam family
    Dioscorea alata..............   Yam

Dicotyledoneae
  Polygonaceae—buckwheat family
    Rheum rhaponticum. . . . .   Rhubarb
    Rumex acetosa. . . . .   Sorrel
    Rumex patientia. . . . .   Patience, or dock
  Chenopodiaceae—goosefoot family
    Chenopodium bonus-henricus . . .   Good-King-Henry
    Beta vulgaris. . . . .   Beet
    Beta vulgaris. . . . . var. *cicla*   Chard
    Atriplex hortensis. . . . .   Orach
    Spinacia oleracea. . . . .   Prickly-seeded spinach
    Spinacia oleracea. . . . . var. *inermis*   Round-seeded spinach
  Aizoaceae—carpetweed family
    Tetrogonia expansa. . . . .   New Zealand spinach
  Cruciferae—mustard family
    Brassica oleracea. . . . . var. *acephala*   Kale
    Brassica oleracea. . . . . var. *gemmifera*   Brussels sprouts
    Brassica oleracea. . . . . var. *capitata*   Cabbage
    Brassica oleracea. . . . . var. *botrytis*   Cauliflower, broccoli
    Brassica oleracea. . . . . var. *italica*   Sprouting broccoli
    Brassica caulorapa. . . . .   Kohlrabi
    Brassica napus. . . . . var. *napobrassica*   Rutabaga
    Brassica campestris. . . . . var. *rapa*   Turnip
    Brassica juncea. . . . .   Leaf mustard
    Brassica juncea. . . . . var. *crispifolia*   Curled mustard and others
    Brassica pekinensis. . . . .   Pe-tsai Chinese cabbage
    Brassica chinensis. . . . .   Pakchoi Chinese cabbage
    Barbarea vulgaris. . . . .   Upland cress
    Nasturtium officinale. . . . .   Water cress
    Armoracia lapathifolia. . . . .   Horse-radish
    Lepidium sativum. . . . .   Garden cress
    Raphanus sativus. . . . .   Radish
    Raphanus sativus. . . . . var. *longipinnatus*   Chinese radish
    Crambe maritima. . . . .   Sea kale
  Leguminosae—pea, or pulse, family
    Pisum sativum. . . . .   Pea
    Pisum sativum. . . . . var. *macrocarpon*   Edible-podded pea
    Vicia faba. . . . .   Broad bean
    Phaseolus vulgaris. . . . .   Kidney bean
    Phaseolus vulgaris. . . . . var. *humilis*   Bush bean
    Phaseolus coccineus. . . . .   Multiflora, or scarlet runner, bean
    Phaseolus lunatus. . . . .   Lima bean
    Phaseolus mungo. . . . .   Urd bean
    Phaseolus aureus. . . . .   Mung bean
    Phaseolus angularis. . . . .   Adzuki bean
    Phaseolus calcaratus. . . . .   Rice bean
    Phaseolus aconitifolius. . . . .   Moth bean
    Phaseolus acutifolius. . . . .   Tepary bean
    Vigna sesquipedalis. . . . .   Asparagus, or yard-long bean
    Vigna sinensis. . . . .   Cowpea, or Southern pea
    Glycine max. . . . .   Soybean

Euphorbiaceae—spurge family
    Manihot esculenta............   Manioc (cassava, yuca, tapioca plant)

Malvaceae—mallow family
    Hibiscus esculentus...........   Okra

Umbelliferae—parsley family
    Daucus carota............... var. *sativa*   Carrot
    Petroselinum crispum..........   Parsley
    Petroselinum crispum........ var. *tuberosum* Hamburg, or root, parsley
    Apium graveolens............ var. *dulce*   Celery
    Apium graveolens............ var. *rapaceum* Celeriac
    Pastinaca sativa.............   Parsnip
    Anthriscus cerefolium........   Chervil

Convolvulaceae—morning-glory family
    Ipomoea batatas.............   Sweet potato

Solanaceae—nightshade family
    Solanum tuberosum...........   Potato
    Solanum melongena...........   Eggplant
    Lycopersicon esculentum.......   Tomato
    Lycopersicon esculentum....... var. *cerasiforme* Cherry tomato
    Lycopersicon esculentum....... var. *pyriforme* Pear tomato
    Lycopersicon esculentum....... var. *commune* Common tomato
    Lycopersicon esculentum....... var. *grandifolium* Potato-leaved tomato
    Lycopersicon esculentum....... var. *validum* Upright tomato
    Lycopersicon pimpinellifolium..   Currant tomato
    Physalis pruinosa.............   Husk tomato
    Capsicum annuum...........   Pepper
    Capsicum frutescens..........   Hot, or pungent, pepper

Martynaceae—martynia family
    Proboscidea Jussieui (Keller)...   Martynia

Cucurbitaceae—gourd family
    Cucurbita pepo..............   Pumpkin
    Cucurbita pepo.............. var. *condensa* (Bailey) Bush pumpkin (summer squash)
    Cucurbita moschata..........   Pumpkin (cushaw and large cheese)
    Cucurbita maxima...........   Squash
    Citrullus vulgaris............   Watermelon
    Cucumis sativus.............   Cucumber
    Cucumis melo...............   Muskmelon
    Cucumis melo............... var. *reticulatus* Netted melon
    Cucumis melo............... var. *cantalupensis* Cantaloupe
    Cucumis melo............... var. *inodorus* Cassaba melon
    Cucumis melo............... var. *chito* Mango melon, or lemon cucumber
    Sechium edule...............   Chayote

Compositae—Composite family
    Cichorum intybus............   Chicory
    Cichorum endivia............   Endive
    Scolymus hispanicus..........   Spanish salsify
    Scorzonera hispanica..........   Black salsify
    Tragopogon porrifolius........   Salsify

Taraxacum officinale............		Dandelion
Lactuca sativa...............		Lettuce
Lactuca sativa...............	var. *crispa*	Curled lettuce
Lactuca sativa...............	var. *capitata*	Head lettuce
Lactuca sativa...............	var. *longifolia*	Cos lettuce
Lactuca sativa...............	var. *asparagina*	Asparagus lettuce
Helianthus tuberosus..........		Girasole, or Jerusalem, artichoke
Cynara cardunculus...........		Cardoon
Cynara scolymus.............		Artichoke

Classification Based on Hardiness. Vegetables are often classified as *hardy* and *tender*. Those classed as hardy will endure ordinary frosts without injury, while those classed as tender would be killed. This implies that frost injury is the chief difference between hardy and tender plants, but there are other distinctions. Some of the hardy plants will not thrive well under hot dry conditions, so that in the North they should be planted early in the spring or late in the summer. Others will withstand frost and also thrive during the hot weather of summer. Some tender vegetables do not thrive in cool weather even if no frost occurs. The terms *cool-season* and *warm-season* crops are used to suggest conditions under which the crops thrive best, rather than their susceptibility to frost injury.

Based on the temperature that the plants will withstand, some vegetable plants are hardy, some semihardy, others tender, and still others very tender. The hardy ones may safely be planted before the date of the last killing frost in spring. The semihardy will not stand a hard frost but will grow in cool weather and are not injured by a light frost. The tender plants are injured or even killed by a light frost but can withstand cool weather and a cold soil, while the very tender are injured by cool weather. This system of classification is of some value in connection with a discussion of time of planting. By grouping all hardy plants together general principles regarding time of planting can be given for the whole group. The semihardy, tender, and very tender plants may be grouped in the same way for discussion. This system is used in Chap. 8.

Classification Based on Parts Used as Food. In this system of classification those crops grown for their leaves or stems are placed in one group. This group includes cabbage, kohlrabi, collards, asparagus, rhubarb, all the salad crops, and all the potherbs or greens. A second group includes those crops grown for their fruits, as melons, tomatoes, eggplant, beans, and peas, while a third group includes those grown for their flower parts, as cauliflower and broccoli. Those crops grown for their underground portions (roots, tubers, bulbs, and corms), as potatoes, sweet potatoes, beets, carrots, parsnips, radishes, turnips, salsify, onions, garlic, and dasheen, constitute a fourth group. In each of these groups the crops cover a great range of cultural requirements, so that grouping them in this way is not of much value.

Classification Based on Methods of Culture. A system of classification based on essential methods of culture is very convenient. In this system all those crops that have similar cultural requirements are grouped together for discussion. This makes it possible to give the general cultural practices for the group without the necessity of repetition in the discussion of individual crops. This system combines some parts of the other three methods. In some of the groups, as cucurbits, beans and peas, bulb crops, and cole crops, all crops considered in each belong to the same family. In other groups as perennial crops, potherbs and greens, salad crops, and root crops, more than one family is represented in each group. In the perennial-crops group of five vegetables, four families are represented.

In teaching principles of vegetable growing this system of classification has been found more satisfactory than any other and is followed in a general way in this book. In some of the groupings the crops within a group do not have much in common, but they are placed together for convenience. The vegetables discussed are placed in 13 groups, and the discussion for each group constitutes a chapter. The grouping is as follows:

Group　1. Perennial crops
　　　　　　Asparagus, rhubarb, artichoke, Jerusalem artichoke, sea kale
Group　2. Potherbs or greens
　　　　　　Spinach, New Zealand spinach, orach, kale, chard, mustard, collards, dandelion
Group　3. Salad crops
　　　　　　Celery, lettuce, endive, chicory, cress, corn salad, parsley, salad chervil
Group　4. Cole crops
　　　　　　Cabbage, cauliflower, broccoli, Brussels sprouts, kohlrabi, Chinese cabbage
Group　5. Root crops
　　　　　　Beet, carrot, parsnip, turnip, rutabaga, salsify, turnip-rooted chervil, skirret, radish, horse-radish, scorzonera, or black salsify, scolymus, or Spanish salsify
Group　6. Bulb crops
　　　　　　Onion, leek, garlic, shallot, ciboul (Cibol), or Welsh onion, chive, or cive
Group　7. The potato
Group　8. The sweet potato

Group 9. Peas and beans

      Pea, bean, broad bean, common, or garden, bean, Multiflora bean, Lima beans, tepary beans, soybean, cowpea, or Southern pea

Group 10. Solanaceous fruits

      Tomato, eggplant, pepper, husk tomato, or physalis

Group 11. The cucurbits

      Cucumber, gherkin, muskmelon, watermelon, citron melon, pumpkin, squash

Group 12. Sweet corn, okra, martynia

Group 13. Chayote, yam, dasheen (taro), manioc (yuca, cassava)

CHAPTER 3

Soils and Soil Preparation

The soil is the storage house of mineral nutrients and water used by higher plants, as well as the home of their roots. Therefore the physical and chemical composition of the soil is of great importance in crop production. The chemical composition can be changed by adding fertilizers and other materials and, to some extent, by drainage and tillage, which favor aeration. The physical condition can be changed by drainage, by tillage, by incorporating organic matter, and by use of lime and other flocculating materials. Unless the soil is in good physical condition large yields cannot be obtained. Good fertilizer practice, good seed, and the best of care will not ensure success unless the soil is of good texture and is well prepared.

There are two general kinds of soils—mineral and organic (muck or peat). Their origin and classification are so different that they are discussed separately.

CLASSIFICATION OF MINERAL SOILS

Mineral soils are classified in various ways and with many divisions. The most useful classification for the average reader is one based on the general characteristics that are important in crop production. In technical publications dealing with soils the terms soil series, soil types, and soil classes, or textural grade, are in common usage.

Soil Series. A soil series is a group of soils having similar profile characteristics, developed under similar climatic conditions, from the same kind of parent material. Variations within the series are confined to the difference in the A horizon. In the United States each series is given a name, usually (but not always) geographic from a village, city, county, or river, as Ontario, Miami, Norfolk, Muscatine. The subdivision of the series based on the characteristics of the A horizon gives the soil type.

Soil Type. A soil that has relatively uniform profile characteristics represents a soil type. Any particular soil of a series is designated by its textural name, as sandy loam, clay loam, or silt loam; before the textural name is added the series name. The type name is, therefore, made up of two parts, the first designating the series and the second the individual within the series, as, for example, Dunkirk clay loam, Norfolk sandy loam. The first word in each of these names designates the series, and the rest the textural grade, or class. Taken together they make the name of the soil type.

Soil Class. The soil class, or textural grade, is a classification based on texture alone. Texture is a term used to indicate the coarseness or fineness of the soil; the textural composition is determined by a mechanical analysis, which is a laboratory process. The system used by the U.S. Department of Agriculture separates the soil particles into seven sizes, as given below.

Name of soil	Size, millimeters
Fine gravel	2 −1
Coarse sand	1 −0.5
Medium sand	0.5 −0.25
Fine sand	0.25–0.10
Very fine sand	0.10–0.05
Silt	0.05–0.005
Clay	0.005 and below

Mineral soils are separated into three groups: sandy soils, loamy soils, and clayey soils, determined by the proportion of the several sizes there given. Sandy soils include gravelly sands, coarse sands, medium sands, fine sands, and very fine sands. Loamy soils include coarse sandy loams, medium sandy loams, fine sandy loams, very fine sandy loams, silt loams, silty clay loams, and clay loams. Clayey soils include gravelly clays, sandy clays, clays, and heavy clays.

All classes of soils are used to some extent for vegetable production, and while no one class can be said to be the best, each class has its advantages and disadvantages. One class may be very desirable for crops grown under certain conditions, but undesirable for the same crops grown under other conditions or for other crops. The soil classes preferred for vegetable production are sandy soils, sandy loams, silt loams, clay loams, and muck or peat soils.

SANDY SOILS. A sandy soil is single-grained, and the individual grains can be seen and felt readily. The different classes of sandy soils are determined on the basis of the proportion of the various sand separates making up the soil. When wet, a sandy soil can be formed into a ball, but it will crumble readily if touched.

Sandy soils are naturally infertile and are not retentive of moisture. They are considered of value for very early crops, but they are not suited to long-season crops or those grown during the warmest part of the growing season. The finer-grained sandy soils are used extensively for growing vegetables. The moisture-holding capacity of sandy soils can be increased by adding organic matter in the form of manure, crop residues, or soil-improving crops.

SANDY LOAMS. A sandy-loam soil contains much sand but has enough silt and clay to make it hold together somewhat. When moist, a sandy loam can be formed into a cast that will bear careful handling without breaking. Sandy loams contain from 20 to 50 per cent of silt and clay. The four classes of sandy loams are separated on the basis of the percentages of the various separates from fine gravel to very fine sand.

Sandy loams are more retentive of moisture and of nutrients than are the sands and, in general, are considered better for vegetable growing. They are not so early as the sandy soils, but are earlier than the loams, silt loams, clay loams, or clays. Both the sandy and sandy-loam soils may be worked soon after a rain or after irrigation without injury. This is a great advantage in early preparation of the soil and in keeping weeds under control by cultivation.

LOAM SOILS. A loam is a soil having a relatively even mixture of different grades of sands and of silt and clay. Loams contain less than 20 per cent of clay, from 30 to 50 per cent of silt, and from 30 to 50 per cent of sand.

SILTY LOAMS. These soils contain less than 20 per cent of clay, 50 per cent or more of silt, and less than 50 per cent of sand. When dry, silt loam breaks up, it is cloddy or lumpy, but the lumps can be broken down readily, and when pulverized it feels smooth and soft. When wet, a silt-loam soil runs together, and when either wet or dry, it will form a cast if squeezed. They are valuable for the production of most kinds of vegetables, especially where large yields are more important than earliness. These soils are naturally more fertile and more retentive of moisture than are the sands or sandy loams. Silt loams are considered by many as one of the best classes for general vegetable growing.

CLAY LOAMS. These soils contain from 20 to 30 per cent of clay. A soil in this group that contains less than 30 per cent of silt and from 50 to 80 per cent of sand is called a sandy clay loam; one with from 20 to 50 per cent of silt and from 20 to 50 per cent sand is known as clay loam; while one containing from 50 to 80 per cent of silt and less than 30 per cent sand is known as silty clay loam. A clay loam usually is fine-textured and breaks up into clods that are hard when dry. Clay loams are more retentive of moisture than are the soils of coarser texture, but they are difficult to prepare and are not considered so good for early crops. These soils can be improved by the addition of organic matter and to some extent by liming. Clay loams are not desirable for small-growing vegetable crops and are particularly objectionable for root crops.

Muck or Peat Soils. Muck or peat soils are composed largely of plant material in various stages of decomposition. The profile of such soils is characterized by layers differing in the nature of the original plant material and the stage of decomposition. The terms *muck* and *peat* often are used indiscriminately to designate soils that are composed largely of organic matter. In some regions all organic soils are called peat, while in other regions all such soils are termed muck.

Some authorities make a distinction between peat and muck, others do not. When a distinction is made it is based either on the percentage of organic matter or the stage of decomposition. In the first case, if the soil contains as much as 50 per cent organic matter, it is called peat; if it contains less than that, it is called muck. By the second method the soil is classed as muck if decomposition has advanced so far that the structure of the organic residue is no longer evident; otherwise it is called peat. Wilson (1935) stated that according to each of these classifications practically all of the organic deposits of New York are peats. It is probable that most of the deposits in the United States should be called peats under either of these classifications. However, in this discussion the term muck is generally used and refers to any organic soil that is used, or may be used, for vegetable production. The term muck as used here should not be confused with those mineral soils of a muck nature that contain considerable organic matter and are dark in color.

CHARACTERISTICS OF MUCK SOILS. Some of the important characteristics of muck soils are as follows:

1. They are predominately high in organic matter.

2. They are brown or black in color, and the more advanced the stage of decomposition the darker the color.

3. They have a high water-holding capacity, absorbing several times their weight of water. However, the unavailable water is high also.

4. They are generally high in nitrogen. Most cultivated muck soils contain from $1\frac{1}{2}$ to $2\frac{1}{2}$ per cent of nitrogen on the basis of dry weight. Some deposits contain more than $2\frac{1}{2}$ per cent.

5. They are usually low in mineral elements, especially potash. Most of the deposits that have been tested are poor in potash, which is an important limiting factor. Some deposits are deficient in phosphorus, and many are low in some of the so-called minor elements.

For the production of certain vegetables, especially celery, lettuce, and onions, muck soils are considered excellent. A large portion of these three crops grown in some of the Northern states is produced on muck soils. In Florida most of the celery and many other crops are produced on these soils. Carrots, beets, spinach, cabbage, potatoes, and other vegetables are grown to a considerable extent on muck soils in many areas. In regions where severe freezes occur and the growing season is short, muck soils are not suitable for tender, long-season crops. Frosts are likely to occur later in the spring and earlier in the fall on these soils than on mineral soils. It has been assumed that the "frostiness" of muck soils is due largely to the low elevation, but it has been observed that crops are sometimes injured by frost on muck soils and not on mineral soils at approximately the same elevation. Results of studies made by Bouyoucos and McCool (1922) in Michigan give an explanation for this. They made temperature studies on clay loam and muck placed at the same elevation. Their results indicate that heat moves more rapidly through a clay loam than through a muck soil; therefore at night the air above the clay loam has a higher temperature than that above muck. McCool and Harmer (1925) comment as follows on the results of those studies:

During the early part of the day the clay loam absorbed heat more rapidly than did the muck, but by the late afternoon the muck had become nearly as warm as the mineral soil even to the depth of 6 inches. On a clear, cool night which followed, heat was lost from both soils by radiation. The temperature of the cultivated muck dropped 8° more than that of the mineral soil, reaching a temperature 4° below the freezing point of water. At a depth of 6 inches, however, the temperature of the mineral soil dropped 5° more than did that of the muck soil. In other words, sufficient heat moved from below to the surface of the mineral soil to keep the surface from freezing. The muck soil was such a poor conductor that the heat below did not move up, consequently the surface layer and the air just above it were cooled to a point at which a crop would have been frosted. The compact muck soil was a better conductor of heat than was the cultivated muck, with a result that the surface temperature dropped to only 1° below freezing. Further, the muck with a light covering of sand gave an even smaller drop in temperature at the surface than did the compact muck.

The "frostiness" of a muck depends on several factors, of which the following are most important: (1) moisture content, (2) compactness, (3) state of decomposition, (4) content of mineral matter, (5) fertilization.

Heat moves up from below to the surface more rapidly in a moist than in a dry muck. If the soil is compact, the movement of heat takes place still more readily. For that reason the heavy roller is a valuable implement in aiding the prevention of frosts. The looser the surface layer, the greater the danger of summer frosts. Frequently when a field of corn or potatoes on muck has been partly cultivated before a frost occurred, the cultivated portion has been frosted while the uncultivated part has escaped. The loose cultivated layer serves as a blanket to keep the heat in the soil so that the air just above it is not kept warm.

Ordinarily the more decomposed a muck becomes, the smaller becomes the probability of frost occurrence. For that reason, old mucks are generally not as "frosty" as those recently reclaimed. A soil fairly high in mineral matter is likewise not as subject to frost as one that is low in these constituents.

Not all mucks are of equal value for vegetable growing. Their value depends on the stage of decomposition, the character of the material from which the soil was formed, the drainage, the location, and other factors. In general, the more decomposed the material, the better the muck for vegetable growing. It is believed by many authorities that muck soils which have supported a growth of deciduous trees and shrubs are better than those which have grown coniferous trees. A peat which contains a large quantity of material from coniferous trees decomposes more slowly than one which does not contain such material. This is probably due to the resins in the conifers, which preserve the woody materials. Some muck soils are toxic, usually on account of the underlying rock, and are nearly useless for growing vegetables.

Drainage and tillage are important factors in the decomposition of the organic material in muck soils. Removing the water and stirring the soil allow air to enter and favor the growth of organisms that cause the breaking down of the plant remains. Oxidation itself is of importance. Lime also favors decomposition when the soils are sour, for the desirable organisms do not thrive well in a very acid soil. Stable manure has been found to be very beneficial on newly cleared muck soils because of the presence of beneficial organisms in the manure. Manure may, therefore, be considered as an inoculant or at least a carrier of beneficial organisms.

IMPORTANCE AND DISTRIBUTION OF MUCK SOIL. Deposits of muck or peat soils (organic soils) are found in all parts of the world where conditions are favorable for their formation. In Germany, Sweden, Ireland, and other parts of Europe there are large deposits. Canada has 20 million acres or more, and Anderson, Blake, and Mehring (1951) estimate that the United States has about 79 million acres. In the United States approximately 75 per cent of the area is in the glaciated region extending from about the southern boundary of New York State westward to nearly the 90th meridian. The largest deposits of this region are in Minnesota, Wisconsin, and Michigan, with smaller areas in New York, Ohio, Indiana, Illinois, and Iowa. Other important deposits are in a strip along the Atlantic Coast from Maine to Florida, in Louisiana, the Pacific Northwest, and the delta area of California. The Everglades of Florida is the largest of the deposits in the Eastern part of the United States and is mainly saw grass peat or muck.

Only a relatively small part of the muck lands of the United States and Canada is in use for agricultural purposes, and a large part of this is in general farm crops and pasture. A large part of the area in many regions is swampland that has not been cleared and drained. Only a very small fraction of the cleared, drained muck lands is used for the production of vegetables. This is as it should be, for if any considerable portion was planted to the vegetable crops commonly grown on such land, there would be serious overproduction with resultant low prices for the products.

SOIL PREPARATION

Soil preparation, as considered here, consists of drainage, plowing, disking, harrowing, dragging, and rolling. For most vegetable crops good drainage and good preparation are essential. For planting small seeds it is important to have the surface fairly smooth and free of clods and trash in order to plant at a uniform depth and to have good coverage of the seed. Seed drills and transplanting machines operate best on a smooth surface.

Drainage. For wet soils the first operation in the preparation should be drainage, as most soils cannot be properly prepared when poorly drained. Good drainage is essential to success in growing practically all vegetables, although some crops stand wet soils better than others, and a few minor ones, such as water cress, thrive in a very wet soil. Good drainage is especially important for early vegetables because earliness is not possible in a wet soil. The sands are of value in growing early vegetables because they are better drained than the heavier soils. On soils not naturally well drained artificial drainage is a profitable investment. It is much better to drain the soil by means of ditches or tiles than to plant the crop on ridges. Drainage not only removes the excess water but also allows the air to enter the soil, and air is essential to the growth of crop plants and of beneficial organisms which make some of the nutrients available to the plants. Drainage also allows the soils to warm earlier in the spring, thus favoring early preparation and planting.

The draining of muck or peat soils presents a special problem. Without drainage the water table ordinarily is too high for the production of most farm and vegetable crops. These soils subside after they are drained and put under cultivation owing to decomposition and oxidation of the plant material from which they are formed, to compaction by the use of heavy machinery, and to the drying of the soil. The rate of subsidence varies according to the type of muck, the depth of the deposit, the length of time it has been drained, the depth of the water table, and the stage of decomposition of the organic material. The rate of subsidence is greater during the first few years after the land has been drained than later. After the initial subsidence the rate is influenced mainly by the drainage method, especially the depth of the water table maintained. Results of studies by Jongedyk *et al.* (1950) in northern Indiana show clearly the relation of the depth of the water to rate of subsidence over the period 1943–1949. In these studies the water table was maintained at average depths during the crop seasons of 17, 27, and

39 inches, and the rate of subsidence was 0.45, 0.70, and 1.20 inches, respectively. It is important, therefore, to maintain the water table at depths that will permit maximum crop production and, at the same time, keep subsidence low.

The drainage of muck deposits is by means of open ditches and by tile drains. Tile has proved satisfactory where it has been laid properly. The use of tile results in the saving of land area, avoids cutting up the fields by ditches, saves labor by eliminating the necessity of cleaning ditches and cutting weeds on the ditch banks, and does away with a source of supply of weed seed. However, where tile is used the lines usually empty into outlet ditches or canals. The need is for a drainage system adequate to remove excess water within a few hours after a heavy rain, without resulting in excessive drainage at other times.

Since new muck subsides rapidly after it is cleared, drained, and put under cultivation, it is considered wise to use open ditches for the first few years and then to use tile where it can be employed satisfactorily. Where tile is used, it is important to lay it at such a depth that it will lower the water table sufficiently for profitable production of crops and will not be reached by the plow in a few years. Where there is a permanent water supply in the outlet ditches, it is desirable to place the tile 3 to 5 feet in depth and to maintain the desired water level by use of dams in the outlet ditches. The actual depth to lay the tiles depends on the character and the depth of the muck, the nature of the subsoil, and the amount of fall in the area to be drained. Jongedyk *et al.* suggest that a water table of about 24 inches below the surface is satisfactory for most crops grown on muck soils.

The distance that is to be allowed between parallel lines of tile depends on the rainfall, the type of muck, and the nature of the underlying material. The greater the rainfall, the closer the lines of tile should be. Where the muck is deep or is underlaid with clay or marl, lines of tile or ditches must be much closer than when the muck is underlaid with sand or gravel. The distance between lines of tile or open ditches varies from 50 feet in an impervious type of muck to as much as ½ mile in an open type of muck underlaid with sand or gravel at a depth penetrated by the main ditches.

Plowing. Soils for vegetables should be fairly deep, but a shallow surface soil should be deepened gradually. A soil that has been plowed only a few inches deep should be deepened by increasing the depth an inch or two a year until the desired depth is reached. Too much of the subsoil turned to the surface usually is injurious. A depth of 6 to 8 inches is sufficient on most soils. In years past it has been thought that the deeper the land was plowed, the better it was for crop production, provided too much raw subsoil was not turned to the surface at once, but experimental results do not indicate that this is true. The roots of most plants go below the depth plowed.

The time of plowing is determined to a considerable extent by the time the crops are to be planted. In many regions it is a common practice to plow the land a short time before the vegetable crop is to be planted. Where a soil-improving crop is to be turned under, it is desirable to allow the crop to grow as long as is feasible in order to get the maximum quantity of organic matter. Where irrigation is not used, it is important, however, to turn under the soil-improving crop before it has depleted the soil of moisture. Regardless of the time of the year when plowing is to be done, care should be exercised not to plow the land when it is too wet. This is particularly important for heavy soils or those containing a considerable portion of clay. When plowed too wet, such soils bake when they dry out and are very difficult to put in good condition by disking and harrowing. On the other hand, heavy soils should not be allowed to get too dry before plowing or they will break up in hard lumps. A heavy soil is in condition for plowing if, after being compacted in a ball in the hand, it can be crumbled. If it cannot be crumbled, it is too wet to be plowed.

Fall plowing is desirable for early planting in the spring in regions where crops are grown only during the summer. It is especially desirable where sod is to be turned under or for heavy soils that dry out slowly in the spring. The advantages of fall plowing are: (1) to reduce erosion by collecting water in the unbroken furrows, (2) to improve the physical condition of heavy soils by exposing them to frost action, (3) to aid in the control of insect pests by exposing them to the weather, (4) to relieve the pressure of spring work, (5) to make possible the earlier preparation of the soil for planting, (6) to bring about the decay of coarse vegetable matter turned under. Coarse material turned under in the spring is of little value to early crops and may be actually injurious, as mentioned in Chap. 4. Sandy and sandy-loam soils are not so much benefited as heavier soils by fall plowing even in regions where freezes occur, because frost action is not very important on soils that are naturally friable. In regions where freezes do not occur and where crops are grown at any time of the year, plowing is done far enough in advance to permit proper preparation for planting.

Disking and Harrowing. It is a common practice to disk or harrow the land soon after it is plowed, except where the plowing is done in the fall, or in the winter in regions where freezes occur. When plowing is done immediately before planting the land is usually disked or harrowed soon after plowing. In fact, a disk or harrow often is attached back of the plow.

The condition of the soil should determine the implements to use after plowing. A disk harrow is valuable for use on heavy soils and on sod land because it cuts the clods and sod to a considerable depth. After disking, it is a common practice to use a spike-tooth, spring-tooth, or Acme harrow. The first is satisfactory for leveling and smoothing the surface, but is not very satisfactory for use where sod has been turned under or the land is cloddy. The spring-tooth harrow is an important implement to use on stony ground but is objectionable for sod land because it brings the sod to the surface. The Acme is good because it leaves the surface smooth and does not bring sods, clods, or trash to the surface. The Meeker harrow is an especially good implement as a finishing harrow for use where planters are used for planting small seeds and where transplanters are employed for delicate plants like celery and lettuce.

Timeliness is of the greatest importance in all soil-preparation operations. The moisture content of the soil determines to a considerable extent the efficiency of the work done by the harrow. If the soil is too dry, many of the lumps will not be crushed, and if too wet, the soil will become puddled.

Dragging and Rolling. Heavy soils often break up in clods and lumps that are very difficult to crumble with any type of harrow. By use of a heavy drag or roller the lumps may be crushed with comparative ease. In preparing the soil late in the season, the drag often is used immediately after the plow, and then followed with the disk or spring-tooth harrow. In some instances the drag or roller is used before and after the harrow in order to crush the lumps brought to the surface by the harrow. The main use of the drag or roller on heavy soils is to crush the lumps, but on light soils both are often used to pack and smooth the soil. On muck soil the usual practice is to use a drag, or planker, as it is often called, just before planting in order to level and smooth the surface. In this case the drag need not be so heavy as when used for lump crushing, unless packing of the soil is also an important consideration.

CONTROL OF SOIL EROSION

Soil erosion by water and by wind is a serious matter in many vegetable-growing regions. Water erosion is prevalent in all rolling and hilly regions where there is sufficient rainfall to cause erosion, but is perhaps most severe in regions of high rainfall and hilly land in the South. Wind erosion is most severe in the Great Plains area but is important on muck soils and on sandy soils in many vegetable-growing regions of the United States.

Water Erosion. Soil erosion by water can be controlled by terracing the land, by contour tillage and planting, and by strip cropping. Growing a cover crop on the land when it is not producing a crop to be harvested and keeping the soil well supplied with humus also aid in the control of erosion.

By the use of terraces, the land is divided into separate drainage areas, with each area having its own waterway above the terrace. The terrace holds the water on the land, thus allowing it to soak into the soil and reducing or preventing gulleying. The terraces follow the contour of the land and should be made broad and of low grade to allow the water to move slowly.

Fig. 3.1. Strip cropping on sloping land following the contour. (*Extension Soil Conservation, Cornell University.*)

In contour farming, row crops are planted on the contour so that they can be cultivated on the level rather than up and down the slope or at right angles to it. Contour cultivation conserves moisture and reduces erosion by holding the water in the little terraces made by the cultivator until it soaks into the soil.

Strip cropping consists of growing crops in narrow strips across the slope usually on the contour (Fig. 3.1). The strips are planted to a series of crops so that sod crops and other noncultivated crops are placed between strips of intertilled crops. The areas of noncultivated crops usually take up the rains that fall on them and also the runoff from the cultivated strips and thus prevent serious erosion. The width of the cultivated strips is determined by the steepness of the slope, the rate of percolation of water into the soil the absorptive capacity of the soil, and the rainfall. Obviously the steeper the slope, the narrower the strips should be.

Wind Erosion. Soil erosion by wind can be controlled by the use of windbreaks of various kinds, by keeping the soil well supplied with humus, and by growing cover crops when the land is not occupied by other crops. In the growing of small-growing crops on muck soils it is necessary to use windbreaks of some kind unless the land is protected by hills or by natural growth of trees and other vegetation. Protection against wind injury is desirable also on very light sandy soils.

Fig. 3.2. Basket-willow windbreak on muck soil. Oak Orchard area, Elba, N.Y.

The types of windbreaks that are in use on muck soils are: (1) trees, (2) shrubs, (3) fences of boards, slats, or cloth of some kind, and (4) plantings of grain or forage crops.

The trees most commonly planted as windbreaks are box elder, willow, poplar, Norway spruce, and white cedar. The large-growing trees such as the poplars and some of the willows are planted only along roadways and along large ditches, as they utilize too much land when planted in cultivated areas. Small-growing willows and other trees that can be kept in bounds by pruning are planted in single rows at somewhat regular intervals through the fields that are subject to wind erosion. In some areas, rows of basket willows (Fig. 3.2) are planted about 200 to 300 feet apart, and in other cases, rows of white cedar trees are planted about the same distance apart. Hedges of privet make good windbreaks where the plants are not winterkilled. Such hedges are used on sandy soils in some areas and, if placed properly, give good protection.

Windbreaks protect the soil and crop by reducing the velocity of the wind. Denuyl (1943) stated that the reduction in wind velocities is dependent on the height and density of the windbreak. The zone of protection extends out horizontally a distance of 8 to 10 times the height of the trees. Denuyl shows that a single row of green willows 40 feet in height gave protection a distance of 320 to 400 feet. Some protection is given beyond this distance. "As the velocity of the wind increases, the zone of protection decreases."

Objections to the planting of trees as windbreaks are that they occupy a considerable area of land and that they are not effective until they have had a few years' growth. These two objections have led many muck-land vegetable growers to use fences of various kinds. Solid board fences 4 to 6 feet high are used in some regions, especially where small areas are operated by individual farmers. Slat fences, similar to snow fences, are more common than the solid board fences, since they do not cost so much and can be removed easily.

Corn, small grains, and some of the hay crops are used as windbreaks on muck soil in several states.

Of the small grains, rye is the best crop under most conditions, but oats, barley, and spring wheat are satisfactory for planting early in the spring. Where rye is sown as a cover crop in the fall, a strip a foot or more in width may be left every 50 or 60 feet; this will give protection before spring-planted grains are well started. This method is followed by some muck-land farmers in New York. On one large farm hedges of willows are planted about 200 feet apart at right angles to the direction of the prevailing wind, and between these, at intervals of about 50 feet, strips of fall-sown rye are left. Another method of using small grains is to sow a row of grain between rows of crops. In some cases one row of grain is sown between every three to six rows of onions or other crops given similar spacing, but where wind damage is severe, a row of barley or other grain is planted for each row of onions. When onions or other crops are planted very early in the spring, the grain should be sown at the same time, but for crops planted later the grain crop should be sown a week or two before the vegetable crop is to be planted. One of the objections to the use of small grains between the rows is the difficulty of destroying the grain plants. Unless they are removed from the field, they are likely to continue to grow after they have been pulled, or up-rooted by cultivating, thus taking moisture and nutrients needed by the crop plants. Some experiments have been conducted to kill the grain plants by use of chemicals, but without much success because of the difficulty of keeping the chemical off the onions or other crop being grown.

Home Gardening Page 5

Soil Preparation ✓ 30
Chapter 3
Manure ch 4 ✓ 37 etc
Green Manure ✓ 44
Potatoes ✓ 372
corn ✓ 553

CHAPTER 4

Manures and Soil-improving Crops

One of the most difficult problems facing a vegetable grower is to maintain the organic-matter content of the soil. Most vegetables are grown on farms that are intensively cropped; that is, one or more cultivated crops are grown on the land each year, and the crop residues are not sufficient to replace the organic matter lost annually. The loss of organic matter is due to the action of microorganisms which decompose it ultimately to carbon dioxide. The rate of loss depends on the soil type, moisture, temperature, and the type of crop grown. Microorganisms need both water and air for their growth and action. The rate of decomposition is slow in dry soil owing to the lack of water and is slow in wet soil owing to the lack of air. The rate of action also depends on the temperature, the higher the temperature the more rapid the decomposition. The type of crop grown is important since crops differ in the amount of refuse left to be turned for the next crop. The rate of loss of organic matter is greater when a crop such as cabbage is grown than when a crop such as sweet corn is grown. Most of the organic matter produced by cabbage is sold, while only a small portion of that produced by sweet corn is removed from the land.

Organic matter is important as a source of plant nutrients and because of its effect on certain properties of the soil. Since it is colloidal in nature, it is a part of the base exchange complex of the soil. In light, sandy soils the contribution to the exchange capacity is important, and increasing the organic-matter content increases the amount of nutrients a soil can hold in a form which resists leaching. In a light, sandy soil it also increases the water-holding capacity of the soil, but does not have a great effect on the soil structure since these soils have a low clay content. In a heavy soil with a high clay content, organic matter does not play an important role in the exchange capacity, but it has an important function in developing a good soil structure. Various compounds formed during decomposition cement clay particles together into aggregates which make the soil more permeable to water and improve the aeration of the soil. Organic matter has only a slight effect on the water-holding capacity of heavy soils. Thus, soil organic matter is the key to soil fertility since it regulates the soil water and air supply, which in turn control the rate at which nutrients are absorbed by the root.

Soil organic matter can be maintained at a fairly high level by growing rotations which include sod crops and few cultivated or intertilled crops. This system of farming is not economically feasible for a vegetable grower because vegetable land is too valuable to be used for low-value crops. The vegetable grower, therefore, must rely on animal manures and soil-improving crops as a means of supplying soil organic matter.

MANURES

At one time manure was the only fertilizer used in vegetable growing. Since there are few horses on farms and in the cities, the supply of manure is limited. Most vegetable growers are specialized and do not have any kind of livestock as a source of manure. In a few areas where poultry is grown intensively there is a plentiful supply of manure for some vegetable growers. In most areas the supply of manure is limited and expensive so the vegetable grower must use the manure efficiently. It is no problem to supply minerals to plants in the form of chemical fertilizers, but the problem is to supply organic matter to maintain the soil structure. One way to meet the problem would be to grow vegetables on cheaper land so that long rotations could be practiced, but this is seldom practical. Where supplies of manure are limited they can be supplemented with soil-improving crops to help maintain the soil organic-matter level. With limited supplies, the manure should be used on crops which give the greatest response or on crops of the highest value. With a limited supply it would be far better to use it on melons and similar crops, which give good responses, rather than on a crop like sweet corn or dry beans, which give relatively small responses. In some areas there is a possibility of using manure substitutes such as composts, sewage sludges, and other organic waste materials.

Benefits of Manure. Manure is of value as a source of humus, a source of both major and minor nutrients, as a carrier and promoter of beneficial organisms, and possibly as a source of growth-promoting substances. On decomposition of the organic matter carbon dioxide is set free, and this may be of direct value in increasing the CO_2 content of the air and of indirect value in making available some of the mineral elements in the soil.

MANURE AS A SOURCE OF HUMUS. Vegetable growers would not be justified in buying manure for the nitrogen, phosphorus, and potash it contained because these elements can be purchased more cheaply in chemical fertilizers. The main benefit of manure in vegetable growing is its organic-matter content. The manure and bedding or litter mixed with it provide one way for supplying organic matter to the soil. It requires fairly large amounts of manure to replace the organic matter lost each year during cultivation. The amount required varies from 10 to 20 tons per acre per year, depending upon the cropping system and the area.

MANURE AS A SOURCE OF NUTRIENTS. The value of manure as a source of nutrient elements depends on the quantity contained and, to some extent, on the form in which the element occurs. The quantity depends on the kind of manure, the quantity and kind of bedding or other material mixed with it, and the care the manure has had before being applied to the land.

Table 4.1. Pounds of Plant Nutrients in 1 Ton of Animal Manures, Including Bedding

Kind of animal	Nitrogen	Phosphoric acid	Potash
Horse..............	13.2	5.1	12.1
Cow................	11.4	3.1	9.9
Pig.................	9.9	6.7	9.3
Sheep..............	15.8	6.7	18.0
Steer..............	15.0	6.0	8.0
Hen (no litter)........	21.6	16.4	10.2
Duck..............	11.4	28.8	9.8

Table 4.1 shows the composition of various manures stated on the basis of number of pounds of plant nutrients in a ton, as calculated by Gustafson (1944) from published analyses. All the manures except hen and duck manure are lower in phosphorus than in potash, and all except duck manure are higher in nitrogen than in phosphorus. These values are not strictly comparable to the same amount of nutrients supplied in chemical fertilizers owing to the difference in availability in the two forms of material. The nitrogen in manure is slowly available, and only about 25 to 50 per cent of it is available to the crop the first year after application. This slow availability is one of the important properties of manure in increasing yields on light sandy soils. The nitrogen in chemical fertilizers is soluble and subject to leaching and may be washed out of the root zone. Since the nitrogen in manure is slowly available and does not leach, it sometimes is the major factor in producing high yields on soils subject to leaching. Slow availability of nitrogen is not always desirable since many vegetables require large amounts of nitrogen over a short period of time. The rate of release of nitrogen from

the manure depends on the soil temperature, the higher the temperature the faster the release, provided there is sufficient water and air for decomposition to occur. Since the growth of vegetables is somewhat related to soil temperature, the periods when the crops make rapid growth coincide with the rapid release of nitrogen from the manure. The recovery of the phosphorus in manure by plants is sometimes slightly higher than that obtained with chemical fertilizers. One possible explanation for this is that the carbon dioxide released in decomposition of the manure makes more phosphorus available from the supply already in the soil. There is little difference in the recovery and availability of potash in manure and chemical fertilizers since it occurs in soluble forms in both cases.

MANURE AS A CARRIER AND PROMOTER OF USEFUL ORGANISMS. Manure contains organisms which break down the organic matter in the manure itself and aid in the decomposition of humus already in the soil. During decomposition of the manure, materials are set free which act on some of the mineral compounds and make them more readily available to the growing plant. Manure has been found to be of value on new muck soils even when applied in very small quantities. This could not be accounted for on the basis of nutrients supplied, since the beneficial effect is often marked where chemical fertilizers are applied in large quantities. It is thought that the marked effect of such a small quantity of manure on new muck is due to the organisms present in the manure. After the initial application, further applications of manure, in many cases, are of little or no value except for the nutrients contained. On high-lime mucks fresh, strawy manures may be beneficial for another reason, namely, preventing nitrates from accumulating in toxic quantities. Under favorable moisture and temperature conditions, nitrification goes on so rapidly in such soils that crops are sometimes injured by excess of nitrates. Coarse manure, straw, or other carbonaceous materials furnish energy for soil organisms which utilize nitrates. The organisms may so reduce the quantity of nitrates as to eliminate injury to crop plants. It should be borne in mind, however, that the nitrates used by the organisms are built up into more complex nitrogen compounds, which upon the death of the organisms are returned to the soil. These microorganisms might, therefore, be considered as conservers of nitrogen since they utilize the nitrates, some of which might otherwise be lost through leaching.

Detrimental Effect of Fresh Manure, Straw, etc. Coarse manure, straw, and other similar materials sometimes have a marked depressing effect on the yield of crops. It was formerly thought that the injurious effects often noticed following the application of fresh manure were due to an excess of soluble nitrogen in the manures. Evidence now available indicates that the injury is due mainly to a deficiency of nitrates owing to their utilization by organisms which decompose the carbonaceous material. Laboratory studies show that such results occur when the added organic matter contains a large quantity of carbon and a small quantity of nitrogen. A ratio of carbon to nitrogen greater than 15:1 usually results in competition between microorganisms and crop plants for nitrates already present in the soil. Where the soil contains little available nitrogen or where nitrification takes place slowly, this competition is serious and results in injury to the crop. One remedy is to turn under manure or other material far enough in advance to allow it to become partly decomposed before the crop is planted on the land. Another remedy is to supply additional nitrogen to take care of the temporary deficiency. As already mentioned, the organisms will return most of the nitrogen to the soil as their source of energy has been expended.

Losses in Manure. The analyses given in Table 4.1 do not take into consideration losses incident to the ordinary handling of manure. There are three causes of losses: (1) loss of urine by drainage from the stable or yard, (2) loss of soluble material by leaching, and (3) loss of nitrogen by fermentation. The loss of nutrients by leaching may be as much as 60 to 70 per cent in 6 months if unprotected. It is safe to say that under the usual careless manner of storing farm manures out of doors, at least 50 per cent of the value of the nutrients is lost. Part of this loss, if not most of it, can be prevented by proper piling to prevent rain water from running through the pile and nutrients being lost in drainage water. This can be prevented by stacking manure in compact, flat piles not less than 4 feet deep. With this depth there is little loss by leaching, provided the sides and ends are nearly perpendicular. By keeping the manure compact and moist, fermentation is controlled and loss of nitrogen is kept down. It is often necessary and is practically always desirable to apply water to the pile of manure to prevent excessive heating or "fire fanging." The manure should be turned two or three times at intervals during the period it is piled in order to have uniform decomposition. In turning the manure, that from the inside of the old pile should be placed on the top or sides of the new one.

Fresh Manure versus Rotted Manure. From discussion of the losses incident to storing, it would seem to be the best practice to apply the manure to the land as soon as it is produced. This is not always feasible or even desirable. Very often crops are occupying all of the land so that the manure must be stored until the crops are removed. The main advantages of applying manure while it is fresh are: (1) there is little loss of valuable materials through leaching and decomposition; (2) some insoluble compounds in the soil are made soluble through the contact with the decomposing manure; (3) desirable organisms are supplied in fresh manure; and (4) heavy soils are improved by the coarse material. The possible disadvantages of fresh manure are: (1) burning effect on the plants, due to rapid decomposition of urine in manure, especially on open porous soils, (2) utilization of nitrates by the organisms in the manure, thus causing nitrogen deficiency in the soil, and (3) interfering with movement of water after being plowed under. The injury from all of these can be obviated by plowing under far enough in advance to ensure decay before the crop is planted. In addition to the disadvantages mentioned, fresh manure usually contains weed seeds and often carries spores of plant diseases. Decomposed manure contains the mineral elements in a more available form and in greater concentration than does fresh manure. The greater concentration is due to the fact that carbonaceous material has been reduced in quantity by the decomposition. The nitrogen in decomposed manure is not so readily available as that in the urine of fresh manure. The main advantages of decomposed manure are: (1) it is more even in action and carries a more evenly balanced combination of nitrogen, phosphorus, and potash than fresh manure; (2) it is not likely to cause burning; (3) the weed seeds are largely destroyed during decomposition; (4) it does not interfere with soil preparation and cultivation; and (5) it does not cause nitrogen starvation due to competition of the microorganisms and crop plants for nitrates.

Time to Apply Manure. The proper time to apply manure depends on the kind, the stage of its decomposition, the crops to be grown, and the rotations to be followed. When cow manure is to be applied, it should be plowed under as far in advance of planting as convenient. Fall application is desirable if the land is to be plowed before winter. In the North it is not desirable to leave manure on the surface of the ground during the winter on account of loss due to leaching when the ground is frozen. Where vegetables are grown in rotation with general farm crops, it is desirable to apply the manure to the vegetable crop or to the crop preceding.

Rate and Method of Application. The rate of application of manure should be governed largely by economic considerations. The supply of manure available, the kind of crops to be grown, and the character and fertility of the soil should also be considered. Heavy applications of manure cannot be justified on crops which bring a relatively low return. Where the supply is limited or the price high, light applications will usually bring the greatest net returns. With most vegetable crops 10- to 15-ton applications of horse or other animal manures that contain a similar percentage of nitrogen, supplemented with chemical fertilizers, will give greater money returns than heavier applications of manure.

The rate of application of hen manure should be lower than that of any of the other kinds that contain less nitrogen. It should be borne in mind that manure is not a balanced fertilizer; for this reason it is more economical to use a moderate quantity and to supplement it with chemicals.

Under most conditions broadcast application is best. The most common practice is to broadcast the manure before plowing the land. This is essential where unrotted manure is used, since it interferes with soil preparation and cultivation unless plowed under. Well-rotted manure may be applied to plowed land and mixed with the surface by harrowing. A manure spreader can be used to advantage where the quantity used justifies the investment. The spreader saves hand labor and spreads the manure more evenly than is feasible by hand.

Manure is sometimes applied in the furrow for melons and cucumbers. There is some advantage in this method where the quantity of manure is limited because it results in greater concentration in the region of the first-formed roots. Some advantage is also claimed for this method of applying fresh horse manure because of the heating of the soil due to the fermentation of the material. This heat hastens the germination and early growth of melons and cucumbers. It is doubtful, however, if the furrow method of application pays for the extra labor of applying except where only a small quantity is available. Better distribution is obtained by broadcasting.

Composts. When manure became scarce on farms because of the decrease in number of horses, there was considerable interest in developing substitutes for manure. Artificial manures or composts received a lot of attention at one time, but the use of such materials is limited.

Piling manure as described is often termed "composting," but in the true sense of the word a compost is a mixture of materials as manure and soil or manure and leaves or other litter. In making a compost, fresh manure is piled in alternate layers with absorbent materials. One method of making a compost heap is to start with a few inches of loose soil or other absorbent material as a foundation and place on this a layer of fresh manure, then alternating layers of absorbent material and manure. Muck and peat are good absorbent materials and are used to a considerable extent in making compost in some of the European countries. In many parts of the United States these materials could be used to good advantage. The details of making a compost heap vary in respect to absorbent materials used, thickness of the layers, depth of the pile, etc. Sufficient absorbent material should be used to take up the soluble material and the gases from the manure. The entire surface of the pile should be covered with a layer of soil to prevent loss of ammonia.

In making a compost heap it is advisable to make use of all valuable material that is available. Trimmings from vegetables, unless seriously diseased, garbage, straw, hay that is not suitable for feed, weeds, lawn clippings, and leaves may all be added to the compost heap. The process of decomposition is hastened by adding a source of nitrogen for the microorganisms which decompose the carbonaceous materials. In many cases a complete fertilizer is added to the compost pile, especially when manure is not used. Since the microorganisms function most efficiently under slightly acid conditions, lime should be added to reduce the acidity when necessary. In a few weeks after the pile is completed it should be turned over and uniformly mixed and again covered with a layer of absorbent, unless it is to be used at once.

Composts are seldom practical for large-scale vegetable operation because of the large amount of labor they require and the inability of the large grower to obtain sufficient organic residues. Compost piles are popular with small-scale vegetable growers and home gardeners. They are very valuable for greenhouse crops and for growing young plants for transplanting. The amount of compost required in these cases is relatively small, and the amount of labor invested is not too great.

SOIL-IMPROVING CROPS

Soil-improving crops are those grown solely for the purpose of improving conditions of the soil for the growth of succeeding crops. The terms *green-manure crops* and *cover crops* are sometimes used. Green-manure crops are those that are grown especially for soil improvement, are turned under while they are still green, and usually are grown during the same season of the year as the vegetable crops. Thus, land in green-manure crops is not available for growing vegetables, at least during part of the year. Cover crops are those which are grown both for protection of the soil and for soil improvement, but are grown during the season of the year when vegetables do not occupy the land. They are commonly grown over the winter in the North and in other regions where vegetables are produced in the summer, and they are grown during the summer in regions where vegetables are produced in the winter.

They may be plowed under as green or as dead material depending on the crop and other conditions, but most of them are plowed under green. Green-manuring is one of the oldest methods to maintain or increase crop production. Green-manure crops were grown by the ancients, and their beneficial effects were known long before it was understood in what ways they acted to increase crop production. Experiments have confirmed and explained the fact that green manures favorably affect succeeding crops. When a soil-improving crop is turned under, the various nutrients which have gone into the making of the crop are returned to the soil and a quantity of organic matter is added. The organic matter improves the physical condition of the soil and serves as food for microorganisms. The organic matter added in a soil-improving crop is usually more effective than an equal quantity added on the surface and plowed down. The increased benefits are due mainly to the distribution of the organic matter. The roots of the soil-improving crop growing throughout the soil profile results in a good distribution of organic matter throughout the root zone. The mechanical action of the roots is thought to play an important role in improving soil structure. Soil-improving crops should be selected as much on the basis of the root system as on the amount of growth produced in the tops.

Soil-improving crops absorb nutrients from the soil which otherwise might be lost by leaching. These nutrients are held in the plants until they are turned under and then are released to the succeeding crop. In the case of legumes, considerable amounts of nitrogen may be added to the soil by the growth of this crop since atmospheric nitrogen is fixed by the bacteria in the nodules on the roots. In many areas one of the most important functions of a soil-improving crop is to control soil erosion. The dense stand of plants and absence of tillage in the soil-improving crop conserve much of the topsoil which might otherwise be lost because of wind and water erosion.

Selection of Soil-improving Crops. In selecting crops for improving the soil the following points should be considered: (1) adaptation of the crop to the climate and soil, (2) quantity of vegetable matter produced in the time available, (3) character of root growth, (4) ease of incorporating the plant material with the soil, (5) the time which the crop is to be planted, and (6) whether the crop is to be turned under while green or as dead material.

Since in vegetable growing the organic matter is of greatest importance, under most conditions, the crop or combination of crops selected usually should be the ones that will produce the largest quantity of humus-forming material in the time available. Under most conditions of intensive culture in the North, nonlegumes, especially rye, come nearest to fulfilling the requirements. In this type of vegetable growing the obtaining of nitrogen through legumes is a secondary consideration. It is cheaper to buy nitrogen in the form of fertilizers than to get it from legumes, if the growing of legumes increases the time necessary for the production of the soil-improving crop. In other words, if rye or other nonlegume will furnish more humus in the time available than a legume crop, it usually would be preferable to grow the nonlegume and to buy the nitrogen. When the time available for growing a soil-improving crop is in summer, a crop which thrives in hot weather should be selected. For cool-season growth, as in late fall in the North and during winter in the cooler portions of the South, some hardy crop, such as rye or rye grass, is desirable.

The primary purpose of these crops is to provide organic matter and conserve nutrients, and they should be grown according to the best agronomic practices of the area. That is, the soil-improving crops should be fertilized as they would be if they were to be grown for a cash crop. Legumes should be fertilized in the same way as they would be if they were to be grown as a hay crop. Nonlegumes should receive the full amount of fertilizer that would be necessary if they were to be grown as a pasture or hay crop. This use of fertilizer on the cover crops does not represent inefficient fertilizer usage since the cover crops will conserve these fertilizer nutrients until they are plowed down for the succeeding vegetable crop. The amount of organic matter produced usually is much greater when the crops receive proper fertilization and care. In many cases it would be more economical to use part of the fertilizer intended for the vegetable on the green-manure crop. In many cases this is more efficient fertilizer usage than applying all the fertilizer on the vegetable and as a result having a poor growth of the green-manure or cover crop.

Legumes. Where all the conditions of weather, soil, and cropping systems are favorable, the vegetable grower would undoubtedly select one of the legumes. Such crops furnish nitrogen in addition to the humus and because of this are more valuable than nonlegumes. Among the leguminous crops grown are red clover, mammoth clover, crimson clover, bur clover, sweet clover, cowpeas, soybeans, several species of vetch, field peas, Austrian winter peas, three species of lupines, two species of lespedeza, kudzu, velvet beans, crotolaria, sesbania, and several others.

Crimson clover is one of the most important soil-improving crops for vegetables since it thrives well on sandy and sandy-loam soil. The crop does not stand severe winters, so it is not grown over the winter north of New Jersey. In regions where it survives over winter, the seed is sown at the last cultivation of late vegetables. Fifteen to twenty pounds of seed should be sown to the acre either at the last cultivation or at least soon enough for the crop to make good growth before cold weather sets in. In some regions better results were obtained when crimson clover was grown with a nonlegume, such as rye grass. In Northern areas it may be seeded early in the spring for a summer crop. A grass is usually included in the seeding and it is plowed down the following spring.

Red clover, mammoth clover, and alfalfa are sometimes used as green-manure crops in the North. These crops usually compete with vegetables for use of the land; however, they may follow early vegetables. Frequently, one of these legumes is planted at the same time as the processing crop of peas. The peas are an excellent nurse crop for seedlings of these legumes. Annual varieties of alfalfa offer considerable promise as a soil-improving crop in vegetable-growing areas since they make more growth the first year than perennial varieties and are not so difficult to eradicate.

The cowpea is the most important green-manure crop in the South because it produces a large amount of material in a short time and thrives in nearly all sections. It requires hot weather for good growth and does not succeed well in cooler portions of the North. This crop is grown mostly after early vegetables have been removed and before starting fall or winter crops. Where the root knot nematode is present, resistant varieties of cowpeas should be planted. The seed is usually broadcast at the rate of about 2 bushels per acre or is planted with a drill.

The soybean thrives better on a heavier soil and in a cooler climate than the cowpea; therefore, it can be used in the North. The growth is coarse and more difficult to plow under and slower to decompose than the finer growth of most other legumes. The seed is usually broadcast or drilled in the same manner as cowpeas.

Hairy vetch is grown to some extent as a soil-improving crop or as a cover crop on sandy soils in the North. It may be sown alone, but under most conditions it is best to sow with rye. The seed should be sown in July or early August at the rate of 60 to 80 pounds per acre when grown alone or 20 to 30 pounds per acre when grown with rye.

Sweet clover is a good soil-improving crop under some conditions. Sweet clover types consist of annual and biennial types both with either white or yellow flowers. The annual yellow type is useful in the South where it does well and is a valuable green-manure and cover crop. The biennial yellow and biennial white are used in Northern regions. The seed may be sown in the fall, winter, or spring, depending somewhat upon climatic conditions. Scarified seed should be used to ensure quick germination, and 15 to 20 pounds of seed per acre is ample. Seed may be drilled or broadcast.

Three species of annual lupines are used to some extent as soil-improving crops. These are the white, yellow, and blue lupines. They require cool weather for best growth and are grown as winter annuals in the South and as spring and early-summer annuals in the North. The blue lupine is probably most widely used mostly on the coastal plain soils of the East coast. While it produces large amounts of organic matter it is attacked by root knot nematode and by several organisms which cause diseases of vegetable crops. It should not precede tomatoes, peppers, melons, and related crops because of the disease factors.

Two species of lespedeza (*Lespedeza striata* and *L. stipulacea*) are good soil-improving crops for the South. *L. striata* is the common lespedeza, and there are two improved varieties, Tennessee 76 and Kobe. *L. stipulacea* is the form known as Korean. Both of these species are adapted to the South, but Korean succeeds farther north than the common lespedeza. They are seeded early in the South from February to April at rates of 20 to 30 pounds of seed per acre. They usually compete with vegetables for the land during spring and early summer but are useful soil-improving crops for vegetables planted late in the fall or winter.

Two species of crotolaria (*Crotolaria spectabilis* and *C. striata*) are used for green-manure crops in the South. Both species behave as annuals and make their best growth during hot weather. They are especially adapted to sandy land in the South and are widely used in Florida as green-manure crops for winter vegetables. The seed is broadcast or drilled in the late spring at rates of 15 to 30 pounds per acre. The crop attains a height of 3 to 6 feet and produces a large amount of organic matter.

Common sesbania (*Sesbania macrocarpa*) is also a popular annual legume for soil-improving crops in the South. It is a subtropical plant and does well in hot weather. It does not grow as well on sandy soils as does crotolaria but is better adapted to the heavier soils. It sometimes is used in California, Arizona, Texas, and Florida as a green-manure crop in the areas which produce winter vegetables. The seed may be broadcast or drilled at rates of about 20 pounds per acre. Under ideal conditions the plant reaches a height of 6 to 8 feet and produces a large amount of organic matter.

Seed Inoculation. When any of the legumes are to be grown on land that has not grown the same crop, or another crop that has the same bacteria in the nodules on the roots, the seed or the soil should be inoculated with the appropriate bacteria. The material for inoculating the seed can be purchased from commercial firms that make a specialty of legume inoculation or from seed dealers.

Nonlegumes. Of the nonlegumes rye is by far the most popular soil-improving crop because it can be grown on nearly all kinds of soils and is not adversely affected by cold weather. Rye may be planted later than any other green-manure or cover crop and, therefore, is a valuable crop after the harvest of late vegetables in the North where no legume except vetch is of much value. When vegetable crops are harvested in late summer, rye should be sown immediately to obtain good growth before winter. Under such circumstances, however, domestic rye grass and field brome grass usually will produce more organic matter than rye. Where late vegetable crops are harvested rye can be planted but will not make much growth until spring. The production of organic matter would be quite small if an early crop was to be planted on this land. To obtain a good crop of rye to turn under, at least 2 bushels of seed to the acre should be broadcast or drilled.

Domestic rye grass and field brome grass are good winter cover crops in the North provided they can be planted 6 to 8 weeks before killing frosts occur in the fall. These two crops are used most successfully when sown between the rows of sweet corn, late cabbage, or other vegetables at the last cultivation. After the crop has been removed the grass should be fertilized with a complete fertilizer supplying 30 to 50 pounds per acre of the three major nutrients. The fertilizer stimulates a large amount of growth in the fall and greatly increases the production of organic matter. The root systems are dense and heavy, and the top growth is fine, so that the material decomposes rapidly.

Many other nonlegumes are used to some extent as green-manure crops, but they are grown in competition with vegetables. These include corn, sudan grass, sunflowers, rape, mustard, buckwheat, and millet. Pearl millet is probably one of the most widely used summer soil-improving crops in the North. It produces a large amount of organic matter in a relatively short time. The nonlegumes do not add nitrogen to the soil except as the decaying organic matter furnishes carbon as food for organisms that fix atmospheric nitrogen. They do, however, furnish large amounts of organic matter and absorb nitrates and other soluble nutrients and prevent their loss by leaching. All of these nonlegume crops respond well to fertilization. Experiments have shown that the plant nutrient content of the soil-improving crop is increased more than can be accounted for by the amount of fertilizer added. The fertilizer stimulates rapid, vigorous growth of the plants, and with a larger root system they are more efficient in utilizing nutrient reserves already in the soil. In many areas, the nonlegumes produce more organic matter in a short period of time than do any of the commonly used legumes.

Turning Under Soil-improving Crops. The best time to turn under soil-improving crops depends on: (1) the time the succeeding crop is to be planted, (2) the kind of soil-improving crop, (3) the season of the year when the crop is grown, (4) the condition of the soil, and (5) the climatic conditions. When the soil-improving crop is to be followed by early vegetables, it must be turned under in the fall, winter, or early spring. If a late crop is to follow the soil-improving crop, the turning under should be delayed as long as is feasible in order to produce a large quantity of humus-forming material. It should be borne in mind, however, that the organisms causing the breaking down of the plant material consume nitrates and may thereby interfere with the growth of the vegetable crop.

The recommended practice is to apply from 40 to 100 pounds of nitrogen in the form of calcium cyanamid, ammonium nitrate, urea, or some other nitrogen fertilizer to the acre at the time a nonlegume soil-improving crop is turned under. This is especially important when material having a wide carbon-nitrogen ratio, such as mature or nearly mature rye, is turned under. Nitrogen applied with the soil-improving crop is utilized by soil microorganisms in decomposing the plant material, and when the material has decomposed, the organisms die and the nitrogen is released to the crop. This release usually occurs a few weeks after plowing depending on the temperature and moisture conditions. It is generally considered that plowing under nitrogen with a soil-improving crop takes the place of a nitrogen side-dressing since the nitrogen is released about the time when a side-dressing would be made.

The soil-improving crop may have an injurious effect on the succeeding crop because of utilization of soil moisture. Warren (1945) has shown a marked reduction in yield of sweet corn in a dry season when rye was turned under in early May in New York, a few days before the corn was planted. That the reduced yield on the rye plots resulted from the rye drying out the soil is shown by the fact that soil moisture was much lower in the rye plots than in those where no rye was grown. Similar results have been obtained on Long Island where a green manure was turned under a short time before planting a late crop of cauliflower. In a wet season, or when irrigation is used, this injurious effect of the soil-improving crop is eliminated. For these reasons it is important to turn under the material far enough in advance to allow for partial decomposition before the next crop is planted. The time required for decomposition depends on the kind of material, the stage of growth, the temperature of the soil, the soil moisture, and perhaps other factors.

In general, the more succulent the material is at the time it is turned under, the more quickly it decomposes. Dry material decomposes much more slowly than green material, and for this reason it is desirable to turn under soil-improving crops before they are mature, unless considerable time is to elapse between the plowing and the planting of the succeeding crop.

There is a common belief that turning under a large quantity of green material will increase the acidity of the soil. While it is true that on decomposition of material of this kind organic acids are set free, the soil acidity is not increased, or if it is, the condition is temporary. Turning under humus-forming material generally does not increase the lime requirement of the soil.

Plant material decomposes most rapidly when the soil is warm and well supplied with moisture. If the soil is dry when the soil-improving crop is turned under, little or no decomposition will take place until moisture is supplied by rain or by irrigation. In regions where summer droughts are prevalent, it is best to turn under the soil-improving crop while the soil is still moist, unless irrigation is practiced.

Sewage Sludge. In some areas the sludge from sewage-disposal plants is available for use on vegetables and other crops. There are two types of sludge, activated and digested. The activated sludge contains about 5 per cent N, 5 per cent P_2O_5, and small amounts of K_2O, while the digested types contain about 2 per cent N, 1 per cent P_2O_5, and a trace of K_2O. Both may contain varying amounts of minor elements and other plant nutrients, depending on the area. The availability of nitrogen in the sewage sludge is about the same as that for manure or cottonseed meal. In most areas, sewage sludge is too expensive to use for commercial vegetable growing as a source of nutrients, and it is doubtful that the organic matter supplied would justify the cost of the material. Digested sludges are usually considered safe (in so far as health is concerned) to use on vegetables if they are plowed down before the crop is planted, but activated sludges need heat treatment before they can be used as a fertilizer. Some states have regulations specifying the conditions under which sewage sludges can be used as garden fertilizers. These materials have their greatest use as fertilizers for turfs since a slowly available source of nitrogen is desirable. This slowly available supply of nitrogen limits their use as a fertilizer for vegetable crops.

CHAPTER 5

Commercial Fertilizers and Lime

COMMERCIAL FERTILIZERS

The term commercial fertilizer is used to distinguish between animal manures and other materials applied to the soil to furnish raw materials to the plant. When the term came into use manure was not considered a commercial product, while the other materials used as fertilizers were so considered, hence the use of the word commercial. A commercial fertilizer may consist of a single chemical compound, as nitrate of soda or muriate of potash; or it may consist of a mixture of several chemical compounds; or of organic materials such as bone meal, tankage, and cottonseed meal. All materials supplied to the soil to furnish plants with raw material except animal manures and other organic wastes are called fertilizers or commercial fertilizers. Lime is a fertilizer although applied mainly to correct acidity of the soil.

Importance of Commercial Fertilizers. In vegetable growing, commercial fertilizers are very important and are increasing in use every year. This increase is due to the shortage of animal manures and to the increasing knowledge of the value of commercial fertilizers. It is possible to grow large crops without the use of commercial fertilizers, provided manure is used in large quantities, but this is not an economical practice. Manure is not a balanced fertilizer, being especially deficient in phosphorus. If manure is applied in large enough quantities to furnish sufficient phosphorus for large yields, it would result in a waste of nitrogen and potash. Even with manure, it is usually economical to use commercial fertilizer in some form. Manure is scarce in most of the vegetable-producing areas, and growers cannot afford to use enough of it to supply the nutrients required for producing large yields.

Chemical Elements Essential to Growth. For many years it was believed that only 10 elements, carbon, hydrogen, oxygen, nitrogen, phosphorus, sulfur, potassium, calcium, magnesium, and iron were essential to the growth of higher green plants. It is now well established that other elements are necessary for the growth of green plants. Experiments have shown that manganese, boron, copper, zinc, and molybdenum are required for all higher plants and that chlorine, silicon, and sodium may be required for some of them. The essential elements commonly supplied by the soil are divided for convenience into two groups, major elements (macroelements) and minor elements (microelements). Minor elements are just as essential for growth as major elements, but the amount required for normal growth is much smaller in the case of minor elements. The major elements are nitrogen, phosphorus, potassium, magnesium, calcium, and sulfur. The minor elements usually include iron, manganese, boron, copper, zinc, molybdenum, chlorine, sodium, and silicon, but many others are included in this classification by some workers even though they are not known to be essential to the growth of plants.

Merely because an element is essential to growth does not mean that it must be supplied to the soil. Most soils contain sufficient quantities of many of the mineral elements, but a large part of the land used for vegetable production must be supplied with nitrogen, phosphorus, and potassium to produce large yields. Soils in many areas are deficient in calcium, others in magnesium, and still others in one or more of the minor elements. Carbon, hydrogen, and oxygen are obtained from the air and from water. Most of the nitrogen comes from the soil since most vegetables cannot utilize atmospheric nitrogen. Bacteria in the nodules on the roots of legumes (peas and beans) utilize atmospheric nitrogen, and this source of supply is of some value to legumes. Other plants must depend entirely on nitrogen in combined form in the soil. All the other elements are obtained entirely from the soil. If the soil does not contain the essential elements in forms that are available to the plant, they must be supplied in fertilizer. In most vegetable growing it is desirable to use fertilizers even though the soil contains a large potential supply of the nutrients. This is due to the fact that the elements usually are present in forms that become available too slowly for the best growth of vegetables.

Commercial fertilizers are purchased mainly for the content of one or more of three major nutrients, nitrogen, phosphorus, and potassium. A fertilizer containing all three of these nutrients is called a complete fertilizer although other mineral elements are essential to growth of the plants and some soils are deficient in one or more of several elements. Some of these elements such as sulfur, sodium, chlorine, and calcium may be present in mixed fertilizer in combination with nitrogen, phosphorus, or potassium. Minute amounts of some of the minor elements may be present as impurities in commercial fertilizers, but generally the amount contained is not sufficient to satisfy needs for crops growing in soils deficient in one of these minor elements. With an increase in use of synthetic nitrogen salts and more pure forms of potash salts, the minor-element content of fertilizers is much smaller than it has been in the past when less pure salts were used.

Many physiological disorders have been shown by experiments to result from a deficiency of one or more of the essential elements. Some of these troubles appear to be increasing in importance, and it seems safe to assume that such disorders will become more and more prevalent as time goes on unless the deficient elements are supplied to the soil. These deficiency troubles result mostly from a deficiency of some of the minor elements. Many factors have contributed to the deficiency of minor elements in the soil. Some of these factors are:

1. Intensive production of crops and continued drain on the supply of mineral elements in the soil by removal in the harvested crop

2. Loss by leaching

3. Decrease in the use of manure in vegetable production (manure contains all the mineral elements that are in the food consumed by the animals, and when manure is used in large amounts minor-element deficiencies are seldom encountered)

4. Increase in purity and concentration of the common fertilizer chemicals (fertilizer elements are supplied mostly from chemical sources rather than organic materials of plant and animal origin such as cottonseed meal, dried blood, and tankage)

Chemical Tests for Determining Fertilizer Needs. For many years there has been great interest in chemical tests of soils, especially rapid chemical tests to determine the soluble nutrients for purposes of estimating fertilizer needs. Many tests have been devised, and some have been commercialized. Most experiment stations and agricultural colleges have a soil-testing service for growers in their locality. These tests have value as an aid in diagnosing nutrient deficiencies and excesses when interpreted by properly trained men. They are particularly valuable in determining cause of unproductiveness of soils, but they should not be expected to give the necessary information for determining the exact fertilizer requirement of any crop on a particular soil. No form of soil analysis will supply this information. The methods of making the tests vary considerably with respect to acidity and other characteristics of the extracting solution. Some extracting solutions consist of only an acid, while others consist of an acid well buffered with salts. The ratio of soil to extracting solution and the time of contact vary also in the different procedures. As might be expected, different procedures do not give the same results even when used on the same soil. The fact that the procedures differ is not of major importance, but rather that one procedure gives consistent results on the same soil. It does not matter what type of extracting solution is used so long as the results from the chemical tests can be correlated with actual crop responses in the field. The limiting factor in the use of these soil tests is the relative scarcity of correlating crop-response experiments. Usually these experiments must be run on many soil types and in many areas before the chemical soil tests have much value. As the various experiment stations accumulate more of this basic information, the value of their chemical soil tests will increase.

Many investigators have described plant tests or tissue analyses for determining fertilizer needs of crop plants. These tests also vary considerably in the type of extracting solution used and in the part or parts of the plant taken for analysis. These tissue tests have much in their favor since they measure the amount of nutrients the plant has taken up from the soil rather than depending on some chemical test to indicate availability of nutrients to plants. The fact that a nutrient is not contained in large amounts in the plant tissue does not necessarily mean that it is lacking in the soil since other factors may have interfered with uptake of the particular nutrient. However, these tests do seem particularly valuable for determining nutrient deficiencies. Chemical tests of both the soil and the plant would seem to be more reliable than tests of either alone. While these soil and plant tests undoubtedly are of value in the hands of trained, experienced persons, they might be worthless or entirely misleading in the hands of amateurs. Experienced workers do not base their diagnosis or recommendations entirely on the results of chemical tests but take into consideration information from many other sources.

Nitrogen. Of the three elements commonly supplied by fertilizers, nitrogen has the quickest and most pronounced effect. It is a constituent of all proteins which are the active components of protoplasm and is a constituent of the chlorophyll molecule. It stimulates vegetative growth and encourages the development of large stems and leaves. Nitrogen tends to produce succulence, a quality of great importance in many vegetables. Since it favors vegetative growth it may delay maturity of fruits and seeds. Nitrogen is more likely to be the limiting factor than either phosphorus or potash on most vegetable soils since it is lost from the root zone by leaching. A nitrogen deficiency is characterized by a stunted, yellow, woody plant. Recovery from the deficiency is usually rapid following application of nitrogen fertilizers.

The main sources of nitrogen used in fertilizers are synthetic compounds. The most important sources of nitrogen in mixed fertilizers are ammonium nitrate, nitrogen solutions, anhydrous ammonia, ammonium sulfate, and urea. Cyanamid and nitrate of soda are used mostly as materials for separate application. Nitrate of soda is mined from deposits in Chile and once was the most important source of nitrogen, but the use of synthetic nitrate of soda exceeds that of the natural material. Cotton-seed meal, linseed meal, blood meal, tankage, fish scrap, and other such products are used to a limited extent to supply nitrogen in fertilizers. They are more expensive than synthetic sources and are used in small amounts, mainly as conditioners. The concentration of nitrogen in these natural materials is so low that they cannot be used in high-analysis fertilizers.

The soil organic matter contains nitrogen, and some of it is made available for crops by the action of microorganisms. Most of the nitro-gen contained in manure is slowly available and is not subject to leach-ing until it is converted to nitrate by soil organisms. Nitrogen deficiency is most likely to occur on light soils that are low in organic matter and subject to excessive leaching. Nitrogen in the nitrate form is rapidly leached out of the root zone as water percolates through the soil. Am-monium forms of nitrogen are adsorbed by the soil colloids and resist leaching. The ammonium ion is converted to the nitrate ion by micro-organisms in the soil and then will be subject to leaching. The rate of conversion of ammonium to nitrate is governed by the temperature, aeration, and moisture content of the soil. Ample moisture with good aeration and high temperatures favor rapid conversion of ammonium to nitrate. While most plants absorb both ammonium and nitrate nitrogen, the absorption of nitrate seems to be most rapid in so far as most vege-tables are concerned. The relative amounts of ammonium and nitrate nitrogen that a plant takes up depends on the pH of the soil, the type of plant, and the age of the plant; however, with most soils that have good enough drainage to ensure good growth of vegetable crops, the con-version of ammonium to nitrate will be quite rapid so that the majority of the nitrogen taken up by the plant will be in the form of nitrate.

Phosphorus. Phosphorus is a constituent of nucleoproteins and plays an important role in many enzymatic reactions. A lack of phosphorus is indicated by slow growth of plants with small leaves of a grayish-green color. The midribs, veins, and petioles of the leaves and parts of the stem show a purple coloration in severe cases of deficiency. Lack of phos-phorus delays maturity of fruits and seeds.

Practically all the phosphorus used in fertilizers is derived from phos-phate rock $[3Ca_3(PO_4)_2 \cdot CaF_2]$, the mineral apatite. The phosphorus in phosphate rock is insoluble in water, and citric acid and is unavailable to plants. When applied as finely ground rock some of the phosphorus is made available by soil acids, but the amount is small. Superphosphate is formed by treating phosphate rock with sulfuric acid. The reaction converts the unavailable tricalcium phosphate to available monocalcium and dicalcium phosphate; thus, superphosphate is a mixture of these materials with the gypsum that also is formed by the reaction. One-half of 20 per cent superphosphate is gypsum. Triple superphosphate is made by treating phosphate rock with phosphoric acid, which forms mono- and dicalcium phosphates, but does not contain gypsum as does regular superphosphate. The available P_2O_5 content of superphosphate is about 20 per cent, while triple superphosphate is 47 per cent P_2O_5. Another source of phosphorus in mixed fertilizers is ammonium phosphate, which is formed by the reaction of phosphoric acid with ammonia.

Many soils are relatively low in available phosphorus although considerable quantities of phosphorus may be present in the soil. On land that has not been heavily fertilized for a number of years, phosphorus usually gives good plant responses when applied as a fertilizer. Most of the soils in the intensive vegetable-growing areas have been heavily fertilized for a number of years, so that the soil reserve of phosphorus has been built up to such a level that response to phosphorus is no longer important. Many soils have a high capacity to fix phosphorus, that is, to tie it up in unavailable forms, and since phosphorus is rapidly tied up by the soil, the amount added is usually far in excess of the amount of phosphorus actually taken up by the plant. The availability of phosphorus is determined to a great extent by the soil reaction. In very acid soils, phosphorus may be unavailable owing to the formation of insoluble iron and aluminum phosphates. In alkaline soils, it may occur as insoluble tricalcium phosphate. Phosphorus is most readily available to plants when the soil reaction is pH 6.0 to 6.5. Manure is low in phosphorus, and almost all of it is combined in proteins. This protein phosphorus is slowly available to the plant and is not effective in producing rapid plant growth.

Potassium. Potassium is thought to be essential for the formation and translocation of carbohydrates and is needed in large quantities by most root crops. A deficiency of potassium results in a stunting of the plants and a marginal chlorosis and firing of the older leaves and also affects secondary thickening of roots and tubers, resulting in slender rather than thick storage organs. The potassium in the plant is in a soluble form and is moved from the old leaves to the young leaves as a shortage occurs; therefore the symptoms of deficiency first appear on the lower or older leaves.

Deficiencies are most likely to occur on light sandy soils and on most muck or peat soils. Most soils contain large quantities of potash, but it is primarily in the form of insoluble minerals. The amount available to the plants appears to be fairly well correlated with the clay content of the soil. Soils that are high in clay usually are high in available potash. While calcium is the predominant cation in the soil complex, potassium is usually the predominant cation in the plant. Many plants absorb far more potassium than they actually need for growth and maintenance of high yields, and this excessive absorption is called "luxury consumption."

The most important source of potash in fertilizers is muriate of potash (potassium chloride). Potassium sulfate is used in some areas, and sulfate of potash-magnesia is used to a slight extent, mainly as a source of magnesium. All of these materials are water-soluble, and there is no difference in their potash-supplying power to the plants. The difference in response to various sources of potash is due to the complementary elements such as chlorine or sulfur rather than to the potash.

Calcium. Calcium plays a major role in cell-wall formation, especially in the middle lamella. Pectic acid reacts with calcium to form insoluble calcium pectate, which cements the cells together. The effects of calcium shortage are noticed first in young tissue since it is not translocated from the old tissues rapidly enough to prevent damage in younger tissue. In severe cases of deficiency the plant is woody and the leaves are pale and brittle and the terminal bud dies. The roots are short, thickened, and usually discolored. These symptoms are easy to produce in sand cultures, but seldom are found in the field. Blossom-end rot of tomato fruit and blackheart of celery are evidences of insufficient calcium in the affected plant part, but the rest of the plant appears normal. These symptoms are associated with low soil moisture or high soluble salts in the soil, which reduces water uptake by the plant.

It is the predominant cation in most soils but is rapidly lost from the soil by leaching, and this results in an increase in soil acidity since hydrogen replaces it on the clay colloid. Shortage of calcium may be one of the reasons why plants grow poorly on very acid soils, but it is not the only factor involved.

Fertilizers made with superphosphate contain calcium both as calcium phosphate and as gypsum (calcium sulfate). Lime is usually the main source of calcium supplied to the soil.

Sulfur. Sulfur is a component of some proteins and amino acids that are essential to normal plant metabolism. It is also contained in certain volatile compounds which impart a characteristic odor and flavor to certain vegetables. A general yellowing and stunting of the plant occurs when sulfur is lacking. A deficiency is seldom observed in the main vegetable-producing areas but most often occurs with other crops in parts of the West, particularly on soils derived from basalt. In heavily populated areas appreciable amounts of sulfur are deposited annually in the rainfall. The sulfur in the atmosphere is derived from burning coal. Fertilizers made with superphosphate contain sulfur as gypsum, and, in addition, ammonium sulfate and potassium sulfate also may be present in mixed fertilizers. Where special applications of sulfur need to be made, gypsum (calcium sulfate) is used. Elemental sulfur can be used, but it acidifies the soil. In most cases the beneficial effects attributed to elemental sulfur have been due to the acidification of the soil rather than to sulfur as a plant nutrient.

Magnesium. Magnesium is essential for chlorophyll formation since it is a component of the chlorophyll molecule. A deficiency of magnesium causes a chlorosis between the veins of the older leaves since it is translocated out of the old leaves and reutilized in the young leaves. A deficiency is most likely to occur on light sandy soil but may occur on very acid soil regardless of texture. It is often a serious problem with potatoes since the soil reaction is maintained below pH 5.4 to control scab. Members of the cabbage family, muskmelons, tomatoes, and beans apparently have a fairly high magnesium requirement. Heavy applications of potash depress magnesium uptake and may accentuate deficiency problems. In water cultures high levels of calcium reduce the magnesium uptake, but liming a soil usually increases the availability of magnesium from soil minerals and may alleviate magnesium deficiency. It has been demonstrated in the laboratory that magnesium toxicity occurs when magnesium in the root medium greatly exceeds the calcium level, but this seldom, if ever, occurs in the field. Magnesium is supplied by dolomitic limestone where liming is desirable. Other sources are sulfate of potash-magnesia and magnesium sulfate (Epsom salts). The former is frequently used in mixed fertilizers, and the latter is used as a foliage spray.

Boron. The exact function of boron in the plant is not known. It is thought to play a role in cell-wall formation and apparently facilitates translocation of sugars. The first visible symptom of boron deficiency is a breakdown of cells in regions where rapid cell division occurs, usually the apical bud or cambial regions. The vascular system of the root and stem is affected so that water movement in the plant is impaired and wilting of the plant is sometimes the first indication of deficiency. The carbohydrate content of roots and storage organs is lower in deficient than normal ones, and this is a result of slow translocation of sugars since the leaves have a high carbohydrate content when boron is deficient. In severe cases, the terminal bud dies, young leaves are malformed, and brown or black corky areas are found in storage organs. Experimental results have shown that heart rot of sugar beets, black spot of beets, cracked stem of celery, and brown rot, red rot, or browning of cauliflower are all symptoms of boron deficiency. These crops have a high boron requirement and may show symptoms of deficiency, while other crops in the same field make normal growth.

Boron deficiency is most likely to occur on heavily cropped sandy soils or on any soil where the soil reaction approaches neutrality. Boron is tied up in unavailable forms in alkaline soils. Deficiency may be severe in dry weather since the uptake of boron by the plant seems to be associated with soil moisture.

Boron is usually mixed with fertilizer for soil applications, but in some cases a foliage spray gives better results. Borax (sodium tetraborate) is the most common source of boron and is very soluble in water. Colemanite (calcium borate) is slowly soluble and sometimes is used for crops that are sensitive to high boron levels. An excess of boron is toxic to all plants, but the amount required to produce toxic effects depends on the kind of plant and the type of soil. Beets, turnips, cauliflower, celery, and broccoli need and tolerate fairly large amounts of boron, but beans, squash, cucumber, and melons seldom show boron deficiency and may be injured by fairly small applications. Toxicity is more likely to occur on acid, sandy soils with a low content of organic matter than on nearly neutral, loam or clay loam with a high organic-matter content.

Iron. Iron is essential for the formation of chlorophyll but is not a part of the chlorophyll molecule. It is a component of several enzymes and probably affects chlorophyll synthesis in this manner. Iron deficiency is indicated by a uniform chlorosis of the youngest leaves. Apparently iron is not translocated out of the older leaves since they remain green and have a high iron content.

Most soils supply enough iron for vegetables to make normal growth, and it sometimes is present in toxic amounts in some very acid soils. It is unavailable to plants in alkaline soils, and in some areas of the West lime-induced chlorosis is an important problem. Soil applications usually do not benefit the plant, but foliage sprays give temporary relief. Ferric sulfate has been the most common source of iron, but ferric citrate is frequently used as a spray. Chelated iron compounds are promising since the iron is combined with a complex organic molecule and is not rendered insoluble in the soil as are the inorganic sources.

Manganese. Like iron, manganese is essential for chlorophyll formation although it is not a part of the chlorophyll molecule. Manganese is also a component of several important enzymes, mostly functioning in oxidation reactions. The first symptom of deficiency is a yellowing or chlorosis of the young leaves. The areas between the veins are yellow, but the veins remain green. The deficiency symptoms are similar to those of magnesium deficiency except that the chlorosis first appears on the young leaves, while in the case of magnesium it first appears on the oldest leaves. Manganese becomes unavailable to plants as the soil reaction approaches neutrality. It is soluble in acid soils and may be present in toxic amounts in some soils. Toxicity is a well-known trouble in some tropical soils but only occurs occasionally in temperate regions. The effect of manganese toxicity seems to be an induced iron deficiency, and spraying the plants with iron compounds tends to reduce the damage. Experiments with nutrient solutions indicate that the iron-manganese ratio in the solution is very important for some plants. This relationship is not as clear with plants growing in the field. There is some evidence that manganese may be tied up by soil microorganisms as well as by a neutral or alkaline soil reaction. The deficiency is common on shallow mucks that have been mixed with underlying marl and is usually the first deficiency symptom to appear as a result of overliming mineral soils. Beans, onions, tomatoes, beets, and spinach have a high manganese requirement. Manganese sulfate is used to correct the deficiency both as a soil application and as a foliage spray. Sprays give better results in some areas, especially on calcareous muck soils. In some areas the deficiency can be overcome by acidifying the soil with sulfur or using an acid-forming fertilizer.

Zinc. Most soils supply enough zinc for vegetables, although tree crops on the same soil may suffer from deficiency. Zinc is a component of enzymes and is necessary for chlorophyll formation and functions in the synthesis of auxins. A deficiency may result from microbiological fixation of zinc or from the formation of insoluble compounds in alkaline soils. Sweet corn and beans have a high zinc requirement, and deficiencies have been reported in Florida and in the West. The young leaves of deficient plants are pale yellow or almost white, which gives rise to the term *white bud* to describe zinc deficiency of sweet corn. Zinc sulfate is used to correct the deficiency either as a soil application or as a foliage spray. Some evidence indicates that fungicides containing zinc may supply appreciable amounts to the plants. Excessive amounts of zinc are toxic, and the recommended amounts should not be exceeded, especially when it is applied to the foliage as a spray.

Molybdenum. Molybdenum is a component of an enzyme involved in nitrate reduction in the plant. Other functions of this element have not been discovered. A deficiency is characterized by a mottling or chlorosis and malformation of the young leaves with eventual death of the terminal bud. The leaf blades do not expand, and the leaf may be straplike or may consist of midrib without any blade. *Whiptail* of cauliflower and broccoli is due to a deficiency of molybdenum. These crops have a high molybdenum requirement, and only a few cases of deficiency have been observed in the field on other crops. Deficiency is most likely to occur on very acid soils, especially those that have been heavily leached. Liming is usually effective in eliminating the deficiency. When it is not practical to maintain pH 5.5 or higher, molybdenum is added to the fertilizer or sprayed on the foliage. Ammonium molybdate and sodium molybdate are the common sources used. One or two pounds of the materials per acre is usually all that is needed. Very large applications may be toxic to the plant, and high molybdenum content in forage is harmful to cattle, so care should be exercised in using this element on vegetables.

Copper. Little is known about the exact roles of copper in plant metabolism except that it is a component of certain enzymes that function in oxidation reactions. Deficiency usually results in a dull, faded-green color of the leaves followed by bleaching of the tips. With onions, the outer scales of the bulb are thin and have a poor color. Frequently copper deficiency appears during hot weather as a scalding of the leaves. Deficiency is most likely to occur on peat or muck soils, but it also occurs, in some areas, on very light, sandy soils. Deficiency is frequently associated with high organic-matter levels of the soil, and it is thought that either the organic matter changes the copper to unavailable forms or there is fixation of the copper by microorganisms. Copper is usually supplied in the fertilizer either as copper sulfate or as finely divided copper oxide.

Sodium. Sodium has never been shown to be essential to the growth of plants although it is beneficial to some plants. The beneficial responses to sodium usually occur where potash is in insufficient supply, and it may indicate that sodium fulfills some of the functions of potassium. Results of experiments reported by Harmer and Benne (1941) and by Sayre and Shafer (1946) indicate that common salt (NaCl) is of value in production of some vegetables. Harmer and Benne showed increased yield of several crops grown on muck soils that were fertilized with phosphate and potash. These crops included garden beets, celery, turnips, sugar beets, and chard. They also showed that there was marked increase in the sodium content of the crop where salt was applied. Sayre and Shafer reported large increases in yield of beets on mineral soils from the use of salt in addition to fertilizer containing nitrogen, phosphorus, and potash.

Chlorine. The first evidence that chlorine is essential for the growth of plants was the experiments of Broyer *et al.* (1954). These experiments showed definitely that chlorine was essential for the growth of tomato plants in water cultures. Some investigators have attributed the responses of crops to common salt, at least in part, to chlorine. Some evidence of this is presented by Tottingham (1919) and Pew (1949). No known cases of chlorine deficiency have been reported in the field. Most fertilizers contain fairly large amounts of chlorine when muriate of potash is used to supply potassium.

Fertilizer Analysis. The analysis is the statement of the percentage of nitrogen (N), phosphorus (P_2O_5), and potash (K_2O) contained in a complete fertilizer or of one of these nutrients in a separate material. In most states, the statement of the analysis is required by law. This statement is printed on a tag or on the bag. The analysis is quite often represented by three figures, as 5-10-5, 3-12-18, or 10-20-10. These figures represent the analysis of the complete fertilizer, the first giving the percentage nitrogen, the second, the percentage available phosphorus, and the third, the percentage water-soluble potash. In many areas a fourth figure is added to indicate the percentage magnesium (MgO). The content of minor elements and other ingredients may be stated on the tag in certain areas.

The average concentration of plant nutrients in commercial fertilizers has been increasing each year. A complete fertilizer containing less than 20 units of nutrients is considered a low-analysis fertilizer, and one containing above 20 units is sometimes called a high-analysis fertilizer. The term high-analysis fertilizer refers to a fertilizer containing 25, 30, or more units such as an 8-16-8 or a 10-20-20, although these are sometimes termed *double strength* or *concentrated* fertilizers. The use of the terms low analysis and high analysis has resulted in some confusion since some users have assumed that the value of the fertilizer depended on the total units regardless of the proportion of nitrogen, phosphorus, and potash. Nitrogen costs more per pound than either phosphorus or potash. Two mixtures may have the same number of total units but differ markedly in price because of the difference in the proportion of the three important constituents. For example, 2-8-10 and 5-10-5 analyses contain 20 units of nutrients each, but the latter costs more and is worth more on most upland soils. The vegetable grower should make his purchase on the basis of analysis and formula rather than on the price. A ton of 10-20-10 fertilizer contains exactly twice the quantity of each of the three important nutrients as a 5-10-5; therefore the former is worth twice as much as the latter. A ton of 10-20-10 usually costs less than 2 tons of a 5-10-5 since many costs such as bags, freight, and handling are essentially the same per ton for the two types. In general, the nutrients cost less per pound when purchased in high-analysis fertilizers than in low-analysis fertilizers. The labor cost involved in application is lower since less fertilizer is handled when a high-analysis fertilizer is used.

Fertilizer Formula. The formula is a statement of the kinds of material and the quantities of each used in making a ton of mixed fertilizer. The fertilizer industry has not chosen to state the materials used in making mixed fertilizers, but there is a trend toward what is known as *open-formula* fertilizers. Users of fertilizers have a right to know the materials used and are coming more and more to demand this information. It is particularly important to know the source of nitrogen since in some areas it is desirable to have it in a readily available form, but in others, in a slowly available form. Some manufacturers would like the grower to believe that a particular brand of fertilizer contains some secret or rare ingredients that others do not contain. However, from the figures published by the U.S. Department of Agriculture giving the annual consumption of fertilizer materials (Table 5.1), it is evident that most fertilizers contain essentially the same ingredients. There are relatively few sources of potash and phosphorus used in mixed fertilizers. There are many sources of nitrogen used, and the main difference between brands of fertilizer is the relative proportion of the various nitrogen sources.

Table 5.1. Amount of Various Fertilizer Materials Used in the United States during the Year Beginning July 1, 1954, and Ending June 30, 1955

Fertilizer material	Amount used	Per cent of total consumption
Nitrogen sources	Tons of N	
Ammonia....................................	582,000	25.8
Ammonium nitrate...........................	530,000	23.6
Compound solutions..........................	458,000	20.3
Ammonium sulfate and sulfate-nitrate...........	324,000	14.4
Other solids................................	320,000	14.3
Natural organics............................	36,000	1.6
Total nitrogen............................	2,250,000	100.0
Phosphorus sources	Tons of P_2O_5	
Normal superphosphate........................	1,494,000	64.6
Concentrated superphosphate..................	602,000	26.4
All others.................................	216,000	9.0
Total phosphorus..........................	2,312,000	100.0
Potash sources	Tons of K_2O	
Muriate of potash...........................	1,705,000	91.4
Sulfate of potash and sulfate of potash-magnesia...	127,000	6.8
All others.................................	33,000	1.8
Total potash.............................	1,865,000	100.0

Many fertilizer materials increase the acidity of the soil. In some states, the potential acidity of the fertilizer must be stated, usually in terms of the number of pounds of calcium carbonate required to neutralize the acidity produced by a ton of fertilizer. In low-analysis fertilizers, the potential acidity is neutralized by using calcium carbonate to replace some of the sand used to dilute the fertilizer materials. In general, it is far more economical to buy high-analysis fertilizers and neutralize the potential acidity by applying lime to the soil. The potential acidity of high-analysis fertilizers seldom exceeds 500 pounds of calcium carbonate per ton of fertilizer. On light soils that are subject to heavy leaching, it would be desirable to have nitrogen in two forms, one readily available and the other slowly available but not subject to leaching. This slowly available nitrogen is usually furnished by materials of plant or animal origin such as cottonseed meal, tankage, fish scrap, and others. Since these organic materials are expensive, it is usually cheaper to purchase a fertilizer containing only readily available nitrogen and to supply extra nitrogen as side-dressings when needed. Organic materials have some benefit as conditioners and driers which prevent caking of the fertilizer during storage.

Most high-analysis fertilizers are produced in pelleted or granulated forms. These are easy to distribute and can be applied at a uniform rate since they do not clog the machine used for application. They can be purchased early in the season (when most companies allow a liberal discount) without danger of caking during storage on the farm.

Complete fertilizers are available in both dry and liquid formulations in some areas. Solutions of various nitrogen compounds have been in use for a long time, and recently, liquid phosphoric acid has been used as a separate material, but liquid complete fertilizers are relatively new. These solutions can be handled rapidly with pumps and can be applied with more precision than most dry fertilizers. They are used at the same rate per acre as dry fertilizers with the same analysis. The solubility of the ingredients is claimed to be an advantage, but this is not always true. On a soil with a high phosphorus-fixing capacity, the soluble phosphorus would be fixed more rapidly than the more slowly soluble phosphorus compounds in superphosphate. The concentration of nutrients in liquid fertilizers is limited by the solubility of potassium compounds, and a 10-10-10 solution is about the limit unless the potash level is reduced. The liquid complete fertilizers have as many advantages and disadvantages as do the dry complete fertilizers. The use of liquid complete fertilizers will increase, especially in those areas near sources of phosphoric acid and where fertilizer has not been used in the past. It is much cheaper to build a plant for liquid-fertilizer manufacture than for dry formulations, and the industry will grow as long as there is a plentiful supply of phosphoric acid.

Fertilizer Ratio. The fertilizer ratio is the proportion of the three principal nutrients in a mixed fertilizer or the quantitative relation they bear to each other. The term fertilizer ratio has come into use because of the large number of possible analyses with the same proportion of nutrients. It is much simpler to base fertilizer practice on a fertilizer ratio than an analysis. For example, if it is desired to use a fertilizer containing twice as much phosphorus as nitrogen and potash, a large number of analyses are possible, such as a 4-8-4, 5-10-5, 6-12-6, 7-14-7, etc., up to 15-30-15. All of these analyses have the nutrients in the ratio 1-2-1. While many ratios are offered for sale, only a few are really necessary, such as 0-2-1, 1-1-1, 1-2-1, 1-3-1, 1-4-1, 0-2-3, 1-2-2, and 1-2-3. The fertilizer ratio that should be selected depends to a considerable extent upon the rate of application and the crop to be grown. In some areas where the land has not been heavily fertilized previously a 1-2-1 or a 1-3-1 ratio may be most desirable, while in adjacent areas that have been fertilized heavily previously, a 1-1-1 ratio would be more economical to use. On soils such as silt loams, loams, and clay loams, the fertilizer ratio used should usually contain more phosphorus than other elements. On light sandy soils, the fertilizer usually contains larger amounts of phosphorus and potash than nitrogen, such as a 1-2-2 or a 1-2-3. Where heavy applications of manure have been made to vegetable-growing soil, a ratio such as 1-4-1 is used to supplement the low phosphorus content of the manure. For vegetables grown on muck soils, the fertilizer used is usually high in potash since most mucks are low in this element. Fertilizer ratios for these soils include 0-2-3, 1-2-3, and 1-4-6.

Rate of Fertilizer Application. Obviously, the rate of application of fertilizer should be considered only in connection with a definite analysis, but there is great confusion in the discussions one hears on this point. It is not uncommon to hear discussions of rates of application without mention of analysis or of analysis without reference to rates of application. With the large number of analyses now available and with what seems to be a necessity to consider ratios, there is need for a change in the terminology. Instead of discussing applications in terms of hundreds of pounds of a mixture per acre, we should discuss them in pounds of nitrogen, phosphorus, and potash to the acre. For example, we might recommend 100 pounds of nitrogen, 200 pounds of phosphorus, and 100 pounds of potash to an acre. An application of 1 ton of 5-10-5 would supply these quantities, or $\frac{1}{2}$ ton of a 10-20-10, or $\frac{1}{3}$ ton of 15-30-15. Similarly, with the other ratios, thinking in terms of the nutrients rather than in terms of the total pounds of mixture to use would simplify matters and avoid confusion.

The rates of application of the important nutrients should be based on the fertility of the soil, the cropping system, the crop to be grown, and the gross return that reasonably might be expected from the crop. Where the land is well supplied with one of the elements in forms available to the crop, it would be poor economy to use much of that element in the fertilizer mixture. On many muck soils, it is a waste to use much nitrogen since such soils are rich in this element. On soils containing considerable amounts of clay, little potash is needed. Large applications of fertilizer are justified only when the soil is well drained, in good physical condition, and has a reaction in the range favorable for growth of the crop. Lime should be used to reduce the acidity of the soil to desirable range for the crop before applying fertilizer. When the gross return from the crop is low, it may not be profitable to use a large amount of fertilizer. On the other hand, the labor involved in producing the crop is the major-cost item in many cases, and a good way to reduce the labor cost is by producing maximum yields per acre. This being the case, heavy applications of fertilizer are frequently justified on crops which require large amounts of labor as a means of reducing the unit cost of labor.

Time and Method of Application. Fertilizers for vegetable crops are commonly applied before or at the time of planting. Where fertilizer attachments are available for the planting machine, this is the most practical way to apply the fertilizer. Under most conditions there is no advantage in making more than one application of fertilizer except where nitrogen is used as a side-dressing. Usually all the phosphorus and potash and part of the nitrogen are applied at the time of planting. Phosphorus does not move in the soil water and must be placed in the root zone of the plant rather than on the surface. Potash is leached slowly in heavy soils, but on very light sands, potash may leach out of the root zone and a side-dressing may be advisable. All chemical sources of nitrogen are soluble and subject to leaching, so it may not be efficient to supply all of the nitrogen for the crop at the time of planting. It may be more efficient to apply part of the nitrogen as a side-dressing after the plants have begun their growth. On a soil well supplied with organic matter or where large quantities of manure have been plowed down, all of the nitrogen is applied at the time of planting.

There are several methods of applying fertilizer, all of which have their advantages and disadvantages. The most important methods are:

1. Broadcasting on the surface before plowing
2. Broadcasting on the surface after plowing and mixing with the surface soil by disking or harrowing
3. Applying fertilizer in a band in the bottom of the plow furrow
4. Applying fertilizer in bands 2 to 3 or more inches from the row and 2 to 3 or more inches below the surface
5. A combination of the broadcasting methods or plow-furrow application with bands at the side of the row at planting time
6. Applying fertilizer with a drill below the surface of the soil before the crop is planted

The results of many experiments show that when small amounts of fertilizer are used the greatest yields are obtained by applying the fertilizer in bands near the row rather than broadcasting the same amount of fertilizer. The fertilizer should be placed far enough from the seed so that injury does not result. A high concentration of soluble materials from the fertilizer in the seed zone causes a delay in germination and injury to the young plants and may result in failure of the seed to germinate. There is more danger of injury to the plants from burning action of the fertilizer on a sandy or sandy loam soil than on loam or clay loam soils or muck soils. Injury from fertilizer is greater from band placement near the row than from any other method of placement because of the concentration near the plant.

In general, the results indicate that no one method of application is best under all conditions. The effectiveness of the various methods depends on the character of the soil, the rainfall, the quantity and concentration of fertilizer used, and the kind of crop grown. If a soil has a high fixing power for phosphorus, for example, band placement would be better than broadcasting, especially for a light application. In the band method the fertilizer would be in contact with much less soil than in the broadcast method; consequently, less of the phosphorus would be fixed with the former method than with the latter method. The moisture supply affects the efficiency of the various methods of placement. When the rainfall is heavy, there is likely to be greater loss of nutrients by leaching when the application is made in the bottom of the furrow than by any other method. This is especially true on light, well-drained soils. On the other hand, this is a good method for a dry season, and application at the surface after plowing is a poor method under the dry conditions. Since it is not possible to know in advance what the moisture supply will be, except where irrigation is used, it is desirable to use methods that are most likely to be satisfactory under average conditions.

For most vegetables at least part of the fertilizer should be applied near the seed so that the young plants have an abundance of nutrients to get them off to a rapid start. Applications of fertilizer that have been broadcast are not utilized efficiently until the plants develop a fairly large root system. The quantity and concentration of fertilizer to be used should be considered in determining the method of application to be followed. For small applications of fertilizer, band applications near the row are likely to give the best results with most crops. With large applications of fertilizer, a combination of banding part of the fertilizer and plowing down or broadcasting the remainder usually gives better results than either method alone. Various kinds of drills and fertilizer distributors are available. The common grain drill does not apply enough fertilizer to be useful on most vegetable farms. Some types of broadcasting equipment do not apply enough fertilizer for vegetables, but other types have a wide range in rate of application and are popular on vegetable farms. Many planters have fertilizer attachments which place the fertilizer in bands near the seed. The fertilizer attachment should apply the fertilizer in bands 2 to 3 inches from the seed and at the depth or slightly below the seed for most vegetables. Some types do not place the fertilizer properly on rough land or when driven at high speeds, and seed damage usually results. If the planter does not band the fertilizer properly, it is safer to apply most of the fertilizer by some other method.

Foliage Application of Fertilizers. In some areas, minor elements are supplied to vegetable crops as a foliage spray. In some cases, this is the most efficient means of supplying the minor element to prevent deficiencies. Only very small amounts of these elements are needed, and the leaf absorbs enough to satisfy the need for normal growth. This practice stimulated a number of workers to investigate the possibility of applying complete fertilizers as a foliage spray. Almost without exception, these experiments have shown that the leaf is not an efficient absorbing organ and high yields cannot be obtained by the use of foliage sprays as the supply of fertilizer. Hester (1951) obtained an increase in yield of carrots receiving three sprays of urea containing 90 pounds of nitrogen per acre. There is no evidence that this was due to foliage absorption since the urea was washed off the plants and into the soil by rain and irrigation water. Brasher *et al.* (1953) reported that tomato plants growing in sand cultures could not absorb enough fertilizer from frequent foliage sprays to maintain normal growth if the surface of the sand was shielded so that the fertilizer applied to the leaves could not reach the roots. Numerous field experiments by these workers in Delaware indicated that soil applications of fertilizer were much superior to foliage applications.

The foliage of vegetables is damaged by high concentrations of fertilizer as a spray, although some plants tolerate higher concentrations than others. In most cases, 5 pounds of fertilizer per acre as a spray is all that can be applied without injury. It is obvious that the large amounts of nitrogen and potash required by most vegetables cannot be supplied as a foliage spray. All the evidence indicates that the major elements can be applied more efficiently and at a lower cost as a soil application than as a foliage spray.

LIME

Lime is used mainly as a soil amendment to neutralize the soil acidity, although calcium, the important element in lime, is a nutrient. The use of calcium by plants has been discussed previously. In addition to neutralizing acidity directly, lime may be of value in rendering harmless toxic materials in the soil and in increasing the availability of certain nutrient elements.

Soil Reaction. Most plants are influenced markedly by the reaction (acidity or alkalinity) of the soil. Acidity may be expressed as total acidity (potential acidity) or by hydrogen-ion concentration. Total acidity (titratable acidity) is measured by titration with a base, and this measures the quantity of H ions that can be made to combine with a base. Determining the H-ion concentration gives a measure of the H ions that are present in a given system at a given time; i.e., it is a measure of the free H ions. Normal solutions of various acids have the same titration values or the same total acidity, but very different H-ion concentration owing to difference in dissociation. For example, in a tenth normal solution of hydrochloric acid nearly all the H ions are active, while in a tenth normal solution of acetic acid less than 1 per cent of the H ions are active. These two solutions have the same total or titratable acidity.

Soil reaction is expressed in terms of pH, which may be defined as the logarithm of the reciprocal of the H-ion concentration. Water is the common solvent, and since it dissociates into H+ and OH— ions, one of which is characteristic of acids and the other of bases, the dissociation constant is very important. This constant is approximately 1×10^{-14}. Neutrality is the point at which H^+ and OH^- ions are in equilibrium, so that, at this point, the H-ion concentration equals 1×10^{-7}. In expressing H-ion concentration in terms of pH only the exponent is used, therefore pH 7 means 1×10^{-7} and represents neutrality. At neutrality there is 1 gram of hydrogen in solution in about 10 million liters. It is essential to remember that the pH scale is a logarithmic one. For each decrease of one unit on the pH scale the H-ion concentration increases tenfold. For example, the concentration of H ions is 10 times greater in a solution of pH 6 than in one of pH 7, and 100 times greater in a solution of pH 5 than in one of pH 7. The fractions of the pH scale also represent logarithmic values.

The soil is not a true solution, and the reaction of the soil is determined by the proportion of hydrogen to bases adsorbed on the clay and organic colloids in the soil. The potential acidity is determined by the proportion of hydrogen on the colloid, the type of colloid, and the amount of colloidal material in the soil. For all practical purposes the potential acidity of the soil is not a logarithmic value. It usually requires about an equal amount of base to change the soil reaction from pH 5.0 to 6.0 as it does to change it from pH 6.0 to 7.0. The soil is so highly buffered that the potential acidity is essentially linear, but the H-ion concentration expressed as pH is logarithmic.

Response of Vegetable Crops to Soil Reaction. Vegetable-crop plants vary greatly in their response to the reaction of the culture medium. Results of many experiments indicate that most vegetable crops thrive better in a soil that is slightly acid than in a soil that is neutral or alkaline. The reaction of the soil determines to a great extent the availability of most plant nutrients. In a soil that is neutral or alkaline, phosphorus availability is low and certain minor elements such as iron, manganese, boron, and zinc may be tied up in forms that are unavailable to the plant. In very acid soils, the availability of phosphorus and molybdenum is low and toxic concentrations of iron, manganese, or aluminum may be present. Maintaining the soil reaction between pH 6.0 and 6.8 usually ensures maximum availability of essential minerals in the soil and eliminates the danger of toxic concentrations of iron, aluminum, and manganese.

It is not possible to give the optimum soil reaction for any crop under all conditions because the character of the soil, the organic-matter content of the soil, the moisture supply, and other functions may influence

Table 5.2. Classification of Vegetables according to Range of Reaction for Satisfactory Growth

Soil reaction	Crops
pH 6.0–6.8........	Asparagus, beets, carrots, cauliflower, celery, lettuce, Lima beans, muskmelons (cantaloupes), onions, parsnips, peas, spinach
pH 5.5–6.8........	Beans, broccoli, cabbage, cucumbers, peppers, radishes, squash, sweet corn, sweet potatoes, tomatoes, turnips
pH 4.8–5.4........	Potatoes

the response of the crop at a given soil reaction. Results of many experiments conducted on a large number of soil types indicate that vegetable crops may be classified roughly as to their response to soil reaction. Such a classification or grouping is given in Table 5.2. The grouping given in this table indicates the range of reaction over which the crops might be expected to make satisfactory growth when other factors are favorable. Under some conditions satisfactory yields are obtained on soils with a lower or higher pH than the range given. In most cases, however, higher yields would be obtained within the ranges mentioned than at either a lower or higher pH provided other conditions are the same. The potato plant produces satisfactory yields over a wide range of reaction, but when the scab organism is present in the soil, injury is severe at reactions between pH 5.5 and 7.0.

Crops may be benefited indirectly by liming an acid soil owing to the effects of lime on: (1) decomposition of organic matter through making conditions more favorable for the organisms, (2) the growth of nitrogen-fixing bacteria associated with leguminous plants, (3) rendering harmless certain toxic substances, (4) increasing the availability of certain elements in the soil, and (5) improving soil structure by flocculating colloids. Cruciferous crops may be benefited by liming owing to the effect of neutralizing the acidity on the organism causing club root. This organism, a slime mold, thrives only on an acid soil.

Effects of Overliming. Under some conditions completely neutralizing the acidity results in reduced yields even with crops that are intolerant to acid-soil conditions. In many cases reducing the soil acidity to near the neutral point by liming may result in minor-element deficiencies. The availability of iron, manganese, boron, and zinc is low in neutral or alkaline soils, and they may be made unavailable to the plant by over-liming the soil. Applying lime to a soil that is to produce potatoes is likely to be detrimental if the soil reaction is pH 5.4 or higher and the scab organism is present. This organism does not thrive on soils that are highly acid, but it should be kept in mind that the potato does not make its best growth on a strongly acid soil. Potato yields are likely to be reduced when the soil reaction is below pH 4.8.

Forms of Lime. The forms of lime most commonly used are ground limestone (calcium carbonate, $CaCO_3$) and slaked lime or hydrated lime (calcium hydroxide, $Ca(OH)_2$). Burned lime (calcium oxide, CaO) is sometimes used. Calcium oxide is made by burning calcium carbonate, the process setting free CO_2 and leaving a residue of CaO. Calcium oxide exposed to air takes up water and forms calcium hydroxide, or slaked lime, which is frequently prepared by adding water to calcium oxide. One hundred pounds of calcium carbonate on burning loses 44 pounds of carbon dioxide, leaving 56 pounds of calcium oxide, or burned lime. Therefore, 56 pounds of unslaked, burned lime is equivalent to 100 pounds of limestone. On slaking, 56 pounds of burned lime takes up 18 pounds of water, making 74 pounds of hydrated lime equal in calcium oxide content to 100 pounds of calcium carbonate. Both calcium oxide and calcium hydroxide on exposure take up CO_2 from the air and change back to the carbonate form according to the following reactions: $Ca(OH)_2 + CO_2 \rightarrow CaCO_3 + H_2O$ and $CaO + CO_2 \rightarrow CaCO_3$. It is generally thought that there are great differences in the speed of the various forms of lime in correcting soil acidity. It should be borne in mind, however, that only calcium carbonate is effective in reducing soil acidity. Calcium oxide and calcium hydroxide are not effective until they have combined with CO_2 in the soil air and have been converted to calcium carbonate since the soil reaction is regulated by the carbonate-bicarbonate buffer system. The difference attributed to the speed of action of the different materials is due entirely to the size of the individual particles. Hydrated lime is usually ground more finely than limestone, but limestone ground to pass through a 100-mesh sieve (100 to the inch) reacts as rapidly in the soil as does any other form of lime. If the soil surface is moist, hydrated lime may cake and form lumps which have little effect on the soil reaction when they are incorporated into the soil. For efficient action, the liming material should be thoroughly mixed with the soil. Land plaster or gypsum (calcium sulfate) is sometimes used in place of lime, but it does not take the place of any of the forms of lime in correcting acidity.

Application of Lime. The quantity of lime to apply depends on: (1) the soil reaction, (2) the crop to be grown, (3) the kind of soil, and (4) the form of lime. Before using lime in any great quantity, one should determine the lime requirement by one of the several methods available. Obviously the rate of application should be higher on a soil that is very acid than on one that is only slightly acid. It has been pointed out that crops differ widely in their tolerance to acidity; therefore liming might not be necessary for many crops grown on soils that are only slightly acid. The kind of soil is of importance because some soils such as clays and mucks have a high exchange capacity and are highly buffered, while sands and sandy loams have a low exchange capacity and little buffer action. Crops grown on the lighter soils may be injured by the acidity contributed by heavy fertilizer application, but this is seldom an important factor on the heavier soils. The potential acidity of the fertilizer should be kept in mind on light soils, and lime should be added before the pH drops below the desired level. Crops grown on soils with a low organic-matter content are more likely to be injured by acidity than crops grown on soils with a high organic-matter content at the same soil reaction. On the other hand, there is more danger of overliming sandy and sandy loam soils than there is with the other soils mentioned.

Recommendations for the applications of lime are usually made in terms of tons of ground limestone per acre. In most areas, ground limestone is the cheapest form of lime available. If slaked or hydrated lime is used, less is required since 74 pounds of slaked lime is equivalent in neutralizing power to 100 pounds of ground limestone. If a ton of ground limestone is recommended, about 1,500 pounds of hydrated lime will do the same job. The various types of lime vary greatly in their magnesium content from practically no magnesium to as much as 25 per cent magnesium (MgO). High-magnesium limestone is desirable on soils where magnesium deficiency is known to occur, and it is usually the cheapest source of magnesium for plants. When high-magnesium limestone is available at the same cost as regular ground limestone it would seem desirable to use it on most vegetables.

Lime is usually applied with the fertilizer attachment of a grain drill or with a fertilizer or lime spreader. A grain drill is satisfactory where only a few hundred pounds are to be supplied per acre. The lime spreader is the best means of applying lime since the machine is made for this purpose and can be regulated to apply at any desired rate. For the best and most rapid action of lime, it should be applied uniformly and thoroughly mixed with the soil. It is desirable to apply the lime as far in advance of planting the crop as possible so that the soil reaction will be at the desired level before the crop is planted. When 1 or 2 tons of ground limestone per acre are to be applied it is usually broadcast after plowing and thoroughly harrowed into the surface. Where larger amounts must be applied, it is desirable to apply half the limestone before plowing and the remainder after plowing and mix it with the surface soil by harrowing. Where a strongly acid soil has been limed, it is best to grow a crop that is not sensitive to soil acidity since it usually takes more than one season to get the lime thoroughly distributed through the soil. The vegetable grower should follow a regular liming program in which moderate amounts of lime are applied frequently rather than allowing the pH to drop to such a low level that crop injury occurs and it requires a large amount of lime to correct the condition.

CHAPTER 6

Seeds and Seed Growing

Good seed is essential to success in vegetable growing. The most careful and efficient gardener cannot achieve success with poor seed, even if he gives the closest attention to all other factors of production. Since the cost of seed is such a small item in the total cost of production of most vegetable crops, the grower cannot afford to take any more chances than necessary. The best seed obtainable should be used.

What Is Good Seed? Seed to be classed as good must be: (1) clean, (2) viable, (3) free from disease, and (4) true to a good name. Seed to be classed as clean must be free from weed seeds, dirt, and other foreign matter. Most vegetable seed is relatively free from impurities, though occasionally it is not well cleaned and contains too much dirt and refuse.

Good seed is viable. It must have sufficient vitality to complete the process of germination. To do this, it must be able to nourish the embryo plant until it can support itself independently of the supply of food stored in the seed. This means more than mere sprouting. Vegetable growers have little trouble with this problem as very few of the better seed houses put out seed of unduly low vitality. Most seedsmen make germination tests of their seeds to be sure that they are viable. Some states require a statement of the percentage of germination and the date the test was made, and many seedsmen supply this information on all of the seed they sell. The buyer of seed should insist on a statement of the percentage of germination, but he should bear in mind that many kinds of seed lose vitality in a relatively short time when held under unfavorable conditions.

Seed should be free from disease. Some diseases, as black rot of cabbage, are carried on the seed coat and can be controlled by seed treatment; others are carried within the seed coat. Some, such as the anthracnose of beans, are not successfully controlled by seed treatment. Blackleg, carried within the seed of cabbage and cauliflower, can be fairly well controlled by hot-water treatment as discussed in connection with disease in Chap. 18.

Seed should be true to a good name; *i.e.*, it should be true to type for the variety in question. This point is of prime importance and is the one which gives the vegetable grower the greatest concern.

Definition of Terms. A horticultural classification of vegetables recognizes the following gradations: (1) the kind, (2) the variety, (3) the strain, and (4) the stock. Work (1925) gives the following definitions of these terms:

KIND. A kind includes all the plants which, in general usage, are accepted as a single vegetable, as for example, tomato, cabbage, bean. This is not the same as the genus or the species of botanical classification. The species, as *Brassica oleracea*, includes several kinds—cabbage, cauliflower, and others. The beans come from more than one species.

VARIETY. A variety includes those plants of a given kind which are practically alike in their important characteristics of plant and product. Each variety should be distinct in one or more prominent and significant features. Named varieties that are not distinct should be classed as strains of a recognized variety, or as mere synonyms.

The line between varieties is not sharply drawn and is mainly a matter of informal consensus of opinion.

STRAIN. A strain includes those plants of a given variety which possess its general characteristics but which differ from others of the variety in one important or two or three minor respects—difference not great enough to justify a new variety name. Thus Red Kidney is a standard variety of bean. Wells Red Kidney is an anthracnose-resistant strain of this variety. The distinction between variety and strain is based simply on degrees of difference.

STOCK. A stock represents all plants of the same parentage or pedigree. Differences between various stocks of a variety or strain should be very slight. A seed grower may maintain more than one stock of a strain, each representing a single pedigree line. Two seed growers may have stocks so nearly alike as to be indistinguishable, but as long as they are separately maintained they are distinct stocks.

The distinctions of these definitions are not hard and fast; in fact, the seed trade is anything but consistent in its use of terms. The idea of a stock as distinct from a strain is based on the concept of parentage or pedigree lines. While some seed houses practically ignore the pedigree idea, many keep careful records and are able to trace parentage through several generations. At the same time, stocks of presumably nearly equal excellence are often used interchangeably.

BUYING SEED

Seed growing is a technical and highly specialized business carried on largely in regions particularly adapted to the production of special crops. Because of these facts most vegetable growers should buy all their seeds and practically all growers should buy most of their supply. In buying, it is usually desirable to get the best seed available, making the cost a secondary consideration. Cheap seed is usually the most expensive in the long run. The vegetable grower should obtain all the information possible on reliable sources of seeds of the varieties and strains of all the crops he grows. Seed source and strain tests conducted by the experiment stations have shown great variations in yield, in earliness, in uniformity, and in other important qualities. This is true for most varieties of all the important kinds of vegetables. After getting such information as is available, the grower would do well to determine for himself on his own land the varieties and strains that prove most satisfactory.

Growers should buy only from reliable dealers, those that have a good reputation to maintain. Commercial growers would do well to deal mainly with houses that cater especially to producers like themselves. Most reliable seed houses make a specialty of some crop or crops, and usually the seedsman who gives special attention to a particular crop develops and maintains superior strains. It usually pays to buy from seedsmen who take pride in certain crops. The better growers have learned to buy from specialists, so that it is not at all uncommon for a gardener to buy tomato seed from one house, cabbage seed from another, sweet corn from a third, and so on.

In buying seed it is well to buy as near the source as possible. The originator, the introducer, or the specialist is more likely to use greater care in maintaining good stocks than is a dealer who has no special interest in the variety or strain. This is not always true as the originator may, after a time, become careless, while another grower may maintain or even improve the stock. Seed dealers have learned that certain seed growers and wholesalers have superior stocks. Some vegetable growers are beginning to learn these sources and inquire for them when buying seed. This trend toward seed of known origin is a wholesome one and should be encouraged. When dealers carry more than one stock of a given variety the buyer should ask for the stock number. This would make it possible for him to get the same or a different stock the next year, depending on whether it proved satisfactory or unsatisfactory.

To be reasonably sure of getting seed that is true to type and is adapted to his conditions, the grower might get samples to test on a small scale a year in advance. He should obtain a stock number or other identifying information from the seedsman so that he could order the same stock if it proved satisfactory. When it is known that growers are testing the seed in advance for performance, reliable dealers are not going to take chances on supplying inferior stocks. Some growers buy seed of celery, cabbage, cauliflower, and others a year in advance and test it on a small scale. If it proves satisfactory, he is assured of having a good stock to plant the following year. Should it not be satisfactory he has saved the labor and expense of growing an unsatisfactory crop. One should not buy seed very far in advance of planting unless good storage conditions and facilities are available.

Cost of Good Seed. Growing good seed is expensive. Seed users must, therefore, stand ready to pay the price for a good product. This does not mean that a high price in itself means high quality or that one should pay more than good seed is worth. With most crops the cost of seed to plant an acre is so small that a difference of 25, 50, or even 100 per cent is hardly significant, provided, of course, greater value is offered for the higher price. The practice of sending the same seed lists to several houses, asking for quotations, and placing the order where the total is lowest is the poorest kind of business. There is no basis of comparing prices unless it is known that the products are of equal quality, and in most cases this is not known in buying seeds.

Certified Seed. Many states now provide certification service for recognized varieties of many kinds of vegetable seeds. Crops being grown for certification are inspected two or more times during the period of growth for seed-borne diseases and for trueness to type. Inspections are made usually by specialists of the State College of Agriculture, State Experiment Station, or the State Department of Agriculture, and certificates are issued to the seedsmen by some official agency. These certificates are attached to the bags or other containers used for the seed certified.

Each state usually publishes rules and standards that must be met before the certificates are issued. Buyers of certified seed should read carefully the statement of scope of certification because the standards are not the same in the various states. Greater uniformity in certification standards is very desirable, and while it might not be feasible to have the same standards apply to all regions, it would be practicable for the states within a region to have the same rules and standards.

VARIETY AND STRAIN TESTING

Testing for trueness to type and for performance is of much greater importance than testing for purity and germination since growers suffer little loss from impurities or from low germination. Most vegetable seeds are clean and have at least fair vitality, but very often the crop produced is not true to type. Some testing of varieties to find those suited to the growers' needs is essential, but after this is determined most attention should be paid to the testing of strains and stocks of the varieties selected.

Great differences in yield, earliness, size, and other performance characters exist between strains of the same variety of many crops, and it is only by trial that the superior strains are found. Many of the agricultural experiment stations conduct variety and strain tests of the important crops and recommend those that appear the most promising. However, the vegetable grower needs to test those recommended in order to determine whether or not they fit his particular conditions and market. A variety or strain may be very satisfactory for some conditions and markets and not for others. In some cases earliness is more important than large yields, while in others the reverse is true. In growing vegetables for processing in many areas earliness is not important but large yields are. Other characteristics, such as size, shape, resistance to disease, and other factors, should be taken into consideration in determining the value of a strain.

While the commercial gardener should make his main plantings of tested and reliable strains and varieties, he should be on the lookout for new and promising things. These should be tested on a small scale, for it is only by trying new or so-called new varieties and strains that the best is discovered. The grower who depends on the highly advertised novelties for his main plantings usually fails. A good rule to follow is to try the new while making a living from the old reliable strains. The grower producing only a few kinds of crops can well afford to try the new listings, for now and then he will find something of distinct merit. He should not be led astray by extravagant language in the catalogue description but should learn to discriminate between "selling talk" and information as to the value of the thing advertised. He should learn to discriminate between statements of opinion and statements of facts.

SEED GROWING

Seed growing is a highly specialized business requiring particular knowledge and skill not possessed by many vegetable growers; therefore most gardeners should buy their seeds through the regular channels. Seeds of many crops are grown commercially in regions where the soil and climate are especially favorable, and some are produced in foreign countries, where the ecological factors are favorable and, in addition, where labor is cheap. Some seed crops are produced satisfactorily in a dry climate. Others like cabbage, cauliflower, and other species of Brassica grow best in a relatively cool climate. California is an important seed-growing state because the climatic conditions are almost ideal for the harvesting, curing, and handling of seeds of many crops. In humid regions, many seed crops grow satisfactorily, but there is danger of loss at harvest time, hence a dry region is preferable, other things being equal.

While most vegetable growers should purchase a large part, if not all, of their seeds, there are many progressive men who are growing all their seeds of certain crops and finding it profitable. Before undertaking to grow seed, the grower should weigh carefully the advantages against the disadvantages. He should be fitted by temperament, knowledge, skill, and situation to do it well, for if the demands are not worth meeting effectively, he had better buy the seed.

Advantages. The man who grows his own seed knows its origin and parentage. He is able to select according to his own ideal and to suit his own conditions. Commercially grown seed is sold on all markets, and the individual should find an advantage in selecting to suit his local climate, soil, and market. One who grows seed learns to know the crop and the plant that produces it. This applies to the details of culture and management of the crop as well as to the characters of the plant itself. Few enterprises offer more in the way of personal satisfaction than seed improvement for the man who is fitted by temperament and training to do the work well. If the grower produces a strain of seed that is better than other strains, he will find that other growers are willing to pay a good price for his product. Some growers have developed a good paying side line in the growing of high-grade seed of some special crop.

Disadvantages. The disadvantages of seed growing outweigh the advantages in most cases. Seed growing is exacting work. It competes with other work at critical times in the vegetable-growing business. It calls for knowledge of the principles of plant breeding, of the technique of growing seed crops, of curing and handling seed. It calls for keen observation and aptness in judging and comparing type and performance. It requires close application to details, such as keeping biennial plants over winter and avoiding danger of crossing in the field.

In seed growing one of the serious problems is to isolate the plantings so that crossing will not take place. While some crops, as beans, Lima beans, peas, lettuce, and tomatoes, are mainly self-pollinated, it has been shown that some crossing may take place in all of these. Rick (1949) has shown that cross-pollination in the tomato varied with the season and location in California. Other crops are normally cross-pollinated. These include cabbage, cauliflower, kale, kohlrabi, Brussels sprouts, turnip, radish, carrot, beet, cucumber, muskmelon, watermelon, squash, pumpkin, parsnip, corn, spinach, salsify, and okra. Varieties of all these cross, and closely related species of some cross readily. Cabbage, cauliflower, and other species of Brassica cross with each other if they blossom at the same time. Muskmelon and cucumber do not cross with the other cucurbits. Watermelon crosses with the citron melon, but not with the other cucurbits. Parsnip crosses with wild parsnip. Pumpkin and squash of the same species cross readily, and, according to Whitaker and Bohn (1950), *Cucurbita moschata* is cross-fertile with *C. pepo* and *C. maxima*.

In growing seed of vegetable crops, it is necessary to isolate plantings if more than one variety of a crop is to be grown or if more than one kind of crop of the genus Brassica is grown. The distances necessary to separate varieties and kinds depend on the crop, the method of pollination, whether by wind or insects, and the kind of insect. Some insects travel only a short distance, while others go long distances. Wind-blown pollen of corn may be carried a considerable distance, while that of other crops may be blown only a short distance owing to the character of pollen itself.

The beginner in seed growing would do well to start with crops that are easily handled, especially such crops as corn, tomato, beans, peas, and the cucurbits. All these crops are annuals so do not need to be carried over winter. He should not attempt to grow seed where the climatic conditions are very unfavorable to production, harvesting, and curing. Not more than one variety of any crop that readily crosses should be grown unless sufficient land is available to enable the grower completely to isolate his plantings.

Since seed growing is a subject in itself, it is not within the scope of this book to do more than point out a few of the factors that should be considered before undertaking the work. Those interested in seed-growing methods are referred to special books and bulletins on the subject.

LONGEVITY OF VEGETABLE SEEDS

It is well known that seeds of some vegetables retain their vitality longer than seeds of others. For example, seeds of cucumber, squash, muskmelon, and lettuce retain their vitality longer than those of carrot, parsnip, parsley, and onion. It is also known that any kind of seed retains its vitality under some conditions better than under others. In some sections of the South and in the tropics it has been found that seeds kept under ordinary storage conditions do not retain their vitality for very long periods. Poor keeping under these conditions has been attributed to high temperature and to high humidity. Studies made by Duvel (1904) indicate that humidity is the main factor. Later studies by Barton (1935 and 1939), Boswell *et al.* (1940), and Beattie and Boswell (1939) bear out the conclusion of Duvel that humidity is the most important factor in deterioration in vitality of seed stored at room temperature but that at high humidity temperature is important. Barton (1939) reported results of storage experiments on seeds of carrot, cauliflower, eggplant, lettuce, onion, pepper, and tomato stored at room temperature and at —5°C. at Yonkers, N.Y. Some lots were air-dried and stored without sealing, some air-dried and sealed, others dried over CaO to remove about one-third of the moisture, still others were mixed with CaO to remove one-third or one-half of the moisture. Germination tests were made after 6 years of storage. The results may be summarized as follows:

All the kinds of seed stored at —5°C. maintained vitality for 6 years under all conditions of storage—open or sealed, air-dried or dried over CaO, or mixed with CaO to reduce moisture. Results of germination tests of the lots stored at room temperature show that tomato and eggplant seeds retained their vitality better than any of the others over the 6-year period. When the moisture of the seed was not reduced before sealing, the sealed seed had a lower per cent of germination than the unsealed seed. Eggplant retained viability for 6 years under all conditions studied. Air-dry, sealed tomato seed showed marked deterioration after 5 years' storage, while air-dry, unsealed seed retained viability (80 per cent) after 6 years. When the moisture was reduced and the seed was sealed, it remained in good condition for 6 years. Carrot seed lost vitality completely in 4 years when stored sealed; when not sealed, the viability was fairly well maintained for 6 years. Air-dry pepper seed, stored sealed, lost viability completely after 2 years; when not sealed germination was low (45 per cent) after 2 years. Lettuce retained vitality for 3 years in both open and sealed containers, but after 4 years there was no germination of air-dry seeds; when moisture was reduced and the seed was stored sealed, viability was maintained for 6 years. Results with onion seed was about the same as with lettuce. Cauliflower seed, stored air-dried and sealed, germinated only 12 per cent after 2 years; when moisture was reduced one-third, germination was 60 per cent after 4 years.

In a study of rapid deterioration of vegetable seeds, Boswell *et al.* stored 10 kinds of seeds at 80 and 50°F. and three different humidities at each temperature—44 and 51 per cent, 66 per cent, and 78 and 81 per cent. The seed stored were Lima bean, kidney bean, sweet corn, peanut (shelled), beet, spinach, cabbage, carrot, onion, and tomato. The mean moisture content of the seed stored at high humidity varied from about 8 per cent for peanut to 15 per cent or above for Lima bean, kidney bean, and beet at equilibrium. At low humidity the mean moisture content varied from about 5 per cent for peanut to about 10 per cent for Lima bean. At high humidity and high temperature at the end of 110 days, the germination of onion and peanut had fallen to zero, spinach and sweet corn to 25 per cent or less, and only beet and tomato maintained a germination above 70 per cent. At 251 days Lima bean germinated 26 per cent, beet 9 per cent, and tomato 68 per cent. All the others were 0 to 1 per cent. At low humidity (51 per cent) and low temperature (50°F.) only kidney bean and sweet corn had fallen significantly in germination by the end of 251 days.

Results of experiments reported by Toole, Toole, and Gorman (1948) showed that onion seed stored at 80°F. and 80 per cent humidity dropped to about 30 per cent germination in 6 weeks. Germination of lettuce seed dropped sharply after 6 weeks and germinated only 30 per cent at the end of 15 weeks. Of 13 other kinds of vegetable seeds only tomato was alive at the end of 36 weeks, and this seed germinated under 70 per cent. The other seeds in this experiment were bean, cabbage, carrot, celery, corn, cucumber, pea, pepper, spinach, turnip, and water-melon. All of these 15 kinds of seeds were stored at other temperatures and humidities, and the results were similar to those reported by Boswell *et al.* (1940) given above.

Toole, Toole, and Gorman found that the moisture content of the seed varied directly with the humidity but was influenced only slightly by temperature. Both the equilibrium moisture content of the seed at a given humidity and the rate of change of moisture with change of humidity were different for the different kinds of seeds.

The results of all the experiments indicate that, when seed is to be stored at room temperature in common storage, it should not be stored in sealed containers unless the moisture content is reduced. Toole (1942) made the following recommendations: (1) for seeds exposed to a temperature of 80°F. for more than a few days, the relative humidity should be no higher than 45 per cent; (2) for seeds exposed to 70°F., the relative humidity should be no higher than 60 per cent; (3) very short lived seeds, such as onion and shelled peanuts, old seed, or seed contaminated by fungi should be kept at lower humidity than is recommended above; (4) for seeds in cold storage at 40 to 50°F., the relative humidity should be no higher than 70 per cent, preferably not above 50 per cent; (5) seeds removed from cold storage at a humidity above 50 per cent should be dried to a moisture content safe for the temperature of later exposure, unless they are planted within a few days.

The results of the experiments mentioned indicate clearly that the length of life of the vegetable seeds studied is determined by the conditions under which they are held in storage.

Seed Testing. The term *seed testing* is ordinarily used in connection with purity and viability. Since vegetable seeds are fairly free from impurities, testing for purity is not of much value but testing for viability or germinating qualities is important, for such a test may be the means of avoiding losses due to sowing seed of low germinating power. By making a germination test the grower knows how much seed to plant to get a good stand of plants and may save time by avoiding the necessity of replanting or of having too few plants. Seed kept over from one year to the next should always be tested for germination before planting, because some kinds of seed lose their viability in a few months under unfavorable conditions of storage. However, under suitable storage conditions viability of any kind of vegetable seed will be maintained for a long period, as discussed previously. Perhaps the best method for the vegetable grower to use in making a germination test is to sow the seed in soil in a seed flat or seed pan. The seed should be counted, then planted in rows, and covered to the proper depth with soil. The flats or pans of seed may be placed in a greenhouse, in a hotbed, or in a moderately warm place in the dwelling. The soil should be kept moist but not wet. Counts made of the plants that come through the soil will give the gardener a good idea of what might be expected of the seed when planted under favorable conditions in the field. A simple method of making a germination test is to count out 25, 50, or 100 seeds of the sample to be tested and to place these between folds of moist blotting paper or moist cloth (cotton flannel). The blotting paper or cloth is placed in a soup plate, and another plate is inverted over the lower one to prevent rapid drying. The seeds should be placed in a warm room and kept moist, but not wet, by sprinkling. As the seeds sprout, they are counted and thrown away. The rapidity of germination and the vigor of the sprout should be noted, for seeds which germinate very slowly and produce weak sprouts may fail to produce plants when planted outside.

Temperature and Germination of Seed. It is fairly well known that some kinds of vegetable seeds will not germinate at low temperatures and that some will rot in cold soil. Kotowski (1926) reported results of studies of the effects of temperature on the germination of 17 different kinds of vegetables, representing eight families. The seeds were planted in coarse quartz sand in flats in electrically controlled, constant-temperature chambers. The seeds used were onion, beet, spinach, radish, cabbage, cauliflower, pea, garden bean, Lima bean, carrot, parsley, tomato, eggplant, pepper, muskmelon, cucumber, and lettuce. The temperatures used were 4, 8, 11, 18, 25, and 30°C.

In general the speed of germination of all kinds of seeds used in this experiment increased as the temperature rose, but at the lower temperatures the percentage germination of spinach, lettuce, cabbage, parsley, and beets was higher than at high temperatures. From this point of view the optimum temperature for spinach was 4°C., and cabbage 8°C., and for beets 11°C. Only lettuce, spinach, radish, and pea germinated at 4°C. At 8°C. all except tomato, eggplant, pepper, cucumber, melon, garden bean, and Lima bean germinated. These did not germinate at 11°C., although the garden bean developed radicles but no hypocotyl. All seeds germinated at 18°C. and, all except lettuce, at the higher temperatures, but the speed of germination was slow at 18°C. for all of the warm-season crops—tomato, eggplant, pepper, cucumber, melon, bean, and Lima bean.

The minima for beet, onion, cabbage, cauliflower, carrot, and parsley are between 4 and 8°C. The minima for eggplant, pepper, cucumber, melon, and bean are between 11 and 18°C.

The viability of tomato, eggplant, pepper, cucumber, melon, and garden bean was not affected by temperatures of 11, 8, and 4°C., for these seeds germinated after being in the germinating chamber at these low temperatures for 35, 45, and 60 days, when placed in chambers held at 30°C. The Lima bean is the only seed that rotted when held at temperatures too low for germination. Lettuce did not germinate at 30°C. Several research workers have shown that lettuce seed may fail to germinate when planted in warm soil (80°F. or above). This is discussed in Chap. 17.

Results of these and other experiments explain why it is feasible to plant some seeds in cold soil and not feasible to plant others under the same conditions. It is not safe, however, to plant many kinds of seed in the field when the soil is too cold to permit germination because, under average field conditions, disease organisms are likely to be present and the soil may become so compacted that seedlings would have difficulty in breaking through the crust. Insects and other animal parasites might also injure the seed.

CHAPTER 7

Plant Growing and Plant-growing Structures

Some vegetable-crop plants usually are started in well-prepared beds, and the young plants are transplanted later in the field, or garden. These include cabbage, cauliflower, broccoli, celery, eggplant, pepper, sweet potato, tomato, and a few others. Whether these are started in outdoor beds or under protection of cold frames, hotbeds, or greenhouses depends on the climate of the region and the time of the year the crop is to be grown. In regions having long cold winters and short growing seasons all of these are started in some kind of plant-growing structure when grown as an early crop. Even in regions where the winters are not so severe, as in the Southern parts of the United States, forcing structures are used to a considerable extent for starting plants for early crops. Other crops, such as lettuce, onion, cucumber, melon, and beet, sometimes are started in cold frames, hotbeds, or greenhouses.

The important advantages of starting plants in greenhouses or other forcing structures are: (1) increasing the length of the growing season and making it possible to grow long-season crops in regions where summers are short, (2) making it possible to grow more than one crop on the same land in one growing season, (3) protecting the plants from unfavorable weather, (4) obtaining larger yields of long-season tender crops when grown where summers are short, and (5) making it possible to produce an earlier crop by planting seed before it would be safe to plant in the open.

GREENHOUSES

Since greenhouse construction and management are specialized subjects taught in special courses in most agricultural colleges, the greenhouse is discussed here only from the standpoint of use by the market gardener and the truck grower as an adjunct to his outdoor gardening. Many up-to-date market gardeners and truck growers in the North have at least a small greenhouse for use in starting plants during winter and early spring. The use of greenhouses for this purpose is increasing. Some

86

vegetable growers combine vegetable forcing with their outdoor gardening. They have entered the forcing business by utilizing the greenhouse for growing crops to maturity when the space is not needed for starting plants. This, however, is not practicable where only one small plant house is available.

In regions that have long cold winters and short growing seasons, greenhouses are superior to hotbeds and cold frames. Some of the advantages are: (1) temperature can be controlled more easily in greenhouses than in other forcing structures; (2) ventilation can be regulated better and with less danger of chilling the plants; and (3) the work of planting and caring for the plants can be done without exposing the workers and the plants to unfavorable weather. During early spring there is danger of chilling the plants in hotbeds and cold frames when the cover is removed for watering, transplanting, and other care. There is no such danger in greenhouses. The greenhouse may be used also for growing crops to maturity during fall and winter before the structure is needed for plant growing.

Sash Houses and Other Small Greenhouses. When a grower expects to use a greenhouse only for growing plants for transplanting, he cannot afford to build an expensive structure since it is used for only a few months each year. For this reason there is a demand for small, relatively cheap greenhouses. Many growers have built cheap frame structures and covered them with hotbed sash. While these sash houses are more expensive than hotbeds, the advantages more than balance the extra cost. Some of these houses are low structures with the eaves within a few inches of the ground level, while others have walls entirely above ground. In the low type of construction the walk between the beds is excavated to the depth of 2 or 3 feet, and the beds or benches are near the ground level. This type is more easily heated than the high type but is less convenient for work. On poorly drained soils the low type is not satisfactory.

The high type of sash house has walls extending 2 to 4 or more feet above the surface of the ground. Some of these have solid concrete walls up to the eave plate, others have wood walls, and still others have part wood or concrete with glass above. Where considerable labor and money are expended for walls, framework, and heating systems it would be wise to build a standard type of greenhouse rather than a sash house. The only advantage of a sash house is its low cost. Two types and sizes of greenhouses are shown in Figs. 7.1 and 7.2. Both are suitable for growing crops to maturity.

Some building concerns are making a specialty of small ready-cut greenhouses to meet the needs of the vegetable growers for plant-growing structures.

Fig. 7.1. A relatively cheap type of greenhouse for plant growing and vegetable forcing. (*Courtesy of Lord and Burnham.*)

Fig. 7.2. A larger and more expensive greenhouse than the one shown in Fig. 7.1. (*Courtesy of Lord and Burnham.*)

The sash house and other small greenhouses can be heated by hot air, hot water, or steam. Steam is not feasible unless a steam-heating system is used for other purposes. In some sections heating by means of hot air carried through vitrified tile flues is very common. The flue is installed in much the same way as described for the flue-heated hotbed. Hot-water heating is the most desirable, although it is more expensive to install than is the flue system. Hot water requires less attention and maintains a more even temperature in the house.

HOTBEDS

Use of Hotbeds. The main use for hotbeds is for starting plants to be grown in the garden or field, although they are used to some extent to grow crops to maturity out of the normal growing season. Before greenhouses came into such general use, nearly all market gardeners depended on hotbeds for starting plants such as cabbage, tomatoes, eggplants, and peppers. Even where they have greenhouses most gardeners still use hotbeds.

Location. The main consideration in locating hotbeds are: (1) nearness to the farm buildings so that they can be cared for with the least trouble, (2) proximity to a good water supply, (3) protection from the cold winds by locating them on the south or southeast side of a hill, on the protected side of buildings, or by means of windbreaks, board fences, or walls. Where no suitable protection is already available, a tight fence about 5 feet high is often constructed on the north and west sides of the frames.

Southern or southeastern exposures are preferable because beds will get more sunshine with these exposures than with others. Where there is more than one row of frames, they should be parallel to each other, with ample spaces between the rows for the handling of the sashes and mats. Eight to ten feet of space between the rows of frames is desirable, if the land is not too valuable.

The Hotbed Frame. The frame may be made of wood, cement, brick, or stone, the first two materials being the most common. Where wood is used in making a permanent hotbed, 2- by 4-inch lumber is used for posts. These posts are driven into the ground at the corners of the bed and at intervals of 4 to 6 feet along the sides of the bed. Boards or planks are nailed to these posts. It is desirable to use a double layer of 1-inch boards or one layer of 2-inch planks for the frame. The frame may or may not extend to the bottom of the pit, but in any case it should extend 12 to 18 inches above the surface of the ground on the back side (usually north side) and 6 to 12 inches on the front, thus affording a slope preferably to the south. Every 3 feet a crossbar or slide should be placed for the sash to rest upon. For these crossbars, 2- by 3-inch pieces are satisfactory. A ½-inch strip nailed in the center of these crossbars to prevent binding of the sash is an advantage. In all permanent hotbeds durable wood should be used. Cedar, locust, or chestnut for the posts and cypress or chestnut for the frame are satisfactory.

Concrete is being used by many gardeners for hotbed frames. This is much more durable than wood and is cheaper in the long run. In making frames of concrete the mixture is poured into forms in the usual way.

Sash. Only the most durable wood should be used in making hotbed sash. Cypress and cedar are popular for this purpose. Sashes differ in size, but the most common size is 3 by 6 feet. A larger sash is too heavy to handle and is more subject to breakage. Most gardeners buy the sash already made, and this practice is usually wise, although it is advisable to inquire into the type of construction and the wood used.

The sash should be painted before being glazed. A good grade of glass is always desirable, although cheaper grades are sometimes used. The glass is generally lapped about ⅛ inch. Some gardeners prefer to butt the glass, but if the ends do not fit closely there will be considerable leakage. Each 3- by 6-foot sash is usually made for three rows of 10- by 12-inch glass, requiring 18 panes for each sash. Putty or mastica is applied in the rabbet of the sash bar, then the glass is pressed into it and held in place by glazing points. These materials prevent water from running down under the glass. After glazing, the sash should be painted again. Each year a coat of paint should be given to protect them against decay.

Hotbed Covers. The ordinary hotbed covered with sash needs some protection during cold weather. It is necessary to cover the beds every cold night and sometimes during the entire day in early spring, especially for tender plants, such as tomatoes, eggplants, peppers, or melons. Old matting, carpets, or heavy burlap may be used, but most gardeners use straw mats. These are sold by dealers in garden supplies but may be made at home.

Manure-heated Hotbeds. In the early days of vegetable growing in the United States fresh horse manure was the main source of heat for hotbeds. In most regions of the United States such manure is not available in any considerable quantity since vegetable growers do not keep horses and the supply formerly obtained from the cities is practically nonexistent. Where fresh horse manure is available it can be used to advantage as a source of heat for hotbeds. The manure must be fairly fresh, or very little heat will be generated. Two parts excrement to one part straw or other litter will give good results. Manure with shavings as litter is not satisfactory.

Preparation of manure for the hotbed should begin 10 days to 2 weeks before the beds are needed. If fresh manure from the stable is used, it should be placed in a flat pile about 4 feet high, 4 to 5 feet wide, and any length desired. If dry at the time of piling, the manure should be moistened in order to start fermentation. In 2 or 3 days the manure will begin to steam. When fermentation is well under way, the pile should be turned to ensure uniform heating throughout. In turning the manure, that from the interior of the pile should be placed on the exterior of the new pile. In 2 or 3 days after turning the manure should be in condition for placing in the pit.

The pit for the hotbed should be well drained since water collecting in it will interfere with the fermentation of the manure. The pit should be as wide as the frame of the hotbed. The depth of the pit depends on the length of time the bed is to be used; the longer the period, the deeper the pit should be because more manure is needed for a hotbed to be used for 3 months than for one to be used for a shorter period. Most pits are from 24 to 36 inches deep, but 12 to 18 inches is sufficient where heat is needed for only 3 or 4 weeks.

In filling the pit the manure should be thrown in layers of 5 or 6 inches and each layer trampled fairly well, especially along the sides and ends of the pit. Since the manure will settle several inches, allowance should be made for this. Sometimes a layer of 3 or 4 inches of straw is put over the manure in order to have a more even distribution of heat and prevent hot spots in the soil. A layer of 4 to 6 inches of good soil is put on the manure or straw, although 2 inches of soil is sufficient if the seeds are sown in flats instead of in the soil of the bed.

Temporary hotbeds are made by placing the frames on the top of a pile of fermenting manure. The frames are usually banked with manure as protection from cold. More manure is required where the frame is set on the pile, because the pile must be considerably wider and longer than the frame. This type of hotbed is desirable where drainage is poor.

Flue-heated Hotbeds. Hotbeds are frequently heated by hot air conducted through flues from a firebox located at one end of the beds. Flue-heated beds are very commonly used for growing sweet-potato plants in New Jersey, but they are also used for growing other plants in many sections of the country. For sweet-potato plants the beds used in New Jersey are open, but for growing other plants they must be covered.

A common type of open flue-heated bed used in New Jersey is 12 feet wide and 60 feet long. The walls commonly are built of concrete blocks or of solid concrete. A firebox is built at one end, preferably at the end facing the cold winds, and deep enough to ensure a good circulation of air under the bed. The inside of the firebox should be at least 3 feet wide, 6 feet long, and 4 feet high if wood is to be used as fuel. The inside of the box is lined with firebrick surrounded by concrete.

For a bed 12 feet wide and 60 feet long two 6-inch flues are used. These flues are made of 6-inch round glazed tile pipe connected to the rear of the firebox as near the top as possible. The flues are placed under the ground to within a few feet of the farther end of the bed where they come to the surface under the bed. In order that there may be good draft, the flues should not be horizontal but slope gradually upward from the firebox to the farther end where it is brought above the surface by an elbow. The soil covering is usually 15 to 16 inches deep near the firebox and 6 to 8 inches at the other end. A 30-foot bed may be heated by means of one 8-inch flue. In a bed of this length the air at the outlet is hot and it is best to protect the floor boards above the outlet with asbestos or with sheet metal. This protection is not necessary in a 60-foot bed.

Two chimneys are constructed for beds of the kind described, one in each corner at the firebox end. The height of these chimneys varies from 3 or 4 feet to 6 or 8 feet high, depending on the location. The smoke and warm air from the firebox go through the flues and pass out into the open space under the bed. They circulate under the bed and finally escape through the chimneys. The floor of the bed is made of boards placed on timbers laid across the bed.

For growing plants other than sweet potatoes, the open hotbed is not satisfactory. A hotbed of the type described can be covered with two rows of hotbed sash, with the upper end resting on a ridge in the center. The width should be less than 12 feet, however, in order to allow sufficient slope to the sash.

Hot-water-heated Hotbeds. Hot water is the most satisfactory heat for hotbeds as the temperature can be controlled more easily than with any other method. It is more expensive to install than hot-air heat as used in the flue-heated beds. Since the installation of a hot-water heating system is more expensive than the other systems mentioned, care should be given in locating and constructing the beds. The hotbed frame should be made of concrete or other durable material.

Where greenhouses or other structures are heated by hot water, it is often possible to use the same boiler for heating the hotbeds.

Electrically Heated Hotbeds. Heating of hotbeds with electricity is common in many regions. Electric-heated hotbeds are used to a considerable extent in Norway and Sweden where the cost of electric current is low. Reports from these countries are favorable for the use of electricity for this purpose. In the United States several experiments have been conducted to determine the practicability of this method of heating. Garver and Vincent (1927), Kable (1932), Currence (1932), Moses and Tavernetti (1934), Stout *et al.* (1936), and others have published results of studies of electric heating of hotbeds. Some of these investigators have given data on the cost of equipment and on the current consumed under different conditions. From these data one can estimate the probable cost of operating an electric hotbed under a given set of conditions. Garver and Vincent compared manure-heated with electric-heated hotbeds at Pullman, Wash., and found relatively little difference in cost between these two types when the cost of construction and equipment was distributed over 3 years. This calculation was based on the actual cost of materials used in construction, manure for heating at $12 per cord, and electric current at 3 cents per kilowatt-hour.

The most common type of heating by electricity is by passing current through specially constructed cable, consisting of electrically insulated resistance wire enclosed in a flexible metal sheath. The temperature in the bed can be controlled automatically by means of a thermostat.

The main advantages of the electric hotbed are as follows:

1. They are always ready for use.
2. They may be converted into cold frames by turning off the electricity.
3. They are easily manipulated and readily moved.
4. They can be used as long as may be necessary, whereas manure loses its heat in a few weeks.

The first cost of an electric hotbed is greater than for a manure hotbed, and it requires some experience with electric apparatus to build and operate an electrically heated bed. Where electricity is available at a low cost, electric hotbeds give promise of being practicable.

COLD FRAMES

Use of Cold Frames. There are four general purposes for which cold frames are used: (1) for starting plants in the spring, (2) for hardening off plants which have been started in the hotbed or greenhouse, (3) for wintering hardy plants started in the fall, (4) for growing crops such as lettuce, radishes, beets, and parsley to maturity. If only a little protection is necessary, cold frames are satisfactory for starting plants. In some regions some crops such as cucumbers, melons, beets, and celery are started in cold frames, and when weather conditions become favorable and protection is no longer needed, the covering is removed. In some cases the frame is removed also and the crops receive field culture.

Cold frames are constructed in very much the same way as hotbeds except that no pit is required. In fact the main difference between a hotbed and a cold frame is the absence of any form of heat in the latter, except that provided by the sun. Permanent cold frames are commonly made of concrete, Fig. 7.3, while temporary ones are made of boards.

Cold frames are covered with glass sash, canvas, or cloth. Where sash is used, the frames are as a rule 6 feet wide, although frames 12 feet wide are not uncommon. When cloth is used, the beds are very often 12 feet wide.

PLANT GROWING

Good plants are essential to success in vegetable growing. To have good plants one must get good seed and use judgment and care in sowing the seed, in the management of the seedbed, in transplanting the seedlings, and in hardening-off the plants before they are planted in the open. Plant growing calls for skill and care. Any neglect may cause a serious loss due to delayed maturity or to a decrease in yield or both. Perhaps no factor is more commonly neglected than the selection and the preparation of the soil for the plant bed.

Vegetable Crops

Soil for the Plant Bed. A good soil for plant growing is of good physical character, friable, retentive of moisture, and free of disease organisms, especially of the "damping-off" fungi. It carries an abundance of nutrients for satisfactory growth. The demand for nutrients is heavy since a 3-inch layer of soil often must support a thick stand of sizable plants before time for setting in the field. There is danger, however, of having too high a concentration of soluble salts where the soil is composted with manure in large quantity or when heavy applications of fertilizer are applied to the soil. The electrical-conductivity method of measuring the total soluble salt content of the soil frequently is used as

FIG. 7.3. A good permanent type of cold frame.

an index of the fertility of the composted soil. This method does not indicate the proportion of the different soluble constituents present, but it serves well as a guide, especially in cases of excessive and injurious contents of soluble salts.

The base soil should be of a loamy nature, preferably a sandy loam well supplied with organic matter for the transplanting soil. Pure sand may be used for starting seedlings that are to be pricked out later into a good loamy soil. It is a common practice to make a compost pile of soil and manure in alternate layers at least a year in advance of the time the material is to be used for plant growing. Where sod is used, the compost pile should be made 2 or 3 years in advance. The proportion of manure to soil varies from one part of manure to three to ten parts of soil depending on the fertility and physical condition of the soil. If the soil is heavy, some sand should be added either to the compost pile or at the time it is to be used. For rapid decomposition of the manure and sod, moisture is essential and water may have to be applied from time to time. The compost should be turned to mix the ingredients, since a poorly blended compost will produce uneven plants.

Before the compost is used for plant growing, it should be run through a soil shredder or put through a coarse screen for mixing and removing, or pulverizing, large particles. The soil should be so stored in the fall that it will be available for use when needed, regardless of the weather. It is usually desirable to sterilize the soil by steam, electricity, formaldehyde, or other chemical treatment.

Sowing Seed. Moisture, oxygen, and congenial temperature are requisites of germination. In greenhouses and hotbeds moisture and a congenial temperature are artificially provided, but to maintain the proper moisture the soil must be of good texture. The soil for the seedbed should be light and friable, but not so light that it dries out quickly. A heavy soil, or one containing considerable clay, is not satisfactory because when the surface becomes dry it gets hard and cracks and if kept wet it puddles. These conditions are not favorable for good germination and growth. A sandy-loam soil is most generally used for seedbeds, but muck is considered almost ideal for celery, lettuce, and some other crops.

The time for sowing seeds in greenhouses, hotbeds, or cold frames depends on the kind of crop and the subsequent treatment it is to receive before the plants are to be set in the field. If they are to be set directly from the seedbed, less time is given than when they are to be transplanted once or twice. In general the length of time between seed sowing and setting the plants in the field varies from 3 or 4 to 12 weeks. When the plants are not transplanted prior to setting in the field, 4 to 6 weeks is usually allowed between the sowing of the seed and setting the plants. A longer time is allowed in outdoor seedbeds than in greenhouses, hotbeds, or cold frames, since the growing conditions are less likely to be favorable in the former than in the latter. When only one transplanting is to be made and the usual spacing is given, the seed of most crops should not be planted more than 6 weeks prior to time for planting in the field. Many growers start plants too early for best results. When started too early, the plants are likely to become stunted or else allowed to get too tall and spindly. Early planting also increases the cost of growing the plants. Plant-growing requirements for specific crops are given under the discussion of individual crops.

Seeds are planted in flats or directly in the soil of the greenhouse bench, hotbed, or cold frame. The flat is filled with a good, friable soil which should be firmed to prevent too much settling. It is particularly important to firm the soil in the corners and along the edges. The firming of the soil is done with a board to leave the surface level and smooth. The surface of the soil should be below the top of the flat to prevent water running off.

Most vegetable seeds are sown in rows and covered with soil. When flats are used, the rows are spaced about 2 inches apart, but in greenhouse benches and in hotbeds, the rows are usually 3 to 6 inches apart, the wider spacing being used when the seedlings are not to be pricked out. A convenient method of measuring and marking the rows to receive the seed is to use a stick about 2 inches wide, $\frac{1}{4}$ inch thick, and of a length to fit the flat. The edge of the stick may be pressed into the soil to the depth desired. After all the rows are made, the seed is planted thinly and is covered by sifting fine soil over the rows and firming it lightly. When sowing seed direct to the soil of the hotbed, greenhouse, or frame, a rakelike marker is often used. After the seed is sown, it is covered by hand by brushing it lightly back and forth over the row to fill the little furrow. There are small hand seeders which are used for sowing seeds in greenhouse benches and in hotbeds. This machine is pulled across the bed by hand in much the same way as one would use a hand weeder. Small seeds are sometimes sown broadcast and covered very lightly with fine soil or merely covered with a piece of cloth or burlap. The latter method is often used for celery and other small seed.

The depth of soil over the seed depends, to a considerable extent, on the size of seed and the kind of soil. Very small seeds should be covered lightly if at all. Cabbage seeds and others of similar size are covered to the depth of about $\frac{1}{4}$ inch, while beets are covered to the depth of $\frac{1}{2}$ inch in light soil. In heavy soil, seeds should have less covering than in light soils.

Care of the Seedbed. Very close attention must be given the seedbed if good results are to be obtained. Only by experience can one learn just how to care for the seedbed under the artificial conditions that prevail in greenhouses, hotbeds, and cold frames. The gardener wants good stocky plants ready at the required season, and to have them great care must be given to the temperature, moisture, ventilation, transplanting, and hardening-off. Things to avoid are: (1) chilling the plants, (2) overheating and lack of ventilation which make the plants soft, (3) overwatering, which makes the plants soft and very susceptible to damping-off, and (4) wilting of plants due to too much heat or too little water.

WATERING. Caution should be exercised in watering the seedbed. Before the seedlings come through the surface, there is danger of washing out the seed and puddling the soil. At this time the seedbed should be watered with a fine spray from a sprinkling can or with a fine rose on a garden hose. Water dashed on the seedbed through an ordinary hose nozzle or through a rose with large holes is likely to wash out the seed.

The seedbed should never be allowed to dry out, nor should it be kept soaked, but sufficient water should be applied to wet all of the soil in the flat. Until the plants are well established, the soil should be kept fairly moist but not wet. After the plants are well established, the watering should be done thoroughly, but not too often. There is usually more danger of overwatering than underwatering. Keeping the surface wet after the plants are up is favorable to damping-off, hence it is best not to water often but to soak the soil thoroughly and then withhold water until the plants show the need of it. Of course more water is required on a bright day than on a cloudy or rainy day because of greater evaporation and transpiration. In fact plants should not be watered on cloudy days unless absolutely necessary. Watering should be done early enough in the day to allow the foliage of the plants to dry off before night. It is best to do the watering in the morning, for if done during the middle of the day there is some danger of sunscald, and if done late in the afternoon the plants may not dry off before night. Watering reduces the temperature in the hotbed, and for this reason it should be done early enough to allow the bed to get warm before the sun goes down. Before the plants are to be taken up to set in the field, the plant bed should be thoroughly soaked so as to have as much soil as possible adhere to the roots.

CONTROLLING TEMPERATURE. In greenhouses and in steam- or hot-water-heated hotbeds the temperature is controlled by turning on and turning off the heat in some or all the pipes and by regulating the ventilation. During bright days in spring it is often necessary to turn off all of the heat and ventilate thoroughly to keep the temperature down. The temperature that should be maintained depends on the kind of crop. Tomatoes, peppers, eggplants, cucumbers, and melons thrive best in a relatively high temperature, while cabbage, cauliflower, lettuce, celery, onions, and beets do best in a relatively low temperature. Slow, steady growth is preferable; therefore the temperature should not be high enough to make rapid, succulent growth nor low enough to check growth until time for hardening the plants.

Ventilation of greenhouses and frames where young plants are growing needs careful attention. Ventilation dries the air and aids in the control of the temperature. In greenhouses ventilation is obtained by opening the ventilators, while in frames the sashes are raised at one end or pulled down a short distance. The tendency is to ventilate too little rather than too much. As plants grow, more and more ventilation should be given until finally on bright warm days the sash may be removed. In ventilating during cold weather the wind should not be allowed to strike the plants. In greenhouses this is obviated by opening the ventilators on the side of the house opposite the direction of the wind. In frames the wínd is prevented from striking the plants by raising the end of the sash on the side of the frame opposite the direction of the wind.

Transplanting. Plants started in the greenhouse, hotbed, or cold frame are usually transplanted at least once, and sometimes twice or three times, prior to being set in the field. The common practice is to sow seeds thickly in flats, or directly in the soil of the greenhouse, hotbed, or cold frame. When the first true leaves are fairly well developed, the seedlings are usually transplanted or pricked out either into flats or into the soil of the greenhouse bed, hotbed, or cold frame. The soil should be loose and friable. The flat is filled with soil, which is firmed a little

Fig. 7.4. Spotting board used in making holes to receive seedling plants.

in the corners and along the sides. A leveling strip is used to remove the surface soil and to leave the surface level, then the soil is compacted lightly. Holes to receive the plants may be made with the finger, with a small dibble, or with a spotting board, similar to the one shown in Fig. 7.4. The use of the spotting board is desirable in order to get the plants evenly spaced. For best results the soil should be moist, but not wet enough to stick to the pegs.

Seedlings are spaced 1 to 2 inches apart each way depending on the size of the plants and the length of time they are to remain in the box or bed. Sometimes plants are transplanted twice before being set in the field. As soon as they begin to crowd after the first transplanting, they are taken up and transplanted again, spacing them farther apart. If they have been planted 2 by 2 inches the first time, they may be spaced 3 by 3 or 4 by 4 inches at the second transplanting. Tomatoes and some other plants are often put in paper bands, veneer bands, flowerpots, tin cans, or other containers at the second transplanting, one plant to each receptacle. The main advantage in using pots, or dirt bands, is that the roots are not disturbed when the plant is set in the field as all of the soil around the roots remains intact. In transplanting, the soil should be pressed down around the roots, with care to see that the hole is closed at the bottom. The stems of young, succulent plants are sometimes injured by pressing with the fingers in transplanting. The pressure should be exerted downward rather than against the plant. After each transplanting the plants should be watered thoroughly to settle the soil round the roots. When the plants are soft, it is an advantage to shade them until they become established. Bright warm sunshine is likely to cause wilting since the roots cannot take up moisture as fast as it is transpired from the leaves.

Seeds of cucumbers, melons, Lima beans, and sweet corn are sometimes planted in pots or plant bands a few weeks before time for setting in the open. Several seeds are planted in each receptacle and the young plants thinned to the desired number either before or after planting in the field. In planting in the field, all of the soil is kept around the roots so as to check the growth of the plant as little as possible.

ADVANTAGES AND DISADVANTAGES OF TRANSPLANTING. The main advantages in transplanting plants prior to setting them in the field or garden are economy in the use of valuable space in the greenhouse, hotbed, or cold frame and economy in the care of slowly developing seedlings. With expensive seed there is the additional advantage of saving of seed. If plants are not to be transplanted, it is necessary to have the seedbed of sufficient size to allow the plants to grow for several weeks without crowding. This would mean utilizing more space than is needed for the first few weeks and also adds to the labor and expense of caring for the seedbed. For example, several hundred cabbage seedlings can be started in a flat 12 by 18 inches in size, whereas when they are transplanted 2 by 2 inches apart, the flat would hold only 48 plants. With other vegetable crop plants similar economy in the use of seedbed space results from growing seedlings thickly and then transplanting them at the proper time.

Increase in root branching results from the transplanting of many plants. This is an advantage when the plants are grown in beds and must be taken up before they are transferred to the field. This is due to the fact that in taking up the plants from the seedbed some of the roots are broken. This results in greater root branching than is the case when the plants are allowed to grow in the seedbed. There are many more short branch roots on transplanted plants of those kinds which are readily transplanted than on nontransplanted plants. This means that, when the plants are taken up for setting in the field, there is a larger absorbing surface in the block of soil around the roots of transplanted plants than in a similar block of soil taken up with nontransplanted plants. There is, however, no advantage in more than one transplanting. In fact, with some plants more than one transplanting results in excessive branching and a reduced spread. A slight increase in the number of branch roots is not accompanied by a decreased spread, but marked increase in branching results in considerable reduction in feeding area.

When pots or plant bands are used, there is no advantage in transplanting, so far as the response of the plant is concerned, since practically all the roots remain intact when the plants are set out. Results of experiments by Cranefield (1899) and Boyle (1913) indicate that transplanting is a disadvantage when pots or plant bands are used.

Many growers and others believe that transplanting results in a more stocky plant with a better root system and that this increases the yield and hastens maturity. Experimental evidence indicates that transplanting in itself generally does not increase the yield or hasten maturity, but that the increase in space and better conditions usually given do have this effect. In most of the earlier experiments the space factor was not eliminated and other factors also were involved, so that the advantages claimed were not due to the transplanting but to more favorable environment for growth. In some cases the plants referred to as transplanted were not taken up and reset but merely were shifted from one receptacle to another. These were compared with nontransplanted plants grown in beds or in flats.

The main disadvantages of transplanting are the extra labor required and the check in growth due to taking up and resetting the plants. The extra labor involved often is offset by the economy in the use of valuable greenhouse space for the seedbed and the saving of labor in caring for the plants. All plants are checked in growth by transplanting, but with those that are easily transplanted, this check may be offset by the increase in root branching. Even with such plants as cabbage and tomatoes, transplanting when the plants are large usually results in delayed maturity and often in reduced yield. With plants poorly adapted to transplanting, such as corn, cucumbers, melons, and beans, the check in growth is very marked and results in serious reduction in yield unless the transplanting is done while the plants are small. A second transplanting of these plants is usually very injurious. It is doubtful if more than one transplanting of any plants is justified as far as crop yields are concerned. It may be desirable from the standpoint of economy in the use of valuable space.

Loomis (1925) in an elaborate series of experiments at Ithaca, N.Y., with several vegetable crops, found that transplanting always resulted in a check in growth, the check being proportional to the size of the plant at the time it was reset. This check in growth did not always result in a reduced yield, because differences due to transplanting in the greenhouse frequently were obscured by the shift to the field or by hardening prior to the shift. The effect generally was more to retard development than to decrease the yield. Loomis concludes as follows:

While there are isolated instances of crops which appear to have made a thriftier growth after an early transplanting, these instances will seldom bear statistical analysis, and the conclusion that transplanting is a harmful but frequently necessary operation seems to be required. On the other hand, the field data do not justify a large expense to avoid early transplantings, since the only shift which has consistently affected either earliness or total yield in cabbage and tomatoes is the final one to the field.

DIFFERENCES IN RESPONSE TO TRANSPLANTING. It is well known that some plants are more injured by transplanting than are others. In fact, it is believed by many that some plants will not withstand the process, but the evidence from Loomis' experiments indicates that any of the common vegetable plants may be transplanted satisfactorily during the early stage of growth. With some kinds of plants, such as corn, beans, and the cucurbits, there is only a short period when they are not seriously injured by being taken up and reset. This is the reason that these plants are usually grown in pots or plant bands when they are started indoors. Even with those crops which commonly are transplanted, such as tomatoes and cabbage, the check in growth is considerable if the transplanting is done when the plants are large.

Results of experiments conducted by Loomis clearly established a correlation between the ease of transplanting and rate of new root formation. Plants which are rather easily transplanted showed a slow rate of root replacement, but also a slow rate of top growth. Plants seriously injured by transplanting normally have a rapid rate of top growth and slow root replacement. Loomis concluded "that root replacement appears to be the largest single factor concerned in transplanting." Figure 7.5 illustrates the difference in root replacement of cabbage and corn plants. Eight days after being transplanted the transplanted cabbage plant had a much greater absorbing surface, owing to root branching, than did the check plant. The transplanted corn plant, on the other hand, had not branched at all, and the total absorbing surface was very much less than that of the plant which had not been transplanted. With increasing age the rate of root replacement decreases with most, if not all, vegetable plants.

The immediate effect of transplanting is a slowing down or stopping of the growth of the plant for a period; this seems to vary directly with the quantity and duration of the reduction of the water supply. While various factors, both environmental and internal, affect recovery from transplanting, they all act through their final effects on the water supply.

This is only slightly influenced by the tops. The roots are the most important factor involved in resistance to, and recovery from, transplanting. Loomis suggests that there are three factors concerned: (1) the proportion of the root system retained in transplanting which depends on the size of the plant and the character of root branching, (2) the effectiveness of the retained roots in absorbing water during the first few days

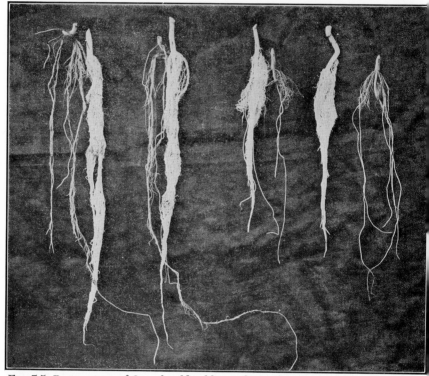

FIG. 7.5. Root systems of 8-weeks-old cabbage plants (four on the left) and 2-weeks-old sweet-corn plants (four on the right), showing effects of transplanting on root development. The plant on the left of each set of two is the nontransplanted plant; the one on the right is the transplanted one 8 days after transplanting.

after transplanting, an effect presumably correlated with the amount of suberization in the older roots, and (3) the rate of new root formation, which depends on the kind of plant, its age, and possibly on the stored food. There is evidence that the roots of some plants which are difficult to transplant are suberized or cutinized at an early age. Deposition of suberin or cutin in the endodermis, or in the periderm layer, would hinder water absorption. This would have a marked effect on the recovery of the plant following transplanting. Loomis found that branch formation in shortened roots was inversely proportional to the extent to which suberization had progressed.

Containers for Plant Growing. Various kinds of containers are used for growing plants, one plant to a container. Clay pots, paper bands, paper pots, peat pots, and wood veneer bands are the most common. Containers made of carbonaceous materials such as wood, paper, or peat frequently give unsatisfactory results. Studies by Knott and Jeffries (1929), Haber (1931), Jones (1931), and Youden and Zimmerman (1936) indicate that the poor growth of plants in these containers is due to deficiency of nitrates. The carbonaceous material of these containers supplies energy food for organisms that cause decomposition of the material itself. These organisms also consume nitrates and thus compete with the crop plants for the available nitrates in the soil. By supplying extra nitrates to the potting soil and by adding nitrogenous fertilizer as need is evidenced by the plant, the difficulty is overcome. New clay pots take up nitrates from the soil solution, and, for this reason, plants grown in them frequently make slower growth than plants grown in pots that have been used. Soaking new pots in a solution of nitrate of soda, or applying nitrogenous fertilizer when needed, will supply the deficiency.

Romshe (1954) reported results of experiments in Oklahoma in which plant bands made of wood veneer, Manila paper, and heavy asphalt paper were compared in growing tomato plants. The bands were of three sizes, 2 by 2, 3 by 3, and 4 by 4 inches, all of them being 3 inches in depth. Romshe found no significant difference in yield of tomatoes for the kinds of material of which the bands were made. There was, however, increase in both early and total yield with increase in size of bands. He found also that plants transplanted both in flats and plant bands consistently produced higher yields than those grown from seed spot-planted in the flats and bands, which is somewhat at variance with results of other experiments.

One advantage of using pots and plant bands is that the roots are not injured or disturbed when the plant is set in the field as the ball of soil is moved with the plant. In the case of peat pots, the pot is set in the soil with the plant and the roots grow through the walls of the container and enter the soil.

Blocking Plants. A method of growing tomato and other plants, known as blocking, is practiced in some parts of New Jersey. The blocking is done about 10 days before the plants are to go to the field and consists of cutting the soil and compost into blocks with a blocking hoe. The shank of a wide-bladed hoe is straightened out to make the blocking hoe, or a cutting tool made from a crosscut saw is used for the purpose.

The bed is specially prepared for the plants before they are "spotted out" by spreading 2 or 3 inches of compost on the spotting bed, then before the compost has had a chance to get dry, sandy-loam soil is spread on it to the depth of 2 or 3 inches. When the material settles, it is of the desired thickness for tomatoes and eggplants.

In blocking, the operator stands on a plank over the bed and cuts between plants so that each plant has a block of soil at least 3 by 3 inches and as deep as the soil and compost. The cutting severs the large lateral roots, and new branch roots form. The cutting of the roots checks growth somewhat, and the check results in the development of more feeder roots.

Hardening Plants. The term *hardening* or *hardening-off*, is applied to any treatment that results in a firming or hardening of the tissues of the plants, thus enabling them better to withstand unfavorable environmental conditions. Many persons speak of hardening only in connection with the processes that enable plants to withstand frost injury, but it is as important to harden them so that they will withstand insect injury, whipping, hot drying winds, or other unfavorable conditions. All experienced gardeners know that soft, tender plants are injured by unfavorable soil, or atmospheric conditions, and make an effort to prevent this injury by subjecting them to some hardening treatment.

Any treatment that materially checks growth increases hardiness. With plants that possess potential hardiness, as cabbage and related crops, hardiness increases in proportion as growth is checked. With tender plants like tomatoes, peppers, eggplants, and the cucurbits, checking growth results in only slight resistance to cold.

The treatments commonly used to harden plants are exposing them to relatively low temperature for a week or more and allowing the soil of the plant bed to become dry, or a combination of these two. Exposing plants to relatively low temperature is perhaps the most common method employed and is usually accompanied by withholding water. Exposure to low temperature is done by reducing the heat and increasing the ventilation in greenhouses and hotbeds or by removing the plants to a cold frame. Since any treatment that checks growth results in hardening, it is evident that low temperature is not essential; therefore removing plants to cold frames is an unnecessary expense unless the greenhouse or hotbed is needed for other plants. In other words, hardening can be accomplished as well in the greenhouse or hotbed by withholding water as by exposing them to low temperature in the cold frame. It is easier to control the water supply than to control the temperature. With some plants, notably celery and cabbage, and probably others, exposing them to relatively low temperature (40 to 50°F.) for 2 weeks may result in serious loss due to premature development of the seed stalk. This subject is discussed in considerable detail under Celery in Chap. 17.

Hardening is accompanied by: (1) decrease in rate of growth, (2) thickening of the cuticle, (3) increasing the waxy covering on the leaves of cabbage and some other plants, (4) increasing the percentage of hydrophilous colloids, (5) increasing the percentage of dry matter, (6) decreasing the percentage of freezable water, (7) decreasing the transpiration per unit area of leaf, (8) increasing the percentage of sugars, and (9) development of a pink color, especially in the stems, petioles, and leaf veins. The leaves of hardened plants are of a deeper green color and smaller in size than similar unhardened plants of the same age. Rosa (1921) emphasized the increase in hydrophilous colloids and the decrease in freezable water in the cells during hardening as the chief factors in reducing or preventing injury of plants by freezing temperature.

Harvey (1918) suggested that the principal effect of hardening cabbage plants is a change in the constituents of the protoplasm which prevent their precipitation as a result of the physical changes incident to freezing. The proteins are changed to forms which are less easily precipitated. This is indicated by an increase in the amino acid content of the cabbage on hardening.

It seems evident that the most important changes occurring during hardening are those which increase the water-retaining power of the cell. The decrease in water and the increase in the colloid content are important factors in increasing the water-holding power. The thickening of the waxy covering on the leaves of cabbage may be important in protecting plants against freezing. Undercooling of the cell solution is of considerable importance, and Harvey found that those plants which have the most bloom on the surface of the leaf are the most resistant to the formation of ice within the tissue.

Levitt and Scarth (1936) suggested that one factor in frost injury is protoplasmic strain and that the greater resistance to plasmolysis and deplasmolysis found in hardened cabbage plants as compared to unhardened plants is due to the greater resistance to the injurious effects of the strain. Levitt (1939) found that the critical freezing temperature of hardened cabbage plants was $-5.6°C.$ and of unhardened plants $-2.1°C.$ Since the unhardened plants retained 3.5 times more water in the liquid state per gram of dry matter than hardened plants at their critical freezing temperatures, Levitt concluded that injury due to dehydration is precluded. He found that reducing the rate of freezing and thawing did not alter the critical freezing temperature of unhardened plants, which indicates that injury was due to cell contraction and not to intercellular ice or to rapid thawing. With hardened plants the critical freezing temperature was lowered by reducing the rate of freezing but not of thawing.

Hardening should be gradual in order to prevent a severe check to growth or the possible killing of the plant. It is better to maintain a moderate rate of growth throughout the plant-growing period than to have rapid growth up to the time of hardening and then check it suddenly. Many growers overharden their plants, and this results in delayed growth after the plants are set in the field. In fact it is doubtful if any hardening treatment is advisable for some warm-season plants such as tomatoes, peppers, and eggplants. Porter (1935), Brasher and Westover (1937), and Babb (1940) have shown that subjecting tomato plants to the hardening treatment may result in reduced early yield. It seems probable that pepper and eggplant plants react in the same way as tomato plants. None of these kinds of plants can be hardened to withstand ice formation in the tissues.

Commercial Plant Growing. The growing of plants for sale is of considerable importance in many parts of the United States, especially in those areas where climatic conditions are favorable for outdoor production. Some of the important areas of commercial production are the Rio Grande Valley of Texas, areas in southern Georgia, parts of South Carolina, Virginia, Louisiana, Arkansas, California, and Arizona. Hundreds of millions of plants, including cabbage, tomatoes, sweet potatoes, onions, cauliflower, peppers, and others, are grown for shipment to other areas. Since these plants are grown, in most cases, in the field and are not transplanted prior to field setting, the cost of production is low as compared with plants grown in greenhouses or hotbeds.

Results of experiments comparing field-grown tomato plants produced in the Southern parts of the United States with home-grown plants in some of the Northern states have been conflicting. These are discussed in Chap. 24. It is suggested that the reasons for conflicting results are differences in: (1) succulence of the plants at the time they are pulled, (2) length of time between pulling and planting, (3) method of packing and transporting, (4) the soil and weather conditions at the time of planting and immediately thereafter, and (5) presence or absence of disease in the plants at the time they are received.

Soft, succulent plants are likely to heat in transit and to reach their destination in such poor condition that many will not survive unfavorable conditions and those that do will start growth slowly. Plants that are too hard and woody will grow slowly at first, and fruit setting will be delayed. Freshly pulled plants are more likely to withstand unfavorable conditions such as dry soil and hot, dry weather at planting time than are plants that are in transit a day or two after being pulled.

The danger of introducing disease into a region should be considered in buying plants from a distance. While many plant growers are careful in all their operations and some of the states furnish good inspection service, the danger of introducing a disease into another area is not eliminated completely.

CHAPTER 8

Planting Vegetable Crops in the Open

The time and method of planting seeds and plants of a particular species in the open determine to a considerable extent the success or failure of the crop. Even with good seeds or good plants satisfactory and profitable crops will not be produced unless the planting is done at the right time and in a proper manner. Attention must be given to the preparation of the soil for the seedbed, to the depth of planting, to the rate of planting, and to various other factors such as thinning and watering to ensure a satisfactory stand of plants. Planting both seeds and plants in the open is considered in this chapter.

Time of Planting. No definite date can be given for planting vegetable seeds and plants because climatic conditions vary widely within relatively small areas, owing to differences in elevation, proximity to large bodies of water, etc. The time of planting should be determined with reference to the soil and weather conditions, to the kind of crop, and to the time the produce is desired. In regions where climatic conditions are favorable throughout the year there is no definite time for planting. Where earliness is an important factor, as in regions of short growing seasons, the first planting is made as early as soil and weather conditions are satisfactory for the crop or crops grown. In sections of the Southern part of the United States and in parts of California and Arizona, where crops are grown for market during the fall and early winter, it is the practice to plant in late summer or early fall. In areas where freezing weather occurs, crops for early-summer market are planted as soon as the danger of frost is past. Vegetable crops may be grouped into three classes with respect to cold resistance: (1) hardy, or those that will withstand hard frost, (2) half-hardy, or those that will withstand light frosts and the seed of which will germinate at relatively low temperatures, (3) tender, or those that are killed or injured by frost and the seed of which will not germinate in cold soil. The hardy group includes kale, spinach, turnips, mustard, onions, and peas; seeds of these may be planted as soon as the soil can be prepared in the spring. Well-hardened cabbage plants may also be planted at this time. Seeds of the half-hardy group may be planted 2 to 3 weeks before the danger of killing frost is over. Beets, carrots, parsnips, celery (seed and hardened plants), lettuce, and chard belong to this group. The third group includes beans, Lima beans, sweet corn, cucumbers, melons, pumpkins, squashes, okra, tomato plants, eggplants, and pepper plants. Sweet corn and beans will withstand more cold than the others in this group and often are planted before danger of frost is over. Where earliness is important, it pays to take chances on most crops that are grown from seed planted directly in the field, since the cost of seed and of labor of planting is not large. Most of the hardy and half-hardy vegetables do not thrive well during very hot weather.

When more than one planting is made of any crop, the second and later plantings should be timed so as to have a continuous harvest for the period desired. This is especially important for the home gardener and for the market gardener who attempts to supply special customers. In timing various plantings, it should be borne in mind that the temperature and other ecological factors have a marked effect on the length of time required from planting to harvest. For example, Magoon and Culpepper (1926 and 1932) and Appleman (1923) have shown that the higher the temperature, the shorter the time required to bring sweet corn to any definite stage of maturity. Magoon and Culpepper found that the number of days from planting to silking in sweet corn at Washington D.C., varied from 63 to 92 days for the Stowell Evergreen variety. Appleman showed that the rate of ripening of sweet corn is directly proportional to the temperature. This is discussed in Chap. 26.

Depth of Planting Seeds. No definite rules can be given regarding the depth to plant seeds of various kinds. The size of the seed, the kind of soil, and the amount of moisture in the soil should be considered. Large seeds are planted deeper than small seeds, although it does not follow that the largest seeds should be planted the deepest. Kidney beans and Lima beans are not usually planted so deep as peas, because unlike the pea the young bean plant pushes the cotyledons up through the soil and, if the covering is too deep, they may be broken off and the plant thereby injured. Small seeds, such as celery, are often merely pressed into the soil or covered with burlap or other similar material. On light soils such as fine sand or sandy loams, seeds are planted to a greater depth than on heavy soils. The more moisture there is present in the soil, the less need there is for deep planting. For this reason seeds are usually given a relatively light covering in the spring. The same kind of seeds planted in late summer requires greater covering because the surface layer of soil is usually drier and it is necessary to place the seed at a greater depth to obtain sufficient moisture to ensure germination and to bring the plant to the surface.

Marking Rows. In growing vegetables on a commercial scale, uniform spacing between rows is important and, except where contour planting is necessary to control erosion, straight rows are desirable. Uniform spacing between rows and straight rows make cultivation and spraying or dusting easier than where the rows are unevenly spaced and crooked. Uniformly spaced rows can be made by measuring accurately and using stakes and a line or by using markers of various kinds. When seed drills or transplanting machines are used for planting, a line is usually set for the first row and the marker attachment on the machine is used for the remainder.

Methods of Planting. Most commercial gardeners plant seeds with machine planters of some kind. Machines do the work much better and more rapidly than is possible by hand sowing. The common seed drills open the furrow, drop the seeds, cover them, and pack the soil at one operation. These drills can be regulated to sow at various rates and at the depth desired. By regulating the rate of seed sowing, thinning can be reduced to the minimum. There are several makes of seed drills on the market, all of which are satisfactory when properly used.

Sowing seed by hand is commonly practiced in home gardens, as too small quantity of any one kind of seed is used to justify the expense of a seed drill. It would be necessary to adjust the drill to the different kinds of seeds, and the time required to do this would often be enough to do the planting by hand. A garden line or marker should be used when planting is to be done by hand in order to have straight rows. The furrow for small seeds may be made with the rake or hoe handle, using the same kind of a motion one uses in sweeping. For large seeds the furrow may be made with the corner of an ordinary hoe, with a heart-shaped hoe, with the plow attachment, or with one of the cultivator teeth of a wheel hoe. The seeds should be distributed uniformly in the furrow. Small seeds such as radish, turnip, and lettuce may be sown direct from the seed packet or from an envelope with the end cut open by moving it slowly over the row and tapping it lightly with a finger. The seeds should be covered immediately to prevent loss of moisture from the soil. After the seeds are covered, the soil, if dry, should be firmed by trampling or by tamping with the back of the hoe. This is especially important when the soil is dry as it brings the seed into close contact with the soil particles. The seed drill has a broad wheel that packs the soil over the seeds.

Rate of Planting. Among the points to be taken into consideration in regard to the quantity of seed to plant are: (1) the viability of the seed,

(2) the time of planting, (3) the condition of the soil, (4) the size and vigor of the young plants, and (5) the possible ravages of insects.

Seeds known to be of low viability should be planted more thickly than those having high percentages of germination. Seed held over from one year to the next should be tested for germination. If the percentage of germination is low or if the sprout is weak, the seed should not be planted, for a poor stand of weak plants would result.

Seeds planted when the soil and weather conditions are unfavorable to quick germination should be planted at a heavier rate than when the conditions are favorable. The longer the time required for germination of any given kind of seed, the heavier should be the rate of planting.

Seeds that produce delicate weak plants, such as carrots and parsnips, should be planted quite thickly to ensure a good stand. Any excess of plants may be removed to prevent crowding.

In planting seeds of melons and cucumbers it is a common practice to plant freely in order to have several times as many plants as are needed. In most regions it is expected that the cucumber beetle will seriously injure, or even kill, many of the plants. Unless large numbers are started, the chances are against saving enough for a good stand of strong plants. After the beetles have disappeared, the plants may be thinned to the desired distance apart.

Thinning. This is an important operation when seeds are planted where the crop is to mature, for more plants usually come up than are needed and unless some are removed, injury by crowding will result. Thinning may be made a process of selection. The weakest plants should be discarded and the strongest left to grow. By thinning, a uniform stand is obtained, but as this is a tedious and expensive operation vegetable growers try to avoid it as much as possible by planting the right quantity of seed and distributing it evenly. There is some tendency to delay thinning too long, and this results in overcrowding and injury to the plants that are left. Thinning should be done as soon as there is reasonable assurance that the plants left will not be killed by unfavorable weather conditions or destroyed by insects that are injurious during the early stages of the plant's growth.

Transplanting. Success in transplanting plants to the field or garden is dependent on good plants, good condition of the soil, and doing the work in the proper manner.

The soil should be thoroughly prepared prior to transplanting. It is very difficult to set plants properly in hard, lumpy soil, and plants set under these conditions are likely to be seriously checked in growth or to become weak and die. Contact between the roots and soil is important because the roots cannot take up moisture unless they are in close contact with fine, loose soil. For the same reason it is essential that the soil be well firmed around the roots.

Some authorities recommend removing part of the foliage when the plants are set in the field, but it is doubtful if this is a desirable practice. Kraus (1942) has shown that pruning off part of the foliage of head lettuce, cauliflower, celery, peppers, and onions did not increase the survival of plants following transplanting to the field. Heavy pruning delayed heading of lettuce and reduced the early yield of cauliflower. With the other crops there was no significant difference in yield between pruned and unpruned plants. Kraus found that loss of water by transpiration immediately after transplanting was greater from unpruned than from pruned plants, principally because of their larger leaf area. The more rapid root growth of unpruned plants resulted in an increase in loss of water as a result of their ability to obtain water from the soil. The greater root growth of unpruned plants resulted from the larger reserve of carbohydrates in the leaves. Removal of part of the foliage by pruning reduced the carbohydrate supply available for root growth and also reduced synthesis. Pruning both tops and roots of onion plants that are to be transplanted is a common practice wherever the crop is grown from transplants. Jones, Perry, and Davis (1949) state that experiments in Texas and California show that a considerable reduction in yield of bulbs results from pruning both tops and roots. However, pruning facilitates planting.

Another type of pruning is practiced with tomato plants in which the terminal bud and part of the stem are removed. When this is done, the lateral branches develop earlier than is the case where the terminal bud is not removed. It is claimed by some that this type of pruning increases the early yield of fruit. Sayre (1945) has shown that when the pruning was done at the 7- or 8-week stage of growth, both early yield and total yield were reduced. When the pruning was done at the 6-week stage, the difference in early and total yield between pruned and unpruned plants was not significant. Topping tall, "leggy" plants aids in transplanting with machine transplanters and reduces injury and loss of plants by wind whipping. It is doubtful if this type of pruning is justified except when the plants are very tall and slender. The development of new roots is dependent on the carbohydrate supply, and the ability of the plant to get water is limited by the growth of new roots, especially when the plants have not been transplanted previously.

Where irrigation is used the water may be applied either before or after setting the plants. If the soil is very dry, it is best to irrigate before transplanting, but care should be taken to prevent puddling heavy soils. When the soil is in good condition for the transplanting operation, irrigation should be given after the plants are set. However,

with soil in good condition, plants that have been previously transplanted and well hardened can be set even during hot, dry weather
without much wilting if they are taken up with a block of earth around
the roots. Plants that have not been transplanted previously and are
pulled from the seedbed without any soil adhering to the roots should
be watered when the soil is very dry.

Where irrigation is not used, the best time to set plants is in cloudy
weather or in late afternoon. Evaporation and transpiration are less in
cool, cloudy weather than in warm, sunny weather. Setting plants in
late afternoon gives them time during the night to recuperate from the
shock of transplanting.

Plants are set by hand or by machines of various kinds. When setting by hand, various methods are used. For plants that have been transplanted prior to field planting, it is usually the custom to take them up
with considerable soil around the roots, and in setting them a furrow
is made with a small plow, or a hole large enough to take in the block or
ball of soil is dug with a trowel, shovel, or spade. For large plants like
tomatoes a turn plow may be used to good advantage for opening the
furrow. The plants are set in the furrow, earth is packed around each
with the hand, and the remainder of the furrow is filled with a cultivator. The plow attachment of a hand cultivator, such as the Planet
Junior, is valuable for opening furrows for cabbage, lettuce, celery, and
similar plants which have been transplanted previously. The depth of
the furrow can be regulated to suit the size of the plants. The best tool
for making a hole for transplanting plants which are taken direct from
the seedbed is the dibble. This too makes a hole without removing the
soil. The dibble is held in one hand and the plant in the other, and after
the hole is made a plant is inserted and then both hands are used to firm
the soil around the roots, or the dibble may be used to press the soil
against the plant. Care should be taken to see that the soil is firmed
around the roots and that no space is left unfilled at the bottom of the
hole. The trowel and spade are also used in setting plants either in the
same manner as the dibble or in digging holes for receiving the plants.
There are small hand planters on the market, which work very satisfactorily in good soil. A small tank on the side for water may be used if
desired. By tripping the lever at the top a small quantity of water is
applied around the roots of the plant, but this method of watering is
practicable only on a small scale.

Large-scale planting of cabbage, tomatoes, celery, onions, and other
vegetables is done mainly by means of transplanting machines (Fig. 8.1).
These machines do the work better and more rapidly than is commonly
done by hand. They open the furrow, apply water, and firm the soil at
one operation. The water is applied from a barrel or tank mounted on

the machine and reaches the roots of the plants through a hose that ends just in front of the shoes of the transplanter. Some of these machines are powered by engines mounted on the frame, while others are pulled by a tractor. Transplanting machines are not used to very good advantage in setting large plants which have soil around the roots as is usually the case with transplanted ones; therefore such plants are generally set by hand.

Plants should be set slightly deeper than they were in the seedbed. It is an advantage to set long slender plants quite deep as this will keep

Fig. 8.1. Transplanting machine in operation. (*Courtesy of Holland Transplanter Co., Holland, Mich.*)

them from being whipped by the wind and, with some plants as the tomato, roots will grow from the stem below the surface of the soil. Care must be taken not to set celery and lettuce plants so deep that the crown will be buried.

Watering. A plant set in very dry soil should be watered unless there is a block or ball of moist soil around the roots. The water should be applied around the roots and the wet soil covered with dry earth to prevent baking. In hand planting a little soil is usually packed around the roots and then the water is poured into the depression. After the water disappears, the hole is filled with dry soil. The transplanting machine applies the water about the roots and in such small quantities that the surface of the soil is not puddled.

When watering is not practicable, the roots of the plant are often puddled prior to setting. This is done by dipping the roots into a thin paste made with clay in water. Puddling prevents drying of the roots and also causes the soil particles to adhere to them when planted. The mud paste should not be allowed to dry on the roots as this would cause injury by preventing the moist soil from coming into contact with them. The puddling should be done just before planting, or else the puddled plants should be covered with moist burlap, moist moss, straw, or other material to prevent evaporation of moisture in the paste. Puddling requires much less labor than watering the plants and gives satisfactory results when properly done. When plants are watered after being planted, it is desirable to cover the moist soil with a little loose, dry earth to prevent rapid drying and consequent baking and cracking.

Starter Solutions. Use of starter solutions instead of water alone at the time of setting out plants has become a common practice in recent years. They are used occasionally also to apply nutrients to plants while they are growing in the field. The starter solution is made by dissolving fertilizer nutrients in water. Although any good complete fertiltizer can be used in making a starter solution, a high-analysis one that leaves little or no insoluble residue is preferred. When a high-analysis fertilizer such as a 13-26-13, 11-32-14, or similar one is used, it is recommended that about 4 pounds of the fertilizer be dissolved in 50 gallons of water. For fertilizers of lower analyses, such as 4-16-4, 5-10-5, 5-10-10, about 10 pounds should be dissolved in 50 gallons of water. Solutions made with the lower-analysis materials will leave considerable insoluble residue. Usually about $\frac{1}{4}$ to $\frac{1}{2}$ pint of solution is used per plant of such plants as cabbage, tomatoes, or peppers. When a transplanting machine is used, the solution is poured into the tank on the machine and is delivered through a hose to the soil around the plant as it is set.

Use of a starter solution usually increases the yield of the crop, especially when grown on land that is not well fertilized. On highly fertilized land the starter solution may not increase yield, but since it is inexpensive, its use is recommended where it is desirable to use water in transplanting.

Number of Plants per Acre. The number of plants required to plant an acre of ground at various spacings can be determined by multiplying the distance in feet between plants in the row by the distance in feet between the rows and dividing the product into 43,560, the number of square feet in an acre.

Use of Plant Protectors. Various kinds of protectors have been used to protect individual plants and hills of plants or seeds in the field. The claim is made that by the use of protectors maturity is hastened, owing to increasing the temperature and protection against light frosts. They also protect the plants from whipping by winds and heavy, dashing rains.

In France, bell jars are used for forcing plants in the field, but these have never come into use in the United States. A type of box covered with a pane of glass has been used to some extent by market gardeners for starting cucumber, melon, and other warm-season crops planted in hills. This type of box is made with a sloping top, and a pane of glass is

Fig. 8.2. Paper plant protectors placed over muskmelon plants to protect them against frosts and to trap heat to germinate seed in cold soil. (*Courtesy of Department of Vegetable Crops, University of California.*)

placed on top and held in place by a stone, or still better, the glass is slid into grooves cut into the top of the side boards. This makes a miniature cold frame.

Various kinds of paper protectors are in use in the United States in starting warm-season crops in the field. Such devices are used on a very large scale in the Imperial Valley of California for muskmelon (cantaloupe) and other tender plants. They are also used by thousands of growers in other sections of the country, especially in the North, for protecting tender plants that are started early.

Some of the protectors are factory-made and are ready for use, and others come in sheets and require special forms to shape the paper.

Glassine paper and oiled and waxed papers of various kinds are used in making plant protectors, and these are superior to untreated paper. Paper protectors, such as are shown in Fig. 8.2, provide some heat and protect plants against light frosts and chilling winds as well as against wind injury by whipping and blowing sand and soil particles. They aid in preventing injury by some insects during the early stages of growth of the plant. On the other hand, the paper protectors reduce the intensity of the light reaching the plants, and when this reduction is marked, growth is not normal. Hibbard (1925 and 1926) presented data on the effect of various materials on light intensity. Using figures representing the light intensities in the greenhouse as 100, the following descending order of light intensities was obtained: cellluloid 91; glassine 81; light parchment 71; heavy parchment 71; oiled paper 64; medium parchment 61; and brown wrapping paper 23. Under another set of conditions out of doors, the following figures were obtained: uncovered 100; cellulose 93; glassine 92; medium parchment 83; light parchment 80; oiled or waxed paper 76.

Results of studies by Ware (1936) in Arkansas, covering a period of 3 years, indicate that good plant protectors hastened germination and early growth and increased early and total yield of muskmelons.

Careful attention must be given to the plants under protectors to provide ventilation and to prevent too soft succulent growth under some conditions. Thompson (1929) has pointed out that protectors might be a disadvantage in a season when the weather is mild for some time and then a frost occurs. Under such conditions the protected plants are more likely to be injured or killed by frost than those that have been growing in the open and are more hardened. Unless some ventilation is provided, moisture accumulates in drops and, on freezing, results in injuring or killing the portion of the plant in contact with the ice crystals. To get rid of excess moisture a 1-inch slit in the paper cones may be made on one side, preferably on the side away from the prevailing wind. This slit is lengthened as the plant grows, and eventually the paper is pulled apart.

While many growers have used paper plant protectors with success and profit, there are conditions under which the protectors are of no advantage and may be actually injurious. On the average, however, the protectors do shield the plants and hasten maturity if careful attention is given the plants while the protectors are in use.

CHAPTER 9

Cultivation, Mulches, and Chemical Methods of Weed Control

There are several methods of weed control used in vegetable growing. These include cultivation or intertillage, mulches, the use of oils and other chemicals, and flaming or burning the weeds. Cultivation is the method most universally practiced, but some of the other methods are becoming of increasing importance and deserve attention. Although cultivation and mulching are practiced primarily for weed control, other benefits may be derived from them.

CULTIVATION

Cultivation is a well-established practice, and its benefits are well known. There is, however, a great deal of misconception as to the reasons for the benefits derived from the practice. Many theories have been advanced and many experiments have been conducted to determine the reasons for the beneficial effects of cultivation of crop plants. Among the factors mentioned are the following:

1. Destruction of weeds, thereby conserving moisture and nutrients and eliminating competition for light and air
2. Conserving moisture by the formation and maintenance of a soil mulch
3. Increasing aeration and thereby favoring nitrification and aiding other chemical changes in the soil
4. Increasing nitrification through conserving moisture, favoring better aeration and raising the temperature of the soil
5. Increasing the absorption and retention of heat

Effects of Cultivation on Yield. Cultivation generally increases the yields of crop plants. This is due mainly to weed control, although the formation and maintenance of a soil mulch by cultivation may be important factors under some conditions. The results of a large number of

117

experiments in cultivating corn carried on in many states show conclusively that weed control is of prime importance.

Data reported by Thompson (1927) and by Thompson, Wessels, and Mills (1931) from experiments carried on in New York as well as results of experiments by Merkle and Irvin (1931) in Pennsylvania show clearly that weed control is of major importance in the cultivation of vegetable crops. The data showing the effects of cultivation as compared with scraping the surface of the soil to control weeds on the yield of six crops grown at Ithaca, N.Y., are shown in Table 9.1. These experiments were

Table 9.1. Effects of Maintaining a Soil Mulch by Cultivation on the Yield of Six Vegetable Crops
(Thompson)

| Crop | Average yield in pounds per plot of marketable portion of crop | | | Odds of significance |
	Cultivated	Scraped	Percentage increase from cultivation	
Beets......................	60.57	58.10	4.25	None
Carrots....................	86.68	84.42	2.68	7:1
Onions.....................	77.55	72.01	7.69	49:1
Cabbage....................	119.03	119.40	None	None
Celery.....................	144.49	116.44	24.00	9,999:1
Tomatoes, untrained..........	187.96	185.92	1.10	None
Tomatoes, trained............	158.61	156.04	1.65	2:1

carried on for 6 years on a sandy-gravelly-loam soil. The treatments were in triplicate. One set of plots was cultivated once a week with a hand cultivator, another set was scraped with a sharp hoe to keep the weeds under control. Weeds were eliminated as a factor in both sets of plots; therefore the comparison of the yields shows the benefits derived from the soil mulch.

The data show little or no benefit from the maintenance of a soil mulch except in the case of the celery crop, the yield of which was increased 24 per cent with highly significant odds. Results of cultivation experiments conducted on a Sassafras silt-loam soil on Long Island are similar to those obtained at Ithaca. In the Long Island experiments two cultivation treatments were employed in addition to the scraping to control weeds. One of the cultivation treatments was discontinued when the crops were about half grown, since it was thought that late cultivation might do more harm than good. A comparison of this treatment with the regular cultivation, which continued throughout the period of growth of the crops, gives some idea of the value of late cultivation under the conditions that prevail on Long Island. All treatments were in triplicate. A summary of the data from these experiments, as reported by Thompson, Wessels, and Mills (1931), is given in Table 9.2.

Examination of the data in Table 9.2 shows no large difference in yield between the plots cultivated throughout the growing season and those cultivated until the crop was about half grown nor between the cultivated and scraped plots. The only crop in which the difference in yield between the regularly cultivated plots and the scraped plots is statistically significant is the potato, and in this case the scraped plots produced the highest yield. Where the weeds were allowed to grow, the yields of all crops were markedly reduced. While late cultivation did not increase

Table 9.2. Yields of Crops in Cultivation Experiment on Long Island

Crop	Number of years	Average yields, pounds per plot			
		Cultivated	Cultivated half season	Scraped	Weeds allowed to grow
Beets.................	7	240.31	239.72	233.21	45.56
Carrots...............	5	505.30	506.41	519.50	29.72
Onions...............	4	67.70	69.60	64.30	3.60
Cabbage..............	4	233.57	234.56	207.46	129.08
Tomatoes.............	7	164.03	166.57	166.82	23.28
Potatoes.............	4	148.35	150.42	158.82	52.67

the average yield, it does not follow that late cultivation may not be of value under some conditions. When weed growth is heavy late in the season, late cultivation might be expected to increase the yield. On the other hand, when weed growth is light, cultivation after the crop is more than half grown may do more harm than good because of injury to the above-ground portion of the plants and to the destruction of the roots to the depth cultivated.

Experiments conducted by Merkle and Irvin on a Hagerstown silt-loam soil in Pennsylvania with potatoes, field beans, cabbage, and mangels gave results similar to those carried on in New York. Mangels was the only crop that gave significantly higher yields from frequent (seven to eight times) cultivation than from scraping the soil. Cultivating three times did not result in higher yields of mangels than did scraping the soil to control weeds. With field beans, cultivating three times, six to eight times, and scraping all gave essentially the same average yields over a period of 4 years. The results with potatoes over a period of 4 years show no significant difference in yields between cultivating three times, cultivating six to eight times, and scraping. Cabbage was in the experiment only 1 year, and while the scraped plots produced the largest yield, the difference may not be significant.

Werner (1933) conducted cultivation experiments on a dark, heavy silt-loam soil in Nebraska with a number of vegetables for a period of 4 years. Cultivation was done with a hand cultivator with teeth or shovel attachments, and scraping was done with a sharp hoe to keep the weeds down and to fill the cracks with loose soil. Both irrigated and unirrigated areas were used for the cultivation experiments, and the results are shown in Table 9.3.

Table 9.3. Relative Yields of Scraped and Cultivated Plots—Yields of Cultivated Plots Taken as 1.00
(Werner)

Crop and varieties	Number of years	Unirrigated	Irrigated
Tomatoes, Earliana............	3	1.14	0.95
Tomatoes, Marglobe...........	2	0.95	1.03
Eggplants....................	3	1.73	1.18
Sweet potatoes...............	4	1.19	1.15
Potatoes....................	4	1.11	0.94
Beans, Lima..................	3	2.13	1.15
Beans, wax...................	4	1.03	0.98
Cabbage, early...............	4	1.18	0.97
Average of all crops..........	...	1.31	1.04

Results of a large number of experiments conducted in England and reported by Russell (1950) are similar to those reported by Thompson and others in the United States. Based on the results obtained in England and in various parts of the world Russell concludes as follows: "The first conclusion which every experiment, capable of showing, has clearly shown, is that seedling weeds can have a very serious effect on the early development of a crop, and once the crop has suffered a check due to such a cause, it will usually never fully recover from it. One of the fundamental criteria that should be used in judging the necessity or value of a cultivation operation is, therefore, its effect on the weeds in the soil."

Results of all cultivation experiments indicate that the main function of cultivation is to control weeds. Maintaining a mulch may be desirable to close cracks in the soil, to reduce surface *runoff*, and, under some conditions, to conserve moisture by slowing up the movement of moisture to the surface and to increase aeration.

Effects of a Soil Mulch on Moisture Conservation. One of the benefits claimed for cultivation is the conservation of moisture due to the formation and maintenance of a soil mulch. The usual explanation is that the mulch decreases or stops the capillary flow, and this slows up the movement to the surface, since the moisture would then move by diffusion. Much recent experimental data seem to show that in semiarid regions drying of the surface soils, after a rain or after irrigating, is so rapid that forming a mulch by cultivating is of little or no value. In humid regions it may be an advantage to cultivate after a heavy rain in order to hasten the drying of the surface soil before there is much water lost from lower depths. Data obtained in humid regions indicate that a mulch conserves moisture in a majority of cases, but by no means in all. Results of moisture determinations made on a Dunkirk sandy-gravelly-

Table 9.4. Effects of a Soil Mulch on Moisture Content* of the Soil under Different Crops and in a Fallow Soil
(Thompson)

Crop grown	Average per cent of soil moisture for the growing season, calculated on dry-weight basis									
	1921		1922		1923		1924		1925	
	C	*S*	*C*	*S*	*C*	*S*	*C*	*S*	*C*	*S*
Beets..............	9.0	8.3	9.8	11.1	8.2	8.0	12.0	11.2	12.1	10.5
Carrots............	8.7	8.2	11.1	11.5	9.0	8.0	13.1	12.3	12.7	11.7
Onions............	8.7	8.2	11.2	11.2	9.5	9.4	12.0	11.2	11.9	11.4
Cabbage...........	10.0	9.6	15.2	14.6	10.5	10.6	11.1	10.3	11.4	10.5
Celery............	10.1	8.8	13.5	11.7	10.8	8.6	10.8	8.6	10.4	10.0
Tomatoes..........	7.9	7.4	14.0	12.9	8.7	9.8	11.7	11.6	15.1	12.9
Fallow (no crop).....	....	...	15.3	14.9	10.3	10.4	11.6	13.2	13.8	12.2
Average..........	9.1	8.4	12.9	12.6	9.6	9.3	11.8	11.2	12.5	11.3

* *C*, cultivated once each week during growing season; *S*, scraped with hoe when weeds appeared.

loam soil at Ithaca, N.Y., during the growing seasons 1921 to 1925, are taken to illustrate this point. Soil samples were taken to a depth of 30 inches during four seasons and to the depth of 18 inches the fifth season from plots producing various crops and from one set of uncropped plots. Table 9.4 shows the average moisture content of the soil for the season under the different treatments.

A consideration of the data in Table 9.4 shows that cultivation, as compared to scraping, resulted in the conservation of moisture in 30 out of 39 comparisons, and in loss in 7 comparisons, while in the others the two treatments were equal. It is interesting to note that the scraped plots reached a lower moisture content in 24 comparisons and the cultivated plots in 13, while in the other two comparisons both reached the same minimum. In the 5 years 280 moisture determinations were made on comparable cultivated and scraped plots. In 188 of these the soil from the cultivated plots contained the higher percentage of moisture; in 79 the soil from the scraped plots was ahead; in the other 13 the moisture was the same under the two treatments.

While the weed plots did not always have the lowest average moisture content for the season, they did reach a lower minimum every year. This suggests that the marked effect of a small growth of weeds may be due to competition with crop plants at a time when moisture is the limiting factor.

There was no definite relation between the average moisture content of the soil for the season and the yield of crop except in the case of celery, where the cultivated soil had the highest moisture and produced the largest yield. With the other crops it did not always follow that the yield was increased by cultivation, even though the soil mulch conserved moisture. In some instances, cultivation resulted in loss of moisture at critical periods; in others, it conserved moisture when a lower water content was an advantage. When the soil was cultivated soon after a light rain, moisture was lost because of hastening of evaporation by exposing more surface to the drying action of the air. In many instances practically all of the moisture from a light rain was lost by cultivating before the water had penetrated below the depth cultivated. Knowledge of these facts enables one to time his cultivating more intelligently and to reduce or to eliminate the detrimental effects.

Whether or not cultivation will conserve moisture depends on the nature of the crop as to the top growth, the extent and distribution of the roots, the humidity of the air, the velocity of the wind, and the quantity of water in the soil. It has been shown by Viehmeyer (1927) and other workers that a compact dry layer of soil is practically as effective in checking water loss at the surface as is a loose dry layer. Since forming a mulch by cultivation is effective in conserving moisture only when it hastens the drying of the surface, it follows that under conditions of rapid drying, cultivating the soil would be of little or no value so far as moisture conservation is concerned. This has been shown to be the case in many experiments in semiarid regions and was apparently true under some conditions in the experiments at Ithaca, N.Y.

Cultivation may conserve moisture by preventing surface runoff as shown by Call and Sewell (1918). It seems probable that, in many cases, this is much more important than any conservation due to checking evaporation by the soil mulch. On the other hand, cultivation may have an injurious effect due to the loose soil being washed away during heavy rains, thus leaving the surface uneven with the plants on a ridge. This happened several times in the cultivated plots at Ithaca when the adjoining scraped plots were not injured at all.

Effect of Cultivation on Soil Temperature. It is often stated that cultivation of the soil increases the absorption and retention of heat. This may be true for the subsoil, but probably is not true for the surface soil. Bouyoucos (1913 and 1916), working with a sandy-loam soil in Michigan, found that uncultivated (scraped) soil at depths of 3, 6, 7, and 20 inches averaged higher in temperature than cultivated soil throughout the growing season. Mosier and Gustafson (1915) found that

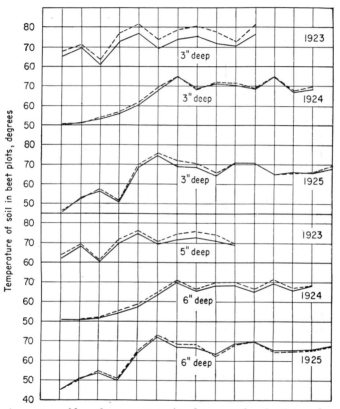

FIG. 9.1. Average weekly soil temperature (in degrees Fahrenheit) in cultivated and scraped plots of beets. The solid line represents the temperature of the cultivated soil, the broken line the temperature of the scraped soil.

at depths of 2 and 4 inches uncultivated silt-loam soil averaged higher than cultivated soil during the summer. These studies were carried on for a period of 5 years. Thompson (1927) reported results covering studies carried on for 3 years at Ithaca, N.Y., on a sandy loam. The temperature of the soil at depths of 3 and 5 or 6 inches was higher on the scraped plots than in comparable cultivated plots through the growing season every year, regardless of the moisture content of the two. The average weekly temperature is shown graphically in Figs. 9.1 and 9.2.

The belief that stirring the soil results in raising the temperature is based on the fact that evaporation of water consumes heat. If this were the only factor involved, stirring the soil would raise the temperature whenever it resulted in conserving moisture and lower the temperature when cultivation increased the loss of moisture. In the experiments at Ithaca the scraped soil had the higher temperature when it contained less moisture and when it contained more moisture than the cultivated soil. The compactness of the uncultivated soil probably accounts for the

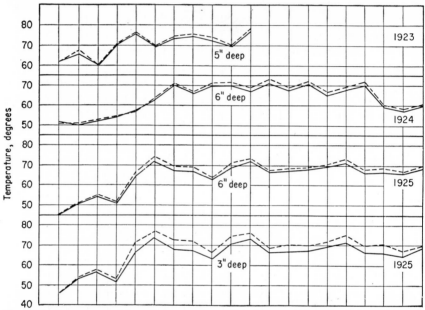

Fig. 9.2. Average weekly soil temperature (in degrees Fahrenheit) in cultivated and scraped uncropped plots. The solid line represents the temperature of the cultivated soil, the broken line the temperature of the scraped soil.

higher temperature. Bouyoucos suggests that the dry layer of loose soil forms poor and imperfect connections with the subsoil and that the heat energy which it receives from the sun is not all conducted downward but that a large amount accumulates in the surface of the mulch and then some of it is radiated back to the atmosphere. Because of the compactness of the surface of uncultivated soil and consequently better heat-conducting power, a greater quantity of heat is carried to lower depths than is the case in cultivated soil. By suspending thermometers 1 inch above the surface of the soil, Bouyoucos found that on some days the temperature was 7 to 10°F. higher over the cultivated than over the uncultivated soil.

Effects of Cultivation on Nitrification. The results of many studies of the effects of the soil mulch on nitrification are somewhat conflicting.

Any increase in nitrates due to stirring the soil would be the result of improving the conditions for nitrification, as by increasing aeration or providing better moisture or better temperature conditions for the growth of nitrifying bacteria. Since the soil mulch does not always have the same effect on moisture conservation, one might expect that it would affect nitrification differently under different conditions. When moisture is limited, any treatment that conserves it would favor nitrification. It is doubtful if cultivation is of much importance from the standpoint of aeration except on heavy soils.

Nitrate nitrogen determinations made at Ithaca, N.Y., every 2 weeks during the growing season of 1925 show no consistent advantage for the soil mulch on a sandy-loam soil. In two comparisons out of eight there was a significant difference in favor of the soil mulch. The growth of crops had a marked effect on the quantity of nitrates. The difference in yield between the cultivated and scraped plots was not sufficient to account for any appreciable difference in nitrates under the two treatments with the exception of celery.

Some investigators have found a positive correlation between soil moisture and nitrates. In the studies reported by Thompson there was a positive relation in 12 out of 17 cases, a definite negative relation in 2, and no relation or a slightly negative one in the other 3. It should be borne in mind, however, that other factors than moisture affect nitrification and nitrate accumulation and might mask the changes produced by increase or decrease in the water content. Temperature has a marked effect on nitrification, and growth of the crop on nitrate accumulation.

While cultivation does not always increase nitrification, it does often have this effect on heavy soils, where stirring the surface may increase aeration and, under some conditions, conserve moisture. On light soils, forming a mulch has relatively little effect on either aeration or moisture conservation.

Cultivating Implements. In many parts of the world where labor is cheap, much of the cultivation is done with hand tools. Such tools are used also where the land is too rough for the use of other types of equipment. Where labor is not cheap and conditions are favorable, vegetables are cultivated by hand cultivators of the wheel-hoe type, by animal-drawn cultivators, and by tractor cultivators. In the United States, hand cultivators are used in commercial vegetable growing mainly for cultivating small-growing crops produced on an intensive scale and in home gardens. Garden tractors are used mainly for similar types of production. Large tractor cultivators are used mainly in cultivating such crops as sweet corn, cabbage, tomatoes, and other large-growing plants, the rows of which are spaced far enough apart to allow ample space for the wheels.

Garden tractors are being used more and more in intensive vegetable growing, where they are taking the place of hand cultivators. A careful operator can do practically as good cultivation with a small tractor as with a hand cultivator and better than with horse-drawn cultivators.

The most successful garden tractors are the relatively small ones used only for cultivation and similar work. A tractor large enough to do satisfactory plowing is too large for the best cultivation, especially for the small crops planted in rows 15 to 24 inches apart. A tractor for cultivating small crops on loose friable soil need not have as much power as one used on heavy soil. Garden tractors and hand cultivators save much hand hoeing and weeding as they can be run close to the row and used when the plants are small, or even before they come up.

Various types of attachments can be used on all of the types of cultivators mentioned. The most common attachments are teeth, shovels, and blades that run just beneath the surface of the soil, cutting off the weeds and leaving a thin mulch. Disks and rakelike attachments are used to some extent on hand and small tractor cultivators. The blade attachments and the "sweep" commonly used in some areas are very efficient in controlling weeds and are less destructive of the roots of crop plants than are the shovel and teeth attachments.

When and How to Cultivate. Since weed control is the most important function of cultivation, it follows that the work should be done at the time most favorable for killing the weeds. This is accomplished most easily before the weeds have become established, and it is important to kill them before they have competed seriously with crop plants for moisture and nutrients. The best time to cultivate is just as the weeds are breaking through the surface because at this time the roots are small and do not have much of a hold on the soil. At this stage shallow cultivation is all that is necessary; if the weeds are allowed to get large, deeper cultivation is necessary unless a blade type of cultivator or the sweep is used. Deep cultivation destroys many roots and prevents the plants from getting the full benefits of the surface soil.

When feasible, cultivation should be given as often as necessary to prevent weeds from injuring crop plants. This means frequent cultivation when conditions are very favorable for the growth of weeds, as after a rain or an application of irrigation water followed by good weather for growth. There is no justification for the practice of cultivating once a week or once in 2 weeks regardless of the conditions. Under some conditions it is desirable to cultivate more often than once a week, and under others a month might elapse between cultivations without harm. When there is no weed growth and a soil mulch is already formed, not only is further cultivation an unnecessary expense but it is usually injurious owing to the destruction of roots and to bringing moist soil to the surface to dry out. If 3 or 4 inches of surface soil is kept stirred, most of the roots are destroyed so that it is impossible for the plants to utilize the nutrients in the richest soil.

Generally, if sufficient cultivation is given to keep weeds under control, it will be enough to accomplish all other purposes.

Cultivation immediately after a rain of ½ inch or less is likely to do more harm than good, because of hastening of the drying of the surface soil, which contains most of the water from such a rain. The destruction of the roots in the wetted surface would also prevent the plants from getting benefits from the rain.

USE OF MULCHES

Many kinds of materials are used to some extent as a mulch for weed control and for other purposes. These include leaves, straw, hay, and other similar materials, sawdust, peat moss, and paper. None of these is used to any great extent in commercial vegetable growing but somewhat in home gardens to keep down weeds and to hold moisture.

The usual practice in using mulches, except paper, is to spread the material evenly over the surface of the soil between the rows and around the plants. The thickness of the mulch varies from 1 to 3 or 4 inches depending on the kind of material and the cost. Mulches of straw and similar material are usually 2 to 3 inches, and peat moss about 1 inch. Sawdust has been applied experimentally 2 to 3 inches in thickness. All of these materials have some value in supplying organic matter, and all tend to deplete the soil of nitrogen, since the organisms that cause decomposition of the organic matter consume nitrogen. Allison and Anderson (1951) point out that sawdust is low in mineral elements, especially phosphorus, as well as nitrogen. Application of nitrogenous fertilizers should be made in sufficient quantity to supply both the organisms in the soil and the crop plants. In the case of sawdust, some carrier of phosphorus should be applied also unless the soil is well supplied with it.

Where any of the materials are available at little or no cost they can be used to advantage, provided the cost of hauling and applying is not too great. According to Allison and Anderson a cubic yard of loose sawdust weighs 200 to 300 pounds or 10 to 15 pounds to the bushel. On this basis it would require over 35 tons to cover an acre of land to the depth of 2 inches. Since sawdust is capable of absorbing water from two to six times its own weight, it would require much more than 35 tons of weathered material to cover an acre 2 inches deep. It seems doubtful that it would be economical to haul sawdust very far.

Johnson (1944) conducted experiments with sawdust as a mulch for tomatoes and potatoes in Alabama. His results indicate that pine sawdust 10 years old or older is satisfactory as a mulch when incorporated with the soil, provided sufficient nitrogen is used to prevent deficiency of this element. The sawdust depressed the nitrates in the soil during the first 18 months, after which time there was an increase. The mulched soil maintained a higher moisture content and a more uniform temperature than the unmulched soil. The sawdust mulch was 3 inches in thickness; when applied for incorporation with the soil it was 2 inches in thickness.

The use of mulch paper in vegetable growing was much discussed from about 1925 to 1935 following its successful use in growing sugar cane and pineapples in Hawaii. Experiments by several workers, including Flint (1928), Thompson and Platenius (1931), Magruder (1930), and Hutchins (1933), showed that the paper mulch increased the yields of many vegetable crops and hastened the maturity of most of them. The paper keeps the product off the ground. This is of considerable importance with some crops, such as tomatoes and melons, under certain conditions. Although the paper eliminates weeds in the covered area and thus cuts down the cost of cultivation, this is offset by the cost of the paper and the labor of applying it.

CHEMICAL WEED CONTROL

The use of chemicals to control weeds has been attempted for many years. Most of the early methods were either not effective or were too expensive to meet with wide acceptance by vegetable growers. Since 1940, new chemicals have been discovered which are effective at a reasonable cost. The increase in cost of labor since that time has speeded up the adoption of chemical methods of weed control. Chemical weed control has become a separate branch of horticultural and agronomic research in many states. New chemicals are being developed each year to do a more effective and cheaper job of controlling weeds. Since the field is growing so rapidly, only the general principles will be discussed here. Local experiment stations should be consulted to determine the best materials, the exact rates, and methods of applying chemicals on vegetables.

The object of chemical weed control is to eliminate hand weeding of vegetable crops. It is not intended to replace all mechanical tillage but only to make mechanical tillage more efficient. The cost of chemical weed control can be greatly reduced by spraying only a band over the row. This band is the area where tractor tillage implements are not effective in controlling weeds. The success of many types of chemical weed killers has made growers more aware of weeds, and they are no longer satisfied to accept weedy fields as inevitable. Weed-free fields of many vegetable crops can be obtained with no hand weeding and a minimum of cultivation.

The chemicals used to kill weeds are called herbicides. The ideal herbicide is one which will kill all weeds infesting a crop and not harm the crop, but few such materials have been discovered. There are many chemicals on the market which are called selective herbicides. This means that if the chemicals are used properly, certain weeds will be killed but the crops will not be damaged. This term is a little misleading, since chemicals used improperly may damage the crop severely. Most of the chemicals used for weed control in vegetables are selective. In other words, the crops on which they are used have a certain degree of tolerance for the specific chemical.

Mode of Action of Herbicides. The exact way herbicides kill plants is not known. Some poison certain essential enzyme systems which disrupt the metabolism of the plant. Others speed up certain plant processes so that the metabolism is out of balance and the plant eventually dies for lack of reserve food materials. Complete coverage of the weed plant is essential for chemicals which kill only the area it contacts. Other chemicals are absorbed by weed roots or leaves and are translocated throughout the plant, so that in these cases complete coverage is not essential for good weed kill. A few chemicals are effective only on germinating seeds, while others may kill plants at any stage of growth. Since so many different types of chemicals are used to control weeds, each material requires special precautions. It is necessary to know the mode of action of the chemical and the nature of the crop tolerance to the chemical.

Crop Tolerance to Herbicides. The amount and type of herbicide that can be safely used on a vegetable depend on its tolerance to the chemical. There are several types of crop tolerance to herbicides, but no vegetable exhibits all types of tolerance to all herbicides. It should be noted that various weeds may have the same type of tolerance to herbicides as do crops. A herbicide may give complete control of one weed, while another species escapes without injury. The four main types of tolerance are as follows:

CROP ESCAPES DAMAGE BECAUSE OF ITS MORPHOLOGY. A good example is the use of dinitro materials to control wild mustard (*Brassica arvensis*) in peas. The herbicide is applied after the peas have emerged. The herbicide spray does not stick on the waxy pea leaves, but since the mustard leaves are hairy, the droplets of spray stay on the leaves. The mustard leaves are killed where the spray is held by the hairs. Weeds which have waxy leaves like peas are not damaged by these dinitro sprays.

CROP ESCAPES DAMAGE BECAUSE OF TIMING OF HERBICIDE APPLICATION. These are the preemergence sprays where the herbicide is applied before the crop comes through the ground. They are used mostly on large-seeded vegetables which take several days to emerge, such as sweet corn, beans, peas, and potatoes. These herbicides are usually not effective by the time the crop comes up, and successful weed control depends on rapid germination of weed seeds.

CROP ESCAPES DAMAGE BECAUSE OF PLACEMENT OF HERBICIDE SPRAY. The ground between the rows is sprayed so that none of the herbicide spray comes in contact with the vegetable plant. In some cases, a shield is needed to prevent crop damage. This method is not widely used.

CROP ESCAPES DAMAGE BECAUSE OF "BIOCHEMICAL TOLERANCE." Probably the best example of this type of tolerance is the use of Stoddard Solvent on carrots. The oil enters both the carrot leaves and the weed leaves. The carrot leaves are not damaged, but most weeds are killed. The exact reason for this is not known and is usually called a *biochemical tolerance*. The successful use of many herbicides depends on crop biochemical tolerance to concentrations of a chemical that will kill certain weeds.

Rate of Application. The amount of herbicide a vegetable will tolerate without damage may vary with the growing area or season. It is essential to consider the factors affecting the crop and weed tolerance to various herbicides. Some of the most important factors to be considered are as follows:

SOIL TYPE. In many cases the soil type determines the type of chemical that can be used or the amount that can be safely applied for weed control. On light, sandy soils certain herbicides may leach down to the crop root zone and cause severe damage to the crop, while on heavier soils this may not be a problem. The organic-matter content of the soil is important since some herbicides are tied up by the soil organic matter. To get effective weed control they must be applied at high rates on soils with a high organic-matter content. If applied at these same rates on a soil with a low organic-matter content, the crop may be damaged. The moisture content of the soil is important if herbicides are used that kill only germinating seeds. They are usually rather short lived materials, and the weed seeds must come up within a short period of time or the chemical will not give effective control. In many cases irrigation can be used effectively to improve the action of these herbicides. The soil temperature is important since it determines the rate of come-up of the crop and weed seeds. When the crop comes up before the herbicide has been dissipated damage may result, while if the weeds come up too slowly, poor weed control may result.

ENVIRONMENTAL FACTORS. Temperature may have a profound effect on crop tolerance or the effectiveness of the weed kill. When volatile herbicides are used, the temperature is obviously an important factor. At high temperatures the herbicide may be volatilized so fast that effective weed control is not obtained, or in other cases, rapid vaporization of the herbicide may damage the crop plant. The temperature, too, affects the rate of growth of both the crop and weeds and may make proper timing difficult. Sunlight influences the rate of growth of the crop and weeds, and some herbicides are more effective when the weeds are rapidly growing. Effective weed kills may be obtained in bright, sunny weather, and poor kills during periods of dark, cloudy weather. Sunlight and temperature also may affect the morphology of the plant. The protective waxy coating of the crop leaf may not be as highly developed under some environmental conditions as under others.

AGE OF THE PLANT. The tolerance of the crop to herbicides may change as the plant grows. Some crops are more susceptible to injury when they are small, while other crops are more susceptible when they are large. The habit of growth of the crop may change so that more spray is intercepted and damage results. Most herbicides kill the weeds quickest when they are small, and it usually takes more chemical to kill large weeds. The most effective weed control is obtained when the weeds are just coming through the ground in most cases. However, there are a few herbicides that kill only germinating seeds and do not control weeds already emerged.

Accuracy of Application. Herbicides must be accurately applied since there is a narrow range of safety. The applications must be uniform over the whole area, otherwise crop damage may result or poor weed control may be obtained. Most herbicides are applied as a spray. The amount of water used with the chemical is of little importance since the water is only a vehicle to ensure uniform distribution of the material over the area. The rates recommended for herbicides are in terms of pounds of active material per acre of ground covered with the spray. When bands of spray are applied over the crop rows, the cost is less since only part of the field is sprayed. If the vegetable is planted in 3-foot rows and a 1-foot band is sprayed, only one-third of the actual land area is covered with the spray. Therefore, for an acre of crop only one-third of the chemical will be necessary.

Different companies may supply the same chemical under a different trade name. These formulations may vary in the concentration of the active ingredient, but the concentration of active ingredient is always stated on the label as required by law. Since the recommendations are made in terms of active ingredient, it is easy to determine the amount of formulation to use. Some herbicides are poisons and should be handled according to instructions on the label. Since they are to be used on plants intended for human consumption, their use is regulated by the

Food and Drug Administration. Only materials that have been proved harmless when used according to the recommendations are cleared for use. It is unlawful to use materials that have not been accepted by the Food and Drug Administration. If the label on the container is carefully followed, there is no danger to the grower or to the ultimate consumer.

Equipment for Applying Herbicides. Herbicides should be applied with equipment especially designed for the purpose. It is difficult to do an accurate job with hand equipment. The most popular type of sprayer is the inexpensive low-gallonage sprayer mounted on a tractor. These apply usually from 10 to 15 gallons of water per acre and are fitted with special nozzles so that a uniform band of spray is applied. The machines must be calibrated at a definite tractor speed, and this speed must be maintained at all times. A speedometer on the tractor is very helpful and almost essential to do an accurate, effective job of spraying herbicides. If the tractor slows down, more chemical will be applied, and if it goes faster, less chemical will be applied. Poor speed control results in either crop damage or poor weed control. It is unwise to attempt to use standard insecticide and fungicide spray machines for weed control since the nozzles of these spray machines are designed to get a maximum amount of spray material on the plant. If herbicides are used with this type of nozzle, the material is concentrated on the crop and poor weed control and crop damage will result. Some types of herbicides are difficult to remove from the sprayer. If a crop sprayer intended for general use is contaminated by some of these herbicides, severe crop damage may result when the sprayer is used on a sensitive crop. For this reason it is generally best to have a low-volume sprayer for herbicide use only.

Chemicals Used for Weed Control. Many chemicals have been used for chemical weed control of vegetables. Most of these are effective only under limited conditions. In the following discussion only those that have been widely accepted for use on vegetables will be discussed.

INORGANIC SALTS. Most inorganic salts are toxic to plants if the solution applied to leaves is sufficiently concentrated. Few of them show any selective action. Common salt, sodium chloride, has been used for controlling weeds in young beets. It is applied as a spray when the beets have about four true leaves. Unfortunately, the salt does not control lamb's-quarters (*Chenopodium album*), which is a common pest in beet fields. Calcium cyanamid dust has been used successfully on controlling weeds in onions and asparagus. It must be applied when the weeds are quite small or have not germinated. The effect is rather short lived, and ample moisture is essential. Potassium cyanate spray has also been used as a weed-control material in onions.

PETROLEUM PRODUCTS. Stoddard Solvent, or dry-cleaning fluid, is extensively used as a herbicide for carrots and related crops. It is a mixture of several petroleum compounds and has a boiling point of 148 to 201°C., of which the 148 to 182°C. fraction is the most active. The unsaturated or aromatic compounds are the most active as herbicides. The oil does not enter the cells of carrots and related crops so that the crop generally escapes without any damage. The Stoddard Solvent is applied without dilution or mixture with water since emulsions with water are generally toxic to the carrots. Injury may result in some cases if sprayed on wet foliage of carrots. The weeds are killed slowly at low temperatures, but the end result is the same. If the temperature is too high when the material is applied, it may volatilize so fast that poor weed control results. Stoddard Solvent sprays are most effective on small weeds since complete coverage of the weeds is essential for good control. The foliage of perennial weeds is damaged, but new growth soon starts from the old roots. Ragweeds (*Ambrosia* sp.) and wild carrot (*Daucus carota*) are not controlled by these sprays.

THE DINITRO COMPOUNDS. These are the alkanolamine salts of dinitro-O-secondary-butyl phenol. They are protein coagulants and are reported to inhibit flavoprotein enzymes. The respiration rate of plants increases greatly when these materials are applied. They are widely used on beans, peas, corn, and potatoes as preemergence sprays and are used on peas after they come up to control wild mustard. When applied before the crop comes up, the dinitro sprays kill most of the weed seeds which germinate or the seedlings which emerge for a relatively short period of time, 1 or 2 weeks. Even though the effective length of time of kill of this material is short, weed control is obtained throughout the whole season if the soil is not disturbed. Perennial weeds are not killed by dinitro sprays. The dinitros are volatile compounds and when applied during periods of high temperature may cause crop damage or be dissipated before the weeds come up. On light, sandy soils they may leach down onto the crop seed and cause damage, especially during hot weather. Closely related compounds are the pentachlorophenols. They have essentially the same action on plants as do the dinitro materials and are used in the same way.

SUBSTITUTED UREAS. These materials have been used by biochemists for many years as a type of specific enzyme poison. The most common material used in weed control is 3-(P-chlorophenyl)-1′,1′-dimethyl urea (CMU or Karmex-W). It is widely used on asparagus, being applied both before and after the cutting season. The material is also used around greenhouses and cold frames at high rates to eradicate completely all plant growth. It is adsorbed on soil colloids and especially by the organic matter of the soil. On heavy soils with high organic-matter content more of the material must be used to get effective weed control than on light soils. It is only slightly soluble, and care must be taken to agitate the solutions while spraying. However, the chemical is rapidly absorbed by plants which quickly become yellow and die. At the specified rates, it does not harm asparagus but gives good weed control on all weeds in asparagus beds except certain large perennial weeds.

CARBAMATES. Two of these materials are in common use. They are IPC (isopropyl-*N*-phenyl carbamate) and Chloro IPC (isopropyl-*N*-3-chlorophenyl carbamate). The action of the two compounds is similar except that IPC is more soluble and more volatile than Chloro IPC. In cool weather IPC is used, and in warmer weather Chloro IPC is used. They act as mitotic poisons and stop cell division at the metaphase. The dehydrogenase enzymes are inhibited, and the initial effect is to reduce respiration, but this is followed by a great stimulation of respiratory activity in the plant. These materials give excellent control of most grasses, chickweed, and purslane and are used mostly on spinach and onions. These materials are adsorbed by the soil and do not leach. They remain in the soil for a long period of time, and poor stands of rye winter cover crops have resulted following their use on onions.

THE 2,4-D-TYPE MATERIALS. These materials are derived from 2-4-dichlorophenoxyacetic acid. They are all powerful herbicides and severely damage or kill most broad-leaved plants. At low concentrations grasses are not markedly damaged. The action of 2,4-D on plants has been studied in greater detail than any other herbicide. The specific manner in which plants are damaged is not completely known. The material brings about both physiological and morphological changes in the plant. Plant leaves and stems become twisted and severely curled following application of 2,4-D. The respiration rate of the plant greatly increases, and death follows within a few days if sufficient material has been applied. It is most active when plants are rapidly growing, so the best weed kill is obtained during warm, sunny weather. 2,4-D is rapidly absorbed by either leaves or roots and is translocated throughout the plant so that complete coverage of a plant is not necessary for good kill. Their use on vegetables is usually limited to sweet corn. Applications at low rates to sweet corn just emerging from the ground are effective and safe. Damage to the sweet corn may result if the corn is fairly large. On light soils it may leach down to the root zone and injure sweet-corn roots. Some formulations of 2,4-D are extremely volatile, and the fumes may drift into other fields and damage sensitive plants. Crops like tomatoes, cucumbers, melons, and beans are very sensitive to 2,4-D. The extreme sensitivity of many vegetables to this material limits its use to areas where sensitive crops are not grown nearby.

A herbicide derived from 2,4-D called Crag-1 has greater value on vegetable farms. This is sodium 2,4-dichlorophenoxyethyl sulfate and is inactive as a herbicide in this form. This chemical requires water to carry it down into the soil where microorganisms break it down to 2,4-D. It is effective only on germinating seeds. When applied to the soil either as a preemergence spray or between the rows at the last cultivation it is rapidly broken down to an active form and gives good weed control. It can be effectively used in conjunction with irrigation to provide conditions favorable for weed-seed germination.

OTHER HERBICIDES. N-1-naphthyl phthalamic acid (Alanap-1) is an outstanding herbicide for vine crops. It is applied either as a preemergence or postemergence spray on cucumbers, muskmelons, and watermelons. Some varieties of squash may be damaged by this material, while others are tolerant. It must be applied before weeds have germinated, since only germinating seeds are killed effectively. Water is necessary for its action. When applied during conditions favorable for rapid seed germination, it gives excellent weed control in vine crops.

CHAPTER 10

Irrigation

Irrigation is essential to successful vegetable production in arid and semiarid regions, and in many humid regions it is an insurance against drought. Some regions have little or no rain during the year and must be irrigated for crop production. Others have rain intermittently for 5 or 6 months and little or none during the remainder of the year. In such regions irrigation is essential for crop production during the dry portion of the year and also at times during the so-called rainy season. Irrigation is recognized as an essential practice in vegetable production under the conditions mentioned, and provision is made for it.

In so-called humid regions, where the annual rainfall averages from 30 to 50 inches and is distributed throughout the year, irrigation has not been considered essential. However, there is seldom a growing season that water does not become a limiting factor in crop production. It is during such periods of water shortage that irrigation is of greatest value. A short period of dry weather often reduces the yield materially and lowers the quality of the product, and a prolonged drought may result in total loss of a crop. The value of irrigation in humid regions varies greatly from year to year depending on the amount and distribution of the rainfall during the growing season. A region might have a heavy annual rainfall and still need supplemental irrigation because of poor distribution, especially shortage of water during a period of rapid growth of the crop. This is illustrated by the results reported by Ellison and Jacob (1954) in experiments with potatoes on Long Island, N.Y. In 1949 with 7 weeks of low rainfall in June and July, 5.9 inches of water applied over a period of 6 weeks increased the yield of U.S. No. 1 potatoes 206 bushels to the acre. The rainfall during the period from planting to harvest was 11.08 inches. In 1950 with 16.33 inches of rain during the growing period, 4.65 inches of irrigation water increased the yield only 10 bushels to the acre. The yield in 1950, of about 400 bushel to the acre, without irrigation was higher than with irrigation in 1949. The temperature during June and July, 1949, was considerably higher than in 1950. Similar results with several crops have been reported by workers in other parts of the Eastern half of the United States.

Irrigation in the United States 1939 and 1949. From 1939 to 1949 the acreage of land under irrigation increased from 17,982,830 acres to 25,787,455, or 43.4 per cent, according to the U.S. Census of agriculture for 1950. About 94 per cent of the irrigated land in 1949 was in the 17 Western states. Of the other states Arkansas, Louisiana, and Florida accounted for 1,364,303 acres, and the other 28 states had only 152,586 acres under irrigation in 1949 (Table 10.1).

Table 10.1. Acres of Land under Irrigation in the United States by Regions and Some Individual States, 1939 to 1949, and Percentage Increase

Area	1939	1949	Increase, %
17 Western states.........	17,243,396	24,270,566	40.8
Arkansas................	159,412	422,107	164.8
Louisiana...............	413,969	576,775	39.3
Florida.................	126,191	365,421	189.6
Other 28 states..........	39,862	152,586	282.8
Connecticut.............	520	8,088	
Massachusetts...........	2,049	18,507	803.2
Michigan...............	2,960	13,901	369.6
New Jersey.............	7,956	28,117	253.4
New York..............	5,948	19,248	223.6
Pennsylvania...........	3,356	7,251	116.1
Wisconsin..............	2,345	9,781	317.1
United States...........	17,982,830	25,787,455	43.4

While only a very small part of the land under irrigation is in the Eastern part of the United States, it has increased rapidly since 1939. In some of the Eastern states irrigation increased more rapidly from 1949 to 1955 than from 1939 to 1949.

There are three general methods of irrigation—surface, subirrigation, and spray or sprinkling. Spray or sprinkling irrigation is in reality surface irrigation, but in common usage the term surface irrigation means applying water by flooding or by means of a trench or furrow.

Surface Irrigation. Surface irrigation is used extensively in arid and semiarid regions of the United States but has not become popular in the Eastern part of the country. This method requires level, or nearly level, land and for this reason is little used where soils are shallow and leveling would be necessary. Two methods of surface irrigation are in use in the United States. One is known as *furrow* and the other as *flooding*. Neither of these is used to any great extent in the Eastern part of the United States. The main advantage of surface irrigation over other kinds is the low cost of equipment. The main disadvantages of surface irrigation are: (1) uneven distribution of water; (2) loss of water in open porous soils, (3) puddling and baking of the soil in the furrows and all of the surface soil in the flooding method following the application of water, and (4) cost of labor in the distribution of water. However, where the land is nearly level and a cheap supply of water is available, this method is satisfactory. Where a stream can be diverted and water run to the field by gravity or where flowing wells are available, surface irrigation is a cheap method.

FIG. 10.1. Furrow irrigation of lettuce at Salinas, Calif. (*Courtesy of G. J. Raleigh.*)

The furrow method of irrigation (Fig. 10.1) consists of running the water through furrows between the rows, or between narrow beds, in such a way that it will moisten all of the soil between the furrows. This method can be used successfully on slightly rolling land if the furrows follow the contour, with enough slope to permit the water to flow slowly.

Irrigation by flooding is used in growing onions and some other crops in Texas and in other regions of the Southwestern and Western parts of the United States. This method is not satisfactory for all crops and is usable only on level, or nearly level, land. Any given bed irrigated by this method must be practically level, hence where the land is uneven it requires leveling. The area to be flooded is diked with soil, and the bed is flooded. The land is prepared for irrigation by making narrow ridges across the area to be planted. The distance between the ridges is determined by the slope of the land; the steeper the slope the closer the ridges should be.

The main laterals, used in the flooding method, should be constructed so as to be slightly above the level of the surface in order to give a good head to the water to the smaller lateral ditches. The bottom of minor laterals should be kept level with the surface of the field so that they may be drained after the field has been irrigated. The size of the minor laterals and main ditches is determined by the quantity of water they are to carry.

Subirrigation. This method consists in delivering the water to the plants from below. The advantages claimed for subirrigation are as follows: (1) the water supply is constant; (2) the surface soil is kept dry which prevents rapid evaporation; (3) the soil is not puddled, therefore the surface does not bake. The main disadvantage is the large quantity of water required. Subirrigation is not satisfactory where the subsoil is porous or where there is a hardpan or impervious subsoil near the surface. For successful subirrigation the land must be level or have a slight and uniform slope.

Spencer and Berry (1916) give the following as essentials for the successful operation of subirrigation systems: (1) an abundant and cheap water supply, (2) a subsoil floor of clay, marl, or hardpan located at a depth of 3 to 5 feet below the surface, (3) a foot or more of coarse sand on top of the subsoil, (4) a top soil of sandy loam which is neither too porous nor too compact and which will convey water freely, (5) land that admits perfect drainage, and (6) land that is level without depressions or raised places.

In the vicinity of Sanford, Fla., where subirrigation is used extensively, the water is supplied by artesian wells, obtained by driving pipes down into the artesian stratum and allowing the water to rise to a height above the surface of the ground. In some instances force pumps are used where the water rises to within easy reach from the surface. The water is conducted through laterals made of 3-inch drain tile with the lines 24 feet apart. These tiles are placed at least 18 inches deep and have a fall of 1 inch or more to every 100 feet.

Spray Irrigation. Spray irrigation is the method most commonly used in the Eastern part of the United States and is replacing other types to some extent in many other regions. In this method the water is applied in the form of spray or mist somewhat similar to a gentle rain. Some of the advantages of spray irrigation are as follows: (1) it can be used on land too uneven for other types of irrigation; (2) it can be used on soils that are too porous for other methods; (3) it distributes water more uniformly than any other type of irrigation; (4) the rate of application can be so adjusted that little or no erosion occurs; (5) light applications of water can be made on soils of low water-holding capacity and shallow depth and for shallow-rooted crops, thus avoiding loss of water and soluble nutrients; (6) in this method ditches and borders required for surface irrigation are eliminated, thus making more land available for crop production and eliminating ditch cleaning.

The main disadvantages of spray irrigation are: (1) initial cost of equipment is high; (2) operation cost is high owing to necessity of supplying water under pressure; (3) labor cost is high where movable lines are used; (4) strong winds may prevent irrigation at critical times, resulting in uneven distribution of water, and cause excessive loss of water by evaporation; (5) mechanical difficulties such as sprinklers failing to rotate, nozzles becoming clogged, sand and gravel lodging in couplings, resulting in excessive leakage; and (6) moving pipelines in soft sticky soil, disagreeable work which may cause a serious labor problem.

TYPES OF SPRAY IRRIGATION. There are three general types of spray-irrigation systems in use. One is known as nozzle line or oscillating pipe-line in which small nozzles are placed in the pipes at intervals of about 3 feet. Another is known as rotary sprinkler, and the third is the per-forated-pipe system.

The oscillating pipeline may be permanent or movable. In the permanent installation the pipelines usually are placed on posts, either high (about 6 feet) or low ($1\frac{1}{2}$ to 4 feet), the former being the most popular because the lines are placed high enough to permit machinery and equipment to pass under them. The portable system consists of one or more nozzle lines that are carried from one part of the field to another as needed. The main advantages of the portable lines are: (1) the cost of pipe and installation is low; (2) the lines are out of the way during land preparation, cultivation, spraying or dusting, and harvesting. The cost of operation is greater owing to the labor of moving, connecting, and disconnecting the lines. The oscillating-pipe system delivers water fairly uniformly, and each unit moistens rectangular areas. One of the disadvantages of the system is the time required to apply a given quantity of water.

The rotary sprinkler system, developed in California, is widely used in various parts of the United States (Fig. 10.2). It is replacing surface irrigation to a considerable extent in many areas and the oscillating-pipe system in areas where this has been in use. Both portable and semi-portable rotary sprinkler systems are in use. In the portable the pump, main line, and laterals are moved from field to field. In the semiportable, the pump and main lines are installed permanently and only the lateral lines are moved. The most common rotary sprinkler system consists of lightweight portable steel or aluminum pipe with sprinklers mounted at varying intervals. In one small-size system sprinkler heads are used that deliver about 4 gallons of water per minute at a pressure of about

20 pounds per square inch. The sprinklers are spaced about 20 feet apart in the line, and the lines are spaced 40 feet apart. A larger system that is in common use employes a sprinkler head that delivers about 18 gallons of water per minute at 45 pounds pressure. The sprinkler heads are spaced 40 feet apart in the line with the lines 60 to 80 feet apart. At 40 by 80 feet one line 400 feet long will supply about 1 inch of water to 3 acres in 10 hours. Schwalen *et al.* (1953) state that to obtain uniform distribution of water it is necessary to overlap adjacent sprinkler patterns; the maximum spacing should be no more than 60 per cent of the wetted area. A common practice is to space the sprinklers on the laterals at

Fig. 10.2. Overhead rotary sprinkler system of irrigation. (*Courtesy of Corrugated Culvert Co., Berkeley, Calif.*)

intervals of 40 per cent of the wetted diameter and to have the distance between laterals not more than 60 per cent of the wetted diameter.

There is another type of rotary sprinkler that delivers from 200 to over 400 gallons of water per minute and covers an area 300 to 400 feet in diameter. This requires high pressure—about 100 pounds at the sprinkler. One of the reasons for the success of this system is the use of lightweight, thin-wall pipes that are put together quickly without the use of any tools. The rotary sprinkler system of irrigation requires less time to apply a given quantity of water than the oscillating-pipe system. No supports are necessary for the rotary sprinkler system since the pipe rests on the soil and the risers are screwed into the pipe.

In some installations of the rotary sprinkler type of irrigation only one line of pipe is employed, which is moved to another location as soon as the area is irrigated. This is somewhat objectionable because workmen moving the pipe must travel on the saturated soil and the system is not in use while the line is being moved. It would be better to have enough lines to make it unnecessary to stop irrigating while a line is being moved and also to allow the water to penetrate below the surface a few inches before moving a line of pipe. On some soils it would be advisable to have two lines set up at the same time and to operate them alternately to prevent runoff and erosion.

The most popular type of rotary sprinkler has two nozzles, one that waters the area immediately around the risers and the other covering the remaining area. These sprinklers are operated by the water pressure and revolve very slowly.

Fig. 10.3. Perforated-pipe system of irrigation in use irrigating potatoes in Montana. (*Courtesy of W. R. Ames Co., San Francisco, Calif.*)

The perforated-pipe system of irrigation (Fig. 10.3) differs from the other overhead spray systems in that no nozzles, risers, or heads are involved. Water is forced out through holes drilled in the pipes, and the pressure used varies up to 20 pounds per square inch, usually from 4 to 15 pounds. In this system the water covers a rectangular area 10 to 50 feet wide, 40 feet being the standard. Lightweight quick-coupling pipes are used and are available in various lengths, with 20 feet being standard. Pipe sizes vary from 2 to 8 inches in diameter for aluminum and from 3 to 10 inches in steel pipe. The size used is determined by the length of the line and the volume of water. The rate of application of water ranges from ½ to 2 inches per hour depending on the size and spacing of the holes. The factors that should determine the rate of application are the slope of the land, the permeability of the soil, the crop grown, and the desired speed of coverage. On slopes, and for heavy soils, a low rate of coverage is desirable in order to prevent runoff and erosion. Light, permeable soils will absorb water at a fairly high rate of application without causing erosion or runoff.

In this, as in other portable systems of irrigation, it is desirable to have more than one line of pipe so that it will not be necessary to stop irrigating to move the pipe nor to move it while the surface of the irrigated area is very wet. On soils that absorb water slowly, it is desirable to have two lines available to operate alternately in order to prevent runoff and erosion.

Planning an Irrigation System. The first step in planning an irrigation system should be to make sure that an adequate supply of water is available during the driest seasons. The next step should be to get all available information in order to determine the kind that would be most feasible under the particular conditions. Irrigation specialists suggest that for the usual kinds of vegetables grown under irrigation in the Eastern part of the United States the spray outfit should be able to deliver at least 1 inch of water per week over the area to be irrigated. This quantity is equivalent to 27,152 gallons per week for each acre. The water should be free from materials that would injure plants and from dirt and sand that would clog the nozzles. If there is a choice of sources of water supply, the cost of the original installation and of operation and upkeep for each source and the dependability should be given consideration before making a choice. When there is any question as to the adequacy of the supply it should be tested to determine the quantity of water available.

Since the laying out and installing of an irrigation system require a considerable knowledge of engineering, the reader is referred to special books and bulletins written by irrigation specialists.

Applying Water. The frequency of watering and the quantity of water that should be applied depend on the class of soil, the depth to hardpan, the depth to which roots penetrate, the utilization or removal of water by the crop, and the loss by evaporation from the surface of the soil. The quantity of water necessary to penetrate a given depth of soil, when all of the available water is exhausted, varies with the kind of soil. Sandy soils require half or less than half as much water to penetrate 1 foot of soil as do clay soils, and the requirement for loam soils is between that for sandy and clay soils. If a hardpan is near the surface, only enough water should be applied to wet the soil to the hardpan. This would require more frequent watering and less water at each application than would be the case where a greater depth of soil is to be penetrated. Where the subsoil is gravelly, only enough water should be applied to moisten the soil above the gravel, since any excess would result in loss of soluble nutrients in the drainage water.

It is obvious from the above that any general statement regarding the quantity of water to apply would be misleading without specifying the conditions. In the Eastern part of the United States 1 inch of water per week has been the general recommendation. Wessels and White-Stevens (1945) state that in the dry season of 1944 an inch was not enough at certain periods during the season. They point out that as the crops increase in size and the weather becomes warmer the loss of water through transpiration and evaporation becomes greater. Peikert (1947) stated that the usual practice in Michigan was to apply 1 to 1½ inches of water at each application for shallow-rooted plants grown on light soils. Deeper-rooted crops and heavier soil applications of 2 to 2½ inches are made. He suggested that it is desirable to apply only enough to bring the soil moisture up to field capacity to the depth of the principal feeding roots. In arid and semiarid regions, especially where the soils are deep, much more water may be applied at one irrigation than is desirable in humid areas and on shallow soils. Without knowing how much available water is in the soil and its water-holding capacity, it is not possible to judge accurately how much water should be applied at one time, or when to apply it. The rate of growth of the crop, the color of the foliage, and temporary wilting give a fair indication of the need of water. However, growth may be checked before wilting is in evidence. There are more accurate guides than the appearance of the plants, one of which is called the plaster-of-paris electrical-resistance method described by Bouyoucos (1950). The principal parts of the equipment consist of porous absorbent blocks made of plaster of paris and a moisture meter. Two electrodes are imbedded in each block with leads. When buried, the block absorbs moisture from and gives it up to the soil, so that the water content of the blocks tends to be in equilibrium with that of the soil. The electrical resistance of the block varies with its moisture content, and that varies with the soil moisture. The leads from the block buried in the soil are connected to the moisture meter which is calibrated to read directly in percentage of available moisture. The blocks should be placed in the most representative part of the field at depths where most of the roots are located. The meter covers a range of soil moisture from field capacity to the wilting point, and Bouyoucos suggests that a field should not be irrigated so long as the reading is 50 per cent or more. As soon as it falls below 50 per cent water should be applied, especially on sandy soils. Heavy soils may not need irrigation until the reading on the meter is considerably below 50 per cent, possibly as low as 20 per cent on clay soil. Bouyoucos gives directions for use of the blocks and meter.

CHAPTER 11

Rotation, Succession, and Intercropping

ROTATION

The term rotation, as applied to crop production, may be defined as a systematic arrangement for the growing of different crops in a more or less regular sequence on the same land. Rotation differs from succession cropping in that the former covers a period of 2, 3, or more years, while the latter refers to the growing of two or more crops on the same land in 1 year. Systematic crop rotation is not so common in vegetable growing as in general farming. It is, however, important in vegetable growing and should be planned and followed as systematically as feasible.

The benefits derived from crop rotation are due largely to the control of disease and insects and to the better use of the resources of the soil.

Rotation as a Factor in Disease and Insect Control. Many serious diseases can be controlled in a practical way by a systematic rotation in which the host plant is grown on the same land not oftener than once in 3 or 4 years. Rotation is effective in disease control mainly with those diseases whose spores or other propagating parts live only 1 or 2 years. Clubroot of cabbage and other crucifers can be controlled by keeping the land free of cruciferous crops and weeds for 3 years. Other diseases, such as the potato scab and onion smut, cannot be controlled by ordinary rotation since the organisms involved live in the soil for several years. In planning a system of rotation from the standpoint of disease control, one needs to know what kinds of crops are affected by a given organism. Some organisms attack only one host plant, others affect only those that are closely related, while still others are not limited even to the same species, genus, or family. Root knot, caused by a species of nematode (*Heterodera marioni*), is a serious disease of a large number of crops representing many different families of plants. It can be controlled by rotation in which resistant or immune crops are grown for 2 or 3 years. These resistant or immune crops include corn, wheat, winter oats, barley, Iron, Victor, Monetto, and Brabham cowpeas, velvet beans, and certain varieties of a few other crops.

145

Rotation is of value in the control of some kinds of insects, especially of species which feed on only one crop and which are unable to move very far. If the host plants are not near at hand when the insects emerge, many will perish before reaching them. With most insects a short rotation is as effective as a long one since they die in a short time after emergence if their food plants are absent. In planning a rotation for insect control one should follow a crop which has been infested by one known not to be attacked by the same insect.

Effect of Crop Plants on Those That Follow. Experimental results obtained by many workers have shown that crop plants have a marked effect on yields of those that followed. In experiments at the Rhode Island Experiment Station it was shown that mangels, rutabagas, cabbage, and buckwheat had a marked depressing effect on the yield of onions that followed. On the other hand, the yield of buckwheat was highest following rutabagas. The plan of this experiment was to grow 16 different crops on as many plots for two seasons and then to grow one of these on the entire area the third year. The first crop grown on the entire area was onions, and the yield varied from 72 to 524 bushels to the acre. The very low yields of onions followed the crops mentioned above, and the highest followed timothy and redtop and redtop alone. The second crop grown on the entire area was buckwheat, and the highest yield followed rutabagas (33.8 bushels to the acre). The lowest yield of buckwheat followed millet, timothy, and corn (4.4 to 5.4 bushels to the acre). These experiments were continued, and other crops were grown over the entire area, but the results mentioned are sufficient to illustrate the effects of crops on those that follow.

In 1930 the experiments at the Rhode Island station were changed, and 5 of the crops grown previously were left out. The experiments were set up in cement frames, and the methods followed were similar to those previously used except that 4 crops were grown every third year instead of one crop as in the earlier experiments. The 11 crops grown were onions, potatoes, mangels, rutabagas, cabbage, buckwheat, corn, millet, oats, rye, and carrots. These were grown on their respective plots for two years, and the third year the 4 uniform crops were grown. In 1930 and 1933 the uniform crops were corn, rutabagas, mangels, and potatoes; in 1936 potatoes, mangels, carrots, and onions; in 1939 and 1942 the uniform crops were potatoes, mangels, rutabagas, and onions. These uniform crops were grown across the strips that had produced the 11 crops the two previous years. Each year the equivalent of 1,000 pounds of 8-10-10 fertilizer was applied per acre, and the soil reaction remained in the range of pH 5.0 to 6.0. The results of these experiments were published by Odland and Bell (1950). The lowest yields of mangels were following carrots, mangels, and millet. The lowest yields of potatoes followed potatoes, rutabagas, and millet. Low yields of rutabagas followed mangels, millet, and rutabagas. The lowest yields of onions followed mangels, cabbage, and rutabagas. These results with onions were similar to those obtained in the earlier experiments. For 3 crops out of 4, millet, mangels, and rutabagas had the most deleterious effect on those that followed. Rye, oats, and onions were usually followed by high yields.

In another series of experiments, the results of which were reported by Bell, Odland, and Owens (1949), there were three types of rotations as follows: (1) silage corn 1 year, potatoes 1 year, alfalfa-timothy hay 4 years; (2) corn 1 year, potatoes 1 year, mixture of alfalfa, red clover, alsike clover, timothy, and redtop 4 years; (3) same as (2) except that there was no legume in the hay mixture. The average yield of potatoes from 1930 to 1946 for rotation 1 was 246 bushels per acre; for rotation 2 the yield was 222 bushels, and for rotation 3 it was 294 bushels to the acre. These differences are significant. It is of interest to note that both organic matter and nitrogen in the soil were lower in rotation 3 than in the others.

Results of an experiment in Connecticut, reported by Janes (1951), are somewhat similar to those obtained in Rhode Island. In the Connecticut experiments two types of rotations were followed. Type 1 involves growing two crops each year of the alternate years of the 4-year rotation. Type 2 is less intensive, involving only one crop every second year, and the one vegetable crop is followed by a cover crop of rye. In type 1 beets and cabbage in the second year and lettuce and cauliflower in the fourth year are used to measure the rotational effect. Beets and lettuce are grown as early crops and are followed in the same season by cabbage and cauliflower, respectively. In type 2 rotation tomatoes in the second year and onions in the fourth year are used to measure the rotational effects. The tomatoes and onions are followed by a rye cover crop.

Beets showed no difference in yield in the early years, but in the last 4 years the yield following sweet corn and a winter cover crop of vetch was much larger than following spinach and carrots. The yield of cabbage was highest after corn and vetch and lowest following soybeans grown as a soil-improving crop. The lowest yield of lettuce was following sweet corn and vetch. The author states that the lettuce plants were badly stunted, the roots were brown and had very few branches; cauliflower yields were not significantly different following the various crops. Tomato yields were lower following sweet corn and vetch, and soybeans, grown as a soil-improving crop the previous year, lower than following carrots and spinach—grown on the same plots. Onion yields were very low following sweet corn and vetch, and pink root was more severe than when the crop followed other crops. The largest yield of onions followed peppers, but not much larger than after beets and spinach.

Many explanations have been offered to account for the divergent effect of crop plants on those that follow. Some of the explanations are as follows:

1. Difference in uptake of nutrients from the soil
2. Difference in effect on soil reaction, especially the greater removal of bases by some crops than by others
3. Difference in quantity of organic matter left in the soil
4. Difference in effect on pathogenic organisms in the soil
5. Difference in toxic materials produced on the decomposition of the plant remains
6. Difference in extent and distribution of the root systems

Results of experiments at the Rhode Island station showed that the lowest yield of onions followed those crops that removed the largest quantity of the deficient nutrients and the highest yield followed red-top, which removed the smallest quantity of the same nutrients. It was not universally true, however, that the crops which removed the largest quantity of the deficient nutrients were the ones that had the most depressing effect on the succeeding crop.

Soil reaction is affected differently by the various crops, and it was found in the Rhode Island experiments that the yield of onions was highest following those crops giving rise to the least acidity. When the acidity was reduced by liming, the effect of the various crops on the yield of onions, an acid-sensitive crop, was much less divergent. Mangels and buckwheat increased acidity, and redtop decreased it. Other acid-sensitive crops probably would be affected in the same way as onions. Odland, Bell, and Smith (1950) stated that those crops that removed the largest quantity of basic materials were generally the least favorable to succeeding crops grown on moderately to strongly acid soils. On slightly acid, neutral, or alkaline soils the effect would be different than on moderately to strongly acid soils. The deleterious effect accompanying acidity may not be due to acidity itself but to increase in soluble aluminum, manganese, and ferrous iron or to effect of acidity on beneficial soil organisms such as nitrifying bacteria.

Crops differ in the quantity and quality of organic matter left after harvest. This organic matter may be beneficial through its effect on the physical condition of the soil and in other ways. On the other hand, it may have a deleterious effect on the succeeding crop. If the organic matter has a high carbon-nitrogen ratio, crop yield may be low because of competition for nitrogen between the crop plants and the microorganisms that break down the organic matter. There is evidence also that toxic materials may be set free on the decomposition of some kinds of plant materials. Janes (1951) suggested that the low yields of lettuce and onions following sweet corn and a cover crop of vetch might have resulted from toxic material from the vetch, as was indicated in a preliminary experiment in the greenhouse.

The importance of crop rotation in the control of diseases has been discussed from the standpoint of the same organisms attacking several crops. There is, however, some evidence that some organisms in the soil develop more following some crops than following others. This was indicated by the effect of different crops on the development of root rot on lettuce and onions in the experiment reported by Janes. This might be due to the effect of the previous crop on soil reaction, quality and quantity of organic matter, and on other factors.

Difference in character and distribution of the root system might account for variation in the effect of crops on those that follow. A crop with a shallow root system might produce a lower yield following another with a similar root system because of having the same area of soil from which to draw nutrients. On a heavy soil, following a deep-rooted crop by one with a shallow root system might be an advantage to the latter through the effect of the deep roots on aeration and water movement in the soil. A crop with a deep root system draws nutrients from the depth reached by the roots.

Order of Crop Rotation. While it is impracticable to outline a definite rotation to follow under all conditions, there are a few principles that should be observed. To utilize fully the resources of the soil it is well to alternate shallow-rooted and deep-rooted crops and to follow crops that furnish organic matter with those whose culture favors its decomposition. In order to grow as much organic matter as is feasible and at the same time not sacrifice money crops, the rotation may be so planned as to give time to grow some soil-improving crop. In regions having relatively short growing seasons this can be done by following a crop harvested in late summer by a crop planted early in the next spring, and by following a crop harvested late in the fall by one planted late the following spring or early summer. In the first case a green-manure crop planted as soon as the money crop is harvested will make considerable growth before winter and may be turned under early in the spring. In the latter case a green-manure crop planted late in the fall will make most of its growth the following spring and may be plowed under in time for a crop to be planted in late spring or early summer. In regions having a mild climate, where the vegetable crops are grown mainly in winter and the soil-improving crop is grown during the summer, the same principle holds.

In many sections vegetable crops are grown in rotation with general farm crops. This is especially true in regions producing late potatoes, late cabbage, and in growing canning crops, such as tomatoes, peas, sweet corn, and beans. In such cases a small grain crop may well follow the vegetable crop; this, in turn, may be followed by a legume hay. The sod land may then be planted to corn and followed by the vegetable crop the next year, or the vegetable crop may follow the hay unless weeds or insect pests are likely to be troublesome. For small-growing vegetables like beets and carrots a clean-culture crop should usually precede.

SUCCESSION CROPPING

Succession cropping is the growing of two or more crops on the same land in one growing season. For success this requires heavy fertilization and good cultural practices. Succession cropping is practiced by all market gardeners and by many truck growers who operate on high-priced land. Under such conditions it is necessary to keep the land occupied with a money crop for a large part of the growing season, and by planning the cropping system carefully, two, three, or even four crops may be grown in 1 year. The number of crops that can be grown depends largely on the kind of crops and the length of the season. In planning for succession cropping the same principles should be observed as in planning a rotation. Special attention should be given to growing soil-improving crops.

As examples of succession cropping the following might be mentioned: (1) early lettuce or radishes followed by beans, and these by fall turnips or spinach, (2) early cabbage followed by late potatoes, where the growing season is long enough, (3) early potatoes followed by late cabbage, (4) early carrots or beets followed by beans, (5) lettuce followed by late celery, a practice often followed on muck land in New York. All kinds of combinations can be worked out to meet the needs of the individual grower and his market requirement. The plan should be worked out in advance so that the land, labor, and equipment may be utilized to the best advantage. It is not to be expected that any definite plan made in advance would always be carried out, as weather, pests, or change in prospective market demand might make a change desirable. Any plan of cropping system should have some flexibility, and this ought to be taken into consideration in making it.

INTERCROPPING, OR COMPANION CROPPING

When two or more crops are grown together on the same land, the system is known as intercropping, or companion cropping. This may embrace succession cropping as in the planting of cabbage, lettuce, and radishes at the same time. The radishes mature and are removed first, and then the lettuce will follow. Both will be out of the way before the cabbage needs all of the space. Intercropping is practiced mainly by market gardeners on high-priced land and where much of the work is done by hand. Gardeners of foreign extraction are more likely to follow this system than are American gardeners. In the United States intercropping is being less and less followed owing to the extra labor required.

The main advantages of intercropping are: (1) economy of space, which is important with high-priced land, (2) saving in tillage as the same plowing and fitting of the land serve for two or more crops, (3) more complete utilization of the nutrients, any surplus applied to one crop being available for another, and (4) increased gross returns from the area cultivated. These advantages may be more than offset by the following disadvantages: (1) increase in labor costs due to the necessity for a large amount of hand labor and the impracticability of using large cultivating implements, (2) larger demand for nutrients and moisture, and (3) greater difficulty in controlling insects and diseases. The increased demand for moisture might be serious during dry periods. In disease and insect control one crop might be injured by the material used for controlling the pests on another. There is also the danger of injuring one crop when another is being harvested.

For intercropping of the intensive kind to be successful, an abundant supply of labor must be available. It is not practicable, under most conditions where land values are low and labor costs high, because large implements cannot be employed to advantage under most kinds of intercropping.

In planning intercropping, the grower should consider the time each crop is to be planted, the habit of growth, the space required by each at various stages of growth, and the time when each is expected to mature. Care should be exercised to prevent one crop from seriously interfering with another at a critical period of development. Intercropping is more likely to be successful where irrigation is practiced than where dependence is placed on rain alone for the moisture supply.

Various plans of intercropping are used by market gardeners, and in nearly all of them small-growing, quick-maturing crops are planted with larger, later-maturing ones. Radishes and lettuce are often planted as intercrops with cabbage or other similar crops. Cabbage and tomatoes may be grown together, the cabbage plants being set early in the season and tomatoes set between the rows. Under this system the rows of cabbage plants are farther apart than under the single-crop system. The early cabbage will be ready to harvest before the tomato plants need the space. On Long Island some growers who produce early potatoes and late cucumbers leave out every other or every third row of potatoes and plant cucumber seed in this space after the potato crop is nearly grown. The potatoes are harvested before the cucumber plants need additional space. Similar methods are followed with other crops in many regions.

Intercropping is frequently practiced in new asparagus beds and in fruit plantings of various kinds. This kind of intercropping is not objectionable if the welfare of the perennial plants is not jeopardized by poor management. In general, small-growing plants should be used as intercrops in the asparagus bed and in plantations of small fruit. The grower should, at all times, consider the welfare of his perennial plants and not allow the immediate money crop to interfere with their growth. The fertilizer applied should be sufficient to care for the needs of both the intercrop and the perennial crop.

CHAPTER 12

Control of Diseases and Insects

Knowledge of control measures for important disease and insect pests is essential to successful vegetable growing. Both diseases and insects are becoming more serious owing to the concentration of vegetable crops in the most favorable areas for production. New pests appear from time to time because of changes in cultural practices which may then favor their development to injurious proportions or they may be introduced from other areas. No subjects taught in agricultural colleges are more important for the student interested in vegetable growing than entomology and plant pathology. The student should learn the methods of control and must be able to identify common insects and diseases. The essential points in the life history of common pests should be known in order to apply control measures intelligently.

Since all agricultural colleges are giving fundamental courses in entomology and plant pathology, these subjects are considered only in their general relation to vegetable production.

Importance of Controlling Pests. Insects and plant diseases cause losses to vegetable growers amounting to many millions of dollars annually, probably hundreds of millions. Exact estimates are impossible because there are so many factors involved. In some cases pests greatly reduce the expected yield so that the price goes up because of the short supply. Damage estimates calculated on the basis of this high price are misleading since the price would not have been so high if damage had not occurred. While the grower applies the control measures, the ultimate consumer pays for the cost of disease and insect control. Control measures greatly increase the cost of production of vegetables, and for some crops, disease and insect control is one of the largest items in the cost of production.

A reduction in quality of vegetables may result from diseases and insects. All grades and standards for market vegetables have strict limits on the amount of disease and insect injury that may be present on vegetables in a designated grade. Excessive damage lowers the market grade and price and may even result in rejection of the vegetable by

153

market buyers. The presence of insect fragments or certain plant diseases may result in seizure of processed vegetables by health authorities. Insects and diseases continue to damage vegetables through marketing and handling processes and even in the consumer's home. With all these factors to consider, it is easy to see that the damage is great but difficult to evaluate in terms of dollars lost annually.

Successful vegetable growers recognize that in many instances spraying, dusting, and other control measures are just as essential as cultivation or any other operation. It is impossible to produce satisfactory crops in most regions without rigorous disease- and insect-control measures. Even when diseases and insects do not appear to be serious, appreciable increases in yield have occurred as a result of spraying or dusting. One of the most striking cases was the early use of DDT on potatoes to control insects. Potato vines sprayed with DDT were greener and stayed green longer and produced yields of 100 to 200 bushels per acre more than those not sprayed. Previously, it had never been realized how much damage was done to potatoes by leaf hoppers and similar insects which did not leave clearly visible marks of feeding. Large increases in yield have followed soil fumigation in cases where soil insects, nematodes, and soil fungi were not thought to be present. Onion yields have been increased as much as 400 bushels per acre through smut-control treatments, even though the grower said smut was not a problem. These illustrations show the importance of testing disease- and insect-control methods even though damage is not severe and to find out if the value of increased production justifies the cost of the treatments.

Methods of Control. Among the means of controlling insects and diseases, the following are important.

ROTATION OF CROPS. The importance of crop rotation in insect and disease control is discussed in Chap. 11.

DESTRUCTION OF REFUSE AND PLANTS HARBORING INSECTS AND DISEASES. Insects of many kinds pass the winter in the refuse left on the field or garden. If this is plowed under most of the insects die, but diseases that live over winter on plant remains are not destroyed by plowing. In many cases, a thorough disking is as effective as plowing in destroying hiding places for insects. Some insects pass the winter in weeds and trash in the fence rows and around the edges of fields; therefore cleaning up these places is important. Many of the virus diseases affecting vegetables overwinter in the roots of perennial weeds. Destruction of these weeds near seedbeds or greenhouses is essential where young plants are being grown for transplanting. Infection of young transplants with a virus is usually disastrous.

GROWING RESISTANT VARIETIES. In the control of some plant diseases the growing of resistant varieties is the most practical means of control. In fact, in some cases this is the only feasible means of controlling certain diseases such as the asparagus rust, fusarium wilt of muskmelons, cabbage yellows, verticillium wilt of tomatoes, and spinach blight. Great progress has been made in developing strains and varieties of various crops resistant to specific diseases. Among the notable examples of resistant varieties, the following should be mentioned: (1) Mary Washington and Martha Washington varieties of asparagus resistant to the asparagus rust, (2) Hollander, Wisconsin Ballhead, and other varieties of cabbage resistant to yellows, (3) Iroquois, Delicious 51, and other varieties resistant to the fusarium wilt of muskmelons, (4) Moscow VR, Loran Blood, and other varieties of tomatoes resistant to verticillium wilt. Hundreds of other varieties and strains resistant to some disease have been developed in recent years, and additional ones are added each year. Many of these are mentioned in the crop chapters, but the reader interested in keeping up to date on new strains and varieties should consult current publications from the experiment stations and the extension services.

Breeding for disease resistance is one of the most promising fields for the plant breeder and plant pathologist. Breeding for insect resistance has not been as successful as breeding for disease resistance. Varieties of several kinds of vegetables show some degree of resistance to insect injury. The Sequoia potato is resistant to leaf hopper injury, and the Butternut squash is resistant to the squash vine borer. Many varieties resistant to various insects will undoubtedly be developed by plant breeders in the future.

SEED TREATMENT TO CONTROL DISEASES AND INSECTS. Seed treatment with fungicides has been practiced for many years to prevent seed rots, damping-off, and certain seed-borne diseases. There are many chemicals available, and the selection of the one to use depends on the crop and the diseases to be controlled. Treatment of specific crop seeds will be discussed in the chapter concerning the crop.

The chemical applied to the seed must give adequate disease protection and must not be harmful to the crop. In many cases, several different chemicals may be used with the same degree of success on seed of a single crop. Also, they may be applied in a variety of ways, such as dry powder, slurries, and dipping or soaking in solutions.

Corrosive sublimate (bichloride of mercury) and formaldehyde have been used for many years for treating seed potatoes and certain vegetable seeds. Two other old chemicals are still used to a limited extent: calomel on the crucifers, celery, and onion, and copper sulfate on tomatoes and peppers. The most popular materials are organic chemicals, such as Arasan, Spergon, Phygon, Tersan, and Captan. The organics containing mercury, such as Ceresan and Semesan, are used on a few crops, but mercury injures many vegetable seeds. Spergon is a good lubricant and is used on all types of beans both to protect the seed from diseases and to prevent seed damage in the planter. Certain antibiotics have shown promise in controlling seed-borne bacterial diseases, particularly as a dip for seed potatoes.

Some seed-borne diseases are effectively controlled by soaking the seed in hot water (122°F.) for 20 to 30 minutes, depending on the type of seed. This treatment kills the organisms causing black rot, blackleg, and alternaria leaf spot of crucifers and bacterial fruit spot and anthracnose of tomatoes and peppers. Hot-water-treated seeds should also be treated with a fungicide before planting to protect the seed from damping-off and seed rots which may be present in the soil.

There are only a few insects which can be successfully controlled by seed treatment. Peas and beans are fumigated with carbon bisulfide or dusted with DDT to control weevils during storage, but this does not protect the seeds from insect damage after planting. Effective control of seed-corn maggot injury can be achieved by treating all types of bean, sweet corn, cucumber, and squash seed with a suitable insecticide such as chlordane, lindane, dieldrin, or aldrin. A fungicide, usually Arasan or Captan, is applied at the same time. The seeds are coated by mixing them with a methocel slurry of the insecticide and fungicide. Treatment of onion seed in a similar manner controls onion smut and onion maggot. Treating carrot seed with aldrin has prevented serious damage from the first brood of the carrot rust fly.

Some of the chemicals that have been used for treating seed are not mentioned here, and new materials are being developed each year. While more than one material may be recommended for the same type of seed, it does not mean that more than one should be applied to the seed since injury may result if more than one is used. When several materials are suggested, it usually indicates that each may be effective under certain conditions. The recommendations of the extension services, agricultural colleges, and departments of agriculture should be followed in each locality. The manufacturer's directions on the label should always be followed regarding the concentration of the material to use on the specific kind of seed.

The use of clean, disease-free seed eliminates the need for seed treatment in some cases. Sometimes this is the only practical means of control when no effective chemical means of control is known. Most of the bean seed used in the humid parts of the country is grown in the West where bacterial blight and anthracnose of beans do not occur because of climatic conditions. Since no practical seed treatments are known, disease-free seed is the only means of control of these diseases in most parts of the United States.

Certified seed is very important in controlling certain diseases of potatoes. When tubers containing a virus are used for seed, the virus is spread to other plants in the field by insect vectors and large reductions in yield may result. Certified seed is produced under a rigid inspection program in the northern part of the United States and in Canada. Diseased plants are removed from the fields, and insect vectors are kept under control. The seed is grown in greenhouses or in the South as a further check on freedom from virus diseases. This strict control and high standards of perfection have made potato growing profitable in spite of the great number of virus diseases that infect the potato. Other types of seed are grown under rigid standards and are labeled as certified seed by local inspection organizations.

CONTROL BY SOIL TREATMENT. Soil pests are usually controlled in greenhouses and in plant-growing soil by heating the soil or fumigating the soil with certain chemicals. Greenhouse soil may be sterilized in place by running steam through drainage tiles and covering the soil with heavy paper or tarpaulins during the steaming. Satisfactory results can be obtained only when the drainage tiles have been laid close enough together to get good heat distribution. Another method of sterilizing the soil in place involves the use of a large inverted pan fitted with steam lines. When the area under the pan has reached the desired temperature, the pan is moved to a new location and the process repeated until the whole house has been steamed.

Soil for growing plants may be sterilized in flats or in bulk in special steam chambers or large autoclaves. Large boxes fitted with electric heating cable have been successfully used for sterilizing soil in bulk. Flash pasteurization of soil involves passing the soil through a revolving cylinder where it is exposed in shallow layers to an intense flame for a short time.

When sterilization is done properly, insects, nematodes, disease organisms, and weed seeds are killed, but care must be taken to prevent contamination of the sterilized soil. When a sterilized soil is reinoculated with a disease organism, it usually causes more damage than in a soil that was not sterilized since there are no competing organisms.

Sometimes plants grow poorly following sterilization of the soil. This has been attributed to killing more beneficial organisms than harmful ones; to the accumulation of excessive amounts of soluble salts; and to puddling the soil by handling when it was too wet.

Soil in greenhouses, in flats, or in piles may also be treated with formaldehyde or other chemicals to destroy soil pests. A dilute solution of formaldehyde is applied as a drench, and the soil is covered with wet bags, paper, or plastic for 1 to 2 days. The covers are removed, and the soil must be aerated for about 10 days to remove the last traces of formaldehyde. Planting too soon may result in death or injury to the seed or plants.

Methyl bromide and similar soil fumigants are much more popular than formaldehyde. The materials are liquified under pressure and penetrate the soil rapidly as a gas when the pressure is released. The fumigant is applied by inserting a tube into the soil at specified intervals to ensure uniform distribution. Soil in piles or in flats or other containers may be successfully treated. The flats or piles are covered for about 24 hours and are safe for planting after 2 or 3 days. The soil temperature should be above 60°F. for best results.

Soil fumigation has been successfully used in the field to control nematodes, insects, certain fungi, and weeds. The four kinds of fumigants in general use are methyl bromide (bromomethane), chloropicrin (trichloronitromethane), dichloropropene (1,3-dichloropropene), and ethyl dibromide (1,2-dibromoethane).

Methyl bromide is frequently used for fumigating seedbeds. The seedbed is thoroughly fitted and prepared for seeding before treatment, and the fumigant is allowed to evaporate from shallow pans placed at intervals under a gastight cover. The cover is supported so that there is an air space between it and the soil and the edges of the cover are buried and held down with a few inches of soil. The amount of methyl bromide used varies from 1 to 4 pounds per 100 square feet, depending on the pests to be controlled. The cover is left in place for 48 hours, and seed may be planted 2 or 3 days after it is removed. Most insects, nematodes, and weeds are killed, and satisfactory control of fungi is obtained. While the methyl bromide is not expensive, the need of a cover and the labor involved make the method somewhat expensive.

Chloropicrin is also used for fumigating seedbeds, but it is expensive and disagreeable to handle. Insects, nematodes, weeds, and all but a few resistant fungi are killed when it is used properly. The material must be applied uniformly over the whole area, usually 2 to 3 cubic centimeters at intervals of 10 inches in each direction. The soil must be watered immediately to seal the surface, and the best results are obtained when the soil is covered with burlap bags, newspaper, or other material sprinkled with water to prevent the surface from drying. The cover may be removed after 4 or 5 days and the soil allowed to aerate. Seed should not be planted until all traces of the gas has disappeared, usually 1 or 2 weeks, depending on conditions. Chloropicrin is extremely toxic to plants both in the soil and in the air.

Chlorobromopropene (CBP) has given good control of nematodes, fungi, and weeds in Florida. It is emulsified with water and applied as a drench. Application is made easy with a small pump which mixes the chemical with water and delivers the emulsion to a sprinkling nozzle through a plastic hose.

Mixtures containing dichloropropene or ethylene dibromide are also used for soil fumigation. They give good control of nematodes and insects but do not control weeds or fungi and are generally used for fumigating fields rather than seedbeds. The soil should be well prepared, free from lumps, and moderately loose. Very light sandy soils must be compacted. A moist, but not wet, soil is essential, and the soil temperature should be at least 50°F. and preferably 60°F. or above. The fumigant is applied at a uniform depth although the desirable depth varies with the soil type and the pests to be controlled. Generally, seedbeds are treated 3 to 4 inches deep and fields about 6 inches deep, and the holes or furrows made by the applicator must be closed and firmly packed immediately.

All fumigants are toxic to plants, and all traces should be allowed to diffuse out of the soil before the crop is planted. The time required for safety varies with the kind of soil, soil moisture, soil temperature, rate of application, weather following application, and the kind of fumigant used. Light soils are safe sooner than heavy soils. Excessive soil moisture may retard diffusion of the fumigant, while warm, sunny weather with some breeze favors rapid disappearance of fumigants. Chloropicrin is extremely toxic and leaves the soil slowly. Methyl bromide is also highly toxic but leaves the soil so rapidly that crops may be planted 2 or 3 days after treatment.

Since the advent of organic insecticides, the control of soil insects by means of applying insecticides to the soil has become increasingly important. There are several methods of application in general use. Suspensions of calomel applied as a drench around the roots of crucifers at transplanting have been used to control the cabbage maggot and also clubroot, a soil-borne disease. Insecticides, such as heptachlor, aldrin, and dieldrin, have been used successfully in the transplanting water to control this insect. Since the cabbage maggot and onion maggot fly lays its eggs on the stem of the plants near the ground surface and the larvae must crawl down to the roots, control can be attained by applying a barrier of insecticide on top of the soil around the stem of the plants. Aldrin, heptachlor, dieldrin, and parathion have been effective both as dusts and sprays. In some areas a formaldehyde drench at planting is used to control onion smut and an insecticide may be added to the solution to control the onion maggot.

Control of many soil insects is possible by applying insecticides to the soil before planting the crop and thoroughly working the chemical into the soil. The insecticide may be applied after plowing as either a dust or spray and mixed with the soil during normal fitting operations. The first insecticide to be so used with success was benzene hexachloride to control wireworms and grubs on potatoes. While insect control was effective, the material imparted an objectionable flavor to the potatoes. However, dieldrin, aldrin, and methoxychlor do not impart flavors to crops and have been used widely to control soil insects. Only a few pounds of insecticide are needed for an acre, and control may extend over a period of 2 or 3 years. While flavor may not be altered, root crops may contain dangerous amounts of insecticide unless the recommendations for their use are followed exactly.

In some areas these insecticides have been mixed with fertilizer for application to field crops. Such a practice is not wise for vegetable growers since all vegetables do not all receive the same rate of fertilization. The danger of harmful residues in vegetables, especially root crops, is too great to risk applying too much insecticide. Most vegetable growers have sprayers or dusters, and the insecticide can be applied more accurately with these machines than with a fertilizer spreader.

CONTROL BY APPLYING CHEMICALS TO PLANTS. Insects are divided into two main groups: (1) chewing insects which eat leaves and other plant parts and (2) sucking insects which damage plants by sucking their juices. In addition, many insects are agents in the transmission of certain plant diseases. Many kinds of chemicals are effective in killing chewing insects, since the insect eats the poison-coated plant parts. Since sucking insects do not chew the plant, insecticides which penetrate the skin or enter through the breathing tubes must be used. These insecticides may also control chewing insects.

Many fungus diseases are controlled by spraying or dusting the plants with fungicides, which are materials poisonous to fungi but harmless to the plant. There are only a few materials which kill bacteria causing plant diseases. The most effective way to control bacterial and virus diseases of plants is to kill the insects which transmit them. Aphids, leaf hoppers, and other insects are known to transmit virus diseases, such as cucumber mosaic, potato leaf roll, and others. The cucumber beetle transmits the bacteria, causing bacterial wilt of cucumbers and other cucurbits. Stewart's bacterial wilt of sweet corn is harbored over winter in flea beetles which infect sweet corn when they begin feeding in the spring.

In spraying or dusting for disease control, the material should be applied before the disease appears, or at least before it has gained much foothold. Once the fungus has entered plant tissue, fungicides are not effective; therefore the spray program should be directed to prevent the development and spread of the fungus before it has entered the plants. Spraying or dusting before a rain is preferable to applying material after a rain since the fungus spores germinate best under moist conditions. If the fungicide is applied after a rain, it may be too late to control the disease. Of course, spray material should be applied far enough in advance to allow it to dry out before rains.

Timeliness and Thoroughness. In all insect- and disease-control measures, timeliness and thoroughness are important considerations. For instance, the fungicide should be applied before the appearance of the diseases, or at least as soon as there is the slightest evidence. It is too late to control diseases after they have seriously injured the crops. Even for insect control, treatment is most effective when the material is applied as soon as the insects make their appearance. If the treatment is delayed too long, the plants may be seriously injured or killed before the insects are destroyed. This is especially true where there is a heavy infestation, as there may be so many insects present as to do considerable damage before getting enough poison to kill them.

Since insects are killed mainly by eating the poison or by coming into contact with the insecticide and since disease spores are killed by contact with the fungicide, it is important to cover all parts of the plants with the spray or dust. For the control of many diseases and insects the underside of leaves, as well as the upper side, should be covered. Spray materials should be applied as a fine mist so as to cover the surface without having the liquid collect in drops and run off. High pressure is necessary to get a fine mist. In order to get good distribution, insecticides in the form of dusts should be finely divided.

Spraying and Dusting Equipment. Many kinds of sprayers and dusters are in use, from small hand equipment to large power machines. A commercial vegetable grower cannot afford to rely on hand equipment, and he should purchase the largest power machine that can be justified by the acreage under cultivation. It is difficult to obtain good coverage and uniform application with hand equipment. For the small grower the most versatile sprayers are small piston pumps or gear pumps attached to the power take-off of the tractor. These can also be used to apply herbicides. The large grower should have this type of sprayer also and, in addition, a large capacity sprayer which may be driven from the tractor or by a gasoline engine. Where a variety of crops are grown it is difficult to find one machine which will be efficient for all types of spraying. Dusters are also available in a wide range of sizes but are used only for insect and disease control. Under ideal conditions, there is no difference in effectiveness of spraying and dusting. A slight breeze greatly reduces the efficiency of a duster, and over a wide range of conditions, spraying probably does a better job of disease and insect control. Both sprayers and dusters can be adapted to many types of crops by changing the position and number of outlets. In fact, it is essential that the outlets be adjusted each time the machine is used to compensate for growth of a crop or for different crops.

The volume of water used per acre is not important for insecticides and most fungicides as long as the foliage is completely covered with the spray material. Low-volume sprayers are designed to give good coverage with small volumes of water (*e.g.*, 30 gallons per acre) while high-volume sprayers may require 100 gallons of water or more per acre. The important factor in control is that the recommended amount per acre of insecticide or fungicide be applied uniformly over the foliage of the crop.

Application of chemicals to crops by airplane is common where large acreages of a single crop are grown. Airplanes can cover large acreages in a short time and permit accurate timing of treatments regardless of the condition of the soil. Plane application in small fields is seldom practicable, and the danger of drift of the materials is greater than with ground equipment. Custom application of pesticides by plane is the general practice, although large operators may own their own plane.

Insecticides. There are three general types of insecticides based on the manner in which they enter the insect's body: stomach poisons, contact poisons, and fumigants. Stomach poisons are those which are effective only when they are eaten by the insect. The other types are effective if they are ingested by the insect, but it is not essential for their action. The most commonly used stomach poisons are the arsenicals, such as lead arsenate, calcium arsenate, magnesium arsenate, paris green, and others. Other stomach poisons include sodium fluosilicate, sodium fluoaluminate (Cryolite), mercuric chloride (corrosive sublimate), mercurous chloride (calomel), and rotenone. Most of these materials remain on the plant for a long time unless washed off by rain. They should not be used near harvest time when there is danger of the insecticide remaining on the edible portion of the plant.

The contact insecticides are materials which enter the body of the insect through the skin. They are valuable for controlling sucking insects which do not chew the plants. They also kill if they are eaten by chewing insects. The contact insecticides are all organic compounds, both naturally occurring and synthetic. Pyrethrum and nicotine are the important naturally occurring contact poisons. The synthetic contact insecticides used on vegetables are mostly chlorinated hydrocarbons and organic phosphates. Among the chlorinated hydrocarbons are aldrin, chlordane, dieldrin, DDD, DDT, heptachlor, lindane, methoxychlor, and toxaphene. Some common organic phosphates are malathion, parathion, and TEPP (tetraethyl pyrophosphate). Most of these synthetic materials decompose to nontoxic compounds when applied to plants, some slowly and others rapidly. The rate of decomposition generally determines the length of time before harvest that the material can be used safely. All of these materials are volatile and may be taken into the insects body as a gas through the breathing tubes. This fumigant action is important in the use of TEPP and parathion.

Another type of insecticide is the systemic insecticide. These chemicals are not especially toxic to insects as they are applied to the plant, but the plant absorbs the chemical and transforms it to highly toxic compounds. Since the insecticide is moved throughout the plant, it is called a systemic insecticide. All insects feeding on plants sprayed with these materials are killed for a few weeks after the material is applied. Some important systemic insecticides are octamethyl pyrophosphoramide (Schradan, Pestox) and a trialkyl thiophosphate (Systox). Systemic insecticides have only a limited use on vegetables for market but can be used on a wide variety of vegetables grown for seed.

All insecticides are toxic to man, and some may injure plants, so extreme care must be taken to follow the directions for their use and to take all recommended precautions. Many are sold under trade names which do not indicate the active ingredient. However, the active ingredients and recommended concentrations are always printed on the label of the container. The grower should read the label and follow the instructions exactly.

Fungicides. The term fungicide is applied to any chemical used to control fungus diseases. Copper compounds are the most commonly used fungicides, and copper sulfate is the most important of them. Bordeaux mixture, made with copper sulfate, lime, and water, is the oldest material used to control plant diseases. Other copper compounds used frequently are called insoluble or fixed copper compounds. While copper compounds are powerful fungicides, they may also injure plants if the soluble copper content is too high. They have been supplanted by synthetic metal carbamate compounds which seldom injure vegetables. These materials are sold under a number of trade names, but a specific type name has been designated for each group of closely related compounds. These groups include ziram, ferbam, zineb, nabam, thiram, captan, and maneb.

Bactericides are materials which kill bacteria, and while many are known, few are adaptable to controlling bacterial diseases of plants. Derivatives of the antibiotic streptomycin have been effectively used to control certain bacterial diseases of vegetables.

Miller Amendment. Public Law No. 518, commonly known as the Miller Amendment, went into effect in 1955. This law establishes tolerances for residues of all types of chemicals used on plants intended for human consumption. No chemical may be used on food plants until a tolerance for that chemical has been established by the Food and Drug

Administration. Vegetables in interstate commerce containing more than the established tolerance of an approved chemical or a chemical that has not been cleared for use may be seized.

This law protects the consumer from indiscriminate use of poisonous chemicals, and it also protects the grower and chemical manufacturer from unknowingly harming the health of himself and the consumer. Therefore it is essential that the vegetable grower follow recommendations exactly as to kind of chemical to use, the amount to use, and the time to apply it. The established tolerances are in keeping with good insect and disease control if the grower does a thorough job at the right time.

General Crop Diseases. Among the more serious diseases that are rather general, the most important are root knot, caused by a parasitic eelworm or nematode; rhizoctonia, which causes cankers on the stems and roots of various plants; and damping-off. Root knot is discussed in connection with cabbage, and rhizoctonia is described in connection with the potato.

Damping-off is often serious on plants in the seedbed and transplanting bed. The plants are attacked at or near the surface of the ground, causing a rotting or damping-off. This may be caused by any one of several species of fungi including those of Pythium, Rhizoctonia, Botrytis, Sclerotinia, Phoma, Phytophthora, Colletotrichum, and Gloeosporium.

Since the growth of these fungi is favored by moisture and relatively high temperature, the trouble may be checked by keeping the temperature down and withholding water. It is especially important to water the plants in the bed early in the day so that the plants themselves and the surface of the soil may dry before night. Thorough ventilation of the greenhouse, hotbed, and cold frame is important. Sterilizing the soil used for the plant bed and treating the seed are recommended. Spraying the surface of the soil and the stems of the seedlings with ziram or captan at 4- to 7-day intervals gives good control when used as a supplement to the other treatments.

General Crop Insects. Insects may be grouped roughly into two classes, from the standpoint of their food plants: (1) those that ordinarily attack only a single crop or a few closely related crops and (2) those that are general feeders and are not particular as to their food plants. Examples of the first class are asparagus beetles, potato beetles, and the large tomato worm, the last two feeding on a few closely related plants. The second class includes cutworms, white grubs, wireworms, blister beetles, grasshoppers, onion thrips, and red spider.

The onion thrip is usually most injurious to the onion crop, although it attacks cauliflower, cabbage, cucumbers, tomatoes, turnips, and kale. This insect is discussed in connection with the onion crop. The other insects are discussed here because they are equally destructive to a number of crops.

CUTWORMS. Cutworms are nearly smooth caterpillars 1 to 2 inches long, the larvae of large-bodied moths. Many species have been reported as pests of vegetable plants. Their greatest injury is done by cutting off the stems of young plants near the surface of the ground, especially of those plants which are transplanted and are spaced considerable distances apart, as cabbage, cauliflower, tomato, eggplant, and sweet potato. Cutworms work mainly at night, and one worm can destroy many plants in a single night.

The best method of cutworm control on small acreages is the use of poison baits. The bait is commonly made from wheat bran, molasses, fruit, and water mixed with an insecticide such as lead arsenate, paris green, toxaphene, chlordane, or DDT. The moist bait is spread at dusk so that it will not dry out before the cutworms start to feed at night. For large acreages cutworms may be controlled by working soil insecticides, such as chlordane, aldrin, or dieldrin, into the top 3 inches of soil before planting. Dusts of DDT, toxaphene, dieldrin, aldrin, or chlordane applied to the surface of the soil around the plant also give good cutworm control.

WHITE GRUBS AND WIREWORMS. White grubs are the larvae of May beetles or June beetles (*Lachnosterna arcuata*). Wireworms are the long, hard-shelled, brownish larvae of click beetles. Both grubs and wireworms are abundant in land that has been in sod for some years, although some species of wireworms may be injurious to crops following only 1 year of sod. Both insects feed on roots and other underground parts of plants. The greatest damage is done to potatoes and root crops, but all crops may be injured to some extent. Short rotations are one means of control. Applications of soil insecticides before planting as described for cutworm control also give good control of these insects, although larger amounts of insecticide may be needed for grubs and wireworms.

GRASSHOPPERS. These insects are troublesome to vegetables, especially in the dry regions of the Middle West and West. The poisoned bait recommended for cutworms is a good control measure for grasshoppers. Spraying or dusting the vegetables and surrounding vegetation with chlordane, aldrin, dieldrin, or toxaphene is effective when baits are not practical.

BLISTER BEETLES. These insects are common garden pests and are often destructive to beans, peas, potatoes, and beets, although they feed on many kinds of plants. The beetles are slender, somewhat softbodied, and variously colored. They are injurious in the adult stage and may be controlled by spraying or dusting with DDT or parathion.

RED SPIDER. The red spider (*Tetranychus telarius*) is not a true spider but a mite. It is widely distributed and often injures all kinds of beans, cucurbits, tomatoes, beets, and celery. It is a serious greenhouse pest. The presence of mites on the undersides of leaves may not be suspected until injury appears. Mites suck the plant juices and cause the leaves to lose their color, shrivel, and die.

In the open, all kinds of mites can be controlled by spraying or dusting with parathion or TEPP and similar materials. These are also effective in greenhouses, but application as an aerosol is usually preferred.

CHAPTER 13

Marketing

Profits in commercial vegetable growing depend as much on proper
harvesting, handling, and marketing as on good production practices.
The grower is largely responsible for the appearance of his products
when they reach the market. Unless he has grown the varieties the
markets demand, has protected the crops from diseases, insects, and
other pests, has graded them carefully and properly packed them in
containers suited to the products and methods of handling, he has not
done all that is expected of him.

Many gardeners are experts as producers and failures as salesmen.
This is natural since the problems are different, but it is essential that
the grower who does his own marketing devote time and study to the
problems of marketing as well as to those of production. Under many
conditions it is probably better for the grower to specialize on production and let others do the marketing than to attempt to become expert in
both lines. However, the grower must know what the market demands
both in products and methods of handling, even if others are looking
after the selling.

Much of the marketing problem belongs to the field of economics,
hence most of the discussion here deals with the product itself and with
the physical handling of it. To understand the problems of transportation, of organization of marketing agencies, of distribution, of factors
affecting marketing costs, and of merchandising requires a knowledge
of the fundamentals of economics. It is probable, however, that the
greatest opportunity for improvement in the quality of the product is
through the use of better strains and varieties, through better production, harvesting, grading, packing, and other handling methods. The
grower is responsible for the marketability and quality of the product
as it leaves his hands, and the improvement that can be made up to this
point largely is dependent on his own efforts. While it may be true that
the cost of distribution of perishables in the large cities is too high,

there is little the individual grower can do about it. The grower can improve the grading, packing, storage, and loading of his produce, and this improvement would go a long way toward solving some of the problems of marketing.

It should be borne in mind that fresh vegetables are living organisms; therefore they undergo normal life processes: they respire, they lose water through transpiration, and they undergo chemical changes. These processes contribute to the gradual deterioration of the product and are influenced by temperature, atmospheric humidity, and other factors. In all handling procedures the aim should be to retard the life processes without stopping them altogether.

The harvesting, grading, packing, and handling methods for the various products are discussed under the individual crops.

Harvesting. The stage of development of vegetables when harvested determines to a considerable extent the quality of the product when it reaches the consumer. No definite rule can be given in regard to time of harvesting since this depends on the kind of crop, on the weather conditions at harvest time, and on the distance to market or the length of time required to reach the consumer. Such crops as beans, Lima beans, peas, and sweet corn deteriorate in quality if not harvested soon after reaching edible maturity; therefore it is always advisable to harvest them as soon as this stage is reached. With products which increase considerably in size after reaching edible maturity there is a tendency to delay harvesting until they have reached full size. This delay often results in lowering the quality of the product. Tomatoes and muskmelons grown for distant markets are harvested long before they reach edible maturity. In fact, in many cases they have not begun to ripen when harvested. This results in poor quality and has a decided tendency to depress the market for these products. Both tomatoes and muskmelons should be allowed to remain on the vines as long as possible and still have them reach the consumer in good condition.

Promptness is of great importance in harvesting and handling many perishable crops. A day's delay may result in heavy losses, especially in hot, sultry weather or in seasons when frosts are likely to occur. Lettuce often becomes almost worthless in a day after the heads have formed, especially if the weather is very hot. The plants may send up seedstalks or become seriously injured by *tipburn* and *drop*. Promptness in removing the products from the field is important with most crops, especially in very hot or wet weather.

Enormous losses occur each year due to carelessness in harvesting and handling vegetables. Much of this could be overcome through instruction of the help in the proper methods of harvesting and handling the products in the field. Bruising or other injury detracts from the appearance of the product and makes it more susceptible to disease injury since germs are more likely to get a foothold if the surface is broken.

Preparation for Market. Many vegetables require special preparation before they are ready for packing. Root crops, asparagus, celery, lettuce, spinach, and other vegetables are often washed to remove any soil that adheres. While water is used mainly for the sake of cleanliness, it has other values. It gives some vegetables a bright appearance and prevents them from wilting. Washing may be injurious, since moisture on the surface is favorable to the development of diseases, especially when the washed product is packed tightly and shipped considerable distances without refrigeration.

Some vegetables are trimmed in preparation for marketing. The dirty, decayed, diseased, and discolored leaves of celery, lettuce, spinach, and other leafy vegetables are removed before the products are packed for market. Removing diseased leaves is of value in checking the development of disease in transit and on the market and also improves the appearance of the product. Part of the foliage of beets, carrots, and other root crops, when bunched for market, is removed by stripping off the older leaves and, in some cases, by cutting back all of them. Since the Second World War there has been a notable increase in marketing of the root crops, especially carrots, with the tops removed entirely and packaged in consumer packages. In the preparation of celery it is a common practice in Florida and in some other areas to cut back the foliage to about 16 inches in length, thus saving considerable in crate material and in transportation.

Waxing of some vegetables, such as tomatoes, peppers, cucumbers, muskmelons, carrots, rutabagas, potatoes, and sweet potatoes, is a fairly common practice. Waxes are used to improve the luster and to control shriveling through reducing loss of moisture from the product. Various kinds of waxes are used, and different methods of application are followed. Canadian rutabagas commonly are given a coating of paraffin by dipping them in the melted wax. Most other products are waxed with a water emulsion, or a hydrocarbon solution of one or more materials applied by dipping, or spraying, or as a foam. Other methods of waxing are used to some extent.

Many products, such as asparagus, celery, green onions, broccoli, beets, carrots, and radishes, are often tied in bunches in preparation for market to facilitate handling in the retail store. The bunches should be tied tightly to present a neat appearance on the market. When vegetables are to be marketed in consumer packages, much greater care is used in washing and trimming than when they are to be sold in bulk. It is the aim in consumer packaging to have the product ready for cooking or for serving raw without additional preparation.

Grading. Well-graded products of inferior quality often sell to better advantage than poorly graded or ungraded products of high quality. A few inferior specimens in a package govern, to a considerable extent, the price paid for the entire contents of the package. Uniformity in size, shape, color, and ripeness is of great importance in disposing of any product, and this cannot be secured without careful grading. Grading means more than separation with reference to size, although this is important. In separating any product into grades all characters that affect the appearance and quality of the product should be considered.

Not only should vegetables be carefully graded, but there should be some recognized standard that applies to a region or preferably to the whole country. Uniform and well-recognized grades make for cheap marketing, for if articles are not graded or are poorly graded, the buyer has to inspect the product before he can know what he is buying. This adds to the cost. By dividing products into uniform grades, sales may be made by grade, thus facilitating the marketing process. Uniformity in grading is absolutely essential to success where products are sold on grade.

Standard grades furnish the basis for trade. Some standard is essential in marketing products at a distance and also for market information and inspection. Lack of grade standards has made market quotations unsatisfactory to the grower because it has not been possible to describe products in terms that are understood. With standard grades the buyer and seller have a common language in the grade name or number. This is especially true if the grades are legalized by state or national laws. Standard grades eliminate a great deal of friction between producer and dealer due to lack of understanding and also reduces loss caused by rejections, delays, and dishonest dealing. They simplify the whole marketing process. Standardizing grades is one of the first improvements attempted by any successful cooperative marketing organization, for it is recognized that the first step in marketing is to have standard products.

The U.S. Department of Agriculture has developed grade standards for most vegetable products, and many of the states have adopted the Federal grades. These grade standards have little to do with consumer preference or nutritional value but are based mainly on general appearance, size, trueness to type, and freedom from blemishes. The Federal grades are not compulsory, but if they are used and the package carries the grade name or number, the contents must meet the grade specifications when shipped out of the state. In the states that have adopted the Federal grades the package carries the grade name or number and the contents must meet the specifications in both intrastate and interstate commerce.

In any set of grade standards the aim should be to make the grading and the descriptive terms as simple as possible. Technical descriptions and complicated grades discourage the use of any set of standards by the average grower. The number of grades should be kept to the minimum, preferably only two for most products. The first grade should include a large part of any well-grown crop. The second grade should usually include the marketable product that does not meet the requirements for the first grade. If any portion of a crop is below the requirements of the second grade and is still marketable, it should ordinarily be sold by sample as "sample grade."

Containers for Vegetables. Containers of some kind are necessary for nearly all vegetables when they are shipped, and for most of them even when hauled direct to the market from the field. Containers perform the following functions: (1) furnish convenient means for hauling products, (2) give protection to the goods themselves, (3) furnish security from pilfering, (4) provide a measure of the contents, (5) prevent loss of small articles, (6) ensure cleanliness, (7) provide a means whereby products may carry identification marks, shipping directions, legal requirements, and advertising matter.

Vegetables are packed in a great range of kinds and sizes of containers from the quart berry box to the barrel, including many kinds and sizes of baskets, hampers, boxes, crates, bags, and paper cartons. Some of the containers are employed for one kind of product only, as, for example, celery crates, cantaloupe crates, cauliflower crates, and asparagus crates. Other kinds, such as the round stave basket, till baskets, handle baskets, hampers, lug boxes, wire-bound crates, and bags of various kinds are, more or less, general-purpose containers used for many kinds of products. Hampers have been replaced to a considerable extent by wire-bound crates because the former do not stack well. On local markets in some areas several kinds and sizes of containers are used for the same product, and in many cases second-hand containers predominate.

Since 1920 considerable progress has been made in standardizing the sizes of some containers. Downing and Spillman (1924) reported that 50 styles and sizes of hampers were in use in the United States. Since that time hampers have been standardized by Federal statute, and only 9 sizes from ⅛ bushel to 2 bushels are standard. Some others that have been standardized according to Carey (1950) are climax baskets; standard berry baskets and till baskets capacity ½ pint, 1 pint, 1 quart, and multiples of the quart, dry measure; round stave baskets of nine sizes from ⅛-bushel to 2-bushel capacity; and splint baskets of 4-, 8-, 12-, 16-, 24-, and 32-quart capacity. Paperboard baskets of the same standard sizes and same general dimensions as the splint baskets have become popular in some regions for packing certain products. Carey described the kinds and sizes of containers used in the United States for packing fruits and vegetables.

One of the striking changes that has taken place since 1950 is the packing of lettuce in paperboard cartons in California and Arizona. In these areas the cartons, holding 2 dozen heads, have replaced to a large extent the wood-shook crate of 4-dozen capacity. Other products, including some in consumer packages, are packed to some extent in cartons.

There is still need for standardization of containers and the elimination of many sizes. The large number of sizes and kinds of containers in use leads to confusion and adds to the cost of the product by increasing the machinery necessary for manufacture.

There appears to be a trend toward smaller containers for many products. This is indicated by the use of "pony" crates for cantaloupes and celery; 8- and 12-quart climax baskets for tomatoes and other products; 50- and 100-pound sacks for potatoes in place of the 150- and 180-pound sacks formerly used; and 50-pound sacks for onions in place of the 100-pound sacks. Consumer-size containers are increasing in importance also. These include special paper bags and cloth bags used for potatoes and holding from 5 to 10 pounds, mesh bags for onions holding from 5 to 25 pounds, and various sizes and kinds of cartons used for celery, rhubarb, tomatoes, and other products.

Packing Vegetables for Market. In packing vegetables for market there are three important considerations: (1) a satisfactory package for the product, (2) honest packing, which includes uniform product throughout the package and full measure, (3) careful placing of the product so that the specimens will remain in position until they reach the market and present an attractive appearance.

The package should be selected for the particular product, bearing in mind the protection of the product itself and also the demands of the market. In selecting a container for vegetables to be shipped long distances, attention should be given to its ability to withstand rough handling and to its desirability from the standpoint of stacking in the car, as well as to the possibility of quick cooling.

Honest packing should be practiced. The packer who puts up a dishonest pack fools no one but himself. The buyer is always on the lookout for dishonest packing and usually penalizes the produce and the producer or packer.

Consumer Packaging. Although consumer packaging or prepackaging has been in use with some products, such as potatoes and onions, for many years, it is only since the Second World War that this method has assumed much importance. In most of the prepackaging operations, the vegetables are washed, trimmed, and otherwise prepared ready to be cooked or served raw. The most common methods in prepackaging vegetables are to place the product in: (1) bags made of transparent film, (2) trays or cartons overwrapped with transparent films, or in cartons with windows of transparent film, (3) mesh bags, and (4) paper bags. Mesh bags are used on a large scale for onions, and paper bags are used for potatoes and sweet corn.

The packaging of produce in consumer packages lends itself to self-service in retail stores. This is one of the advantages claimed for consumer packaging. Other advantages claimed are that packaging (1) increases the shelf life of the product, (2) reduces waste because of increase in shelf life and because of less handling by the clerk and customer, (3) decreases work of preparation in the home, (4) increases sales, and (5) decreases number of help required in the retail store. Some of the advantages claimed for prepackaging have not been proved by actual experiment or in practice. The increase in store life of the product claimed for prepackaging in some cases may be due more to the use of refrigeration than to the packaging. The reduction in clerk hire may be offset by the extra work in the preparation and packaging of the product. The savings in waste and spoilage and all the other savings may not be enough to cover the cost of packing materials and labor used in prepackaging.

When transparent films are used for prepackaging, either as bags or as overwraps, it is important that the material be flexible and strong. It is important also that ample ventilation be provided by perforations in the films in order to prevent oxygen deficiency and accumulation of carbon dioxide. When the free oxygen is used up, anaerobic respiration will take place and carbohydrates will be broken down to carbon dioxide and alcohol, which impart an undesirable taste and odor to the product. While films differ in degree of permeability to gases, it is the general rule to perforate all kinds of films with small holes so that the product will have an ample supply of oxygen. Even though perforated, the films prevent rapid loss of moisture and may maintain too high humidity for some products. There are marked differences in oxygen requirement of vegetables, hence difference in the amount of ventilation that should be provided for various kinds of products packaged in plastic films. Onions, for example, require much more ventilation than broccoli.

Most of the consumer packaging has been done in or near the consumer centers by persons specializing in this business alone. There is considerable difference of opinion as to the best place for prepackaging, whether in the producing region or in or near the market. The main advantage in packaging in the producing region is saving in cost of packages and transportation by the elimination of portions of the product that are not usually eaten, such as the foliage of carrots and the basal portion of the leaves and part of the stem of cauliflower. Elimination of the portion of the product that usually goes into the garbage pail would result in large savings in packages and transportation for many kinds of produce.

To be economically successful the prepackaging facilities must be operated through a large part of the year. This is not feasible in most producing regions unless produce is purchased from other areas when local produce is not available. Another drawback to consumer packaging of some products in regions located long distances from the market is the danger of some decay of the product in transit. Should decay set in, the product would have to be removed from the container, sorted, and repackaged before being offered for sale. It seems to the author that packaging of the very perishable products in consumer packages will likely be done mainly at the market end. However, improvement in packaging, refrigeration, and transportation may make it feasible to do consumer packaging in the producing region.

Transportation of Vegetables. A large part of the produce grown for market is transported by rail and by auto truck. Vegetables grown within 100 miles of the market are hauled almost entirely in trucks. In fact, a large part of the produce grown within 500 miles of the large markets is delivered by trucks, and hauls of 1,000 miles, as from Florida to New York and other Eastern cities, are common. Much longer truck hauls are not uncommon.

Railroads haul a large part of the produce grown more than 600 to 800 miles from the market. They have the advantage of good terminal facilities in most of the large cities of the United States, and fewer men are required to move a trainload by rail than by truck. The railroads have good refrigeration facilities. Trucks can pick up produce from the field or packing house and deliver it to the store. However, most market centers are not well provided with terminal facilities for trucks.

For most products shipped long distances refrigeration must be used, and during very cold weather it is often necessary to provide heat in the car or truck to prevent freezing injury. These items of expense are almost unknown to the market gardener who delivers his produce to a local market.

Good transportation facilities have made it possible to extend the area of production of perishable vegetables to areas 3,000 miles from the market. Producers have taken advantage of climatic conditions to grow crops for the large markets when these markets could not be supplied with local products. This has had the effect of extending the season of consumption, since most vegetables are now available in the fresh condition practically throughout the year.

While most of the fresh produce marketed in the United States is shipped to market by truck or by rail, water transportation is still used to some extent. Some of the produce grown in Michigan is shipped by boat to Chicago, Milwaukee, and other lake ports; produce from Norfolk, Va., is shipped to Washington, Baltimore, New York, and Boston by boat. Water transportation is cheaper than rail transportation, but it usually takes longer than by rail or truck.

The use of the motor truck has made more difficult the problem of estimating the quantities and kinds of produce that will be available for sale on the important markets at any time. There is need for a system of reporting probable arrivals of produce by truck before the opening of the market each day. There is also need for truck terminal facilities in most large city markets.

Considerable interest developed in air transportation of produce immediately after the ending of the Second World War, and some experiments were being conducted. Not enough information is available to justify any definite statements regarding the feasibility of the use of the airplane in transporting vegetables. However, it seems safe to say that this method will be practicable only for handling perishable produce of relatively high value per ton. Airplanes are being used successfully for transporting vegetable plants from some of the Southern and Southwestern states to other parts of the United States.

Precooling of Vegetables. When vegetables are harvested during hot weather, it is desirable to remove field heat as soon as is feasible in order to retard ripening and deterioration. This is accomplished by precooling the produce either before or immediately after loading. The common methods of precooling are as follows:

1. Placing the produce in a storage room, refrigerator car, or truck refrigerated with ice or by machine. This method is slow but can be used satisfactorily if there is forced air circulation.

2. Cooling in ice water (hydrocooling). Two methods of cooling with water are in use—immersing in ice water and passing the produce through a spray of cold water.

3. Placing ice in the package with the produce. This method has been in use for a long time and is satisfactory for many products. This method is being replaced to a large extent for lettuce in California and Arizona in favor of vacuum cooling.

4. Vacuum cooling has developed very rapidly since 1950. According to Welch and Whitaker (1953) there has been a very striking change in packing and cooling methods used for lettuce in California. Much of the lettuce formerly packed in packing houses with ice in the package is now packed in the field in cartons and is vacuum-cooled to refrigeration temperatures in less than 30 minutes. When this method is used, top icing in the car or truck is eliminated.

After the produce is precooled it is desirable to keep it cold by shipping in refrigerator cars or trucks, by storing in cold-storage rooms, by use of refrigerator cases in retail stores, and by use of the refrigerator in the home.

Selling Vegetables. Vegetables are disposed of by producers by many different methods, both at retail and at wholesale. Retail sales are made directly to the consumer through house-to-house calls, through city retail markets, and through roadside stands. Wholesale sales are made: (1) to retail stores, restaurants, and hotels, (2) to country buyers and shippers, (3) to trucker dealers, at the farm and at city and regional markets, (4) to wholesale dealers and jobbers in the market, (5) through auction markets in the producing regions, and (6) through cooperative organizations of producers. The cooperative organization may use any or all of the wholesale selling methods mentioned. In addition to outright sales, producers may consign produce to merchants who sell on commission.

Retail selling is not popular with growers, except with those who have good locations for roadside markets. All retail methods of sale are expensive, and most growers believe that their time is of more value on the farm than in selling produce in small lots to the consumer.

Market gardeners sell most of their produce at wholesale to retail stores, to various types of buyers on local markets in nearby cities or on regional markets. Growers who are located long distances from market sell largely to wholesale dealers or jobbers. These may be local buyers or representatives of buyers in distant markets who buy outright at the shipping point. Produce may be sold by wire subject to inspection on arrival, but most growers prefer to sell to buyers at the shipping point rather than to take chances subject to inspection on arrival.

Cooperative marketing by farmers has been employed to a limited extent for many years, but within the past 50 years hundreds of cooperative organizations have been formed for selling all kinds of agricultural products and for buying supplies. While these associations can accomplish more for the farmer than he can accomplish for himself, it should be remembered that there have been many failures and relatively few successes in this field. This fact should be a warning to go slowly and to study thoroughly the need of a cooperative organization, the reasons for success and failure, and the methods followed by successful organizations. Many failures have been due to the fact that the growers did not see the need of a cooperative organization, to lack of cooperative spirit, to poor management, and to poor business methods.

Cooperative associations, to be successful, must be organized because of a real need, and the members must have the proper attitude toward cooperation. In addition to these there must be a sufficient volume of business to make economical operation possible, there must be capable management, good business methods, and loyalty to the association on the part of the members.

Some of the important services that a cooperative organization can render to the grower are: (1) to standardize the product, (2) to improve the grading and packing, (3) to develop old markets and find new ones, (4) to effect savings through large-scale handling, better distribution, etc., (5) to obtain and disseminate crop and market information, (6) to advertise the products of the members, and (7) to buy needed supplies. Most of these things can be accomplished by an organization because funds are available to obtain the services of experts along the

Fɪɢ. 13.1. Roadside market of Leon Stanisewski, Westfield, Mass. (*Courtesy of Paul Work.*)

various lines. This is impossible for most individual growers, since the volume of business is too small to bear the burden of all the services that a cooperative association can render.

Roadside Markets. Since about 1920 there has been a marked development in roadside marketing in the vicinity of nearly all cities in the United States. This development has coincided with the great expansion of travel by automobile. Hauck (1954) reported that in 1939 seven counties in New Jersey had 246 roadside markets, and by 1953 the number had increased to 1,400 in these same counties. The state of New Jersey had 2,100 roadside markets in 1953. Similar development has taken place in many other areas.

Roadside markets range in size from a small table in the front yard to large stores selling hundreds of dollars worth of produce per day (Fig. 13.1). Some of these markets sell only the produce grown by the seller, others buy all they sell, and still others sell their own produce and also buy many products for resale; some roadside-market managers sell only local products, others buy shipped-in produce of all kinds to sell along with the home-grown vegetables.

Some of the essentials of success in operating roadside markets are as follows:

1. A location on a much-traveled road
2. A location with adequate driveways and parking facilities
3. An adequate volume of business to justify devoting the time and effort necessary to operate the business
4. An attractive stand and display of products
5. Good-quality produce and a continuous supply
6. Good signs that can be easily read from some distance
7. Reasonable prices and good salesmanship
8. An honest pack
9. Courteous service
10. A real interest in the customer

A roadside market should be located well off the edge of the road, preferably where the road is level, or at the top of a hill, as motorists do not like to stop on a hill or at the bottom. A location where the market can be seen from a distance is desirable. It has been found that a location on the right side of the road leading into town sells much more produce than one located on the opposite side. This is due to the fact that most persons buy produce on returning from a drive and prefer not to have to cross a traffic lane to reach the stand.

The question of price at which products should be sold at roadside markets is one on which there is considerable difference of opinion. In general, it would seem that the producer who operates his own market should get most of the profit usually taken by wholesaler and retailer. On the other hand, the price should not be higher than the retail price in city markets for the same quality of produce.

Some students of roadside marketing suggest that the price the consumer pays should be above the wholesale price, but somewhat below the retail price since there are no delivery charges and little loss of product. The buyer should gain some advantage since he is performing part of the function of distribution. Bond (1941) reported results of a study in New York State in which 234 operators out of 454 set prices between city wholesale and retail prices, 113 set prices at city retail, 55 set prices at city wholesale or below, and 13 set prices above city retail.

CHAPTER 14

Storage of Vegetables

Storage of vegetables is of great importance since it tends to stabilize prices by carrying over produce from periods of high production to periods of low production. Without storage the producer would be forced to put his products on the market soon after harvest, regardless of the demand. This would cause a glut and market stagnation with consequent loss to the producer. While the consumer would benefit by lower prices during the glut, this would be offset by higher prices later when the demand became greater than the supply.

The large production of vegetables in the South, Southwest, and California in late fall, winter, and spring has nearly eliminated long-period storage of most products grown in the northern part of the United States. The only vegetables stored in considerable quantities for long periods are potatoes, sweet potatoes, onions, winter pumpkins, and winter squashes. The only stored vegetables of much importance that do not have to compete with the fresh product are sweet potatoes, winter pumpkins, and winter squashes. Late-crop potatoes from storage must compete with new potatoes from the milder sections of the United States during a considerable part of the storage period. Stored onions come into competition with the freshly harvested product in the latter part of the storage period. The late crops of celery and cabbage produced in the Northern part of the United States are in competition with the new crops produced in milder regions. Because of this competition, the quantity of these crops put in storage is much less than formerly.

With most vegetables, the main need of storage is for short periods—in many cases for a few weeks only.

Requirements of Storage. Successful storage requires a good product, the proper temperature and atmospheric humidity, the right stage of maturity for the products to be stored, and freedom from disease and other injury. A diseased or injured product usually deteriorates rapidly in storage, especially under conditions favorable for the development of storage rots.

Specific rules for the best conditions for storage that will apply to all products cannot be given because of difference in the requirements. Most of the root crops such as beets, carrots, parsnips, rutabagas, and turnips keep best in a relatively cold, humid atmosphere, while sweet potatoes, pumpkins, and squashes keep best in a relatively warm, dry atmosphere. The last three deteriorate rapidly under cool, moist conditions; control of temperature and humidity is therefore very important and is obtained by both natural and artificial means. Recommended storage conditions and approximate length of storage period for many vegetables, as reported by Rose, Wright, and Whiteman (1949), are given in Table 14.1.

Storing in the Field. Field storage, in trenches and pits and by mounding on the surface of the ground, is still practiced to some extent. Trenches are used for storing cabbage and celery; pits for cabbage, turnips, beets, carrots, parsnips, potatoes, and sweet potatoes. All the crops mentioned, except celery, are sometimes placed in piles on the ground and covered with hay, straw, or other litter and then with soil. The covering of soil should be heavy enough to prevent severe freezing.

Field storage is unsatisfactory and is giving way to other methods. The main disadvantages of this type of storage are: (1) the temperature and moisture cannot be controlled, hence under unfavorable climatic conditions large losses are likely to occur; (2) the produce can be removed only with difficulty when the ground is frozen, and this may prevent marketing at the time desired; (3) the product not removed may be injured when the pit or mound is opened during cold or wet weather; and (4) the labor required to store and remove the products from pits or mounds is large.

The only advantage in field storage is that it is always available, and any amount of space can be used as required. Many growers use field storage because they believe it is cheap, but when labor is taken into consideration it is an expensive method.

For short storage periods the mound above the surface of the ground is fairly satisfactory. A well-drained location should be selected so that no surface water runs about the base of the mound. The surface should be leveled, and it is desirable to have two small trenches across the bed, at right angles to each other, to provide for ventilation at the bottom. Boards or troughs are often placed over the trenches, and at the intersection of the trenches, a small open box is set on end to form a flue up through the pile of vegetables. The earth floor is covered with 4 or 5 inches of hay, straw, or other litter, and the product is placed on this in a conical pile around the flue. A covering of straw, hay, or similar material is put over the pile, and over this a layer of soil. The covering of soil should be only a few inches thick at first, but increased as the weather

Table 14.1. Recommended Storage Conditions and Approximate Length of Storage Period for Commercial Storage

Vegetable	Temperature, °F.	Relative humidity, %	Approximate length of storage
Asparagus........................	32	85–90	3–4 weeks
Beans, Lima:			
Unshelled......................	32	85–90	2–4 weeks
	40	85–90	10 days
Shelled........................	32	85–90	15 days
	40	85–90	4 days
Beans, snap......................	32–40	85–90	2–4 weeks
Beets:			
Topped........................	32	95–98	1–3 months
Bunch.........................	32	85–90	10–14 days
Brocolli, Italian..................	32–35	90–95	7–10 days
Brussels sprouts..................	32–35	90–95	3–4 weeks
Cabbage........................	32	90–95	3–4 months
Carrots:			
Topped........................	32	95–98	4–5 months
Bunch.........................	32	85–90	10–14 days
Cauliflower......................	32	85–90	2–3 weeks
Celery..........................	31–32	90–95	2–4 months
Corn (green).....................	31–32	85–90	4–8 days
Cucumbers......................	45–50	85–95	10–14 days
Eggplants.......................	45–50	85–90	10 days
Endive..........................	32	90–95	2–3 weeks
Garlic (dry).....................	32	70–75	6–8 months
Horse-radish....................	32	95–98	10–12 months
Jerusalem artichoke...............	31–32	90–95	2–5 months
Kohlrabi........................	32	95–98	2–4 weeks
Leeks (green)....................	32	85–90	1–3 months
Lettuce.........................	32	90–95	2–3 weeks
Muskmelons.....................	32–34	75–78	7–10 days
Honey Dew melons...............	36–38	75–85	2–4 weeks
Casaba and Persian melons.........	36–40	75–85	4–6 weeks
Okra...........................	50	85–95	2 weeks
Onions.........................	32	70–75	6–8 months
Onion sets......................	32	70–75	6–8 months
Parsnips........................	32	90–95	2–4 months
Peas (green).....................	32	85–90	1–2 weeks
Peppers (sweet)..................	32	85–90	4–6 weeks
Potatoes, late...................	38–50	85–90	5–8 months
Pumpkins, winter.................	50–55	70–75	2–6 months
Radishes, winter.................	32	95–98	2–4 months
Rhubarb........................	32	90–95	2–3 weeks
Rutabagas.......................	32	95–98	2–4 months
Salsify..........................	32	95–98	2–4 months
Spinach.........................	32	90–95	10–14 days
Squashes:			
Summer........................	40–50	85–95	2–3 weeks
Winter........................	50–55	70–75	4–6 months
Sweet potatoes...................	50–55	80–85	4–6 months
Tomatoes:			
Ripe..........................	40–50	80–85	7–10 days
Mature green..................	55–70	80–85	3–5 weeks
Turnips.........................	32	95–98	4–5 months
Watermelons....................	36–40	75–85	2–3 weeks

gets colder. The ends of the trenches and flue should be kept open for ventilation until it is necessary to close them to prevent freezing the product. It is better to make several small mounds rather than to make one large one because, when a mound is opened, it is best to remove the entire contents.

Storing in Cellars. The ordinary house cellar is used to a considerable extent for the storing of root crops for home use. If it contains a heater, this is one of the poorest places in which to store vegetables, as it is likely to be so warm and dry that the products will shrivel. However, by partitioning off a room, which can be kept cool and fairly moist, the house cellar is satisfactory. The storage room should have an opening to the outside for ventilation.

Outdoor cellars, made especially for storing root crops, usually give better results than the house cellar. With proper construction the temperature and moisture can be controlled to some extent. This type of storage structure may consist of a pit with a gable roof covered with sods or soil, or a more elaborate structure. Some of the more elaborate are built in a depression or ravine and covered with soil except at the ends. The structure built into a sidehill, or in a ravine and covered with soil, is preferable to the pit type since the soil on the sides and top prevents rapid changes in temperature. In any case the entire structure should be well insulated, and it is desirable to have the exposed end face the south.

Storage cellars are best suited to the storage of beets, carrots, parsnips, turnips, and potatoes since these products keep best where the humidity is relatively high.

Storing in Aboveground Houses. Common storage houses built entirely above the surface are extensively used in storing sweet potatoes, onions, and cabbage, and also to some extent for other products. Where it is necessary to have a dry atmosphere in the storage house, the cellar or structure of the semicellar type is not satisfactory since it is difficult to control the moisture in structures of this kind.

The advantages of this type of storage over any of the others mentioned are: (1) moisture can be controlled more readily; (2) products can be put in and taken out with less work and less discomfort; (3) grading and packing can be done to better advantage than from field storage or even in most types of cellars.

The character of construction of storage houses depends mainly on the type of product and the region in which it is to be stored. The colder the region, the greater the insulation needed. Sweet-potato storage houses in the South differ considerably from the cabbage and onion houses in the North, yet the same general principles of insulation and ventilation are applied in the two regions.

Cold Storage. The main advantage of cold storage over common storage is in the control of temperature and humidity, especially the former. In cold-storage warehouses the temperature can be kept at the desired point regardless of the weather condition, provided the building has been constructed and equipped properly. This ready control of temperature is not possible in any other type of storage, consequently less loss is sustained under refrigeration than in common storage. For this reason cold storage is being used even for products which keep fairly well in common storage. Cold storage is used for a large part of the celery that is stored, and to some extent for lettuce, onions, potatoes, carrots, beets, cabbage, cauliflower, and other vegetables.

Location of Storage Houses. In the early development of storage, the houses usually were built on the farm for use by the owner for his surplus for home use, or for sale. While farm storage is still used to a considerable extent, the tendency is toward commercial storage houses in the cities or at some central point in the producing region. The change from storage on the farm to use of large, commercial houses makes for more efficient storage. The main advantages of the large commercial houses over the small storage structures on the farms are: (1) lower cost per cubic foot of storage space, (2) lower maintenance and management cost, (3) usually more efficient management, because large-scale storage permits employment of efficient managers who devote their time to the business, (4) usually better equipment for handling produce at the storage house and, therefore, less labor required in doing the work, and (5) better location with reference to transportation facilities to markets. One of the disadvantages of farm storage houses is that in regions where winters are severe there are times when it would be unsafe to haul the produce to the market or shipping point because of danger of freezing injury. It is during long cold periods that the demand for the stored products is likely to be the greatest. These factors often cause the producer to miss good markets for his stored products. When the produce is stored in consuming centers, or on a good transportation line, it can be placed on the market at any time. For this reason central storage houses are more popular than isolated farm storage houses.

Common storage houses, those having no artificial means of cooling, are usually located on the farms or at some central point in the producing region. Cold-storage houses are located mainly in the cities, although a small percentage are located in small towns or villages in fruit and vegetable regions. The main advantage of locating storage houses in the cities is the convenience of marketing.

Cold-storage space in the cities is usually controlled by dealers, hence the producer gets only an indirect benefit from such houses. This has led growers, in many sections, to build cold-storage plants in the producing region. There is an advantage in having cold-storage houses near the producing region, especially for very perishable products such as celery and lettuce. The sooner perishable products are placed in storage after they are harvested, the longer they will keep.

Effects of Storage on the Vegetable Industry. Storage extends the period of consumption of many vegetables, and this increases the demand. Without storage the consumer would be able to obtain vegetables only during the time that they are available from the field in various sections of the country. With some crops this would cover a considerable portion of the year, while with others it would cover only a short period. Sweet potatoes would be available for only 4 or 5 months, and Irish potatoes and onions for 6 or 7 months. Without storage the acreage of many vegetables would have to be reduced because it would be impossible to consume, during the harvesting period, all that is now grown. Storage therefore increases consumption by lengthening the period of availability of many standard vegetable products.

In general, storage increases the price the farmer receives for his products, even if they are stored by middlemen, because it helps to prevent market gluts and makes for more uniform distribution. Storage also benefits the consumer. Assuming that storage is essential, the producer must decide whether to build his own storage, rent storage space, or sell to someone who will do the storing. If the producer is located a considerable distance from the market or a good transportation line, he probably should not build his own storage.

The farmer has to decide whether to sell his storageable produce at harvest time or to store it for later marketing. In making this decision he should take into consideration the probable increase in price, the cost of storage, the loss of produce due to shrinkage and decay, the cost of resorting and packing, the cost of removal from storage to the car or truck for shipment to market. The loss from shrinkage is greater than commonly supposed. This loss is dependent on the condition of the product at the time of storage and on the care in handling and on the storage conditions, especially the temperature and humidity of the atmosphere. It is frequently stated that the time for the farmer to store onions, potatoes, cabbage, and other products is when the price is high at harvest time, and the time to sell at harvest, or soon thereafter, is when the price is low. The farmer is more likely to store his products when the price is low at harvest time. While it is generally true that the farmer loses money by storing when the price is low at harvest, it is evident that it would be still lower if all of the crop were dumped on the market as soon as harvested. In other words, the advice to the individual farmer not to store potatoes or onions when the price is low in the fall may be safe, but it would be disastrous if all farmers followed it. Both the producer and the consumer would suffer.

The storage period for most products in the United States is shorter than it was formerly, because of the availability of fresh produce for a large part of the year. Much of the demand for storage is for short periods to carry produce over temporary gluts on the market. Retail stores that handle vegetables need some storage facilities for the very perishable products since they deteriorate rapidly in the relatively dry atmosphere and the temperature maintained in the stores.

CHAPTER 15

Perennial Crops

Asparagus	Jerusalem artichoke (Girasole)
Rhubarb	Sea kale
Artichoke	

Perennial crops occupy the land for a period of years and therefore should be located where they will not interfere with the usual tillage operations. It is advisable to grow these crops in an area to themselves. In the home garden they should be planted on one side, or at one end, so that the remainder of the garden can be treated as a unit in plowing and harrowing. For the same reason, on commercial vegetable farms the perennial crops should be grouped together in one field, or in one portion of a field. After perennial crops have been planted, manures and fertilizers are applied to the surface. Except for the points mentioned the perennial crops have little in common as far as cultural practices are concerned.

ASPARAGUS

Asparagus is one of the most delicate, wholesome, and appetizing products of the garden. Its early appearance in the spring, together with the fact that an asparagus bed when once established will produce for many years, makes it of special importance in the home garden as well as in the market garden and on the truck farm. As a processed product it is an important one, being canned and frozen in large quantities.

Statistics of Production. The production of asparagus for fresh-market sale and for processing is an important industry. The average annual acreage has increased from 48,000 acres for the period 1918–1927 to 127,596 acres for the years 1948–1952. The average annual farm value has increased from $9,492,500 to $34,572,000 for the periods mentioned. The acreage grown for fresh market decreased sharply from the average of the period 1928–1937 to the average for 1948–1952, but the increase in acreage grown for processing has increased as shown in Table 15.1. The leading states in total acreage in 1952 were California with 69,400 acres; New Jersey, 26,000; Washington, 10,600; Illinois, 8,600; and Michigan, 7,500 acres. It should be borne in mind that the figures of acreage, production, and farm value, as reported, include only commercial production for the important producing states. They do not include production on a small scale by market gardeners or production for home use.

Table 15.1. Estimated Average Annual Acreage, Production, and Farm Value of Asparagus Grown for Market and for Processing (*Agricultural Statistics*)

Years	Acres	Production	Value (000 omitted)
For market			
1918–1927	23,455	2,345,500 crates	$ 6,647.5
1928–1937	62,825	5,175,500 crates	8,737
1938–1947	48,526	6,253,900 crates	13,906.5
1948–1952	41,298	3,715,000 crates	14,164.4
For processing			
1918–1927	25,336	34,545 tons	$ 2,845
1928–1937	42,145	54,249 tons	4,008
1938–1947	60,058	70,904 tons	9,969
1948–1952	86,298	100,300 tons	20,407.6

History and Taxonomy. Asparagus is indigenous to Europe and Asia where it has been in cultivation for over 2,000 years. It was prized as a food by the Greeks and Romans and valued for the medicinal properties of all its parts. Asparagus has been grown in the gardens of America ever since the earliest settlements were established.

Asparagus, a genus of the lily family, has at least 150 species native of Europe, Asia, and Africa. Some of these are herbaceous and some woody; both erect and climbing forms are common. In addition to the edible asparagus, the genus contains the so-called "smilax" used by florists and the ornamental plants known as "asparagus ferns." The species of this genus are devoid of ordinary green leaves, the green branches functioning as leaves. The small scales or spines on the stems are the true leaves.

The garden asparagus, *Asparagus officinalis* Linn. var. *altilis* Linn., is a perennial, dioecious herb 4 to 10 feet tall. The male flowers are yellowish green and conspicuous, while the female flowers (on separate plants) are less conspicuous. The fruit is a three-celled berry which becomes red as it matures. The seeds are large (⅛ inch or less in diameter), rounded at the back but more or less flattened on one side, black in color.

Soils and Soil Preparation. Asparagus can be grown on nearly all kinds of soil, but a deep, loose soil is preferred. Sandy, sandy-loam, and silt-loam soils are used to a large extent in many asparagus-growing regions, although some of the muck lands are considered excellent. For fresh-market asparagus, where earliness is of importance, sandy and sandy-loam soils have an advantage. The soil should be well drained.

Asparagus does not grow well on a highly acid soil; when such soils are used liming is desirable. On mineral soils, it is desirable to maintain the reaction between pH 6.0 and 6.7. On natural limestone soils and others that are neutral or slightly alkaline, asparagus is grown successfully, but it is not desirable to bring an acid soil to neutrality because of the expense involved and also because the lime might render unavailable some essential element. When asparagus is grown on a soil that has a favorable reaction it is desirable to use fertilizers that are neutral in reaction.

The soil should be well prepared since the crop occupies the land for many years and there is no opportunity for further preparation after the plants are planted. It is desirable to have the land freed of noxious weeds as weed control is expensive in an established planting. The land should be well plowed to the depth normally practiced on the tract to be used. On most upland soils a depth of 8 inches is sufficient, but on deep, alluvial soils a greater depth is desirable. After being plowed, the land should be well fitted by harrowing and dragging, if necessary to break up clods, so that the roots can be covered with loose soil.

Manures and Fertilizers. The experimental data on fertilizing asparagus are conflicting and generally inconclusive. Wessels and Thompson (1937) reported results of experiments on a Sassafras silt-loam soil in which manure at the rates of 10 and 20 tons, plus a liberal application of phosphorus, did not produce such large yields as a moderate application of a complete fertilizer during the first 4 years. In the next 5 years, however, 20 tons of manure plus phosphorus produced a significantly higher yield than the complete fertilizer. In spite of the large yields on the heavily manured plots, the use of manure was not profitable. From the results of these and other experiments, it appears that one could not afford to pay very much for manure (probably not over $2 per ton) for use on the asparagus bed. The results of these experiments indicate that on the Sassafras silt loam on Long Island, 100 pounds of nitrogen, 125 pounds of phosphorus, and 160 pounds of potash would give good results. It might well be expected that these quantities would be satisfactory on similar soils elsewhere. On rich silt loams smaller quantities of the nutrients are required. Apple and Barrons (1945) reported that the largest yields in experiments on a light soil in Michigan were from an application of approximately 120 pounds each of nitrogen and phosphorus and 180 pounds of potash to the acre. On the peat-sediment soils in one of the producing areas in California experiments showed no response to any fertilizer regardless of kind, rate, or time of application. This is an exceptional case. In nearly all other asparagus-growing areas of the United States the crop responds to liberal applications of fertilizer.

There is considerable difference of opinion as to the best time to apply fertilizer to a producing bed, and results of experiments are conflicting. Some experiments have shown no significant difference in yield of asparagus fertilized before the start of the cutting season and that fertilized at the end of harvest. Other experiments have shown advantages for application at the beginning of the season, and still others indicated better results for application made at the end of harvest. Under many conditions it would be better to apply part of the fertilizer before growth starts, and the remainder at the end of harvest. One serious objection to applying all of the fertilizer at the end of harvest is that a long period of dry weather may occur and the fertilizer not become available until too late to be of the greatest value. Where irrigation is used this difficulty would be removed. Regardless of the general fertilizer practice, it is desirable to apply part of the nitrogenous fertilizer before growth starts and part at the end of harvest.

Common salt (sodium chloride) has been considered by some growers as essential to success in growing asparagus. Experimental results have been conflicting and inconclusive. It is certainly not essential, as good asparagus is grown without the use of salt. There is some evidence that when insufficient potash is used salt may increase the yield. Working (1924), using solution cultures, found that seedlings grew better where sodium was used in low concentration than in solutions without sodium. Chlorine did not show beneficial effects that might have been expected from fertilizer experiments reported by others. While applications of salt may be beneficial under some conditions, it is doubtful if its use is justified when the asparagus is well fertilized with a complete fertilizer containing muriate of potash. More experimental evidence is needed on the problem.

Growing Asparagus Crowns. Asparagus crowns are grown from seed planted in a well-prepared seedbed where the plants are allowed to grow for one full growing season before being planted in the permanent bed. The asparagus grower may grow the crowns or may buy them from some plant growers. Where the crop is to be grown on a large scale, it usually is cheaper to grow them than to buy them; there are some other advantages in growing them at home. If the grower produces his own seed, as well as the crowns, he has knowledge of the source and of the productiveness of the parent plants, has opportunity for rigorous selection of the crowns, and has the crowns available when wanted for planting and can plant them soon after digging—a decided advantage.

While many growers of asparagus crowns take special care in selecting the seed, in growing the crowns, and in selecting only the well-developed vigorous ones, some growers pay little attention to the source of the seed or to the grading of the crowns. Crowns should be purchased only from sources known to be reliable.

Under average field conditions asparagus seed is slow to germinate, the time required varying from 2 to 6 weeks depending on the temperature and moisture of the soil and the depth of planting. Some authorities have thought that the seed had a period of dormancy, but Borthwick (1925) showed that germination will take place immediately after maturing if the environmental conditions are satisfactory. Germination is very slow at temperatures below 20°C. The rate of germination at different temperatures under laboratory conditions is given in Table 15.2. The optimum

Table 15.2. Effect of Temperature on Rate of Germination of Asparagus Seed
(*Calif. Agr. Exp. Sta. Tech. Paper* 18)

Temperature of germinating chamber, °C.	Percentage germination in given number of days:							
	3	4	5	6	8	10	12	17
10	0	0	0	0	0	0	0	0
20	0	0	2	4	11	14	. . .	27
25	0	25	65	84	98	98	98	98
30	0	50	74	83	91	95	96	97
35	0	5	. . .	16	31	55	67	
40	0	0	0	0	0	0	0	0

seems to be about 30°C. (86°F.), although the difference between 25 and 30° was slight in the experiments mentioned. At 40°C. there was no germination in 17 days. The slow germination at low temperatures probably is due to low rate of water absorption. Borthwick showed that water absorption increased with rise in temperature between 10 and 40°C. Soaking hastened germination, even when planted in cold soil. Seed soaked at 25 to 35°C. germinated more quickly than that soaked at higher or lower temperatures. Soaking for 3 to 5 days at 30 to 35°C. is recommended. After soaking, the seed should be spread out to dry, and during the drying it should be stirred to hasten evaporation of water on the surface and to have it dry uniformly.

The land for the seedbed should be well prepared and well supplied with nutrients. Unless the soil is rich, it should be liberally fertilized with a complete fertilizer approximating a 1-1-1 ratio. Planting the seed for commercial production usually is done with seed drills, preferably those that drop one seed in a place and spaces evenly, since thinning is difficult. The rows may be spaced 24 to 36 inches apart, depending on the tools used for cultivation. The plants should be 3 or 4 inches apart in the row.

Weeds should be kept under control by shallow cultivation, by use of herbicides, or by a combination of the two methods. Deep cultivation is undesirable as this destroys some of the roots and thus checks growth of the plants.

Under most conditions, well-grown 1-year-old plants are best. Older crowns are difficult to dig and are injured in digging if they have made good growth. Old stunted crowns are inferior to younger ones.

Male versus Female Plants. Asparagus is dioecious; *i.e.*, it has pistillate (female) and staminate (male) flowers on different plants. Occasionally perfect flowers occur, but this is rare. Field-run plants will average about 50 per cent males and 50 per cent females. While it has been shown by Tiedjens (1924) and Jones and Robbins (1928) that male plants produce larger yields than female plants, the economic advantage is not sufficient to justify discarding half of the plants. The female plants produce larger spears. In regions having short growing seasons asparagus plants do not blossom the first season; therefore it would not be possible to select plants on the basis of sex without growing them 2 years in the nursery. This would be uneconomical use of land since 1-year-old crowns are better than older ones, as mentioned previously.

Digging the Crowns. The crowns may be dug in the fall after growth has ceased and stored in a good storage or left in the ground until time for planting. Where they are grown for sale, they usually are dug and stored so as to be available for shipment at any time. When left in the ground over winter, it is desirable to cover them lightly with straw or other material to protect against alternate freezing and thawing which may result in heaving the crowns.

The crowns may be plowed out with a moldboard plow which turns them upside down. They are lifted out of the loose soil with a short-handled fork. Another implement, similar to the bean harvester, is used for digging. The digging part consists of a U-shaped knife that runs under the mass of fleshy roots. The knife should be at least 8 inches wide at the bottom with an upward tilt toward the rear so as to lift the crowns and make it easy to take them out with a fork. Care should be taken in digging to injure them as little as possible. If the digging is to be done in the fall, the tops should be cut off and removed or burned so as not to interfere with the operation.

The best storage temperature for asparagus crowns is about 40°F., but they can be kept for a considerable period at higher temperature if the atmosphere is fairly dry. On the other hand, the crowns should not be allowed to dry out, since growth is slow after they have become desiccated. It is best to plant the crowns as soon as feasible after they are dug.

Planting Asparagus Crowns. As has been suggested, 1-year-old crowns are recommended, since experience seems to indicate they give better results than older ones. If the crowns are left for 2 years, they become checked in growth by crowding and also the roots become so intertwined that they can be separated only with difficulty and with considerable injury. One-year-old crowns can be dug with less injury to the roots and consequently with less interruption to growth.

Only well-grown crowns of good size, containing large buds, should be planted, since many of the small weak ones do not survive. This results in a poor stand of plants and low yields. Results of experiments carried on in Pennsylvania and reported by Myers (1915) show that the yield from the small crowns was much below that for the larger sizes. The average annual value of the first six crops was $539, $520, and $418 per acre from grade 1, grade 2, and grade 3, respectively. Obviously, it would have paid better to have discarded the grade 3 crowns since the gross return was over $700 less per acre for the 6 years from grade 3 plants than from grade 1. Results of experiments conducted for 12 years in California and reported by Jones and Hanna (1940) showed that for the first 7 years the grade 1 crowns of the Palmetto variety significantly outyielded the grade 3. In the Mary Washington variety the mean yield for the 12 years was significantly greater for grade 1 and grade 2 crowns than that for the grade 3. Over the 12-year period the Mary Washington outyielded the Palmetto. In this experiment there was no significant relation between the size of crown planted and the weight of spear. It should be borne in mind that the crowns grown in California average larger in size at the end of one season's growth than they do in most other sections of the United States because of a longer growing season there. Two sizes are shown in Fig. 15.1.

In most sections of the United States the crowns are planted in the spring as early as the soil can be put in good condition. It is desirable to do this before growth begins. Fall planting is practiced to some extent in the South.

The depth of planting varies from 6 to 14 inches depending on the physical characteristics of the soil. According to Hanna (1947) the depth of planting on sandy-loam and peat soils of the delta region of California is 8 to 12 inches, 10 inches being the most common. In Ryers Island experiments, Hanna reported no great difference in yield from crowns planted 5, 8, and 12 inches deep, while on a heavy soil at Davis yield of spears was higher from crowns planted 8 inches deep than for those planted 12 inches deep. On the other hand, Young (1940) reported from Massachusetts results in which crowns planted 2 inches deep produced a larger yield per acre of spears over a period of 9 years than crowns planted 6, 4, and 8 inches deep. The soil used in this experiment is classed as Merrimac gravelly sandy loam and is about 10 inches deep and underlaid with gravel. The crowns were all covered to the depth of

Fig. 15.1. Two sizes of 1-year-old asparagus plants grown at Ithaca, N.Y. The two on the left are satisfactory; the two on the right are rather small.

2 inches at planting. Young states that the loss of plants was much less in the 2-inch plot than in the others. He found no significant difference in the depth of the crowns from the various planting depths at the end of the twelfth season of growth. On upland soils it is probable that 8 inches should be the maximum depth of planting; on heavy soils the covering should not be over 6 inches deep. Regardless of the depth of the furrow, the crowns should not be covered over 2 or 3 inches deep at planting time.

The furrow in which the crowns are set is made with a turnplow running twice in the row and throwing the furrows in opposite directions or with a double moldboard plow. The distance between the rows varies considerably. In growing green asparagus, in most sections of the East, the rows are spaced 4 to 5 feet apart, although some growers prefer 6 feet. When the asparagus is to be blanched, the rows are spaced 6 to 8 feet apart, the wide spacing being desirable for the purpose of ridging the soil over the rows. The usual spacing between the plants in the rows is from 18 to 24 inches, although some growers give less space and others more. Jones reported results of spacing experiments covering a period of 7 years in which plants were spaced 12, 18, 30, and 36 inches apart in rows 7.5 feet apart. There was no significant difference in total yields between 12- and 18-inch spacing; above 18 inches the yield decreased considerably. In size of spear, the 18-inch spacing was superior to the 12-inch and about equal to the wider spacings. Haber (1935) reported results of experiments in which plants were spaced 1, 2, and 3 feet apart in the row with rows 3, 4, and 5 feet apart. His results indicate that rows 3 feet apart are too close and that spacing 1 foot apart in the row results in a decrease in size of spear as compared with wider spacing. Plants spaced 3 feet apart showed no significant superiority over those 2 feet apart. Thompson (1945) reported results of a spacing experiment covering a period of 13 years in which there were 10 full harvests. These experiments were conducted on a Dunkirk fine sandy loam of moderate fertility and slightly acid (about pH 6). The spacings in the row were 12, 18, and 24 inches with the rows spaced 4 and 5 feet apart. The average annual yield per acre of marketable asparagus increased as the distance between the plants in the row decreased. The differences are statistically significant. The difference in yield between the two row spacings over the three spacings in the row is not significant. However, at the 24-inch spacing in the row the yield was significantly higher from the rows 4 feet apart than from those spaced 5 feet apart. The yield of grade 1 spears followed, in general, those of total marketable. The yield varied markedly from year to year and apparently was not related to temperature, to rainfall during the growing season, or to the length of the harvest period. The average number of spears per plant increased as the spacing in the row increased. Also, the number per plant was greater for the 5-foot spacing between rows than for the 4-foot spacing except for those 24 inches apart in the row. The average weight per spear was greater from rows spaced 5 feet apart than from those 4 feet over each of the three spacings in the row. The weight per spear for the three spacings in the row over the two-row spacings was small and not significant.

Since asparagus crowns increase in size throughout the commercial life of a planting, it does not appear desirable to set the plants closer than 18 inches apart in the row; this distance might be increased to 2 feet under some conditions. The distance between rows should not be less than 4 feet for unblanched asparagus and not less than 6 feet where the spears are to be blanched. The spacings should be increased when the crop is grown on good silt-loam or muck (peat) soils. Hanna states that the rows should not be less than 7 feet apart for blanched asparagus in California.

After the furrows are made, the crowns are dropped by hand, care being taken to see that the buds are up. In small plantings the large roots are spread out by hand; where large acreages are set, this is seldom done. As soon as feasible after the crowns are placed in the furrow, they are covered to the depth of 2 or 3 inches with loose soil. When the crowns send up shoots through the soil covering, more soil is added and this is repeated at intervals, so that before the end of the season the furrow is filled. The filling of the furrow is done as the land is cultivated. The crowns should never be covered to the full depth of the furrow at first as many of the buds would be smothered before reaching the surface.

Intercropping. In many sections no spears are harvested from a new planting until the beginning of the third year, or after the plants have had two seasons' growth. This has led to intercropping in order to get some money return from the land every year. Where the rows are far enough apart to allow ample space for the intercrop and the asparagus, intercropping is a satisfactory practice during the first 2 years, provided sufficient nutrients are available for both crops and a suitable crop is grown. Snap beans, early cabbage, lettuce, or any other small-growing crop may be planted between the rows of asparagus. Tall-growing or long-season crops should not be grown with asparagus on account of shading and competition for moisture and nutrients. The cultivation required for a good growth of asparagus will be sufficient for the companion crop, and the return from the latter should go a long way toward paying for the cost of growing both.

Cultivation and Care. The general care given asparagus is very different from that given most other vegetable crops, because the plants occupy the same area for many years. This makes it impossible to plow the land to destroy weeds and to loosen the soil while the planting remains in production.

Every year after the first it is desirable to disk and harrow thoroughly each spring before growth begins. If the tops have been left standing over winter, they can be broken over by a drag on a bright clear day and then disked into the soil. This may require disking lengthwise and across the rows, or diagonally. Part or all of the fertilizer may be applied before the final harrowing. In some regions it is a common practice to apply cyanamid at the rate of 200 to 500 pounds to the acre over the rows before growth starts to control weeds and to supply nitrogen.

Cyanamid dust at the rate of 100 pounds to the acre applied when the weeds are about 1 inch high and wet with dew will also control weeds. Several other herbicides have been used successfully in controlling weeds both in the asparagus nursery and in established plantings. In several experiments in various parts of the United States CMU has given good control of both broad-leaved weeds and grasses.

Weeds between the rows can be kept under control by proper cultivation, which should be shallow and frequent enough to keep weeds cut back. Some hand hoeing may be desirable to keep down weeds during the cutting season. A satisfactory method of destroying weeds at the end of the cutting season is to run over the rows with cultivators equipped with knife or blade attachments that run a little below the soil surface, cutting off all weeds. This cultivating will also cut off all asparagus spears, but if done on the last day of harvesting, little or no injury will be done and the asparagus plants will get a start ahead of the weeds.

Hanna (1947) stated that in the delta region of California flooding of old asparagus beds has become a general practice. The flooding is done for 4 to 6 weeks in December and January, and the depth of water is 6 to 12 inches.

Where blanched asparagus is desired, it is necessary to mound the soil over the rows in order to bleach the young spears. On large plantations this is done by means of a plow, a disk harrow, or with an asparagus hiller. The hilling is started in the spring before growth begins or at any later time when blanched asparagus is desired. It is a common practice in California to cut green asparagus for the fresh market for a few weeks and then to mound the soil over the row for blanched asparagus for canning. The mounds must be kept up as long as blanched spears are desired. After the cutting season is over, the mounds are leveled by means of a plow, disk, or other implement. If any of the fertilizer is applied at the end of the cutting season, it should be applied between the rows and mixed with the soil by cultivating. It should be borne in mind that the treatment given the asparagus bed during the growing season determines, to a very large extent, the quality and quantity of the crop the following year. The plant food used in the production of shoots in the spring and early summer is manufactured in the foliage and stored in the roots during the previous season's growth. For this reason a strong, healthy growth of foliage is essential to a good yield of shoots.

Green versus Blanched (White) Asparagus. Green asparagus is preferred on most of the markets in the United States, although a considerable part of the canned product is blanched or white. The demand, however, has been increasing for green asparagus for canning and freezing, owing perhaps to the increasing knowledge of the value of green vegetables in the diet. A study by Waugh (1929) on the Boston market showed that the price paid increased as the length of the green portion of the spear increased. With spears 9 inches long, the price increased on an average 38½ cents a dozen bunches for every additional inch of green from 3 to 9 inches. Most of the fresh asparagus sold on the markets in the United States is green.

Hanna (1947) reported results in California covering a period of eight full harvests in which there was no significant difference in yield between white and green spears grown under the same conditions except for the ridging required for the blanched spears. The white spears averaged higher in weight than the green ones, but there were fewer of them.

Removing the Tops. Formerly, some authorities advised cutting and burning the asparagus tops as soon as the berries turn red. It was argued that if the berries are allowed to ripen, they fall off and the seeds germinate and the seedlings become troublesome. It was suggested also that burning destroyed the rust on the old plants. It is now known that if the tops are removed while they are still green, the roots are deprived of a large quantity of manufactured food. For this reason it is desirable to let the tops stand until they are dead. The tops are a great protection to the roots in regions where low temperatures occur, since they hold the snows and thus often prevent deep freezing and rapid changes in soil temperature. Under such conditions it is best to let the tops stand until spring and then to disk them into the soil. Burning the tops is wasteful since an acre of asparagus tops is equivalent in humus-forming material to several tons of average stable manure.

Morse (1916) has shown that early removal of asparagus tops decreases the quantity of reserve food material stored in the roots and also that most of the material used in growth of shoots is stored in the roots during the previous season. Samples of tops were taken for analysis in August, after blossoming but before berries were formed, and in October, when the stalks had turned yellow. To determine how fast translocation took place, the branches were removed and analyzed by themselves.

It was found that both sugars and protein disappeared with ripening. The disappearance of sugars as they are formed is indicated by the higher percentages in the stalks than in the branches, both in midsummer and in autumn. Analyses of the roots showed that most of the reserve food stored in them in the fall is sugars. Morse suggested that neither sugar nor protein is completely transferred to the roots, because until killed by frost the cells contain active protoplasm and its supply of food.

Duration of a Plantation. The length of time an asparagus bed will produce profitable yields depends on the treatment it receives. A well-established bed, which receives good cultivation to keep down weeds and good fertilizing each year, should produce profitable crops for 15 to 20 years. In practice, however, usually it is found desirable to renew the planting about every 10 to 15 years. When an old bed produces nothing but small, spindling shoots, it should be plowed up. Of course, in order to have a supply of asparagus every year, a new bed should have been started in another location some years before the old one is destroyed.

Varieties. True varieties of asparagus are few, and the characteristics of these are not well defined since there is mixing of strains due to crossing in the field. Mary Washington is the principal variety grown in the United States, but others grown to some extent are Martha Washington, Reading Giant, Palmetto, and Argenteuil. The Washington varieties are more resistant to rust than are the other varieties and are fully equal, or superior, in market quality to the best of the others mentioned. Martha Washington is somewhat more resistant to rust than Mary Washington, but is not so good in other respects. A selection of Mary Washington known as Paradise and some numbered strains developed in California are said to be superior to the standard strain in some regions, but they have proved to be more susceptible to rust in some areas of the Eastern part of the United States than the standard strain.

Until superior, rust-resistant strains or varieties are available the Washington varieties should be planted in most of the asparagus-growing areas of the United States.

The Washington varieties were developed by Norton (1913) at a time when the asparagus rust was so serious as to threaten the entire asparagus industry in this country. They were developed from a cross between a male plant of unknown American origin, grown from seed at Concord, Mass., and a female plant of Reading Giant obtained from England. The male plant was remarkable in transmitting vigor and rust resistance. From this pair was produced the Martha Washington. The male plant was named Washington, and a cross between this and a giant female, taken as a seedling from a bed of Reading Giant at Concord, Mass., resulted in the Mary Washington.

Asparagus Rust. The asparagus rust (*Puccinia asparagi*) is the most serious disease of asparagus in all the United States. It appears on the plant as small reddish-yellow spots on the main stem and on the branches. As the disease develops, the spots enlarge into patches until the whole plant has a reddish-brown or orange color, which becomes darker later in the season.

The damage caused by the rust is not seen directly in the marketed product but reduces the yield by weakening the plants during the summer after the cutting season is over and often killing them. No practical control measures have been developed for this disease except the se of rust-resistant varieties. Results of studies by Kuhn *et al.* (1952) in llinois indicate that stocks of the Washington varieties are the most esistant of a large number tested, but none was completely resistant. It eems probable that a new strain of rust has appeared, since in the llinois experiments no strain or variety, of a large number tested, was ound to be resistant.

Fusarium Wilt. This disease, caused by a fungus (*Fusarium* sp.) in he soil, has been reported from most of the asparagus-producing regions of the United States. Spears affected with wilt may show a brown discoloration of the surface and become wilted and stunted. Losses in some plantings occasionally are severe, but the disease is not so common as he rust. No control measures have been developed except to avoid planting on infected soil and to use healthy planting stock. New plantings should not be made near old infected beds.

Asparagus Beetles. Asparagus is attacked by two species of beetles, he common asparagus beetle (*Crioceris asparagi* L.) and the 12-spotted asparagus beetle (*Crioceris duodecimpunctata* L.). The adult of the common asparagus beetle is slender, blue black with red thorax, and emon yellow and dark-blue wing cover. The length of the body is about $1/4$ inch. The full-grown larva is dark gray with shiny black head and egs. The 12-spotted asparagus beetle can be distinguished from the common species by its broader back and orange-red color. Each wing cover is marked with six black dots. The larva of this species is orange in color and about $3/10$ inch long.

Injury by the common asparagus beetle is due to the work of both the adults and larvae to the tender shoots, and to the plants later in the season. The larvae feed on the tender portion of the tops, but the beetles gnaw the epidermis or rind of the stems as well as the tender portions. This injury to the asparagus tops results in weakening the roots. The chief damage inflicted by the 12-spotted asparagus beetle is by the adult on the young shoots in the spring. Later both the adults and larvae feed on the berries.

Injury to the asparagus shoots may be reduced or prevented by cutting all shoots every 3 or 5 days. This will remove all eggs deposited on them. When infestation is heavy during the harvesting season, a dust containing $3/4$ of 1 per cent rotenone dusted on the spears will kill the beetles. If this dust is used heavily on the spears, it may be advisable to wash off the dust residue before marketing or using the asparagus. This dust is effective against the larvae if their bodies are well covered with the dust. An 85–15 calcium-arsenate-hydrated-lime dust is as effective as rotenone, but it should not be used during the harvest period; it may be used on young plants that have not reached cutting age and on summer foliage after the cutting season. Spraying with 4 pounds of 4 per cent rotenone to 100 gallons of water and a suitable spreader is considered somewhat more effective than the dust, but the dust treatment is more commonly used.

Garden Centipede (*Scutigerella immaculata*). According to Hanna (1947) the garden centipede is by far the most serious pest of asparagus in California. These animals when mature are about ¾ inch long. In feeding, they make a large number of small, round holes in the spear below the surface of the ground. Hard fibers develop around these holes and make the spears unfit for canning. Hanna states that only green asparagus is cut from badly infested fields; the green portion is not injured. When infestation is heavy, the yield is reduced and often the plants are killed. Wymore (1924) stated that where infestations are scattered throughout the field, flooding is the only practical means of control. A levee is built around the field, and water to the depth of 1 foot or more is held on the field for 3 or 4 weeks during December and January. All parts of the field infested must be covered and no stubble left above the water.

Harvesting. In most asparagus-growing sections of the Eastern and Middle Western states, the first cutting is made at the start of the third season, or after the plants have had two full growing seasons in the permanent bed. In some regions having a longer season, as in South Carolina and in California, asparagus is harvested during the second season, or after one season's growth in the field. During the first cutting season the harvesting period is short, usually from 2 to 4 or 6 weeks. After the first cutting season the period of harvest runs from 8 to 12 or 14 weeks. In regions having a relatively short season, 8 weeks' cutting is long enough, for the plants must be allowed to make good growth before frost in order to produce a satisfactory yield the following season.

Asparagus is usually harvested every day during the main portion of the cutting season, but if the weather is cold, every other day or even every third day may be often enough. On the other hand, in very hot weather when the growth is rapid, it is necessary to go over the bed twice a day, especially where blanched shoots are desired. Culpepper and Moon (1939) have shown that for temperatures between 52.5 and 87.5°F. the relationship between growth rate and temperature is represented by lines that are almost straight. The rate of elongation approximately doubled with each increase of 10°C. (18°F.) over a limited range of temperature. They found that growth was slow at first, increased rapidly to about 65 centimeters in height when it was at a maximum, and then slowly decreased as the stalks became taller. The cutting is done with a knife made especially for this purpose. In cutting, one takes hold of the shoot with one hand and with the other inserts the knife to the desired depth (1 or 2 inches below the surface of the soil for green asparagus) and severs the shoot with a downward stroke. Care should be exercised to avoid injuring the crown and the other shoots; hence the knife should be inserted almost straight down beside the shoot, and then tilted slightly to cut off the stalk. One thrust with the knife should be sufficient.

If white asparagus is desired, it is necessary to cut the shoots soon after they force their way through the surface of the soil. They turn green on exposure to the light. White shoots are cut several inches below the surface of the mound of soil, but they should be severed 1 or 2 inches above the crowns to avoid injury to the crown.

Owing to acute shortage of labor during the Second World War and immediately after, interest developed in reducing the labor required for harvesting asparagus by snapping off the spears instead of harvesting by the usual method. To test the feasibility of snapping asparagus to be canned, Barrons (1945) conducted some tests in Michigan in 1944 and 1945. The results of these tests indicate that: (1) there was saving in labor in harvesting and a still greater saving in the preparation of the spears in the factory; (2) the yields of cannable spears from the two methods of harvesting were not significantly different; and (3) the snapped asparagus was cleaner than the cut when it reached the factory. It was found also that the yield of cannable asparagus the second year was essentially the same for the two methods of harvesting. Results of later experiments in Michigan reported by Carolus (1949) are similar to those reported by Barrons. Carolus states that pressure must be applied with the thumb and fingers not far below the top. If the spear is grasped too low down, the break may occur one-half to more than an inch below the point where fiber development occurs. Hanna (1950) reported that at Davis, Calif., snapping resulted in lower yield than the usual cutting method of harvesting. Snapping is practiced in some areas, especially where the crop is grown for processing, and it results in considerable saving in labor.

Since asparagus loses its quality quickly after it is harvested, it should be prepared and put on the market as soon as possible. For the very highest quality, asparagus should be cooked within a few hours after being cut, but this is impossible except where it is produced at home. However, the local gardener has a decided advantage over the grower who lives a long distance from his market.

Washing Asparagus for Market. The asparagus shoots are taken to the packing shed where they are washed, bunched, and packed. This preparation may be done in almost any kind of building. The necessary equipment and supplies consist of stationary benches or tables, tubs or tanks, brushes, and wire-bottom trays for washing, machines for bunching, knives, tape or raffia, shallow pans, crates or boxes, labels, nails, and a supply of water. The shoots are usually washed before bunching; this can be done easily by dousing the tray of shoots a few times. Green asparagus does not always need washing, but the butt ends usually require some rinsing to give the bunch a clean appearance. This is sometimes done after the shoots have been bunched. Some growers prefer to scrub the outside of the bunch of shoots after they have been bunched and tied. For this a stiff brush is used.

Grading. Asparagus is taken from the field to the packing shed where it is separated into grades, based mainly on size. The number of grades varies considerably. In some sections no grading is done except to throw out unmarketable spears; in others the marketable spears are separated into two grades; in still others, as in California, as many as six grades are used. Where two grades are used, it is desirable to follow the specifications of the U.S. Department of Agriculture.

If the spears are separated into more than two grades, those that meet the requirements of U.S. grade No. 1 should be separated mainly on the basis of size. For most markets three grades are sufficient, the best grade being a fancy product, the second including spears which meet the requirements of U.S. No. 1, and the third corresponding to U.S. No. 2.

Bunching. After being separated into the different grades, the shoots are placed in a bunching machine with the heads all one way, only one grade being put into a bunch. When the bunching apparatus is full, the clamps are closed and the asparagus is tied near each end with tape or raffia. The butts are cut off evenly with a sharp knife and the bunches packed immediately or else placed in a cool place not exposed to currents of air. The size of bunches ranges from 1 to 3 pounds, depending on the market. Bunches of 2½ pounds are common in California. For local retail trade in many parts of the United States, small bunches, usually 1 pound, are preferred. After bunching the bunches are stood in shallow pans in 2 to 3 inches of water until packed. Many growers and shippers wrap the bunches in parchment paper with only the tips of the spears extending above the paper. The wrapper usually bears the name of the grower or shipper.

Packaging in film bags without bunching has been tested, and it has been found by Carolus, Lipton, and Apple (1953) that the films helped to maintain: (1) market quality by reducing moisture loss, (2) edible quality by checking development of fibrousness, and (3) nutritional value by reducing loss of ascorbic acid. Carolus emphasizes that impermeable film bags cannot be recommended because of the danger of anaerobic decomposition, which would result in the development of off flavors, as has been reported by other workers.

Asparagus is sometimes packed in boxes or crates without bunching. When the loose pack is used, the butts are cut off and the spears are laid in boxes lined with oil paper with a layer of wet moss on the bottom. The box is laid on its side during packing. When the box is full, the oil paper is folded over the asparagus and the side boards are nailed on. The loose pack may include ungraded spears or only those that are difficult to bunch.

Packing. Several types of packages are used for asparagus, the most popular one being a box having solid ends and made especially for this product. These boxes are made to hold 1 or 2 dozen bunches. A popular crate used in California is a pyramidal one with two compartments holding six bunches of 2½ pounds each. The pyramidal crate is a good shipping container as it conforms to the taper of the bunches and thus prevents their shifting in handling and shipping. The bottoms of the crates usually are lined with paper on which is placed damp moss. The butts of the bunches are set on the moss. When packed in this manner and kept under good refrigeration asparagus can be shipped long distances without serious loss in quality.

In some areas part of the asparagus, especially that sold on local markets, is packed without bunching. In some cases field-run and low-grade spears are so packed, but in others even first-grade asparagus is packed without bunching. However, most of the crop shipped to sell as fresh asparagus is bunched as described above.

Changes in Quality after Cutting. Asparagus undergoes marked changes in structure and chemical composition after it is cut, and the rate of these changes depends on the temperature. The most important changes concern growth in length and weight, in sugars and crude fiber. All these changes are markedly influenced by the temperature at which the spears are kept after they are harvested. Bisson, Jones, and Robbins (1926) have shown that the spears grow in length if the butts are in water or are placed on moist moss. The growth rate was least 33°F. and increased as the temperature was raised to 41, 56, 77, and 95°F. The greatest increase in length occurred during the first 24 hours. There was an increase in weight also due to the absorption of water. Chemical analyses show a loss in reducing substances and in total sugars. The losses were especially pronounced at the higher temperatures. The maximum rate of loss occurred during the first 24 hours. Crude fiber increased during storage at all temperatures. The greatest increase in crude fiber at all temperatures was during the first 24 hours after the spears were cut, but was least at the lowest temperature and greatest at the highest temperature. Lignification took place throughout the length of the spear.

The results given above show the importance of getting the asparagus graded, bunched, packed, and cooled as soon as possible. Pentzer *et al.* (1936) have shown that precooling as soon as the car is loaded results in a marked reduction in temperature during the first 4 days in transit from California to Eastern markets. The transit temperature of a precooled car averaged 45°F. the first day and 47°F. the first 4 days, as compared with 61 and 56°F., respectively, for the nonprecooled car. Refrigeration was used in both lots. Precooling results in a reduction in transit refrigeration costs and, if well done, assures a satisfactory condition on arrival. Precooling was accomplished by fans that circulated the air in the car through the ice bunkers, reversing the natural circulation.

RHUBARB

Rhubarb is grown for its large, thick leafstalks, or petioles, which are used for sauces and pies. It is used in the diet in the place of fruit. Since rhubarb is available early in the season, it is a popular article of food.

In the home garden, the rhubarb bed should be located on one side or at one end along with the other perennials so that it will not interfere with preparation of the remainder of the area. Commercially, it should be planted in a block by itself or with other perennials for convenience in tillage operations.

The rhubarb plant is a herbaceous perennial, the underground portion of which consists of large, fleshy, and somewhat woody rhizomes and a fibrous root system. The first leaves grow from the crown, and it is the petioles of these that are used for food. Later the flower stem develops and may grow to the height of 4 to 6 feet. This stem is hollow and has conspicuous nodes and relatively small leaves. The flowers are numerous in successive panicles, small, greenish white in color, on slender pedicels. Self-pollination within the individual flower does not occur because the anthers ripen and shed their pollen before the stigma is receptive (protandry). Pollen may fall from flowers on the upper part of the stem, which open later, to the stigmas of lower ones.

History and Taxonomy. Rhubarb is a native of the colder portions of Asia, probably Siberia. It was introduced into Europe about 1608 and was first grown in Italy. According to Sturtevant, the first mention of its use in America was in 1778, but by 1806 it was in common use.

Rhubarb belongs to the buckwheat family, Polygonaceae, and to the genus Rheum, which contains perhaps 25 so-called species. The common cultivated rhubarb belongs to the species *Rheum rhaponticum* L.

Climatic Requirements. The rhubarb crown and rhizomes are resistant to cold and to dry conditions. The plant thrives in regions where the crowns remain frozen all winter and where the soil remains dry throughout the summer, as in California. In regions where the summers are rainless or practically so and the winters are mild, rhubarb grows during the winter and early spring and is dormant during the summer. In other regions the plant is dormant during the winter and grows during the spring and summer. A dormant period does not seem to be essential as the plant grows throughout the year in the Imperial Valley of California when irrigated as water is needed. The vegetative parts of the plant are killed at 26 or 27°F. At relatively low temperatures for growth, the stalks develop the pink color, while at high temperatures the green color predominates.

Rhubarb does not grow well in regions where the mean temperature during summer is above 75°F. or the winter mean is much above 40°F. In the United States the crop is not well adapted to the Southern states, except at relatively high altitudes where the climatic conditions are similar to the regions much farther north.

Soils and Soil Preparation. Rhubarb is grown on many kinds of soils from sands to peats and clays but does best on rich, well-drained loams that are well supplied with organic matter. Where earliness is important a sand-loam soil is preferred. The plant is tolerant to soil acidity and grows well on soils that are slightly to moderately acid. However, it is grown on neutral to slightly alkaline soils in some areas.

The soil should be plowed to a good depth and thoroughly prepared before the crop is planted. If the soil is low in organic matter, it is desirable to grow a soil-improving crop to turn under in preparation for the rhubarb. Preparation should begin a year in advance of planting.

Manures and Fertilizers. Rhubarb requires large quantities of nutrients for good growth and large yields. Where manure is available on the farm it can be used to advantage at the rate of 20 tons to the acre on mineral soils. On peat or muck soils, manure is not important since such soils are high in organic matter. If manure is used, it is desirable to supplement it with superphosphate to supply 100 to 150 pounds of phosphorus (P_2O_5) and some readily available nitrogen. Since manure is not available in large quantities in many of the vegetable-growing regions, rhubarb growers must depend mainly on commercial fertilizers to supply nutrients and soil-improving crops for organic matter. A fertilizer approaching a 1-1-1 ratio should give good results on sandy-loam soils if applied at a rate to supply 100 to 150 pounds each of nitrogen, phosphorus (P_2O_5), and potash (K_2O) to the acre. On rich silt loams or clay loams the rate might be reduced.

The application of manure and fertilizers the first year should be made before the rhubarb is planted. If fresh, strawy manure is used, it should be applied before the land is plowed. Well-rotted manure may be applied either before or after plowing with a small quantity applied in the furrow and mixed with the soil before the plants are set. Fertilizer may be applied broadcast before the land is plowed, applied in the bottom of the furrow as the land is plowed, broadcast after plowing, or part by one of these methods and part in the furrow into which the plants are to be set.

In an established planting, the fertilizer usually is applied broadcast and mixed with the surface soil by harrowing or cultivating. In addition to the application of a complete fertilizer, many growers apply some readily available nitrogen carrier to supply 25 to 50 pounds of the element to the acre. This material is applied usually at the end of harvest. When manure is used on an established planting it is applied usually after growth has ceased and the leaves have died.

Planting. Rhubarb is propagated mainly by division of the crowns. In dividing, the crowns may be cut into as many pieces as there are good, strong buds. When old crowns are used, only the vigorous outer portions should be planted. In most regions where hard freezes occur planting usually is done in the spring. Where severe freezes do not occur and the autumn season is long, planting may be done to advantage during the autumn after the foliage has been killed by frost.

The pieces are planted at a depth at which the buds will be about 2 inches below the surface. Soil is filled in and firmed well around the roots, but the soil above and around the bud is left loose. The distance between plants in the row varies from 2 to 4 feet and the rows 4 to 6 feet, depending on the richness of the soil and the vigor of the varieties planted. In home gardens 2 by 4 feet is satisfactory.

Rhubarb grows readily from seed, but this method is not recommended because the seedlings do not come true to type of the parent plants. This method is used in the development of new varieties.

Cultivation and Care. Clean, shallow cultivation should be given as often as necessary to control weeds. Before growth starts, the bed should be harrowed thoroughly, but with care to avoid injuring the crowns. It is desirable to apply the fertilizer at this time so as to mix it with the surface soil by harrowing. In some sections of California the rows are bedded with soil as soon as growth starts. The leaves grow up through several inches of soil, resulting in longer stalks and a good pink color.

Varieties. There are relatively few varieties of rhubarb. The old varieties Victoria and Linnaeus are the best known, but some of the newer varieties have become popular because of their attractive red stalks. Among these are the Canadian varieties McDonald, Ruby, Valentine, and Sunrise. According to Robb (1952), McDonald, developed at McDonald College in Quebec, is best known of the Canadian varieties. These highly colored varieties are replacing the older Victoria to a considerable extent because the latter does not develop a red color in field plantings. In some regions, however, the Victoria is the principal variety for forcing since it produces large yields of good-size stalks with good color when grown in the dark. Other varieties are also used for forcing. Strawberry, Cherry Red, and other varieties are grown in California.

Diseases and Insects. The most serious disease of rhubarb is crown rot or foot rot caused by a fungus which attacks the base of the stalks, causing them to fall over. When the disease is severe it may kill the plants. Diseased plants should be removed and destroyed to lessen the chance of spreading the organism to healthy plants. Spraying the bases of healthy plants may give some protection. Preventive measures recommended are the use of disease-free plants and planting them on land which has not grown rhubarb for 3 or 4 years.

The rhubarb curculio, a rusty snout beetle, often causes damage to the plants by boring into the stalk, crowns, and roots. It also attacks wild dock. The insect may be kept in control by hand picking, by burning infested plants, by destroying dock plants growing in the vicinity after the beetles have laid their eggs, and by dusting the plants with ¾ per cent rotenone.

Harvesting. In regions with a fairly long growing season, rhubarb is harvested for a short period during the second year and for the full harvest period in the third year. Where the growing season is relatively short, the first harvest is made at the beginning of the third season. For best results over a period of years the harvest period should not be longer than 8 to 10 weeks. Harvesting both in spring and in late summer is not advised except when the bed is to be discontinued. Usually after 10 to 12 years the plants become so crowded and the leaf stalks so small that it does not pay to maintain the old bed.

In harvesting, the stalks are pulled (not cut) and the leaf blades are cut off. The stalks usually are washed before being packed for market. For local markets the stalks often are tied in bunches of 1 pound or more, but for shipping they are packed in bulk in boxes lined with paper.

Forcing. Rhubarb forcing on a commercial scale is important in many sections of the United States, in Canada, and in many parts of Europe. The practices vary in the various regions and with different growers, but the principles are similar. The term "forcing" as used here means the production of rhubarb stalks during the winter from large crowns that have been taken from the field into a forcing structure that can be heated. It is confined largely to regions where the climate is most suitable for field production of good vigorous crowns. When the plants are grown exclusively for forcing, 2- or 3-year-old ones are preferred, although some growers use 1-year-old crowns. When forcing is a side line to outdoor production, older roots often are used. Experimental results reported by Sayre (1927) indicate that 3-year-old roots produce larger yields than younger ones. Roots 4, 5, and 6 years old produced about the same yield as those that were 3 years old.

With any method of growing and forcing, the roots are dug or plowed out late in the fall and left outside until they are thoroughly frozen, after which they are ready for forcing. When the roots are left out of doors to freeze, they should be covered lightly with soil or with some other material to prevent too rapid evaporation of moisture. Freezing seems to be essential, but Sayre's results show that light freezing is better than severe freezing. He found that severe freezing (2 weeks at −10°F.) was injurious and reduced the yield, while brief thorough freezing, followed by a rest period, was as effective as freezing throughout the dormant period. On this point Sayre reports as follows:

Soon after digging in the fall, roots of various ages were frozen for 2 weeks in cold-storage chambers at 20°, 10°, and -10°F. Half of each lot of roots was then forced immediately. The remainder of each lot was kept dormant for an additional month before forcing. Regardless of the freezing temperature, the roots of each lot which received the longest rest period, produced a two- to threefold greater yield and make a more rapid growth than roots which had not been given the rest period. Severe freezing was not effective in shortening the rest period needed for maximum growth.

Rhubarb can be forced in house cellars, in hotbeds, in specially constructed forcing structures, or in any dark or semidark location where moderate temperatures can be maintained. Light is not essential or desirable. If windows are present in the structure they should be covered to exclude the light. If light is present, the stalks will grow toward it and become so curved as to render them unattractive and difficult to pack for market. When forced in darkness or semidarkness, the stems develop a rich pink or red color and good quality and the leaf blade expands very little. Heat for forcing may be supplied by stoves or by hot-water furnaces, the latter being more satisfactory than the former in commercial-forcing structures. A temperature of about 60°F. is considered very satisfactory. At higher temperatures the crop is earlier, but the color and quality are not so good as when forced at 60° or below. At 50°F. growth is too slow.

The crowns are placed on the floor of the forcing structure as close together as practicable and are covered with 2 or 3 inches of soil. The soil should be worked down between the clumps. It is desirable to leave narrow aisles at intervals of 5 or 6 feet for convenience in harvesting the stalks.

Forced rhubarb is harvested when it reaches the length of 18 inches or slightly more. The stalks are packed in attractive cartons, mainly holding 5 pounds of stalks. For transporting to market, 10 of these cartons are placed in heavier cardboard containers.

ARTICHOKE

The artichoke, or globe artichoke (*Cynara scolymus*), is a herbaceous perennial plant grown for its flower head or flower bud (Fig. 15.2). It is a coarse, thistlelike plant of the sunflower family, native of the Medi-

Fig. 15.2. Globe artichoke plant showing edible portion being harvested. (*Courtesy of Henry Washburn, University of California Agricultural Extension Service.*)

terranean region, and common in the wild form in southern Europe and in northern Africa.

The aboveground portion of the plant dies down each year, and the crowns of individual plants decay after a year's growth but are renewed by offshoots from the rootstocks. The flowers are borne terminally on the main stem and the laterals. The edible portion consists of bracts which are fleshy at the lower end. The plant grows to the height of 4 to 5 feet and bears several buds.

The artichoke will withstand temperatures several degrees below freezing. However, if freezing occurs during the growing period the plants will be injured or killed. For this reason the crop is grown mainly in regions having mild winters. Hot weather causes the buds to open, thereby reducing the tenderness of the edible portion. In the United States the crop is grown commercially mainly in three counties near the Coast, south of San Francisco, where the winters are mild and the summers are relatively cool.

The artichoke will grow on a wide range of soils, but it produces best on a deep, fertile, well-drained soil. According to Tavernetti (1954) it is important to keep the soil well supplied with organic matter. Many growers apply 10 to 12 tons of manure to the acre immediately after the stalks are cut in the summer. Nitrogenous fertilizer is applied at the rate of 60 to 85 pounds of nitrogen to the acre, as sulfate of ammonia, nitrate of soda, or other carrier, just before harvesting begins.

The acreage of artichokes grown in California has varied from 6,400 to about 10,400 acres over the period 1939–1952, with lowest yields in 1944 and 1945. The yield per acre has varied from 80 to 125 boxes of approximately 40 pounds, and the price from $1.70 per box in 1939 to $4 in 1951. The average annual farm value for the 5-year period 1948–1952 was $2,762,800.

Propagation. Vegetative propagation by means of suckers or offshoots from the old rootstock or by dividing the old crown into pieces with a stem and a piece of the crown. The latter method has the advantage of providing the new plant with more reserve food than the offshoot would contain. When offshoots are used, it is desirable to select them from plants of high productivity and other desirable characteristics. They are selected and removed when 12 to 18 inches high, and care is taken to save as much of the root system as possible.

Planting and Care of the Crop. In California planting is done during the fall and winter. The distance of planting varies, depending on the fertility of the soil and the methods of culture. Tavernetti states that the rows usually are 8 feet apart and the plants 6 feet apart in the row in California, although these distances vary somewhat. The plants are set 6 to 8 inches deep.

The crop in California is irrigated several times (usually three to five) during the growing period, the first irrigation being applied in early summer to start growth for fall harvest.

Clean cultivation is given as needed during the growing season. After each irrigation the soil between the rows is disked or harrowed to kill the weeds and to smooth the surface. After the last harvest in spring, the stems are cut off below the level of the ground. There are three different methods of disposing of the old stems and leaves. Some growers make silage of them, others place them in a dead furrow between the rows and cover them over, and still others allow them to dry and then burn them.

According to Tavernetti, maximum production occurs during the second and third years following planting. After about 4 years, it is usually found desirable to renew the planting.

Harvesting, Grading, Packing, and Marketing. Harvesting begins when the first buds reach maturity in the fall and continues until spring, the peak coming in early spring. The buds are harvested before they become loose and fibrous. The stem is cut 1 or 1½ inches below the base of the bud. The buds are separated into five or six sizes, usually by machine graders, then they are graded for quality. They are then packed in layers in paper-lined boxes of three sizes: large, 9¾ by 11 by 20⅝ inches; half size, 4⅞ by 11 by 20⅝; and a box used for local shipments 8½ by 14 by 22⅜. The large and half-size boxes are used for long-distance shipments. Large buds are the most desirable.

For long-distance shipments refrigerator cars are used with the usual icing. Most shipments are in mixed cars with lettuce and other vegetables.

JERUSALEM ARTICHOKE

The Jerusalem artichoke (*Helianthus tuberosus*) is a herbaceous perennial arising from fleshy rootstocks that bear oblong tubers. When grown under cultivation, it is handled as an annual. This plant belongs to the Compositae family and is a native of North America, where it was grown by the Indians at the time the early settlers arrived in the United States.

The Jerusalem artichoke has been recommended as feed for hogs and as a garden vegetable for human consumption but has not become popular for either purpose in the United States. One objection to it is that in digging it some of the tubers are left in the ground and the plants become weeds that are difficult to control.

An interesting characteristic of the Jerusalem artichoke is that the carbohydrate inulin is stored in the tubers. Inulin on hydrolysis yields fructose (levulose). Fructose, or fruit sugar, bears the same relation to inulin that glucose (dextrose) bears to starch. Fructose is of interest because of its reputed value in the diet of persons suffering from diabetes.

The Jerusalem artichoke is adapted for production over a wide range of climatic and soil conditions. It is grown in many parts of Europe, in parts of Asia, and in many of the temperate regions of the Southern Hemisphere. It can be grown in nearly all parts of the United States.

Culture. The Jerusalem artichoke will grow on all kinds of soils but does not thrive in a wet soil. It will grow better on poor soils than most crops. In France this crop is planted on soil too poor for potatoes or beets. Of course, larger yields are obtained when the crop is grown on good soil than when grown on poor soil. Sandy or sandy-loam soil has the advantage over heavier soils of not adhering to the tubers when they are dug.

Little is known about the fertilizer requirements of the Jerusalem artichoke, but results of French and German experiments indicate that potash is important. The fertilizer practice followed for potatoes would probably be satisfactory for this crop.

Planting may be done in the fall at harvest time or in the spring before growth begins. Boswell (1936) recommends planting as early in the spring as the soil can be satisfactorily worked. He suggests planting whole tubers or pieces of about 2 ounces in size and to the depth of about 4 inches. The usual distance of planting recommended is 2 feet apart in the row with the rows 3 to 3½ feet apart, except under very favorable conditions for growth where the distance between plants in the row might be as much as 4 feet and between rows 4, 5, or 6 feet.

Less cultivation is required for the Jerusalem artichoke than for most cultivated crops as the plants choke out weeds. Little or no hand weeding and hoeing are required.

Harvesting. The large woody tops of the plants must be cut and removed before the tubers can be harvested. The tubers grow in such a wide area of soil that the ordinary potato digger is not satisfactory for harvesting; when a plow or middlebuster is used, a relatively large proportion of the tubers is left in the ground. Hand digging with forks probably gets the largest percentage of tubers, but this is laborious and expensive.

Storage and Handling. The tuber of the Jerusalem artichoke does not develop a thick corky layer as does the potato tuber, but only a thin skin which is very easily injured. The thin skin allows moisture to be lost, thus causing the tuber to shrivel on exposure to the air so that in common storage the tubers cannot be kept for more than a few weeks. However, good sound disease-free tubers can be kept successfully for several months in cold storage at high humidity and a temperature of 32°F. They keep well in the soil also.

SEA KALE

Sea kale (*Crambe maritima*) is a hardy perennial of the Cruciferae, or mustard family, native of western Europe. It is grown for its young leaves and shoots, which are blanched with earth or with a sea-kale pot.

A large flower pot, with the hole in the bottom plugged, will serve the purpose of a regular kale pot.

Sea kale may be propagated by seeds or by cuttings. When seeds are used, they are planted in a well-prepared seedbed to the depth of about 1 inch. After the plants are well up, they are thinned to 5 or 6 inches apart in the row and given good cultivation and care during the season. The following spring they are taken up and planted in the permanent bed. When cuttings are used, pieces of roots 4 to 5 inches long are planted in their permanent location early in the spring, spaced 3 feet each way.

The bed should be well fertilized each year, either with manure or with chemicals. The care of the bed should be about the same as described for rhubarb. At the close of the season the dead leaves are cleared away and the crowns of the plants are covered with a mulch of compost or manure.

Shoots from plants which have made a strong growth may be harvested for a short period during the second season, but a full crop should not be taken until the plants are 3 years old. The young shoots are cut when 4 to 5 inches tall and used much in the same manner as asparagus. The cutting season usually lasts 3 to 6 weeks. This vegetable is popular in England but is little grown in the United States.

CHAPTER 16

Potherbs or Greens

Spinach   Kale
New Zealand spinach   Mustard
Orach   Collards
Chard   Dandelion

Potherbs, or greens, are grown for their foliage; their culture is relatively simple. Most of them will withstand freezing temperatures and are grown mainly in the cooler parts of the growing season. Chard and New Zealand spinach are exceptions; they are relatively tender and are grown during the summer in the North. Spinach is the only crop in the list that is grown on a large scale for shipment to distant markets and for canning and freezing.

To the plants listed many others might be added. Some crops used for greens such as turnips, beets, and sea kale are discussed in other chapters. Many wild plants such as dandelion, several species of docks, lamb's-quarters, wild cress, pokeweed, milkweed, and others are used as greens.

The need for green food is being greatly emphasized owing to the increase in knowledge of the value of essential minerals and vitamins, especially vitamin A, found in green plants.

SPINACH

Spinach (*Spinacia oleracea*) is the most important potherb, or greens, grown in the United States and has increased greatly in importance since about 1918. The commercial acreage in the important producing states has increased from an annual average of 18,139 acres in the period 1918–1922 to an average of 84,252 acres for the five years 1948–1952. The total acreage was less during the period 1948–1952 than in the 5 years 1938–1942 owing to a sharp reduction in spinach grown for the fresh market. The average annual acreage grown for processing increased from 6,285 in the period 1918–1922 to 33,396 for 1948–1952. The average annual farm value increased from $3,489,000 in 1918–1922 to $17,022,000 for the 5 years 1948–1952. The figures given for acreage and farm value include only the commercial spinach grown in 17 states in 1948–1952. Many other states grow some spinach for sale, and large numbers of home gardeners grow it for family use.

The leading states in acreage of spinach grown in 1952 were Texas with 23,000 acres; California, 11,200; Oklahoma, 6,800; Arkansas, 5,900; Pennsylvania, 5,400; New Jersey, 4,800; and New York, 4,100 acres. California was in the lead in the production of spinach for processing in 1952 and was followed by Texas, Arkansas, and Oklahoma (Fig. 16.1).

Fig. 16.1.   A large field of spinach near Crystal City, Tex.

Spinach is one of the important vegetables processed by freezing, with an estimated 91,464,000 pounds frozen in 1952.

Spinach is rich in vitamin A and contains appreciable quantities of ascorbic acid, riboflavin, and a small quantity of thiamine. It is also rich in iron and calcium, but the calcium is said to be unavailable owing to the fact that it unites with oxalic acid to form calcium oxalate.

Plant Characters. The spinach plant, soon after germination, develops a rosette of leaves from a much-shortened stem near the surface of the ground. When the plant reaches a certain size, under favorable conditions, the stem begins to elongate and lateral branches arise from the axils of the rosette leaves. Secondary lateral branches arise from the leaf axils of both the central and the lateral stems. The flower clusters are borne axially on both the larger stems and on the smaller branches. Rosa (1925) states that flowering usually begins on the middle portion of the larger stems and proceeds toward the base and the top. From 6 to 12 flowers develop in each cluster, but they do not all develop at the same rate.

While spinach usually is dioecious, occasionally monoecious plants are found. Rosa has described four types of plants with reference to sex expression: (1) extreme males, (2) vegetative males, (3) monoecious, and (4) females. The monoecious plants may be predominantly staminate, predominately pistillate, or purely pistillate early but with some staminate flowers later, or almost equally staminate and pistillate throughout the season.

Rosa's experimental results indicate that environmental influences have no effect on sex expression. In general culture the ratio of staminate and pistillate plants is 1:1. The male plant dies after flowering, while the female continues to develop and ripen its seed.

Climatic Requirements. Spinach thrives best during relatively cool weather and will withstand freezing better than most vegetable-crop plants. In regions having mild winters the crop is grown mostly during the winter and early spring, while in other regions it is grown both as a spring and as a fall crop. Spinach does not do well during hot weather. The length of day has a marked effect on its development. Garner and Allard (1920) found that lengthening the period of light artificially during the short days of late fall resulted in flowering within a few weeks. Plants from seed sown Nov. 1, when grown under artificial light for 6 hours, in addition to normal daylight, blossomed between Dec. 8 and 23, while those that had only daylight had no blossoms as late as Feb. 12.

Knott (1939) has shown that the photoperiodic response of spinach is altered by temperature. Thus he shows that plants of the Old Dominion variety that were grown at relatively low temperature (40 to 50°F. and 50 to 60°F.) for a month under the normal length of day of winter developed seedstalks earlier than those grown for the same length of time at 60 to 70°F., or 70 to 80°F., regardless of the subsequent temperature in which they were grown (Fig. 16.2). When plants were grown for a month at 40 to 50°F. under a 15-hour photoperiod and then moved to higher temperature ranges under the same day length, the higher the temperature to which the plants were subjected, the sooner did the seedstalks develop. The higher temperatures used were 50 to 60°F., 60 to 70°F., and 70 to 80°F. When grown under a 15-hour day, the optimum temperature range for seedstalk development was found to be 60 to 70°F.

The above results may explain why certain varieties go to seed when grown in the spring in the North and do not go to seed when planted in late summer. Spring-planted spinach is subjected to relatively low temperature early and then to rising temperature and increasing length of day. Spinach for fall harvest is planted in warm weather and makes most of its growth as the weather becomes cooler and the length of day gets shorter. It should be kept in mind, however, that there are variety and strain differences in regard to seedstalk development. The Virginia Savoy and Old Dominion shoot to seed quickly when planted in the spring in the North, while Long Standing Bloomsdale and others do not develop seedstalks so rapidly.

Soils and Soil Preparation. Spinach can be grown on any good soil, but sandy loams and mucks are better than heavier soils. Sandy loams are desirable where earliness is important in the spring as well as for fall and winter crops in some regions. Silt loams are good where earliness

Fig. 16.2. Old Dominion spinach plants grown during winter under normal length of day at 70 to 80°F. following treatments for 1 month at the following temperatures: left to right, 40 to 50°F., 50 to 60°F., 60 to 70°F., 70 to 80°F.

is of less importance than large yields. Muck soils are good also where earliness is not of great importance, as when the crop is grown for processing. When the spinach is grown on muck soil there is less grit in the processed product than when grown on mineral soils.

Good drainage is important especially where the crop is grown under irrigation or grown during the wettest part of the year in humid regions. In some areas, where the land is flat and not well drained, the land is bedded in low flat beds with space between the beds to ensure drainage. In some regions these beds are 5 to 6 feet wide with a space 18 to 24 inches between beds. Where furrow irrigation is used the beds are 18 to 24 inches wide with the furrow between the beds.

Soil Reaction. Spinach is known to be susceptible to injury by high acidity, or to conditions accompanying acidity, such as aluminum toxicity. Zimmerley (1926) reported results of experiments at Norfolk, Va., in which optimum growth was at soil reactions between pH 6.0 and 7.0. He found marked retardation in growth at lower pH than 5.5; Wessels (1932) reported similar results from experiments on a silt-loam soil on Long Island. In the Long Island experiments, the yield of spinach was less than half as much on plots with a reaction of pH 5.0 as on plots with pH 6.0 to 6.3. At Norfolk and on Long Island there was practically no growth at pH 4.5 and most of the plants died in the seedling stage. Burgess and Pember (1923) attribute the injurious effects of acid soils to aluminum toxicity rather than to the H-ion concentration in itself. Under some conditions chlorosis develops when spinach is grown on soils that are only slightly acid, neutral, or alkaline. McLean and Gilbert (1925) reported chlorosis on spinach grown as a spring crop in Rhode Island soils with reaction values between pH 6.2 and 6.9. Zimmerley also reported chlorosis of spinach in alkaline soils in Virginia, but states that none was observed where the crop was grown on soils more acid than pH 6.5. McLean and Gilbert attributed chlorosis to lack of available manganese on alkaline or slightly acid soils and were able to overcome this condition by spraying the plants with 0.004 per cent manganous sulfate solution. Zimmerley found that the use of manganous sulfate was effective in reducing chlorosis only during the early stages of the trouble. Where the entire plants were yellow, the treatment was of no apparent benefit.

Considering all the experimental data, it would seem that completely neutralizing the acidity is not desirable. On the other hand, where the soil is more acid than pH 5.5 (possibly 6.0) liming probably would prove beneficial.

Manures and Fertilizers. In most regions where spinach is grown on a large scale little fertilizer is used. Hawthorn (1932) reported that on the rich alluvial soils of southern Texas, growers rarely used fertilizers but were using new land that had not been impoverished by cropping. It is probable that with continued cropping it will be necessary to use fertilizer to maintain profitable production. Where manure is available on the farm or can be purchased at a low price, it may be used profitably on infertile mineral soils. If fresh strawy manure is used it is desirable to apply it for the crop preceding spinach or to plow it under well in advance of planting the spinach seed. When manure is not used, it is desirable to grow soil-improving crops to maintain the organic matter.

Commercial fertilizer is used in fairly large quantities in growing spinach in most parts of the United States, except in Texas and in California. If manure is not used, the fertilizer for sandy and sandy-loam soils should supply 100 to 125 pounds each of nitrogen, phosphorus (P_2O_5), and potash (K_2O). On silt loams and clay loams, both nitrogen and potash may be reduced. Where manure is used, the quantity of nitrogen and potash might be reduced by half. Many spinach growers apply all of the fertilizer after the crop is planted, making several applications. Zimmerley's results indicate that part of it should be applied before the crop is planted. From these results it would seem desirable to apply from one-half to two-thirds of the fertilizer before planting the crop and the remainder as top-dressing on sandy or sandy-loam soil. On heavier soils it would seem to be unnecessary to make more than one application.

Planting. Spinach is grown mainly as a winter crop in regions where winters are mild, as in parts of California, Arizona, and some of the areas of the Southern states. In such regions seed is planted at intervals during the fall and early winter. Where winters are severe, spinach seed is planted as early in the spring as soil and weather conditions become favorable for an early summer crop, and in late summer or early fall for fall harvest. In regions having relatively cool summers plantings are made for summer harvest also. Planting in the fall and overwintering are common in some regions where winters are not very severe but too cold to permit much growth until spring.

The rate of seeding varies greatly depending on the method of production and the distance between the rows. Hawthorn states that when the seed is sown broadcast on irrigated land in Texas the rate is 8 to 10 pounds to the acre, but when sown in rows the rate is 4 to 6 pounds. In many other regions, heavier rates of seeding are used, ranging from 15 to 30 pounds according to the spacing of the rows, which varies from 7 inches to about 24 inches apart. In the vicinity of Norfolk, Va., the rows are spaced about 10 inches, while in other regions the spacing is 12 to 15 inches between rows for hand cultivation or for special power cultivators.

In the home garden spinach seed is usually planted by hand, but in commercial plantings seed drills are used. Gang drills, four or more drills attached to a common frame, are used by growers in many sections.

Thinning. When spinach is grown on a large commercial scale, thinning is seldom practiced, but in some regions the plants are thinned to stand 4 to 5 inches apart in the row. Where thinning is not practiced, the spacing should be regulated by adjusting the rate of seeding. Thinning can be done readily by using a narrow, sharp hoe to cut out the plants. The main advantage derived from thinning is the development of large, uniform plants. The main disadvantage is the cost involved. In the home garden the common practice is to remove the largest plants as soon as they get large enough for use and to continue this operation until the plants have sufficient space for full development.

Cultivation and Chemical Weed Control. Weed control is very important because the spinach plant cannot compete well with weeds.

Harvesting is made more difficult where weeds are present. The weed problem is particularly serious in overwintered spinach. Clean, shallow cultivation, the use of a herbicide, such as Chloro IPC, or a combination of the two should be used.

Varieties. The varieties of spinach now being grown are not very different from those studied by Goff (1887) and by Kinney (1896). Kinney collected and studied all the available varieties. He classified them into four groups as follows:

Group 1. Norfolk or Bloomsdale
Group 2. Round-leaved
Group 3. Thick-leaved
Group 4. Prickly-seeded

Jones and Rosa (1928) reported tests of 121 varieties obtained from American and European sources and concluded that there are only five distinct varietal types, one of which they believed had been developed since Kinney had made his studies. Geise and Farley (1929) and Drewes (1932) also described the varieties and followed in a general way the classification given by Jones and Rosa. Geise and Farley classified varieties into two classes or groups: A, flat-leaved type, and B, savoy-leaved type. Each of these classes was subdivided into three groups as follows: I, Short Season Group; II, Long Standing Group; and III, Slow Growing Group. More recently Magruder *et al.* (1938) published a classification and description of the principal American varieties of spinach. This classification is as follows:

A. Leaves savoyed
   B. Leaves heavily savoyed
      C. Plants late seeding
         D. Leaves blue-green—Juliana
         D.D. Leaves dark green—Long Standing Bloomsdale
      C.C. Plants not late seeding
         D. Plants very early seeding—Virginia Savoy
         D.D. Plants medium-early seeding—Dark Green Bloomsdale
   B.B. Leaves medium-savoyed—Old Dominion
A.A. Leaves not savoyed (or slightly savoyed in cool weather)
   B. Plants early seeding
      C. Seeds prickly—Hollandia
      C.C. Seeds not prickly—Viroflay
   B.B. Plants not early seeding
      C. Seeds prickly—Amsterdam Giant
      C.C. Seeds not prickly
         D. Leaves blue-green—King of Denmark
         D.D. Leaves medium green—Nobel

The varieties of spinach studied by Magruder *et al.* were grown and described at Ithaca, N.Y. (2 years); Arlington, Va., and Beltsville, Md. (5 years and seven crops); Winter Haven, Tex. (three crops); and Davis, Calif. (five crops). Complete descriptions and brief characterizations of the important varieties are given by Magruder *et al.* Since new varieties come on the market from time to time and some of the old varieties are discarded, it does not seem worthwhile to describe them here.

Spinach Blight, or Yellows. This is a virus disease caused by the cucumber mosaic virus. It is very widespread and is serious in many areas. The virus is transmitted from several wild and cultivated host plants to spinach by aphids. It is most severe on fall and winter crops because of the build-up in other hosts during the summer.

Plants affected by the disease show a light yellowing and malformation of the young leaves in the early stages. In later stages the plants become completely yellowed, stunted, twisted, and the blade curves backward toward the base of the plant.

The most feasible means of control is to grow blight-resistant varieties such as Virginia Savoy and Old Dominion. The Virginia Savoy was developed in 1920 from a cross between Bloomsdale Savoy and a type obtained from Manchuria by F. N. Meyer. The Old Dominion was developed by selection following a cross of Virginia Savoy and King of Denmark. Both Virginia Savoy and Old Dominion are savoy varieties widely grown for the fresh market. While these two varieties are generally resistant, J. P. Fulton (1950) reported that a strain of cucumber virus 1 has been isolated in Arkansas to which both Virginia Savoy and Old Dominion are susceptible.

Downy Mildew. This disease, also known as blue mold, caused by *Peronospora effusa,* is one of the most serious diseases of spinach and is prevalent in most regions where the crop is grown. It develops in cool, moist weather and generally is most severe in coastal areas. The disease appears on the leaves of plants of any age and is first seen as large yellow spots or blotches. The affected parts finally decay or dry up, and the whole leaf dies. The underside of the leaf becomes covered with a fuzzy growth that is white at first and later becomes bluish purple.

Richards (1939) reported results of elaborate studies made on this disease. He found that 35 varieties of spinach tested were equally susceptible to the mildew. He stated that the most important source of the inoculum on Long Island was from diseased spinach plants; that the soil and the seed may be sources of the primary inoculum; but that their importance had not been determined. Richards suggested the isolation of the overwintered plants from the winter- and spring-planted spinach as the best control measure on Long Island. The use of fungicides as protectants and the selection of varieties for resistance to the mildew proved unsuccessful in his studies. Pound (1953) reported that a foreign introduction (P.I. 140467) carries a single dominant gene for immunity. The best hope for control seems to be the development of resistant varieties.

Correction of any unfavorable environmental conditions is important in the control of this disease. Good drainage, weed control, preventing crowding of the plants, and good fertilization are important.

Heterosporium Leaf Spot. This is an old disease and is found almost everywhere spinach is grown. The disease appears as small brown spots, which enlarge and multiply until so much of the leaf is affected that the remainder turns yellow and dies. Greenish-black mold appears in the spots on both surfaces of the leaf.

No definite control measures are recommended except to keep the plants in a thrifty growing condition by good cultural practices.

Other Diseases. In addition to the diseases mentioned, there are others that are of importance under some conditions. These include Cercospora leaf spot, anthracnose, fusarium wilt, rust, scab or black mold, smut, crown rot, damping-off, and root knot. Damping-off can be controlled by seed treatment. Seed treatment for damping-off and seed rot is generally recommended where these troubles are of importance. The treatments used disinfect the seed and give some protection to the sprout as it emerges. New materials come on the market from time to time and recommendations change; therefore it is not desirable to suggest specific treatments. Experiment stations and extension services can supply specific and up-to-date information on the best treatments.

Spinach Aphid (*Myzus persicae*). This insect is a pale-yellowish-green plant louse that often causes serious injury to the spinach crop. It injures by sucking the juice out of the leaves and also carries spinach blight from diseased to healthy plants. Since this insect lives largely on the underside of the leaves, it is very difficult to control by spraying.

Control of the aphid can be by dusting with 3 per cent nicotine dust, 1 per cent rotenone, 7 per cent parathion, or 1 per cent TEPP, provided the treatment is started while infestation is small and the dusting is well done. Parathion should not be used within 15 days of harvest. Spinach for processing must be completely free of aphids.

Beet Leaf Miner (*Pegomyia hyoscyami*). This insect is a serious pest of early spinach in many sections of the United States. For discussion see under Beet.

Harvesting and Handling. Spinach may be harvested from the time the plants have 5 or 6 leaves until just before the seedstalks develop. A larger yield is obtained when the plants are allowed to develop to full size than when harvested while they are small. They should be harvested before the seedstalk develops.

Spinach, for fresh market, is harvested usually by cutting the taproot just below the lowest leaves, using a sharp knife, a sharp hoe, or some other cutting implement. For processing the plants are cut off about an inch above the soil surface. Implements have been developed for both methods of harvesting. One type cuts the whole plant for market, and another cuts off the leaves for processing. When the latter method is used for spinach grown during short days more than one harvest can be made before seedstalks develop. Since Friedman, Lieberman, and Kauffman (1951) have shown that for prepackaging, "clip-topped" spinach is preferred by some packers, it would seem that the same method of harvesting might be used for market as for processing. They showed that less labor is required for packaging for clipped spinach than for the crown-cut product and that the former yielded more packages than the latter.

It is best not to cut the plants immediately after a rain or heavy dew because the leaves are crisp and break easily when wet. A slight wilting will prevent this breaking.

Yellowed and diseased leaves should be removed and the product handled carefully to prevent bruising or breaking the leaves and stems. Washing in tanks usually results in injury, but spraying the plants on moving belts does not have this disadvantage.

Spinach is packed for shipment in various types of containers, including the round bushel basket, hamper, and crate. For long hauls, crushed ice is placed in the container and shipment is made in refrigerator cars or trucks. As a rule the quantity of ice placed in the container is about equal to the weight of the spinach.

A considerable portion of the spinach sold in retail stores is prepackaged in bags made of transparent films which allow gas exchange but maintain high humidity by reducing evaporation of water.

NEW ZEALAND SPINACH

New Zealand spinach (*Tetragonia expansa*) is not a true spinach but belongs to a different family, Aizoaceae. The leaves resemble spinach leaves to some extent, and the product is used in the same way. The plants are much branched, spreading often 3 or 4 feet across, and grow to the height of 1 to 2 feet. The leaves are thick, dark green, and somewhat triangular in form. The seeds are enclosed in a hard rough pod.

New Zealand spinach thrives in hot weather when ordinary spinach will not grow satisfactorily. It is not seriously injured by the leaf miner and does not go to seed quickly. The tips of the branches are harvested for food, and since these do not come in contact with the soil, there is no sand or soil to be washed off and no waste in preparing for the table.

Culture. Seed may be planted in a greenhouse or hotbed during late winter. The plants should be pricked out while still small, preferably into pots, so that they can be set out later without disturbing the roots to any great extent. These plants should be set 2 to 3 feet apart in rows 3 to 4 feet apart, but only a few plants are required for a family of five. Commercially, the seed is sown in the open in rows very much like spinach, but more space must be given. New Zealand spinach is not so hardy as spinach; therefore it should be planted later in the spring.

Harvesting. When grown for home use, the tips of the branches, 3 to 4 inches long, are snipped off. This is continued throughout the season. When grown for market, a more common practice is to cut off the entire plant 2 or 3 inches from the surface of the ground. A bunch is grasped in one hand and is cut off with a large, sharp knife held in the other hand. Two, three, or more cuttings are made in this way. The product is handled in much the same way as spinach, for which it is a substitute. This main harvest period is during the summer when spinach is not available.

ORACH

Orach, or mountain spinach (*Atriplex hortensis*), has long been used as a kitchen-garden vegetable in Europe but is rarely grown in the United States, except in the Great Plains and intermountain regions, where it is grown in home gardens as a substitute for spinach. Babb and Kraus (1939) state that for the regions mentioned orach has several advantages over spinach, which shoots to seed before the plant makes sufficient growth to furnish an edible product. Orach is easily grown, is drought-resistant, and is tolerant to alkaline and saline soils, according to these investigators. They state that the plant continues to develop large tender leaves on the upper portion of the plant, thus supplying a continuous supply of greens throughout the growing season.

Orach belongs to the family Chenopodiaceae. Babb and Kraus describe four varieties as grown in the Great Plains area. These are Triumph, which grows to the height of 6 to 9 feet; Gelbe, 6 to 9 feet; Lee Giant, 7 to 10 feet; and Deep Blood Red, 4 to 6 feet. They state that the Triumph is the variety most widely grown in the Great Plains and intermountain regions.

The seed is planted in the open early in the spring in rows 18 to 24 inches apart and the plants thinned to stand 10 to 12 inches in the row. The plants are used while young and tender, and although they stand hot weather fairly well, they soon run to seed; therefore, for a continuous supply, successive plantings should be made at intervals of 2 weeks until summer weather arrives.

The general culture of orach is about the same as for spinach, for which it is a substitute.

CHARD

Chard, or Swiss chard (*Beta vulgaris* var. *cicla*), is a foliage beet which has been developed for its large, fleshy leafstalks and broad, crisp leaf blades. It is one of the best potherbs for summer use since it withstands hot weather better than most greens. The leaves are prepared for the table like spinach, while the leafstalks and midribs are often cooked and served like asparagus. Chard is not so rich in iron as spinach but is a good addition to the list of potherbs and deserves more general planting, especially in the home garden. It may be canned in the same manner as spinach.

Culture. Chard is easily grown. The plants may be started in the greenhouse or hotbed and transplanted to the open as soon as the danger of hard frosts is over, or the seed may be sown in the garden or field where the plants are to grow. The rows should be about 18 inches apart for hand cultivation and from 30 to 36 inches for tractor cultivators. When the plants are set out, they should be spaced 10 to 12 inches apart, and when seed is sown in the garden, the plants are at first thinned to 3 inches, and later when they begin to crowd they are thinned to 8 to 12 inches apart in the row. The plants removed to thin the rows may be used as greens.

A planting made in the spring will produce greens throughout the season until hard freezes occur, and with a little protection the plants will live throughout the winter. Any good garden soil is satisfactory for chard. Unless the soil is rich and well supplied with humus, a medium application of manure is desirable. Where manure is not available, a green-manure crop may be used to supply humus. In addition to manure an application of a little readily available nitrogen and about 500 pounds of superphosphate to the acre is advised. Where no manure is used, a complete fertilizer should be applied on most soils.

Chard is grown to some extent as a forcing crop in greenhouses.

Varieties. There are only a few varieties, the most important one being Lucullus, which has very large crumpled, dark-green leaves, with greenish-white leaf stems. Giant Perpetual has broad light-green leaves. Lyon, a new variety selected for its broad stem and midrib, is listed by some seedsmen. Large Ribbed White has broad, white stalks and white midrib. Rhubarb chard has dark-green, crumpled leaf blades and bright-crimson petioles, or leafstalks.

Harvesting. The usual method of harvesting for home use is to cut off the outer leaves 1 or 2 inches from the ground while they are still tender, using a large, sharp knife. Care should be taken to avoid injuring the bud. For market, a more common method of harvesting is to cut off all the leaves above the growing point in the center. Subsequent harvestings are made in the same way when the leaves reach marketable size. The leaves often are bunched and tied in preparation for market, and the product sold by the bunch or by the pound. Chard, however, is not an important market vegetable.

KALE

Kale (*Brassica oleracea* var. *acephala*) is a minor crop although it ranks high among the greens in nutritive value. It has a high content of vitamin A and contains appreciable contents of thiamine and ascorbic acid. It is an important crop in home gardens in many areas in the southern half of the United States. As a commercial crop it is of importance only in Virginia, mainly in the region around Norfolk, and it is only from this region that statistics of acreage, production, and farm value are available. In the period 1939–1952 the acreage varied from 2,100 to 3,100 acres; the yield from 260 to 490 bushels, of approximately 18 pounds; average annual production from 572,000 to 1,260,000 bushels; and the price per bushel has varied from 23 cents to $1.05 per bushel. The farm value in 1952 was $1,013,000.

Kale is hardy to cold, but does not thrive in hot weather, hence it is seldom grown as a summer crop, except where summers are cool.

Kale has been under cultivation for a very long time. It was known to the ancient Greeks. Several varieties were described by Cato, who lived about 200 B.C. It was known in the United States during the seventeenth century.

Many types of kale are known, but they all probably belong to the same species. The chief characteristics of all are that the plants do not form heads like cabbage or produce edible flowers like cauliflower and broccoli. Some are grown as ornamentals, being variously curled and of beautiful colors.

Soils and Fertilizers. Kale will thrive on any good garden soil, but a well-drained sandy loam is considered best. On flat land that is not naturally well drained the crop is sometimes planted in low flat beds with drainage between the beds.

Kale is a fairly heavy feeder, and unless grown on rich soil, it should be liberally fertilized with a complete fertilizer. On infertile sandy-loam soils the application of 100 pounds each of nitrogen and potash (K_2O) and 200 pounds of phosphorus (P_2O_5) to the acre should give good results. On heavier, more fertile soils the rate of application might be reduced by one-half.

Planting. Kale is grown as a fall, winter, and early-spring crop in the South, and the seed is planted in late summer and fall. In the North the crop is grown either in the fall or early spring. Seed for the fall crop is planted in July and August depending on the locality, elevation, etc. Spring planting should be done as early as the soil can be prepared.

Seed is sown with a drill, and the rows are spaced about 18 inches apart for hand cultivation and 24 to 30 inches apart for tractor culture. After the plants are well established, they are thinned to stand about 6 inches apart. When grown for home use, the plants removed in thinning are usually used as food.

Cultivation and Care. Clean cultivation is given kale, and the general care is about the same as for spinach.

Kale is attacked by the same insects as cabbage, especially by the false cabbage aphid (*Aphis pseudobrassicae* Davis), the true cabbage aphid (*A. brassicae* Linn.), the cabbage worm, the cabbage looper, and the harlequin cabbage bug. The same sprays suggested for the control of these insects on cabbage will control them on kale, but for successful kale spraying a specially rigged sprayer should be used. The nozzles should be near the ground and arranged in such a way that two of them spray the same row so that the material strikes the plants from the sides.

Varieties. The varieties of kale grown in the United States belong to two groups, Scotch and Siberian. The foilage of the former is grayish green in color and very curled and crumpled, while that of the Siberian is of a bluish-green color and curled, but not quite so much as the Scotch. Both dwarf and tall forms are grown, but the former is the more popular. The most common varieties are Dwarf Curled Scotch, or Norfolk, Early Curled Siberian, Tall Scotch, and Dwarf Green Curled.

Harvesting. For home use the leaves are often picked from the plant, while for market the entire plant is cut off near the ground with a large knife. The discolored and injured leaves are removed, and the plants packed for shipping without washing. Some of the commercial crop is prepackaged in bags of transparent films for the retail trade. The films permit gas exchange but maintain high humidity, thus preventing drying of the product.

MUSTARD

White mustard (*Brassica juncea*) is grown for salad and greens to some extent but has been replaced largely by spinach and kale. This plant is a hardy annual of the Cruciferae family. Seed is sown very early in the spring for spring use and in the fall for a winter crop. The plants go to seed quickly in the spring. The seed is sown thickly in drills 12 to 15 inches apart, and the plants thinned as they crowd in the row. The White London is one of the well-known varieties of this species.

On a good sandy-loam soil 50 to 75 pounds of nitrogen, 100 to 150 pounds of phosphorus, and 50 to 75 pounds of potash per acre should produce good results even without manure, provided the humus supply is maintained by turning under soil-improving crops. Where manure is used, an application of 25 to 30 pounds of nitrogen and about 80 pounds of phosphorus should be sufficient.

Giant Curled and Ostrich Plume are varieties of *B. Japonica* grown to some extent in the South. Both produce large curled leaves. The Ostrich Plume, or Giant Ostrich Plume, is the most important variety of mustard in some sections of the South.

Black mustard (*B. nigra*) is grown largely for its seed, which is made into the mustard of commerce.

COLLARDS

The collard (*B. oleracea* var. *acephala*) is an important green vegetable in Southern gardens and on Southern markets in the winter months. The edible portion is the green rosette of leaves, resembling cabbage leaves prior to heading (Fig. 16.3).

Fig. 16.3. Cross section of head of collard. (*Courtesy of J. C. Miller, La. Experiment Station.*)

The collard will withstand a greater range of temperature, both heat and cold, than any other vegetable crop grown in the South. Miller (1934) states that it will withstand 15°F. unless this temperature follows a period of warm weather.

There are two methods of planting the crop. One is to sow the seeds in cold frames or on row beds and to transplant the plants to the garden or field when they reach a height of 6 to 8 inches. The plants are spaced 18 to 24 inches apart in rows 3 to 3½ feet apart. The second method is o sow the seed in a well-prepared permanent row, thinning the plants to the desired spacing. The planting season in the coastal region of Louisiana is from July to November. In most interior regions of the South, planting is done in the spring.

The collard is grown on all kinds of soil, but sandy loams and silt loams are considered best. Soil preparation, fertilization, and cultivation recommended for the cabbage crop are satisfactory for collards.

Miller describes the harvesting and the preparation for market as follows:

There are three methods by which the collard is prepared for market. The first and the one most commonly used in the market-garden areas is to cut the mature head, or rosette. The rosette may be pulled together and tied with a string. The second method and the one most extensively used by the market gardeners and truck growers along the Gulf Coast is to cut the plants when they are about one-eighth to one-fourth their normal size and to tie them together into a bunch. This method of bunching lends itself to the use of smaller shipping containers, and the product also gives a better appearance on the market. The third method is to cut the lower large leaves of the plant and tie them into a bunch, weighing from 1½ to 2 pounds.

DANDELION

The wild dandelion is a great favorite for spring greens. For this purpose it is cut from meadows and lawns, where it is considered a noxious weed since it drives out grasses and other plants.

The dandelion has been improved in size and vigor by culture and is grown to a considerable extent as a potherb in Europe and in a small way in the United States. Some of the varieties or strains resemble endive. The cultivated dandelion has been developed from the wild species, *Taraxacum officinalis,* a member of the Compositae, or sunflower family.

Dandelion seed is usually sown in the place where the crop is to mature, although the plants may be started indoors and transplanted to the garden in the spring. The plants should stand 10 to 12 inches apart in the row with rows 15 to 18 inches apart for hand cultivation. A sandy or light loamy soil is preferred. The crop is usually harvested like spinach. The plants are sometimes blanched by tying the leaves together or by covering to exclude the light.

Dandelion plants are sometimes forced in hotbeds or in greenhouses for winter and early-spring markets.

CHAPTER 17

Salad Crops

Celery	Parsley
Lettuce	Chervil
Endive	Cress
Chicory	Water cress

Salad plants, in general, thrive best during the cooler parts of the growing season; to be of the highest quality their growth must be fairly rapid and continuous. Celery and lettuce are the only crops in this list that are grown on a large commercial scale, and they are found on the market throughout the year.

Salad crops are appreciated now more than ever because of the increase in knowledge of their value in the diet. They are especially valuable for the ash constituents and for their vitamin content, as well as for supplying bulk. These crops generally are eaten without cooking and are the main ones so consumed.

CELERY

Celery is second in importance of the salad crops in value and popularity, being exceeded only by lettuce. Until comparatively recent times celery was considered a luxury, but it is now a common article in the diet and is available throughout the year. A large part of the celery crop grown in the United States is consumed in the raw state, but considerable quantities are used in vegetable juices, soups, stews, and as a cooked vegetable. In England some celery is canned.

Statistics of Production. Celery production increased fairly consistently from 1918 to 1952. The average annual acreage, production, and farm value of celery grown commercially in the important producing states are shown in Table 17.1.

The leading states in acreage of celery grown in 1952 were California with 15,700 acres; Florida, 10,400; New York, 2,450; Michigan, 1,900; Colorado, 1,100; New Jersey, 1,100; and Ohio, 1,000 acres.

Table 17.1. Average Annual Acreage, Production, and Farm Value of Celery
Grown in Important States, 1918–1952
(*U.S. Dept. Agr. Statistical Bull.*, 1938 and *Agricultural Statistics*)

Years	Acres	Production, crates (000 omitted)	Farm value, (000 omitted)
1918–1927	19,803	5,366*	$10,861
1928–1937	33,855	9,146*	14,398
1938–1947	41,323	14,973†	38,758
1948–1952	37,972	22,397†	50,502

* Crates of approximately 90 pounds.
† Crates of approximately 60 pounds.

History and Taxonomy. Celery is a plant of marshy places, and according to Sturtevant its habitat extends from Sweden southward to Algeria, Egypt, Abyssinia, and in Asia even to the Caucasus, Baluchistan, and the mountains of India. It has been found growing wild in Tierra del Fuego, in California, and in New Zealand. The wild plant was probably used for medicinal purposes hundreds of years before it was used for food. There is no evidence that it was grown by the ancients as a food plant, but if it was planted at all it was for medicinal purposes. The first mention of its cultivation as a food plant was in 1623 in France. The first cultivated celery differed little from the wild plant.

Celery, *Apium graveolens,* is a biennial plant, although grown as an annual crop. Under some conditions the plant behaves as an annual, developing flowers and seeds during the first year, as mentioned under Premature Seeding. Celery belongs to the family Umbelliferae. The flowers are small, white, and borne in compound umbels among the leaves of the flower stalk, which grows to the height of 2 to 3 feet.

Climatic Requirements. Celery thrives best when the weather is relatively cool and with a moderate, well-distributed rainfall during the growing season. Of course, the crop can be, and is, grown in relatively dry regions by supplying water artificially. Even in so-called humid regions irrigation is used to advantage. Few crops suffer more than does celery from deficiency of water. Celery requires a relatively long growing season. Celery production is confined largely to regions having either a mild winter climate, as in parts of Florida and California, a relatively cool growing season during summer, or a long growing period in the fall. Some regions, influenced by large bodies of water, such as portions of New York, Michigan, and Ohio, have both a relatively cool growing season in summer and a long growing period in the fall. Other regions, such as the mountain valleys in Colorado and other states, pro- duce celery during the relatively cool summers.

Soils and Soil Preparation. A good well-drained muck or peat soil is considered almost ideal for celery, and a considerable part of the crop grown in the United States is produced on such soil. However, any good sandy loam or silt loam will produce a satisfactory crop if weather and moisture conditions are favorable and the crop is given good care. A sandy loam, well supplied with organic matter, is preferred to any other mineral soil. A heavy clay should be avoided.

Celery does not thrive well on a soil more acid than pH 5.5. Lime should be used where the soil has a higher acidity than mentioned, but it is not desirable to raise the pH above 6.7.

The soil for celery should be well prepared by plowing, harrowing, and dragging or rolling where there are clods or lumps. Compacting loose muck or peat soil by rolling or dragging is desirable. The time for plowing is determined to some extent by the previous use made of the land. If a soil-improving crop is grown just ahead of the celery, the land should be plowed long enough in advance of planting to allow the material turned under to become partly decomposed. At the time of planting the surface of the soil should be smooth and even. This is especially important where machine planters are used because it is im- portant that the plants be set at the proper depth, neither too deep nor too shallow. It is not possible to set them at a uniform depth where the surface is very uneven.

Fertilizers. Celery is a heavy feeder and a poor forager; therefore, on any but rich soils, large quantities of fertilizers are applied. Where manure is available on the farm, its use is recommended on mineral soils. If manure can be purchased at a moderate price, it would probably be desirable to use it. Results of experiments in Rhode Island on a fine sandy-loam soil, reported by Crandall (1937), indicate that stable ma- nure was superior to green manures in both yield and profit. The manure was priced at $10 a cord, or about $5 per ton. In these experiments, two vegetable crops were grown on the manured plots each year, while only one vegetable crop was grown on the green-manured plots. Yearly ap- plications of 16 tons of manure to the acre, supplemented with approxi- mately 1,000 pounds of a 4-8-6 fertilizer, or with 1,500 pounds of a 6-8-6, produced larger yields and greater profits than green manures and 1,500 pounds of 6-8-6 or the same quantity of 6-10-8 fertilizer.

The fertilizer practices recommended vary widely depending on the soil class, soil fertility, previous manure and fertilizer treatments, and the cropping system followed. For mineral soils, ratios approximating 1-1-1, 1-2-1, and 1-2-2 are recommended for many areas and the rate of appli- cation usually varies from 75 to 100 pounds to the acre of nitrogen. In

Florida the recommendation[1] for sandy soils is 5,000 pounds of 6-8-6 to the acre and 2,250 pounds for marl soils. On loam soils the application usually is less than for sands or sandy loams. In some areas, as in parts of California, there has been no response to applied phosphorus or potash, but great response to nitrogen. In other areas, nitrogen and phosphorus have increased yields and potash has not. In most celery-growing regions, side-dressing with 40 to 50 pounds of readily available nitrogen to the acre in one or two applications, in addition to the complete fertilizer, is recommended.

The fertilizers used on muck or peat soils usually contain a high proportion of potash, since most of such soils are low in this element. Some of these soils are low in phosphorus also. The fertilizer recommendations for celery grown on muck soil vary considerably because of difference in the stage of decomposition of the organic matter, difference in drainage, in pH, in the previous fertilizer practice, and in time the crop is grown. On poorly drained muck soil in Michigan a 1-4-4 ratio is recommended, while on a well-drained muck a ratio of 0-1-2 is suggested. In well-drained mucks nitrification is much more rapid than in a poorly drained one. Nitrification takes place more rapidly when the soil is warm than when it is cold, hence the difference in recommendation for early and late celery. The analyses used on muck soils in the various celery areas of the United States are 0-10-20, 0-9-27, 0-12-12, 0-12-18, 3-12-12, 3-9-18, and 5-10-15. The rates of application of nitrogen vary from none to as high as 100 pounds to the acre, of phosphorus from 120 to 240 pounds of P_2O_5 to the acre; potash from 120 to 300 pounds of K_2O to the acre. However, the highest rates of nitrogen and potash recommended are for close-culture celery (rows 18 inches apart).

Common salt (sodium chloride) is used at the rate of 500 to 1,000 pounds to the acre by some growers in Michigan. Experimental results reported by Harmer (1941) indicate that salt increased the yield on muck soils in Michigan, and he recommended its use. However, the use of salt is not a general practice in other celery-growing regions of the United States.

OTHER NUTRIENTS. Several nutrient elements, in addition to nitrogen, phosphorus, and potash, are essential to the growth of celery, and where there is a deficiency of any element it should be supplied. Some of the troubles listed as diseases are known to result from deficiencies of certain elements, as calcium, magnesium, and boron.

Calcium deficiency seems to result in the trouble known as "blackheart," which is called a physiological disease. This trouble occurs in most regions where celery is grown. It first shows as a tipburn on the young leaves and spreads quickly to most of the heart tissues. This is

[1] *Ext. Circ.* 121.

followed by drying, blackening, and in severe cases the killing of the entire heart. Results of experiments by Geraldson (1954) in Florida indicate that blackheart develops because of a deficiency of calcium in the young leaves. Chemical analyses showed that the calcium content of the young leaf tissue affected by blackheart was markedly lower than that of similar tissue of plants unaffected by the disorder. Results of field and greenhouse experiments showed that control was obtained by foliar application of calcium nitrate or calcium chloride. In Geraldson's experiments in the field treatments were begun 5 weeks before harvest and made weekly thereafter. Application was made directly to the heart area at the rate of 150 gallons to the acre with concentrations of 0.05, 0.10, and 0.25 molar. The soil in these experiments varied from muck to sandy muck with a pH of about 6.0 and containing a relatively large quantity of soluble calcium. Geraldson stated that the calcium chloride treatment at 0.25 concentration was slightly injurious to the older leaves when hit by the spray. In the field experiments, blackheart was increased markedly by application of sodium oxalate, sodium citrate, or magnesium sulfate. From these and other results, it seems that blackheart may be caused by a lack of balance, or antagonism between certain cations (sodium, potassium, and magnesium) and calcium.

In solution culture in the greenhouse, Geraldson reported that every plant dependent on the nutrient solution for its calcium supply was affected by blackheart regardless of the amount of calcium in the solution. Duplicate cultures receiving foliar application were free of blackheart.

Boron deficiency results in a trouble generally known as cracked stem, but also called brown checking and scratch. The symptoms are brown lesions with transverse cracks on the inner surface of the petioles and usually over the vascular bundles on the outer side of the petioles. The epidermis and adjoining tissue curl outward, followed by a dark-brown coloring of the exposed tissue, as shown in Fig. 17.1.

Experimental results reported by Purvis and Ruprecht (1937) in Florida showed that cracked stem can be controlled by the application of borax. They recommended 10 pounds of commercial borax to the acre applied in solution near the base of the plant. Satisfactory results have been obtained in New York and in other areas by applying borax in the dry form. It may be mixed with the fertilizer. On muck soils in New York 25 to 30 pounds of borax ($Na_2B_4O_7 \cdot 10H_2O$) per acre are recommended where it is known that cracked stem is a problem. On mineral soils less borax is required to control the disorder than on most muck soils. Lachance, Bertrand, and Perrault (1942) reported results of experiments in Quebec in which 15 pounds of borax to the acre gave good control and 5 pounds reduced cracked stem considerably. These experiments were conducted on an acid muck. More borax would be required to control cracked stem on a neutral or alkaline muck than on an acid one.

Some varieties, such as Utah 10-B and Utah Special, are more susceptible to cracked stem than some others. Utah 52-70, Utah 16-8, Utah 16-PC, and Summer Pascal have been shown to be less susceptible in field tests in California than are Utah 10-B and Utah Special.[2]

Fig. 17.1. Cracked stem of celery, a symptom of boron deficiency. (*Courtesy of A. G. Newhall, Cornell University Agricultural Experiment Station.*)

A chlorosis resulting from a deficiency of magnesium is common in many celery-growing regions of the United States. This chlorosis affects the yield and market quality of the crop. Pope and Munger (1953) and Davis and McCall (1953) have shown that there is a marked varietal difference in susceptibility, Utah 10-B being the most susceptible.

[2] *Calif. Agric.*, December, 1952.

Chemical analyses, reported by Pope and Munger, of four varieties grown on muck soil in New York showed a much higher content of magnesium in Tall Fordhook and Utah 15 than in Utah 10-B or Emerson Pascal. The latter two varieties developed chlorosis, and the other two did not. Results of field experiments in Michigan, reported by Davis and McCall, indicated that Utah 10-B is very susceptible, Utah Top Ten and Utah Ten Grand developed considerable chlorosis, whereas Summer Pascal seemed to be much less susceptible. Emerson Pascal and Utah and Utah 52-70 were intermediate. In the Michigan experiments magnesium applied to the soil at various rates failed to control the development of the chlorosis. However, spraying the plants with magnesium sulfate practically eliminated chlorosis. On the basis of these results, Davis and McCall made a tentative recommendation of 10 pounds of magnesium sulfate applied every 10 days throughout the growing season.

Inheritance studies made by Pope and Munger indicate that a single gene conditioned the utilization of magnesium and that the normal condition is dominant.

Growing Plants. Celery plants for an early crop in regions of short growing seasons are started in greenhouses, hotbeds, or cold frames. The late crop in such regions and most of the celery grown in mild climates, as in California and Florida, are started in outdoor seedbeds. However, direct seeding in the field where the crop is grown to maturity is practiced in some areas, as in the coastal region of California. The direct-seeding method is feasible only where irrigation is available, since it is necessary to keep the soil surface moist during germination and early growth of the seedlings.

The time of sowing seed is determined largely by the time the crop is desired for use. If the plants are not to be transplanted before being set in the field, 8 to 10 weeks is sufficient in most cases, although in some regions large plants are desired for setting out during hot weather, especially where furrow irrigation is used, in which case a longer period in the seedbed is required. In Florida, where celery is grown in the fall, winter, and spring, seed sowing begins in July and continues at intervals during the fall and winter. The chief problem there is to get the plants started during the hot weather of summer. Partial shading of the seedbed helps in bringing the seedlings through the hot weather. It is not desirable to sow any earlier than is necessary to get plants large enough for planting at the proper time. When the plants are transplanted once before being set in the field, 10 to 12 weeks should be allowed.

Soaking the seed, prior to planting, hastens germination and is practiced by some growers, especially for the late crop of celery. A common method is to moisten the seed in a pan or other receptacle and put it in a warm place where it is kept for several days or until the sprouts begin to appear. Another method is to place the seed between folds of cloth. The cloths are kept moist. Care must be taken to prevent the seeds from drying out as this would injure their vitality. As soon as the sprouts appear, the seeds should be planted because if the sprouts are allowed to grow too long there is danger of breaking them in planting. When ready for planting, the seed is spread out in an airy place to dry, but complete drying should not be allowed. Many growers mix the seed with ashes, dust, corn meal, or other substances to take up the moisture and to aid in distributing the seed.

Celery seed may be sown in rows or broadcast; both methods are used. Broadcasting gives a better distribution of plants, but sowing in rows gives an advantage in watering, thinning, and weeding. When plants are started in the greenhouse or hotbed, the seed is sown broadcast or in rows about 2 inches apart and covered with pieces of burlap or with about ⅛ inch of soil. Sometimes the burlap is used even when the seed is covered with soil. The burlap prevents washing the seed into piles when watering and also prevents rapid drying of the surface of the soil. As soon as the seedlings appear, the covering should be removed to prevent injury to the plants. When the seed is sown in outdoor beds, broadcasting is sometimes practiced and the beds are covered with burlap. Sowing in rows 12 to 18 inches apart with a seed drill is popular in some sections. By this method the plants can be kept well cultivated with hand cultivators. Thinning can be done more easily when the plants are grown in rows.

When the plants are grown in a greenhouse or hotbed and are transplanted prior to setting in the field, 2 ounces of seed of good germination is sufficient for 1 acre planted about 6 inches apart in rows 3 feet apart. When the plants are grown in outdoor beds and are taken direct from the seedbed to the field, ¼ pound of seed is the usual quantity, although some growers use more. Where the direct seeding method is followed, a pound or more seed is used per acre. Of course, the viability of the seed should be taken into consideration in determining the quantity to sow for a given area.

After the seed is sown, close attention should be given to watering before the seed germinates and while the plants are small. The surface soil should never be allowed to dry out until the plants become well established, but keeping the soil soaked should be avoided in order to reduce the chance of damping-off of the seedlings.

Plants for an early crop of celery are often transplanted 4 or 5 weeks after the seed is sown. They are set into flats or into the soil of the hotbed or greenhouse bed, spacing them 1½ by 1½ or 2 by 2 inches.

For a large portion of the celery acreage, the plants are taken direct from the seedbed to the field since transplanting is expensive and is of little advantage.

Setting the Plants. Before the plants are taken up for setting in the field, the plant bed should be watered, preferably a few hours in advance of lifting the plants. This is especially desirable with plants that have been transplanted, as the watering will make the soil adhere to the roots. It is desirable to set the plants when the soil is moist and the air rather humid, as there is less wilting of the foliage under these conditions than when the soil and air are dry. When it is necessary to

Fig. 17.2. Celery plants set on edge of irrigation furrow in California. Note large size of plants with most of foliage removed. (*Courtesy of J. E. Knott, University of California.*)

plant in dry soil, it is desirable to apply water at the time of setting. Machine planters are equipped to apply water in the small groove made to receive the plant; this is an excellent method as the roots come into direct contact with the moist soil. If plants are set by hand, water may be applied either before or after planting, preferably after, unless the soil is very dry. In irrigated regions the soil may be irrigated either before or after planting, but when the soil is very dry some wetting before setting the plants is desirable.

Plants generally are set on the level in unirrigated sections, but in some cases they are set below the level of the surface. In irrigated sections the plants sometimes are set on the side of the irrigation furrow (Fig. 17.2).

Trimming both the foliage and the roots is a common practice in some regions, especially where the plants are allowed to get large before being set in the field. The cutting back of the taproot is practiced only when the plants have been allowed to grow in the seedbed until ready for field planting. The object of this pruning is to stimulate the development of lateral roots. There is difference of opinion regarding the desirability of pruning off part of the foliage. Results of experiments reported by Kraus (1942) indicate that removing part of the foliage is more likely to result in loss than in gain. These experiments were conducted at Cheyenne, Wyo., for 2 years with four varieties, and although the differences in yield were small and in many instances not significant, the trend is in favor of not pruning. In no comparison were pruned plants significantly superior to unpruned ones, while the mean of all varieties showed a significant increase in weight at odds of 19:1 for the unpruned plants. When conditions are favorable for growth, removing part of the foliage is likely to delay development and possibly reduce yield.

Celery plants are spaced 4 to 10 inches apart in the row, with 6 to 8 inches being the most common distance. The space between the rows varies from 18 to 24 inches for close culture to as much as 5 feet if the celery is to be blanched with soil. A common distance is $2\frac{1}{2}$ to 3 feet between rows for blanching with paper or boards and $3\frac{1}{2}$ to 4 if soil is used for blanching. However, much of the celery is not blanched. Generally the closer the spacing in the row the larger is the yield of marketable celery. Davis (1950) has shown that for Cornell 19 and Utah 15 varieties, spacing the plants 4 inches apart in the row produced larger yields than those spaced 6 and 8 inches apart. The percentage of marketable celery was considerably higher with the 4-inch spacing than with wider spacing. These experiments were conducted on muck soil for 2 years with two rates of fertilizer application (1,500 and 2,500 pounds of 0-10-30 to the acre). With varieties that produce suckers freely, wide spacing increases the tendency, thus resulting in a greater percentage of trim, since the suckers are removed in preparation for packing.

Celery plants are set by hand and by machine. Machine planters do a very satisfactory job on level or nearly level surface, provided the soil surface is smooth. The plants must be set at a fairly definite depth, deep enough to prevent drying of the roots but not so deep as to cover the growing point. Plants that have been transplanted prior to setting in the field usually are taken up with a block of soil; such plants can be set by hand in a shallow furrow made with a small hand plow. Nontransplanted plants, when set by hand, are set in openings made with a small dibble or with the forefinger.

It is important to have fairly straight rows equal distances apart for convenience in planting with a machine and for spraying or dusting. The use of a line or marker is desirable. Where a machine planter is used the marker attached to the planter is used to mark the rows after the first one.

Cultivation. Good clean cultivation throughout the growing season is important, since weeds are troublesome on most soils used for celery growing. The celery plant grows slowly and is soon injured by weeds. Celery responded more to cultivation for the purpose of maintaining a soil mulch than any of the other crops grown in the cultivation experi-

Fig. 17.3. Roots of celery plant grown on sandy-loam soil at Ithaca, N.Y. Note limited distribution of roots.

ment at Ithaca, N.Y. Celery roots do not have so much spread as most other vegetable-crop plants, and it is thought that because of this less moisture is intercepted by celery roots than by roots of cabbage, for example. Figures 17.3 and 17.4 show the distribution of roots of full-grown celery plants in a sandy-loam soil at Ithaca, N.Y.

When the plants are small, hand cultivators or small tractor cultivators are used near the rows, and larger implements for cultivating the centers. When weeds are troublesome, knife or blade attachments generally are used, although small disks are employed to some extent when the plants are small. When the disks are used, the row is straddled with a two-wheel cultivator, one set of disks running on each side of the row. These disks throw the soil away from the plants and leave them on a little ridge, which is leveled down in hand weeding. The disks are employed only in preparation for hand weeding.

In all cultivation the surface soil should be left as level as possible; therefore it is desirable to use small-toothed cultivators. Shallow cultivation is desirable at all times, especially near the plants, as many of the roots grow near the surface and within 6 to 12 inches of the row.

Weeds can be controlled in the celery-plant beds by spraying with herbicidal oils listed in Chap. 9.

Fig. 17.4. Roots of celery plants uncovered by washing off the surface soil to the depth of 2 inches. Note the large number of coarse roots confined to a limited zone.

Blanching. The term blanching means the loss of green color in the petioles, or stalks, and is accomplished by excluding the light from them. Since it is known that the green of plants contains a higher vitamin A content than nongreen parts, the demand for blanched celery has decreased markedly. A considerable portion of the crop grown in the United States is harvested without blanching. When blanching is done the methods employed include the use of paper, boards, and soil. Paper has taken the place of boards in most regions because it requires much less labor to place in position and also because the first cost is less than with boards. When blanching is done in warm weather paper and boards are used almost exclusively, because celery banked with soil is likely to rot in hot weather. In fact, soil is used mainly to protect against freezing injury.

Two types of paper are used for blanching celery, ordinary building paper and a paper similar to heavy roofing paper but without the objectionable tar. The latter type is much more durable than the former, and if given the proper care, will last for several years. The paper is cut into strips 10 to 12 inches wide and is bought in rolls. In applying the paper to the celery, two rolls are used at a time, one on each side of the row. It is unrolled and set on edge against the celery plants and is held in place by wires bent in the shape of an inverted U, with each leg about 18 inches long. The wires are placed over the row with one leg on each side, and the ends are pushed into the soil to the depth of 6 or 8 inches.

Banking with soil is the most economical method. The soil is worked up to the plants gradually in order to avoid getting it into the center of the plant. The banking is usually done by means of a celery hiller, which pushes the soil against the plants. The wings of the hiller are adjustable so that the soil can be pushed to any desired height. As cold weather approaches, the soil is usually worked up to the tops of the plants.

Varieties. There are not many distinct varieties of celery grown in the United States, and not more than 10 or 12 are grown on a large scale. Green varieties have increased in importance since about 1920, and the yellow, or self-blanching, varieties have decreased in importance. The most important green varieties are Utah, of which there are several strains, Giant Pascal, Emerson Pascal, Summer Pascal, and Fordhook. The varieties, and strains of the same variety, differ in resistance to diseases and bolting (premature seeding), in seasonal adaptation, and in other characters. All of the green varieties have resistance to fusarium yellows. Emerson Pascal is resistant to early and late blights and to fusarium yellows but has a tendency to bolt. Summer Pascal, Utah 52-70, and Tall Fordhook are resistant to brown spot. Utah 10-B is more subject to a chlorosis resulting from magnesium deficiency and to cracked stem, a symptom of boron deficiency, than other strains and varieties.

Some of the important yellow, or self-blanching, varieties are Michigan Improved Golden, Cornell 19, Supreme Golden, Golden Plume, or Wonderful, Golden No. 15, Golden Self-blanching, and Cornell 619. These varieties and strains of some of them differ markedly in resistance to diseases and in many other characteristics. Cornell 19 and Cornell 619 have thick petioles of the Utah and Pascal types, are resistant to fusarium yellows, but have a tendency to bolt. According to Newhall (1953), Cornell 19 is susceptible to brown spot. Michigan Golden, Michigan Improved Golden, Supreme Golden, and several other varieties are resistant to fusarium yellows.

Since no list of varieties is up to date longer than a year, no recommendation is made.

Premature Seeding of Celery. Premature seeding, or "bolting," of celery plants frequently results in large loss in many regions, especially in the North in summer and in Florida during late winter and spring. The plants develop seedstalks before they reach marketable size. Figure 17.5 shows a field of celery grown on muck soil at Williamson, N.Y., in 1924. In that year celery growers in New York suffered severe financial losses because of premature seeding. Again in 1945 losses were very heavy in New York and in other states, some fields being a total loss.

Fig. 17.5. Premature seeding of late celery at Williamson, N.Y. Over 60 per cent of these plants produced seedstalks and were worthless for market.

Celery growers and others have attributed premature seeding to various factors, such as poor seed, especially seed lacking in vitality; early sowing of the seed; check in growth due to freezing, to drouth, to crowding, to disease, and other things; and to exposure of the plants to relatively low temperature, but not freezing, for a considerable period. Results of experiments in Montana, as reported by Starring (1924), and in New York, reported by Thompson (1929 and 1933), show that exposure of the plants to relatively low temperature (40 to 50°F.) is the main factor involved in premature seeding. In the experiments carried on at Ithaca, N.Y., checking growth of the plants by freezing, by allowing them to become crowded in the transplanting flats, and by allowing the soil to get dry, delayed seedstalk development and resulted in a lower percentage of seeders. The experiments on the effect of checking growth by drying were carried on for 4 years. The method used was to withhold water from some lots of plants for 10 days to 2 weeks before they were set in the field. The soil was allowed to become dry enough to permit the plants to wilt. At the time of planting these plants were yellowish green in color and considerably checked in growth as compared to the check plants, which were kept well watered.

In the 4 years during which these experiments were carried on, there was not a single instance in which drying hastened seeding or increased the percentage of seeders. Starring obtained similar results.

Exposing celery plants to relatively low temperatures (averaging 40 to 50°F.) for periods of from 10 to 30 days results in premature seeding when the plants are grown subsequently under conditions favorable for growth. Thompson (1933) reported results of experiments carried on for 3 years in which the plants that were subjected to 40 to 50°F. for 10 days or longer always, produced some seedstalks in the field before they were half grown. Similar plants (check) kept in the greenhouse at 60 to 70°F. until set in the field produced no seedstalks. The data from these experiments are shown in Table 17.2.

Table 17.2. Effect of Exposure to Relatively Low Temperature (40 to 50°F.) for 10, 20, and 30 Days on Subsequent Development of the Seedstalk in Celery

Preliminary temperature treatment, °F.	Number of plants	Per cent of seedstalks
Check, 60–70	550	0.00
10 days, 40–50	550	7.63
20 days, 40–50	550	44.36
30 days, 40–50	550	74.00

In experiments conducted entirely in the greenhouse for several years, celery plants that were grown continuously at 60 to 70°F. (medium temperature) produced no seedstalks; similar plants grown for 15 or 30 days at 40 to 50°F. or at 50 to 60°F. produced 100 per cent seedstalks in the greenhouse held at 60 to 70°F. (Figs. 17.6 and 17.7). The only difference in treatment of the check and cold-treated plants was that the latter were subjected for 15 and 30 days to the lower temperature 6 to 8 weeks after the seed was sown. Both before and after the cold treatment, the cold-treated plants were grown at 60 to 70°F. Plants grown at 50 to 60°F. following the preliminary temperature treatments went to seed 100 per cent regardless of the previous treatment; however, the previous low-temperature treatment hastened seedstalk development. Plants grown at relatively high temperature (70 to 80°F.) following the preliminary treatment produced no seedstalks, regardless of the previous treatment as shown in Table 17.3. The high temperature seems to nullify the effect of the low-temperature treatment given previously.

Fig. 17.6. Celery plants showing effect of temperature on growth. Left, plants grown at 60 to 70°F. for 2½ months from seed sowing; right, at 60 to 70°F. for 1½ months and at 40 to 50°F. for 1 month. All those grown at 40 to 50°F. went to seed in the field.

Fig. 17.7. Effects of relatively low temperature on flowering of celery. Plants in full flower were grown at 40 to 50°F. for a month prior to setting them in the field; those not in blossom were grown at 60 to 70°F. prior to field planting.

The evidence clearly points to the danger of growing celery plants in a cool greenhouse and to subjecting them to low temperature (40 to 50°F.) in the cold frame for 2 weeks. The practice of *hardening off* plants in the cold frame is a dangerous one and is not necessary. Hardening can be accomplished by withholding water. The earlier the plants

Table 17.3. Effect of Exposure to Relatively Low Temperature for 15 and 30 Days on Subsequent Development of Seedstalks of Celery under Three Ranges of Temperature

Preliminary treatment, °F.	Number of plants	Per cent of seedstalks on dates given			
		Mar. 20	Apr. 3	Apr. 25	May 8
In medium-temperature house					
Check, 60–70	20	0.00	0.00	0.00	0.00
15 days, 50–60	20	0.00	0.00	65.00	100.00
30 days, 50–60	20	0.00	0.00	65.00	100.00
15 days, 40–50	20	0.00	85.00	100.00	100.00
30 days, 40–50	20	25.00	45.00	100.00	100.00
30 days, 70–80	20	0.00	0.00	0.00	0.00
In cool house					
Check, 60–70	20	0.00	0.00	100.00	100.00
15 days, 50–60	20	5.00	65.00	100.00	100.00
30 days, 50–60	20	10.00	60.00	100.00	100.00
15 days, 40–50	20	88.00	100.00	100.00	100.00
30 days, 40–50	20	80.00	100.00	100.00	100.00
In warm house					
Check, 60–70	10	0.00	0.00	0.00	0.00
15 days, 40–50	10	0.00	0.00	0.00	0.00
30 days, 40–50	10	0.00	0.00	0.00	0.00

are started, the more likely they are to go to seed the first season, especially when they are grown in what is considered a cool greenhouse.

Heredity is involved in premature seeding as is indicated by variety and strain differences with reference to seedstalk development. Some strains produce few or no seedstalks even under conditions favorable for their development, while others produce 100 per cent under the same conditions. However, the conditions under which the plants are grown, especially during the early stage of growth, determine whether or not variety and strain differences in seedstalk development appear.

Most of the commercial crop of celery in the important producing states is grown from plants started in outdoor seedbeds with little or no protection against cold. If these plants go through a period when the temperature averages 50 to 55°F. for 2 weeks or more, or about 40 to 45°F. for a week or 10 days, losses from premature seeding may be expected to be heavy. In the Northern states early sowing of seed in open beds is likely to result in premature seeding. In the main celery-growing areas of New York sowings made before the middle of April are likely to bolt to seed to some extent every year, and to a large extent when the temperature in the latter part of April and in May is relatively low. Normally, plants grown from seed sown the last of April or the first part of May do not develop seedstalks.

Attempts have been made to control bolting by the use of growth regulators. Wittwer, Jackson, and Walton (1954) studied the effect of maleic hydrazide on seedstalk development on Cornell 19, a variety that is subject to premature seeding. They found that concentrations of 50 to 100 parts per million applied before cold induction to young plants having 8 to 10 leaves induced flowering in many plants which otherwise would have remained vegetative. Concentrations of 250 parts per million resulted in death of young plants. Higher concentrations (500 to 1,000 parts per million) applied at much later stages of growth (37 true leaves) did not kill the plants but retarded development of seedstalks.

Pithiness. Pithiness, or *hollow stalk*, has been ascribed to check in growth, to too rapid growth, and to poor seed, especially to seed produced on pithy plants. Sandsten and White (1902) and Austin and White (1904) presented evidence to show that pithiness is an inherited character. Emsweller (1932) stated that there are two types of pithiness: one in which the entire plant is pithy even when very young, and the other in which the outer petioles become pithy when the plant approaches maturity. Emsweller's evidence indicates that the former type is inherited, and he states that it is dependent on a single dominant gene. Since the solid-petiole condition is recessive, it is a simple matter to establish nonpithy strains. By removing pithy plants from the celery-seed field, the inherited type of pithiness could be eliminated in a short time.

Diseases. Celery is subject to a large number of diseases caused by fungi, bacteria, nematodes, and viruses. Some diseases are widespread and very destructive, others are more limited in distribution but destructive, and still others are serious under some conditions. Among the most widely distributed are the early and late blights.

EARLY BLIGHT. The fungus causing this disease is *Cercospora apii.* The name early blight is somewhat misleading since in some regions it appears later than septoria blight and bacterial blight. The organism may be seed-borne and hence occurs almost everywhere celery is grown. It requires hot weather for rapid development and is checked by temperatures below 40°F. The disease appears first on the leaves as small circular, yellowish-brown spots. These spots enlarge rapidly under favorable conditions, and in a few days they have a light-brown central area, gradually turning to dark brown surrounded by a band of yellow. It attacks leaves in all stages of growth but is most prevalent on the older leaves.

Treatment of fresh seed to kill the pathogen is one of the control measures recommended. Newhall (1953) suggested hot-water treatment for 30 minutes at 118 to 120°F.; a dip in formaldehyde solution (1 to 300) for 3 hours at room temperature; a preliminary soak in tepid water for 30 minutes followed by a dip in mercury bichloride solution (1:1,000) for 5 minutes and rinsing for 15 minutes in water. The hot-water treatment is considered the best. Dusting or spraying seedbeds with a copper fungicide is an economical method of delaying the development of the blight in the field. Field treatment to control this disease varies considerably depending on climate, on the extent of local experimental work, and on other factors. Various kinds of copper compounds are used as dusts or sprays, including Bordeaux mixture and copper-lime dusts and other dust formulations. So many materials are in use that it is not feasible to make specific recommendations that would be generally applicable. The use of blight-resistant varieties is the most economical means of control. The Emerson Pascal is fairly resistant to both early and late blight and is highly resistant to fusarium yellows.

LATE BLIGHT. This disease is caused by the fungus *Septoria apii* var. *graveolentis* and occurs in all countries where celery is grown. The fungus is seed-borne and also lives on the debris from a previous crop. The disease may start in the seedbed where it forms small circular water-soaked spots on the leaves. A little later the spots turn nearly black and become filled with black dots, which are the fruiting bodies of the fungus. It can attack any part of the plant above ground. The disease develops most rapidly in cool, wet seasons and is most serious on the late crop in the Northern part of the United States.

The control measures for late blight are similar to those for early blight. Seed over 2 years old is likely to be free of the organism, and such seed is used by some celery growers. However, unless the seed has been stored in good storage, the germination would be very low, or nil. Emerson Pascal is resistant to this disease.

BACTERIAL LEAF SPOT. This is a bacterial disease caused by a soil-inhabiting bacterium *Pseudomonas apii*. The disease appears as small circular reddish-brown spots with pale-yellow borders. It can be distinguished from late blight by the absence of black fruiting bodies. The disease develops most rapidly in hot, humid weather.

Control measures for this disease are similar to those used for the early blight except the seed treatment. The bacterium is not seed-borne.

FUSARIUM YELLOWS. In 1937 Nelson, Coons, and Cochran described two forms of the pathogen, I and II, to which they gave the name

Fusarium apii n.sp. for form I and *F. apii* var. *pallidum* for form II. A third form has been found, but its identity seems not to have been determined. Stunting of the plant, vascular discoloration, and rotting of the crown and roots are common to all three forms. The fungus lives in the soil for many years and accumulates as celery is grown on the same land year after year.

Growing of yellows-resistant strains or varieties is the only satisfactory way of preventing losses from this disease. Most, if not all, of the dark-green varieties, such as Giant Pascal, Utah, and others are fairly resistant. Resistant self-blanching, or yellow, varieties include Michigan Improved Golden, Cornell 19, Cornell 619, Emerson Pascal, Golden Pascal, Florida Golden, and several others that have varying degrees of resistance.

PHOMA ROOT ROT. The fungus that causes this disease is *Phoma apiicola,* which also attacks carrots, parsnip, parsley, and caraway. It may attack the plants in the seedbed, where it causes stunting, yellowing of the outer leaves, and rotting of the roots. The disease usually starts at the base of the stems, and the tissues turn bluish green but gradually become dark brown. The fungus causes rot in storage also.

No satisfactory control measures have been devised for this disease. Long rotations, deep plowing to bury the fruiting bodies, and sterilization, or changing the soil in the seedbed, aid in keeping the disease in check. Storage at 32°F. helps to hold back the development of decay.

BROWN ROT. This is a fungus disease, caused by *Cephalosporium apii,* and was found in Colorado in 1943. Smith and Ramsey (1951) described the chief symptoms of brown spot as irregular tan to brown shallow lesions on any of the aboveground parts of the plant. The lesions often are so numerous that they coalesce to form a brown streak extending the full length of the petiole. Some distortion of the mature petiole may occur.

No thoroughly satisfactory control measures have been developed. According to Newhall (1953) growers in New York failed to get good control with either a low-soluble copper or with a liquid Dithane spray applied as for blight control. Some varieties apparently are resistant. These include Utah 52-70, Utah 15, Utah 16, and Tall Fordhook.

VIRUS DISEASES. Newhall states that there are at least nine virus diseases of celery, three or four of which are widespread and cause heavy losses. Most of the viruses have several wild and cultivated host plants. Aphids are the most common carriers (vectors), but thrips carry spotted wilt and leaf hoppers carry virus yellows.

Cucumber mosaic virus is widespread in the United States and causes heavy losses in some cases. The early symptoms of this disease is a grayish cast and some mottling of the inner leaves. Later the plants are stunted, and some of the leaflets are fernlike. A closely related virus causes Southern celery mosaic that is established in Florida, Cuba, Puerto Rico and occurs in some of the Northern states.

Western celery mosaic is present in California and Colorado. It resembles Southern celery mosaic, except that leaf mottling is usually followed by spotting. This virus seems to be restricted to the members of the Umbellifereae family and mainly cultivated species.

Spotted wilt occurs mainly in the cool coastal fog belt of California where a large number of vegetables are attacked by the virus.

Celery virus yellows is caused by the aster yellows virus which is common also on carrots and lettuce. This disease should not be confused with fusarium, which is caused by a fungus in the soil. The symptoms on celery are shortening, twisting, yellowing, and some mottling of the inner leaves and petioles. Usually there is stunting and a general yellowing of the foliage.

Control of the virus diseases includes elimination of the wild host plants near the seedbeds, control of perennial weeds along ditch banks, roads, and fence rows, and destruction of the insect carriers where feasible. Spraying and dusting to control the insect vectors have not always been successful, especially where large numbers migrate to the celery field and are not killed before they have inoculated the plants at the first feeding. Development of resistant strains or varieties of celery is the best solution.

OTHER DISEASES. Celery is subject to several other diseases including pink rot (*Sclerotinia sclerotiorum*), several species of nematodes, black crown rot (*Centrospora acerina*), damping-off (*Pythium* sp.), rhizoctonia crater spot, a bacterial soft rot (*Erwinia caratovora*), and perhaps others.

Insects. While celery is attacked by a large number of insects it is seldom that most of them cause serious losses. However, under some conditions any of them may cause considerable injury. In many celery-growing areas the carrot rust fly and tarnished plant bug are most likely to be very injurious. Others that cause losses in some areas under some conditions are aphids, flea beetles, mole crickets, springtails, army worms, wireworms, green-celery worm, celery leaf tier, celery looper, celery caterpillar, thrips, red spider mite, and perhaps others. Wilson and Hayslip (1951) listed and described the insects that are injurious to celery in Florida, including all of those mentioned above, except carrot rust fly. Only carrot rust fly and tarnished plant bug are discussed here.

CARROT RUST FLY. This insect is an imported one, being first noticed as injurious to carrots in Canada in 1885. Since that time it has spread through the Northern part of the United States.

The larva, or maggot, attacks celery, carrot, and parsnip, eating off the small roots and burrowing into the edible roots of the carrot and parsnip. The adult is a small shining dark-green fly, and the larva is a slender, straw-colored maggot about $\frac{3}{10}$ inch long.

Celery seedbeds may be protected by screening with cheesecloth during the period when the flies are active. This period varies from region to region and from year to year in the same region. In western New York the flies are active from about May 25 to June 10. Screening the seedbed would be of no value where the plants are set before the flies become active. Where screening of the seedbed would give no protection, 1 pound of pure flake naphthalene spread over 100 square feet of bed surface will give protection as it is an effective repellent of the flies. This treatment should be given as soon as the flies begin to emerge and repeated once or twice a week apart. Other insecticides, such as chlordane and parathion, may prove effective.

TARNISHED PLANT BUG. This is a sucking insect that feeds on a large number of plants. The main injury to celery results from the feeding of the adult bugs, which puncture the stalk, especially at the joints, and cause a blackening of the tissue. The injury is known by celery growers as black joint.

The adult is a brownish bug about $\frac{1}{5}$ inch long, mottled with various shades of red and yellow-brown spots. The insect hibernates as an adult in leaves and other trash. They emerge in the spring, and the female inserts her eggs in the green tissue of her food plants, sometimes celery plants. When eggs are deposited in celery plants the larvae cause serious injury to the hearts of the plants.

DDT in either dust or spray form will give control, but a health hazard might be involved if the insecticide was applied a short time before harvesting the crop. It should not be used on celery within about 25 days of harvest.

Harvesting. There is no definite stage of maturity at which celery must be harvested to be of satisfactory quality. If harvested before the plants reach full size, the yield is lower than when allowed to complete growth, but the price received for the early-harvested crop may more than compensate for the lower yield.

In harvesting celery, the plants are cut off below the surface soil with a large knife or with various types of home-made cutting implements. A large part of the crop grown in the United States is cut by hand because it is difficult to cut off the plants at a uniform depth by any other method. Various kinds of cutting implements and machines have been used, but none has been very satisfactory because of the difficulty of regulating the depth at which the plants are cut where the soil surface is very uneven or varies much in compaction. If the plants are cut too low, hand trimming is necessary, and if cut too high, there is shattering or dropping of the outer leaves.

Preparation for Market. The preparation for market includes stripping to remove suckers and diseased and damaged leaves, washing, grading, packing, and precooling. All of these operations, except precooling, may be done in the field, or they may be done in packing houses.

When celery is to be shipped without washing, it is stripped, graded, and packed in the field. If it is to be washed before shipping, it may be put in field crates and hauled to the packing house where it is stripped,

Fig. 17.8. Assembly in use in Florida for preparing celery for market. All preparation is done as the machine moves slowly through the field. (*Courtesy of G. J. Stout, University of Florida.*)

washed, graded, and packed, or all of these operations may be done in the field in a specially designed assembly. A packing house on wheels has been developed in Florida (Fig. 17.8) and is used for preparing for market a large part of the celery crop grown in that state. The celery is cut by hand and placed on moving belts which convey the bunches past a cutter which cuts them to the desired length (usually 16 inches), then on to the main floor or platform. The celery is washed, graded, packed, and the packages closed for shipment to market. This field packing house moves through the field at slow speed, propelled by an automobile engine. A truck, towed by a cable attached to the rear of the machine, brings empty containers and hauls away the packed crates. About 65 persons are employed for one machine, and as many as 26 rows of celery are harvested at a time as the machine moves through the field. It is claimed that this method of preparing the celery for market results in large savings, as compared with the packing-house method.

Celery is graded to some extent in all producing areas of the United States, but in some sections the grading is not so well done as it should be. The U. S. Department of Agriculture has formulated grades of celery based on market quality, including size and other factors. Some of the states have established grades also, and in most cases they conform to the U.S. grades. Grade specifications are changed from time to time and for this reason are not given here.

A large part of the celery crop shipped from the important producing centers to market is clipped to 16 inches in length and packed with tops and butts reversed in alternate layers. This clipping reduces transportation and handling costs as compared with celery packed with full foliage. Celery prepared in this way requires little or no trimming when it reaches the market. However, celery packed flat, as mentioned, is more susceptible to damage from pressure than celery packed upright.

According to Carey (1950) the crate most commonly used for clipped celery has become virtually standard in all important producing regions. Some of these crates are wire-bound, and some are nailed with some variation in inside dimensions, but generally $9\frac{3}{4}$ by 16 by 20 inches. The crates used for celery that is not clipped vary somewhat in dimensions with the producing areas. Most of the crates in use are much smaller than those formerly used and are termed "half-crate," usually 10 or 11 inches in width, about 20 inches long, and mainly about 20 inches in depth.

The importance of rapid cooling of celery soon after it is harvested is recognized, and most of the crop to be shipped long distances is precooled before it is loaded. The important thing is to remove field heat and to get the temperature down to refrigeration temperatures as soon as feasible. Various methods of precooling have been devised to accomplish these objectives. One method of precooling followed in some areas is to immerse the celery in water at a temperature a little above freezing for a sufficient length of time to lower the temperature to the degree desired. Another method is to place the packed crates of celery in precooling rooms where the cooling is done by cold air blasts. Where cold air is used for precooling it is necessary to spray the celery with water to prevent wilting.

Prepackaging celery is practiced to some extent in all producing regions. The number and size of stalks and the kind of shipping container used vary considerably. Film bags, film wraps, and trays overwrapped with film are in use to some extent. When the stalks are completely covered, the film must permit the movement of air and gases in order to prevent anaerobic respiration. In some cases, celery for nearby markets is tied into bunches of 12 stalks and handled without packing in containers. This method is satisfactory for truck hauling to nearby retail outlets, where there is very little handling.

Storage. Commercial storage of celery for long periods of time is not as important as it was formerly, because it is available from producing areas during most of the year. It is stored mainly for short periods in regions where late celery must be harvested before freezing weather arrives in the fall and at other times when there is likely to be a glut on the market.

Various methods of storage are in use including: (1) trenching in the field, (2) storing in pits, and (3) storing in cold-storage warehouses. Trenching in the field is practiced mainly in the fall when there is danger of freezing before the crop can be harvested and usually for only a short period of time. By this method a trench is opened with a plow and the loose soil in the bottom is shoveled out. Several rows of celery are packed in each trench with the stalks standing upright. When the trenching is done to protect the celery against freezing for a short time, soil is thrown against and over the stalks with a plow. For longer periods of storage, 6 weeks or more, boards are set against the sides of the trench and the celery is placed between them. Soil is banked against the sides of the trench, and a covering of boards is placed over the top. A layer of straw or other material is placed over the boards, and over this a layer of soil to prevent the material from being blown away. As the weather gets cold, more soil is added to protect the celery against freezing. Another method of covering the trench is to nail boards together in the form of a V and invert them over the trenched celery. The boards are banked with soil as needed to prevent the celery from freezing. These methods of storing celery for any considerable period are in use mainly by market gardeners who supply local markets and by the home gardener.

Storage in a cold-storage warehouse is the most satisfactory since it is the only method in which temperature and humidity can be controlled. Other advantages of cold storage are: (1) less labor is required than in the other methods; (2) it is more convenient, as the warehouses are equipped with elevators, trucks, and other facilities for handling the celery; (3) the celery can be shipped to market regardless of the weather, which is not true of the field type of storage. It is unsafe to remove celery from field storage when the temperature is very low because of the danger of freezing, and besides it is disagreeable work under such conditions.

Most authorities recommend a temperature of 32°F. for the celery storage room, and most managers of storage warehouses aim to maintain this temperature. This is a safe recommendation since there is considerable variation in temperature in different parts of the storage room in most storage houses, owing to inadequate air circulation. The temperature is lowest usually near the floor and near the walls and highest near the ceiling. It should be borne in mind, however, that when the air is at 32°F., the temperature of the celery, especially in the center of the crate, is higher and also that celery does not freeze at the freezing point of water.

Celery in storage, even at an air temperature of 32°F., is active. During the early part of the storage period normal ripening processes are going on, and later there is a breaking down of the cells which is followed by decay. Corbett and Thompson (1925) showed that changes take place in the cell walls and that there is translocation of sugars and other products from the outer stems to the inner ones. Microchemical studies made at weekly intervals during storage indicate a marked change in the pectic compounds of the middle lamella. The more resistant pectic compounds change to less-resistant ones, and these changes are correlated with the observed changes in the celery.

Chemical analyses showed marked changes in sugars and in nitrogen. Both reducing and total sugars showed a marked decline in the leaf blades from harvest time to the end of storage. This decrease was accompanied by an increase in the petioles until toward the end of storage when there was a marked decline. Soluble nitrogen increased in both the leaf blades and petioles until toward the end of storage when there was a marked decrease in the blades and a slight decrease in the petioles. Insoluble nitrogen was high in the blades at harvest time and, in general, decreased from then to the end of storage. At low temperature all these changes take place slowly and increase as the temperature is raised.

LETTUCE

Lettuce is the most popular of the salad crops, being grown in nearly all home gardens and by large numbers of commercial growers. In 1952, the farm value of the commercial crop was exceeded only by potatoes and tomatoes of the vegetables grown in the United States. While a large part of the commercial production is centered in California and Arizona, it is grown for market in many states and is available throughout the year.

Statistics of Production. The average annual acreage, production, and farm value of lettuce grown commercially in the important producing states of the United States from 1918 to 1952 are given in Table 17.4.

Acreage, production, and farm value have increased greatly since the 1918–1927 period, and the farm value increased much more than acreage and production. California is the leading state in lettuce pro-

Table 17.4. Estimated Average Annual Acreage, Production, and Farm Value
of Lettuce Grown in the United States 1918–1952
(*Agricultural Statistics*)

Years	Acres	Production, crates* (000 omitted)	Farm value (000 omitted)
1918–1927	58,887	11,158	$ 17,110
1928–1937	154,316	19,457	29,242
1938–1947	163,829	26,485	63,658
1948–1952	209,702	36,678	114,701

* Equivalent Western crate (approximately 70 pounds).

duction, accounting for a little over 60 per cent of the acreage in 1952
with 128,600 acres. Arizona was second with 27,900 acres. Other states
producing over 2,000 acres are Texas, 11,700 acres; New Jersey, 5,300;
Colorado, 5,000; New York, 4,500; Florida and Washington, 2,200 acres
each. As with other crops, the figures given do not include the lettuce
grown on a very small scale by market gardeners nor that grown in home
gardens.

History and Taxonomy. Lettuce is probably a native of Europe and
Asia and has been in cultivation at least 2,500 years. It is mentioned
frequently by ancient writers, some as far back as 500 B.C.

Cultivated lettuce *Lactuca sativa* is related to the wild lettuce *L.
scariola,* a common weed in the United States. The two cross readily and
are considered by some botanists as belonging to the same species.
Lettuce is an annual and belongs to the Compositae, or sunflower family.

There are four distinct types of lettuce grown in the United States.
These are known as head; cutting, or leaf; cos, or romaine; and asparagus, or stem, lettuce. The four types are recognized as subspecies or
botanical varieties and are known under the following names: head,
variety *capitata;* cutting, or leaf, variety *crispa;* cos, or romaine, variety
longifolia; asparagus lettuce, variety *asparagina.* There are two classes
of head lettuce known as crisphead and butterhead.

Climatic Requirements. Lettuce thrives best in a relatively cool
growing season with monthly mean temperature of 55 to 60°F. It is
grown in the Southern part of the United States, in the Imperial Valley
of California, and in Arizona mainly in winter. In areas having a mild
winter climate and cool summers, as the Salinas Valley of California,
lettuce is grown during a large part of the year. This general region, the
coastal area of Washington, and some of the valleys at high altitude in a
few of the Western states produce a large part of the summer supply of
lettuce marketed in the United States. These regions have relatively
cool summers and grow the crop under irrigation.

Madariaga and Knott (1951) showed that the length of time from planting to harvest varied from 70 to 150 days. They found that it took longer to grow a crop in the Salinas Valley when planted in November and December than when planted later, with a shortening of the time to April. The temperature and length of day probably are the main factors, but they do not seem to be the only ones involved. It is possible that the minimum temperature of 40°F. used by Madariaga and Knott in their calculations is too high. However, they found that the degree-day summations multiplied by the average length of days were fairly consistent for plantings made from March to August in the Salinas Valley area.

Soils and Soil Preparation. Lettuce is grown on many kinds of soils from clay loams to sandy loams and muck or peat. It reaches its highest development on sandy loams and silt loams well supplied with organic matter and on a good well-drained muck or peat soil. Where earliness is important a sandy loam is preferred because it warms up earlier than other soils. Where earliness is not important silt loams and muck are preferred.

Lettuce does not grow well on mineral soils that are strongly acid, but it is not desirable to completely neutralize the acidity by liming. Hester, Parker, and Zimmerly (1936) reported results of an experiment on a Sassafras loam soil in Virginia in which the yield increased as the acidity decreased from pH 5.0 to 6.5. At pH 7.0 the yield was less than at pH 5.8, 6.0, or 6.5, probably because lime renders unavailable some essential element such as manganese or iron, since chlorosis developed. Lettuce is grown satisfactorily on natural alkaline soils in some regions, but it is not desirable to use lime to bring the reaction to neutral, or alkaline. It is usually desirable, however, to use lime on mineral soils more acid than pH 6.0.

The soil for lettuce should be well drained but retentive of moisture. Thorough preparation to obtain a good seedbed is important. The surface should be smoothed with a smoothing harrow or drag and be free of clods or lumps since it is difficult to sow the seed where the surface is lumpy and uneven. On loose muck soil a drag or roller usually is used to compact the surface before planting. Where furrow irrigation is used, the land is bedded into low flat beds (4 to 8 or 10 inches) with irrigation ditches between them. The width of the beds varies considerably, but a common width is 18 to 20 inches, with similar space between them. With beds of this width two rows usually are planted on each bed.

Fertilizers. The lettuce plant is a poor forager with a small root system, therefore the surface soil should be well supplied with nutrients. The soil should have a good supply of organic matter also. When lettuce is grown on mineral soils, manure or soil-improving crops should be used to maintain the soil in good physical condition. Where manure is available on the farm or can be purchased at a moderate price, it may be used to advantage on mineral soils but should be supplemented with some commercial fertilizer. Applications of 10 to 15 tons of stable manure supplemented with 50 pounds each of nitrogen and potash and 180 pounds of phosphorus should produce good results even on an infertile soil. The manure will benefit the crop, or crops, following the lettuce. When soil-improving crops alone are used to maintain the organic-matter supply, more nutrients are needed than where manure is used. On sandy and sandy-loam soils without manure, 75 to 100 pounds of nitrogen and 150 to 200 pounds each of phosphorus and potash should give good results. On silt loam and clay loam 50 pounds each of nitrogen and potash and 100 to 150 pounds of phosphorus should supply the needs of the lettuce crop.

Fertilizer practice on muck soils differs considerably from that on mineral soils. On newly cleared mucks with a favorable reaction nitrogen usually is not needed, but both phosphorus and potash are required in considerable quantities. On such soils an application of 100 pounds of phosphorus and 150 pounds of potash should give good results. On muck soils that have been cropped and well fertilized for 10 years or longer a complete fertilizer to supply about 25 pounds of nitrogen and 75 to 100 pounds each of the other two nutrients should give good results.

In many cases, especially on mineral soils, it is desirable to apply extra nitrogen as a side-dressing during the growing season, using a readily available form to supply 25 or 30 pounds of actual nitrogen. The aim should be to maintain a steady growth of the plants.

In addition to nitrogen, phosphorus, and potash, it is necessary under some conditions to supply other elements such as boron, manganese, magnesium, and copper. The quantities of these required for good growth vary greatly, depending on the character of the soil, soil reaction, and other factors.

Growing Plants for Transplanting. For an early crop of lettuce in regions where the growing season is short, the seed is sown in a greenhouse or hotbed several weeks before time for planting in the field. The usual practice is to sow the seed 6 to 8 weeks in advance of field planting and to transplant the seedlings into flats, spacing them 1½ by 1½ or 2 by 2 inches apart. Before setting the plants in the field they are given a hardening treatment for a period of a week or 10 days. Some growers follow the practice of cutting off some of the foliage at the time of setting the plants in the field, but results of experiments reported by Kraus (1942) indicate that this is not a good practice. The removal of part of the foliage delays the growth of the plant.

Planting in the Field. Hardened plants and seeds may be planted as soon as hard freezes are over. In regions where hard freezes do not occur, but where the summers are hot, as in Arizona, in the Imperial Valley of California, and in the milder sections of the South, lettuce is grown during the winter and seed is planted in the fall and early winter. In the Salinas-Watsonville district of California the cool summers and mild winters make it possible to mature lettuce throughout the period from the latter part of March to late December. In this region planting is done in late winter and at intervals through the spring and summer. Lettuce is grown in summer also in the Puget Sound region of Washington and at high elevations in Colorado and some of the other Western states. In most other sections of the United States, planting is done as early in the spring as possible for an early-summer crop and in mid-summer or later for a fall crop.

Lettuce seed usually does not germinate well at high temperatures (above 30°C.). Old seed will germinate at a higher temperature than will fresh seed. Several workers have shown that moist lettuce seed may go into dormancy when exposed to high temperature in the dark, as when planted. Shuck (1934) found that fresh seed failed to germinate at 20°C. unless given a pretreatment and that exposure of moistened seed to light or to low temperature will break dormancy. Exposing moist seed to chilling at 4 to 6°C. for 3 to 5 days results in breaking dormancy. Shuck (1934), Thompson (1938), Barton (1939), and Griffiths (1942) have shown that, if the early stages of germination are initiated at low temperatures, growth is uninhibited at high temperatures. Thus Barton found that the seed germinated at 30 to 35°C. after pretreatment. It is common practice of many growers to chill lettuce seed to be planted in warm soil by placing it between folds of moistened cloth in a refrigerator or on blocks of ice. This prevents the seed from going into dormancy when planted or breaks dormancy in case the seed is dormant. The pretreated seed may be dried for planting if the sprout has not emerged from the seed coat.

Commercially, the seed is sown with drills—either single drills operated by hand or gang seeders, with two, three, four, or more drills drawn mostly by tractors. With rows spaced 14 to 18 inches apart, 1½ to 2 pounds of seed should be sufficient to plant an acre; for rows spaced farther apart less seed is required. As soon as the plants are well established, they are thinned to stand from 10 to 18 inches apart, the closer spacing being allowed for small-growing varieties and the wider spacing for large-growing lettuce. The thinning should not be delayed or crowding will produce weak spindling plants. In some cases, the plants removed in thinning are transplanted to other beds, but it is doubtful if this is an economical practice in commercial plantings. The taking up and resetting of the plants results in checking growth, thus delaying maturity as compared with those not disturbed.

Where plants are set out, the spacing is about the same as is given plants grown from seed sown in the field. The plants usually are taken up with a block of soil and are planted by hand in a shallow trench or furrow since machine planters are not adapted to such planting.

Cultivation and Care. Shallow cultivation to control weeds is very important for lettuce as the plants cannot compete successfully with weeds. The root system is small, and many of the roots are near the surface, therefore deep cultivation is likely to be detrimental. When weeds are troublesome, the knife or blade attachments of cultivators are better than the cultivator teeth. The blade attachments cut off the weeds below the surface of the soil and leave a thin mulch, without injuring the roots. Some hand weeding or hoeing usually is necessary to control weeds between plants in the row.

In desert areas, where there is little or no rainfall, as in the Imperial Valley of California and in Arizona, lettuce is grown entirely under irrigation. In other areas where there is little or no rain for several months, the crop grown during this period is produced under irrigation also. Irrigation practice varies considerably under the conditions mentioned. According to Veihmeyer and Holland (1949) the number of irrigations may be as many as 6 to 8, or as few as 2 or 3 on crops receiving no rainfall. They suggest that summer- and fall-maturing lettuce in the Monterey Bay region of California be irrigated three times: (1) at the time of planting, to germinate the seed, (2) at the time of thinning, and (3) 30 days after thinning. In other areas with higher temperature and drier atmosphere more frequent irrigation may be necessary. In many humid regions irrigation is important to supplement rainfall.

Varieties. According to Thompson (1951) there are about 150 distinct varieties, of which 20 or 25 are commercially important. There are, however, more than 1,100 names, owing to the fact that some varieties are known under many different names. Tracy (1904), in his classification of lettuce, recognized over 100 distinct varieties, many of which are still listed in the seed catalogues. Tracy classified the varieties into three general classes, with subclasses, as follows:

Class I. Butter varieties
    Subclass I.   Cabbage-heading varieties
    Subclass II.   Bunching varieties
Class II. Crisp varieties
    Subclass I.   Cabbage-heading varieties
    Subclass II.   Bunching varieties

Class III. Cos varieties

Subclass I.   Spatulate-leaved varieties

Subclass II.   Lanceolate-leaved varieties

Subclass III. Lobed-leaved varieties

Thompson divides the varieties into five general classes: crisphead; butterhead; cos, or romaine; leaf, or bunching; and stem.

The most important commercial varieties are in the crisphead class (Fig. 17.9), of which there are many, and new ones are added from

FIG. 17.9. Great Lakes, a popular variety of the crisphead type of lettuce. (*Courtesy of Associated Seed Growers, Inc.*)

time to time, but old ones are discarded so that the number that are important does not increase appreciably. Among the best known names of the crisphead varieties are New York and Imperial. New York 515 is the most important of the New York varieties. The Imperials of importance are Imperial 44, 152, 456 (also called Cornell 456), 615, and 847. Great Lakes and Pennlake are other important varieties of the crisphead type. There are several strains of Great Lake designated by numbers 407, 428, 6238, 97145, and A36. Premier is a named strain.

Big Boston (Fig. 17.10), White Boston, May King, Salamander, and Wayahead are the best-known varieties of the butterhead type. White Boston is the only variety that is grown to any considerable extent, having replaced Big Boston. The butterhead varieties are of relatively little importance commercially because they do not stand up as well in shipping and handling as do the varieties of the crisphead type.

Fig. 17.10. A good head of White Boston lettuce, a variety of the butterhead type. (*Courtesy of Associated Seed Growers, Inc.*)

Fig. 17.11. Three varieties of leaf lettuce. Foreground, Oakleaf; center, Salad Bowl; rear, Slobolt. (*Courtesy of Joseph Harris Seed Co.*)

Black-seeded Simpson, Early Curled Simpson, Grand Rapids, and Slobolt are the main varieties of leaf, or bunching, lettuce (Fig. 17.11). This type is the most important for home gardens as it can be grown where the temperature is too high for head lettuce. Leaf lettuce is the type most commonly grown in greenhouses, and strains of the Grand Rapids are most popular for this purpose.

Of the cos type (Fig. 17.12) there are two varieties known as Paris White (White Cos) and Dark Green. While the total acreage of the

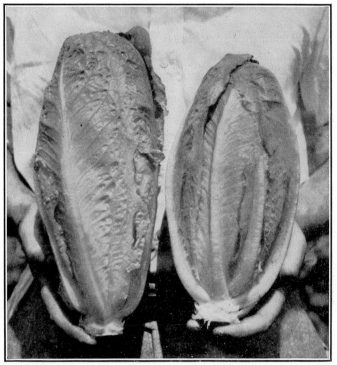

Fig. 17.12. Two varieties of cos lettuce. Left, Eiffel Tower; right, White Paris. (*Courtesy of Associated Seed Growers, Inc.*)

cos type is small it is of importance in some areas where it is grown for nearby markets.

Celtuce is a large-leaved, thick-stemmed lettuce that is slow to shoot to seed. It was introduced as "celery lettuce" and is grown for the thick stem which is eaten either raw or cooked. It has not become very popular in the United States. The leaves are edible, but are inferior to the leaves of the other types.

Descriptions of the types and varieties mentioned are given by Thompson (1951).

Diseases. Lettuce is subject to a large number of diseases, but only a few of them cause serious losses under most conditions. Most of them are difficult to control since the nature of the lettuce plant makes it difficult to apply the common fungicides. The known diseases include sclerotinia drop, botrytis rot, bottom rot, downy mildew, slime, or bacterial, rot, mosaic, aster yellows, big vein, brown blight, redheart, tipburn, and several others of minor importance. Only a few of the most important are discussed here. For a good discussion of the most important lettuce diseases in the United States, including descriptions and control measures, see Bohn (1953).

SCLEROTINIA DROP. This disease, caused by soil-inhabiting fungi, *Sclerotinia sclerotiorum* and *S. minor*, is found in practically all parts of the United States and causes severe losses in some areas. The organisms attack many other vegetable plants and can persist in the soil for a long time.

This disease usually begins on the stem near the ground and spreads both upward and downward. Plants attacked by it show a characteristic drooping or dropping of the leaves. The attack of the fungus cuts off the water supply to the leaves when the petioles are invaded, and this results in wilting and a dropping of the leaves. The parasite rapidly ascends the stem and kills the leaves. Under moist conditions the fungus produces a white mycelial growth on the foliage. In this growth appear small black sclerotia.

Control measures consist of crop rotation of 3 or more years using nonsusceptible crops such as corn, other cereals, onions, and beets; frequent shallow cultivation to keep the soil surface dry; and dusting with a fungicide containing 7 per cent metallic copper.

BOTTOM ROT. The organism causing this disease is now known as *Rhizoctonia solani* Kuhn. The fungus causes damping-off of seedlings as well as other diseases on many host plants. On lettuce plants in the field the first parts affected are the leaves that touch the ground. Two characteristic symptoms are the rusty, slightly sunken lesions on the petioles and midribs and the slimy brown rot on the leaf blade. The disease may spread throughout the head. Later the tissue dries up, leaving a black mummified plant.

The parasite lives in the soil on growing plants and on plant refuse. It develops rapidly under moist, warm environment.

Control measures recommended include: (1) long rotation with crops such as sweet corn, potatoes, onions, tomatoes, beets, and other crops not attacked by the fungus, (2) removal of all refuse as soon as the crop is harvested, (3) shallow cultivation after rains to hasten the drying of the surface, and (4) dusting with a fungicide. Good results have been obtained by dusting the soil under the plants with ethyl-mercury phosphate dust and New Improved Ceresan. Two or three weeks before harvest, the dust is blown under the plant with a special lettuce duster applying 12 to 15 pounds of dust to the acre.

GRAY MOLD ROT. This is caused by a species of *Botrytis*. It is not serious, generally, but under some conditions it is of great importance, for the mold rot may attack the plants at any stage of growth in the field, in the greenhouse, or in transit. When it attacks the plants in the seedling stage, the disease resembles common damping-off. More commonly the rot is found on fully developed or partly developed plants. The disease appears as a soft, dark, decayed area on the base of the stem. It develops rapidly, and when the petioles are rotted the leaves wither. On the mature head the inner, tender leaves often become a slimy mass. Sometimes the disease appears on one side of the plant.

In the greenhouse this disease can be controlled by regulating the temperature and the ventilation. The fungus grows best at temperatures between 68 and 75°F., so that a relatively low temperature at night is desirable. Keeping the surface of the soil relatively dry during the day will aid in controlling this trouble in the greenhouse.

BROWN BLIGHT. The cause of this disease is unknown. Plants affected by it in the early stage of growth assume a mottled, yellow color, become rosetted, and do not head. If the disease appears after the heads form, the entire plant may become yellowish, and dead, brown, irregular streaks may appear in the outer leaves. Infected leaves usually dry up and turn brown.

Brown blight is known to occur in Arizona and California. It was so severe in the Imperial Valley about 1920 that it was thought that lettuce could no longer be grown profitably in that area. Loss from this disease has been nearly eliminated by the development of varieties and strains that are resistant to the disease. The varieties and strains resistant to this disease, according to Bohn, include Imperial 17, 44, 152, 410, 456, 615, 847, 850, and Great Lakes.

DOWNY MILDEW. This disease, caused by *Bremia lactucae*, is not serious in the field in many sections of the United States, but in the coastal regions of California it has caused considerable losses, especially in the winter crop. There are numerous races of *B. lactucae*, and Bohn states that some of the strains can attack all varieties that are resistant to some of the races. The resistant varieties include those listed as being resistant to brown blight except Imperial 17. Resistance to the different races is specific so that control of downy mildew at a given location "can best be determined by trying it out in that location." Crop rotation, eradication of wild lettuce, clean cultivation, and avoiding excessive irrigation will aid in the control of this disease in the field.

YELLOWS. This disease is known as aster yellows since it was first found on aster plants. Yellows is a virus disease that produces a similar disease in many other species of plants. On young lettuce plants the new leaves are the first to show the characteristic yellowing. On older plants that have formed heads the inner-head leaves become yellow and finally nearly white. If the disease appears early, no head will develop. In some areas, as in New York, this is by far the most destructive disease of lettuce during warm weather. In some seasons entire fields are rendered worthless by it.

The virus causing the disease is spread mainly, if not entirely, by a species of leaf hopper which carries the disease from infected to uninfected plants. Since the disease is found in a large number of species of plants, including many weeds, its spread is difficult to control. Eradication of all weed hosts within 300 feet of the lettuce field will reduce the severity of the disease. Spraying young lettuce with 5 per cent DDT to control leaf hoppers is recommended by some authorities. The DDT should not be used on lettuce within 30 days of harvest because of the danger of residues on the heads.

MOSAIC. The mosaic generally is not a serious disease of lettuce, but in a dry season when aphids are abundant there may be considerable loss. Jagger (1921) has shown that it is transmitted from diseased to healthy plants by aphids, and Newhall (1923) showed that the virus also lives on the seed. While no definite control measures are practiced, the use of clean seed and controlling the insect carriers would seem to be the logical methods to employ.

TIPBURN. This disease frequently is very serious in the field, causing severe losses under some conditions in all the important lettuce-producing sections. Tipburn is a physiological breakdown of the older internal head leaves and inner wrapper leaves of head lettuce. It may affect leaf lettuce but seldom does severe damage. The breakdown is generally followed by a soft rot which renders the lettuce unsalable, although it may not be seen on the outside of the head.

Much experimental work has been conducted to determine the cause of tipburn. There is fairly general agreement that the trouble is most likely to occur when the head approaches marketable size. Many believe that plants that are making rapid growth are more susceptible than those that have made slower growth. It is generally believed that the environmental conditions under which the plants are grown are the important factors. Results of studies by Andersen (1946) indicate that water deficiency, as shown by high soil-moisture tension, is the primary cause of tipburn. He found a highly significant correlation between severity of tipburn and the difference between maximum soil and maximum air temperature, tipburn being most severe when the difference was greatest. The greatest difference between soil and air temperature occurs when a cool moist period is followed by a sunny dry period. Newhall (1929) and others observed that tipburn was most severe under such conditions. During a warm, dry period transpiration is high, and since the soil temperature would rise more slowly than that of the air, the difference between maximum air and soil temperature would be great at the beginning of the warm period. This might result in a water deficit in the plant.

No satisfactory control measures have been developed, except to grow varieties that are somewhat resistant to tipburn. The varieties that are most resistant are Imperial 456 (Cornell 456), Progress, and Great Lakes. Moderately resistant varieties include Imperial 410, 615, 847, and 850. Resistance to tipburn is not complete since all varieties develop the trouble when conditions are favorable. Those that are resistant develop little or no tipburn under conditions that render susceptible varieties unmarketable. Growing lettuce during the cooler parts of the season on soils that do not favor excessively rapid growth; limiting the quantity of fertilizer, especially nitrogen; and limiting the use of irrigation water as the plants approach maturity will aid in controlling tipburn.

BIG VEIN. This disease, caused by a soil-borne virus, is very widespread and results in serious losses in some areas, especially where lettuce is grown on the same land for several years. The first symptom of this disease, observed in young plants, is a yellowing along the veins. This is followed by thickening and crinkling of the entire leaf. The plant continues to grow, but produces smaller, less firm heads than normal plants.

The virus does not penetrate the aboveground part of the plant, but is confined to the roots where it multiplies. It persists for a long time in the soil.

Growing lettuce in virus-free soil and rotation with crops that do not harbor the virus are control measures suggested for field-grown crops. In greenhouses and hotbeds, big vein can be controlled by heat and by some of the soil fumigants such as D-D, formalin, and chloropicrin.

Premature Seeding. Seedstalks often develop before the plant is full grown, and this results in loss to the grower. Results of experiments reported by Thompson and Knott (1933) indicate that high temperature is the most important factor involved in premature seeding of lettuce. Seeding may take place during the cool weather of early fall if the plants have been subjected to high temperature for a considerable period earlier in their growth. In these experiments, length of day had no appreciable effect on seedstalk development.

Insects. The most important insect pests of lettuce are various species of plant lice, or aphids. Control measures for these are the same as for the spinach aphid. The cabbage looper also attacks lettuce. For description of this insect and control measures suggested see under Cabbage.

Cutworms sometimes injure lettuce early in the season and may be controlled by poison mash as recommended in Chap. 12.

Harvesting. The stage of development at which lettuce is harvested depends on the type and the purpose for which it is grown. Head lettuce, when grown for market, is allowed to grow to full size and to develop a solid head. When grown for home use, it is often harvested before the head is well formed, but when used as leaves there is no advantage in growing a heading type. Leaf lettuce grown for home use is harvested at any time after the plants get large enough for use. A common practice is to thin the plants at various times, removing the largest ones for use and leaving the small ones to develop. In this way one planting will supply the table for a considerable period. When grown for market, leaf lettuce is usually allowed to develop to full size, unless the price is very high prior to that time, in which case the plants are cut any time after they become half grown. Of course, a larger yield will be produced on a given area if the plants are allowed to develop to full size than if cut earlier, but the returns may be as high under the latter practice.

Lettuce is cut usually with a long-handled sharp knife. Where the lettuce drop is serious, it is best to make the cut above the leaves resting on the ground so as to eliminate the disease spores and prevent their spread throughout the crate.

It is best not to harvest the lettuce immediately after a rain or while the dew is on it. When the plants are full of water, the leaves are crisp and brittle and break easily in handling.

Since 1950 a marked change has taken place in the method of harvesting and handling of lettuce in California and Arizona, as a result of the use of the vacuum-cooling method. This process has resulted in a change from the shed packing of 4 to 6 dozen heads of lettuce in wooden crates with ice to the dry pack of 2 dozen heads in paperboard cartons. The cartons are packed in the field, thus eliminating the use of the equipment formerly employed in the packing sheds. Some of the ice houses have been converted to vacuum cooling at great expense.

In the vacuum-cooling method, according to Welch and Whitaker (1953), about 320 dry-pack paperboard cartons (equivalent to one-half carload) are mechanically placed in a large steel precooling tube at one time. They state that with this method of cooling, the center of the head is cooled to about 34°F. in less than 30 minutes. The temperature should not go below 32°F. After being precooled, the cartons should be transferred immediately to refrigerator cars that have been precooled with ice in the bunker. Only bunker ice is used during transit.

The vacuum-cooling method and the use of paperboard cartons have resulted in combining harvesting and packing into a single operation. The methods of harvesting and packing in the field have been described by Welch and Whitaker.

Lettuce grown in the large producing areas of the United States is well graded for shipment to distant markets, and usually only the best grade is shipped. In some of the other areas grading is not done so well as it should be. All head lettuce should be graded, and only solid heads reasonably free from disease and other injury should be put on the market. The U.S. Department of Agriculture has formulated grades, the specifications of which can be obtained from the Department and from the state marketing agency in most of the states where the crop is grown commercially.

Packing. As mentioned above a large part of the commercially grown lettuce is packed for shipment in paperboard cartons. Usually 2 dozen heads are packed in a carton, and no ice is used either in the container or over the load, as has been the common practice where the standard wooden crate is used. The so-called standard vegetable crate is still used in some areas, and it holds from 4 to 6 dozen heads packed in three layers with crushed ice between the layers and over the top. In some of the areas of the Eastern part of the United States, a crate smaller than the standard vegetable crate is used for crisphead lettuce. As a rule 2 dozen heads are packed in this crate, but when the heads are very large, only 18 heads are packed per crate. The heads are packed in two layers, the bottom layer placed with the stem end down and the top layer with the stem end up. The butterhead type of lettuce, as Big Boston or White Boston, is packed 2 dozen to the crate as mentioned above, but the crate is smaller than the one used for crisphead varieties. Leaf lettuce grown in greenhouses in some of the states is packed in splint baskets, usually of 24 quarts capacity, which deliver about 10 pounds of lettuce.

Storage. Lettuce is not usually considered a storage product, but under good refrigeration it can be kept for a period of 3 to 4 weeks provided it arrives at the storage house in good condition. For storage it is packed as for market and is placed in cold storage where the temperature is kept at about 32°F. Storage is of great importance since it often happens that the market is glutted for a few weeks and then is nearly bare for a period. Storage prevents this glut and tides the market over the period of slack production. This helps both the producer and the consumer.

ENDIVE

Endive, or escarole (*Cichorium endivia* Linn.), belongs to the Compositae, or sunflower family, and is probably of East Indian origin. It was used as food by the Egyptians at a very early period, being referred to by Pliny, who states that it was eaten as a salad and potherb in his day. As now grown, endive is eaten mainly as a salad. With the great increase in the serving of tossed salad in the home, in restaurants, and in hotels, commercial production has increased. It is grown on a small scale by market gardeners in many parts of the United States and on a relatively large scale in some areas, as in parts of Florida and the Winter Garden region of Texas. Statistics are available only for Florida and these show an increase from 1,000 acres in 1939 to 4,800 acres in 1952 and production from 550,000 to 2,400,000 bushels.[3]

Culture. The general methods of culture are similar to those used for lettuce. In regions having mild winters, it is grown as a winter crop since it does not thrive well in very hot weather. It can be grown, however, in many regions as a spring and early-summer crop and as a fall crop. Where growing seasons are short, the plants may be started in a greenhouse or hotbed and the plants set out as soon as hard freezes are over. Endive will withstand light freezes.

Any soil suitable for lettuce is satisfactory for endive. Since rapid, continuous growth is important, the crop should be well fertilized, and in most regions irrigation is desirable. The fertilizer practice suggested for lettuce is suitable for endive.

Blanching to reduce bitterness of the leaves was practiced in the past but has been discontinued where the crop is grown on a large scale. Since endive is used to a considerable extent in a mixed salad the bitterness is not objectionable. Furthermore, when grown rapidly the mass of leaves in the center lose much of the green color and bitter taste.

Varieties. There are two types of endive, the curled, or fringed-leaved, and the broad-leaved varieties, the latter type being marketed under the name *escarole*. The fringed-leaved type is more ornamental and more popular as a salad vegetable than is the broad-leaved type. The important varieties of the former are White Curled, Green Curled, Pancalier, and Deep Heart Fringed. Broad-leaved Batavian, Full-heart Batavian, and Florida Deep Heart are varieties of the broad-leaved type and are sold on the market as escarole. These are used as a potherb as well as a salad.

Harvesting and Packing. In harvesting, the plant is cut off near the surface of the soil and any diseased, discolored, or injured leaves are removed. The outer leaves are folded over the centers of the plants as they are packed. The containers used for shipment are 1-bushel round-bottom, or tub, basket and the vegetable crate. For long hauls, refrigeration should be used. Precooling and icing as practiced for shipping lettuce and other leafy crops are desirable for endive.

[3] *U.S. Dept. Agr. Agricultural Statistics.*

CHICORY

Chicory (*Cichorium intybus* Linn.), also known as French endive, Witloof, Witloof chicory, and succory, is probably a native of Europe and Asia. It has been in use as a salad plant from time immemorial but was probably not cultivated by the ancients. It was not mentioned in the descriptive lists of vegetables until the thirteenth century.

At the present time chicory is grown mainly for its leaves used in salad and for its root as an adulterant for coffee. In Europe the green leaves are used as potherbs to some extent.

Culture. When grown for salad, the seed is usually planted in spring or early summer in rows 15 to 18 inches apart and the young plants thinned to 4 or 5 inches. Too early planting may result in development of the flower stalk and a root of no value for forcing. Any soil suitable for beets, carrots, and parsnips is satisfactory for chicory. The cultivation and care throughout the growing season are the same as for parsnips. On the approach of cold weather the roots are lifted, or plowed out, and the tops cut off about 2 inches above the crown. The roots are then stored in a cool place where they will remain until needed.

Forcing. When chicory is used as a food in the United States, it is grown largely as a forced crop, and a pure forcing strain should be selected. The crop may be forced under greenhouse benches, in cellars, or out of doors. A temperature of 50 to 60°F. is usually maintained. At a higher temperature the heads are not so solid, and there is a tendency to shoot up too rapidly.

The roots usually vary considerably in size and should therefore be graded before they are planted. It is desirable to make three or four grades based on length and size. Roots of each grade should be cut to a uniform length so that all the crowns will be covered to the same depth. The size of the head corresponds to the size of the root used. Very large roots produce large heads, many of which are often made up of small divisions. Some good, solid heads develop from the very large roots, but they are generally too large for the best market use. Medium to large roots produce heads of the best market size, while small roots yield too many small straight heads. A head 4 to 5 inches long and weighing 2 to 3 ounces is the most desirable.

In preparing the roots for forcing, the slender tips are cut off. They may be taken from storage for forcing at any time from late fall until spring; for a succession of heads, new plantings should be made every 2 or 3 weeks. The roots are set in a trench in a sloping direction with the crown about even with, or below, the surface. They are placed close together, and the crowns are covered with fine soil, sand, or sawdust to the depth of 6 to 8 inches. This covering excludes the light and prevents the leaves forming the head from spreading, making the head solid and compact. Before covering, the roots and the soil below should be watered. One or two later waterings may be necessary, but the soil above the crowns should not be soaked. With the proper temperature 3 to 4 weeks is usually required to develop good heads, but at high temperatures the heads will push through the covering earlier.

Good chicory may be grown in outdoor trenches. These trenches should be at least 18 inches deep and 12 to 18 inches wide. The roots are set and covered as described above. Over the covering of sand, soil, or sawdust is placed fresh horse manure to the depth of about 2 feet and extending about 1½ feet on either side of the trench. The manure furnishes the heat and protects the heads against freezing.

Chicory is harvested by cutting off the head at the base. The outside leaves are pulled off, and the heads are packed in baskets. The French and Belgian product is shipped in 20-pound baskets with the heads packed in layers. A smaller package is desirable, and the 3-pound climax basket has been used.

PARSLEY

Parsley (*Petroselinum hortense*) is the most popular of the garden herbs grown in this country. The leaves are used for flavoring, for garnishing, and to some extent for salads. The plant is a biennial, or short-lived perennial, of the Umbelliferae family and is a native of Europe. It has been in cultivation for over 2,000 years. Parsley is very high in iron, vitamin A, and ascorbic acid (vitamin C).

Culture. Parsley seed is slow to germinate. For this reason it is often sown in the greenhouse, hotbed, or specially prepared bed in the open. The young plants are then transplanted where they are to grow to edible maturity. The plants are hardy and may be set out as early as cabbage. In the North, seed is commonly sown outdoors early in the spring and at intervals during the growing season. In the South, the crop is grown mostly during the winter and spring. When grown commercially, the rows are spaced about 15 inches apart and the plants given a space of 4 to 8 inches in the row.

Parsley is grown as a forcing crop in greenhouses, hotbeds, and cold frames in winter and spring in some areas. In some regions where winters are relatively mild, the crop is grown in cold frames.

Field culture of parsley is similar to that given other small-growing plants. Weed control is very important, and this can be accomplished by frequent shallow cultivation or by a combination of cultivation and use of herbicidal oils.

Varieties. There are two distinct forms of parsley grown for its foliage, the plain-leaved and the curled, the latter being the most popular in this country. The best-known varieties are Moss Curled, Extra Double

Curled, Fern-leaved, and Curled Dwarf. The plain-leaved parsley has as good flavor as the curled, but is not so attractive, hence is little grown. In addition to the forms grown for their foliage a turnip-rooted parsley is grown for its edible root. This is grown in the vicinity of some of the large cities, where it is sold mainly to the foreign population. The culture of turnip-rooted parsley is about the same as for carrots.

Harvesting. In harvesting parsley the outer and larger leaves are removed and tied in bunches for market. By this method the plant continues to produce a marketable product for many weeks. The bunches are packed for shipment in a small-size vegetable crate, in which are packed 4 dozen bunches, and in bushel baskets. Crushed ice usually is placed in the package, and shipment is made under refrigeration to distant markets.

CHERVIL

Chervil, or salad chervil (*Anthriscus cerefolium*), is an annual plant very much like parsley, popular in Europe but little grown in this country. It is used for garnishing and flavoring. The curled-leaved varieties are the most popular because of their attractive appearance.

The plant is grown in very much the same way as parsley, and the leaves are ready in 6 to 8 weeks from seed sowing. It does not thrive in hot weather, therefore should be grown as a spring or fall crop. It is hardy and will withstand the winters in the North if given the protection of a cold frame or even a covering of straw or similar material. The plant grows to the height of 18 inches to 2 feet, but the foliage is usually harvested when young.

CRESS

Cress, or garden cress (*Lepidium sativum* Linn.), is an annual of the Cruciferae, or mustard family, and is a native of Europe. It is a cool-weather plant grown for its root leaves. Seeds are sown as soon as the ground can be prepared in the spring. A cool, rich soil should be chosen, for rapid growth is essential to good quality. The plant quickly runs to seed in hot weather. Cress seed is usually planted in rows 12 to 15 inches apart, and the plants thinned as needed for the table.

The leaves are used in salads and garnishings and are usually ready for use in 6 to 8 weeks from the sowing of the seed. If the leaves are removed without injuring the crown, the plant continues to bear.

Other species of cress, belonging to the genus Barbarea, are rarely grown in this country, although they are cultivated to some extent in Europe. The spring cress (*B. verna*) is a biennial, but when grown under cultivation it is treated as an annual or as a winter perennial; the seeds dropping in summer produce plants that send up flower stalks the following spring.

WATER CRESS

Water cress (*Nasturtium officinale*) is a perennial belonging to the Cruciferae family. It carries several other Latin names, as *Roripa nasturtium-aquaticum*, *Sisymbrium nasturtium-aquaticum*, and *Radicula nasturtium-aquaticum*. It is a prostrate, or trailing, plant, native of Europe and extensively naturalized in other parts of the world. It thrives in ditches, pools, and stream margins, but can be grown in greenhouse, hotbed, cold frame, or other places where the soil can be kept moist. Water cress is readily propagated by seed and by pieces of stem.

Culture. When grown commercially out of doors watercress is planted in beds supplied with water from springs in limestone regions. When grown in this way, the beds must be carefully made so that all parts of them will be covered with slowly flowing, clean, uncontaminated water. Shear (1949) has described the construction of the beds and the methods of production, harvesting, and handling the crop in Virginia. He states that the shape and size of beds are determined to a great extent by the flow of water from the spring and the contour of the adjoining land. A bed should be so constructed that surface floodwater cannot run through it, since it would injure both the bed and the cress.

Planting usually is done in early spring in regions where the crop is grown outdoors in the United States, using either seed or cuttings. When seed is used, usually it is mixed with dry sand and sown broadcast in a well-prepared bed and then covered lightly. The soil is kept moist until the plants have developed the first true leaves, when enough water is let in the beds to cover the plants. Plants are set about 1 foot apart in the permanent beds, and immediately after planting enough water is turned into the beds to cover the plants. After the plants are well established, more water is run into the beds, and the depth is increased as growth increases.

Water cress can be grown in rich moist soil in the garden, but provision should be made for watering in order to assure rapid, continuous growth.

Harvesting and Marketing. In harvesting, the tops of the plants are cut off at a length of about 6 inches with a long sharp knife. The pieces are tied into bunches near the tops, and the butts trimmed off, so that the finished bunch is about 4 inches long. The bunches are kept in water until ready for packing, which should be done as soon as possible. It is important to keep the cress cool until it reaches the consumer. When shipped considerable distances precooling and shipping under refrigeration are desirable.

Water cress is a good source of calcium, iron, vitamin A, and riboflavin and contains an appreciable quantity of ascorbic acid.

CHAPTER 18

Cole Crops

Cabbage	Brussels sprouts
Cauliflower	Kohlrabi
Sprouting broccoli	Chinese cabbage

All cole crops are hardy and thrive best in cool weather, being grown in the South mainly during the winter. The crops in this group are closely related, belonging to the same genus (Brassica), most of them to the same species. The cultural requirements for all the crops in the group are very similar, and many of the same diseases and insects attack them all. Kale and collards are cole crops, but for convenience they are included with other potherbs or greens.

CABBAGE

Cabbage is by far the most important member of the genus Brassica grown in the United States and, in fact, is one of the important vegetable crops. It is grown by market gardeners in all sections of the United States and by special vegetable growers and general farmers in many regions. Cabbage is grown in home gardens, both on the farms and in villages and cities.

Statistics of Production. The general trend of cabbage production has been upward, as shown in Table 18.1, although the greatest increase

Table 18.1. Average Annual Acreage, Production, and Value of Cabbage
Grown for Market and Manufacture, 1918–1953
(*Agricultural Statistics*)

Years	Acres	Yield per acre, tons	Production, tons	Price per ton	Value (000 omitted)
1918–1927	129,897	8.1	1,054,230	$17.65	$18,573
1928–1937	165,609	6.6	1,082,910	14.89	16,052
1938–1947	191,739	7.5	1,377,640	19.50	32,087
1948–1953	170,897	9.6	1,400,670	26.01	44,163

275

occurred during the 1942–1947 period. Some of the increase in price has been due to the increase in acreage in the South for winter and early-spring cabbage, which brings a higher price than fall cabbage. This increase in winter production has drastically reduced the demand for stored cabbage grown in the Northern states. In 1953, 25,000 acres of cabbage was grown in Texas, 22,000 acres in New York, 19,600 acres in Florida, 10,200 acres in North Carolina, 9,700 acres in California, and 9,500 acres in Wisconsin. Georgia, New Jersey, and Louisiana each grew more than 5,000 acres, and many other states grew some cabbage for market. New York produced the greatest tonnage of cabbage with 253,800 tons, Florida was second with 192,100 tons, Texas third with 125,000 tons, and California and Wisconsin each produced about 100,000 tons.

History and Taxonomy. Cabbage is found in the wild state on the chalk rocks of the seacoast of England, on the coasts of Denmark and northwestern France, and in various other localities from Greece to Great Britain. It has been known from earliest antiquity and was probably in general use 2000 to 2500 B.C. It was held in high esteem by the ancient Greeks and is said to have been worshipped by the Egyptians. Cabbage was introduced into European gardens in the ninth century and into the United States in the early days of colonization.

It belongs to the Cruciferae, or mustard family, and is known by the technical name *Brassica oleracea* var. *capitata* Linn. The wild cabbage plant is herbaceous, usually perennial, but sometimes biennial. The cultivated cabbage is biennial, although grown as an annual crop. There is great variation among the cultivated types of cabbage. They differ in size, shape, and color of the leaves, and in size, shape, color, and texture of the head.

Climatic Requirements. Cabbage thrives best in a relatively cool, moist climate. The crop is grown in the South mainly during the winter and early spring. The main, or late, crop is grown almost entirely in the Northern states where summer temperatures are relatively low. Fresh cabbage is on the market in the United States every month of the year. Most of the winter cabbage is produced in Florida and Texas with appreciable amounts in California. As the weather warms up, cabbage is harvested progressively northward through the spring and summer. States east of the Mississippi River produce most of the cabbage during the early spring and summer. The largest part of the cabbage crop is harvested in the early fall, with New York, Wisconsin, and Michigan the largest producers. In the late fall, the production areas are located further southward down the Atlantic Coast until winter production begins in the extreme Southern states. California produces sizable amounts of cabbage during all seasons except the summer.

Soils and Soil Preparation. Cabbage is grown on all types of soils from the sands and mucks to the heavy soils. For a very early crop, sandy or sandy-loam soils are considered best; for a late crop, where a large yield is the most important consideration, clay loams and silty soils are preferred. A good muck soil is very satisfactory for late cabbage. A sandy soil is excellent in the spring, when moisture does not become a limiting factor, but in late summer such a soil is not desirable unless irrigation is available. Early crops are grown mostly on light soils, while the late crop is grown on heavy soils, which are most retentive of moisture and are richer.

Cabbage does not grow well on a highly acid soil. Hester, Parker, and Zimmerley (1936) reported results on a Norfolk sandy-loam soil showing a marked increase in yield as acidity decreased from pH 4.3 to about 6.0. They state that maximum availability of phosphorus may be expected between pH 5.5 and 6.5, and since the phosphorus supply is important, they consider this reaction range as most satisfactory. Where clubroot is very serious, some authorities recommend application of caustic lime or hydrated lime to bring the soil to a neutral or alkaline reaction. Under most conditions lime should be used on soil more acid than pH 5.5, but it does not seem desirable to decrease acidity beyond pH 6.5 except where clubroot is very serious and can be controlled by no other means.

For early cabbage in the North, fall plowing is important since it is desirable to plant very early in the spring. In the South, cabbage is planted in the fall or winter, depending on the locality and climate; therefore summer or fall plowing is practiced. Fall plowing in the North is desirable where sod land is to be used. The vegetative matter will then be partially decayed by spring, and the soil in a good condition to receive the crop. Where cabbage is transplanted into the field, a minimum amount of fitting is necessary after plowing, since transplanting machines make a good bed for the plant as the furrow is opened. If cabbage is direct-seeded, the ground should be fitted thoroughly so that there are no clods or lumps that interfere with the placing of the seed at the desired depth and spacing.

Fertilizers. Cabbage is a heavy feeder, especially of nitrogen and potash. It is considered a hard crop on the soil, and there is experimental evidence to substantiate this belief. Farmers often report that corn following cabbage produces a smaller yield than when it follows corn. A major portion of the vegetative growth made by the cabbage plant is harvested and sold off of the farm; therefore there is a heavy removal of nutrients from the soil.

The amount and type of fertilizer used vary in different parts of the country, depending on the soil and the climatic conditions. In the Northeast, the usual fertilizer for early-market cabbage is 800 to 1,000 pounds per acre of an 8-16-16 supplemented with nitrogen side-dressings. In the Southeastern states, the general fertilizer application of cabbage is about 1,000 pounds of an 8-8-8 per acre supplemented with nitrogen side-dressings. In Louisiana, it is recommended that manure or a green-manure crop be plowed down and the cabbage fertilized with 600 to 800 pounds of a 4-12-4 per acre supplemented with 1 or 2 nitrogen side-dressings. On most soils in California, 50 to 100 pounds of nitrogen per acre or 10 tons of manure per acre is considered adequate fertilization for cabbage, but in a few areas phosphorus is also applied. On the sandy soils in Florida, a ton of 6-8-8 is usually applied, while on the peat and muck soils about 500 pounds of a fertilizer like 0-12-16 or 0-8-24 is used. Copper sulfate is added to the fertilizer on peat and muck soils. On all soils in Florida if the pH is above 6.0, manganese, zinc, and borax are also added to the fertilizer.

Late cabbage for processing usually is fertilized at the rate of 750 to 1,000 pounds of an 8-16-8 with nitrogen side-dressings where manure is not used. In most regions where cabbage for processing is grown, it is grown on general farms in rotation with other farm crops, and manure is available for the cabbage crop. Heavy applications of manure before planting eliminate the necessity for heavy nitrogen side-dressings and reduce the amount of fertilizer that must be applied. At one time, it was thought that growers could not afford to use heavy applications of fertilizer on cabbage for processing. However, since the Second World War the price of farm labor has increased so much that the only way to reduce the cost of labor is to produce maximum yields. Fertilizer is relatively cheap when compared to labor, and therefore growers who produce cabbage for processing usually apply maximum amounts of fertilizer to cut down the unit cost of labor for the crop. Many experiments have shown that cabbage gives a good response to manure, and most of the older experiments indicate a superiority of manure over commercial fertilizers. However, these experiments did not involve supplemental nitrogen as side-dressings. The greatest benefit of manure or soil-improvement crops for cabbage seems to be the slowly available supply of nitrogen which the cabbage utilizes efficiently throughout its growth. Even if a large amount of chemical nitrogen is applied at planting time, the losses from leaching are so great that the cabbage suffers from nitrogen deficiency later in the season.

Volk, Bell, and McCubbin (1947) reported that the nitrate level in sandy soils of Florida was the most important factor influencing cabbage yields in that area. When the nitrate level in the soil dropped below 15 pounds per acre, the yield was reduced. It was difficult to maintain this optimum level of nitrate in the soil by means of a single application of nitrogen. In seasons of low rainfall, the application of large amounts of nitrogen at planting would maintain a high nitrate level in the soil throughout the growing period, but with more rainfall nitrogen side-dressings were essential to produce high yields.

The cabbage plant produces a dense, although shallow, root system which efficiently utilizes broadcast applications of fertilizer. However, best results are obtained when part of the fertilizer is placed in bands 2 to 4 inches from the young plants. This supplies readily available nutrients to the plant while the root system is still small and gets the plant off to a good start so that it makes better use of soil reserves and broadcast applications of fertilizer.

Vittum and Hervey (1952) found that increasing the rate of fertilization of cabbage resulted in more burst heads. However, an effective insect-control program reduced the number of burst heads by about 50 per cent. Unsprayed cabbage that was not fertilized yielded about 16½ tons of marketable heads per acre, while that fertilized with 1,800 pounds of 5-10-10 yielded 20½ tons per acre. When the plants were sprayed to control insects, the yield of cabbage fertilized with 1,800 pounds of 5-10-10 was increased to more than 26 tons per acre. Most of this increase in yield of marketable cabbage was due to the reduction in the number of burst heads.

Growing Plants. There are several distinct methods of growing cabbage plants for the early crop: (1) sowing seed outside in the fall in the South, (2) sowing seed in the cold frame late in the fall or early winter and transplanting to the field direct from the seedbed, (3) sowing seed in a hotbed early in the spring and transplanting direct from the seedbed, (4) sowing seed in the greenhouse or hotbed and transplanting the plants at least once before setting them in the open.

In many sections of the South, especially along the Atlantic Coast, from the eastern shore of Maryland south to Florida and along the Gulf Coast, the most common practice is to sow seed in open beds in late summer, or in the fall, and to set the plants in the field in 6 to 10 weeks. On the eastern shore of Maryland the seed is sown the latter part of August or early in September so that the plants are large enough to put out before cold weather sets in. In the coast section of South Carolina, the seed is sown early in October. In cooler sections of the South and in regions where there are great variations in temperature, seed often is sown in cold frames in late fall and early winter and the plants set out in February.

Sowing seed in the hotbed in March and setting the plants directly in the field without transplanting is practiced to some extent in the North, but this method is not satisfactory where earliness is of prime consideration. Plants grown in this way are usually not well hardened and therefore will not withstand freezing. Those that survive are likely to be weak and spindly.

The most common method for growing early plants in the North is to sow the seed in a greenhouse or hotbed 8 to 10 weeks before they are to be set in the field: The seedlings are transplanted when small, spacing them 1½ to 2 inches apart each way. Some growers transplant cabbage plants twice before setting them in the field, giving them more space at the second transplanting. If more space could be given at the first transplanting, better results would be secured without additional transplanting.

Cabbage plants for the late crop in the North are grown in the open. The seed is sown about 6 to 8 weeks before time for planting in the field. A good, loose soil should be selected for the seedbed, which should be thoroughly prepared. Heavy fertilization of the seedbed is not desirable since a rich soil is likely to produce too rapid growth.

The quantity of seed required for an acre of land depends on the viability of the seed, the care taken in preparing the seedbed, and the method of growing plants. If the seedbed is well prepared and given good care, more plants will be available from a given quantity of seed than if the soil is not well prepared and poor care is given. A pound of seed of high viability will furnish ample plants for 4 acres if they are grown in greenhouses or hotbeds and the seedlings are pricked out. When seed is sown in outdoor beds and the plants are transplanted directly to the field, it is not safe to expect more than enough plants for 2 acres from 1 pound of seed. Many of the plants, because of crowding in the seedbed, do not develop properly and are thrown away.

Planting. Cabbage plants which have been well hardened will withstand a temperature of 10 to 15° below freezing if not of long duration. In regions where freezes do not occur, planting may be done at any time of the year if water is available for growing the crop. In regions where hard freezes occur, well-hardened plants may be set out as early in the spring as the ground can be prepared or as soon as the danger of hard freezes is over. Late cabbage in the Northern states is set out the latter half of June and in July, depending on the earliness of fall freezes. About 4 months should be allowed for late cabbage to mature.

The spacing of the plants in the field depends largely on the variety. Small-growing varieties like Jersey Wakefield are set 12 to 15 inches apart in the row, with the rows 2 to 3 feet apart. During recent years the market has preferred small heads of cabbage, and objection has been raised to the large size of Danish Ballhead grown in New York State. The size can be regulated by spacing the plants. Where the demand is for small or medium-sized heads, the spacing in the row should not be greater than 15 inches; 12 inches might be better. The yield per acre would be increased by close spacing under ordinary conditions.

Vittum and Peck (1954) found that the greatest yield of Danish cabbage was produced when the plants were irrigated and spaced 12 inches apart in the row. Irrigated cabbage yielded 35 tons per acre at the 12-inch spacing and produced 6 pound heads, while at the 36-inch spacing the yield was only 26 tons per acre with 11-pound heads. Without irrigation the 12-inch spacing produced 30 tons per acre and the heads weighed a little less than 5 pounds each. These would be considered large heads on most markets, since the most desirable size is about 3 to 3½ pounds per head.

Cabbage plants are set by hand and by transplanting machines. By the hand method, the opening for the plant may be made by use of a dibble, trowel, or a small plow. When the plow is used, the plants should be set immediately before the soil dries out. Hand transplanters are also used. These have attachments so that water may be applied around the roots as the plant is set. Machine transplanters are used to a large extent where considerable areas are planted. These machines do a better job than is usually done by hand. They open the furrow, apply water around the roots, and pack the soil around the plant, all in one operation.

When setting out cabbage plants from the seedbed during the summer, only the strong, stocky plants should be used because many of the weak ones do not withstand the shock of transplanting and many others make slow growth. In an experiment in Pennsylvania (Myers, 1916) plants were graded according to size at the time of planting in the field. The experiment covered 3 years, 2 years with Enkhuizen Glory and 1 year with Danish Ballhead. The average of the yields from the different grades was as follows: small plants, 12.7 tons per acre; medium, 17.7 tons; ungraded, 18.5 tons; and large, 21 tons per acre.

Cultivation. In the cultivation of cabbage great care should be exercised to prevent destruction of the roots; therefore only very shallow cultivation should be given after the plants have attained considerable size. Many of the roots of the cabbage plant grow within 2 inches of the surface of the soil, and these run almost horizontally (Fig. 18.1). Before the plant is half grown, the roots cross in the center between the rows, and if deep cultivation is given, more harm than good may be done. Sufficient cultivation should be given to keep down weeds and probably to maintain a soil mulch while the plants are small. After the plants are half grown, cultivation is not so important unless weeds are troublesome. Cultivation should cease when it is impossible to perform the operation without injuring the plants, since there is evidence that little moisture is lost from the soil by evaporation from the surface, when the plants are large. There is also evidence that cultivation destroys the roots near the surface.

Experimental evidence obtained at Ithaca, N.Y., indicates that on a sandy-loam soil the soil mulch is not of great importance. The average yield for the 6 years was the same on the scraped plots as on the cultivated plots, and the only difference between these treatments was in the presence and absence of a soil mulch. Weeds were kept down in

Fɪɢ. 18.1. Roots of cabbage plants uncovered by washing off the surface soil to the depth of 2 inches.

both cases. A soil mulch was maintained on the cultivated plots throughout the growth of the crop. On a heavier soil the mulch might be of greater value, but even under such conditions, root destruction by deep cultivation may offset any benefit derived from the mulch. Results of cultivation experiments at two locations in New York, at State College, Pa., and at Lincoln, Nebr., are discussed in Chap. 9.

Hand hoeing or hand weeding is usually necessary to keep the weeds down between the plants in the row. This is especially important in the spring when weed growth is rapid.

Varieties. Seedsmen list a large number of varieties of cabbage, but only a few of them are of much importance. Myers and Gardner (1919) reported that, in 1915, 54 representative seedsmen listed 243 varieties, but of these only 35 were listed by more than 10 seedsmen and 174 varieties were listed by not more than two seedsmen. Boswell, *et al.* (1934) estimated that 9 varieties of cabbage, which they described, include 85 to 90 per cent of all varieties of cabbage grown in the United States.

The different varieties grown in the United States have been classified in various ways. No classification that has been attempted is entirely satisfactory, but the one suggested by Myers (1915) is probably the best. This is similar to the one suggested by Allen (1914), but three groups are added to those mentioned by Allen. Myers suggest eight groups as follows:

1. Wakefield and Winningstadt group
2. Copenhagen Market group
3. Flat Dutch or Drumhead group
4. Savoy group
5. Danish Ballhead group
6. Alpha group
7. Volga group
8. Red Cabbage group

The Wakefield or Winningstadt group includes varieties having small pointed heads (Fig. 18.2). The plants mature early and are grown chiefly

Fig. 18.2. Three varieties of early cabbage: (1) Jersey Wakefield; (2) Charleston Wakefield; (3) Copenhagen Market.

for the early crop over most of the country. The best-known varieties of this group are Jersey Wakefield and Charleston Wakefield. Jersey Wakefield is popular in California for planting during the winter since it is somewhat resistant to bolting. Charleston Wakefield is grown in Louisiana for winter harvest for the same reason.

The Copenhagen Market group is important largely because of the variety Copenhagen Market (Fig. 18.2, variety 3) which is the most important early roundhead cabbage grown in the United States. It is nearly as early as Jersey Wakefield, and the heads are much larger. The head is round and compact, having few outer leaves and a small core. The leaves are small to medium-sized, light green in color, and covered with a heavy bloom. The stem is short. It is one of the most important early varieties in the North and is also used for a midseason and early-fall crop and is popular throughout all of the cabbage-growing areas in the United States as an early-maturing, quick-growing, roundheaded cabbage. The Golden Acre, an early strain of Copenhagen Market, has become popular because it produces a smaller head than most strains of Copenhagen Market. The Copenhagen Market types are likely to bolt after exposure to cold weather and are not suited for growing during seasons of the year when temperature may drop below 50° for any extended period of time.

Other varieties in this group with a midseason maturity include Glory of Enkhuizen, Marion Market, Globe, and Bonanza. Glory is a popular midseason variety in the North, parts of the South, and in California. It is likely to bolt if subjected to low temperatures. Bonanza is a high-

Fig. 18.3. Three varieties of midseason cabbage: (4) Enkuizen Glory; (5) Early Summer; (6) Succession.

yielding, fast-growing cabbage which produces hard heads when quite small but will stand in the field for a long time without splitting.

The Flat Dutch group is distinguished from all others by the flat heads (Fig. 18.3, varieties 5 and 6). The plant is medium to large and the outer leaves are very numerous, curving inward and closing the head loosely. The color is light green. The head is large, flat, and solid. The leaves forming the head fold over each other at the center. Varieties in this group differ considerably in the length of time required to mature, but the most popular varieties are those which mature early. Early Round Dutch (Early Dwarf Flat Dutch) has a fairly round head and is widely grown in Florida and along the Atlantic Coast during seasons of the year when low temperatures are likely to occur. Slowbolting Flat Dutch has good resistance to seedstalk development and is preferred in California. All Head Early is grown in Louisiana for the winter crop since it also resists cold weather.

The Savoy group is characterized by foliage very much blistered or wrinkled. The foliage is dark green and has very little bloom. The quality of this group is considered superior to all others, but it is not of much commercial importance, although long cultivated. The most important varieties are Chieftain and Drumhead Savoy.

The Danish Ballhead group contains the most important varieties of cabbage, the best known being the Danish Ballhead, also known as Hollander, Danish, Danish Roundhead, and many other names. Many new strains are designated by the place they originated, such as Wisconsin Hollander, Wisconsin Ballhead, and Penn State Ballhead. The mature plant is medium-sized, the outer leaves are few in number, curving inward to some extent, light green in color, and are covered with fairly heavy bloom. The head leaves are of fine texture and reach well past the center of the head. The head is of medium size and very solid. It is the best-keeping variety grown in the United States and is used to a greater extent than all other varieties of cabbage for fresh market, kraut manufacture, and storage. It is grown principally in the Northeast and Middle West for late-fall production. It is seldom grown in the other areas because of the late maturity.

The Alpha group contains the earliest varieties. The heads are smaller than Wakefield, round and very solid. The plants are small and may be planted close together. This group is of little commercial importance since no well-known varieties are included in it. St. John Day and Badger Market are perhaps the best-known varieties.

The Volga group is best represented by the variety Volga. The mature plant is large and has a few outer leaves which curl outward. The leaves are large and thick and steel blue in color. The head is of medium size, globular but somewhat flat. The head leaves extend a short distance past the center, thus giving it a bald appearance. The head is solid on top, but rather open below. It is a late-maturing cabbage and is not widely grown.

The red cabbage group is distinguished from all others by its deep purplish-red color. Otherwise, the plants show a considerable resemblance to Danish Ballhead, but the yield is usually smaller. Red Rock (Red Acre), Red Danish, and Round Red Dutch mature a little earlier than Danish Ballhead, while Mammoth Red Rock and Large Red mature about the same time as Danish Ballhead.

Market reports classify cabbage into five distinct types: Danish, domestic, pointed, red, and savoy. Danish, red, and savoy groups are the same as those discussed above. The pointed cabbage includes the Charleston and Jersey Wakefield and similar types. All other types of cabbage are considered domestic cabbage. This grouping includes the Copenhagen Market, Alpha, Flat Dutch, and Volga groups.

Premature Seeding in Cabbage. Growers of early cabbage frequently suffer financial losses because of the development of the flower stalks before the plants head. In some sections of the South, the plants are set in the field in the fall and the crop is put on the market in spring or early summer. Under these conditions, the plants are in the field throughout the winter and in some seasons a considerable percentage shoot to seed. In the North premature seeding is not uncommon, especially when the plants are started early and grown at relatively low temperatures for several weeks. Various factors have been mentioned as possible causes of bolting, including (1) early sowing of the seed, (2) warm, open winters, (3) cold winters, (4) extreme changes in temperature, (5) checking growth of the plants in the plant bed, (6) poor seed, especially seed of low vitality, (7) poor soil, (8) influence of heredity, and (9) various cultural practices that affect the rate of growth.

Results of studies made by Miller (1929) and by Boswell (1929) indicate clearly that growing the plants at relatively low temperature is associated with premature seeding. This exposure to relatively low temperature seems to be essential to flower-stalk formation, but other factors have considerable influence on it. Both Boswell and Miller found that the size of the plant at the time it is exposed to low temperature is of considerable importance. The larger the plants are (other factors being the same) at the time growth is checked by low temperature, the greater is the tendency for wintered-over cabbage to shoot to seed in the spring. Boswell found that the percentage of seeders increases with increasing size of plants above a stem diameter of 6 millimeters. The earlier the seed is sown, the higher is the percentage of seeders, mainly because the early plants are larger than the others at the time of exposure to low temperature. Increasing the size of the plant by fertilizing the plant beds increases the percentage of seeders, but Boswell found that the fertilizer treatment in the field had no effect on flowering. This is due probably to the fact that the plants are set in the field so late in the fall that the fertilizer has little or no effect on growth before winter.

Strains exhibit significant differences in tendency to shoot to seed, even when grown under identical conditions. Zimmerley (1922) found that the strains of Wakefield varieties which produce small, compact heads and head uniformly are less likely to shoot to seed than are those that are somewhat open-headed, leafy, and later-maturing. This indicates that shooting to seed is hereditary, but experimental results show clearly that environmental conditions determine the expression of the hereditary tendencies.

Seeding of Mature Cabbage. The effect of temperature on reproduction in cabbage is well illustrated in results of experiments with mature plants conducted by Miller (1929). Mature plants taken up in the fall before they were subjected to low temperature did not seed when grown subsequently in a warm greenhouse (60 to 70°F.), while those grown in a cool greenhouse (50 to 60°F.) produced flowers and seeds. The plants grown continuously in the warm house produced three heads in succession during the first year (Fig. 18.4). One of these plants was kept in the warm house for 2 years after it was brought in from the field in October, 1925, and this plant produced six heads (the fourth is shown

Fig. 18.4. Effect of a rest period on seeding of mature cabbage when grown in a warm greenhouse. Plants 1 and 2 were stored at 40°F. for 2 months; plants 3 and 4 were brought directly from the field to the greenhouse.

in Fig. 18.5). After the sixth head had developed and the plant was about 3 years old, it was moved to a cool greenhouse and within a few months it flowered. The plants used in this experiment represent a pureline strain so that all of them had the same genetic constitution. The difference in behavior of the plants grown under the two ranges of temperatures could not have been due to hereditary differences, but to the environment.

After being stored at 40°F. for 2 months, the plants flowered in the warm greenhouse a month earlier than similar plants grown in the cool house. Storage at 40°F. for 2 months hastened flowering in the cool greenhouse. Storage for 15 and 30 days had little effect on flowering.

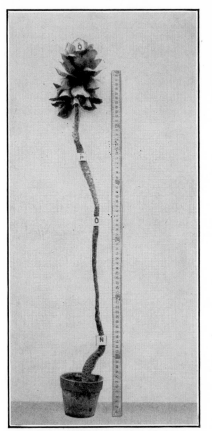

Chemical analyses of the tissues surrounding the growing point indicate a marked increase in the quantity of elaborated foods in this region. It seems probable that this increase is associated with the development of the flower stalk.

Increasing the length of day by use of electric lights had little or no effect on flowering. Etherizing the plants had no effect on time of flowering.

The results of these studies show that the type of growth can be controlled by temperature and that it is a relatively simple matter to produce one generation of plants each year. In one experiment 10 plants produced two crops of seed and two crops of heads in 2 years, but the normal order was reversed. In improvement work it is feasible to grow heads to maturity in the field during the summer and to produce seed in the greenhouse during the winter. The quickest method seems to be to store the plants for about 2 months at a temperature around 40°F. and then to grow them in a warm greenhouse (60 to 70°F.).

Fig. 18.5. Effect of temperature on seeding of mature cabbage. This plant was grown in a warm greenhouse for 2 years and produced six heads; it was then transferred to a cool greenhouse, and within a few months it flowered.

Diseases. There are several very serious diseases of cabbage, the most important being clubroot, root knot (nematodes), yellows, blackleg, and black rot. A serious infection of some of these is sufficient to make cabbage growing unprofitable and in many instances results in total loss of the crop.

CLUBROOT (*Plasmodiophora brassicae* Wor.) is produced by the invasion of a slime mold on the roots. Plants affected by this disease show, in the earlier stages of growth, a wilting of the foliage on sunny days, with recovery toward evening. The roots of affected plants show characteristic swellings, which often become very large. The mass of thickened malformed roots presents a clubbed appearance.

The organism is a soil parasite which thrives best in an acid soil. Walker (1938) summarizes the control measures as follows: (1) Badly infested areas should be abandoned for cruciferous crops. (2) Select clean soil for plant beds to avoid infestation of new areas and avoid contamination of new areas by implements, farm animals, plants, and surface drainage water. (3) Keep the soil alkaline if possible. Walker and others suggest pH 7.2 as a desirable soil reaction for control of clubroot. The lime, preferably hydrated, for clubroot control should be applied in the spring rather than during the previous fall. Chupp and Leiby (1947) suggest calomel (8 ounces to 50 gallons of water) applied in the planting water at the rate of 400 gallons per acre for cabbage and 700 gallons for cauliflower. A long rotation, in which no cruciferous plants are grown, is of value in controlling the disease in the field.

ROOT KNOT. This disease affects cabbage and many other kinds of vegetables and is caused by various species of nematodes of the genus *Meloidogyne*. These root knot nematodes invade the roots of plants and cause galls to form on the roots. These irregular swellings are sometimes confused with clubroot. More of the small roots are affected, and the knots are located nearer the tips of the roots than in the case of clubroot. Root knot is not usually serious in the North, but is very destructive to many crops in the South.

Crop rotation was the only means of control for many years, but many soil fumigants are now used for control. The nematode lives on more than 500 species of plants, and complete eradication of all host plants for a period of 3 years is almost impossible. Small grains, most grasses, corn, velvet beans, and some varieties of cowpeas and soybeans are nearly immune to the nematode. Fumigation is the only practical means of control. Seedbeds should be fumigated with methyl bromide, chloropicrin, or chlorobromopropene. The first two mentioned are applied as undiluted liquids which volatilize rapidly, while the latter is applied mixed with water as a drench. Several other types of fumigants are satisfactory, but in every case the whole area of the seedbed should be treated.

Ethylene dibromide and mixtures containing dichloropropene are generally used for field fumigation. Both are good nematocides and insecticides. The entire field is sometimes fumigated by applying the material below the soil surface in rows about 12 inches apart. This requires from 15 to 25 gallons per acre depending on the formulation used. In other cases, only the rows or hills where the plants are to grow are fumigated. A single stream is applied along each row and requires only about 8 gallons of fumigant for rows 3 feet apart. The beneficial effect of fumigation may last for more than one season in some areas, but annual applications are needed where nematodes are numerous. Row applications are effective only on the crop that immediately follows fumigation.

YELLOWS. This disease is recognized in the field by the lifeless, yellowish-green color which shows up in 2 to 4 weeks after transplanting. The plants are stunted and often warped and curled because the attack is more severe on one side of the plant than on the other. The vascular bundles of the stem and lower leaves become darkened, the color deepening as the disease progresses. Diseased plants shed their lower leaves while the plants are still attempting to grow.

This disease is caused by *Fusarium oxysporum* f. *conglutinans*. When the soil is seriously infested with the fungus, a large part of the crop may be destroyed. Walker states that this disease is confined to members of the cabbage tribe (cabbage, cauliflower, broccoli, Brussels sprouts, kohlrabi, kale, and collards). It is especially destructive to cabbage and is a serious menace when cabbage is grown as a summer crop. It is seldom destructive to winter-grown cabbage in the South. Tisdale (1923) has shown that the fungus does not develop at temperatures lower than 68°F. and that it is at its maximum rate of growth when the temperatures reach 80 to 90°F. At 95°F. growth is inhibited.

The organism persists indefinitely in the soil; therefore ordinary crop rotation does not control the disease. Seedbed infection is one of the worst dangers; hence care should be taken to plant the seed in clean soil. Where the disease is present and is serious, the only practicable control measure is to grow resistant strains or varieties. There are resistant strains of the various important cabbage types: Jersey Queen (Wakefield type); Resistant Detroit, Resistant Golden Acre, Racine Market, Marion Market, Medium Copenhagen Resistant (all of the Copenhagen Market type); All Head Select, Globe, Improved Wisconsin All Seasons (all of the Glory type); and Wisconsin Ballhead, Wisconsin Hollander, Bugner, Empire Danish, and Red Hollander (all of the Danish type). Other resistant strains are introduced from time to time.

BLACKLEG. This disease is caused by a fungus parasite (*Phoma lingam* (Tode) Desmax). It may invade almost any portion of the plant, but the worst damage occurs when it kills the stems of the young plants in the seedbed or in the field. Infection often occurs on the stem near the ground, causing dark sunken areas. The disease spreads from these areas, gradually killing the base of the stem and roots, so that the plant wilts. The wilting of the entire plant is characteristic of the advanced stages of this disease, and the leaves adhere to the stem instead of falling off as in the yellows. In the advanced stage of the blackleg, the dead areas are covered with very small black specks, which are the fruiting bodies. These live in the soil on parts of diseased stems and leaves and may persist for 2 years or more. Humid, rainy weather encourages spread of the disease. The fungus may invade the seed without affecting germination, and the fungus borne in the seed is frequently the primary source of infection in seedbeds.

Crop rotation and seed treatment are the methods of control generally recommended. The rotation should cover at least 3 years. Hot-water treatment, 122°F. for 25 to 30 minutes, is effective in destroying the parasite on the inside as well as on the outside of the seed.

BLACK ROT. This is caused by bacterium (*Xanthomonas campestris*) and appears in the plant at any stage of growth. The yellowing of affected leaves followed by a blackening of the veins is the first indication of the disease. Later the plants show a dwarfing or one-sided growth of the head, or if the disease is severe and starts early in the season, there may be no head formed. The heads sometimes rot and fall off. A cross section of the stem of affected plants shows a brown or black ring corresponding to the woody tissue. Often the blackening of the veins of the leaf can be seen through the outer tissues.

This disease is a serious pest of cabbage, cauliflower, Brussels sprouts, and rutabagas. Cauliflower is more susceptible than any of the other crops. Seed infection is the major means of overwintering, but it may also live over in the stems of the diseased cabbage and Brussels sprouts. Seed treatment by the hot-water method described for blackleg destroys the bacteria on the seed. The use of clean seed, crop rotation, and seedbed sanitation are recommended. The rotation should be one in which no cruciferous crops or cruciferous weeds are allowed to grow for at least 3 years.

OTHER DISEASES. Many other diseases attack cabbage, including alternaria leaf spot, wire stem, bacterial leaf spot, sclerotinia rot, white rust, downy mildew, anthracnose, and several others. It is seldom that these cause serious losses; therefore no discussion of them is given here.

Insects. Cabbage and closely related plants are attacked by many insects, including both those with chewing and those with sucking mouth parts. The important chewing insects of cabbage are the cabbage maggot, green-cabbage worm, Southern cabbage butterfly, cabbage looper, diamondback moth, cross-striped cabbage worm, cabbage webworm, garden webworm, purple-backed cabbage worm, and zebra caterpillar. The important sucking insects attacking cabbage are cabbage aphid, turnip aphid, and harlequin cabbage bug.

CABBAGE MAGGOT. (*Hylemyia brassicae*). The cabbage maggot is a small whitish larva of a black fly a little smaller than the common housefly. The fly deposits eggs just below the surface of the ground, on or near the roots of cruciferous plants. The eggs hatch in a few days, and the larvae feed on the plants for about 3 weeks. They first attack the rootlets and then burrow into the main root, causing the plant to wilt and, in most cases, to die. Even if the plant is not killed outright, its vitality is often so weakened that only a small head, or no head at all, is formed. In the North the maggots are most destructive to early cabbage in the field and late cabbage in the seedbed.

Calomel has been used for the control of the cabbage maggot for a long time. It is applied as a dust on the stems of transplants, as dusts in the furrow at time of planting or dusted on the surface around the plant, and as a water suspension in the setting water when a transplanter is used. More effective and cheaper control can be accomplished using heptachlor, aldrin, or dieldrin, which are effective in a number of ways. They may be sprayed or dusted into the furrow at the time of setting or applied in the setting water when a transplanter is used. Some growers have dusted the stems of transplants with these materials with good success. A broadcast application thoroughly fitted into the soil for control of wireworms and other soil insects also gives good control of the cabbage maggot. The exact amount of material to use varies with localities, and local authorities should be consulted before using these materials on crops.

GREEN CABBAGE WORM, OR IMPORTED CABBAGE WORM (*Pieris rapae*). This worm is the larva of a small white butterfly. The larva is about 1 inch long and velvet green in color. It is the most destructive of the common cabbage insects, eating holes in the leaves and often burrowing into the head.

The most popular materials are DDT, methoxychlor, and parathion or mixtures of parathion with other insecticides. These materials cannot be applied to the cabbage within 2 or 3 weeks of harvest, but rotenone and pyrethrum sprays or dusts can be used the day before harvest. If an effective job has been done with the more powerful insecticides, rotenone and pyrethrum will protect the cabbage during the last stages of growth. Since the cabbage plant has a waxy leaf, best results are obtained when a wetting reagent is used in the spray mixtures.

SOUTHERN CABBAGE WORM (*Pontia protodice*). In the adult stage this insect resembles the adult of the green-cabbage worm but is pure white in color. The larva is strongly colored, purplish-and-yellow-striped, with black spots. The injury done by this insect is identical with that of the green-cabbage worm; therefore the same control measures are used.

CABBAGE LOOPER (*Autographa brassicae*), the larva of a moth, resembling the cutworm moth, feeds on the foliage of cabbage and related plants. This worm can be distinguished from the others by its peculiar looping, or doubling up, as it crawls. It is more active than the other worms previously considered and is therefore more difficult to control. In addition to attacking all cole crops it sometimes injures peas, beets, celery, and lettuce. The control measures are much the same for the looper as for the green cabbage worm, except that rotenone is not very effective against the looper. Pyrethrum is effective if applied properly.

OTHER CABBAGE WORMS, including the diamondback moth, cross-striped cabbage worm, cabbage webworm, purple-backed cabbage worm, and zebra caterpillar, injure the crop in much the same way as those already discussed and are controlled by the same measures. The cross-striped cabbage worm bores into the head in the same manner as the green-cabbage worm.

CABBAGE APHID (*Aphis brassicae*). This is one of the species of insects commonly called plant lice. These insects are more injurious during the latter part of the season than earlier. The cabbage aphid is covered with a coat of fine waxy powder, very much like the bloom on cabbage leaves. This covering protects the insects from spray material since the liquid runs off their waxy surface. Spraying with nicotine sulfate solution, to which soap has been added as a sticker, has been recommended in the past. Sprays or dusts of parathion and TEPP are effective in controlling cabbage aphids. Parathion cannot be used within 2 weeks of harvest, but TEPP can be used a few days before harvest. Timeliness is very important in aphid control; the plants should be sprayed before large populations of aphids build up.

TURNIP APHID (*Aphis pseudobrassicae*) is closely related and similar in appearance to the cabbage aphid. The character of damage, life history, and means of control are the same as for the cabbage aphid.

HARLEQUIN CABBAGE BUG (*Murgantia histrionica*) is a true bug about ⅖ inch long, mottled red, black, or yellow. Both the adult and the young suck the juices and inject a poison into the plant. In many sections of the South this insect is one of the most important pests. The young insects are much more easily killed than the adults, but both young and old are difficult to kill by ordinary sprays and dusts. Dusts or sprays containing sabadilla, rotenone, or pyrethrum will control the insects in the younger stages. The sprays should be applied as soon as any insects appear because the adult, or nearly mature, bug is difficult to control by any insecticide mixture. Sanitary measures are important in controlling this bug, and all refuse should be disked or plowed under as soon as the crop has been harvested.

Harvesting. Cabbage which is grown for the early market is harvested as soon as it has attained sufficient size to be placed on the market, since earliness is usually more important than size. The first shipments from the South usually consist of small, immature heads, but as the season advances the quality improves and the heads are closely trimmed. Midseason and late cabbage are not harvested until the heads are full and hard.

In harvesting, the heads are cut with a large knife or, in some cases, with a hatchet. The head is grasped in one hand, and the plant is bent over so that the head can be cut above the outer leaves. Usually the cutter takes two rows at a time, and as he cuts the heads he places them on the row to be gathered by others or he tosses them to a man on a wagon or truck. For late cabbage, care is taken to prevent bruising the heads; for this reason the cutter usually places them on the row to be gathered by others, who toss them to a man on the wagon or truck. They are carefully placed and are hauled to the packing shed or to the storage house.

Grading and Packing. A large part of the cabbage crop is graded and sold according to U.S. Department of Agriculture standards. Marketing quotations and prices are commonly based on the various standards. The U.S. standards are based on solidity, trimming, freedom from withering, puffiness, bursting, soft rot, and seed stems, and damage caused by discoloration, freezing, disease, and insects. There are grades for all types of cabbage, both fresh and stored. Most markets prefer a small-to-medium-sized cabbage head; usually 3 to 4 pounds is the most desirable. The cabbage should be uniformly trimmed to the same number of wrapper leaves and should be packed according to size. Since many retail stores price cabbage by the head, uniformity of size is very important. The detailed grade specifications are changed from time to time, and for that reason they are not given here.

Most of the cabbage crop is shipped in open-mesh bags holding 50 pounds of cabbage. Many markets require that the bags be labeled with count as well as weight of cabbage in the bag. Bags containing 16 heads are the most popular sizes on most markets. Some cabbage is shipped in various types of wooden containers. The Los Angeles lettuce and vegetable crates are the most popular. Cabbage shipped during warm weather should be loaded in refrigerated cars with pulverized ice blown over the load. For winter-time shipments in the North, the cars should be heated to prevent freezing of the cabbage.

Storing. Production of late cabbage for storage in the North was once very important, but the proportion of the crop devoted to storage is becoming smaller each year. Fresh cabbage can be obtained on most markets every month of the year. Consumers show a definite preference for fresh green cabbage over the white stored cabbage even though the price of the former may be much higher. The essentials of success in keeping cabbage in storage are: (1) a good storage variety, (2) freedom from disease or injury of any kind, (3) a relatively uniform temperature near the freezing point, and (4) a moderate degree of humidity, enough to prevent wilting but not so moist as to cause condensation. A good storage variety of cabbage is one with compact, hard heads such as Danish Ballhead. Heads that are diseased when harvested will not keep so well in storage as those that are free from disease. Even if the particular disease present does not continue to develop in storage, the diseased areas give a good opening for some of the storage rots. For this same reason injury which is caused by rough handling is likely to increase loss and shorten the storage period. The lower the temperature, the longer the cabbage will keep, provided the heads do not actually freeze. In fact, slight freezing does not cause serious injury. Since cabbage will not freeze in a room where the air temperature is 32°F. it is safe to maintain that temperature. Moderate humidity in the storage house is important since the common storage rots develop rapidly in a very moist atmosphere and wilting occurs under very dry conditions. In many storage houses, the greatest problem is to control the humidity. Various types and methods of outdoor storage are employed for keeping cabbage for home use and for market for a relatively short period. Heads are sometimes stored in outdoor pits, in much the same manner as root crops. Another common method is to pull the plants, roots and all, and place them in a pit with their heads down. It is impossible to control the temperature and humidity completely in any type of outdoor storage; in addition, it is very inconvenient to remove the cabbage when wanted. For these reasons, most commercial cabbage is stored in specially constructed warehouses. The cabbage is stored on slatted shelves or in slatted bins with ample room for air circulation up through the piles. This prevents pockets of high humidity which would allow diseases to develop. Cabbage shrinks considerably in storage, and the longer it is kept in storage the greater is the shrinkage. Shrinkage is also greater when disease and insect and mechanical injury are present when the heads are put into storage.

CAULIFLOWER

Cauliflower is grown for its white, tender head, or *curd*, formed by the shortened flower parts. While the crop is grown in much the same way as cabbage, it is much more difficult to grow successfully than cabbage.

Statistics of Production. Cauliflower is not one of the most important of the vegetable crops, ranking about twentieth in the list from the standpoint of total value. While statistics are available for the important producing states only, these supply most of the crop and show the trend in production and price (Table 18.2).

Table 18.2. Average Annual Acreage, Production, and Farm Value of Cauliflower Grown in the United States, 1918–1953

Year	Acreage	Yield per acre, crates	Production, crates (000 omitted)	Price per crate	Value (000 omitted)
1918–1927	12,083	257	3,036	$1.36	$ 4,036
1928–1937	28,459	245	6,948	0.77	5,320
1938–1947	32,220	313	10,340	1.12	11,915
1948–1953	31,820	405	12,831	1.27	16,061

The average acreage of cauliflower reached a peak in 1946 and has declined somewhat since that time although the production has been more than 12 million crates yearly since 1945. The production did not drop because the yield per acre increased and offset the decline in acreage. The frozen pack of cauliflower increased from 4,821,000 pounds in 1944 to 35,710,000 pounds in 1953. Diverting part of the production to processing helps prevent market gluts and consequent low prices. The increase in yield per acre is due to many factors but primarily to better production practices resulting from specialization by growers. The small marginal producers have dropped out, leaving the more efficient growers who have increased their acreage and produce the crop more efficiently. California was the leading state in cauliflower acreage in 1953 with 12,300 acres, and New York was second with 7,000 acres, mostly on Long Island. Oregon, Texas, Michigan, Colorado, and Florida grew from 1,400 to 1,800 acres each. About three-fourths of the cauliflower for freezing was grown on the West Coast.

Climatic Requirements. Cauliflower thrives best in a cool, moist climate. It will not withstand so low temperature or so much heat as will cabbage. Cauliflower heads will not develop well in hot weather; for this reason it is grown mostly in the fall and winter. Few sections of the United States have the combination of climatic conditions that is favorable for its production. Sections of California have favorable conditions during the fall and winter. Two sections of New York, Long Island and Erie County, have relatively long cool autumns, because of the tempering influence of nearby bodies of water—the Atlantic Ocean and Lake Erie. A third section of New York, the Catskill Mountain region, has a relatively cool summer season and a good rainfall during this period, so that cauliflower can be grown successfully during the summer. Early-fall freezes prevent successful cauliflower production as a late-fall crop in the Catskill section. Most of the California crop is harvested from the first of November to the last of March. New York cauliflower is harvested mainly from the first of August to the last of November. The Texas and Florida crop is harvested during the winter and early spring.

Soils and Soil Preparation. When other conditions are favorable, cauliflower can be grown on any good soil, but a fairly deep, loamy soil is desired. Sandy loams and silt loams are preferred, although good clay loams are used. The soil should be well supplied with organic matter and well drained. Good drainage is particularly important where the crop is grown during the fall or in the winter.

FIG. 18.6. Magnesium deficiency in cauliflower.

Cauliflower is sensitive to high acidity. Wessels (1932) has shown that maximum yields on a Sassafras silt-loam soil on Long Island were obtained at soil reactions between pH 5.5 and 6.6. As the acidity was reduced from pH 4.5 to about 5.5, the yield of most strains increased markedly. When the reaction approached neutrality, there was a tendency for the yields to decrease, probably because of decreased availability of boron. Workers at the Rhode Island station obtained similar results. Wessels reported very striking differences in the behavior between varieties of cauliflower in their response to varying degrees of acidity. Some varieties developed severe whiptail, while other varieties made more or less normal growth when the pH was below 5.0.

Cauliflower has a high requirement for magnesium, and deficiency symptoms may be apparent when grown on very acid soils (Fig. 18.6). This condition develops on Long Island where cauliflower is grown in rotation with potatoes on very acid sandy soils. The most satisfactory remedy is liming the soil with dolomitic limestone to bring the soil reaction up to about pH 6.5. This is not practical on Long Island because it results in scab on the following crop of potatoes, so the magnesium requirement is met by using a fertilizer containing soluble magnesium.

Fertilizers. Jones, Ernst, and Tavernetti (1935) reported that manure is used at the rate of 10 to 20 tons per acre in some sections of California, while in other sections heavy applications of nitrogenous fertilizers are used. It was not often necessary to use a complete fertilizer in California, but in some areas there was a good response to phosphorus as well as nitrogen.

In New York, the three major sections of cauliflower production follow different fertilizer practices. In the Catskill Mountain region, cauliflower is grown for 1 or 2 years and followed by 3 to 5 years of hay before cauliflower is planted again. Occasionally, manure is used on the cauliflower, but usually the fertilization practice is 1 or 2 tons of a 5-10-5 or a 5-10-10 fertilizer per acre. In Erie County, 5 to 10 tons of manure is usually applied, and in addition 1,000 to 2,000 pounds of a 5-10-10 fertilizer. On Long Island, the usual fertilizer application is 2,000 to 2,500 pounds of a 5-10-10 fertilizer per acre. Manure is seldom used for cauliflower on Long Island, although a rye cover crop may be grown to turn under. While cauliflower gives good response to fertilization, the rates used in most of New York are excessive. The same yields could be obtained by using smaller amounts of complete fertilizer and supplementing it with more frequent and heavier applications of nitrogen side-dressings. On most New York soils, all common sources of nitrogen are equally effective, but on the acid soils of Long Island nitrate of soda seems to give the best results.

Band placement of complete fertilizer is frequently recommended, especially when only a small quantity is applied. Jacob and White-Stevens (1941) conducted experiments for 3 years on Sassafras silt-loam soil on Long Island in which broadcast applications gave better results than banding on both sides of the row. When 1,500 or 2,000 pounds of a 4-8-6 fertilizer was applied in bands, the cauliflower plants were injured so that the same quantities applied broadcast produced a larger yield. Applying part in bands and part broadcast might be better than applying all broadcast.

Results reported by Robbins, Nightingale, and Schermerhorn (1931) and by Carew (1947) indicate that a marked deficiency in nitrogen may result in *buttoning* of cauliflower. Carew showed that other factors are involved, as discussed under Buttoning.

Seed. The importance of good seed can scarcely be overemphasized. Poor strains are expensive at any price, for these will not produce good marketable heads under the most favorable conditions. Prior to the Second World War a large part of the seed of early- and medium-maturing types was imported, mainly from Denmark. However, seed of the large-growing late-maturing types grown during the winter and spring in California has been produced in California for many years. During the war, when importations were cut off, all types of cauliflower seed were produced in the United States, and this has continued to a great extent since the war. In 1953 American seedsmen produced 14,000 pounds of cauliflower seed and imported only 4,600 pounds from Europe. Although the retail price of cauliflower seed is high (sometimes $30 to $40 per pound), seed cost represents only a small part of the cost of production. From 2 to 4 ounces of seed will produce enough plants to set out an acre, the quantity depending upon germination of the seed and the method of growing the plants.

Varieties. Cauliflower varieties differ in plant size, time of maturity, range of maturity, and certain foliage and curd characteristics. There are few primary producers of seed, but almost all seed companies offer it for sale, and frequently a single lot of seed may be sold under a number of different synonyms.

Super Snowball is one of the earliest varieties of cauliflower to mature. Early Snowball A, Super Junior, and Snowcap are similar varieties. The plant is dwarf with medium-large leaves, and the inner leaves curl over the head while the outer leaves curl outward at the tip. The plants are fairly uniform in maturity, and the curds soften if not harvested at the proper time. The curd is of moderate size but tends to be flatter and thinner than later varieties. The Super Snowball types are more likely to develop whiptail than the Erfurt types.

Erfurt or Snowball types are mostly later and larger than Super Snowball types. The leaves tend to be more erect and sometimes longer, and the curds are more rounded, thicker, and heavier than Super Snowball types. The various strains cover a fairly wide range in both time and uniformity of maturity. Early Snowball (Catskill, Dwarf Erfurt) is nearly as early as Super Snowball, but the leaves are short and erect and the plant is somewhat larger. Snowdrift, White Mountain, and Snowball X are a week or more later in maturity, and the plants are larger and curds heavier than the early varieties. The harvest period is not concentrated, but Snowball M and Snowball Imperial have a concentrated harvest period and are similar to the other strains. Improved Holland Erfurt has been a favorite variety of Long Island, and the growers prefer imported seed. There are many strains of this variety, and many are similar to, or the same as, the various strains of Snowball which are grown from seed produced on the West Coast.

Late-maturing varieties of cauliflower, sometimes called heading broccoli, are grown for winter harvest in California. These are vigorous, tall-growing, firm-headed plants that grow well during the winter in mild climates. There is a wide range of maturity between these varieties. Varieties such as November-December, Christmas (January), and February mature at the time indicated by their names when the plants are set out in August. Late Pearl, Cossa, and April mature in the spring when the plants are set out in the fall. Some of these varieties are over-wintered in England, but California is the only growing region in the United States.

There are varieties of cauliflower with purple heads which do not require blanching. Early Purple Head is popular in home gardens but is not grown to any extent commercially. The purple color disappears upon cooking, and the cooked head is pale green, tender, and mild-flavored.

Growing Plants. Cauliflower plants are grown in very much the same manner as cabbage plants. In the North, seed for the early crop is sown in the greenhouse or hotbed and the plants transplanted as described for cabbage. Cauliflower seed is not sown quite so early as cabbage. In the Eastern part of the United States the seed for the late crop is sown about the same time or a little later than late cabbage and the plants are handled in much the same manner. In California, seed is planted at various times in the spring, summer, and fall, depending on the type grown and the region in which the crop is produced. The seed of broccoli type, grown in the Salinas region, is sown in late summer and early fall for winter and early-spring crops.

Since seed is expensive, it is well worthwhile to use those measures which will result in the greatest number of plants from a given amount of seed. Marvel (1952) increased plant production by treating the seed-beds with methyl bromide and lindane before planting. The methyl bromide fumigation controlled all weeds and damping-off, and the lindane controlled cabbage maggots and other soil insects. Plant beds handled in the regular manner produced about 40 plants per square foot, while those grown with soil fumigation and soil insecticide produced 60 plants per square foot. The plants from the treated beds were more uniform and more vigorous since they did not compete with weeds and were not damaged by insects and diseases.

Planting. Plants for the early crop in the North are usually set out as soon as the danger of hard frosts is over. The late crop, in regions where severe freezing occurs, is planted in time for the heads to mature before the arrival of very cold weather. On Long Island and in the Buffalo, N.Y., region, the planting is done the latter half of July and the first part of August; in the field in California at various times through the summer, fall, and early winter. Planting is done by hand or with machines, the latter being used where the acreage justifies the expense.

The distance for planting varies, depending on the variety and the fertility of the soil. The rows are usually about 3 feet apart, and the plants are set 18 to 30 inches apart in the row. The methods of planting are the same as for cabbage.

Cultivation. In the cultivation of cauliflower the same precautions should be taken as suggested for cabbage, for the root systems of the two crops are similar. The weeds should be kept down at all times.

Physiological Disorders. The most important physiological disorders of cauliflower are whiptail, browning, buttoning, and blindness. The first two are deficiency symptoms of specific essential elements, while the last two may result from a variety of causes.

WHIPTAIL. Whiptail results from a deficiency of molybdenum. This condition of cauliflower has long been known, but the cause of the trouble was discovered only recently. Many workers have reported that cauliflower developed whiptail on very acid soils and the condition could be corrected by liming the soil. Molybdenum is unavailable in very acid soils, and availability is increased by reducing the acidity with lime. Whiptail seldom occurs when the soil reaction is pH 5.5 or higher. The Super Snowball types are much more sensitive to molybdenum deficiency than are the Erfurt types. The discovery of molybdenum deficiency as the cause of whiptail was made by workers in Australia. The leaf blades do not develop properly and may be straplike and severely savoyed. In severe cases only the midribs develop, which accounts for the name whiptail. The growing point is usually severely deformed and does not produce a marketable head. In severe cases there is a stimulation of sprouts on the base of the plants. Waring *et al.* (1949) reported that whiptail could be prevented by liming the soil to a pH of 6.5 or by applying 1 pound of sodium or ammonium molybdate per acre. The molybdenum compound may be mixed with the fertilizer, applied in irrigation water, or applied in water when the plants are set in the field. Spraying the plants in the seedbed with $\frac{1}{10}$ ounce of sodium molybdate per square yard 2 weeks before transplanting gave good control of whiptail when the plants were subsequently set into the field. Since fertilizer efficiency is low on very acid soils, the best remedy is liming the soil to pH 6.5 where it is practical.

BROWNING (BROWN ROT, RED ROT). This is a physiological trouble resulting from a deficiency of boron. It has been known in the Catskill Mountain region of New York for several years and has been found in other parts of that state. The trouble first appears as water-soaked areas in the stem and in the center of the branches of the curd, as shown in Fig. 18.7, but the first external appearance is on the surface of the curd (Fig. 18.8). Later, these areas change to a rusty-brown color. In this stage the trouble is known in the Catskill Mountain region as brown rot or red rot. Browning is associated with hollow stem, but many fields of cauliflower with hollow stem have been found to be free of browning. Curds affected with browning are bitter, both in the raw and in the cooked state. Other symptoms resulting from deficiency of

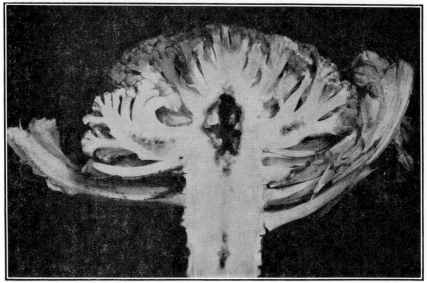

Fig. 18.7. Head of cauliflower showing hollow stem and browning symptoms of boron deficiency.

boron are changes in color of foliage, thickening, brittleness, and downward curling of the older leaves, followed by the development of blisters on the upper side of the midrib. The first color change is a change to a dull green followed by a fading of the green to a greenish-yellow color in a band along the apical margin of the older leaves. Later the edges of the older leaves develop a purple color, and the greenish-yellow band, mentioned above, turns orange-yellow and extends inward from the edge of the leaf for ½ to 1½ inches. In severe cases of boron deficiency the small leaves and the growing point may die. Dearborn (1942) and Chandler (1940 and 1942) have given more complete descriptions of boron-deficiency symptoms on cauliflower.

Results of experiments reported by Dearborn in New York (Table 18.3), by Purvis and Hanna (1940) in Virginia, and by various other workers have shown that the application of common borax (sodium tetra-borate, $Na_2B_4O_7 \cdot 10H_2O$) controls browning and the other symptoms described. The quantity of borax needed to control the trouble depends on the character of the soil, the soil reaction, and the extent of the deficiency. On acid soils, 10 to 15 pounds to the acre usually is sufficient;

FIG. 18.8. Boron deficiency in cauliflower. Both heads were produced on boron-deficient soil: the one on the left without boron; the one on the right with 10 pounds of borax to the acre applied to the soil.

on neutral or alkaline soils, a larger quantity may be necessary, but this can be determined only by experiment. Since in acid soils the boron, applied in the form of borax, is readily available, there is danger of injury to plants when too large a quantity is applied. On neutral or alkaline soils much of the boron may be rendered unavailable.

Table 18.3. Effect of Borax on Grade and on Browning of Cauliflower on Two Types of Soil, in Per Cent

Borax per acre, pounds	Lackawanna silt loam			Culvers silt loam		
	Grade 1	Grade 2	Browning	Grade 1	Grade 2	Browning
0	43.7	25.5	24.4	21.6	5.2	49.3
5	56.0	30.6	1.3	53.0	18.3	0.0
10	58.1	32.2	0.5	50.2	21.0	0.0
25	55.2	33.4	0.0	60.3	15.2	0.0

Boron-deficient cauliflower usually has hollow stems, but hollow stems are not always a symptom of boron deficiency. Heavily fertilized, rapidly growing cauliflower develops hollow stems even though boron is applied in adequate amounts. In the case of boron deficiency, the hollow areas are surrounded by water-soaked, discolored tissue, while in vigorous plants the stem is perfectly clear and white with no signs of disintegration. The normal type of hollow stem may be controlled by spacing the plants closer together or by reducing the fertilizer applied. Attempting to correct this condition by applying more boron in the fertilizer is dangerous since toxicity may result.

BUTTONING. The term *buttoning* is applied to the development of small heads, or buttons, while the plants are small. It has been considered by

Fig. 18.9. Buttoning of cauliflower, plant on the left. The plant on the right is a normal heading plant.

most authorities as premature heading, but Carew (1947) has shown that the curd of normal plants begins to develop as early as that of the so-called button. The main difference is that the developing head of a normal plant is hidden by the foliage until it is of considerable size, while the button is exposed as soon as development begins, as shown in Fig. 18.9. The plants that develop buttons are small and have small leaves which do not cover the developing head.

Robbins, Nightingale, and Schermerhorn (1931) and Carew have shown that a marked deficiency of nitrogen in the culture medium is likely to result in buttoning. Carew has shown also that crowding of the plants in the flats and certain other factors that markedly restricted vegetative growth increased the trouble. It seems probable that nitrogen deficiency is involved in most cases where buttoning is pronounced. Young plants or those about 6 weeks old when set in the field are much less likely to develop buttons than are older plants. Growers are therefore advised to start plants about 6 weeks before they expect to plant them in the field and to follow those practices which will result in rapid vegetative growth. These include maintaining an adequate supply of nutrients and good control of weeds, diseases, and insects, especially the cabbage maggot. It is desirable to delay planting until weather conditions are likely to be favorable for growth.

BLINDNESS. Blind cauliflower plants are those without terminal buds. The leaves that develop are large, dark green, thick, and leathery. In some cases, axillary buds may develop, but the plant does not produce a marketable head. In England, blindness is most common on over-wintered cauliflower plants and is thought to be an effect of low temperature on the small plants. It occurs to some extent in all cauliflower regions in the United States but is due to different causes. The terminal buds may be broken during handling of the plants or eaten by insects or rodents. Certain species of cutworms eat the terminal buds of the plants, and the resulting injury is sometimes confused with whiptail. The insect eats part of the young, unexpanded leaves, and later, when these leaves expand, they may consist of only midribs with parts of the leaf blade attached. Some growers have attributed this to molybdenum deficiency and have made unnecessary applications of molybdenum to their cauliflower plants.

Insects and Diseases. The same insects and diseases that attack cabbage also injure cauliflower. The control measures used on cabbage are satisfactory for cauliflower.

Blanching. A perfect head of cauliflower is pure white. To obtain this it is necessary to exclude the sunlight. While the head is small, it is protected by the small inner leaves which curve over it, but before it is full grown these leaves begin to lift and some other means of covering is necessary. The usual method is to bring the outer leaves up over the head and tie them with twine or rubber bands. By using a different-colored twine or band each day for several days it is easy, when cutting, to select those that have been tied the longest. Sometimes two outer leaves are broken over to protect the head, but this method is not so satisfactory as tying.

The length of time for the blanching of the head depends on the weather. In the hotter part of the season when the plants are growing rapidly, 2 or 3 days will be sufficient, while in cold weather 8 to 12 days may be required. If left too long during hot weather, the leaves begin to rot and discolor the head. In cool weather the heads begin to push up their flower stalks and assume a "riced" condition if left too long. This reduces their value. They may even begin to branch, and this renders them worthless except for pickles. Examination of the heads should be made every day during hot weather and at intervals of every 2 or 3 days in cool weather. It is seldom necessary to examine more than an occasional head of any particular day's tying, as all the heads will be ready about the same time. However, if the heads are developing unevenly, it is necessary to examine every one.

In some of the large, late varieties in which the leaves are very long and upright, the heads or curds are fairly well protected and no artificial protection is required, especially when the crop matures during cool weather. This is true of the large-growing varieties produced in some regions of California during the winter. These varieties belong to the type formerly called broccoli or cauliflower broccoli. Since the sprouting broccoli has become of importance, the name *broccoli* is seldom used for the cauliflower-broccoli type.

Harvesting. Cauliflower is harvested when the heads attain the proper size and before they begin to rice or become discolored. Medium-sized heads are in greatest demand. In harvesting, the plant is cut off well below the head with a large sharp knife.

The heads are trimmed with a long sharp knife cutting squarely across the leaves, leaving ½ to 1 inch projecting above the head. The stubs left protect the head from injury by rubbing against the crate. The stem of the plant is cut off so as to leave at least one circle of outer leaves and the smaller inner leaves.

In a study of factors affecting the price paid for cauliflower sold at auction on Long Island, Hartman (1939) showed a relation between closeness of trimming and price. In general, it was found that the more the curds were covered by surrounding leaves, the higher was the price per crate. Hartman found also that crates packed with from 10 to 13 heads generally sold for a higher price than those containing a larger number.

Grading. Cauliflower heads are usually graded into at least two grades and sometimes three. The U.S. Department of Agriculture has promulgated standards for cauliflower, and it would seem desirable to use these where careful grading is feasible. Unstandardized grading may be unprofitable, as was shown by Hartman (1939) to be the case with cauliflower sold on an auction market on Long Island. In this case, the best cauliflower was packed as No. 1 regardless of quality, provided it was marketable, so that one grower's No. 2 might be as good as another grower's No. 1, and a given grower's No. 2 might be as good at one time as his No. 1 at another time.

Packing. Cauliflower is packed in various types of containers; the slatted cauliflower crate and wire-bound box are the most popular. Some are flat crates for packing one layer of heads, but most are deeper so that two layers of heads may be packed. When two layers are packed the heads of both layers face outward. Tight packing is important since it is desirable to have all the heads about the same distance from the slats and to prevent shifting of the heads within the crate.

Prepackaging cauliflower is gaining in popularity. All of the outer leaves are cut from the curd so that only a few of the small leaves remain and the curd is wrapped in a transparent film and packed in various types of paper or fiber cartons. Another popular pack is individual florets cut from the heads and packed in cardboard trays overwrapped with cellophane. For successful prepackaging, the cauliflower should be hydrocooled to remove the field heat and kept refrigerated at all times. The packaged cauliflower spoils more rapidly than conventionally packed cauliflower unless strict attention is paid to refrigeration.

Storing. Cauliflower is not ordinarily stored, but good sound heads can be kept for a short period in cold storage. Results of experiments by Platenius, Jamison, and Thompson (1934) indicate that good cauliflower can be kept for at least 30 days in cold storage at 32°F. In one experiment cauliflower remained in marketable condition for 40 days. When stored at 40°F., deterioration began in about 12 days.

Lee and Carolus (1949) found that treating cauliflower with naphthaleneacetic acid or 2,4-D prevented leaf abscission and increased the length of storage life. These materials prevented leaf abscission when they were sprayed on the plants within a week before harvest or if they were sprayed on shredded paper and packed around the heads in storage. A combination of one of these materials with low-temperature storage resulted in cauliflower remaining in marketable condition for about 6 weeks. Hruschka and Kaufman (1949) reported similar results.

SPROUTING BROCCOLI

Broccoli has become of considerable importance since 1940 and is increasing in popularity. It is grown by a large percentage of home gardeners, by many market gardeners in various sections of the United States, and for processing, mainly freezing. In 1953, 44,050 acres of broccoli with a value of $17,240,000 was produced in the United States. California produced 23,700 acres; Texas, 6,500 acres; and New York, 2,900 acres. Other important states are Pennsylvania, New Jersey, Washington, Virginia, and Oregon. In 1944, only 6,840,000 pounds of broccoli was frozen, but in 1953, the frozen pack was 89,043,000 pounds.

These figures indicate the rapid rise in popularity of broccoli in the United States. Broccoli is fairly high in vitamin A and ascorbic acid and contains appreciable quantities of thiamine, riboflavin, niacin, calcium, and iron.

Climatic Requirements. Broccoli has about the same climatic requirements as cauliflower although it is not as sensitive to hot weather. Broccoli is harvested over a longer period of time than cauliflower since, with broccoli, the lateral shoots develop marketable heads after the center head has been removed. Hot weather during the harvest period results in an undesirable leafiness in the heads, and the heads develop so rapidly that it is difficult to harvest at the proper time. It is grown as a winter crop in Texas and other Southern states. California produces broccoli in the early spring and fall. It is a fall crop in most of the Northern states, although in some regions it can be produced earlier in the summer. The plant is hardy and will withstand fairly heavy frosts without any appreciable damage.

Planting and Culture. The plants are grown in outdoor seedbeds in much the same manner as cabbage or cauliflower. A pound of seed should produce enough plants to plant 4 acres of broccoli in the field. In some areas direct seeding is practiced and the plants are thinned to the desired spacing after the seeds have germinated, but this requires 1 or 2 pounds of seed per acre. Broccoli is fertilized in much the same manner as cauliflower and is subject to the same physiological disorders.

Broccoli may need more nitrogen than cauliflower, especially late in the growing season. A high yield of side shoots can be obtained by liberal nitrogen side-dressings after the central head is cut. A short period of dry weather reduces the yield markedly, and broccoli has responded well to supplemental irrigation in most of the growing areas. Manure and soil-improving crops which increase the water-holding capacity of the soil are desirable for the broccoli crop whenever they can be used.

Broccoli has a fairly high requirement for molybdenum and boron. The symptoms of molybdenum deficiency are a whiptail condition similar to that of cauliflower. The first external symptom of boron deficiency in broccoli is a browning of individual florets in the head. The symptoms within the plant are exactly the same as cauliflower, beginning with water-soaked areas in the stem which later discolor and extend upward into the head.

In the Eastern states, broccoli is planted in rows 36 to 42 inches apart and spaced 18 to 24 inches apart in the rows. Zink and Akana (1951) reported much higher broccoli yields in California from spacing considerably less than those used in the East. They grew broccoli in double rows 13 inches apart in beds 43 inches apart on centers. The spacing in the row was varied from 8 to 20 inches. The greatest yield of center heads was obtained with the 8-inch spacing. As the plants were placed closer together the size of the center head decreased and the production of lateral heads decreased. With Midway or Medium Italian Green Sprouting, about 6½ tons of center heads per acre was harvested from the plants spaced 8 inches apart while only half as much was obtained from the plants spaced 20 inches apart. There is some justification for close spacing for the production of central heads alone since this would greatly reduce the number of harvests and the handling costs of the crop. Zink and Akana also found that plants spaced 16 and 20 inches apart had very large stems and many of them were hollow. The hollow stem was not a symptom of boron deficiency, but merely a result of the rapid growth of the plant at the wider spacing. Hollow stems did not occur in those plants spaced 8 inches apart.

Varieties. Italian Green Sprouting, or Calabrese, is the most widely grown variety of broccoli. Many strains are available, and some have been named by seedsmen. Midway, Green Mountain, and Grand Central are early- to medium-maturing varieties of Italian Green Sprouting. These types are characterized by a dark bluish-green color and produce large compact heads and many smaller lateral shoots after the center head is cut. The late-maturing strains of Italian Green Sprouting are grown only in California over winter for early-spring harvests.

De Cicco is earlier than Italian Green Sprouting and is light green in color and produces an abundance of small lateral shoots. It is the main variety grown in Texas for winter broccoli. Texas 107 is similar but earlier and more uniform in maturity. It has a light-green head and tends to turn yellow sooner than De Cicco.

Waltham 29 is the most popular variety in the East and is widely adapted. It is medium-maturing and outstandingly uniform in maturity and plant characteristics. The color is a dark bluish green, and it produces large compact heads with small flower buds and a moderate number of large lateral shoots.

The variety to grow depends on the climate and the use for which the crop is intended and market preferences. At one time, processors preferred lateral shoots for freezing since it was easier to separate the flower clusters for packaging. With the increase in popularity of chopped broccoli, the size of the broccoli head is of less importance.

Harvesting. The plant resembles cauliflower except that the leaves are more ragged and the central inflorescence develops a longer stem. A cluster of green flower buds, 3 to 6 inches in diameter, develops in the center. At first this head, or cluster, is compact but gradually spreads. The cluster, with 8 to 10 inches of stem, should be harvested before the flower buds open. Lateral shoots develop in the axils of the leaves, and these develop into marketable heads from 1 to 3 or 4 inches in diameter (Fig. 18.10). These lateral shoots produce a continuous harvest for several weeks.

In the packing house the broccoli heads are usually trimmed to a length of 6 inches and tied in bunches weighing about 1½ pounds using a form similar to that used for packing asparagus. In the West, the bunches are usually packed in a flat crate which holds 28 bunches, or 42 pounds, but a variety of packages are used for marketing broccoli in other areas.

Fig. 18.10. Plant of sprouting broccoli showing three heads produced from lateral shoots after the central bud had been removed.

Packing. The flowers on the broccoli heads continue to develop after harvest, and the product is considered unsalable when the flowers begin to open or turn yellow. At room temperatures broccoli becomes yellow in about 3 days; therefore it is very important that broccoli be kept refrigerated at all times. Best results are obtained when the broccoli is hydrocooled to a temperature of about 40° and then packed with snow ice in the crate and kept in refrigerators until offered for sale.

Marth (1952) found that 2,4,5-trichlorophenoxyacetic acid sprayed on the broccoli 3 or 4 days before harvest prevented the loss of chlorophyll from the heads for about 1 week. This material at very dilute concentrations also prevented dropping of the florets during subsequent handling operations.

Some broccoli is wrapped in transparent films for market. The main problem in prepackaging broccoli is the yellowing of the heads in the packages. Lieberman and Hardenburg (1954) found that yellowing could be delayed by storing the broccoli in an oxygen-free atmosphere. Flushing the packages with oxygen-free gas retarded yellowing appreciably and led to the suggestion that ethylene accumulation in the package may be one of the causes of rapid yellowing. Lieberman and Spurr (1955) found that ethylene was one of the important volatile compounds emitted by broccoli in storage. Production of ethylene and the ensuing yellowing were reduced by refrigerating the packaged broccoli. Packaged broccoli had a very strong odor, and much of this odor was due to methyl mercaptan, acetaldehyde, and ethyl acetate, which were emitted from the broccoli. Packaging does not eliminate the need for refrigeration but may actually accentuate the necessity of keeping broccoli cold.

BRUSSELS SPROUTS

The edible portions of this plant are the buds, or small heads, that grow in the axils of the leaves (Fig. 18.11). The heads, or "sprouts," when fully developed, are 1 to 2 inches in diameter. They are prepared for the table in the same manner as cabbage and are a popular frozen product. They are fairly rich in vitamin A and ascorbic acid and contain appreciable quantities of riboflavin, niacin, calcium, and iron.

This crop has been grown in the vicinity of Brussels, Belgium (from whence it gets its name) for hundreds of years and is an important vegetable in most European countries. It is a minor crop in the United States but seems to be increasing in popularity, especially the frozen product. In 1944, about 5 million pounds was frozen, while in 1953 nearly 41 million pounds was frozen, mostly in California. The major producing areas are California with 5,100 acres and New York with 800 acres, mostly on Long Island. The 1953 production was 26,100 tons of sprouts valued at $5,415,000.

Culture. The general cultural requirements for Brussels sprouts are about the same as for cauliflower. The plant will stand considerable freezing and can be harvested late into the fall until severe freezes occur. The best-quality sprouts are produced in the fall with sunny days and light frosts at night. Hot weather results in soft and open sprouts which are undesirable. In California the planting season is May to July, with the peak of harvest occurring October to December, but continuing until March. On Long Island plantings are made in June and July and the harvest ends in December with the peak period in October and November.

The plants are spaced 2 to 3 feet apart in rows 3 feet apart. The plants are usually grown in outdoor seedbeds and transplanted to the field when they are 6 to 8 weeks old. One pound of seed should supply enough plants for 5 or 6 acres. Sometimes 1 or 2 pounds of seed per acre are sown directly in the field and the plants are thinned to the proper spacing.

Brussels sprouts grow best at a soil reaction of pH 6.0 to 6.8, but are not as sensitive to high acidity as cauliflower. Fertilizer requirements are

Fig. 18.11. Plant of Brussels sprouts showing a large number of heads, or "sprouts," on the stem.

similar to cauliflower. In California, manure and nitrogen supply the fertilizer needs, but in New York a common practice is 1 ton of 5-10-10 containing 20 pounds of borax. Nitrogen side-dressings are made in all areas since the crop has such a long growing period.

Dwarf varieties, such as Catskill and Long Island Improved, are grown in New York. Larger-growing varieties are used in California, and Half Dwarf has been the standard variety for some time. A new selection of this variety called 50A produces more uniform and darker-green sprouts than the standard variety.

English gardeners remove the terminal buds after sprouts have begun to form, but this is not practiced in the United States. Metcalf (1954) in Montana studied the effect of removing the terminal bud and lower leaves after sprouts started to form. Removing the terminal bud increased the total yield and average size of sprouts but reduced the number produced. Pruning the lower leaves before the sprouts were ready for harvest greatly reduced the total yield. While terminal-bud removal was beneficial under the short Montana growing season, it is doubtful that it would be of any benefit in the major producing areas. Under favorable climates all the sprouts produced by the plant mature for harvest, and limiting the number of buds for sprout formation would result in lower yields.

Harvesting. Harvesting begins usually in 3 to $3\frac{1}{2}$ months after setting the plants. Early sprouts should be picked over several times, the lowest on the plant being taken each time, otherwise these will open out and become yellow. The first picking should not be delayed after the lower leaves begin to turn yellow as the sprouts get tough and lose their delicate flavor. In picking, the leaf below the sprout is broken off and the sprout removed by breaking away from the stalk. As the lower leaves and sprouts are removed, the plant continues to push out new leaves at the top, and in the axil of each leaf a bud, or sprout, is formed. The sprouts are placed in baskets or other containers as picked and carried or hauled to the packing house. In New York, they are packed in quart berry boxes and are shipped in the ordinary 16- or 24-quart berry crate. The individual boxes are sometimes overwrapped with a transparent film which delays wilting and seems to prolong their shelf life. In California, most of the crop is packed in plastic film bags holding 12 ounces of sprouts, and 12 bags are packed in fiberboard boxes.

The sprouts keep well in storage at 32°F. and high humidity (95 to 98 per cent) for 6 to 8 weeks. For home use in regions where severe freezes occur, the whole plant may be stored in a cool cellar and the sprouts removed as needed. In mild climates the plants are left in the field or garden throughout the winter. In fact, the California crop is grown mainly in the winter and is harvested as the sprouts mature.

Diseases and Insects. Most of the pests of cauliflower also attack Brussels sprouts, and the control measures are much the same.

KOHLRABI

Kohlrabi is grown for the turniplike enlargement of the stem aboveground (Fig. 18.12). It is little known and not appreciated in the United States, although it is an excellent vegetable if used before it becomes tough and stringy. For good quality the growth should be rapid and without check. The plants may be started in the greenhouse or hotbed for an early crop, but the more common practice is to plant the seed where the crop is to mature.

Culture. The seed is sown in rows 18 inches apart for hand cultivation or 24 to 30 inches for tractor cultivation. The plants are thinned to stand 6 to 8 inches apart in the row. Planting at intervals of 2 to 3 weeks will secure the proper sequence and ensure a continuous supply of tender kohlrabi.

A rich garden soil will produce excellent kohlrabi. If the soil is not already rich, a liberal dressing of manure is desirable. If manure is not available, green-manure crops and commercial fertilizer may be used as

Fig. 18.12. Kohlrabi plants ready for harvest. (*Courtesy of Joseph Harris Seed Co.*)

substitutes. A fertilizer similar to that suggested for cauliflower would be satisfactory for this crop.

Cultivation similar to that given cabbage or cauliflower is satisfactory for kohlrabi, but when planted in rows less than 24 inches apart hand cultivators are used.

Varieties. The most popular varieties are White Vienna, Green Vienna, Purple Vienna, and Earliest Erfurt. The White Vienna is probably grown to a greater extent than all of the others combined.

Harvesting. Kohlrabi should be harvested when the swollen stem is 2 to 3 inches in diameter and before it becomes tough and woody. In preparation for market, the root is cut off and the plants are tied together in bunches like beets or sold in bulk.

CHINESE CABBAGE

Chinese cabbage is little grown in the United States and is considered a new vegetable although it has been known by authorities in this country for many years. It is grown as a potherb and also as a salad plant. It requires a rich soil, abundance of moisture, and a cool season. Quick, continuous growth is important.

This plant is probably a native of China where it has been in cultivation since the fifth century.

Chinese cabbage is an annual and has few characteristics of common cabbage. Two more or less distinct species are grown: pe-tsai (*Brassica pekinensis*) and pakchoi (*B. chinensis*). The pe-tsai resembles cos lettuce but produces a much larger head which is elongated and compact; the leaves are slightly wrinkled, green, thin, and much veined. The midrib is broad and light in color. The pakchoi varieties resemble Swiss chard in habit of growth. The leaves are long, dark green, and oblong or oval. This type does not form a solid head. The most popular varieties are Chihili and Wong Bok.

Culture. Chinese cabbage thrives best during the cooler portion of the growing season; therefore in the South it is grown as a winter crop and in the other portions of the country as a fall crop. Hundreds of attempts have been made to produce Chinese cabbage as an early summer crop, but in most seasons the plants go to seed before forming a head. It has been assumed that shooting to seed in summer is due to high temperature, but results reported by Lorenz (1946) from experiments in California indicate that length of day is the important factor. He found that flowering was inhibited at temperatures averaging 80 to 90°F., also that flower induction was hastened as the temperature was lowered from 70 to below 50°F. at equal day lengths. He says that high-quality Chinese cabbage can be produced only under moderate to cool temperatures (60 to 70°F.). Below 60°F. seedstalks may form before good heads can be produced.

When Chinese cabbage is started as a spring crop, the seed is sown in a greenhouse or hotbed and the plants are handled about the same as cabbage. It is important, however, to prevent a check in growth, and for this reason the plants should not be allowed to get too large before being set out. It is best to set them in the field within 4 weeks of the time the seed is sown.

As a fall crop the seeds are often sown where the crop is to mature, and after the plants become established they are thinned to stand 12 to 15 inches apart, depending on the variety and richness of the soil. Some growers prefer to grow the plants in an outdoor seedbed and to transplant the young plants to the field. If they are to be transplanted, the work should be done while the plants are small.

Any rich soil retentive of moisture and in good physical condition will produce a satisfactory crop of Chinese cabbage when the other conditions are favorable. Market gardeners select either a good loam or a sandy loam for this crop. A good muck soil is almost ideal for Chinese cabbage since this type of soil is rich in nitrogen and is retentive of moisture. The largest crops seen by the author were produced on mucks.

The general care of the crop is about the same as that given cauliflower, but the length of time required to grow a crop of Chinese cabbage is less than for cauliflower.

Fig. 18.13. Heads of Chinese cabbage with the outer leaves removed. (*Courtesy of U.S. Department of Agriculture.*)

Harvesting. Chinese cabbage is harvested when the heads are fully developed. The heads are cut from the stalk in the same manner as cabbage or cauliflower. The loose, outer leaves are removed as shown in Fig. 18.13, and the heads are packed in various ways. All kinds of packages are used since the crop has not become of sufficient importance to demand a special package. Some growers use flat baskets, others use boxes and crates of various kinds. Lettuce boxes, used to some extent, are fairly satisfactory for the long-headed varieties. The heads are usually laid in the package rather than placed upright, although the latter method has been used in packing in celery crates.

Chinese cabbage has been grown mainly for local markets, but the industry is developing at considerable distances from the consuming centers; therefore a good shipping package is needed.

Storage. In China on the approach of winter, the plants are pulled, the outer leaves are removed, and the heads are stored in an outside cellar. In the United States storage of Chinese cabbage has not been practiced to any great extent, although it can be kept for several weeks in cold storage at 32°F. and relative humidity of about 95 per cent. At higher temperature the storage life is shortened. In preparation for storage the head is cut from the plant, the outer diseased or injured leaves are removed, and the heads packed loosely in crates or boxes and placed in storage in such a way that there is air circulation around the container in all directions.

CHAPTER 19

Root Crops

Beet	Rutabaga
Carrot	Radish
Parsnip	Horse-radish
Salsify	Turnip-rooted chervil
Scorzonera, or black salsify	Skirret
Scolymus, or spanish salsify	Celeriac
Turnip	

Root crops thrive best in a cool season and in a deep friable soil. When produced in the South, they are grown during the winter. Those requiring only a short growing period do better in spring and fall than in midsummer. Since all the root crops are hardy, they may be planted early in the spring in the North and may be left in the field or garden until late in the fall.

All the root crops listed above have similar cultural requirements. When grown for market, they are produced on an intensive scale. Seeds are nearly always sown where the crop is to mature, the only exception being the beet, seeds of which are sometimes sown in a greenhouse or hotbed for a very early crop.

BEET

The garden beet is an important home-garden crop and is grown by many of the market gardeners. The beet is grown also for shipping to distant markets and for processing. The average annual acreage for the fresh-market crop for the 5-year period 1949–1953 was 8,700 acres with an estimated farm value of $2,040,000. The leading states in production for the fresh market in 1953 were Texas with 5,500 acres and New Jersey and Pennsylvania with 900 acres each. The average annual acreage of beets for processing during the 1949–1953 period was 17,150 acres, and the crop was valued at $3,157,000 annually. The leading states in acreage in 1953 were Wisconsin with 7,300 acres, New York with 4,400 acres, and Oregon with 1,150 acres.

History and Taxonomy. The garden beet is probably a native of Europe, and while it has been known since about the third century it is essentially a modern vegetable. The first appearance of the improved beet in Germany is recorded about 1558 and in England about 1576. It was mentioned by McMahon in 1806 as being grown in the gardens of America at that time, although it is not definitely known when it was first brought over.

The beet is a member of the Chenopodiaceae, or goosefoot family. The garden beet, stock beet, or mangel, sugar beet, and chard belong to the same species, *Beta vulgaris*. It usually behaves as a biennial, producing a thickened root and a rosette of leaves the first year, and flowers and seed the second year. Under some conditions, mentioned later, the plant produces flowers and seed the first year. The flower stalk grows to a height of about 4 feet. The calyx continues to grow after flowering, becomes corky, and completely covers the seeds. This forms what is commonly called the beet seed; in reality it is a fruit containing usually two to six seeds. The true seeds are small, kidney-shaped, and brown in color. They retain their germinating power for 5 or 6 years under ordinary storage conditions.

Soils and Soil Preparation. While beets are grown on nearly all types of soil they thrive best on a fairly deep friable loam, moist but well drained. Where large yields are most important, as for processing or for the fall or winter market, a deep rich alluvial soil, such as a silt loam, is considered very desirable. Muck soil is almost ideal for late beets since it is loose and moist. Light sandy soils are satisfactory when proper fertilization is carried out if water is available for supplementary irrigation. Heavy soils are not satisfactory for beets since the roots are likely to be unsymmetrical in form when grown on such soils.

The results of many experiments indicate that the beet plant is sensitive to soil acidity. Hester, Parker, and Zimmerley (1936) showed marked increases in yield at Norfolk, Va., as the acidity was reduced from pH 5.0 to 5.8. The yields at pH 5.8, 6.5, and 7.0 were essentially the same. Results of experiments in other states are in agreement with those obtained in Virginia. The soil for beets and all other root crops should be thoroughly prepared, and the surface should be loose and smooth. The soil surface must be free from clods and trash for the seeders to function properly. It is impossible to do a uniform job of planting on a poorly prepared soil. After the soil has been thoroughly pulverized it is desirable to smooth the surface with a Meeker harrow or drag just before planting the seed.

Climatic Requirements. Beets are fairly hardy and are generally considered a cool-weather crop. They grow well in warm weather, but the best-quality beets are produced under cool-weather conditions. Good-

quality beets have a high sugar content and dark internal color throughout the root. Under unfavorable conditions beets show alternate white
and colored circles when sliced. This "zoning" of beets is most pronounced in hot weather. Lorenz (1947) found that beets grown in
California and planted in February had a high sugar content and good
color until July when the internal color was rated poor. Beets planted in
May had poor or fair color throughout the summer months until October when the color was classed as good. September plantings had beets

Fig. 19.1. Premature seeding of beet plants. The plants in the row marked with a
hat were grown in a greenhouse at 60 to 70°F. prior to planting in the field and
produced no seedstalks. The plants in the next row to the right were grown at 50
to 60°F. prior to planting in the field, and 94 per cent of them produced seedstalks.

of excellent color and quality by November and continued to be so
until seedstalks started to develop in the spring. Good color was not
directly related to high sugar content, but low sugar content was always
associated with poor color.

Beet plants sometimes shoot to seed before the roots reach marketable size. Results of experiments reported by Chroboczek showed that
if the plants are subjected to relatively low temperature of 40 to 50°F.
for 15 days or longer, some seeding is likely to occur in the field. When
the treatment was 30 days at 40 to 50°F. 47.69 per cent of Crosby
Egyptian plants went to seed in the field before the beets reached a
marketable size. When plants were grown in a cool greenhouse for 2
months or more and then grown subsequently in the field, most of them
went to seed, as shown in Fig. 19.1.

Fertilizers. Beets must make rapid and continuous growth to develop the highest quality; therefore a good supply of available nitrogen, phosphorus, and potash is necessary. On sandy and sandy-loam soils, manure is valuable to supply humus as well as fertilizing elements. On heavy soils it is of importance in improving the physical condition by making them more friable. It is best, however, to apply fresh manure to a crop preceding beets on account of the weed factor. Well-rotted manure may be applied to the land without danger of introducing weed seed. When manure is used at the rate of 10 to 15 tons per acre on heavy soils, the fertilizer should be relatively high in phosphorus. An application of fertilizer supplying 50 to 60 pounds each of nitrogen and potash and 100 to 120 pounds of phosphorus should give good results. Used on light soils with applications of manure the fertilizer should supply 60 to 80 pounds of nitrogen and 120 to 140 pounds of phosphorus and potash. In case manure is not used it is desirable to use soil-improving crops to maintain a humus supply and to apply liberal quantities of fertilizer. On sandy and sandy-loam soils, 75 to 100 pounds of nitrogen and 150 to 200 pounds each of phosphorus and potash should prove satisfactory. On heavier soils less nitrogen and potash would be required. Beets have a fairly high nitrogen requirement, and it is best to apply part of the nitrogen as a side-dressing after the plants are 4 to 6 inches tall. Nitrate sources of nitrogen are usually preferred for beets and seem to give better results than the ammonium sources.

On muck that has been well fertilized for several years an application of 40 to 60 pounds of nitrogen, 80 to 120 pounds of phosphorus, and 120 to 180 pounds of potash is recommended. Harmer (1943) made fertilizer recommendations for muck soils in Michigan based on differences in soil reaction and soil drainage. For poorly drained muck soils below pH 6.5 he recommends 600 to 1,000 pounds per acre of 3-9-18. For well-drained muck of similar reaction he recommends 600 to 1,000 pounds per acre of an 0-9-27. For slightly acid or alkaline muck soils pH 6.6 or higher Harmer suggests 500 pounds of a 0-10-20 for well-drained and 500 pounds of a 3-9-18 for poorly drained mucks. Results of experiments reported by Harmer in 1941 show a marked increase in yield by applying 500 to 1,000 pounds of common salt to the acre in addition to the regular fertilizer used on muck soils in Michigan. Shafer and Sayre (1946) also reported marked responses of beets to salt on mineral soils in New York. Results of other experiments by Sayre and Shafer (1944) and Pew (1949) led them to conclude that the stimulation from salt resulted from the sodium ion rather than from the chloride ion as had been suggested by Tottingham (1919).

In some areas it is important to apply other elements than those mentioned; for example, it has been shown that applications of boron as borax or boric acid are important in certain areas of New York, Wisconsin, and Oregon, as discussed later in this chapter under Physiological Disorders.

Planting. A large part of the beet crop is grown from seeds planted where the plants are to mature, but a few early beets are grown from plants started in the greenhouse or hotbed. In growing plants for transplanting, the seed is sown several weeks prior to the time for outdoor planting. Plants may be allowed to grow in the seedbed until time to set them into the field, or they may be transplanted into flats. It is possible to get beets large enough for market 2 to 3 weeks earlier by growing the plants in the greenhouse. The transplanting method is expensive and is justified only where high prices can be obtained.

Beet plants are fairly hardy, so in regions where hard freezes do not occur seed may be planted during the late summer, fall, and winter. Where hard freezes occur planting should be delayed until danger is over. For a succession of young tender beets, several plantings should be made, the number depending on the length of the growing season. The main crop grown for processing or for fall and winter market in the North is planted during May or early in June. Beets are usually planted in rows 18 to 24 inches apart, and it usually requires 4 to 6 pounds of seed to plant an acre. The seed should be planted about ½ inch deep. Poor stands frequently result on heavy soils which crust after a hard rain and prevent emergence of the small plants. The seedlings emerge over a fairly long period of time, and it is difficult to get a uniform stand of beets of the same age. Since the seed (beet ball) is uneven in size and irregular in shape it is difficult to get even distribution. Fairly good distribution can be obtained by sowing seed that has been screened to separate the seed into various sizes. Hand thinning is usually necessary for the market crop since each fruit contains more than one seed and the plants tend to come up in clumps. Frequently, thinning is delayed until some of the beets are large enough to use, and when the large ones are removed the small ones are left to develop. Those left to mature should be spaced 3 or 4 inches apart. Thinning is seldom practiced with the crop grown for processing because of the high cost of hand labor involved. Processors usually pay a premium for small beets, so that close spacing of the plants is desirable to keep down the size of the individual plants.

Cultivation. Clean, shallow cultivation should be given as needed to control weeds. Experimental results given in Chap. 9 indicate that yields of beets were not increased materially by maintaining a soil mulch. Cultivating after the crop was about half grown was of little or no value. When there are no weeds, late cultivation is likely to do more harm than good because the destruction of roots more than offsets any benefits that might be derived from the soil mulch. Many of the roots of the beet plant are found near the surface, as shown in Fig. 19.2. Cultivation to the depth of 2 inches would have destroyed all the roots shown in the illustration. Most cultivation of beets is done by hand cultivators or small tractor cultivators. The knife attachments of these machines are efficient in killing weeds and destroy few roots, so that these are recommended for most cultivating. Hand weeding sometimes is necessary to keep down weeds in the row.

Chemical Weed Control. Many weeds found in beet fields can be controlled by a spray of common salt. The spray should be applied when the beet plants have three to five true leaves. The most common con-

FIG. 19.2. Roots of the garden beet uncovered by washing off the soil to the depth of 2 to 3 inches.

centration is 2 pounds of salt in each gallon of water, and 200 gallons of the solution is sprayed on each acre. Some growers add ammonium nitrate or nitrate of soda to the salt spray when the beets need a nitrogen side-dressing. Borax may be used in the spray at rates of 20 to 40 pounds per acre to supply boron to the beets as well as to increase the effectiveness of weed control since the borax is toxic to many weeds. All weeds should be thoroughly drenched with the spray. The beets may wilt after spraying, but they recover after a few days. Some weeds, especially lamb's-quarters (*Chenopodium alba*), are not harmed by the salt spray. When lamb's-quarters is severe, a preemergence spray of Stoddard Solvent applied just before the beets emerge helps control this pest. Annual grasses can be controlled by a preemergence spray of 8 to 12 pounds of TCA per acre. In some areas CMU (Karmex W) has been used successfully as a herbicide in plantings of beets. The rate must be carefully controlled, or the beets will be severely damaged. Local agricultural officials should be consulted for local recommendations before using it on beets.

Varieties. The most popular varieties of early beets for market are Crosby Egyptian and Early Wonder. Crosby Egyptian is a flat globe with a small taproot and a smooth exterior. The internal color is dark purplish red with some indistinct zoning. Early Wonder is a flattened globe with rounded shoulders with a smooth, dark, red skin. The interior is dark red with some lighter-red zoning. The leaves of both varieties are mostly green with red veins. These varieties are likely to show pronounced white zoning when grown during hot weather. The most widely grown variety of beet is the Detroit Dark Red and strains derived from it. It is globular with dark-red smooth skin, and the internal color is a uniform dark blood red with indistinct zoning. The leaves are dark green tinged with red or maroon. It is a good all-purpose beet and is used for bunching and for processing. Perfected Detroit is the favorite beet for processing. The interior color is darker than Detroit Dark Red, and the large leaves with strong petioles make it well adapted to mechanical harvesting. Perfected Detroit roots attain their globe shape at an early age and are preferred by canners for small whole beets. They are also used for sliced and diced beets since the color is uniformly dark red and flavor and tenderness are outstanding. Detroit Short Top, a strain of Detroit Red with small leaves, is used for bunching in areas where tops are likely to grow quite large. The long types of beets such as Half Long Blood and Long Dark Blood are grown in Europe, but are not widely grown in the United States. The Long Dark Blood beets may grow a foot or more long.

Physiological Disorders. INTERNAL BLACK SPOT of beets is caused by a deficiency of boron. The hard or corky black spots are scattered throughout the root but are always found in the light-colored zones. The light-colored zones are the youngest cells in the beet and are actively dividing while the beet is enlarging. Boron deficiency characteristically affects the young cells and tissues first. The younger leaves on the plants tend to be more straplike than the older leaves and may be malformed or one-sided in shape. The younger leaves and sometimes the older leaves develop more dark-red color than plants not showing the deficiency. During hot spells the plants show a tendency to wilt quickly during the day. Experiments in the control of internal black spot have been conducted by Walker (1938), Walker et al. (1943) in Wisconsin, Powers and Bouquet (1940) in Oregon, Raleigh, et al. (1941) and Lorenz (1942) in New York, Purvis and Hanna (1940) in Virginia, and by several others in the United States and in Europe. All these investigators have shown that applications of borax give commercial control of internal black spot and other symptoms associated with it. Boron deficiency is most likely to occur on soils that are neutral or alkaline in reaction, since it is held in an unavailable form when the soil reaction rises above pH 6.8. Light, sandy soils that have been cropped intensively and are subject to heavy leaching may show boron deficiency regardless of the soil reaction. The quantity of borax needed for satisfactory control varies with the nature of the soil, the soil reaction, and to some extent, with soil moisture. On a heavy soil or an organic soil more borax would be required than on a light sandy or sandy-loam soil, other conditions being the same. Generally, more borax is needed on a neutral or alkaline soil than on a moderately acid or strongly acid soil. Lorenz has shown that the moisture content of the soil is an important factor in boron deficiency. In greenhouse experiments using a silt-loam soil of limestone origin, he found that when the soil was kept at a low moisture content applying borax at rates as high as 300 pounds per acre injured the beet plants only slightly. On the other hand, when the soil moisture content was kept high 100 pounds of borax was toxic to the beet plants and the young seedlings grown in moist soil. Plants grown in soil kept at a low moisture content and supplied with borax at the rate of 200 pounds per acre showed symptoms of boron deficiency. This explains why boron deficiency is more evident in a season of low rainfall than in one of high rainfall. Walker suggested 40 pounds of borax per acre for areas in Wisconsin where boron deficiency is a problem. On limestone soils in New York the recommendation is 50 pounds of borax to the acre, and about 20 pounds to the acre on acid soils where boron deficiency is known to exist. Harmer (1943) recommended 5 pounds of borax per acre for acid muck soils in Michigan and 10 pounds for mucks that are above pH 6.6. Purvis and Hanna recommended 10 pounds for the acid mineral soils in eastern Virginia.

Varieties of beets show great differences in susceptibility to boron deficiency. Walker *et al.* (1945) grew several varieties in Wisconsin on a soil with a low boron supply. Flat Egyptian made poor growth, and 70 per cent of the plants showed deficiency symptoms while only 50 per cent of the plants of Morse Detroit and Detroit Dark Red was affected. Crosby Egyptian was moderately affected with 20 per cent of the plants showing deficiency symptoms. The most resistant variety was Long Dark Blood which made normal growth, and none of the plants showed evidence of deficiency.

Harvesting. Beets for bunching are harvested as soon as they attain a diameter of $1\frac{1}{4}$ to $1\frac{1}{2}$ inches. After they reach 2 inches in diameter, bunched beets are not in great demand. In some areas, the beets are pulled by hand and the injured or dead leaves are removed before bunching. Four to six beets are tied together with the tops on and are washed to remove any adhering soil. A more popular method is mechanical harvesting of the beets and packaging the topped, washed beets in transparent film bags. The topped beets in transparent film bags have a longer shelf life than bunched beets with the tops on. The late crop of beets grown in the North and those grown for processing in various areas are practically all harvested with a mechanical beet harvester. This machine lifts the beets, cuts off the tops, and conveys the topped roots into a truck which moves along with the harvester. The beets then are hauled to the processor or to the storage house. Some of the beets from this late crop reach the market as topped beets in transparent bags or in bulk; usually in bushel baskets or similar containers. The beets are harvested when most of the crop has a root diameter of ¾ to 2½ inches. Processors pay a premium price for this size of beet. Oversized beets are not in great demand since they can be used only for diced beets or baby food rather than as whole beets or whole slices.

Storing. Beets are often stored in outdoor pits or banks or in common storage houses as the types described in Chap. 14. The best temperature for beets is near the freezing point, but they should not be allowed to freeze. The air in the storage house or cellar should be kept rather humid to prevent wilting and withering of the roots. Beets keep well in a cold storage at a temperature of 32°F. with a humidity of about 90 per cent, which is a common practice where beets are stored for processing.

Diseases and Insects. The beet crop is not seriously injured by many diseases and insects. The scab, leaf spot, and internal black spot are diseases sometimes injurious, and the beet leaf miner and webworm are insects that cause considerable loss under some conditions.

SCAB. This is caused by the same organism as the potato scab. It does not thrive on a soil that is very acid, but it is not safe to make the soil sour enough to control the scab because this would interfere with the growth of the beet crop.

LEAF SPOT. Leaf spot (*Cercospora beticola*) is very widespread in the Eastern and Middle Western states, especially in rainy seasons. The spots are ashen gray surrounded by a purple border. The spot often drops out, and the leaf presents a shot-holed appearance. A large part of the green tissue of the leaves may be destroyed or the leaves may die, in which case they blacken and remain standing. As the leaves die, new ones are formed, thus elongating the crown.

Cleaning up the refuse after harvesting the crop and practicing rotation are beneficial. Thorough spraying with fungicides affords some control, but it is seldom practiced.

BEET LEAF MINER. The larva is a white maggot (*Pegomyia hyoscyami* Panzer) about ⅓ inch long, which burrows in the tissue of the leaves of beets, chard, spinach, and lamb's-quarters. It feeds on the tissues between the upper and lower layers of the leaf and often causes serious injury by rendering the foliage unfit for food and checking the growth of the plant. Infested leaves present a blistered appearance.

Destruction of fallen leaves and other refuse by plowing immediately after harvesting of the crop will aid in controlling this pest since it passes the winter under rubbish in the field. Destruction of lamb's-quarters is also advised.

The fly lays her eggs on the underside of the leaves, and the maggot hatches and enters the leaf. Spraying the underside of the leaves with Parathion or TEPP is helpful if properly applied. It must be applied when the first tiny tunnels are noticed.

WEBWORMS. At least 2 species of webworms attack beets by eating the leaves. The eggs are deposited on the leaves, and the larvae attack the foliage, either spinning small webs among the tender leaves or else feeding on the underside, protected by a small web or with no protection whatever.

Spraying or dusting with DDT will control this insect if care is taken to cover the underside of the leaves.

CARROT

The carrot (*Daucus carota*) is a very popular vegetable and is increasing in importance, owing to the fact that its value in the diet is better understood than it was formerly. It is rich in carotene, a precursor of vitamin A, and contains appreciable quantities of thiamine and riboflavin. The carrot is also high in sugar.

Statistics of Production. Carrot production increased markedly during the period 1923–1945. The acreage in the important states increased from 7,860 acres in 1923 to 97,300 acres in 1945. The acreage decreased after 1945, but production remained about the same, about 30 million bushels. The estimated average annual acreage, production, and value of the commercial crop are given in Table 19.1.

Table 19.1. Average Annual Acreage, Production, and Value of Carrots, 1923–1953

Years	Acreage	Yield per acre, bushels	Production, bushels (000 omitted)	Price per bushel	Value (000 omitted)
1923–1932	20,670	342	7,237	$0.61	$ 4,243
1933–1942	45,580	339	15,150	0.68	10,750
1943–1952	88,670	350	30,939	1.43	43,225
1953	81,990	381	31,230	1.69	51,658

The leading states in acreage of carrots in 1953 were Texas with 28,000 acres; California, 24,600 acres; Arizona, 4,900 acres; and New York, 4,300 acres. About half the carrot acreage is devoted to the winter crop grown in Texas, California, and Arizona. A large portion of the acreage in New York, Wisconsin, Michigan, Washington, and Oregon is grown for processing.

History and Taxonomy. The carrot is a native of Europe, Asia, and northern Africa, and possibly North and South America. It was probably cultivated by the ancients but was not a common food plant. It is now grown throughout the world but is more appreciated in Europe than in America.

It is a biennial of the Umbelliferae, or parsley family. The genus Daucus, to which the carrot belongs, contains about 60 species, some of which are native in North America. Very few of them are cultivated. During the first year a thickened root and a whorl of leaves are formed; at the beginning of the second year the flower stalk starts from the crown and grows to the height of 2 to 3 feet.

Soils and Soil Preparation. The carrot, like the beet, thrives best on a deep, loose, loamy soil. It is grown commercially on sandy-loam, silt, silt-loam, and muck soils. For an early crop a sandy loam is preferred, but for large yields silt, silt loam, or muck is preferred, the last-mentioned being especially desirable because of its fine loose texture. The long smooth slender carrot desired for fresh market can be successfully grown only on deep, well-drained, light soils. Carrots grown on muck soils tend to be more rough and coarse than those grown on light sandy soils. Carrots do not grow well on a soil that is highly acid. Experiments in Virginia and New York indicate maximum yields around pH 6.5. Yields were extremely low at pH 5.2 or below; in fact, there was practically no yield at pH 5.0 at Riverhead, N.Y.

Fertilizers. The discussion of fertilizers for beets applies equally well to carrots. The carrot is considered by many growers to be especially hard on the land, probably because of its heavy draft on the supply of potash. Growers on muck soils report smaller yields of celery and onions following carrots than any other crop. A yield of 10 tons of carrots will remove about 100 pounds of potash, 32 pounds of nitrogen, and 18 pounds of phosphorus from the soil used. Fresh manure should not be applied immediately before planting carrots. Raleigh (1942) has shown that application of fresh manure to carrots may result in branching of the roots, which makes the carrot unfit for market. The substance causing the roots to branch was found in the liquid portion of the manure. Similar responses were obtained in pots by watering carrots with uric acid, urea, and ammonium carbonate. Growth-promoting substances, such as indoleacetic acid, did not produce branching of carrot roots. If manure is to be used, it should be applied to the crop preceding carrots, or only well-rotted or leached manure should be used.

Planting. The carrot is grown from seed planted where the crop is to mature. Since the plant is hardy, seed may be planted in the spring as soon as hard freezes are over in those areas that have severe winter weather. In sections of the South and West where hard freezes do not occur, the crop is planted mainly in the fall or winter, but in certain coastal areas in California, the carrot is an important summer crop because of a relatively cool summer season. Carrot plants sometimes develop seedstalks before the roots reach marketable size, and this results in some loss. Carrots with developing seedstalks have a bitter, undesirable flavor. Results of experiments reported by Sakr and Thompson (1942) indicate that exposure to relatively low temperature during the early stage of growth is an important factor. Fifteen days exposure at 40 to 50°F. resulted in 100 per cent of the plants going to seed when subsequently grown at 60 to 70°F. A small percentage of the plants went to seed when grown at 60 to 70°F. without any cold treatment, but when grown under 70 to 80°F. no seedstalks developed.

Carrot seed is sown in rows 1½ to 2 feet apart in most cases, and it requires 2 to 4 pounds of seed to plant an acre. Mann and MacGillivary (1944) found that lots of seed of the same variety varied greatly in number of seed per ounce and in percentage germination. The amount of Long Imperator seed required to plant an acre varied from 1.8 to 4.6 pounds per acre depending on size of seed and percentage germination. The seed should be planted ½ to ¾ inch deep, the greater depth on light, dry soils. The seed germinates slowly, and the seedling is rather weak, so that soils which crust badly are likely to prevent a good stand of carrots. The seeds germinate irregularly, and seedlings may emerge for a period of 1 to 2 weeks.

Thinning. Since hand thinning is so expensive, commercial plantings of carrots are seldom thinned. The seed should be planted as uniformly as possible so that there is a fairly uniform stand within the row, but the evidence does not justify expensive hand thinning to increase the size of individual carrots. Warne (1948) working in England found that the greatest number of marketable carrots was produced at the closest spacing. Thinning carrots 2 or 4 inches apart in the row increased the average size of roots but decreased the total yield of marketable carrots per acre. Mann and MacGillivary (1949) found no relation between spacing of carrots in the row and size of roots. The seed germination was not uniform, and germination extended over a 10-day period even in germination chambers. The come-up in the field extended over a period of 2 weeks or more. The first seeds to emerge produced the largest roots; however, there was a large variation in root size among those carrots which came up on the same day. This variation was probably genetic.

Environmental Factors on Growth and Color. The orange color of carrots is mostly due to the occurrence of alpha and beta carotene in the roots. These carotenes are precursers of vitamin A, and, in general, the darker the color of the carrots, the higher the nutritive value. Young carrots are light yellow in color and become darker yellow or orange as they grow older. Booth and Dark (1949) studied a number of varieties

Fɪɢ. 19.3. Effect of temperature on the shape of carrot roots. Plant on left was grown at 50 to 60°F., the one in the center at 60 to 70°F., and the one on the right at 70 to 80°F.

in England and found that the rate at which the color increased depended upon the variety and the growing season as well as the age of the root. The intensity of color increased until a maximum was reached, and then the color remained about the same throughout the remainder of the life of the carrot. The maximum carotene concentration that developed depended on the variety but was also influenced by growing season. Red Cored Chantenay developed the highest carotene content of all the commercial varieties studied. Since carrots for the fresh market are usually harvested at an immature stage they are lighter in color than those grown for processing which are harvested when mature. In sections of the South where carrots are grown during the winter the roots sometimes fail to develop a good color. Results of study by Barnes (1936) indicate that low temperature is the main factor responsible for poor color development. Carrots grown in the greenhouse at 50 to 60°F. developed poor color. Those grown at 60 to 70°F. were good in color, while those grown at 70 to 80°F. did not have so good a color as those grown at 60 to 70°F. Temperature had a marked effect also on the shape of the carrot root, the highest temperatures producing the shortest root and the lowest temperatures 50 to 60°F. producing the longest root, as shown in Fig. 19.3. Shape and color of the root were affected

Fig. 19.4. Roots of carrot uncovered by washing off the surface soil to the depth of 2 inches.

somewhat by soil moisture, but not so much as by temperature. At low moisture the roots were longer than at medium or high moisture.

Cultivation. Cultivation to keep down weeds is very important especially in the early stages of growth. Since the carrot grows very slowly for the first few weeks, it cannot compete successfully with weeds. Shallow cultivation with hand cultivators is usually given, and the knife attachments are used when there is considerable weed growth. Cultivation for the purpose of maintaining a soil mulch does not seem to be of much value. Experiments carried on at Ithaca, N.Y., for 6 years showed insignificant difference in yields between plots on which a soil mulch was maintained and those without a mulch. Similar results were obtained in an experiment carried on for 6 years on a silt loam on Long Island. Deep cultivation is likely to be injurious as many roots are found within 2 inches of the surface, as shown in Figs. 19.4 and 19.5.

Chemical Weed Control. Most commercial crops of carrots are sprayed for weed control with Stoddard Solvent, a petroleum product also used as dry-cleaning fluid and paint thinner. The Stoddard Solvent is sprayed over the rows or over the whole area of the field at rates of 50 to 100 gallons per acre. Best weed control is obtained by spraying when the weeds are quite small (Fig. 19.6). All annual weeds and grasses are killed with the exception of wild carrot and ragweed (*Ambrosia* sp.). The carrots may have an oily flavor if the spray is used too near harvest. Usually spraying should not be done after the carrot roots are ¼ inch in diameter. Spraying when the air temperature is very high or when the carrot foliage is wet may cause some injury. The first spray is applied when the carrots are just breaking through the soil if weeds have germinated. Normal tractor cultivation should be followed until weeds begin to appear in the row, when another spray should be applied. One or two sprays should give good weed control for the whole season.

Fig. 19.5. Roots of carrot growing down into the soil to the depth of 2 feet or more.

Varieties. Seedsmen list a large number of varieties of carrots, but only a few of them are of any great importance. The most popular bunching carrots are Imperator, Gold Spike, and Gold Pak. These are all long slender carrots with a good, smooth exterior. The color is fairly good, but not as good as the types used for processing such as Red Cored Chantenay and Royal Chantenay. Red Cored Chantenay has long been the standard processing variety owing to its uniform, dark-orange color. It tends to be thick at the shoulder and tapers to a blunt tip and is shorter than the bunching types. Royal Chantenay grows about an inch longer and is more nearly cylindrical than Red Cored Chantanay. Nantes is a good home-garden variety of carrot. It is long and cylindrical with a blunt tip. The color is not as good as the processing types, but the carrots are tender and have a good flavor. The tops and the roots are brittle and break easily, which makes it unsuitable for bunching.

Diseases and Insects. CARROT YELLOWS. This is a virus disease caused by the yellows virus. The young leaves become yellow and very twisted. Side shoots develop which are also yellow and malformed and give the plant a bushy appearance. The root is covered with many fine roots so that it has a very hairy appearance. Roots from infected plants have a

Fig. 19.6. Weed control in carrots with spray of Stoddard Solvent, 100 gallons to the acre, applied when plants had two to four leaves. Photographed 1 week after application. (*Courtesy of W. H. Lachman, University of Massachusetts.*)

bitter, astringent flavor. This virus is transmitted by the six-spotted leaf hopper in most areas although other species may transmit the virus. The only feasible method of control of this disease is to spray or dust the plants with DDT to control the leaf hopper.

CARROT RUST FLY. The larvae of the carrot rust fly (*Psila rosae* Fab.) cause serious injury to carrots in many sections of the United States and Canada. They also feed on the roots of celery and parsnips. The larvae burrow into the roots of these vegetables and, when present in large numbers, often render them unfit for market. The injury to celery is caused by the larvae eating the small roots, thus causing a weakening of the plant. The adult fly is about ⅙ inch long, dark green, almost black in color. The maggot, or larva, is yellowish white in color, slender, and a little over ¼ inch long. The insect passes the winter in the pupa stage in the soil, and sometimes as larvae in carrots in storage. The adult fly emerges late in spring or early summer (in May in New York) and deposits eggs in cracks in the soil close to the plants and sometimes on the plants themselves. The first brood of carrot rust fly usually does not cause much damage, but the second brood is present in sufficient numbers to cause severe damage. Good control of the first brood has been accomplished by blowing an insecticide into the furrow at the time of planting seed. Parathion, aldrin, and chlordane have all given good results. No safe method has been found to control the second brood, which usually is responsible for most of the damage to processing carrots.

Harvesting. Carrots for fresh market are harvested when the roots are ¾ inch in diameter or larger at the upper end. The carrots are loosened in the soil by means of a special type of plow, called a carrot lifter, or with an ordinary plow. The roots are pulled by hand and partially graded; all split and branched roots are left in the field. Where the carrots are to be sold as bunched carrots, much of the bunching may be done in the field. The bunches are then hauled to a packing house where they are washed and iced and packed for market. Most of the carrots go to the market with the tops cut off and the roots packaged in transparent film bags. Hardenburg *et al.* (1953) found that topping and bagging carrots greatly reduced the loss of weight and water during transportation to the market. The shelf life of the product was greatly increased by topping and bagging. All the tops should be removed since they wilt and darken and begin to decay first. Many types of film can be used successfully for packaging carrots so long as the packages are perforated to prevent development of off flavors. For prepackaging, the topping and washing of the carrots is done mechanically and they are sorted into various sizes for packaging. Carrots grown for processing are harvested with a beet harvester in many areas. This machine lifts the roots, removes the tops, and conveys the roots into a truck moving alongside the harvester. In some areas the carrots are loosened with a carrot lifter and the roots are pulled and topped by hand. They are usually packed in crates or hampers in the field and delivered to the processor in these containers. If they are to be stored they are usually left in the field crates.

Storage. Carrots are stored in the same manner described for beets. They will keep in good condition for 6 months at high humidity (93 to 98 per cent) and at a temperature of about 32°F. Hasselbring (1927) reported that carrots deteriorate in quality in storage owing to slow loss of sugar in respiration. Platenius (1934) showed that the loss of sugar is slow and that carrots retain a high degree of quality and food value for at least 5 months under good storage conditions.

PARSNIP

The parsnip (*Pastinaca sativa*) is not a very important commercial crop, owing largely to the fact that it requires a long growing season, so that no other crop can be grown on the land during the same season. On high-priced market-gardening land, growers produce two, three, or more crops a season. In 1949, 2,565 acres of parsnips was grown in the United States. Pennsylvania, Illinois, California, and New York were the major producing states.

History and Taxonomy. The parsnip is a native of Europe and Asia. It is found growing wild in America, but only as an introduced weed. It has been used as food from an early period and was undoubtedly known to the ancient Greeks and Romans. It was brought to America by the early colonists and was in cultivation in Virginia as early as 1609 and in Massachusetts in 1629.

The plant is a biennial of the Umbelliferae, or parsley family, but the crop is grown as an annual. The second year the seedstalk develops from the enlarged root produced during the preceding season.

Soils and Soil Preparation. A deep, rich soil is essential for successful growing of this crop. On a shallow soil the roots become crooked and often branched. Heavy soils are objectionable because of the difficulty of securing a good stand of plants and smooth roots. Since the seeds are very slow to germinate, the surface of a heavy soil becomes baked before the plants have a chance to break through, hence a poor stand usually results.

The methods of preparing the soil for the parsnip are the same as for the beet.

Fertilizers. The fertilizer treatments suggested for beets should give satisfactory results for parsnips under similar conditions.

Planting. Parsnip seed is planted where the crop is to mature. Since the seed is slow to germinate and the crop requires a long season, planting is usually done fairly early in the spring when the soil is moist. The seed retains its vitality only 1 or 2 years and should be planted thickly. It is usually sown in drills about 15 to 18 inches apart for hand cultivation and 24 to 30 inches for tractor cultivation. One ounce of seed will plant about 200 feet of row, and 3 to 4 pounds is usually planted to the acre when the rows are about 15 inches apart. The seed is covered ½ to ¾ inch deep. In the home garden it is desirable to sow some radish seed with the parsnips so that cultivation can begin before the parsnip plants break through the surface of the soil.

After the plants are well established, in 5 or 6 weeks, they are usually thinned to stand 2 to 4 inches apart in the row.

Cultivation. Cultivation should begin as soon as weed growth starts, or as soon as a crust begins to form. It can begin in a few days after planting if radish seed has been sown with the parsnip seed. It is important to keep down weed growth by cultivating and weeding until the plants are large enough to smother the weeds in the row. During the early stages of growth, parsnip plants are delicate and cannot compete successfully with weeds.

Hand cultivation is commonly given, and the knife attachments are used to a considerable extent, especially when the parsnip plants are small.

Lachman (1946) and others have shown that some of the petroleum products used for weeding carrots are satisfactory for use in controlling weeds in plantings of parsnips. Lachman stated that parsnip plants were generally severely damaged when sprayed after they reached a height of 6 inches but were not adversely affected when the spray was applied in the cotyledon stage.

Varieties. Very few varieties of parsnips are listed by American seedsmen. Hollow Crown, Model, and All American are used by a large percentage of growers. Long Dutch, Offenham Market, and Guernsey are grown to some extent.

Harvesting. Parsnips are usually left in the ground until late in the fall or even throughout the winter. In many sections they are left in the garden until wanted for use, but where severe freezing occurs this is not satisfactory because it is difficult to dig them when the ground is frozen. The common practice in the North is, therefore, to harvest the roots late in the fall and store them where they are available when wanted. Since parsnip roots grow to considerable length, 10 to 12 inches, they are difficult and expensive to dig. They may be dug by hand with a spading fork, or they may be loosened with a plow. When a plow is used, it is best to run it close to the row and throw the furrow away from the plants and then loosen the roots by pushing them toward the furrow. Care should be taken to prevent breaking the roots.

After digging, the tops are removed, and if the parsnips are to be marketed immediately, they should be washed. A large portion of the crop is packed in transparent film bags in the same manner as carrots.

Storage. The same methods of storage are used for parsnips as for beets and carrots. A large part of the crop is sold during the winter and early spring, hence storage is important in regions where the soil remains frozen during most of the winter.

It is believed by many that freezing is necessary for the development of good quality in parsnips, but Boswell (1923) has shown that this is not true. Parsnips stored for 2 weeks at 34°F. attained a quality equivalent to those left in the field for 2 months in late fall at College Park, Md. At 34°F. the change from starch to sugar, mainly sucrose, was rapid and resulted in a marked increase in quality.

SALSIFY

Salsify (*Tragapogon porrifolius*), also known as "vegetable oyster" because of its flavor, is of minor importance in this country but is deserving of greater use. It is a native of southern Europe and is of recent culture, probably not being grown as a food plant until about 1600. It is a hardy biennial belonging to the Compositae, or sunflower family. The leaves are very narrow, resembling those of the leek, but smaller.

Culture. Salsify requires a long growing season for full development; its culture is practically the same as that given parsnips. The seeds are sown in drills 12 to 15 inches apart, and the plants thinned to stand about 2 inches apart in the row.

As salsify is hardy, it can be harvested throughout the winter in most regions, but in order to obtain a continuous supply for use or for market it is desirable to store a part of the crop. It may be stored as described for beets.

The roots are prepared for market by cutting away all but 2 or 3 inches of the leaves, washing the roots, and tying 10 or more plants in a bunch. The bunch is usually tied tightly near both ends.

SCORZONERA, OR BLACK SALSIFY

Scorzonera (*Scorzonera hispanica* Linn.), also known as black salsify, is a perennial, native of central and southern Europe. It belongs to the Compositae family and is grown in the same manner as salsify, except that it is given more room. The roots are long and black and are boiled after being soaked in water to remove the bitter taste.

This plant was known in Spain about the middle of the sixteenth century for its medicinal properties. It is grown in Europe as a food plant but is practically unknown in America.

SCOLYMUS

Scolymus, or Spanish salsify (*Scolymus hispanicus* Linn.), is also a native of Europe and a member of the Compositae family. It is grown and used in the same way as salsify. The root is longer and produces a larger yield. When cooked its flavor is less pronounced than that of salsify, but it has an agreeable flavor and is worthy of attention in this country. It can be dug and stored in the fall or harvested as needed during the winter and spring. The leaves of this plant are prickly and somewhat unpleasant to handle on this account.

TURNIP

The turnip (*Brassica rapa*) is an important crop in most of the Southern states and is generally grown in the early spring and the late fall. In regions where hard freezes do not occur it is grown as a winter crop. It is grown as a summer crop in areas that have cool summers. The turnip is grown both for its enlarged root and for the foliage. In some cases crops are sown especially for the greens, but in other cases the thinnings from the root crops are used for greens. In 1949, the acreage devoted to turnips for greens was 4,289 acres, mostly in Southern states. The acreage grown for roots was 22,414 acres in 1949, and the leading states were Georgia with 4,188 acres and Texas with 3,061 acres, with all the other Southern states growing appreciable amounts. Other important producing areas were California, Pennsylvania, and Ohio, which grew between 800 and 1,000 acres of turnips in 1949.

Turnip greens are considered valuable in the diet, primarily because of the content of minerals, calcium and iron, and vitamins A and C. They also contain appreciable amounts of thiamine and other B vitamins. Various investigators including Bernstein, Hamner, and Parks (1945), Hamner and Parks (1944), and others have shown that environmental conditions affect the content of carotene and ascorbic acid. Thus, Hamner and Parks have shown that light intensity is an important factor in the content of ascorbic acid. In general, the higher the light intensity up to 5,000 foot-candles, the greater was the content of ascorbic acid. According to Bernstein, *et al.*, both ascorbic acid and carotene content seem to be influenced primarily by environmental variables associated with season and location. There was some evidence in their studies that the conditions leading to high ascorbic acid content resulted in low carotene content and vice versa. Fertilizer treatments had little effect on ascorbic acid or carotene content of plants grown in soil.

History and Taxonomy. It is not definitely known where the turnip originated, but it is said to be found growing wild in Russia and Siberia. It has been in cultivation since ancient times and was brought to America at an early period. It was known in Virginia in 1609.

When planted in the spring, the turnip is an annual, but when planted later it is a biennial. It belongs to the genus Brassica and the family Cruciferae and is, therefore, closely related to cabbage, cauliflower, rape, kale, etc.

Soils and Soil Preparation. While the turnip is grown on all types of soil, it thrives best on a deep rich loam.

The method of preparation suggested for beets and carrots would be satisfactory for turnips. In fact the turnip is not nearly so exacting in this respect as either beets or carrots since the seeds germinate quickly and the plants make rapid growth.

Fertilizers. The fertilizer treatments suggested for beets would be satisfactory for turnips, although beets are usually more heavily fertilized. Turnips do not seem to need so much potash as most of the other root crops, but require as much phosphorus and nitrogen (Page and Paden, 1949).

Planting. The turnip is grown almost entirely from seed sown where the crop is to mature. Since it does not thrive in hot weather, the seed is planted very early in the spring and in late summer in the North and during the fall and winter in the South. For the fall crop in the North, the seed should be planted about 2 months before hard freezes are expected. Seed for the spring crop should be planted as soon as the soil can be prepared.

Turnip seed is generally planted in rows 12 to 15 inches apart for hand cultivation and about 24 inches apart for tractor cultivation. Seed drills are used where a considerable area is to be planted, and the seed is covered about ½ inch deep. The usual rate of planting is 2 pounds of seed to the acre for hand cultivation and a little less for tractor cultivation. Broadcast seeding is not practiced to the extent that it was formerly, but when this method is followed more seed is required than under the row method.

Thinning. After the plants become well established, they are thinned to stand 2 to 6 inches apart in the row, the distance depending on the type and purpose for which the crop is grown. If small-growing varieties are grown for bunching, the smaller distance is sufficient, while the large varieties require the greater distance if they are to develop to large size. In the South the thinning continues over a considerable period and the plants removed are used as greens.

Cultivation. Cultivation is usually given turnips when they are grown in rows, but when the seed is sown broadcast cultivation is impossible. The methods of cultivation suggested for beets are satisfactory for turnips.

Varieties. The most popular varieties are the Purple Top Globe, White Milan, White Flat Dutch, White Egg, Yellow Globe, Golden Ball, and Yellow Aberdeen. The most popular variety grown for turnip greens is Shogoin (also called Japanese by some seedsmen), a relatively new variety. In addition to its value for greens, the roots are quick-growing and of good quality. The Seven Top is an old variety grown for greens, but the roots are woody and of poor quality.

Diseases and Insects. Most of the diseases and insects affecting the turnip are also injurious to cabbage and have been discussed under the latter. Clubroot and black rot are the most serious diseases; turnip aphid, root maggot, and flea beetles are the most injurious insect pests.

Harvesting. Turnips are harvested in the same manner as beets. For use as greens the plants are pulled or cut at the surface of the soil and the foliage is cooked in the same way as kale. Young turnips are sometimes bunched as described for beets, but most of them are topped and packed in transparent film bags. A large part of the crop is harvested in the fall, and the tops are cut as they are pulled. In some areas a beet-harvester type of machine is used. The turnips are then packed for market or stored the same as other root crops. Haller (1947) reported that washing Purple Top turnips improved the appearance and reduced decay. Application of wax emulsion to the roots neither improved appearance nor retarded weight loss in storage, but dipping in hot paraffin retarded shrinkage and greatly improved the appearance. The paraffin film on the roots lowered the rate of respiration of the roots and tended to reduce the occurrence of internal breakdown.

RUTABAGA

The rutabaga (*Brassica napobrassica*) is similiar in appearance to the turnip, but differs from it in having a denser root, which is usually rounded or elongated instead of being flattened; the leaves are smooth and covered with a bluish bloom, whereas the leaves of turnip are hairy and green. The roots arise from the underside of the enlarged root as well as from the taproot in the rutabaga, and the crown is long and leafy as compared to the turnip. The rutabaga (Swede, or table turnip) is grown to a large extent in Canada and where the annual production is about 20 million bushels. The production in the United States in 1949 was 3,434 acres, most of this acreage in Minnesota, Wisconsin, and Washington. It is a cool-season crop and is grown in those areas that have a cool summer and fall. It is planted in June and harvested in October and November.

The fertilization is similar to that described for beets. In Canada the usual fertilizer application is 500 to 1,000 pounds of 2-12-10 fertilizer in addition to plowing under heavy applications of manure. The seed is sown in rows 24 to 30 inches apart, and the plants are thinned to stand 6 to 8 inches apart in the row. Usually ½ to 1 pound of seed is sufficient to plant an acre. The leading variety is Laurentian. Cultivation should be shallow and done only when weeds are present.

Under some conditions in parts of Canada, the plants produce seedstalks before the roots reach marketable size. This results in loss. Peto (1934) reported results that indicate that exposure to relatively low temperature (50 to 55°F.) is an important factor in bolting.

In parts of the United States and Canada, as well as in some parts of Europe, brown heart, water core, or raan has caused considerable loss. Results of numerous experiments by many experimenters, including O'Brien and Dennis (1935 and 1936) and MacLeod and Howatt (1935), have shown that this trouble results from a deficiency of boron. Hansen, Coleson, and Raymond (1948) found that spraying the plants with 8 to 16 pounds of borax per acre when the roots were 1 to 1½ inches in diameter gave better control of brown heart than did soil applications of borax. The trouble usually does not occur until August or September when the roots are making rapid growth. Spraying with borax at this time gives satisfactory control.

Fig. 19.7. The waxed rutabaga on the left has a better appearance and longer shelf life than the unwaxed one on the right. (*Courtesy of F. M. Isenberg.*)

The roots are pulled by hand, and the taproot and crown are trimmed with a knife in the field. They are stored at low temperatures and high humidities like other root crops. Practically all of the rutabagas that are marketed are waxed. The roots are trimmed, washed, dried, and dipped for 1 second in hot paraffin wax at a temperature of 250 to 270°F. The paraffin is usually diluted with resin, beeswax, petroleum jelly, or mineral oil to make it less brittle. Waxing greatly enhances the appearance of the root and markedly reduces shriveling and loss of weight during marketing, as is shown in Fig. 19.7.

RADISH

The radish is a favorite crop of the home gardener because it is easily grown and is ready for use in 3 to 6 weeks from time of seed sowing. It grows best in rather cool weather and is a spring and fall crop in the

North and a spring, fall, and winter crop in Southern areas where hard frosts do not occur. It was once grown on a small scale by many market gardeners in all areas and as a greenhouse vegetable. Because of mechanization of harvesting and marketing operations, the size of planting is now larger and fewer market gardeners grow the crop. In 1949, 16,265 acres of radishes was grown on 3,931 farms in the United States. The leading states were Texas with 3,532 acres, Florida with 1,831 acres, and Ohio with 1,530 acres.

The radish is probably a native of Europe or Asia. It has been in cultivation for a long time, being highly prized by the Egyptians at the time of the Pharaohs, and was also known and highly prized by the ancient Greeks. The radish (*Raphanus sativus* Linn.) is both annual and biennial and belongs to the Cruciferae, or mustard family. It is related to the cabbage, mustard, etc., but does not belong to the same genus.

Soil Preference. The radish is grown on all types of soils, but a light, friable soil is considered best. Since it requires only a short time to grow a crop of the varieties commonly grown in America, it can be produced on types of soil that are not satisfactory for other root crops. For an early crop, sandy or sandy-loam soils are preferred, but for summer radishes a cool, moist soil gives better results. Muck soils are used for growing radishes in some areas. The soil must be free from stones and in good condition. The soil should be thoroughly prepared so that there are no clods to interfere with planting operations. After thorough fitting the land is sometimes dragged with a plank drag to smooth the surface before seeding, which ensures uniform planting depth of the seed.

Fertilizers. Since the crop grows so rapidly a rich fertile soil is essential. High-quality radishes can only be produced with an abundance of fertilizer nutrients. Usually a broadcast application of 1,000 pounds of a 5-10-10 or similar fertilizer is made before the crop is planted. If radishes follow a crop which has been heavily fertilized, the amount of fertilizer is reduced.

Planting. The radish is hardy, and the first planting is made very early in the spring in the North and during the winter in the South. For a succession of crisp, tender roots several plantings should be made at intervals of about 10 days. By the proper selection of varieties, radishes may be had throughout the season and even during the winter since the winter varieties can be kept in storage. However, most of the radishes grown in the United States and Canada are the quick-maturing varieties, which do not thrive well in hot weather. In commercial plantings the seed is drilled ½ to ¾ inch deep in rows about 15 inches apart. It usually requires from 10 to 12 pounds of seed to plant an acre, depending upon the number of plants per foot desired. Seed is usually sown to supply

12 to 18 plants per foot of row. For commercial plantings graded seed should be used. This seed has been screened to remove all the small seeds, and the large uniform-sized seed can be planted with greater precision and the plants come up more uniformly. The large-growing varieties, especially those known as winter radishes, are thinned so they stand 2 to 4 inches apart in the row. In the home garden the radishes are often grown as an intercrop or a companion crop and are planted between the rows of other vegetables. A few market gardeners grow radishes between the rows of cabbage and other such crops. The hand operations required in harvesting make this practice too expensive to compete with mechanically harvested radish crops.

Varieties. Varieties of radishes are divided into classes with reference to the season of the year in which the crop is grown and with reference to the shape of the root. The former system has the advantage of bringing together those varieties planted at the same time, but does not aid in identifying them. Most of the commercial crop of radishes are the quick-maturing spring varieties; however, these varieties may be planted at any season of the year. The most popular market types are bright-red globular radishes such as Cavalier, Cherry Belle, Comet, Sparkler, and Early Scarlet Globe. French Breakfast is an olive-shaped spring radish and is not widely grown. The long-rooted spring types are represented by Cincinnati Market, White Icicle, and Long Scarlet Short Top. The later-maturing summer varieties are not widely grown and are usually long-rooted, such as Strasburg, Stuttgart, and White Vienna, but Golden Globe is round. The winter varieties require about twice as long to mature as the spring varieties and are usually grown as a fall crop for storage. The most popular varieties are White Chinese, China Rose, Long Black Spanish, Round Black Spanish, and Sakurajima. The Sakurajima grows to enormous size and has solid, firm flesh of good flavor.

Insects. The insects most commonly attacking radish are plant lice, or aphids, cabbage root maggot, and flea beetles. Aphids can be controlled by spraying with nicotine or one of the organic phosphates such as parathion, malathion, or TEPP. The flea beetle is commonly controlled by spraying or dusting the foliage with DDT or malathion. The cabbage-root maggot can be controlled by a soil application of chlordane, heptachlor, or dieldrin before the crop is planted.

Harvesting and Marketing. Harvesting begins as soon as the roots reach marketable size. The quick-maturing spring varieties become strong and pithy if they are not harvested as soon as they reach edible size. The summer varieties remain edible much longer than the spring varieties. The winter varieties remain edible for several months if stored properly. With small plantings the radishes are pulled by hand and are usually tied in bunches of 6 to 12 in the field. After bunching they are washed to remove the soil and give them a fresh bright appearance. They are usually packed in baskets, hampers, or crates and iced for transport to the market. Winter radishes are handled in much the same way as turnips; the tops are removed before the roots are put in storage. Most of the commercial acreage of radishes is harvested by machine. The radish harvester lifts the radish and removes the top and drops the roots into containers on the machine. Other types of harvesters only lift the radishes, and the tops are removed by machinery in the packing shed. The topped, washed radishes are packaged in transparent film bags for marketing. Practically all of the radish acreage is marketed in transparent bags and is harvested by machines.

HORSE-RADISH

Horse-radish (*Armoracia rusticana*) is found in many farm gardens where it is allowed to grow along fences or walks. The commercial acreage was 2,563 acres in 1949, and Illinois was the leading state with 1,572 acres. Other important producing states were Wisconsin, Missouri, Pennsylvania, and New Jersey.

Horse-radish is indigenous to eastern Europe and is now spontaneous in the United States. Both leaves and roots were used as food in Germany during the Middle Ages. Prior to the sixteenth century, it was probably grown for medicinal purposes only.

It belongs to the Cruciferae, or mustard family, and is known as *Armoracia rusticana*. It is a hardy perennial that produces a tuft of large leaves similar in appearance to the leaves of dock. The flower stem grows to a height of 2 to 3 feet and bears small white flowers in panicled racemes. Seed is produced, but it seldom matures and is never used for propagation.

Soils and Soil Preparation. A deep, rich, moist, loamy soil is desired for growing horse-radish. On hard soil the roots become much branched and crooked. In the vicinity of St. Louis a rich river-bottom soil is used.

In the preparation, the soil should be deeply plowed and thoroughly pulverized so that long straight roots can be grown.

Fertilizers. Unless the soil is already rich and in good physical condition, it should be heavily manured, preferably with well-rotted manure. Some commercial fertilizer is often applied in addition to a heavy coating of manure. A fertilizer containing about 50 pounds each of nitrogen and potash and 70 to 100 pounds of phosphorus to the acre should be sufficient. Where no manure is used, the fertilizer should supply at least 100 pounds of each of the three important ingredients.

Planting. The plant is propagated from root cuttings made from the side roots which are trimmed off in preparing the roots for market. These vary in size from ¼ to ½ inch in diameter and from 2 to 8 inches in length. The long cuttings are best. As these roots are nearly uniform in diameter throughout their length, they are cut off square at the top and oblique at the lower end to denote which end is to be planted up. They are then tied in bundles, packed in sand, and stored in a cool, moist place until spring. The cuttings may be planted in a deep furrow made with a large plow, or a dibble may be used to make holes for them. In either case the cuttings are set in a slanting position with the square end up and about 3 or 4 inches below the surface of the soil. The soil should be well packed around the cuttings. The distance of planting is about 10 to 15 inches apart in the row with the rows 3 to 4 feet apart. Planting is usually done early in the spring so as to give the crop a full growing season.

Cultivation and Care. The crop makes most rapid growth during the latter part of the summer; therefore thorough cultivation should be given throughout the growing season.

In order to secure large, straight roots some growers remove the side roots early in the season. This is done by removing the soil and stripping off the side roots from the upper part of the main root. The soil is then replaced. This treatment results in the production of large, compact roots, but unless the work is carefully done serious injury may follow. The earlier in the season the trimming is done, the less check there is to growth. It is claimed by some that a larger yield is obtained when the roots are trimmed than when they are allowed to grow without being disturbed. Certainly trimming results in a large percentage of straight roots of good size.

Harvesting. The roots are hardy and may be left in the ground all winter, but it is better to dig them in the fall and store them so that they will be available when wanted. The roots are plowed out, the tops and side roots removed, and the marketable product sold or stored. Since the horse-radish is likely to become a bad weed, it is important to remove all the roots in harvesting. The roots are washed and packed in barrels for shipping to market. For special trade they are sometimes tied in bunches of six or eight roots. Only the large, straight roots bring a good price.

The roots are stored in a cool, moist cellar or storage house. Care should be taken to prevent the roots from becoming withered.

TURNIP-ROOTED CHERVIL

Turnip-rooted chervil (*Chaerophyllum bulbosum* Linn.) is a small-rooted plant, native of Europe and Asia. It is a biennial, belonging to the Umbelliferae family, and is of recent culture. The root is swollen, much like a short carrot but smaller, dark gray in color, with yellowish-white flesh.

In Europe the seed is usually sown in autumn since it does not germinate well if kept over winter in the ordinary manner. Spring planting may be followed if care is taken to stratify the seed in sand. If this is done, the seeds germinate immediately after they are sown. The crop gets its growth in a relatively short time, but it improves in quality if left in the ground after the leaves wither and die. The roots may be taken up and stored if the land is needed for another crop. They keep well through the winter if properly stored.

The roots are eaten boiled and have a sweet, aromatic flavor. This plant is little known in America.

SKIRRET

Skirret (*Sium sisarum* Linn.) is a hardy perennial of the Umbelliferae family, although it is grown as an annual. The plant produces numerous swollen roots, forming a bunch from the crown. The roots are grayish white in color with firm white flesh.

It may be propagated from seeds, offsets, or division of the roots. The seed is often sown in a prepared bed, and the seedlings transplanted to the permanent bed when four or five leaves have developed. Plants propagated from offsets and division of the roots are treated like those raised from seed. Skirret is very hardy, and the roots may be left in the ground throughout the winter.

The roots are tender and have a sweet taste. They are used in the same manner as salsify.

CELERIAC

Celeriac, or turnip-rooted celery (*Apium graveolens* Linn. var. *rapaceum* DC.), is grown for its thick, tuberous base, which is used as a salad or as a cooked vegetable. It has the flavor of celery and is popular in Europe but is little grown in America. The plant does not develop so much foliage as celery.

Seed is usually sown in a greenhouse or hotbed for an early crop and in a well-prepared outdoor bed for a late crop. The plants are handled exactly like celery except that they are not blanched since the leaves are not eaten. European seedsmen list several varieties. Giant Prague, Apple, and Early Paris probably are the most popular. In America, the Giant Prague is the most common, and many seedsmen list no other variety.

CHAPTER 20

Bulb Crops

Onion	Garlic
Leek	Shallot
Cibol (ciboule), or Welsh onion	Chive

All the bulb crops are hardy. When grown in the South, they are usually planted in fall or in winter and harvested in spring or early summer. The onion is the only member of this group grown to any great extent in this country. The others are grown chiefly for sale in large cities where there is a considerable foreign population.

All these crops belong to the same genus, Allium, of the family Amaryllidaceae, and their cultural requirements are similar.

ONION

The onion is by far the most important of the bulb crops and is one of the important vegetable crops. It is grown commercially in nearly all parts of the United States. The crop is grown for consumption in the green state and as mature bulbs. The main area of production of the Bermuda type is in Texas, principally in the southern part, but some are grown in the northern part of Texas and in California. The Spanish type is grown mainly in the Northwest and in California, while the domestic varieties are produced in most of the Northern states and in California. The onion is one of the important vegetable crops of the United States, and the production has increased markedly during each period, as is shown in Table 20.1.

The leading states in acreage of onions grown for mature bulbs in 1953 were Texas with 54,900 acres; New York, 14,500 acres; California, 14,100 acres; Michigan, 9,500 acres; and Colorado, 5,900 acres. Oregon, Minnesota, Idaho, New Jersey, and Wisconsin were important producing areas also. New York led in production, followed by California and then Texas. Texas produced mainly the Bermuda type during the winter,

Table 20.1. Average Annual Acreage, Production, and Value of Bulb
Onions, 1918–1953

Years	Acres	Yield per acre, 100-lb. sacks	Production, sacks (000 omitted)	Price per 100 pounds	Value (000 omitted)
1918–1927	64,681	164	10,599	$1.82	$19,157
1928–1937	88,952	155	13,785	1.15	15,840
1938–1947	140,620	259	36,798	1.51	52,635
1948–1953	123,640	346	42,611	1.41	57,460

while New York produced domestic types during the summer. Another reason for the low yield in Texas is the practice in one section of growing onions under dry-land production (without irrigation) with the rows spaced about 3 feet apart. In this area the yield is very low and thus reduces the state average.

Green bunching onions are not included in these estimates, but they are grown by many market gardeners. The estimated acreage of green bunching onions in 1949 was about 8,000 acres, and Texas and California were the leading areas of production.

History and Taxonomy. The onion is probably a native of Asia, perhaps from Palestine to India. It has been in cultivation and used as a food from the earliest period of history. It is mentioned in the Bible as one of the things for which the Israelites longed in the wilderness. It is mentioned as being cultivated in America as early as 1629.

The onion belongs to the genus Allium, which contains about 300 species widely distributed in northern temperate regions, biennials and perennials, mostly bulbous. Many species are native to North America. Some of the wild species produce bulbils instead of seed in the flower cluster, as does the tree onion. All but a few of the plants of this genus have the characteristic onion odor and flavor. The common onion grown for dry bulbs is *Allium cepa*.

Temperature and Photoperiod on Growth. Garner and Allard (1920) and McClelland (1928) have shown that length of day affects flowering and bulb formation in certain varieties of onions. Garner and Allard found that the Silver Skin variety grown from sets, planted May 19 at Washington, D.C., developed normal bulbs and showed the first blossoms July 14 under the normal length of day. Under a 10-hour day, the plants remained green for 12 months and formed no bulbs and no flowers. McClelland grew Prizetaker, Bermuda White, Yellow Globe Danvers, and Silver King under different lengths of day in Puerto Rico. Prizetaker remained in the green-onion stage for 15 months under an 11-hour day; under a 13.5-hour day bulbs were not formed; under a 15-

hour day all had formed bulbs at 30 weeks. Silver King and Yellow Globe Danvers responded about the same to length of day as did the Prizetaker. On the other hand, the Bermuda White developed well-formed bulbs, and the tops were dead in 22 weeks under the 13.5-hour length of day.

Magruder and Allard (1937) and Thompson and Smith (1938) have reported results on effects of length of day on bulbing similar to those of Garner and Allard and of McClelland, but Thompson and Smith have

Fig. 20.1. Effect of temperature on bulb development in Ebenezer variety of onion, grown under long-day conditions. Left, 50 to 60°F.; center, 60 to 70°F.; right, 70 to 80°F.

shown that relatively high temperature, as well as a long photoperiod, is essential for bulb formation in certain varieties of onions that are commonly grown under long-day conditions (Fig. 20.1). Figure 20.2 shows the effect of photoperiod on bulb formation of plants grown under high temperature. Garner and Allard, McClelland, and Magruder and Allard did not study the temperature factor.

Thompson and Smith have shown also that temperature is more important than length of day in seedstalk development. At relatively low temperature (50 to 60°F.) under a short day (9 to 12 hours) onion plants went to seed readily, while under high temperature (70 to 80°F.)

they did not go to seed under either a short day or a 15-hour day. Table 20.2 gives the results of one experiment out of several conducted.

Results of studies by Heath (1943 and 1945) in England are in general in line with those reported by Thompson and Smith. Heath pointed out that there is an interaction between day length and temperature with respect to flowering of onions grown from sets. At temperatures high enough to favor bulbing, long days discouraged flowering. When the temperature was low enough to prevent or delay bulbing, long days accelerated the appearance of flower stalks. Day length did not affect flower initiation but only influenced the rate of development and elongation of seedstalks.

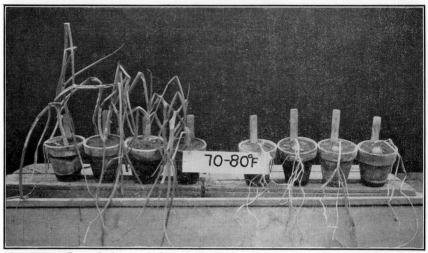

Fig. 20.2. Effect of photoperiod on bulb development in Ebenezer variety of onion. Left, normal length of day from Oct. 29 to Mar. 11; right, 15-hour length of day from Dec. 3 to Mar. 11.

Results of the various studies mentioned explain why many varieties of onions do not produce a satisfactory crop when grown in the South during the winter and early spring. These varieties have been developed in regions where they are grown during the long days of summer when the temperature is relatively high. Bermuda onions, on the other hand, were developed in regions where the relative length of day and night varies but little and are now grown as a commercial crop during the relatively short days of fall, winter, and early spring.

Soils and Soil Preparation. Onions are grown on nearly all types of soils from the sandy loams and mucks to heavy clays. The clays are not satisfactory unless well supplied with humus to lighten them. The greatest difficulty encountered in growing onions on clay is the tendency of this type of soil to run together and bake after hard rains. This is es-

Table 20.2. Effect of Temperature and Length of Exposure to Light on Seedstalk Development in Onion Plants

Treatment	Red Wethersfield			Ebenezer		
	Number of sets	Number of sets producing seedstalks	Number of seedstalks	Number of sets	Number of sets producing seedstalks	Number of seedstalks
50–60°, normal day	20	20	26	20	20	33
50–60°, long day	20	20	30	20	20	25
60–70°, normal day	20	0	0	19	2	2
60–70°, long day	20	2	2	17	1	1
70–80°, normal day	20	0	0	20	0	0
70–80°, long day	20	0	0	20	0	0

pecially injurious after the seed has been sown and before the plants have attained sufficient size to permit cultivation. Sandy-loam soils, when well supplied with humus and heavily fertilized, are satisfactory for onion growing, especially for the early crop. Muck soils are considered the very best type for the production of bulb onions in the North. A very large part of the dry-bulb crop grown in New York, Wisconsin, Minnesota, Michigan, and California is produced on muck. Since muck soils are almost ideal in texture, they are easily prepared and cultivated. They are organic in nature, rich in nitrogen, and have a high water-holding capacity.

The onion plant is sensitive to high acidity and produces maximum yields over a fairly narrow range of soil reaction. Haliburton (1956) on a sandy-loam soil on Long Island reported that maximum yields of onions were produced at pH 5.8 to 6.5. The poor growth at soil reactions below pH 5.8 was due to the toxic effect of soluble aluminum. The decrease in yield above pH 6.5 was probably due to the unavailability of some essential element, probably manganese. Good yields are produced on muck soils over a wider range of soil reaction than on mineral soils.

Soils for onion production should be thoroughly prepared. The seedbed should be well pulverized and have a smooth surface. It is a common practice to drag or roll the land just prior to planting. This is especially important for muck soils.

Manures and Fertilizers. Manure is important in growing onions on mineral soils, especially those poor in humus, but on muck soils the humus is not necessary and nitrogen, phosphorus, and potash can be supplied more economically in chemical fertilizers. When manure is used, it is advisable to apply it to the crop preceding onions, especially if it is not well rotted. Fresh manure usually contains weed seeds and, unless plowed under, interferes with planting and cultivating. An application of 15 to 20 tons of manure per acre should be sufficient. Fresh manure should be turned under in the fall, or as early in the spring as possible. On most soils it is advisable to use commercial fertilizer in addition to manure. For silt-loam and clay-loam soils that are well manured, an application of fertilizer supplying 50 pounds each of nitrogen and potash and 100 pounds of phosphorus to the acre should give good results. However, on sandy and sandy-loam soils, both the nitrogen and the potash should be increased. Where no manure is used, 75 pounds each of nitrogen and potash and 150 pounds of phosphorus are suggested. In the irrigated regions of the West and in Texas, no potash is needed in the fertilizer. In Texas fertilizers such as 6-12-0 and 6-18-0 are applied at rates of 600 to 1000 pounds per acre on light soils and extra nitrogen is added by side-dressing. Nitrogen is the element most needed in California, but some soils need phosphorus also. The initial fertilizer application of 500 to 600 pounds of 16-20-0 per acre is supplemented with liberal nitrogen side-dressings, especially on light soils.

Fertilizer for onions is broadcast or drilled before planting in most areas, but Lorenz *et al.* (1955) reported superior results from banding the fertilizer on an alkaline mineral soil in California. Phosphorus in bands 4 to 7 inches under the row gave much higher yields than equivalent amounts of soluble phosphorus applied in the irrigation water. Liquid phosphoric acid and treble superphosphate were equally effective when banded. Greater yields were obtained with ammonium sulfate banded under the onion rows than with a number of other sources of nitrogen applied in the irrigation water. Applications of aqua ammonia in bands resulted in much lower yields than equivalent amounts of ammonium sulfate in bands because of the toxicity of free ammonia. Split applications of aqua ammonia or placing it farther from the row reduced the toxicity. Ammonia toxicity is most likely to occur on light, alkaline soils when large amounts of aqua ammonia or anhydrous ammonia are applied, and it is due to free ammonia rather than to the ammonium ion.

Fertilizer requirements vary with the type of muck, the length of time it has been under cultivation, the previous treatments, the drainage, and the reaction of the soil. In general, poorly drained and strongly acid mucks require more nitrogen than well-drained, slightly acid, neutral, or alkaline mucks. Newly cleared muck soils usually require less nitrogen and more phosphorus and potash than similar soils that have been under cultivation and well fertilized for several years.

On muck soils used for onions, potash is the main limiting element, but usually there is a good response to phosphorus, and, in some cases, nitrogen is needed. The fertilizer recommendations differ considerably in the various states. In New York the usual application is 1,000 pounds of a

5-10-15 fertilizer per acre on old muck. In Michigan a common application is 1,000 pounds of an 0-10-20 on well-drained muck, but poorly drained muck may receive an equivalent amount of a 3-9-18. After the muck has been fertilized for several years and a reserve has been built up in the soil, the rate of fertilization can be reduced. Fertilizer for onions on muck soils is usually broadcast or drilled, but Davis *et al.* (1950) found that the most efficient way to apply fertilizer for onions was to band it 2 inches below the seed and 1 inch to the side. Applications of 1,000 pounds of 0-10-20 to the acre were safe when banded in this way, but larger amounts should be applied broadcast or with a drill.

Onions grown on muck soils in certain areas sometimes suffer from a deficiency of copper or manganese. The organic matter is thought to complex copper in some manner so as to make it unavailable to the plant. The deficiency is indicated by bulbs of poor color with thin, fragile scales which come off in handling. According to Knott (1933) applying 200 to 300 pounds of powdered copper sulfate to the acre corrects the deficiency. The effect of this application lasts for several years, and no additional copper is needed until the bulbs show the need of it. Manganese is made unavailable to plants as the soil reaction approaches neutrality. A deficiency frequently occurs on muck deposits that have been mixed with underlying marl. In some cases an application of sulfur, which makes the muck more acid, will release enough manganese for normal plant growth. In most areas 150 pounds of manganese sulfate per acre mixed with the fertilizer is the preferred practice. Nylund (1952) corrected manganese deficiency of onions on an alkaline muck soil in Minnesota by spraying the plants with a solution of manganese sulfate. A total of 30 pounds of manganese sulfate applied in 3 sprays of 10 pounds each gave as good control of manganese deficiency, as did 150 pounds of manganese sulfate applied to the soil.

Propagation. The onion is propagated by seed sown where the crop is to mature; by seed sown in a greenhouse, hotbed, or outdoor seedbed; by sets grown from seed sown in the year previous; by top sets, which are produced in the flower cluster of the Egyptian, or tree, onion; and by bottom sets in the multiplier, or potato, onion. The multiplier seldom produces flowers and seeds. The small bulb or set grows into a large one which again breaks up into small ones.

A large part of the bulb onion crop produced in the United States is grown from seed sown where the crop is to mature. In some of the areas in Texas and California, where the Bermuda and certain other early varieties are grown, seedlings are used to a large extent for growing bulb onions. For the production of seedlings, seed is sown in outdoor seedbeds 6 to 10 weeks before transplanting to the field. In the Winter Garden area of Texas the rate of seeding in seedbeds has been from 20 to 30 pounds to the acre. Hawthorne ⟨1938⟩ states that 17 pounds of seed per acre of seedbed provided sufficient plants to set 10 acres in rows 14 inches apart and resulted in 45 to 50 per cent of medium-sized plants. Transplanting gave better results than direct field sowing in Hawthorne's experiments.

Sets are used for the production of green bunching onions; for the production of an early crop of dry bulbs for market in the North; to a considerable extent, for bulbs for home use in nearly all sections of the country; and in growing common varieties for home use and for market in the South. Sets usually produce a larger yield than seeds on ordinary upland soil, but on muck soil it is doubtful if this is true.

Planting. The best time for planting depends on the locality, the type of onions, and the method of propagation used. In the North, sets for green onions or for dry bulbs are usually planted as early in the spring as the soil can be prepared, since light freezes do not injure them. When the multiplier onion is used, the sets are usually planted in the fall. Seeds of the common onion, when planted where the crop is to mature, are sown as soon as hard frosts are over in the spring in regions where severe freezes occur. In the South, the onion is grown during the winter, and seeds, sets, and seedlings are planted in fall or winter depending on the locality and the type of onion. In parts of Texas, seed is sown direct in the field in September or later; where seedlings are used, they are set in the field during the latter part of November or early in December. In some small areas of north Texas, seedlings grown farther south are planted in early spring. In California, according to Davis (1943), early varieties (Crystal Wax, Bermuda, and San Joaquin) and intermediate varieties (Early Grano, Stockton G36, and Red 21) are grown mainly from transplants set in the field from November to March. Davis and Jones (1944) have shown that the early plantings produced larger bulbs and heavier yields per acre than later plantings. Seed for the transplants is usually sown 6 to 10 weeks before they are to be set in the field. Planting of seedlings is done mainly by hand, and the plants usually are spaced 3 to 4 inches apart in rows 14 to 16 inches apart. Davis and Jones have shown that spacing the transplants more than 2 or 3 inches apart in the row results in increase in size of bulbs and a decrease in yield per acre. It is the usual practice to trim the roots and tops before the plants are set in the field. Results of experiments by Hawthorne covering a period of 5 years showed a slightly larger yield for unpruned plants over severely pruned plants, but the unpruned are a little more difficult to plant. Similar results were reported by Davis and Jones from experiments in California. Pruning both tops and roots had a greater depressing effect on yield than pruning either alone.

Clarke *et al.* (1952) reported that onions could be overwintered successfully in Utah if planted between June 1 and Sept. 1. Onions planted after Sept. 1 produced small bulbs and were damaged by heaving over the winter. There were marked differences in the amount of bolting that occurred with the different varieties. The earliest plantings of all varieties produced the greatest number of bolters, but Crystal Wax bolted less than Sweet Spanish and White Portugal when planted in June or July. The performance of the San Joaquin variety was outstanding in survival, yield, and resistance to bolting when planted during August. Seedings made during the first 2 weeks of August produced marketable bulbs the first week of June. Earlier plantings had excellent survival over the winter, but the increase in number of bolters reduced the yield.

Early planting is important in all regions where the crop is grown during the long, warm days of summer. Since bulbing is controlled by the photoperiod and temperature, the plants begin to form bulbs at about the same time regardless of when they were planted. Leaf initiation ceases when bulbing starts, and the growth of the bulb depends on the leaves already present when bulbing commences. Early planting results in higher yields because it permits more leaves to develop before bulbing starts than in the case of later planting.

Methods of planting are very much the same in the various regions. Seed is sown with a drill when the crop is grown commercially, and 4 to 6 pounds is used to the acre if sown where the onions are to mature. Gang planters that sow four or more rows at a time are often used for large acreages. Onion sets are planted by hand or with a machine which opens the row, drops the sets, and covers them with soil. To do satisfactory planting with a machine it is necessary to grade the sets into about three sizes. At the distances ordinarily used 15 to 30 bushels of sets are required to plant an acre, the quantity depending on the size of the sets. The larger the sets, the greater the quantity required to plant an acre of land. If onion sets were true spheres, it would take eight times as many bushels of sets 1 inch in diameter as of sets ½ inch in diameter to plant an acre of land, the spacing being the same. Beaumont *et al.* (1935) give data on the number of bushels of sets of three sizes to set an acre, as shown in Table 20.3.

Table 20.3. Effect of Size of Sets on Quantity Required to Plant an Acre at a Given Distance

Size of sets	Size, inches	Weight, grams	Sets per acre, bushels
Large	¾–1	6.3	94.98
Medium	½–¾	1.4	25.08
Small	¼–½	0.5	8.18

Thinning. The practice of sowing onion seed thickly and then thinning the seedlings to the desired distance was common many years ago. At the present the tendency is to sow the seed more thinly and dispense with thinning since this is an expensive operation. On muck soil, thinning is of less importance than on mineral soils since muck is very light and there is no danger of producing deformed bulbs even where they are crowded. Large yields are obtained where the onions are grown thickly, and since large size is of no importance for common onions, thinning is seldom justified.

Fig. 20.3. Roots of onion uncovered by washing off the surface soil to the depth of 2 to 3 inches.

Cultivation. To produce a good crop of onions, it is essential that weeds be kept under control. This is of special importance during the early growth of the onion as the plant grows slowly at first and is readily injured by weeds. Experimental evidence reported by Thompson, Wessels, and Mills (1931) shows the importance of weed control but no very marked benefit from the maintenance of a soil mulch. Eliminating cultivation after the tops began to fall over did not result in a decrease in yield but in considerable saving of labor. The onion plant has a relatively sparse and poorly distributed root system as shown in Fig. 20.3.

Cultivation usually begins as soon as the plants appear above the surface of the soil and continues until the tops seriously interfere with the work. Hand cultivation with wheel hoes was once a standard practice, but it has been largely replaced by cultivation with small garden tractors or special models of regular farm tractors made for closely spaced crops. For weed destruction, blade attachments which cultivate about an inch deep are superior to other types of cultivator attachments.

Chemical Weed Control. Hand weeding was for a long time the most laborious and expensive operation connected with growing onions, but it has been largely eliminated through the use of chemical methods of weed control. A number of different materials have been used for chemical weed control in onions. Dilute sulfuric acid was one of the first materials to give good weed control in onions, but the method was never widely used because of corrosion of equipment and the danger to the workmen in handling the solution. Special-grade cyanamid applied at the rate of about 75 pounds to the acre before the onions come up gives effective control of early-germinating weeds. A spray of potassium cyanate at the rate of 5 pounds of the chemical per acre applied when the seedling onions have passed through the bend stage is sometimes used. The effectiveness of these two materials depends on the stage of growth of the weeds and the climatic conditions at the time of application. The most widely used material for weed control in onions is Chloro-IPC. It is not effective for all kinds of weeds but is especially effective when purslane (*Portulaca oleracea*) is the major weed problem. The sprays are applied at the rate of 4 to 6 pounds of the chemical per acre and are directed at the base of the plant to prevent wetting the leaves. Usually three sprays are applied: the first, before the onions come up; the second, when the plants are tall enough to permit directed spraying without wetting the leaves; and the third, just before the tops begin to fall over. Chloro-IPC persists in the soil for some time and may damage crops that are sensitive to the material. It is difficult to get a good stand of winter cover crops following onions sprayed with Chloro-IPC.

Varieties. Onion varieties are in a state of rapid change. The old standard varieties are being replaced by F_1 hybrids, and the number of hybrid varieties is increasing rapidly each year. They are produced by making use of male sterility in one of the parent lines. There are hybrids which are similar to all the important types of onions but are higher-yielding and more uniform than the old varieties. There are two general types of onions grown in the United States for use as dry bulbs. They are usually designated as the "American," or pungent type, and the "foreign," or mild type. Three distinct colors are recognized in each class, red, white, and yellow. In general the American onions produce bulbs of smaller size, denser texture, stronger flavor, and better keeping quality. They vary in shape from oblate to globular, the latter being preferred on the market. Probably 75 per cent of the bulb crop consists of yellow varieties of the American type. The most important are Brigham Yellow

Globe, Yellow Globe Danvers, Early Yellow Globe, and Mountain Danvers. Ebenezer is the most popular yellow variety grown from sets. Red Wethersfield and Southport Red Globe are the best-known red varieties. Southport White Globe is the most popular white variety for storage and is well adapted to dehydration and processing because of its excellent white color and high flavor, or pungency. White Portugal, or Silverskin, is grown from sets for green onions and is a good pickling onion because the young sets are almost round.

Of the foreign types, the Bermuda is the most popular, and many acres are devoted to it in Texas. Yellow Bermuda and various strains of it are the most important; all have flattened bulbs with a mild flavor. Crystal Wax is a white Bermuda type. Early Grano and its various strains are very early maturing, globular, yellow onions grown in Texas along with the Bermudas. It is also grown in the Southwest and California. Yellow Sweet Spanish is available in many strains and is a large, globular, mild onion grown mostly in the Western states. Among the white varieties are White Grano, or White Balbosa, and White Sweet Spanish. Italian Red, or Italian Bottle, and Red Creole are grown to a limited extent as winter onions in the South.

Among the varieties grown for green onions, Beltsville Bunching is the most widely grown. It does not form dry bulbs and originated from a cross between *Allium cepa* and *A. fistulosum*. Nebuka, or He-Shi-Ko, or Japanese Bunching (*A. fistulosum*) is popular since it is a hardy plant that overwinters in most localities. White Lisbon is grown exclusively as an early green onion. White Multiplier, Yellow Multiplier, and the Egyptian, or Perennial Tree, onion are also grown for early bunching onions. These are very hardy.

Diseases and Insects. The onion is attacked by many diseases, the most important being smut, downy mildew, pink root, and neck rot, although some others often cause considerable losses. The only insects that are injurious to onions in most regions are onion thrips and onion maggots.

ONION SMUT. Onion smut (*Urocystes cepulae*) is probably the most destructive disease of onions grown in the North. The disease is caused by a fungus which lives from year to year in the soil. The fungus is inactive at temperatures of 85°F. and higher, and for that reason is seldom a problem in the South where onions are grown during warm weather. The fungus attacks only young seedling plants. The disease appears as a dark thickened area on the first leaf soon after it emerges. Later, other leaves are involved and are swollen and tend to bend downward. Small black pustules soon appear and break open, exposing the black powdery masses of spores. If a plant escapes infection until the first leaf has made its full growth, it will continue free from the disease. Most of the infected seedlings die within 3 or 4 weeks, and those that survive do not produce marketable bulbs. Onions produced from healthy sets are not susceptible to infection by smut. Sets are commonly used in some areas where smut is severe. The disease is controlled on seeded onions by a dilute formaldehyde drench which is applied in the furrow at the time of planting. The amount to use varies with the moisture present in the muck, but generally about 1½ gallons of formaldehyde per acre is applied in about 100 to 120 gallons of water. A less cumbersome means of control is to pellet the seed with a fungicide such as Tersan or Arasan. The fungicide is applied with a methocel sticker, and treating the seeds in this manner has given good control of smut. Usually 1 pound of fungicide is used to treat 1 pound of seed. The Nebuka type of Welsh onion (*A. fistulosum*) is resistant to onion smut, and the Beltsville Bunching onion has good resistance also.

DOWNY MILDEW. Mildew (*Peronospora destructor*) is a common disease of onions, especially during cool, wet weather. The fungus coats the outer surface of affected leaves, and they soon turn yellow and die. The disease usually appears at a few points in the field and spreads rapidly under favorable conditions. The pathogen overwinters most commonly in the bulbs of perennial types of onions. These perennial multiplier onions are common in home gardens, and the spores are spread to commercial onion plantings by the wind. There is some evidence that the fungus also can live over winter in the bulbs of several kinds of onions in storage. Spores are produced abundantly when the temperature at night is about 55°F. They are spread by the wind, and as dew accumulates on the plants at night the spores germinate and penetrate the onion leaf. Moisture is required for germination and penetration, and mildew usually appears first in those areas where air drainage is poor. The Calred variety is resistant to the disease and is grown in California. The disease can be controlled by spraying with a zineb type of fungicide at frequent intervals. Usually 6 to 10 applications are made at intervals of from 6 to 8 days.

PINK ROOT. This disease is caused by *Pyrenochaeta terrestris* and is present in many growing sections of the United States and Canada. It is especially destructive in the Rio Grande Valley and in central California. The roots of the affected plants turn pink, shrivel, and die. The bulb continues to produce new roots, and this depletes its food supply so that it fails to reach marketable size. The organism lives in the soil, and there is no practical way to control the disease once the soil becomes infested. In some areas, calcium cyanamid is applied at rates of about 1,000 pounds per acre and is thought to lessen the severity of attack. The disease is most serious in hot, dry weather at the time the bulbs are forming. The Yellow Bermuda is fairly tolerant to pink root. Chives, the Nebuka type of Welsh onion, and the Giant Musselburgh leek are resistant to pink root. The Louisiana Evergreen shallot and the Beltsville Bunching onion are resistant also.

NECK ROT. The neck rot (*Botrytis alii*) is a disease of mature onion bulbs and sets found in all regions where onions are stored. The disease seldom occurs on the bulbs while they are in the ground, although the fungus may attack injured leaves. The lesions on the bulbs appear as sunken, dried areas about the neck and may involve the whole bulb. The fungus lives over winter in the diseased onions in storage. The piles of cull onions dumped outside of storage usually provide the inoculum for the disease. The fungus only attacks onions that have been injured or wounded in some manner. Onions should be allowed to mature until the tops are completely dry before topping. Bruising during harvest should be kept to a minimum. Thick-necked onions should not be stored since they are slow to cure and succumb quickly to neck rot. Artificial drying during early storage reduces severity of neck rot. All varieties of onions are susceptible, but the white varieties are more easily infected than the yellow or red varieties. The mild varieties such as Sweet Spanish are more susceptible than pungent varieties such as Yellow Globe. Onions should be stored at a temperature as near 32°F. as possible, and the relative humidity maintained at about 65 per cent with good air circulation through the piles.

ONION THRIPS. Onion thrips (*Thrips tabaci*) are small, yellowish sucking insects which attack the leaves of onion plants, giving them a blanched appearance. The tender center leaves become curled and deformed, and the outer leaves turn brown at the tips. Thrips are most injurious during dry weather and are seldom very destructive during rainy periods. Dusts containing ¾ of 1 per cent of rotenone have proved satisfactory for use on bunching onions where the fresh green tops bring a market preference. These dusts are most effective when they are used at weekly intervals as soon as thrips appear on the plants. For dry bulb onions, dusts or sprays of DDT, parathion, or malathion have given excellent control of onion thrips. The insecticide should be applied as soon as the first thrips are noticed.

ONION MAGGOT. The onion maggot (*Hylemyia antiqua*) is the larva of a small fly resembling the housefly, but smaller. The eggs are laid on the plants near the base or in cracks of the soil. Small maggots, about ⅓ inch long, kill the young plants and later burrow into the bulbs, causing decay. The onion maggot can be controlled by pelleting the onion seed with an insecticide such as aldrin, heptachlor, parathion, or dieldrin. About 1 pound of insecticide is required for each 100 pounds of seed. The insecticide is applied with a methocel sticker and usually is applied with a fungicide for control of onion smut. In areas where the formaldehyde drench is used for smut control, an insecticide may be included in the drench to control the onion maggot. Blowing an insecticide dust in the furrow at planting also has given good control.

Premature Seeding. In regions where onion sets are used for growing onions and in Texas where plants are grown during the winter, it is common for seedstalks to develop before the bulb reaches marketable size. In some years this premature seeding results in large losses because most of the plants that produce seedstalks fail to develop marketable bulbs.

Premature seeding has been attributed to many factors such as the use of large sets, to unfavorable storage conditions under which the sets

Table 20.4. Average Percentage of Seedstalks Developed from Large, Medium, and Small Sets of Three Varieties of Onions after Being Stored at Various Temperatures

Variety and size	30°F.	32°F.	40°F.	50°F.	60–70°F.
Ebenezer:					
Large...........	2.20	9.14	40.98	35.02	1.58
Medium.........	0.18	0.34	2.05	1.33	0.08
Small...........	0.00	0.00	0.00	0.06	0.08
Yellow Globe:					
Large...........	33.37	42.72	79.98	68.64	18.51
Medium.........	4.69	4.88	21.58	14.07	2.70
Small...........	0.11	0.00	1.28	0.88	0.08
Red Wethersfield:					
Large...........	40.36	68.10	84.38	78.86	24.58
Medium.........	8.25	9.72	26.60	20.56	6.25
Small...........	0.10	0.37	1.13	0.30	0.29

had been kept prior to planting, and to unfavorable weather during the growth of the onion crop; especially to conditions that result in checking growth. Results of experiments reported by Boswell (1923) and by Thompson and Smith (1938) show clearly that size of sets and storage temperature are very important. Boswell showed that sets stored at 50°F. produced a larger percentage of seeders than similar sets stored at 32°F. and that the larger the sets, the greater the percentage of seedstalks. Table 20.4 gives the results of experiments, reported by Thompson and Smith, on the effect of size of sets and storage temperature on premature seeding of three varieties of onions.

A glance at Table 20.4 will show that large sets produced a much larger percentage of seedstalks than did either the medium or the small. The storage temperature that resulted in the highest percentage of seeding was 40°F., and 50°F. was next. The 60 to 70°F. range of temperature was less favorable to seedstalk development than was the 30 or 32°F.

temperature, but the high temperature was not satisfactory because of shriveling and sprouting in storage. The best storage temperatures used were 30 and 32°F. The Ebenezer sets produced a smaller percentage of seedstalks than did the other varieties.

The largest yield of marketable bulbs was produced by sets that had been stored at temperatures least favorable for subsequent seeding. Small sets produced a lower yield than the medium in every comparison, and a lower yield than the large, with the exception of the sets stored at 40 and 50°F.

If the sets were stored at 30 or 32°F. and then all sets over 1 inch in diameter were discarded, the loss from premature seeding would not be serious. Sets less than ½ inch in diameter ordinarily will not produce so large a yield as will those from ½ to 1 inch in diameter.

Hawthorne (1938) has shown that large seedlings are much more likely to develop seedstalks than are the small or medium ones grown under the same conditions.

Harvesting. Onions for use in the green stage are harvested as soon as they reach edible size. The plants are pulled by hand, the roots trimmed, and the outside skin peeled off, leaving the stem clean and white. The onions are then washed and sorted and tied in bunches; the size of the bunch depends on local market preferences. The bunches are packed in crates of various types for the market. The crates should be packed with crushed ice if the onions are to be shipped any distance since they wilt and discolor rapidly at high temperatures.

Onions that are to be stored should be harvested after the tops have begun to break over but before the foliage has dried down completely. If left in the ground until the tops are dead, the bulbs are likely to develop roots. This results in reducing the market value of the onions. Davis (1943) suggested that the best time to harvest onions in California is when from 15 to 25 per cent of the tops have broken over. In the Eastern part of the United States harvesting is delayed until most of the tops are broken over. In some areas, the onion crop is pulled by hand and thrown into windrows to dry before being topped, but most are harvested by a machine that removes the bulbs from the soil and cuts off the tops. When the onions are pulled by hand, they are so placed in the windrows that the tops partly cover the bulbs to prevent sunscald. They are usually left in the windrows long enough for the tops to become dry; the length of time required depends on the weather and may be from 3 to 10 or more days. Lorenz and Hoyle (1946) have shown that under natural conditions in California the onion bulbs lose weight during the curing in the windrow whether or not they are topped, but more weight was lost during the first few days when the tops are left intact. They found also that bulbs with the tops intact were much higher in percentage of dry matter after curing than bulbs with the tops cut off. This difference might be due to greater loss of water from the bulbs with intact foliage, or to movement of materials from the tops to the bulbs, or to both loss of water through the tops and the translocation of sugars from the tops to the bulbs. Lorenz and Hoyle state that the gain in dry matter by the bulbs was of the same magnitude as the loss from the tops.

After the tops are fairly well dried down, they are cut off by hand with shears or with a knife or by a topping machine that sorts the bulbs into sizes as well as removes the tops. It is desirable to leave ½ to 1 inch of the tops attached to the bulb. If cut too close, the neck does not close well and decay organisms have easy access to the bulb.

Curing. Onion bulbs that are to be stored in crates are usually thoroughly cured before being placed in storage. The bulbs are placed in crates as soon as the tops are removed. The filled crates are usually stacked in the field, where they are covered with boards, roofing paper, or other covering to protect the onions from injury by sun and rain. Sometimes the crates are stacked in open curing sheds instead of being covered in the field. The length of time required for curing depends largely on the weather conditions, and thorough curing requires 3 or 4 weeks and even longer in some seasons. Very often they are left in the field or curing shed until marketed, or until freezing weather when they are put into storage houses. Curing and storing onions in crates is practical for hand harvesting, but it does not fit in well with a mechanized operation since it requires so much hand labor. In many areas, crate storage is being replaced by bulk storage. The onions are harvested and topped in the field with a machine and conveyed into a wagon or truck. They then are hauled to the storage and stored in bulk piles 8 to 10 feet deep. The bulk storage has slatted floors with air ducts throughout the lower part of the storage area. Large fans force air up through the piles of onions, and the curing takes place in the storage. The fans bring in outside air when the humidity is low and recirculate the air in the storage during wet periods. Boyd and Davis (1952) found that the shrinkage in bulk-stored onions due to curing was no greater than that occurring in crates in the field. There was no difference in loss due to rots and no reduction in market quality due to storing in bulk rather than in crates. They obtained the best results by storing untopped onions in bulk and drying the tops by means of forced ventilation. The dried tops were easily removed as the onions were graded out. The tangled tops sometimes make removal from the storage difficult.

Cleaning and Grading. Onions cured in crates sometimes are run over a grader before they go into storage. The "thicknecks" and injured and decayed bulbs are picked out, and the dirt and small bulbs fall through the grading machine. The loose outer scales are rubbed off, leaving the onions bright and clean. Bulk stored onions are graded when they are ready to go to market. Undersized and diseased onions are sorted out, and the dry tops are removed. The outer scales usually rub off during the grading process, giving the onions a better appearance for market.

The U.S. Department of Agriculture has worked out grades for Northern-grown domestic onions and for Bermuda onions. These grades should be used under most conditions. Copies of the grade specifications can be obtained from the Department and, in many states, from the state marketing agency.

Packing. The standard package for onions is a 50-pound open-mesh bag. Some growers pack onions in 5- or 10-pound mesh bags for the retail market. No special method of packing is used, but it is important that the bag be well filled to keep the onions from rolling around. If the onions have been in storage for some time, they should be regraded before packing to remove any that have begun to decay or are otherwise injured.

Storage. Onions should be well ripened and thoroughly cured to keep well in storage. Immature, soft, and thick-necked bulbs should be sold as soon as harvested.

The essentials for successful storage are thorough ventilation, uniform, comparatively low temperature, dry atmosphere, and protection against actual freezing. Wright, Lauritzen, and Whiteman (1935) recommended a temperature of 32°F. and a relative humidity of about 64 per cent. They state that sprouting in stored onions was influenced little by the humidity but was increased with increased temperature. Rooting increased with increase in humidity and was little influenced by temperature. Decay showed only a slight tendency to increase as both temperature and humidity increased. The temperatures maintained in the studies were 32, 40, and 50°F., and the humidities were high, medium, and low with the per cent varying with the temperature.

In bulk storages and in some crate storages, large fans with a well-designed air-duct system provide ventilation. In some, heaters are used in connection with fans to assist in the curing process and prevent the onions from freezing during cold winter weather. To maintain a low degree of humidity well-insulated houses should be built entirely above-ground and the ventilation system should be closed during cloudy or rainy periods. During a prolonged period of high humidity, the air is recirculated in the houses to prevent accumulation of moisture in certain areas. The temperature in the storage is gradually reduced by blowing in outside air during cold periods. The temperature in the house should be lowered to equal the mean temperature for the current month of storage. Most of the stored onions are grown in Northern areas, and the outside temperature is low enough to keep the onions satisfactorily if the ventilation is done in the proper manner. Texas onions begin to come on the market in March, which makes storage unprofitable after this time.

In cold-storage warehouses it is possible to maintain a low temperature throughout the storage period, thereby keeping the bulbs in a dormant condition. The temperature should be kept at or below the freezing point to prevent drip from the pipes. If the temperature goes up for a short period of time, the melting of ice on the pipes will raise the humidity in the house. There is no danger of freezing the onions unless the air temperature goes below 28°F. and remains there for a considerable period. Onions usually are stored in crates in these houses, and the labor required in handling makes it expensive. The cost and upkeep of the crates is so great that this type of storage cannot compete with modern bulk storages.

Results of storage experiments conducted at Arlington, Va., Columbus, Ohio, Amherst, Mass., Winter Haven, Tex., and Davis, Calif., as reported by Magruder *et al.* (1941), show marked varietal difference in keeping quality. Italian Red was classed as very poor; California Red, the varieties of the Bermuda type, and Early Grano were classed as poor keepers; White Sweet Spanish, Sweet Spanish, and Prizetaker were given the rating fair. The varieties commonly called "domestic" or "American" are classed as good keepers, and White Creole, Red Creole, and Australian Brown are ranked as very good keepers. It is of interest to note that nearly all the varieties classed as very poor and poor keepers are considered mild onions and the good and very good keepers are "strong," or pungent. Platenius and Knott (1941) showed that the pungency is associated with the content of volatile sulfur; the higher the content of volatile sulfur, the greater the pungency, or the stronger the flavor. The relative pungency of varieties appears to be related to some extent to the concentration of dry matter. During storage, the content of volatile sulfur increased. Foskett and Peterson (1950) found a good correlation between the dry-matter content of onion bulbs and the refractive index of juice from the bulbs and, in addition, a correlation between the refractive index of juice of different varieties and their storage quality. Storage quality was indicated by the percentage of bulbs with sprouts after storage from October until April. The varieties having juice with the highest refractive index showed the least sprouting in April. They suggest the use of the refractive index of the juice as a means of selecting breeding lines with good storage quality. High dry-matter content and high volatile-sulfur content (pungency) are associated with good keeping quality, but the exact relationships involved are not known.

Many chemical sprout inhibitors have been tested on onions, but maleic hydrazide is the only one that was effective. Wittwer *et al.*

(1950) sprayed onion foliage 2 weeks before harvest with 500 parts per million and 2,500 parts per million maleic hydrazide solutions and observed differences in sprouting of onions after a period of storage. The low concentration reduced sprout growth, but the high concentration completely inhibited sprout growth. There were no adverse effects as-

Fig. 20.4. Onions sprayed with maleic hydrazide 2 weeks before harvest did not sprout after 8 months in storage and 22 days at room temperature. (*Courtesy of F. M. Isenberg.*)

sociated with the chemical treatment. Commercial use of this material was not successful at first because the importance of time of treatment was not recognized. Spraying the plants too early resulted in puffy onions, and spraying too late gave no inhibition of sprouts. Isenberg (1956) reported that spraying with 2 pounds of acid-equivalent maleic hydrazide when 50 per cent of the tops were down gave excellent control of sprouting and no puffy onions (Fig. 20.4). Dipping dry bulbs in a solution of maleic hydrazide did not affect sprouting, but dipping bulbs with green necks resulted in some reduction in sprout growth. The most efficient method of application was spraying in the field while the foliage was still green. Chemical sprout inhibitors should not be used on onions intended for seed production.

The storage requirements of onions to be used for growing seed are different from those of bulbs to be used as food. It has been shown by Jones and Emsweller (1939) that the best storage temperature for mother bulbs is from about 45 to 55°F. At either higher or lower temperature of storage, seed yield is reduced. If it is necessary to hold the mother bulbs for several months before planting them in the field, a temperature of 30 to 32°F. might be used for a large part of the period, then shift to a higher temperature (45 to 55°F.) for a few weeks during the latter part of the storage period. This shift to the higher temperature will stimulate the development of seedstalks.

Growing Onion Sets. Onion sets are the small bulbs produced from seed sown very thickly. Ninety-five per cent of the set crop of the United States is produced in the vicinity of Chicago, although a few are grown near Greeley, Colo., Corvallis, Ore., and at a few other points.

The best soils for them are loose sandy loams and silt loams. While rich soils are not especially desired, the areas devoted to onion sets contain soils much above the average vegetable soil in fertility. The size of sets on these soils is controlled largely by very thick seeding. Even with a heavy rate of planting some of the bulbs grown are too large for sets and are usually sold as "picklers." Bulbs over 1 inch in diameter should not be used as sets.

The quantity of seed used for growing sets is determined by the richness of the soil. On poor soils 40 to 60 pounds is used, on medium rich soils 60 to 80 pounds, and on rich soils 80 to 100 pounds of seed is planted to the acre.

The seed is sown by hand seed drills or by gang drills of the types used for planting seed for large onions. Some growers use special seeders which distribute the seed in several rows about 1 inch apart; others place a funnel-shaped spreader on the spout, which distributes the seed over an area 3 or 4 inches in width. The distance between rows is usually 12 to 14 inches, although closer planting is sometimes practiced.

The general methods of culture are the same for onion sets as for large bulbs.

In harvesting, the sets are first loosened by means of an onion harvester, an attachment for the wheel hoe, which runs under the row. They are gathered in bushel baskets and dumped into shallow, slatted trays to dry. Topping is seldom necessary since the small tops shrivel. The trays of sets are left spread for 1 or 2 days, then they are piled one above the other in the field with a space of 3 or 4 inches between. A temporary roof is placed over the pile of trays. The sets are left in the field until they are dry, then they are screened and removed to the storage house. The sets are stored under conditions similar to those used for large bulbs.

LEEK

The leek (*Allium porrum* Linn.) is a biennial grown for its blanched stem and leaves. It is believed to be a native of the Mediterranean region, where it has been in cultivation since prehistoric times. It was known by the ancient Greeks and Romans. It is not grown in this country to any great extent but is produced on a small scale by market gardeners near large cities and is consumed largely by the foreign population.

Leeks are propagated entirely from seed, which may be sown in a greenhouse or hotbed, the young plants being transplanted in the garden at the proper time, or seed may be sown in rows where the crop is to mature. The method of planting and the distance are about the same as for the onion. In fact, the general culture of the crop is very similar to that given the onion, except that leek plants are blanched by banking with soil. The soil is worked up to the plants gradually as they grow, care being taken not to bank up too early as the plants decay easily when young.

The varieties of leeks listed by American seedsmen include London, or American Flag, Elephant, or Monstrous Carentan, Giant Musselburgh, and the Lyon. These varieties are not very distinct.

Leeks are marketed in bunches like green onions. They are eaten raw alone or in mixed salads and cooked as flavoring in soups and stews.

CIBOL (CIBOULE), OR WELSH ONION

Cibol (*A. fistulosum* Linn.) is a perennial but is grown as an annual or biennial. It is a native of Siberia or the East and was introduced into England about 1629. It does not form a real bulb but only a small enlargement at the base. This plant may be propagated by division or by seeds, the latter being preferred. The seeds are sown where the plants are to grow and are grown in the same manner as green bunching onions. The Nebuka (He-Shi-Ko, or Japanese Bunching) variety is grown commercially as a green onion. It is hardy and resistant to pink root and onion smut.

GARLIC

Garlic (*Allium sativum* Linn.) is a hardy perennial plant native of southern Europe. It was known to the ancients and is said to have been disliked by the Romans on account of the strong odor but was fed to their laborers and soldiers. It was used in England as early as the first half of the sixteenth century.

Most of the garlic produced in the United States is grown in California, and the production is about 2,000 acres annually. Small quantities are grown in Texas and Louisiana and in a few other states. Garlic differs from the onion in that, instead of producing one large bulb, it produces a group of small bulbs called cloves. This group is covered with a thin skin. The seedstalk is similar to that of the onion and bears both seeds and bulblets in the same head. Seed, however, is seldom used for propagation as the cloves and bulblets give satisfaction. Cloves are more commonly used.

Garlic thrives best on fertile, well-drained, loamy soils, but any soil on which onions grow well would be satisfactory for garlic. Heavy clay soils may result in misshapen bulbs and make harvesting difficult. The two main varieties grown in California are Late and Early. The Late variety has pink or pinkish brown cloves and matures 2 or 3 weeks later than the Early variety. It yields less than the Early variety but is considered to be of higher quality. The Early variety has tan cloves and is a poor keeper in storage. In planting, the cloves are separated and planted in the same way as onion sets, requiring from 800 to 1,000 pounds of cloves to plant 1 acre. It is planted in California from late October until January. Later plantings are not successful. Mann (1952) found that long days and high temperatures favored bulb development in the garlic plant. As soon as bulbing commences leaf initiation ceases, and to get high yields it must be planted early enough so that a large vegetative plant will develop under the short photoperiods and cool temperatures. The yield potential of the plant depends on the amount of vegetative growth made before bulbing commences. Late plantings do not permit adequate vegetative development of the plant and thereby result in low yields.

The cultivation, fertilization, and general care of the crop are about the same as for onions. The crop is harvested when the tops are partly dry and begin to fall over. This occurs in June and July in California. The plants are loosened by running a cutter bar under the bulbs and are pulled by hand and placed in small bunches in windrows. The windrows are made with the tops up to facilitate drying and to protect the bulbs from the sun. The plants are allowed to dry a week or more in the field, and then the tops and roots are removed by hand with shears. The top is cut an inch above the bulb, and the roots are trimmed about $\frac{1}{2}$ inch below the bulb. The bulbs may be piled in the field and covered with tops to cure longer if necessary. When completely dry, they are graded and packed in 50- or 100-pound open-mesh bags for market or storage. For retail trade 1 or 2 bulbs are packed in small film bags or in small paper boxes with a film window.

Garlic stores well under a wide range of temperatures but sprouts most quickly at temperatures near 40°. The humidity in the storage should be low at all times to discourage mold development and formation of new roots. Garlic is used largely as a condiment as flavoring in soups, stews, pickles, and salads. Only about half the garlic consumed is grown in the United States, and the remainder is imported from southern Europe. The garlic plant is attacked by most of the insects and diseases of onions.

SHALLOT

The shallot (*A. ascalonicum* Linn.) is believed to have come from western Asia. It is a perennial and seldom produces seeds, but the bulb when planted divides into a number of cloves, which remain attached at the bottom. It has been in cultivation from a remote period. It is mentioned and figured in nearly all old works on botany.

It is sometimes grown for the dry bulb but usually for the young plant which is used in the same way as green onions. In some sections the term "shallot" is used for any green onion. Practically all of the commercial crop is grown in southern Louisiana, and, in 1953, 5,200 acres was grown and the crop was valued at $1,500,000. Shallots are grown as a winter crop for bunching green, but as a summer crop for the dry bulbs.

According to Montelaro and Tims (1951) Louisiana Pearl, which is tolerant to pink root, is the main variety of shallot grown in southern Louisiana. Some plantings are made in August, although the bulk of the crop is planted during October with later plantings until January. April plantings usually are made for the production of dry bulbs for seed the following fall and winter. The common fertilization is 600 to 800 pounds of 4-12-4 to the acre mixed with the soil before the crop is planted followed by one or two nitrogen side-dressings. The dry bulbs are planted in hills 6 to 8 inches apart, and one large bulb or two small bulbs are planted in each hill. The rows are 3 to 6 feet apart and are ridged to ensure drainage. The bulbs are covered with only about ¼ inch of soil. Shallow cultivations are made for weed control until about 5 weeks before the plants are ready for harvest, when 2 inches of soil is banked around the plants. Two weeks later another 2 inches is added so that the blanched portion of the shallot will be about 2½ inches long. The harvest season begins in November and ends in May. The shallots are pulled by hand after they have obtained a diameter of at least ¼ inch. The outer skin is peeled off, and the roots trimmed. Then they are washed, bunched, and packed for market. Barrels containing 20 dozen bunches were the standard containers for many years. Shallots are also packed in 1-bushel and 1⅓-bushel crates which hold 5 or 8 dozen bunches. The bunches must be packed with crushed ice since they heat and spoil rapidly unless iced.

When grown for the dry bulb the method of handling and harvesting is similar to that used for onions. Jenkins (1954) reported that high temperatures favored bulbing of the shallot. Plants grown at temperatures of 70°F. and higher all formed bulbs, but larger bulbs were produced with a 15-hour photoperiod than with a 10-hour photoperiod. When the temperature was lower than 70°F., no bulbs were formed regardless of the length of day. For maximum yield of dry bulbs, they should be planted early in the spring to permit a large amount of vegetative growth before bulbing commences. The individual bulbs are about 1 inch in diameter and have a more delicate flavor than onions. They are sold in small containers of various types, but few dry bulbs are grown for the market.

CHIVE

Chive, or cive (*Allium schoenoprasum* Linn.), is a perennial, probably a native of Europe. It is a popular plant in home gardens but is not grown to any great extent commercially. The plant grows in thick tufts and produces very small oval bulbs forming a compact mass. It has a showy lavender flower which, in part, accounts for its popularity among home gardeners. It is propagated by seed and by division of the tufts. Although the plant is perennial, it is a good plan to take up the clumps and replant them every 2 or 3 years. In commercial plantings the seed is sown in the spring in much the same manner as for onions. The fertilization, culture, and general care of the crop are the same as for onions. The plant is grown for its leaves, which are cut by hand with a knife. This cutting stimulates fresh growth, and several harvests can be made once the plants have formed a thick clump. On Long Island and in a few other areas, the clumps are lifted in the fall and potted in paper pots or berry boxes and placed in a cold frame. At intervals some of the plants are placed in a warm greenhouse for 2 or 3 weeks and then are sold as potted plants. These pots will supply fresh chive leaves for a period of several weeks if given good care. Chives are used as a seasoning in salads, in omelettes, and in other dishes. Most of the commercial production is sold to processors, and the finely chopped leaves are mixed with cottage cheese or cream cheese for the retail market.

CHAPTER 21

The Potato

The average annual world production of potatoes is a little over 8 billion bushels, which ranks it with wheat and rice as the world's leading food crops. It is the world's leading vegetable crop. The average composition of the potato is about 80 per cent water, 2 per cent protein, and 18 per cent starch. As a food, it is one of the cheapest sources of carbohydrates and furnishes appreciable amounts of vitamins B_1 and C as well as some minerals.

Statistics of Production. Potatoes are grown in nearly every country in the world, but the European countries, including the U.S.S.R., produced about 89 per cent of the world production in 1953. The leader in production was the U.S.S.R., with about 30 per cent of the world production, followed in decreasing order by Germany, France, the United States, the United Kingdom, and Spain. It is an important crop in all the countries of North and South America; the important producing areas being Canada, Peru, Argentina, Brazil, Chile, and Colombia, but all produce less than the United States. The reported acreages are probably too low for many countries since the potato is a common garden vegetable and the garden production may sometimes exceed the so-called "commercial" production.

Table 21.1. Average Annual Acreage, Production, and Value of Potatoes
Grown in the United States, 1918–1953

Years	Acreage (000 omitted)	Yield, bushels per acre	Production, bushels (000 omitted)	Price per bushel	Farm value (000 omitted)
1918–1927	3,298	106	349,128	$1.20	$405,886
1928–1937	3,342	111	372,142	0.72	254,094
1938–1947	2,783	147	395,170	1.07	431,130
1948–1953	1,635	241	387,579	1.35	516,408

The potato leads all other vegetables grown in the United States in value and is exceeded in total acreage only by dry beans. The potato

372

acreage was relatively stable from 1918 to 1936 when a decline began which was halted during the Second World War (Table 21.1). The acreage has declined steadily since 1943, but the production has dropped only slightly. The yield per acre increased slowly until 1945 when a marked increase in yield per acre began with the introduction of DDT as an insecticide. Many other factors were involved in this sharp rise, but DDT was undoubtedly the major one. The average yield per acre was 138 bushels in 1944 and rose to 157 bushels in 1945, 193 bushels in

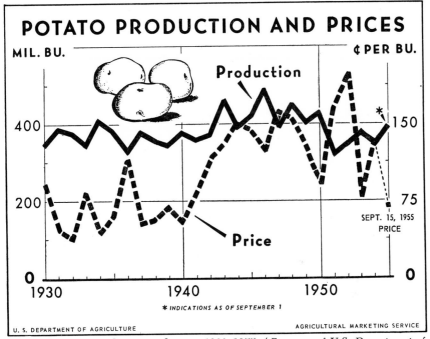

Fig. 21.1. Potato production and price, 1930–1955. (*Courtesy of U.S. Department of Agriculture.*)

1946, 227 bushels in 1948, and 248 bushels in 1953. Some of the increase in acre yield was due to the reduced acreage as a result of marginal growers going out of production. The 1,359,000 acres grown in 1951 was the first time the acreage dropped as low as 1,400,000 acres since 1868. The production in 1951 was 320,519,000 bushels compared with 120,-292,000 bushels in 1868.

There is an inverse relationship between production and price, as shown in Fig. 21.1. In years of low production the total value of the crop is likely to be greater than in years of high production. The per capita consumption of potatoes has declined markedly (Fig. 1.3) but probably not as much as the figures indicate. The consumption figures are based on market receipts of potatoes and do not take into account the marketing losses that occurred when potatoes were shipped in bulk in freight cars and unloaded with shovels. The potato now competes with high-quality vegetables the year round and is no longer the mainstay of the winter diet.

Maine was the leading state in production with nearly 58 million bushels in 1953 and was followed by California, Idaho, New York, Colorado, North Dakota, and Wisconsin. These six states accounted for about 60 per cent of the 1953 production, although potatoes are grown commercially in every state. In California the average yield was 375 bushels per acre; Maine, 370; Colorado, 335; Idaho, 300; New York, 290; Wisconsin, 235; and North Dakota, 165 bushels per acre.

Certified-seed production is a specialized branch of the potato industry. These potatoes are grown under an inspection program to ensure a supply of disease-free seed for commercial production. The main growing areas are those where high yields can be obtained and where the insect vectors of virus diseases can be controlled easily. Maine grew almost one-half of the 1953 certified-seed crop of 44,585,000 bushels. Other important areas were Minnesota, North Dakota, California, Idaho, Wisconsin, and Oregon. These states produced about 87 per cent of the certified seed grown in 1953. The Maritime Provinces of Canada grew more than 10 million bushels and exported about 10 per cent of the crop to the United States.

History and Botany. The potato is a native of South America and was cultivated by the Incas. It was introduced into Europe by the early Spanish explorers during the sixteenth century and is mentioned and described in many of the old herbals but was not cultivated to any extent as a food crop until late in the seventeenth century. It probably reached the North American colonies from Europe. The first important cultivation of the potato in the United States was in Londonderry, N.H., in 1719. Once the prejudices against the crop had been overcome, the cultivation of the potato as a food crop spread rapidly. Some areas were almost completely dependent upon the potato, as is evidenced by the Irish famines of 1845–1847 as a result of the total loss of the potato crop from late blight, *Phytophthora infestans*. Today the potato is one of the important food crops of the world.

The potato is a member of the family Solanaceae, which includes tomato, tobacco, pepper, eggplant, petunia, black nightshade, belladonna, Jimson weed, and others. There are several hundred species of Solanum, but only the potato (*S. tuberosum*) and a few others are tuber-bearing. Salaman (1949) presents considerable evidence that the modern potato was derived from hybrids of *S. tuberosum* and *S. andigenum*. Some of the varieties with resistance to late blight have resulted from crosses with *S. demissum,* but for all practical purposes, the potato is considered to be *S. tuberosum.*

Potato varieties include a wide range of plant characters with the tops (vines, haulms) ranging from prostrate to erect types, all bearing compound leaves with opposite leaflets, but the number and size of leaflets vary greatly. The stems may be green or may contain an anthocyanin which gives them a purple or reddish color. Some flower sparsely, others profusely, and the color of the corolla varies from pure white to deep purple or violet. The fruit is spherical, ½ to 1 inch in diameter, and usually green although it may be purple or black at maturity. Some varieties are very fertile and under proper conditions set many seed balls, but others bear only an occasional fruit. The true seeds are not used for propagation except in the development of new varieties. Most varieties of potatoes have an upright and erect stem until flowering. The flower cluster is borne terminally, and the axillary bud beneath the flower cluster develops a lateral branch which becomes an extension of the main stem. Since flowering eliminates apical dominance, several of the lower axillary buds also produce lateral branches. The weight of these lateral branches usually bends the stem over and gives the plant a semiprostrate habit of growth. These lateral branches comprise about two-thirds of the foliage area and two-thirds of the weight of the plant top. Under favorable conditions lateral branches produce flowers and still more lateral shoots.

The stolons are slender, underground lateral stems arising from buds on the underground portion of the stem. There is considerable variation in the number, length, and diameter of stolons produced by different varieties or under different growing conditions. Initially one stolon is produced at each node, but others may emerge later. The tubers are greatly enlarged tips of stolons, but some of the stolons may not form tubers. The size, shape, and color of tubers vary greatly, and only a few of the possible types are grown commercially. For example, the flesh color may be white, yellow, pink, red, or blue, but only the white types are acceptable in the United States. In most regions tuberization occurs at about the same time as blossoming, but there is no cause-and-effect relationship between the two processes. Under adverse conditions the plant may blossom several times before any tubers are formed. Some workers contend that all the tubers are set at about the same time, but Smith (1931) has shown that tuber setting may take place over a considerable period of time. Werner (1934) reported that the time, duration, and extent of tuber setting for any one variety may be altered considerably by environmental and nutritional factors.

While there is no direct relationship between initiation of flowers and tuberization, flowering and fruiting have an effect on the growth of both tops and tubers, according to Bartholdi (1945). The suppressing effect of flowering and fruiting on vegetative growth has been studied by other workers with tomatoes, cucumbers, and similar crops. Bartholdi studied three plant types: those allowed to flower and fruit (fruiting plants), those with flowers removed after anthesis (flowering plants), and those with the flower buds removed as they appeared (nonflowering plants). The greatest weight of tops and tubers was produced by the nonflowering plants. Flowering reduced the top weight 9 per cent and the tuber weight 10 per cent, and fruiting reduced the top weight 18 per cent and the tuber weight 23 per cent. These results were the average of three experiments which included varieties that flowered and fruited profusely as well as some which flowered and fruited sparsely. The depressing effect of flowering and fruiting on growth was observed with both varietal types and is similar to that observed in other crops. This does not mean that areas where fruiting is uncommon produce higher yields than those where fruiting is profuse, because the opposite is usually true since fruiting and flowering are favored by the same climatic factors that favor high yields of tubers. These favorable environmental conditions more than offset the detrimental effects of flowering and fruiting.

Climatic Requirements. The potato is a cool-season crop but is only moderately tolerant of frost. The temperature during the growing season has long been recognized as one of the most important factors influencing the yield of potatoes. Many workers have studied this relationship and have found that maximum yields were obtained with the growing-season temperature averaging between 60 and 65°F. The high yields obtained in the regions of the world with cool summers lend support to these studies. Bushnell (1925) was one of the first to point out the importance of temperature on tuber production. He grew potatoes in thermoregulated chambers in the greenhouse and found that increasing the growing temperature decreased the production of tubers. Respiration in the aboveground portions of the plant increased with the temperature, thus reducing the amount of carbohydrates available for translocation to the tubers. The yield of tubers depended on the amount of carbohydrates produced over and above the needs for growth and respiration of all other plant parts. Respiration was the critical factor since the rate of photosynthesis was not greatly influenced by temperature. Other workers have shown that the temperature at which maximum yields are obtained depends on the light intensity. The amount of sunlight the plant receives determines to a great extent the rate of photosynthesis and directly influences the amount of carbohydrates available for tuber growth. Tubers are produced at high temperatures only when the plant receives a high rate of illumination, the higher the light intensity during the growing season the higher the maximum temperature allowing tuberization. High potato yields are obtained in some regions which have high daytime temperatures, but the high light intensity in these areas tends to compensate for the high temperature and, in addition, the temperature during the night is low enough to greatly reduce respiration. The soil temperature is also important since this determines the rate of respiration of the tubers. A number of workers have obtained increased yield by mulching, and some of this beneficial effect is due to reducing the soil temperature. Irrigation, also, may reduce the soil temperature.

Some varieties are sensitive to photoperiod, while others produce tubers over a wide range of photoperiods. Garner and Allard (1923) found that the McCormick variety produced many tubers with a 10-hour day; only a few with a 14-hour day; and none with an 18-hour day. Other workers have demonstrated that there is a wide range of response of potato varieties to photoperiod although, in general, tuberization is accelerated by short days. Some of the varieties developed in South America near the Equator do not produce tubers during the long days of summer in Northern areas. Obviously, there are varieties which produce high yields under the long days in Northern areas since these are the most important producing areas for the crop.

Werner (1934) conducted a series of studies on the effect of temperature and photoperiod on tuber production and vegetative growth. The growth of the top was favored by high temperatures and long days, but early tuberization was favored by low temperatures and short days. Under cool and short days the plants were small and had a very high ratio of tubers to tops. The greatest yield of tubers was produced at low temperatures and intermediate day lengths, but the tuber-top ratio was lower than with the previously mentioned plants. As the days became longer or warmer, the tops of the plants were larger and tuber production was lowered. At very high temperatures and long days the plants were devoid of tubers and sometimes produced no stolons. Similar plants were produced in the greenhouse during the short, dark days of winter with moderately high temperatures. Werner also found that the nitrogen supply had an influence on the production of tubers. Restricting growth by withholding nitrogen resulted in tuberization at higher temperatures than when nitrogen was supplied abundantly. An abundant supply of nitrogen resulted in plants with large tops and few tubers when conditions were favorable for growth of the tops, but there was no detrimental effect of an abundance of nitrogen when the plants were grown under cool and short days. The highest yield of tubers was obtained with an adequate nitrogen supply when the photoperiod was relatively long early in the season, favoring a large top growth, and relatively short later in the season, favoring maximum tuber development.

The initiation and growth of stolons are also affected by environment. At temperatures most favorable for potato growth, stolons are initiated and have begun to elongate by the time the plant emerges from the soil. At high temperatures, stolon development may not occur until several leaves have been formed aboveground. The initiation of stolons is associated with an accumulation of carbohydrates in the underground stem, but the level necessary for stolon initiation is lower than the level required for tuberization. Elongation of the stolon ceases when a tuber starts to develop, and conditions favorable for tuber setting limit the growth of stolons. It is frequently reported that high temperatures favor stolon elongation, but it may mean only that the high temperature delays tuber formatfon. During hot, dry periods the stolons may emerge from the ground and form leafy shoots. The growth characteristics of stolons vary considerably with variety.

The potato is a shallow-rooted crop and gives good response to irrigation in most areas. A dry period of only 2 or 3 weeks may reduce the yield enough to make irrigation profitable. In arid regions, potatoes are irrigated at frequent intervals until the tubers are well formed, and then the interval is gradually increased. Excessive irrigation after the tubers are formed may reduce the yield because of rotting of the tubers. Irrigation in these arid areas greatly increases the total yield as well as the percentage of marketable tubers. In most humid areas, irrigation is becoming more common. Pratt *et al.* (1952) reported that irrigation was profitable in upstate New York each year of a 4-year study. It has been a common practice on Long Island for many years. The best results were obtained by irrigating when the soil moisture had dropped to 50 per cent of field capacity. The number of tubers set was increased by irrigation, but the average tuber weight was not affected with most varieties. The increase in tuber set was greatest when the nonirrigated plots were dry at the time of tuber formation.

Many tuber abnormalities are the result of a widely fluctuating moisture supply. During a period of low soil-moisture supply, the tuber makes little if any growth and the cells tend to mature. A sudden increase in soil moisture may result in growth cracks, second growth, or rough, knobby tubers which are not marketable. Sometimes the dry period is accompanied by high soil temperature and the rest period may be broken, so that the tubers sprout in the ground. After sprouting, if conditions are favorable, the sprouts may tuberize and form double tubers or chains of tubers. Many of these abnormalities are eliminated when irrigation is used to ensure a continuous supply of available soil moisture for growth of the plant.

Soils and Soil Preparation. Potatoes are grown on a wide variety of soils from light sands to fairly heavy clay loams and on muck soils; the most popular are light-textured mineral soils and muck soils. The potato plant is very sensitive to drainage and aeration, and it is essential that the soil be well drained. Tubers produced on light soils and muck soils generally have a more desirable shape and brighter skin color than those grown on heavy soils. Heavy soils and stony soils require more power for digging and are generally becoming less popular as a result of mechanized harvest. Light sandy soils are excellent potato soils with proper fertilization and rotation if irrigation is available to prevent reductions in yields due to lack of water. Bushnell (1953) reported that the porosity and aeration of the soils in Ohio limited the yield of potatoes. High yields were obtained when a virgin soil was plowed, but the yield of potatoes decreased in the following years, while the yield of other crops remained fairly high. He found that potato roots did not grow in the portions of the soil that were compacted because of the impact of raindrops or of wheels of machinery. Plowing down green-manure crops in alternate years over a period of 16 years failed to improve the soil structure. The greatest increase in yield was obtained by placing a shallow tile line directly under the potato row to ventilate the soil. The pore space and the percentage of water-stable aggregates in the soil decreased steadily under continuous cropping with potatoes. The maintenance of high yields was not as difficult on light soils, which are more porous because of their texture. Experiments in many other areas agree that fairly long rotations are necessary to maintain high yields of potatoes on heavy soils. High yields can be maintained on light soils by growing winter cover crops each year, but with increased mechanization of cultural practice, the maintenance of soil structure is more difficult. Timing of cultural operations is very important. Plowing, fitting, and planting should be done when the soil moisture is optimum for these operations even though it may cause a delay in planting. Many have observed that good yields of potatoes are never obtained if they are planted when the soil is a little too wet. Greater yields are obtained by delaying planting until soil moisture is optimum for cultural operations which may puddle and compact the soil if the soil moisture is too high. The importance of maintaining a high soil organic-matter content was emphasized by Chucka *et al.* (1943) in Aroostook County, Maine. Over a 13-year period the average yield of continuous potatoes fertilized annually with a ton of 4-8-7 was 351 bushels per acre. Potatoes receiving the same rate of fertilization but with a green-manure crop in alternate years yielded 370 bushels per acre where the green-manure crop was cut and removed, 410 bushels where the green-manure crop was plowed under, and 456 bushels where the green-manure crop was plowed under with 20 tons of manure per acre. These increases in yield were probably due to soil structure and organic matter since nitrogen side-dressings and heavier applications of fertilizer did not increase the yield. In Idaho, it is recognized that potatoes yield more following alfalfa than when they follow a cultivated crop and that this difference in yield is not affected by applying more fertilizer.

It is usually recommended that potatoes be grown at a soil reaction between pH 4.8 and 5.4. This is recommended to control potato scab, and not because the highest yields are obtained at this soil reaction. Wessels (1932), working on Long Island, found that the total marketable yield of potatoes decreased considerably as the pH was allowed to drop below 5.0. The total yield of potatoes was highest in the range of 5.2 up to 6.4, but the marketable yield was reduced at the higher pH because of scab. Smith (1937), working on a heavy soil in New York, found that there was no appreciable difference in the total yield of potatoes grown at soil reactions from pH 4.8 to 7.1. He found that the incidence of scab was lowest in those potatoes grown at pH 4.8, but scab was also reduced when the soil reaction exceeded pH 7.5.

A thorough job of plowing should be done so that all refuse is turned under and will not interfere with planting. Harrowing and disking should be kept to a minimum since these operations tend to destroy the soil structure. It is important that the soil be plowed and fitted when the moisture content is optimum for these operations, because puddling and compaction will result if the soil is too wet. The potato planter makes a good seedbed as it opens the furrow, so a finely pulverized soil is not necessary. Sometimes potatoes are planted immediately following the plow without harrowing or disking. In some areas ridges are made with special tools before the planting, but in most areas the planter forms the ridge.

Fertilizers. Potatoes are usually heavily fertilized since they have a high nutrient requirement and a high gross value per acre, which makes heavy fertilization economical. Lorenz *et al.* (1954) found that a good potato crop in California removed about 150 pounds of N, 35 pounds of P_2O_5, and 250 pounds of K_2O from the soil. The tubers accounted for 60 to 90 per cent of the total nutrients removed. This does not mean that all these nutrients must be added in the fertilizer, but that the fertilizer should supplement the natural fertility of the soil. The wide variations in fertilization in the different areas of production reflect differences in native fertility of the soils. Potatoes grown on most California mineral soils responded to 160 pounds of nitrogen per acre, but there was a small response to phosphorus and no response to potash. On the peat soils in the San Joaquin delta, large increases in yield were obtained with all three fertilizer nutrients, while on the organic soils in the Tule Lake area, there was a response to low rates of nitrogen but little or no response to phosphorus and potash. In Idaho, the soils are well supplied with potash, and potatoes are fertilized with 80 to 100 pounds of N and 60 to 80 pounds of P_2O_5 per acre, but if alfalfa is plowed down or manure is used, the application of nitrogen is reduced. In New York and similar areas, the common practice is 1,500 pounds of 8-16-16 or 1,200 pounds of 10-10-10, while on Long Island, it is 2,000 pounds of 7-7-7 or 5-10-5 per acre. On most organic soils a 1-2-2 or 1-2-3 ratio is used at rates supplying 80 to 100 pounds of nitrogen per acre. The standard fertilizer application in Maine is 1,250 to 1,500 pounds of 8-12-12 per acre. With varieties such as Kennebec, oversize may be a problem, and less fertilizer is recommended than for Katahdin and Chippewa and similar varieties.

Nitrogen has given the most consistent response in all potato-growing areas, and the time of application and source of nitrogen have been studied by many workers. Terman et al. (1951) reported that potatoes grown in Maine should be fertilized with 100 to 120 pounds of nitrogen per acre at planting. A combination of ammonium and nitrate sources gave the best results, and there was no advantage in using natural organic sources of nitrogen. Delayed application of part of the nitrogen resulted in a decrease in yield. Very high applications of nitrogen lowered the starch content and quality of the tubers and delayed maturity, which made the tubers more susceptible to skinning and bruising during harvest. Lorenz et al. (1954) found that ammonium sulfate and aqua ammonia were the best nitrogen sources on the alkaline mineral soils of California. Higher yields were obtained by banding all the nitrogen at planting than by delaying part of the application. Both the nitrate and phosphorus content of the petioles increased with increasing nitrogen applications to the soil. The acidifying effect of the ammonium sulfate apparently made more phosphorus available to the plant on these alkaline soils. The highest levels of nitrogen sometimes resulted in a slightly lower starch content of the tubers than in the plots which received no nitrogen, but the rate of fertilization had no effect on storage losses. Smith and Kelly (1946) also reported that increasing the rate of fertilization resulted in an increase in the nitrate content of the petioles and a lower starch content of the tubers. Their work indicated that a high nitrate content in the petioles early in the season was essential for high yields. This conclusion is borne out by many other experiments which indicate that delayed applications of nitrogen are not effective in increasing the yield in most potato-growing areas. On the other hand, Ware and Johnson (1955) reported a beneficial effect of delayed application of part of the nitrogen and potash on a sandy loam in Alabama. Increases in yield were obtained by side-dressing some of the nitrogen and potash 4 weeks after planting rather than applying all the fertilizer at planting. This increase in yield was greater in seasons with high rainfall.

Similar results have been obtained by other workers on light-textured soils that are subject to excessive leaching, but all indicate that the fertilizer should be applied before tubers are formed.

In most areas potatoes grown on mineral soils receive all the fertilizer at the time of planting in bands 2 to 3 inches to the side and slightly below the seed. Fertilizer mixed with the soil near the seed piece may injure the young plant and reduce the stand and yield. On organic soils in the North Central states, drilling or broadcasting the fertilizer before planting has given as good results as banding, but banding is nearly always superior on mineral soils. Terman *et al.* (1951) reported that in Maine the highest yields were obtained by applying all the fertilizer in bands and that broadcasting part of the fertilizer before planting always resulted in lower yields. In New York, Smith and Kelly (1946) obtained higher yields by broadcasting one-half of the fertilizer before plowing and banding the remainder than by banding all of the fertilizer. The effect of placement was the same at both rates used, 1,200 pounds and 2,400 pounds of 5-10-10 per acre. Tissue tests indicated that the main response in yield was due to nitrogen and that the nitrate content of petioles was lowest when all of the fertilizer was applied in bands. This might indicate that some root damage resulted from the heavy applications of fertilizer near the seed, thereby restricting the nitrogen uptake. The response of potatoes to different methods of placement varies with the soil type and from season to season. Soil moisture at the time of planting and during the early growth of the plants is probably the important factor influencing the response to different methods of placement.

Manure is used for potatoes in many areas where it is available. It is generally applied to a sod crop in the fall previous to planting potatoes. Fresh manure applied immediately before plowing tends to increase the damage from scab. Well-decomposed manure can be applied safely in the spring or just prior to plowing for potatoes. The application of fertilizer is usually reduced when more than 10 tons of manure per acre is applied.

Potatoes do not have a high requirement for most of the minor elements, and deficiencies are seldom a problem. Magnesium deficiency is probably the most common trouble. Since potatoes are grown on strongly acid soils to control scab, the soil supply of magnesium may be limited. Fertilizer supplying 40 to 50 pounds of MgO per acre is used in most areas. Dolomitic limestone in the fertilizer is used frequently in potato fertilizers, but part of the magnesium should be water-soluble.

Manganese deficiency may occur on alkaline mucks which are mixed with the underlying marl. It can be corrected by supplying about 150 pounds of manganese sulfate per acre in the fertilizer. Since potatoes are sprayed frequently to control diseases, inclusion of 5 to 10 pounds of manganese sulfate per acre in each spray should eliminate the deficiency.

Seed. Potatoes are propagated vegetatively from tubers, either whole or cut into pieces. Many diseases are carried by seed potatoes, and disastrous results may follow the use of diseased seed. Most of the potato acreage is planted with "certified" seed which was produced under strict inspection and is certified to be essentially free of certain diseases. The cost of certified seed is usually greater than that of table stock, but the potato grower can hardly afford to use anything but certified seed.

Immediately after harvest tubers have a rest period, or dormant period, during which they will not sprout even though placed under favorable conditions for sprouting. The rest period is longer for immature than for mature tubers and is influenced by the variety and by storage conditions. Many workers have studied methods of shortening this period of dormancy. Appleman (1914) reported that dormant potatoes could be induced to sprout at any time by peeling the tuber. He also found that wrapping the tuber in cotton saturated with hydrogen peroxide shortened the rest period, as did ethyl bromide gas. Denny (1926) shortened the rest period of potatoes by treating them with ethylene chlorohydrin, thiourea, or potassium thiocyanate. Cut seed pieces were soaked in solutions of thiourea and potassium thiocyanate for varying periods of time. Ethylene chlorohydrin was applied as a gas in a tight storage or by dipping the potatoes in a solution of it and storing them in a tight container for 24 hours. Loomis (1927) found that storing freshly harvested tubers at temperatures of 20 to 30°C for 3 to 4 weeks was as effective in breaking the rest period as ethylene gas. In areas where potatoes are grown during the winter, the seed obtained from the summer crop in Northern areas may still be dormant. Several chemicals are used to break the rest period of the seed potatoes in these areas. Cut seed may be treated by soaking in a 1 per cent potassium thiocyanate solution for 1 hour or by dipping in a 1.2 per cent ethylene chlorohydrin solution and storing in a tight place for 16 to 24 hours. Whole tubers are treated with 1 pound of ethylene chlorohydrin per ton of potatoes in a tight storage for 3 days.

When the rest period ends, sprouting begins if conditions favor sprouting. The first sprouts appear at the apical end, and sprouting is suppressed in the other buds as long as the apical sprouts are present; thus the tuber exhibits typical apical dominance. If the apical sprouts are removed, sprouts will appear from the more basal buds. When potatoes are cut into seed pieces, sprouts appear from buds on each piece since apical dominance is no longer a factor. The buds in the eyes of potatoes are multiple buds, and usually one bud sprouts and suppresses the growth of the other buds, but removal of the first sprout permits other buds to produce sprouts. Many workers have studied the relative value of apical and basal seed pieces, with divergent results. If the seed potatoes were sprouting when cut and were planted immediately, the apical pieces usually produced a larger crop since sprouts were already present on these pieces and the plants emerged from the ground sooner than did those from the basal pieces which had no sprouts. If the tubers were cut before sprouting had begun, there was no difference in rate of emergence or in yield from the two types of seed pieces. In other words, there was no difference in the seed value of the different parts of the potato so long as there was an eye on each seed piece. This holds true for the old varieties with many eyes, but for new varieties such as Chippewa, Sebago, Kennebec, etc., this is not always correct since the basal eyes on these varieties are definitely weaker in vigor than the apical eyes. The basal eyes are not well developed, and poor stands sometimes result when large tubers are cut for seed since one or more seed pieces may include one of these weak eyes. A further reduction in stand may result from treating the seed with hot formaldehyde or hot corrosive sublimate to control scab and rhizoctonia. These seed treatments are without effect on the older varieties, but they may have a detrimental effect on the basal eyes of new varieties. Seed growers plant these new varieties close and harvest early to keep down the size of the tuber so that seed pieces can be cut with at least one strong eye.

Many workers have observed that the number of tubers produced per hill is positively correlated with the number of stems per hill. Bushnell (1929) studied some of the factors influencing the number of sprouts produced from a seed piece. The number of sprouts produced on a tuber increased as the length of storage increased. Mature potatoes produced more sprouts than immature potatoes that were harvested at the same time, and tubers stored at 40°F. produced more sprouts than those stored at 32°F. Removal of the first sprouts increased the number of subsequent sprouts, as did treating the seed pieces with thiourea. Smith (1937), summarizing experiments conducted over a 4-year period, found that the largest number of stems per hill was produced by seed tubers stored at the highest temperature studied. Irish Cobbler and Smooth Rural potatoes were stored at 50, 40, 35 and 32°F., and the rate of emergence of plants in the field was in the order of the storage temperatures: the first plants to come up were from seed stored at the highest temperature. There was some reduction in final stand from seed that had been stored at 32°F. The greatest yield was produced from seed that had been stored at the two highest temperatures, but there was some difference in the response of the two varieties studied. The Smooth Rural produced the highest yields after storage at 50°, and the Irish Cobbler, after storage at 40°F. He concluded that in localities where early planting results in high yields, it would be desirable to store seed at temperatures that permit sprout growth before planting, but in areas where later planting results in highest yields, storage at lower temperatures which delay sprouting would probably result in increased yields.

Some workers have reported a superiority of seed that has been allowed to sprout in the light, usually called *green-sprouted* seed. McCubbin (1941) found no difference between green-sprouted seed and seed sprouted in the dark in either the rate of come-up, number of stems per hill, or yield. Most of the previous comparisons had been made between tubers sprouted in the light at high temperatures and tubers left in storage at low temperatures. McCubbin stored potatoes at various temperatures both in the light and in the dark, and some were planted with sprouts intact while others were desprouted. There was no difference in either the time of come-up, number of stems, or yield from seed tubers stored in the light or in the dark so long as the temperature was the same in each case. Desprouting the seed pieces resulted in more stems per hill and a greater number of tubers, but not necessarily a greater total weight of tubers. The delay in plant emergence and the effect on subsequent growth and maturity resulting from removal of sprouts were due to the loss of the sprout as a plant part rather than to a loss of food reserves in the seed piece.

Potatoes are grown from cut seed and small whole tubers, and both are satisfactory provided they came from disease-free stock. Small whole tubers have certain advantages in that they save the labor of cutting and are less likely to rot in the ground. The supply of small whole tubers is not sufficient to plant all of the potato acreage so that some tubers must be cut for seed. The usual size of the seed piece is $1\frac{1}{2}$ to 2 ounces. Many workers have shown that the vigor of the young plant is directly related to the size of the seed piece, the larger the seed piece the more vigorous the plant. The number of stems per hill increases as the size of the seed piece increases. The $1\frac{1}{2}$- to 2-ounce seed piece is a satisfactory compromise between vigor and number of stems per hill and the cost of seed required to plant an acre. Small whole tubers should weigh about the same as cut seed pieces. Tubers $1\frac{1}{2}$ to $1\frac{7}{8}$ inches in diameter usually weigh between $1\frac{1}{2}$ and 2 ounces. Smaller tubers are not desirable for seed since the early growth of the plant is weak. Blocky pieces with square cuts and a minimum of cut surface are most desirable, as illustrated in Fig. 21.2. The number of stems per hill is not related to the number of eyes on the seed piece, since usually one of the eyes will sprout and suppress sprouting from the other eyes. It is essential that each seed piece have at least one eye; it does not make any difference how many it has so long as it has one. The most important factor in cutting seed is to cut pieces of a fairly uniform size and shape so that they can be handled easily by the planter.

Cut seed pieces should be cured to encourage rapid suberization and wound-periderm formation on the cut surface. The wound periderm protects the seed piece from drying after planting and is also protection against rot organisms which may be present in the soil. Artschwager (1927) reported that periderm formation was most rapid at 50 to 65°F. with 85 to 95 per cent relative humidity. The cut seed should be stored under these conditions for a period of 4 to 6 days to allow the wound periderm to form. If the cut seed must be held after curing, it should be stored at about 40°F. until planting. The importance of planting whole tubers or curing cut seed is illustrated by the work of Denny (1929). He grew potatoes in pots in a greenhouse and amputated the seed piece

Fig. 21.2. Tubers cut according to size. Tuber weight, left to right, 3 ounces, 5 ounces, 7 ounces.

from the growing plant at various stages of growth. Removal of the seed piece before the plants reached 10 to 12 inches in height and before tuber setting had begun reduced the yield, and the earlier the seed piece was removed the greater was the reduction in yield. This experiment simulates conditions that occur when seed pieces rot in the ground. Bushnell (1936) found that the seed piece played an important role in the recovery of potatoes from frost injury. Small potato plants injured by frost are likely to die if the seed piece has rotted. If the seed piece is still sound, the plants recover quickly and continue growth. This was observed in the field and verified in the greenhouse by amputating the seed pieces and subjecting the plants to freezing temperatures.

Planting. In areas where hard freezes occur, potatoes are planted after the danger of hard frost is past. In areas where frost does not occur, the time of planting the crop is determined by the time it is to be marketed. In areas where high summer temperatures occur, potatoes are planted so as to bring the crop into maturity at a time when the temperature is lower and more favorable for high yields. In the large potato-producing states in the country's Northern areas, such as Idaho, Maine, New York, Minnesota, and Wisconsin, they are planted in May or sometimes in late April. In Florida, the planting is done in November for spring harvest. In the intermediate states two crops may be grown, one planted in February or March and the other in August or September. In some parts of California, potatoes are planted during the winter for spring and summer harvest, and in other parts, in the spring for fall harvest. Planting potatoes in a cold, wet soil increases the length of time it takes them to emerge from the soil and increases the danger of damage due to rot and insects. Seed stored at low temperatures planted in a cold soil may form tuber sprouts and never emerge from the soil. The small sprouts develop tubers instead of plants.

All of the commercial acreage of potatoes is planted with mechanical planters which are pulled by a tractor. Most planters apply fertilizer in bands at the same time as the seed is planted. The quantity of seed required to plant an acre depends on the spacing and the size of the seed pieces, but in most areas 20 to 30 bushels of seed per acre is planted. The spacing of the plants depends on the fertility of the soil, the variety, and the amount of water available for growth. More seed should be planted with varieties that tend to produce oversized tubers than with those which produce small tubers. With irrigation and high fertility potatoes can be planted closer together than on infertile soils or where water is likely to be limiting growth. The spacing of the plants varies from 8 to 12 inches, and the rows are 30 to 48 inches apart, depending on local conditions. The depth of planting depends on the soil type and usually varies between 4 to 6 inches and tends to be shallow on heavy soils and deep on light soils.

Potatoes are planted on high ridges in Maine, in the South, and in regions where furrow irrigation is practiced. The ridges are necessary for irrigation and give better results than level culture where excessive rainfall may occur early in the season or during harvest. Since the soil dries out rapidly with ridges, a more nearly level culture is practiced in areas where soil moisture might be a limiting factor. The soil is level after planting, but small ridges are formed during cultivation to prevent greening and sunburning of exposed tubers.

Cultivation. The primary object of cultivation is weed control. Cultivation should be often enough and just deep enough to control weeds. Deep cultivation is detrimental since it destroys the roots in the surface few inches of the soil, as shown in Figs. 21.3 and 21.4. Small weeds may be present before the potatoes come up and can be easily eradicated with a weeder or harrow. Weeders can be used until the plants are several inches tall. Row cultivators with points, shovels, or sweeps are used until the foliage begins to cover the ground between the rows. Several cultivations may be made, and the last one is usually combined with hilling or ridging. Hilling covers weeds in the row with soil and also provides additional protection against tubers greening as a result of exposure to light. Hilling is especially important with shallow setting varieties like Katahdin. The hill should be formed with a broad sweep which gathers soil from most of the area between the rows. Large ridges made after the plants are fairly well grown result in severe root pruning

Fig. 21.3. Root distribution of potato plants 95 days after planting. Roots pruned to a depth of 4 inches and 4 inches from either side of row when plants were about 6 inches high, repeated once a week for 3 weeks.

which may reduce the yield. In areas where ridge culture is practiced, the ridges are formed at planting and are built up only slightly by cultivation. Moore (1937) found that soil moisture was lower and soil temperature was higher around the tubers grown with ridge culture than with level culture. Ridging produces conditions which may be favorable with cool, wet soils but unfavorable with warm, dry soils. The beneficial effects of higher soil moisture and lower soil temperature with level culture are frequently nullified by deep cultivation and root pruning.

Chemical Weed Control. Good methods of chemical weed control in potatoes are available, but they have not been used as widely as with certain other crops. Excellent annual weed control can be obtained with a preemergence spray of a dinitro compound plus diesel oil in water, or sodium pentochlorophenate plus diesel oil in water, or of a high concentration of a dinitro alone. The spray is applied just before the potatoes emerge through the soil, and annual weeds are controlled for the season unless untreated soil is turned up. In some areas high yields have been obtained with a preemergence spray followed by only one cultivation and hilling, but in other areas regular cultivation has given higher yields than chemical weed control. On some soils cultivation may

Fig. 21.4. Root distribution of potato plants 95 days after planting. Roots not pruned. Compare with Fig. 21.3.

have a beneficial effect in breaking the crust and thereby increasing water infiltration and aeration of the soil.

Varieties. Varieties differ greatly in time of maturity, appearance, yield, quality, and resistance to diseases and insects. Some varieties are grown in many parts of the country, while others are grown primarily in a single producing area. Some of the present potato varieties have been grown for more than 50 years, and most of these old varieties originated as chance seedlings or through hybridization by amateur breeders. They have many deep eyes, tend to be rough and irregular in shape, and have little if any resistance to diseases or insects. The "new" varieties are those introduced by the U.S. Department of Agriculture and various state experiment stations since 1925. They have only a few, shallow eyes;

smooth, uniform shape; usually higher yields than the old varieties; and, in addition, resistance to some diseases and insects. Both groups of varieties represent a wide range of maturity and appearance.

Since most potatoes are propagated from certified-seed stocks, the amount of certified seed produced of a variety is a good indication of its relative importance. In 1955, 59 potato varieties were grown for seed certification in the United States and about 20 additional varieties in Canada. Of this large number of varieties, 12 varieties account for more than 90 per cent of the certified-seed potatoes grown in the United States and Canada.

The leading potato variety is the Katahdin, the first of the new varieties to be introduced. It is late-maturing, with an oval to round tuber with a smooth white skin and shallow eyes. It yields well over a wide range of conditions and is resistant to mild mosaic, net necrosis, and brown rot and is immune to wart. It has only fair cooking quality but has a good market appearance.

Red Pontiac is the most popular red-skinned variety. It is late-maturing and high-yielding and has oblong to round tubers with a smooth red skin and shallow eyes. It is not resistant to diseases but seems to be fairly drought-resistant and free from misshapen tubers. It is well adapted to muck soils in many of the North Central states and is widely grown on mineral soils in the Red River Valley, in Florida, and in other areas where a red-skinned variety is desired.

Russet Burbank, or Netted Gem, is a very old variety introduced by Luther Burbank. The main area of production is Idaho and Montana, with a limited production in other areas. The long tubers have a russeted skin and many eyes of medium depth and excellent cooking quality. It is not widely adapted and can be grown successfully in only a few places. It has some resistance to scab but is very susceptible to verticillium wilt. Unless growing conditions are ideal it is likely to produce many rough and misshapen tubers.

Irish Cobbler is an old variety of wide adaptation, being grown in every state. It is early-maturing and is well adapted to muck and light soils. The white, smooth-skinned tubers are round with blunt ends, often deeply notched, and have many deep eyes. The market appearance is only fair, but the cooking quality is good. It is susceptible to most virus diseases and very susceptible to scab, but has resistance to mild mosaic and is immune to wart.

White Rose is an old, late-maturing variety, producing long white-skinned tubers with many eyes. The eyes sometimes protrude, making the tuber appear very knobby and rough. This is the leading variety in most sections of California and produces outstanding yields. The market appearance of the variety is poor, and the quality is only fair, but it is harvested during the early summer when potatoes are in short supply.

Bliss Triumph is an early-maturing red-skinned variety and has been grown for a long time. The tubers are round and thick with many deep eyes. It is widely adapted, but it is important mainly in the South and Middle West and in Colorado. It is susceptible to most diseases and is very susceptible to hopperburn caused by leaf hoppers feeding on the foliage. It has good quality for an early-maturing potato but is being replaced by newer varieties.

Kennebec is a new, late-maturing variety which has a fairly wide adaptation. The tubers are large, oblong, with a few shallow eyes and smooth white skin. It produces very high yields and must be planted close in the row to prevent development of oversized and rough tubers. It is resistant to the common strains of late blight, mild mosaic, and net necrosis. It has good cooking and processing quality.

Cherokee is a new, medium-early variety that is replacing Irish Cobbler in some sections. The tubers are medium in size, round with blunt ends, and white-skinned with a few eyes of medium depth. It has resistance to the common strains of late blight, common scab, mild mosaic, and net necrosis. The cooking quality compares favorably with that of Irish Cobbler. It is most popular on the muck soils of the North Central states because of its resistance to scab.

Chippewa is a new, midseason variety producing large, elliptical tubers, medium in thickness, white-skinned, with a few shallow eyes. It has a wide distribution and is especially adapted to muck soils in the North Central and Northeastern states. It is susceptible to leaf roll but does not show net necrosis and is resistant to mild mosaic. The cooking quality is poor to fair.

Sebago is a new, late-maturing variety, with large oblong tubers with a white skin and a few shallow eyes. Under some conditions the lenticels are large, and this gives the tuber a speckled appearance. It is resistant to mild mosaic, net necrosis, brown rot in Florida, yellow dwarf, and has moderate resistance to late blight. The cooking quality is good if the tubers are allowed to mature before being dug. It is popular in the Southern states, especially in Florida for a winter crop, and in some of the North Central and Northeastern states.

A number of other old varieties are grown in various areas, but the total acreage is not great. Russet Rural is produced in Northeastern states primarily for the potato-chip industry. Red McClure is a red-skinned variety which is grown mainly in Colorado. Green Mountain was once the standard variety in Maine and many other sections and was noted for its excellent cooking quality. It is still grown to some extent in New England and Canada, but its popularity is declining because of its extreme susceptibility to net necrosis and its tendency to produce rough misshapen tubers when conditions are not ideal. Many other varieties which have resistance to certain diseases are mentioned under Diseases and Insects.

Diseases. The potato is subject to many fungus, bacterial, and virus diseases. The severity of injury from any particular disease depends on the season and the region in which the crop is grown. Many of the diseases cause damage only in exceptional years, but a few are prevalent in many sections each year and cause varying amounts of damage. Only the most common potato diseases are discussed here.

LATE BLIGHT. This disease is caused by a downy mildew fungus, *Phytophthora infestans*, and is one of the most important potato diseases. The Irish famines during the 1840s were a result of the potato crop being destroyed by the late blight fungus. Infection usually occurs late in the season in Northern areas, but it can occur at any time when moisture and temperature conditions are favorable. The disease is first noticed as irregular water-soaked areas which enlarge rapidly and then turn brown or black as the leaf dies. The white downy mildew sometimes is seen on the lower side of the leaves around the dead areas. The fungus spreads rapidly, and the entire plant may be killed. The tubers are also attacked and may become infected in the soil but usually are inoculated with the fungus during harvest. The disease appears on the surface of the tubers as irregular brown areas, and directly beneath these areas the flesh is reddish brown extending inward for a short distance. The late blight fungus produces a dry rot, but other organisms may follow and produce a soft rot. The fungus lives over winter in diseased tubers, and cull piles outside of storage houses serve as the primary source of inoculum. Elimination of cull piles helps in preventing the disease.

In most areas the plants should be sprayed with a fungicide as soon as they are a few inches high until harvest. Bordeaux mixture is the most common fungicide used, although certain other copper compounds and some of the carbamates are effective. Plants should be sprayed at intervals of 6 to 10 days or more frequently when the weather is conducive to blight infection. The disease is most destructive when a warm period follows a period of cool, wet weather since infection takes place during the cool, wet period and the fungus grows rapidly during the following warm weather. Some of the varieties having resistance to some races of the fungus are Boone, Cherokee, Delus, Kennebec, Merrimac, Plymouth, Pungo, Virgil, Essex, and Placid.

COMMON SCAB. The disease is recognized by the rough, corky lesions on the tubers caused by *Streptomyces scabies*. The raised, corky spots vary in size and number from a few small dots to large lesions covering most of the surface. Scab does not cause a rotting or decaying of the tubers. The fungus is capable of living in the soil for many years and also lives from year to year in the scabby spots on tubers. The scab organism is not active at a soil reaction below pH 5.4 or above pH 7.0. In most areas scab is controlled by maintaining the soil reaction at pH 4.8 to 5.2. Scab is more severe in dry than in wet seasons and usually is more severe in warm than in cool seasons. Applications of manure immediately preceding potatoes usually result in an increase in the amount of scab. In regions where scab is not present in the soils and where scabby tubers must be used for seed, the tubers should be treated with hot formaldehyde or hot corrosive sublimate to kill the organism on the tubers. The varieties of potatoes highly resistant to common scab are Cherokee, Cayuga, Menominee, Ontario, Pungo, Plymouth, and Seneca. Two of the old varieties, Russet Rural and Russet Burbank, have some resistance to scab.

VERTICILLIUM WILT. This disease also is called *early dying,* or *pink-eyes,* and is caused by *Verticillium albo-atrum.* The disease is recognized by a wilting of the plants and a discoloration of the vascular tissue of the stems, tubers, and roots, but does not cause a rot of the infected tissues. The eyes of tubers from infected plants may be pink, especially at the apical end of the tuber. The disease is prevalent in New England and in the North Central and Northwestern states. The fungus lives over in the soil for many years and is difficult to control. Wilt-free soils may be inoculated by using infected tubers as seed, and seed free from this disease should be used. Long rotations, with potatoes only once in 3 or 4 years, give reasonably good control of the disease. It is an especially troublesome disease in Idaho because the Russet Burbank is very susceptible. Houma, Menominee, Ontario, and Saranac are varieties having resistance.

BLACKLEG. Blackleg is a bacterial disease caused by *Erwina atroseptica.* The disease is most prevalent under warm, moist conditions. The plants are severely stunted, and the leaves are yellowed and tightly rolled. The base of the stem develops brown or black rotted areas, and these black areas may continue inside the stem to the tip without being evident on the outside. The disease progresses through the lower parts of the plant to the stolons, eventually reaching the tubers. The tubers show darkened areas both inside and outside and an interior soft rot which may continue to develop in storage. The disease is carried over in tubers produced on infected plants and is controlled by planting seed from disease-free plants. Whole tubers or suberized cut seed should be planted where this disease is prevalent.

RING ROT. Ring rot is a bacterial disease caused by *Corynebacterium sepedonicum.* Ring rot was discovered in eastern Canada in 1931 and in

Maine in 1932, and by 1940 it was present in most of the potato-growing areas of the United States. It is recognized by a wilting and yellowing of the leaves and a lemon-yellow to light-brown discoloration in the vascular ring of the tubers. When the cut tuber is squeezed, a yellow exudate is forced out of the vascular ring in small drops on the surface. A soft rot may follow infection with ring rot, leaving only the outer shell of the tuber. The bacteria live from year to year only in diseased tubers. They can be spread easily by the cutting knife, planters, grading equipment, and containers or other material that has come in contact with diseased potatoes. Only certified seed that is free from all ring rot should be used. Once the disease occurs on a farm, all equipment should be sterilized with formaldehyde or copper sulfate to eradicate the organism. Teton, Merrimac, and Saranac have good resistance to ring rot.

VIRUS DISEASES. There are many diseases of potatoes caused by viruses, but only a few of the important ones are discussed here. Latent mosaic is caused by virus X and is prevalent in all of the old varieties of potatoes, but many of them are symptomless carriers. There are many races of the virus, and some of the more virulent races can cut yields as much as 50 per cent. The leaves are usually light green and may be rugose when the weather is cool. Many other plants closely related to the potato harbor this virus. The virus is transmitted mechanically by the contact of diseased with healthy plants or by the cutting knife. Insect transmission is not important. The only practical control is to use healthy seed. The Saco variety is resistant to latent mosaic.

Mild mosaic is caused by virus A alone or in combination with virus X. Virus A alone produces light-green rugose leaves that are very similar to latent mosaic. Some varieties may show dead spots on the foliage. There is a distinct mottling and crinkling of the leaves with some varieties when both viruses are present. Virus A is transmitted by several species of aphids. Varieties resistant to mild mosaic are Cherokee, Chippewa, Earlaine, Houma, Katahdin, Kennebec, Merrimac, Saco, Sebago, Teton, and Sequoia.

Rugose mosaic, or vein-banding mosaic, is caused by virus Y alone or in combination with virus X. The plants are severely stunted, and the leaves are severely wrinkled and deformed and sometimes mottled. Thin necrotic streaks may be present on the stems and leaves. The leaves and petioles become brittle, and the plants are stunted and die prematurely. Aphids are vectors for this disease, and there are no resistant varieties.

Leaf roll is a common virus disease which causes considerable losses in many areas. In some sections all plants are infected and the growers assume that the leaf-roll symptoms are characteristic of the crop. The leaves are cupped or rolled upward and have a light-green color and a leathery texture. Often there is a reddish discoloration on the margins of the leaves of some varieties. The symptoms are very severe in plants that have grown from infected seed pieces. The virus is transmitted by the green pea aphid (*Myzus persicae*). Plants infected during the current season by inoculation by aphids show the leaf rolling on only the upper leaves. The current-season infection causes a necrosis of the phloem of the tubers of some varieties. This net necrosis is commonly found in Irish Cobbler and Green Mountain tubers. Varieties resistant to net necrosis are Cherokee, Chippewa, Earlaine, Houma, Katahdin, Kennebec, Merrimac, Saco, and Sebago.

Damage from all the virus diseases can be almost eliminated by using disease-free certified seed. The certified-seed grower controls the dis-

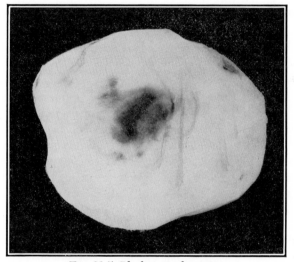

Fig. 21.5. Black spot of potato.

eases by removing all infected plants from the field and by following a rigorous spray program to control the insect vectors.

INTERNAL BLACK SPOT. This appears to be a physiological disorder, a breakdown of tissue just beneath the skin of the tuber, which turns black or bluish black, as shown in Fig. 21.5. Generally the blackening does not show up until after the potatoes are removed from storage and have been graded or otherwise handled. The first appearance of the trouble in the United States, so far as is known, was on Long Island about 1935. Mention was made of it by Bratley and Wiant (1940) and Smith (1940). A similar trouble has been reported in England and Holland, and since 1945 it has been reported in most of the important producing areas in the United States.

Black spot has resulted in losses of hundreds of thousands of dollars to potato growers on Long Island during the past few years. One grower estimated the loss to Long Island growers from about 1940 to 1946 at over a half million dollars. The financial loss results from the fact that lots of potatoes that show black spots are lowered in grade, and consequently in price received. If the spotting is severe, the potatoes may be discarded.

All writers agree that mechanical injury, especially bruising, is the most important factor in the development of black spot. It is evident, however, that the environment under which the potatoes are grown is a conditioning factor since the methods used in handling and storage on Long Island are not very different from those employed in many other regions. Furthermore, potatoes from several farms on Long Island have shown marked difference in the incidence and severity of spotting when handled alike and stored under identical conditions in the same storage houses. White-Stevens and Smith (1945) reported that the injury resulting from bruising was predisposed by the conditions under which the crop was grown, harvested, and stored.

Experiments conducted on Long Island for several years include variety, fertilizers, irrigation, storage temperature, type of storage, time of harvest, and bruising. Heavy applications of nitrogen and high soil moisture seem to increase the tendency of potatoes to blacken following the breaking of the rest period and bruising. Large application of potash tends to reduce the susceptibility to and the severity of blackening. There appears to be some varietal difference as to the amount of blackening, but all commercial varieties used in the experiments have blackened. Green Mountain has appeared to be one of the most susceptible varieties. Rough handling and bruising seem to be the main contributing factors to the occurrence of black spot and the severity of blackening. Applications of the various minor elements have not had any significant effect on the incidence or severity of blackening.

Insects. Potatoes are attacked by many insects, and only those that are widespread and common in occurrence are discussed here.

COLORADO POTATO BEETLE. This is one of the most widespread and destructive potato pests, and it also attacks related plants such as tomato and eggplant. Both the adults and larvae feed on the leaves of potatoes and unless controlled may completely defoliate the field. The beetle also may transmit some of the potato diseases. The adult is a hard-shell beetle about ⅜ inch long with black and yellow stripes running lengthwise on the wing covers. The orange egg masses are laid on the undersides of the leaves. The larvae, known as slugs, have soft, dark-red bodies when young but become orange as they grow older. There are two conspicuous rows of black spots along the side of the body. The larvae enter the soil to pupate. The adults overwinter in the ground and under trash in fence rows and emerge about the time the first potatoes are up and begin feeding and laying eggs. The plants should be sprayed or dusted with an insecticide as soon as the first adults are noticed. Several applications may be required throughout the growing season. Among the insecticides commonly used are DDT, calcium arsenate, rotenone, dieldrin, and heptachlor.

FLEA BEETLES. There are several kinds of flea beetles which feed on potatoes and related plants, but the two most important are the potato flea beetle and the tuber flea beetle. The adult flea beetles are about $\frac{1}{16}$ to $\frac{1}{8}$ inch long, dark brown or black in color, and spring from the plants when disturbed. Both types chew small holes in the leaves of potatoes. The adults lay their eggs in cracks in the soil, and the larvae hatch and feed on the underground portion of the plant. The larvae of the potato flea beetle feed mainly on the roots, but the larvae of the tuber flea beetle feed on the tubers. The adult flea beetles may be controlled by spraying the foliage with an insecticide such as DDT, rotenone, cryolite, or one of the arsenicals, but DDT is the most popular material. They cause the most severe damage when large numbers attack the young plant just coming through the soil. Soil applications of insecticides to control other soil insects noticeably reduce the population of flea beetles in potato fields.

LEAFHOPPERS. Leafhoppers are small green wedge-shaped insects that feed mostly on the undersides of the leaves. Several types of leafhoppers attack the potato and weaken the plant by sucking sap from the leaves and stems. The insect injects a toxin into the plant, and in severe cases the leaves curl upward and turn yellow, finally becoming brown and brittle. This condition is known as hopperburn. Bliss Triumph is susceptible to hopperburn, but Sequoia is resistant. The leafhopper lays its eggs on the plants, and the nymphs are wingless and smaller than the adults. The adults overwinter under trash in fence rows. They are controlled by spraying or dusting with DDT at intervals of 6 to 10 days throughout the growing season. Parathion and malathion are also effective insecticides. Before the introduction of DDT, hopperburn was a common occurrence everywhere potatoes were grown, and it hastened the death of the potato vines. Much of the large increase in average yield per acre of potatoes in the United States that occurred after 1945 was due to the control of the potato leafhopper by the use of DDT.

APHIDS. There are several kinds of aphids, or plant lice, that feed on potato plants. The pink and the green potato aphids and the green peach aphid are the most common. Most aphids are wingless, but winged forms develop through the growing season. The winged forms fly to other potato fields and lay eggs on the plants. The wingless aphids which hatch from these eggs bear living young, and the number of aphids increases rapidly, especially during warm dry weather. The aphid overwinters as an egg on various perennial host plants. Aphids transmit virus diseases and cause severe damage to the plant by sucking the juice from the leaves and young stems. The plants may be stunted, with the leaves tightly curled and rolled when aphids are numerous. Most of the damage has already been done by the time the deformed leaves are noticed. Aphids are controlled by spraying or dusting the plants with parathion, malathion, TEPP, or nicotine sulfate. The entire plant, including the underside of the leaves, should be covered with the insecticide, and it should be applied as soon as aphids are noticed and repeated about once a week until danger of damage has passed. Where aphids are troublesome every year, the first spray should be made as soon as the plants come through the soil.

WIREWORMS. There are several kinds of wireworms which attack potatoes, but usually only one kind is important in an area.. Wireworms are the larvae of click beetles and have hard jointed bodies $\frac{1}{2}$ to 1 inch long and may be white, yellow, or dark orange. They feed on potato seed pieces and sometimes cause enough damage so that the field has to be replanted, but the major damage is feeding on tubers. The feeding holes may extend deep into the tuber and afford entrance for several types of fungi which may cause rotting of the tuber. The feeding damage alone makes the tubers unmarketable. The larvae live 1 or more years in the soil before transforming into adults. They feed in the upper layers of the soil during the spring and summer and migrate downward to pass the winter. Usually they are more abundant following a sod crop than after a cultivated crop. They can be controlled to a certain extent by rotations and by avoiding planting potatoes after a sod crop. In some areas the control is soil fumigation with ethylene dibromide or similar chemicals. A more common practice is to treat the soil with an insecticide such as chlordane, dieldrin, aldrin, or heptachlor. These insecticides are mixed with the top 3 or 4 inches of soil before planting and give good control of wireworms and other soil insects.

Harvesting. Potatoes are harvested in some parts of the United States almost every month of the year, but about 80 per cent of the crop is harvested in September and October. In Northern areas it is essential to harvest before hard freezes occur which may damage the tubers still in the ground. Where frost is not a hazard they are harvested after the tubers reach a satisfactory size, but the time varies according to the market price. The spring crop in warm areas is harvested usually before high summer temperatures begin. Certified-seed growers in Maine and similar areas usually harvest, or at least kill the tops, early in August. Large populations of aphids may build up late in August, and early harvest reduces the incidence of virus diseases transmitted by these insects.

Before the introduction of DDT, potatoes were harvested as soon as the tops were dead. DDT controls the insects which contribute to the early death of the vines, and most potatoes must be harvested while the vines are still green unless a frost has occurred to kill the tops. Harvesting when the tops are green increases the danger of inoculating the tubers with the late blight organism which is usually present on some of the leaves. The tubers on living vines are likely to skin and bruise severely during harvest, and the heavy foliage interferes with the harvest machinery. These factors have all stimulated the use of chemical and mechanical vine killers. Mechanical removal of the tops is popular in many areas, and several types of machines are used which beat or chop the vines into small pieces. Several chemicals, phenolic compounds, sodium arsenite, and others, are used in some areas to kill the tops. Harvesting a week or 10 days after the tops have been killed allows the periderm to set and reduces the amount of skinning and scuffing and lessens the danger of tuber infection with late blight. Vine killing usually reduces the potential yield, but the advantages are considered worth the yield reduction in most cases. It helps to spread the harvest over a longer time in Northern areas where a large grower, waiting until frost has killed the tops, might not be able to get the crop out before a hard freeze. McGoldrick and Smith (1948) found that there was a great variation in the rate of kill with different methods available. The yield was usually lowest with the methods that produced a rapid kill since the tubers continue to increase in size until the tops are completely dead. Rapid kill often resulted in a lower specific gravity of the tubers than did a slow kill; however, the specific-gravity reduction was due to early harvest and not to a specific chemical effect. They observed that vascular discoloration or stem-end browning was more pronounced with those treatments which gave a rapid kill. Meadows (1950) found that the vascular discoloration was not associated with chemical injury since it occurred when the tops were removed mechanically. Severing the stems at the surface of the ground resulted in as much vascular discoloration as did chemicals giving a rapid kill. The least vascular browning occurred when the tops were killed by pulling the stems from the ground or by severing the roots. The amount of discoloration varied greatly with location and season, and it is a potential problem wherever the vines are killed prematurely. The discoloration is most pronounced at the stem end of the tuber, but in some cases it may appear through most of the vascular system. It does not increase in storage and does not affect storage quality, but it does reduce the market value of the potato if known to be present.

All commercial plantings of potatoes are dug with potato diggers or combines of various types. The digger plows the potatoes out of the ground and elevates them on a continuous apron which allows the soil to drop through and then drops the potatoes on the loose soil in the row. The potatoes are then picked up by hand in various types of containers and hauled to the storage or packing shed. The high cost of hand picking has increased the use of potato combines or potato harvesters. The combine digs the potatoes the same way as a digger but elevates them directly into containers or trucks. Usually several men on the machine pick out the vines, stones, and other debris as the potatoes are being elevated. The harvester follows a digger and picks up the potatoes from the surface and feeds them into a truck or container after the debris has been picked out by men on the machine. Combines and harvesters

Fig. 21.6. Potato-storage house built aboveground.

have been most satisfactory in those areas where the soil is level and free from stones.

Potatoes should be picked up as soon as possible to prevent sunburn and similar injuries. Many injuries and bruises occur in the digging operation, and machines should be adjusted so that the potatoes are not subjected to extreme agitation or to drops of any distance. Careless digging and handling increase the storage loss and reduce the grade and market value of potatoes.

Storage. A large part of the potato crop must be stored since most of it is harvested in September and October. Most of the crop is stored in bulk and is handled with loaders and conveyors as much as possible. The storage houses are well insulated and may be built aboveground or partly or entirely underground (Fig. 21.6). Houses built at least partly underground take advantage of the low soil temperature in cooling the potatoes. Occasionally potatoes are stored in refrigerated houses, but most storages use the outside air to maintain the desired temperature. In very cold areas, heaters may be required some of the time. The old storages depended on gravity and convection to obtain air circulation. This is cheap, but not very efficient. The best storages have some type of forced air circulation. Cool outside air is brought in with fans and forced through air ducts under the piles of potatoes. The rate of air exchange can be controlled, and the piles can be cooled rapidly. During periods of warm weather the air in the storage is recirculated.

The storage requirements depend somewhat on the use for which the potatoes are intended. Some of the effect of storage temperatures on seed potatoes has been discussed under Seed. Potatoes for the fresh market should be stored under conditions that preserve the market and culinary quality with a minimum of loss from sprouting, shriveling, and rotting. This is achieved by regulating the temperature, humidity, and ventilation of the storage. To prevent excessive shrinkage and rotting the potatoes should be stored for the first week at a temperature of 50 to 60°F. and a relative humidity of 85 to 95 per cent to permit suberization and wound-periderm formation. Most of the shrinkage takes place during the first month of storage, and it is important to allow the cuts and bruises to heal rapidly and then lower the temperature of the storage. Appleman *et al.* (1928) found that the shrinkage was greater at low temperatures during the first months than at temperatures high enough to permit wound-periderm formation. Most of the shrinkage was water loss, and even though the rate of respiration was high, it did not account for much of the shrinkage. The relative humidity should be high to reduce water loss, but not so high that water condenses on the tubers. Many rot organisms are favored by the high humidity, but proper curing eliminates much of the danger.

Following the curing period the temperature is lowered to 38 to 40°F. to prevent sprouting after the rest period is over. Most varieties of potatoes can be stored for 6 months or longer without sprouting if the temperature does not rise above 40°F. Potatoes freeze at about 29°F., but there may be low-temperature injury from prolonged storage below 35°F. Mahogany browning is a low-temperature injury that affects Chippewa and Katahdin tubers stored at temperatures below 35°F. All potatoes accumulate sugar at low temperatures and have a definite sweet taste. In the normal metabolism of the potato, starch is converted to sugar and the sugar is used in respiration. At low temperatures the rate of respiration is reduced more than the rate of conversion of starch to sugar so that the sugar accumulates. It is important to keep the temperature low after the curing period even though the tubers will not sprout during the rest period. Smith (1933) reported that the shrinkage increased as the temperature increased even though sprouts were not present. The greatest shrinkage in storage occurs when sprouts appear. There is translocation of carbohydrates from the tuber to the sprout as well as an increase in respiration and a large increase in water loss from the tender sprouts.

Storage at 40°F. is not desirable for potatoes to be used for potato chips or frozen French-fries. The brown color that develops when the potato is fried is the result of a chemical reaction between sugar and soluble nitrogen compounds. Sufficient sugar is accumulated at 40°F. to give the fried product an undesirable dark-brown color. The accumulated sugar may be used up in respiration if the potatoes are stored at 60 to 70°F. for a short time. This "reconditioning" is not successful with all varieties. Prolonged storage at high temperatures may cause blackheart. Stewart and Mix (1917) found that blackheart was a physiological breakdown resulting from a lack of oxygen. The high rate of respiration at the high temperature causes an oxygen deficiency in the center of the tuber. Poor ventilation may cause blackheart even at a low temperature. Potatoes for the chip industry should be stored at 50°F. with a high humidity to reduce shrinkage. Sprouting will occur at 50°F. as soon as the rest period is over unless a sprout inhibitor is used.

The first sprout inhibitor to be used was the methyl ester of naphthaleneacetic acid (MENA) discovered by Denny, Guthrie, and Thornton (1942). It was used commercially as a talc dust applied to the tubers in storage, or paper confetti was impregnated with MENA and sprinkled over the tubers. It was used by growers until it was found that losses from rotting were greatly increased by using MENA to inhibit sprouting. The MENA prevented wound-periderm formation, and if rot organisms were present, losses were great. Recently it has been found that MENA can be used safely if applied to the tubers as a gas after the wound periderm has formed. Smith, Baeza, and Ellison (1947) inhibited sprouting of tubers in storage by spraying the foliage before harvest with MENA and similar materials. This seems to be the easiest way to apply such materials. A number of materials sprayed on the plants inhibited sprouting in storage, but maleic hydrazide, reported by Kennedy and Smith (1951), is the most outstanding. They found that 3 pounds of maleic hydrazide per acre as a foliage spray prevented sprouting of potatoes stored at 50°F. It should be applied when the lowest leaves begin to turn yellow and die. Sprays of maleic hydrazide at the time of tuber setting resulted in reduced yield and many malformed tubers, but no effect on yield or quality was noted when the spray was applied when the tubers were well formed. It should never be applied to seed potatoes. Marth and Shultz (1952) reported that the herbicide 3-Cl-IPC applied to the tubers in storage prevented their sprouting for several months. Sawyer and Dallyn (1955) and others found that irradiation of tubers with 10,000 roentgens of gamma rays kept them in a dormant condition for a year or more. These methods may be used more in the future, but maleic hydrazide is the only one that is widely used.

Grading and Packing. Potato grade standards have been promulgated by the U.S. Department of Agriculture, and many states have grades also. These grades are based on size and freedom from defects due to disease, insect, mechanical, and other types of damage. The tubers are separated into size groups by machines, but the defects must be picked out by hand. Potatoes stored at low temperatures should be warmed to about 50°F. before grading since the cold potatoes are likely to be severely bruised during the grading operation. Grading is frequently preceded by washing, which improves the market appearance and exposes defects that otherwise might be missed by the grading crew. Many types of washers are used, but most of them spray water on the tubers as they are tumbled by rollers. The wet tubers are dried in a stream of warm air before grading and packing. In some areas potatoes are waxed before packing to improve the appearance. Waxing is used most widely on red-skinned potatoes, and a red dye is added to improve the color of the skin. All of these operations improve the external appearance, but they have no influence on the internal quality.

The internal, or culinary, quality is not related to external appearance. Good cooking quality is difficult to define, but most consumers desire potatoes that are white after cooking, golden brown when fried, mealy when baked, and firm and in one piece after boiling. The dry matter and starch content of the tuber as measured by the specific gravity is related to the cooking quality. High-specific-gravity tubers are high in dry matter and starch and are likely to be mealy when baked but to slough or break apart when boiled. On the other hand, low-specific-gravity tubers hold their shape when boiled but are likely to be soggy when baked. It is not possible to have one potato that will meet all the requirements for cooking. Several workers have marketed potatoes experimentally that were separated into specific-gravity groups and labeled "boilers" and "bakers." The results of these tests were encouraging, and a premium was obtained for the labeled potatoes. Kunkel *et al.* (1952) described a machine that separates large quantities of potatoes into two specific-gravity groups by using brine of the desired specific gravity. This method of grading may increase in the future. Some difficulty may be encountered since the specific gravity is influenced by growing conditions and by variety. Mature tubers grown in cool climates have a higher specific gravity than immature potatoes or those grown during warm weather. Russet Burbank, Green Mountain, and Mohawk usually have a much higher specific gravity than Pontiac and Chippewa.

Potatoes are packed in bags of various sizes, depending on the market and buyer. Large bags of 50 or 100 pounds capacity are used for the institutional and restaurant trade and retail stores selling potatoes from bulk displays. Most of the potatoes for the retail trade are packed in 5-, 10-, or 15-pound bags. The bags may be paper, paper with transparent windows, or transparent films of various types. Transparent films are most desirable when the tubers are washed and are well graded. Fancy bakers from Idaho are wrapped individually in tissue and packed in lugs. Other areas use similar methods for extra-high-quality potatoes.

Marketing. Early potatoes from Florida begin to move into Northern markets during the month of February, Carolina potatoes in May, Virginia potatoes in June, and New Jersey and Long Island potatoes in July and August. The late crop of potatoes comprises about 80 per cent of the total production. Late potatoes are found in our principal markets during all months of the year except June, July, and August. During the summer months, the market is supplied with so-called early potatoes, mostly from California, Colorado, Nebraska, Virginia, North Carolina, and New Jersey. Long-distance shipments in hot weather are subject to discoloration and decay in transit. The use of vine killers helps avoid this damage if harvest is delayed until the periderm sets. Careful harvesting and handling are especially important. Barger *et al.* (1942) reported that hydrocooling California White Rose potatoes to 50°F. and icing the freight car gave the best control of discoloration and decay. The potatoes should be dried before packing. In cold weather, potatoes may require heating in transit to prevent damage from low temperatures.

Fresh potatoes have been traditionally the main market outlet except for those used for seed. Since 1940 many new methods of marketing have been introduced, and the volume sold by these new methods is increasing each year. About 10 per cent of the potatoes consumed in 1955 were eaten as potato chips. Frozen French-fries are one of the leading frozen-food items, and the volume increases each year. Large quantities of potatoes were dehydrated during the war period 1941–1945, but they were not accepted by civilian consumers. Since then new methods of dehydration have been developed, so that a high-quality reconstituted product can be obtained. Canned small whole potatoes have been available for a long time, and many potatoes have been used as an ingredient in canned soups, stews, etc. Many other frozen, canned, or dehydrated potato products have been introduced, and the volume will probably increase rapidly. Processed potato products are more expensive than fresh potatoes, but convenience is the most important factor since they must compete with other easily prepared processed items. In many areas prepeeled potatoes are sold in large quantities to the restaurant trade and some are sold through retail outlets. They may be whole, cut for French-fries, or sliced as an added convenience for the buyer. In Maine and Idaho, potato starch is manufactured from surplus potatoes. Some of the crop is used as livestock feed, especially culls and waste products from processing.

CHAPTER 22

The Sweet Potato

The sweet potato is a very important crop in tropical and subtropical countries, as in Africa, India, China, Japan, the Malayan Archipelago, the Pacific Islands, tropical America, and southern United States. In the Southern part of the United States the sweet potato is a standard article of food and is more important than the Irish potato. In that area, it is commonly called "potato" and the potato is called "white potato," or "Irish potato."

Some varieties of sweet potatoes, especially those having a moist, soft texture when cooked, are often called "yams" to distinguish them from the dry-fleshed varieties. It is unfortunate that the term yam has been used in this connection since the true yam is an entirely different plant, belonging to the genus Dioscorea. These two plants are not even closely related.

Statistics of Production. The sweet potato ranked fourth in farm value among the vegetables in 1952, being exceeded by the Irish potato, tomato, and lettuce. The acreage, production, and value of the crop fluctuate considerably, as shown in Table 22.1. Acreage and production have decreased markedly since about 1940. The yield per acre has not fluctuated greatly, and in the 5-year period 1948–1952 the average yield was about the same as for the period 1918–1927.

Table 22.1. Estimated Average Annual Acreage, Production, and Farm Value of Sweet Potatoes Grown in the United States, 1918–1952

Years	Acres	Yield per acre, bushels	Production, bushels (000 omitted)	Price per bushel	Farm value (000 omitted)
1918–1927	717,500	93.2	66,901	$1.32	$88,577
1928–1937	835,500	84.6	70,723	0.85	59,837
1938–1947	704,300	88.2	62,149	1.47	91,720
1948–1952	411,800	94.7	39,003	2.37	92,435

405

It is of interest to note that in the period 1948–1952 less than half of the sweet-potato crop was sold, or approximately 19 million bushels. Household use on farms where produced accounts for nearly 11 million bushels; shrinkage and other loss after harvest and use as feed for live-stock and for seed account for the remainder of the crop.

The leading states in production in 1952 were Louisiana with 7,920,000 bushels; North Carolina, 3,900,000; Virginia, 2,210,000; New Jersey, 2,100,000; and South Carolina, 2,080,000. Other important producing states with production of more than 1 million bushels were Georgia, Texas, California, Tennessee, Alabama, and Mississippi.

History and Taxonomy. The sweet potato is probably a native of tropical America and was carried to the islands of the Pacific very early. According to Cooley (1951) it was used for food in prehistoric times in two widely separated regions—tropical Americas and some of the islands of the Pacific. There is no evidence that the sweet potato was known to the ancient civilizations of Egypt, China, Babylon, Persia, India, Greece, or Rome. There is evidence, however, that it was introduced into New Zealand long before the beginning of the Spanish explorations, probably from some of the Polynesian islands. Columbus found the natives of Cuba using the sweet potato as food, and later Spanish explorers found it in Mexico and South America. Oviedo (1526) mentioned it as being grown in the West Indies, and it was carried by him to Spain, from where it was introduced into other parts of Europe. It was known in Virginia in 1648, possibly earlier. There is no evidence that the sweet potato was grown by the Indians in pre-Columbian times in the area that is now the United States of America.

The sweet potato (*Ipomoea batatas* Poir.) belongs to the Convolvulaceae, or morning-glory family. It is a tuberous-rooted perennial. The stems are usually prostrate and slender, and the juice of both vines and roots milky. The blossoms resemble those of the common morning-glory, being almost white or pale violet in color. Studies by Teng and Kehr (1953) and King and Bamford (1937) indicate that the sweet potato is extremely heterozygous. The evidence indicates that it is a hexaploid and that the somatic chromosome number is 90.

Climatic Requirements. The plant is tender and requires a long, warm growing season. It cannot be grown successfully in a region having less than 4 months frost-free period, with warm weather and sunshine for a greater portion of this period. Even with a season of that length, the sweet potato does not produce a satisfactory yield unless the nights, as well as the days, are warm for a considerable portion of the time.

While the sweet potato is more drought-resistant than most other vegetable crops and will produce a fair crop without irrigation in semi-arid regions, it is grown mainly where the annual rainfall is 40 inches or more. Very few are grown in regions receiving less than 35 inches, except where irrigation is used. Minges and Morris (1953) state that in most sections of California where the crop is grown, 4 to 8 irrigations, supplying 18 to 24 acre-inches of water, give the best yields. This quantity of water is as much as the rainfall during the growing season in many sweet-potato regions of the United States.

Soils and Soil Preparation. Well-drained sandy, sandy loam, and loamy sand, with a clay or clay-loam subsoil, are considered almost ideal for sweet potatoes. However, loams and silt loams are used with good results in some areas. Good soil drainage is essential for successful sweet-potato production; therefore the subsoil should be of such a nature that water will penetrate it. Heavy clay soils are not satisfactory because the roots grown in such soils are usually rough and irregular in shape. On the other hand, very light soils, without a fairly compact subsoil, tend to produce long slender roots. The sweet potato does best on a soil that is slightly to moderately acid (pH 5.2 to 6.7). Soils more acid than pH 5.0 should be limed to raise the pH slightly.

Land for sweet potatoes should be plowed 6 to 8 inches deep, provided that depth does not bring more than an inch or two of raw subsoil to the surface. Heavy cover crops, or remains from a previous crop of corn, or cotton should be chopped and worked into the surface soil before plowing so as not to interfere with other preparation and planting. After plowing, the land should be well fitted by disking and harrowing, preferably 3 to 4 weeks before transplanting time. In most of the sweet-potato-growing areas in the United States the plants are set on ridges. These are made with a plow throwing two or more furrows together to form the ridge, with disk hillers, or with other special equipment. Boswell (1950) suggested ridges 10 inches high for most soils. Results of experiments in South Carolina, Georgia, Mississippi, and Texas, reported by Edmond *et al.* (1950), indicate highly significant increases in yield of No. 1 grade sweet potatoes from the use of high or medium ridges as compared with low ridges in most comparisons. The low ridges were 3 to 4 inches high, medium 8 to 9 inches, and high 14 to 15 inches. It might be expected that medium to high ridges would be advantageous on poorly drained soil when there are heavy rains. Low ridges might be better on well-drained soil, especially where rainfall is not high. The ridges should be as wide and flat as practicable because narrow pointed ones dry out rapidly in dry weather. In some areas, where drainage is good and rainfall not very heavy, sweet potatoes are grown on the level or on low ridges.

Fertilizers. The sweet potato requires liberal application of a complete fertilizer for high yields on most of the soils used for the crop. Fertilizer practices in the United States vary considerably, and many growers use too little for best results. On the sandy, sandy-loam, and fine-sand soils recommendations are 40 to 80 pounds of N, 80 to 120 pounds of P_2O_5, and 80 to 160 pounds of K_2O to the acre. Larger quantities of nitrogen and potash are recommended in some cases for the poorer sandy soils. On the other hand, smaller quantities are suggested for silt and silt-loam soils. The quantity of nutrients to apply should be based on the fertility of the soil, the cropping system followed, and the use of manure and soil-improving crops. Where manure is used for the sweet-potato crop or for other crops in the rotation, less fertilizer would be required than where no manure is used. If a leguminous soil-improving crop is turned under, the quantity of fertilizer nitrogen may be reduced.

Soils very rich in nitrogen tend to produce excessive vine growth, and, according to Schermerhorn (1924), such soils produce long, slender potatoes. However, results of other experiments, including those of Edmond *et al.* (1950), indicate that nitrogen must be supplied in considerable quantities for high yields. In the latter experiments, conducted in South Carolina, Georgia, Mississippi, and Texas, on sandy loam, loamy sand, and fine sandy loam, two rates of application of nitrogen termed "high" and "low" were used. The high and low varied considerably and were as follows: in South Carolina, high 50, low 10 pounds to the acre; Georgia, 64 and 16; Mississippi, 80 and 20, 2 years, and 100 and 20, 1 year; Texas, 48 and 12 pounds to the acre. In these experiments the high-nitrogen treatment (48 to 100 pounds to the acre) usually produced significantly higher yields of No. 1 and Jumbo grades than the low-nitrogen application (10 to 20 pounds to the acre).

According to results reported by Schermerhorn, potash produced shorter and more chunky sweet potatoes than were produced without this element on sandy loam and fine sand in New Jersey (Fig. 22.1 and 22.2). On the other hand, Boswell, Beattie, and McCown (1938) reported results from experiments in South Carolina that are not in agreement with those of Schermerhorn. It should be noted, however, that in South Carolina the yields were not increased greatly by the application of potash from 15 to 75 pounds of K_2O to the acre each year for 4 years and 0 to 75 pounds for 3 years. Nitrogen was applied at the rate of 15 pounds of N and phosphorus at the rate of 40 pounds of P_2O_5. It is possible that nitrogen was a limiting element in these experiments and that potash was not limiting. When the soil is not deficient in available potash, one should not expect any marked effect on either yield or shape of sweet potatoes by applying the element in varying quantities.

Most authorities recommend applying part of the fertilizer in the furrow over which the ridge is made, and the remainder as a side-dressing after the plants are set. Where ridges are not used, it is suggested that part of the fertilizer be plowed under and the remainder applied broadcast after plowing or as a side application after planting.

FIG. 22.1. Sweet potato grown with fertilizer containing ample potash. Compare with Fig. 22.2. (*Courtesy of N.J. Agricultural Experiment Station.*)

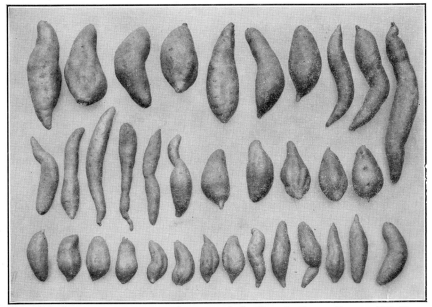

FIG. 22.2. Sweet potato grown without potash fertilizer in Ocean County, N.J. Compare with Fig. 22.1. (*Courtesy of N.J. Agricultural Experiment Station.*)

Manure generally is not recommended for sweet potatoes, although it is used in light applications by some growers. Where manure is used, it is better to apply it to some other crop in the rotation. Other vegetable crops usually give better returns for the manure.

Under some conditions it may be desirable to apply nutrient elements other than nitrogen, phosphorus, and potash. Boron deficiency has been reported on sweet potatoes in North Carolina. Reeve, Prince, and Bear (1944) reported that sweet-potato plants grown in the greenhouse without borax produced potatoes having dark-streaked centers.

Propagation. Sweet potatoes are grown from plants or sprouts produced from seed roots of the previous crop and from vine cuttings. In regions of short growing seasons the crop is grown only from plants produced from seed roots bedded in a hotbed. This method is used also in many of the sweet-potato growing areas of the United States where the growing season is long, especially for an early crop and for vine cuttings. In the warmer regions of long growing seasons, open beds, without artificial heat, are used. Vine cuttings are used for the market crop only where the growing season is long, as in the South Atlantic and Gulf Coast states of the United States and in subtropical and tropical areas.

The quantity of seed roots required to produce enough plants to plant an acre of land depends on the size of roots, the distance of planting in the field, and the number of pullings that can be made without too great delay in planting. According to Boswell (1950), 10,000 to 12,000 plants are planted per acre at the commonly recommended distances of spacing. To obtain this number of plants at one pulling requires 10 to 12 bushels of good-quality seed roots. If, however, sufficient time is available for two more pullings at weekly intervals, 5 or 6 bushels of roots would be enough to plant 1 acre from plants. But, as Boswell pointed out, delay of 2 weeks in planting is likely to result in reduced yield in most producing areas in the United States. Large roots produce fewer plants from a bushel of seed than small or medium-sized roots. One bushel of small to medium-sized roots should produce 2,000 to 2,500 plants from three pullings.

Where vine cuttings are used for planting part of the crop, enough seed is bedded for about one-sixth of the acreage to be planted. These plants are planted in the usual manner, and when they reach sufficient length cuttings 10 to 12 inches long are taken for planting. In some regions where the growing season is too short to produce a good crop for market from vine cuttings, they are used to some extent for growing seed for the following year. Vine cuttings have the advantage of being free from some serious diseases that are carried from the seedbed to the field on the plants. In some tropical areas, where sweet potatoes can be grown at any time during the year, it is a common practice to take vine cuttings from one crop to produce the next one. In this way sweet potatoes are available all of the time without storage and without the necessity of bedding seed roots.

Most varieties of sweet potatoes and many breeding lines produce sprouts mainly at the proximal end (Fig. 22.3), and this tends to restrict the number of sprouts per seed root. Several investigators have shown that treatment of the seed roots with certain chemicals increases the

Fig. 22.3. Sprout development of untreated sweet-potato root showing proximal dominance. (*Courtesy of Tex. and of Calif. Agricultural Experiment Stations.*)

number of sprouts per root and per bushel. Hernandez, Miller, and Fountenot (1950) reported that 10 parts per million of 2,4-D used as a dip significantly increased the number of sprouts of the Puerto Rico variety from two and four pullings. Michael and Smith (1952) showed a highly significant increase in number of plants from treatment of the seed roots with ethylene chlorohydrin at 20 milliliters per 100 pounds of roots and at 40 milliliters per 100 pounds. This treatment was made in a sealed container for 72 hours and was given to All Gold, Puerto Rico, and Cliett Bunch Puerto Rico. Michael and Smith did not obtain a significant increase from 10 parts per million of 2,4-D, but 2,4,5-T at 10

FIG. 22.4. Sprout development of treated sweet-potato roots: upper, exposed for 72 hours to ethylene chlorohydrin at the rate of 20 milliliters per 100 pounds of roots; lower, heated to 110°F. for 12 hours. (*Courtesy of Calif. Agricultural Experiment Station.*)

parts per million resulted in some increase, and heat at 110°F. also had a stimulating effect. Both the chemical and heat treatments destroyed the proximal dominance, as shown in Fig. 22.4. Marked varietal differences in tolerance and degree of response to the treatments were reported.

Where open beds are used for growing plants, a location is selected that is protected from the prevailing cold winds by a building, a tight fence, or a windbreak. Similar protection is desirable for hotbeds also. The drainage should be away from the beds. In making an open bed without any heat an excavation about 6 inches deep is made. The width of the bed usually is 5 or 6 feet and of a length sufficient for the quantity of seed roots to be bedded. It is important that the area selected for the open beds should not have grown sweet potatoes for several years because of the danger of disease. Likewise, the soil, or sand used in hotbeds, should be free from organisms that cause diseases of sweet potatoes. The various types of hotbeds described in Chap. 7 are used for growing sweet-potato plants. Flue-heated beds are, perhaps, the most common, but electric-heated beds are becoming popular where electricity is available at a moderate price.

The best medium to use in the propagating bed is fresh clean sand that has not produced sweet potatoes and has not received drainage water from a field or bed of sweet potatoes. If sand is not available, a loose friable soil may be used. The floor of the bed should be covered with a layer of sand or soil on which to bed the seed roots. Before bedding them, however, it is desirable to treat them with a disinfectant to kill disease spores on the surface. A standard treatment is a 10-minute dip in a 1:1,000 mercuric chloride (corrosive sublimate) solution. It is suggested that about 24 gallons of the solution be made for treating 10 bushels of seed roots. After treating this quantity, add ½ ounce of mercuric chloride and bring up to the original volume; repeat the process for another 10 bushels, then discard the solution and make a fresh one. Mercuric chloride is very poisonous; therefore the chemical itself and the solution should be kept out of reach of children and animals. Sweet potatoes treated with this solution should not be fed to animals or used as food. Another disinfectant that is effective, according to Leukel (1953), is Semesan Bel at the rate of 1 pound to 7½ gallons of water. Both of the disinfectants mentioned sometimes delay or reduce production of sprouts.

The roots should be bedded immediately after treatment. It is desirable to bed roots of similar size together so that they can be covered to the same depth. The seed roots are placed by hand close together, but not touching. They should be pressed down into the sand or soil and covered to the depth of about 1 inch with clean sand or soil. The bed is watered to settle the sand around the roots. As soon as the plants come through the surface, more sand or soil is added in order to develop a good root system along 3 or 4 inches of the stem. Where hotbeds are used the covers are put on as promptly as possible to avoid chilling of the roots.

At the time of bedding the roots, the bed temperature should be about 80°F. and maintained thereafter between 70 and 80°F. At these temperatures a good supply of plants is produced in about 6 weeks. Careful attention is given to watering the bed and to controlling temperature by ventilation of hotbeds or other covered structures.

Planting. The sweet-potato plant is tender and will not withstand a frost; therefore planting should be delayed until the danger of frost is past. In regions having a relatively short growing period it is advisable to set the plants as early as weather conditions will allow. For an early crop in the South early planting is also desirable. Results of many experiments have shown that early planting in the field is essential for maximum yields. Although early planting results in a larger percentage of very large roots (Jumbo) than later plantings, the yield of No. 1 roots is also greater. Beattie, Boswell, and McCown (1938) showed a marked and significant reduction in both total and No. 1 yield when planting was delayed after May 15 in a 4-year study at Florence, S.C. In this experiment plantings were made May 15, May 30, June 15, June 30, and July 15, and there was a drop in yield for each successive planting of approximately 30 bushels of No. 1 and 50 bushels total per acre per 15-day interval. Similar results were reported by Anderson *et al.* (1945) in experiments conducted for 3 years in four locations (Blackville, S.C., Experiment, Ga., Laurel, Miss., and Gilmer Tex.). In these, five successive plantings were made, beginning soon after the last killing frost in spring and extending by intervals approximately one-twelfth of the growing season at each place. Delay in planting reduced significantly the production of the important grades, regardless of place, variety, year, or spacing in the row. Two varieties, Triumph and Puerto Rico (Unit 1 strain) and spacings of 8, 12, 16, 24, 32, and 42 inches in the row were used. Late-planted Triumph had a lower starch content than early and midseason plantings. The carotene content of the roots of the Puerto Rico variety was less from late plantings than from early and midseason plantings. There was a significant change in root shape from chunky to slender as planting time was delayed, the Puerto Rico being affected more than the Triumph. Date of planting had a greater effect on yield than did spacing of plants in the row.

With hand planting it is desirable to set the plants when the soil is wet so as to avoid the extra labor and expense of applying water. If the soil is dry when the plants are set, water should be used if at all practicable. If watering is not practicable, the plants should at least be dipped in a thin paste made with mud and water to prevent the roots from drying out before being set and to make the soil adhere to them. This is called "puddling" and is usually done as the plants are pulled from the bed. The paste should not be allowed to dry on the roots as this would prevent them from coming into contact with the soil and delay growth. After puddling the roots, the plants should be kept covered with burlap, old carpets, blankets, hay, straw, or other material that is kept moist.

The spacing between rows and of plants in the row varies considerably. The most common distance between rows is 3 to 3½ feet, but if ridges need to be more than 10 to 12 inches high for adequate drainage, it may be desirable to space the rows 4 feet apart.

Plants are set at varying distances apart in the row, but mostly from 12 to 18 inches. Experimental results by many workers indicate that close spacing increases the yield of marketable roots. Miller and Kimbrough (1936) in Louisiana obtained higher total and No. 1 yield from 12-inch spacing in the row than from 9-, 15-, 18-, or 20-inch spacing. Beattie, Boswell, and McCown (1938) in experiments at Florence, S.C., found no significant difference in yield or percentage of No. 1 roots from 6-, 9-, 12-, or 15-inch spacing in rows 4 feet apart. Anderson *et al.* (1945) reported results of experiments conducted in South Carolina, Georgia, Mississippi, and Texas in which plants were spaced 8, 12, 16, 24, 32, and 42 inches apart over five dates of planting. Above 8 inches the spacing had little effect on total yield up to and including 16 inches, but, in general, the No. 1 yield decreased as the spacing increased.

Sweet-potato plants are set by hand or by transplanting machines. When planted by hand, the various methods described in Chap. 8 are used. Wooden tongs, with which the plants can be caught by the root and thrust into the soil, are used by some growers. The tongs cannot be used alone to good advantage unless the soil is well prepared and is loose at the time of setting. An implement known as a "shovel," consisting of a piece of lath sharpened to a flat point, is sometimes used in connection with the tongs. This is used to open the hole for the plant. The operator carries the tongs in the left hand and the shovel in the right. Vine cuttings are usually pressed into the soil with a long notched stick. The cuttings are dropped at the proper distances, and the planter places the notch of the stick over the middle of the cutting and forces it into the soil to the depth of 3 or 4 inches. With any of the hand methods of setting plants or cuttings it is important to pack the soil around them to prevent rapid drying.

Cultivation. The methods of cultivating sweet potatoes are not very different from those employed with other farm crops. In a large part of the South they receive less cultivation than most other vegetables, in many instances less than cotton and corn. They should, however, be cultivated often enough to keep the weeds under control. Cultivation is done with one-horse cultivators, sweeps, or with gang cultivators drawn by two horses or by a tractor. As a rule the soil is worked toward the row to widen the ridge. Cultivation should be continued until the vines meet in the middle, but after this no attention is needed except to pull the large weeds by hand.

Difference of opinion exists regarding the advisability of moving the vines so that cultivation can be continued late in the season. Many growers turn the vines first to one side of the row and then to the other while cultivation is going on. Since it is impossible to cultivate without moving the vines after they meet in the centers between the rows, it would seem desirable to move them aside if weed growth is serious. After the cultivation, the vines should be turned back. If there is little or no weed growth, it would be better not to disturb the vines.

Varieties. There are many varieties of sweet potatoes and many more variety names, since some varieties have several names. Because of the confusion in variety names, several attempts have been made to classify the varieties grown in the United States. Price (1893) classified the varieties into three groups based on the shape of the leaves and described most of the varieties grown at that time. Groth (1901) worked out a system based on the main characteristics of leaves, stems, and roots. He then made a key based on the various characters and followed this with brief descriptions. A more complete system of classification was published by Thompson and Beattie (1922), in which the varieties showing a marked similarity were grouped into eight well-defined groups. By means of a simple key the group to which any variety belongs can be determined. Group and variety description given makes identification of the old varieties possible. However, so many new varieties have been developed since 1922, and so few of the old varieties are of much commercial importance, that classification and description are not given.

Most of the varieties of sweet potatoes grown in the United States are what Boswell (1950) called "food types" because they are grown primarily for human consumption. There are, however, at least two varieties that are classed as "feed types" since they are not as desirable for food as are those varieties grown specifically for food. The food type usually is divided into the so-called "dry-fleshed" and the "moist-fleshed" varieties. The terms describe the characteristics of the cooked sweet potato and have no relation to the water content of the raw product. In fact, the so-called "dry" varieties commonly contain a higher percentage of moisture than the "moist" varieties. The terms "soft" and "firm," suggested by Boswell, describe the characteristic of the cooked potato better than the terms dry and moist. Unfortunately, the term "yam" is used in the United States to designate the soft-fleshed varieties. The true yam is a different plant, belonging to another family. The edible roots of the true yam do not resemble the soft-fleshed varieties of sweet potatoes either raw or cooked.

The soft-fleshed varieties are of greater commercial importance in the United States than the firm-fleshed varieties. The most important variety of soft-fleshed type is the Puerto Rico, including Unit I and Cliett Bunch Puerto Rico. The Unit I was developed at the Louisiana Experiment Station and the Cliett Bunch, a Puerto Rico mutation, was found by a grower in Georgia and reselected at the Georgia Coastal Plain Experiment Station. Nancy Hall, an old variety, is important in some areas. Nancy Gold is a deep-orange-fleshed mutation of Nancy Hall found in Kansas. Red Nancy was developed from Nancy Gold. Many other relatively new varieties have been developed both by selection of mutations and by crossing. These include Ranger, Earlyport, Goldrush, Heart-o-Gold, developed by the Louisiana Experiment Station; All Gold and Red Gold developed by the Oklahoma Experiment Station; and Australian Canner obtained by the U.S. Department of Agriculture as an unnamed seedling from the Department of Agriculture of New South Wales, Australia, and introduced jointly by the Mississippi Experiment Station and the U.S. Department of Agriculture. Triumph, an old variety, is grown in some areas but is inferior in edible quality to most of the soft-fleshed varieties.

The important firm-fleshed varieties include Big Stem Jersey, Yellow Jersey (Little Stem Jersey), both old varieties, and several relatively new ones of the Jersey type. The relatively new varieties include Maryland Golden introduced by the Maryland Experiment Station; Orlis, a mutation of Little Stem Jersey (Yellow Jersey), introduced by the Kansas Experiment Station and known under the names of Orange Little Stem and Jersey Orange in New Jersey and adjoining districts; and Rols, a red-skin mutation of Orange Little Stem (Orlis).

Two nonfood varieties, the Pelican Processor, developed by the Louisiana Experiment Station, and Whitestar, developed by the U.S. Department of Agriculture in cooperation with several state experiment stations, are grown to some extent. These varieties produce larger yields and have a higher starch content than the so-called food varieties. The flesh of both of these varieties is white and is low in carotene.

The U.S. Department of Agriculture and several of the state experiment stations are engaged in intensive improvement programs, and new varieties are introduced from time to time. Breeding and selection for resistance to the most serious diseases are of major interest in these programs, but high yields, good market quality, and high food value are included. It is probable that resistance to the important diseases will be incorporated into the most desirable types of sweet potatoes.

Diseases. Sweet potatoes are subject to many diseases in the field and rots in storage, in transit, and in the market. Field disease may be divided into root, stem, and leaf diseases. Stem rot, black rot, foot rot, scurf, pox, and root rot affect the stems and roots, while leaf blight, leaf spot, and white rust affect the foliage. The leaf diseases have not been serious enough to require control measures and are not discussed here. Storage diseases include black rot, Java black rot, soft rot, internal cork, and a few others.

Only brief discussions are given of these diseases. Readers desiring more information are referred to bulletins of the U.S. Department of Agriculture and the 1953 Yearbook and publications of the experiment stations.

STEM ROT. This disease, caused by *Fusarium oxysporum, F. batatas,* or *F. hyperoxysporum,* is very widespread and is very destructive in many areas. The leaves of infected plants become dull in color, then yellowed between the veins and somewhat puckered. The yellowing is followed by wilting of the vine. Diseased stems become blackened inside, and this discoloration may extend almost to the end of the vine. The organisms may invade the roots, producing a blackening of the fibrovascular bundles.

The fungi can live indefinitely in the soil, and they overwinter also in stored sweet potatoes that are diseased. The disease is spread from one locality to another by sale of diseased roots or plants and by soil carried on farm implements.

Varieties of the Jersey Group (Big Stem Jersey, Little Stem Jersey, and Maryland Golden) and of Nancy Hall are reported to be very susceptible. The Puerto Rico is intermediate in susceptibility, while Southern Queen, Triumph, and Yellow Strasburg are quite resistant, according to Cook (1953). The last three varieties mentioned are not of good quality. Breeding for resistance along with high quality is under way.

BLACK ROT. Black rot, caused by *Cerastomella fimbriata,* is a serious disease in the seedbed and field and is very destructive to the potatoes in storage and in transit. The most conspicuous symptom is the small circular dark-brown or black spots on the sweet potato. The spots vary in size from specks to 1 to 2 inches in diameter and, under conditions favorable to growth of the fungus, may cover nearly the whole potato.

The fungus may live in the soil for several years. It lives also in infected sweet potatoes. The disease is spread in much the same way as mentioned for stem rot. The fungus grows best at a temperature of 73 to 85°F. but makes good growth at 55°F. No commercial variety is known to be immune, but some seedlings have been found that are highly resistant or possibly immune.

SOFT ROT. This disease usually is caused by the common bread mold fungus *Rhizopus nigricans,* but other species of *Rhizopus* may cause it. The spores are universally present since the fungus of bread mold grows on many kinds of vegetable material. Infection generally takes place at wounds, such as where the root is broken from the stem and in cuts and bruises incident to harvesting and handling. Less injury occurs in injured potatoes held at high humidity and at 85°F. for a few days after the handling, because healing is so rapid under these conditions that the fungus cannot get established. All varieties are susceptible, but some rot more rapidly than others. Southern Queen and Nancy Hall are resistant; Puerto Rico, Triumph, and Big Stem Jersey are reported to be intermediate in resistance; and Yellow Jersey is very susceptible.

SCURF. This disease, also known as soil stain, is caused by the fungus *Monilochaetes infuscans.* It has little effect on yield but causes a brown stain on the surface of the potato and increases shriveling in storage. It does not spread to other potatoes in storage or cause decay. It persists in the soil for several years and overwinters on the roots in storage. If the roots are bedded, the fungus grows from the seed root to the base of the sprouts and, after planting, spreads down to the new potatoes. Apparently most of the infection comes from the seed roots and is carried to the field on the sprouts.

POX OR SOIL ROT. The fungus causing this disease is *Streptomyces ipomoea.* Pox is a widely distributed field disease that reduces the yield and the proportion of salable potatoes. The most conspicuous symptom is the pits on the potatoes. The pits vary from about ¼ inch to more than an inch in diameter and have a jagged margin. In the early stages the spots are dark-colored and water-soaked. Later the skin over the spots breaks and the contents fall out, leaving a cavity or pit. The disease also kills the feeding roots and develops dark lesions on the stem below the soil line. Affected plants usually are stunted and have yellow leaves.

The fungus lives in the soil indefinitely and is spread by soil adhering to farm implements, by wind-blown soil, by water, and by plants. The organism grows best in a soil less acid than about pH 5.2.

INTERNAL CORK. This is a new virus disease discovered in South Carolina in 1944. Since that time it has been found in many other areas but is most serious in South Carolina, Georgia, and North Carolina. Sweet potatoes affected by this disease appear normal on the outside but have dark-brown or blackish corky spots scattered through the interior. The spots vary in size up to about ¹⁄₁₀ inch in diameter and ⅕ inch long. The corky spots may be so grouped together that large areas of the flesh are affected. The affected tissues remain firm during cooking. Usually only a little internal cork is found when the crop is harvested, but the corky spots increase in number and size during storage. The rate is more rapid at 70°F. than at 55 to 60°F. According to Hughes and Aycock (1952) the Puerto Rico variety is very susceptible to internal cork. Results of their studies indicate that Allgold, and several unnamed clones, are resistant to the disease.

JAVA BLACK ROT. This disease, caused by *Diplodia tubericola,* ranks next to soft rot and black rot as a storage disease. It is present in all sweet-potato areas in the United States and in many other countries. It was discovered on sweet potatoes sent from Java; hence its name. The disease appears as a dry rot of the potatoes, brown at first, then turns black and becomes hard. Decay usually starts at the ends, but sometimes at injuries on other parts of the roots. It develops slowly at first, and there is little evidence of the disease until about a week after infection. The potato rots in a few weeks.

SURFACE ROT. This is a storage disease caused by a species of Fusarium, *F. oxysporum,* that is involved in stem rot. It appears as shallow circular depressed spots on the surface. The spots usually are not more than ¾ inch in diameter and seldom penetrate below the fibrovascular ring. They usually are grayish brown, but sometimes they may be so dark that they resemble black rot spots.

Infection takes place usually through the broken end of the sweet potato. The disease does not become conspicuous until the sweet potatoes have been in storage for about 2 months. It is usually worse in potatoes dug when the soil is wet than when it is dry. Delay of several days in starting curing results in increase of the rot.

CONTROL MEASURES. The main control measures for sweet-potato diseases include: (1) use of disease-free seed roots and plants; (2) crop rotation of 4 or 5 years; (3) seed treatment to destroy fungus spores on the surface of the roots, as described under Propagation; (4) use of disease-free sand or soil for the plant bed, (5) careful handling to keep injury as low as possible, (6) prompt curing at about 85°F. and relative humidity of approximately 85 per cent, (7) storing at 55 to 60°F. following curing, and (8) growing disease-resistant varieties where available.

According to Cook (1953) crop rotation of 4 years generally rids the field of the fungi that cause black rot and scurf. These two diseases can be kept under control by using vine cuttings or sprout cuttings. Stem rot and pox cannot be controlled by ordinary crop rotation or use of disease-free planting stock because the organisms live indefinitely in the soil. Losses in storage and transit from soft rot, Java black rot, and surface rot can be reduced greatly by proper curing and storing under good storage conditions.

Insects. The sweet potato is attacked by relatively few insects, and except for the sweet-potato weevil, the injury done usually is small. Other insects that may cause damage are the sweet-potato flea beetle, striped beetle, sweet-potato plume moth, sweet-potato white fly, leaf folder, and cutworms. Termites, or white ants, have been mentioned as feeding in sweet potatoes in Florida. Only the sweet-potato weevil is discussed here.

SWEET POTATO WEEVIL. The sweet-potato weevil (*Cylas formicarius elegantulus*) is the most destructive insect pest attacking the sweet-potato crop in the United States. It is known to exist in Alabama, Florida, Georgia, Louisiana, Mississippi, South Carolina, and Texas. The adult weevil is about $\frac{1}{4}$ inch long and resembles a large ant. The head, snout, and wing covers are a dark metallic blue. The prothorax and legs are reddish orange.

The adult deposits eggs in small cavities, which it makes in the stem near the ground or into the potato. The eggs hatch in about a week in warm weather, and the larvae feed in the vine or in the sweet potato for 2 or 3 weeks. The pupa is formed in the vine or the potato, and in about a week the adult emerges. The adult may live for several months. In a year six to eight generations may be produced. The weevil continues to breed in stored sweet potatoes and in potatoes left in the ground.

Outbreaks of the weevil in a new locality, in nearly all cases, may be traced to the transportation of propagating material. However, the weevil can be distributed through movement of table stock from infested areas. Strict quarantine of all infested areas should be enforced to prevent introduction of the weevil into uninfested areas. Most of the important sweet-potato-growing states have laws prohibiting the transportation of sweet potatoes, sweet-potato plants, and morning-glory plants, or parts of plants, from infested to uninfested areas. Such laws, strictly enforced, delay, if not prevent, the spread of the weevil.

According to Roberts (1952) the sweet-potato weevil can be eradicated by depriving it of its food for 1 year. Its only known food plants are the sweet potato and some species of morning-glories. It is known to breed in the seaside morning-glory (*Ipomoea littoralis*) and, more rarely, in the marsh morning-glory (*I. sagittata*). These two species of wild morning-glories are found in limited sections of the sweet-potato-producing areas in the United States, mostly in coastal and tide-marsh margins. In some tropical regions other species of Ipomoea are fairly common, and it is possible that the sweet-potato weevil feeds on them. The wild morning-glories can be destroyed by herbicides, discussed in Chap. 9. Where eradication is attempted, no sweet potatoes should be grown within $\frac{1}{2}$ to 1 mile from any known infestation.

Control measures where the weevil is established consist in cleaning up the sweet-potato field, storage house, storage banks, and plant beds;

planting only plants known to be free from the weevil; following good crop rotations; treating infested roots with an insecticide; and spraying or dusting the storage place with an insecticide.

In cleaning up the fields, the vines should be destroyed and all pieces of the potatoes and roots should be removed. Storage houses and banks should be cleaned up at least 1 month before the new crop is planted, and all infested potatoes destroyed by feeding or burning. Following the removal of the potatoes from storage, the storage place should be dusted with 10 per cent DDT at the rate of 1 pound to each 1,600 square feet of surface, or sprayed with DDT using 8 pounds of 50 per cent wettable powder in 100 gallons of water at the rate of $1\frac{1}{2}$ gallons to 1,000 square feet of surface. If infested seed roots are to be used for producing plants, treat thoroughly with 10 per cent DDT dust at the rate of 1 pound to 6 to 8 bushels soon after harvest. Destroy all plants and potatoes in the plant beds as soon as enough plants have been obtained.[1]

In some tropical regions, where sweet potatoes are grown continuously, the sweet-potato weevil is more destructive than in the United States and control is more difficult. Viale and Thomas (1951) conducted experiments in Costa Rica on the control of a sweet-potato weevil by the use of certain insecticides applied to the soil. While good control was obtained with some of the insecticides, no recommendation was made for their use. The weevil present in Costa Rica is thought to be different from the one found in the United States, although the damage caused is similar.

Harvesting. When grown for the early market, sweet potatoes may be harvested as soon as the roots reach marketable size, regardless of the stage of maturity. The main crop, which is intended for storage, should be well matured before digging. When the potatoes are mature, a broken or cut surface dries on exposure to the air, while an immature one remains moist and turns dark in color. However, in regions where early frosts occur the potatoes should be dug about the time of the first hard frost regardless of their stage of maturity. If frost kills the vines, the potatoes should be dug immediately as decay sets in on the dead vines and may pass down to the roots. Edmond *et al.* showed that the yield increased with each successive harvest date in their experiments in South Carolina, Georgia, Mississippi, and Texas. Their recommendation was to harvest as near the first killing frost, fall rains, or low temperatures as practicable without risking danger of cold injury. They stated that flesh color improved with delay in time of harvest. Results of studies by Ezell, Wilcox, and Crowder (1952) indicate that maximum concentration of carotene and total carotenoid pigments occurred about the time of the

[1] For more complete information on the sweet-potato weevil and methods of control see *U.S. Dept. Agr.* Leaf. 121, rev. 1954.

usual harvest for storage. These studies, made at Beltsville, Md., with Yellow Jersey, Nancy Hall, Puerto Rico (Unit I strain), and Orange Little Stem, showed some varietal difference. In general, however, carotene and total carotenoid pigments increased in the first part of the harvest period and then decreased. The ascorbic acid content followed a similar pattern to that of the carotenoids in Nancy Hall, Puerto Rico, and Orange Little Stem, but Yellow Jersey showed little change when the others were increasing. The authors state that ascorbic acid decreased late in the harvest period. Roots from the harvests of Sept. 6 to 15 (early), Oct. 3 to 12 (midseason), and Nov. 6 to 15 (late) were cured, stored at 60°F., and analyzed at intervals during the storage season. The authors summarize the results as follows:

The time of harvest (early, midseason and late) appears to be of less importance in determining the post-harvest behavior of the carotenoid pigments than do the pre-harvest environmental factors. In the Nancy Hall variety the only increase in carotene after harvest occurred during curing of roots from the early harvest. Total carotenoids did not increase after harvest in this variety. The roots of the other varieties from the early and midseason harvests increased in both carotene and total pigments, but relatively little, if any, increase occurred in roots harvested after frost killed the foliage. Time of harvest had relatively little effect on the behavior of ascorbic acid during storage.

The digging implement should be one that keeps cutting and bruising to the minimum. In a study conducted for 4 years by Lutz, Park, and Deonier (1951) in Mississippi it was found that a 16-inch turn plow and a rod-wing middlebuster were better implements than a 12-inch plow, a middlebuster without rod wings, or a mechanical digger. The highest average loss was with the mechanical digger, but the loss was somewhat reduced by removing most of the shakers. The Puerto Rico variety was used in these experiments, and storage was 4½ months. The loss by decay and the total loss (decay and shrinkage) in the studies mentioned are given in Table 22.2.

Lutz, Park, and Deonier found that picking up soon after digging was better than leaving the sweet potatoes in the heap row overnight and that crates were far superior to sacks. Where the potatoes were put directly into crates the total loss by decay and shrinkage was 11.7 per cent; when left in the heap row overnight and placed in crates the next day the loss was 14.7 per cent; when handled in sacks the loss was 30.3 per cent.

Sweet potatoes should be graded somewhat as they are gathered so as to eliminate extra handling. Where they are marketed as soon as harvested, it is common practice to grade and pack in the field. If the potatoes are to be stored, it is a good plan to go over the rows and pick

Table 22.2. Effect of Harvesting Implement Used on the Loss of
Sweet Potatoes during Storage

Implement	Loss by decay, per cent	Total loss, per cent
16-inch plow:		
Fast................................	8.08	19.53
Slow...............................	9.05	20.47
Middlebuster......................	13.08	25.88
12-inch plow......................	11.92	24.35
Rod-wing middlebuster............	8.58	19.98
Mechanical digger................	14.52	29.10

up the sound marketable ones in one basket, then gather the seed stock
in another, and put the injured ones in still another. This eliminates extra
handling and thereby reduces the loss by decay, since in any handling
there is some bruising, which hastens decay. The baskets or other containers used should be loaded on a truck or a wagon with springs and
hauled direct to the storage house. The potatoes should never be
dumped into the truck or wagon.

Preparation for Market. Preparation of sweet potatoes for market includes careful grading, cleaning, and packing. In grading, all characteristics that affect market quality should be considered. Most markets
demand uniform, medium-sized potatoes that are free from cuts, bruises,
and rots. Roots that are too large, too small, misshapen, cut, or bruised
should not be packed for market but used for feed or for other use. It is
desirable to use standard grades that are recognized on the markets.
When the potatoes are sold at harvest time, they may be graded in the
field or in a packing house, preferably the latter. Grading at the packing
house generally is done on portable tables, which consist of frames of a
suitable height and with canvas or burlap fastened to the frames. As
the potatoes are delivered they are dumped on to the tables, and the
graders sort out and pack those that conform to the grade specifications.

In most of the sweet-potato-growing areas of the United States it is
the general practice to wash the potatoes before they are packed for
market. Special equipment (Fig. 22.5) has been designed for washing.
According to Lutz and Simons (1948) a washing and grading line of
common type consists of the following equipment: (1) an overhead
spray washer with underneath rollers, (2) a roller-conveyor type of sort-
ing table, (3) an underneath brush and overhead spray washer, (4) a
10- or 12-foot section roller-belt conveyor for drainage, and (5) a roller-
or flat-belt conveyor for grading. Where black rot is present, washing
spreads the disease.

After sweet potatoes have been stored for a considerable period they should be regraded before being sent to market no matter how carefully they were graded before. If they were carefully graded at harvest time and little or no rot has developed in storage, the regrading may be done by partly emptying the container and picking out damaged or diseased specimens. Better grading can be done, however, by dumping all the potatoes from the containers and repacking. The graders and packers should wear gloves to prevent injuring the surface of the potatoes with

Fig. 22.5. Sweet-potato washer. (*Courtesy of La. Agricultural Experiment Station.*)

the fingernails, and all handling should be carefully done to prevent bruising.

Packing. Sweet potatoes are packed in various types of containers, including hampers, round stave baskets, crates, and boxes. It is important that the container be strong and rigid to eliminate breakage and to prevent bruising of the potatoes.

Sweet potatoes should be packed in clean, neat, substantial containers that show off the product to good advantage when opened for inspection. The container should be well filled when packed. Unless it is more than level full when packed, the constant jarring and jolting of a long freight haul cause it to reach its destination only partly full. Loose packing allows the potatoes to shift about, resulting in bruising, and this is often followed by decay. The shape of the sweet potato does not lend itself to a jumble pack (Fig. 22.6). To carry properly, each potato should be placed by hand and each layer so arranged that the vacant spaces are filled. With any type of container it is desirable to face the top layer, but the potatoes in this layer should be representative of the contents of the container.

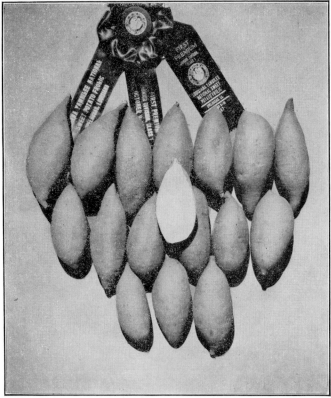

Fig. 22.6. Blue-ribbon sweet potatoes. (*Courtesy of La. Agricultural Experiment Station.*)

Storage. To keep well in storage, sweet potatoes must be: (1) well matured before harvesting, (2) free from diseases causing storage rot, (3) carefully handled to prevent scratching and bruising, (4) well cured after being put in the storage house, and (5) kept at the proper temperature and atmospheric humidity after they are cured.

The stage of maturity at which sweet potatoes should be harvested is discussed under Harvesting.

Careful handling is important since the sweet potato is very easily bruised and organisms causing decay often enter the injured surface. Even if decay does not set in, the bruised areas become discolored and hard, thus injuring the appearance and reducing the quality. The sweet potato will not stand so much rough handling as the Irish potato. In fact very few products are more easily injured than the sweet potato, and it should be given as careful handling as apples and oranges.

Curing is essential for good keeping of sweet potatoes in storage and is accomplished best by maintaining a temperature of about 85°F. and a relative humidity of approximately 85 per cent. At either lower temperature or lower humidity the time required for curing is increased and the loss in storage is likely to be greater. High humidity promotes healing of wounds by favoring wound-cork formation and also reduces shrinkage of the roots through water loss. During curing there is loss in weight varying from 5 to 10 per cent through loss of water by evaporation and loss of solids through respiration. The length of the curing period varies from a few days to 4 weeks, depending mainly on the temperature. At 85°F. curing is accomplished in less time than at 80°F. and much less than at 75°F. Lutz (1952) found that curing for 4 days at 84°F. was sufficient and that this temperature was better than 74, 80, 90, or 95°F. While high temperature is important in curing, it is safer to have the room at about 70°F. than at 85°F. when the potatoes are brought into the house. If they are cool when brought in, moisture will condense on the surface of the potatoes, especially when the humidity is high. After the danger of sweating is past, the temperature should be raised.

Storage Temperature. Results of several experiments indicate that 55 to 60°F. is better than either a higher or a lower temperature. Cooley, Kushman, and Smart (1954) reported results of experiments conducted for 4 years with Big Stem Jersey, Yellow Jersey, Maryland Golden, Nancy Hall, Orange Little Stem, and Puerto Rico stored at 50, 55, and 60°F. for 3, 5, and 7 months. The potatoes were cured at 85°F. and relative humidity near 85 per cent. Their results for all varieties, given in percentage of sound potatoes after 3, 5, and 7 months storage, are shown in Table 22.3.

Table 22.3. Effect of Storage Temperature on Keeping Quality of Six Varieties of Sweet Potatoes after 3, 5, and 7 Months Storage

Temperature, °F.	Per cent sound potatoes after:		
	3 months	5 months	7 months
50	82.4	49.3	20.3
55	87.0	82.3	74.6
60	86.1	83.8	80.2

The data in Table 22.3 are calculated on the basis of original weight and include weight loss in curing and storage and loss from rots. Marked varietal differences were found with greatest loss in Orange Little Stem and the least in Puerto Rico. Over the three storage temperatures and the three lengths of storage, the percentage of sound potatoes was as follows: Big Stem Jersey, 74.7 per cent; Yellow Jersey, 70.8; Maryland Golden, 69.1; Nancy Hall, 70.7; Orange Little Stem, 61.9; and Puerto Rico, 83.4 per cent. Loss in weight from decay was greatest in the potatoes stored at 50°F, and the difference increased with length of storage. After 5 months of storage all varieties except Puerto Rico had significantly smaller percentage of sound potatoes at 50°F. than at 55 or 60°F. The difference between 55 and 60°F. was not significant.

The sweet potato is injured by chilling at temperatures above freezing. Lutz (1944 and 1945) showed that 2 days at 32°F. and 4 days at 40°F. resulted in injury. Potatoes that had been cured before being exposed to the low temperature were much less injured than those that had not been cured prior to the exposure. Kimbrough and Bell (1942) reported injury to sweet potatoes held for 1 week at 40°F.

CHANGES DURING CURING AND STORAGE. Attention has been called to the loss in weight of sweet potatoes during curing and storage. Most of the loss in weight is due to loss of water, but this is masked by loss in sugars in respiration and by the water formed in the same process, as shown by Kimbrough (1929). The percentage of water fluctuates very little during the storage period of as much as 6 months. Other changes that take place in storage are transformations of carbohydrates, especially a decrease in starch and an increase in sugar. This change takes place rapidly during curing and continues slowly during a considerable portion of the normal storage period. In studies by Hasselbring and Hawkins (1915) it was found that the carbohydrate changes took place at temperatures as low as 4°C. and as high as 30°C. At the lower temperature there was a rapid disappearance of starch and an accompanying increase in cane sugar, but the sweet potatoes rotted before equilibrium was reached. These studies were made on Big Stem Jersey and Southern Queen. Similar changes probably take place in other varieties, although some of the important varieties develop a higher sugar content than those used in the studies mentioned.

The changes that take place during curing and storing, especially the decrease in starch and increase in sugar, account for the difference in taste and consistency of the cooked product, between freshly dug potatoes and those that have been stored. The soft-fleshed varieties have a lower starch content and a higher sugar content than the hard-fleshed ones. Culpepper and Magoon (1926) showed that not only do marked changes take place during curing and storage but that further alterations take place during cooking.

The chemical changes taking place are evidenced by a transformation of part of the starch to dextrin and sucrose, thus altering the starch moisture ratio, and during cooking, a splitting of a portion of the starch to maltose.

These changes are responsible for the altered physical consistency of the canned product and its increase in sweetness. The ratio of starch to moisture determines the consistency, and the chief factor causing the difference in sweetness is the amount of sucrose formed.

Storage Houses. Sweet-potato storage houses should be well built, well insulated, and provided with adequate heating and ventilating systems. It is important to have them tight so that there is little or no leakage of air around the openings or through the walls, floor, and roof. Good insulation helps in maintaining a fairly uniform temperature regardless of the fluctuations outside.

Sweet-potato storage houses may be built of any of the ordinary building materials, but most small houses, and many of the larger ones, are built of wood. Wood is a fairly good insulator and may be used to advantage to insulate walls and roof of a sweet-potato storage house if there is a sufficient number of layers with building paper between to prevent the passage of air through the cracks. Insulating boards are more efficient than wood of equal thickness and may be used. Where wood is used for the walls, it is not desirable to fill the space between the layers of boards with sawdust, shavings, or any similiar material, for these will absorb moisture and when once wet will not dry out. This will result in keeping the atmosphere damp and rotting the wood. Furthermore, these materials settle and leave open spaces in the wall. Other material, such as brick, hollow tile, and concrete blocks are used and are satisfactory if the building is properly constructed.

A good ventilation system should be provided so that the air can be changed quickly when desired. This is very important during the curing period.

All doors and windows and ventilators should be made to close tightly. Double doors are desirable, and shutters should be provided for the windows. preferably on the inside. Windows should be as few as will provide sufficient light for the workmen. Excessive light favors sprouting, and large glass areas permit rapid loss of heat.

Large storage houses should be divided into rooms of such size that one room may be filled in 2 or 3 days. If the rooms are too large it is difficult, if not impossible, to cure the potatoes evenly. It is desirable to store the seed stock in a separate room so that it may remain undisturbed until planting time. Each room should have separate heat control.

HEATING THE STORAGE HOUSE. The type of heating apparatus used depends to a considerable extent upon the size of the house. For a small house, a small sheet-iron, wood-burning stove or a small coal stove may be used. Oil stoves are used for small houses in some areas, but these are not entirely satisfactory. For large houses, hot-water or steam heat is preferable since the heat can be more evenly distributed than with stoves or even with hot-air furnaces. Some houses are heated by hot-air furnaces with the air pipes placed under the bins. Electricity is used successfully in both large and small houses in some areas. Where it is available at moderate cost its use may be economical. It has some advantages over other heating methods, including nearly complete automatic control, resulting in less labor for operating, more even distribution of heat, less storage losses, less space for the heating equipment, and less danger of fire.[2]

Storage Banks. While this type of storage is not recommended, it is used on many farms where storage houses are not available. The main disadvantages in the bank method are: (1) large losses from decay, (2) low quality of the potatoes due to lack of proper curing, (3) loss on the market because banked roots will keep for such a short period after removal from the bank or pit, (4) inconvenience of getting the sweet potatoes when needed, especially during cold or rainy weather, and (5) danger of rats getting into the sweet potatoes. In spite of all the disadvantages, it is better to store sweet potatoes in banks than not to store them. By using the best methods of making the banks, the loss can be greatly reduced, but not eliminated, because it is impossible to control moisture and temperature. The term "pit," as used for common outdoor storage, is not a correct one since sweet potatoes generally are stored in banks aboveground.

Storage banks should be made where the drainage is good. A level bed of soil should be made a few inches above the ground level. It is desirable to make two shallow trenches at right angles to each other, to use inverted troughs to provide ventilation at the bottom. If trenches are used, they should be covered with boards. At the intersection of the trenches, or troughs, a small box with open ends should be placed to form a flue up through the pile of potatoes. Cover the earth floor with 4 or 5 inches of straw, hay, leaves, or pine needles and place the sweet potatoes in a conical pile around the upright flue. Place a covering of 3 or 4 inches of straw, hay, or other similar material over the pile and cover with a layer of soil a few inches thick at first. As the weather gets cool the soil covering should be increased. The ends of the trenches, or troughs, and the flue should be kept open until it is necessary to close them to keep out the cold.

It is better to make several small banks rather than one large one, because it is desirable to remove all of the potatoes when the bank is opened.

[2] For full information on storage-house construction, heating, and management the reader is referred to *Farmers' Bull.* 1442.

CHAPTER 23

Beans and Peas

Broad bean	Scarlet runner bean
Soybean	Kidney bean
Mung bean	Lima bean
Tepary bean	Peas
Southern pea	

While beans and peas belong to the same family, Leguminoseae, their cultural requirements have few points in common. All the beans grown in America, except the broad bean, are warm-season plants, while the pea is relatively hardy and grows best under cool conditions. The beans and peas, in common with other legumes, are capable of utilizing atmospheric nitrogen by the aid of bacteria found in the nodules on the roots of the plants.

BEANS

The term *bean,* as used here, includes the following species representing six genera: (1) kidney bean (*Phaseolus vulgaris*), (2) Lima bean (*P. lunatus*), (3) scarlet runner, or multiflora, bean (*P. coccineus*), (4) tepary bean (*P. acutifolius* Gray var. *latifolius* Freeman), (5) Metcalfe bean (*P. Metcalfei*), (6) urd bean (*P. mungo*), (7) mung bean (*P. aureus*), (8) adzuki bean (*P. angularis*), (9) rice bean (*P. calcaratus*), (10) moth bean (*P. aconitifolius*), (11) Southern pea, or cowpea (*Vigna sinensis*), (12) broad bean (*Vicia faba*), (13) hyacinth bean (*Dolichos lablab*), (14) velvet bean (*Stizolobium Deeringianum*), and (15) soybean (*Soja Max*).

The soybean is grown on a large scale in the United States for oil and feed and as a soil-improving crop. Velvet beans and cowpeas are used for soil-improving crops, although the latter is grown for human consumption in the South. The hyacinth and scarlet runner beans are grown mainly as ornamentals in the United States. The urd, adzuki, rice, and moth beans are little known in America; the tepary bean is grown mainly in the Southwest; and the mung bean is grown in Oklahoma.

BROAD BEAN

The broad bean (*Vicia faba*) is a hardy plant, native of Europe and Asia. It is one of the most ancient of the cultivated esculents, having been grown by the ancient Greeks, Romans, Hebrews, and Egyptians. It is said to have been introduced into China about 2822 B.C. This bean is seldom grown in the United States since the summers are too hot in the South and the winters in the North are so cold that it cannot be planted in the autumn and carried over. In some sections of the South and of the Pacific Coast, the seed may be planted in the autumn or the winter for a spring crop, but other types of beans are so easily grown that the extra effort necessary to produce the broad bean does not seem to be justified. In southern Europe, the seed is often planted in the fall and the young plants are protected during the winter. Broad beans are used as green-shell and dry beans and as feed for livestock. It is grown to some extent in California where it is planted in February and March in the warmer sections and later in the cooler regions near San Francisco. It is grown mostly for local use and is not of much importance.

The broad bean is an important food crop in Latin America. The estimated acreage devoted to the broad bean in 1953 was over 400,000 acres, of which Brazil produced 225,000 acres and Mexico 100,000 acres. It is grown mainly at higher altitudes where the climate is relatively cool. The beans are harvested at the green-shell stage as needed for home use or for market, and those remaining on the plant are used as dry-shell beans.

SOYBEAN

The soybean (*Soja Max*) is a native of southeastern Asia and has been cultivated in Japan, India, and China since ancient times. Hundreds of varieties are grown in these countries, and the soybean is second in importance to rice as a food crop, especially in China and Japan. The soybean was first introduced into the United States as early as 1804, but it took nearly 100 years for it to become of much importance. It is grown in the Middle West and the South for feed, forage, and green-manure crops, but its most important use is as a seed for oil and by-products. In 1953, the total cultivation in the United States was 16,510,000 acres, of which 14,366,000 acres was grown for seed production. The value of the crop exceeded 704 million dollars. Many varieties have been developed for oil and feed purposes. There are a few varieties grown for human consumption in the green-shell stage, but there is no commercial production in the United States for use as a vegetable.

MUNG BEAN

The mung bean (*Phaseolus aureus*) is an important food crop in the Orient but is not widely grown in the United States. The sprouted beans are consumed as a cooked vegetable, usually in Oriental dishes, or eaten raw in salads. The dry beans are soaked in water overnight, drained, and placed in containers in a fairly warm, dark room. They are sprinkled every few hours with warm water to encourage growth of the sprouts and are ready for use in about a week. A pound of dry mung beans yields 6 to 8 pounds of sprouts. About 25 million pounds of mung beans is used annually in the United States, mostly as canned bean sprouts.

Mung beans are grown mainly in Oklahoma for hay, for the beans, and as a green-manure crop. The acreage increased greatly during the Second World War when imports from the Orient were cut off. The highest acreage for harvest was 110,000 acres in 1945. The acreage has dropped since then, and in 1953 only 20,000 acres was harvested. Yields of 12 to 15 bushels of dry mung beans per acre are not unusual, although the average yield is only 5 or 6 bushels per acre.

There are two main varieties, Golden and Green, the names denoting the color of the dry seed. Both varieties are grown for hay and green-manure crops, but only the Green is grown for dry-bean production. There are many strains of the Green variety, and those with hard, shiny, dark-green seed coats are preferred for sprouting.

The mung bean has about the same climatic and soil requirements as the Southern pea and is grown in much the same manner. In Oklahoma, the seed is planted in May and early June in 3-foot rows with a bean or corn planter using 5 to 8 pounds of seed per acre. The cultivation and fertilization are the same as for Southern peas or beans. Mung beans germinate well in dry soil and are fairly drought-resistant. The plants grow 14 to 24 inches tall, and the pods are borne at, or above, the top of the foliage, which makes them easy to harvest with a combine; however, the plants are usually pulled and allowed to dry in windrows and threshed. The pods shatter easily, and careful handling is essential for maximum recovery of beans. The mung bean is resistant to most of the diseases and insect pests of cowpeas, soybeans, and common beans.

TEPARY BEAN

The tepary bean (*Phaseolus acutifolius* var. *latifolius*) is probably a native of Southwestern United States and northern Mexico and was domesticated by prehistoric Indian races. Freeman (1912) states that 47 distinct types have been isolated and grown at the Arizona Experiment Station. Two types of beans have been collected from the Indians of southwestern Arizona, which were recognized by them as distinct types, commonly known by the Mexican names frijoles and teparies. Frijoles belong to the group of common kidney beans (*Phaseolus vulgaris*), while teparies belong to the large and variable group described by Gray as *P. acutifolius*. The Pink bean and the Bayou are selections from these early domesticated frijole-type beans. Teparies were probably not domesticated from the type form of *P. acutifolius* Gray, but from the larger, more vigorous broad-leaved variety *P. acutifolius* var. *latifolius*.

The tepary differs from both the kidney bean (*P. vulgaris*) and the Lima bean (*P. lunatus*) in several botanical characters. The seeds are shaped like a Lima bean but are much smaller, and the seed coat of the tepary lacks the characteristic glossiness of the kidney bean. The first pair of aerial leaves of the tepary are smaller and narrower than those of the other two species. The petioles of the first aerial leaves are much shorter than those of kidney or Lima beans, and the leaf has a truncate rather than a cordate base. Tepary beans are especially valuable in arid regions of the Southwest and in northern Mexico. They withstand extreme heat and dry atmosphere and produce a crop under conditions where other types of beans are a complete failure.

The culture of the tepary bean is not very different from that given the common kidney bean under similar conditions. They are usually planted in rows about 3 feet apart with the seeds spaced 6 inches apart in the row and covered to a depth of 3 to 4 inches. They are sometimes grown in hills 18 inches apart with two to four seeds in a hill. The seeds take up water rapidly and germinate under fairly dry soil conditions where other varieties would not come up. They are grown mainly as a dry-shell bean. In preparing for cooking the dry beans absorb water faster and absorb more water per unit weight than other types. This may be due to the fact that the tepary bean has a higher specific gravity than other types of beans.

SOUTHERN PEA

The Southern pea, or Cowpea (*Vigna sinensis*), is probably a native of central Africa. Piper (1913) reports that a wild plant differing little from the Southern pea occurs throughout a large part of Africa and hybrids of this plant and cultivated Southern peas are readily obtained. According to Morse (1920), the cultivated cowpea consists of three main groups: the asparagus bean (*V. sinensis* var. *sesquipedalis*), the catjang (*V. sinensis* var. *cylindrica*), and the Southern pea, each of which represents a group of varieties having much in common. The Southern pea is the most important in the United States, but the other two types are important in other parts of the world. Because of the large number of varieties throughout Africa and southern Asia it is probable that the Southern pea is of ancient cultivation for human food. It was introduced in the early Spanish settlements of the West Indies and was grown in North Carolina in 1714, probably coming from the West Indies. Its culture in Virginia was reported about 1775 and no doubt was quite general in the United States early in the nineteenth century.

It has been known by a number of names in the United States, such as "callivance," "Indian pea," "southern field pea," "cornfield pea," and "cowpea," but Southern pea is the preferred name. In the Southern states the Southern pea is often called "pea" and the garden pea (*Pisum sativum*) is called "English pea." The term pea, however, is incorrect since the Southern pea is not a pea but a bean. It is used as food in both the green-shell and dry stage. It is also grown for hay, ensilage, pasture for all types of stock, and as a soil-improving crop mainly in the Southern states.

It is of special importance to the vegetable grower in the South since it fits in well with the usual cropping system. It can be grown during the summer after the spring or early-summer crop of vegetables has been harvested and before the winter vegetables are planted. In 1949, 150,600 acres of Southern peas was grown for harvest in the green-shell stage and the farm value of the crop was slightly over 4 million dollars. Most of this acreage was grown in the Southeastern states, and the leading states were Texas with 37,422 acres, Georgia with 35,887 acres, and Alabama with 25,447 acres. The production of dry Southern peas for human consumption was estimated at 380,000 acres in the Southern states in 1949. California produces large quantities of the "blackeye" variety of Southern peas for harvest as dry-shell beans. The average annual production of blackeyes in California for the period 1946–1953 was about 660,000 100-pound bags.

Culture. The Southern pea is a warm-weather crop and is therefore grown mainly in the South, although it is grown with success in southern parts of Ohio, Illinois, and New Jersey, parts of Michigan, and other Northern states. It is also successfully grown in parts of California. The crop is very tender and is injured by the lightest frost.

Southern peas are grown on a wide variety of soils and grown best on soils that are well drained. When grown for forage or as a soil-improving crop the seed is usually broadcast or sown in drills 6 to 8 inches apart, and about 90 pounds of seed per acre is required. When the crop is to be harvested as dry beans or as green-shell beans, it is frequently planted in rows 3 feet apart with plants spaced 2 or 3 inches apart in the row. Usually 30 to 40 pounds of seed per acre is required. When grown for dry-shell beans, the Southern peas are harvested and threshed in the various ways mentioned for other dry-shell beans. When used in the green-shell stage they are picked and shelled by hand in some areas. Mechanized harvest is becoming more popular, and the plants are cut with a mowing machine and threshed in a viner similar to that used for peas and green Lima beans. The Southern pea is difficult to thresh in the green-shell stage, and yields are somewhat lower than can be obtained by hand picking.

Hoover and Dennison (1953) studied the rate of maturity of Southern peas in spring and early-summer crops in Florida. As the seed matured the percentage of water decreased and the starch and alcohol-insoluble solids increased. The seed remained green until about 15 days after flowering. About 19 days after flowering all green coloring had left the pods. The usual time of harvest for green-shell beans is when most of the green has left the pods.

Brittingham (1946) described the most commonly grown varieties of Southern pea in the United States. The asparagus, or yard-long, bean (*V. sinensis* var. *sesquipedalis*) is grown mainly as a curiosity and is a climbing plant. It has flabby inflated pods 15 to 30 inches long which shrink around the widely spaced seeds when dry. The Southern pea is a bushy or procumbent type of plant which is twining but not climbing. The pendant pods are from 3 to 12 inches long, are not inflated, and do not shrink around the seeds. Most varieties have purple anthocyanin on stems, leaves, flower parts, or the seeds. The seeds may be solid-colored, speckled, or have an eye pattern. The purple-hull varieties have purple mature pods, and the seeds have an eye pattern of buff or maroon. The plants have anthocyanin on stems and leaves. The blackeye group of varieties has anthocyanin on stems and leaves, but the mature pods are yellow and the seeds have a black eye pattern. This is probably the most widely grown group, and many strains and varieties are grown. California No. 5 is resistant to nematodes, and California 8152 is resistant to wilt as well as nematodes. The other groups are black, speckled, or browneye types. In each of these groups there is a crowder type. For example, the only difference between the blackeye and blackeye crowder varieties is that the seeds are tightly crowded in the pods of the blackeye crowder type. The cream and cream crowder types have white seeds without any pigmentation, and there is no anthocyanin anywhere on the plant. The Lady Cream and similar varieties belong to the catjang group (*V. sinensis* var. *cylindrica*). The pods are erect rather than pendent and are only 3 or 4 inches long and are less than $\frac{1}{4}$ inch in diameter. The seeds are small and spherical and are always tightly crowded in the pod.

SCARLET RUNNER, OR MULTIFLORA, BEAN

The scarlet runner (*Phaseolus coccineus*), also called multiflora bean, is probably a native of Central America or South America, although it was formerly supposed to have been indigenous to Asia. In America it is grown mainly as an ornamental climber; the spikes of rich scarlet flowers and the deep green foliage make it one of the most showy and attractive plants. In Europe this bean is used as food. The tender, green pods only are eaten in some localities, while in others the green and dry seeds are used.

The plant grows 12 feet or more in height and requires 115 to 120 days to mature its seeds. In germinating, the scarlet runner differs from other species of Phaseolus in that the cotyledons remain in the ground and the germination is known as hypogeal. The plant produces a thickened root somewhat like the Dahlia, though smaller.

COMMON, OR KIDNEY, BEAN

The kidney bean (*Phaseolus vulgaris*) is the most important species of bean grown in the United States; in common usage, the term *bean* applies to types and varieties belonging to this species. This crop is grown by a large percentage of home gardeners, and as a market crop it is produced for market as snap beans, green-shell beans, and dry beans. It is also grown on a large scale for processing.

Statistics of Production. The acreage of snap beans for market has increased greatly since 1918, reaching a high of 215,400 acres in 1944 (Table 23.1). The acreage has declined since 1944, but the production

Table 23.1. Estimated Average Annual Acreage, Production, and Farm Value of Snap Beans, Grown for Market, 1918–1953

Years	Acres	Yield per acre, bushels	Production, bushels (000 omitted)	Price per bushel	Farm value (000 omitted)
1918–1927	46,180	112	4,849	$1.32	$ 8,926
1928–1937	135,700	84	11,293	1.18	13,057
1938–1947	184.690	94	17,399	1.76	30,670
1948–1953	178,280	104	18,402	2.09	43,629

has remained about the same because of increases in the average yield per acre. Fresh beans are on the market every month of the year, being produced in the Southern states in the winter, in the Northern states in the summer, and in the intermediate states in the spring and fall. The total market bean acreage in 1953 was 158,620 acres, and Florida was the leading state with 52,600 acres. The other main areas of production were North Carolina with 13,200 acres; New York, 12,500 acres; South Carolina, 12,100 acres; and Virginia, 11,120 acres.

The acreage devoted to snap beans for processing increased greatly during the period 1940–1944 with an acreage of 162,340 acres in 1944 (Table 23.2). The acreage declined to 137,520 acres in 1953, but the

Table 23.2. Estimated Average Annual Acreage, Production, and Value of Snap Beans Grown for Processing, 1918–1953

Years	Acres	Yield per acre, tons	Production, tons	Price per ton	Value (000 omitted)
1918–1927	20,550	2.10	40,100	$ 60.78	$ 2,464
1928–1937	51,960	1.46	75,490	50.62	3,807
1938–1947	109,300	1.67	180,350	103.50	15,211
1948–1953	121,590	2.09	255,360	116.05	29.519

production of 298,580 tons was much higher than any previous year. The leading states in 1953 were New York with 33,600 acres; Florida, 17,300 acres; Wisconsin, 13,700 acres; Maryland, 11,000 acres; and Oregon, 7,650 acres. New York led in production with 57,100 tons, and Oregon was next with 55,100 tons. Pole beans are grown for processing in Oregon, and the yield per acre is much greater than for bush beans grown in other areas. The quantity of snap beans canned has been about the same since 1943 with 22,611,000 cases canned in 1953. The frozen pack has increased each year since 1943, reaching a high of 114,781,000 pounds in 1953, and ranked fourth among frozen vegetables.

The dry-bean industry is of greater importance in the United States than the snap-bean industry. The dollar value of snap beans in 1953 ranked fourth among the vegetables grown in the United States. If the value of dry beans is added, the value of all beans produced exceeded all vegetables except potatoes. There have been yearly variations in acreage and production with few definite trends; however, the acreage has decreased since 1949, but the production has remained much the same as previous years. In 1943, nearly 2,500,000 acres of dry beans was grown and the production was 21 million bags (100-pound) of dry beans. The 1953 crop of 16,761,000 bags of dry beans was valued at $138,750,000 and was produced on 1,437,000 acres. The important production areas were Michigan with 384,000 acres; California, 283,000 acres; Colorado, 234,000 acres; Idaho, 152,000 acres; and New York, 135,000 acres. Part of the dry-bean crop produced in the Western states is for seed purposes.

Dry beans furnish a large part of the protein food in Latin America.

The combined production of dry beans in South America, Central America, Cuba, Haiti, and the Dominican Republic was twice that of the United States in the period 1945–1949 and nearly 2½ times more in 1952 and 1953. Most of those produced in Latin American countries are consumed in the countries where produced or in other countries of Latin America. The United States, on the other hand, exports considerable quantities to other countries of the Hemisphere. Since the population of the United States is about equal to that of the other countries mentioned,

Fig. 23.1. Field of snap beans grown on muck soil in Florida Everglades. Note windbreak of old cornstalks and weeds.

it can be inferred that the per capita consumption of dry beans in Latin American countries is several times that of the United States.

History and Taxonomy. The common bean is probably a native of South America and is undoubtedly of ancient origin. Many varieties were grown by the American Indians before they became generally cultivated in Europe.

It belongs to the family Leguminoseae and is, therefore, related to the peas, clovers, and many other plants of great economic importance.

Soils and Soil Preparation. Beans are grown on practically all types of soils from light sands to heavy clays. In California, peat soils are used for growing dry beans with very satisfactory results. In Florida, snap beans are grown on a large scale on the peat soils of the Everglades and on light sands during the late fall, winter, and early spring (Fig. 23.1).

In regions where freezing weather occurs, sandy and sandy-loam soils are preferred for an early crop, but heavier soils are desired for the mid-season crop.

The bean plant does not produce large yields when grown on extremely acid soils. It is sensitive to high concentrations of soluble aluminum and manganese. At Norfolk, Va., Zimmerley obtained the highest yields at soil reactions between pH 5.3 and 5.8 or 6.0. Similar results were obtained by Wessels on a silt-loam soil on Long Island. Forsee and Hoffman (1950) also obtained maximum yields on organic soils in Florida when the reaction was pH 5.5 to 6.0. Liming should not be necessary for beans if the soil reaction is above pH 5.5 unless the soil contains high levels of soluble aluminum or manganese.

A good job of plowing under green-manure crops and crop residues is essential for proper operation of planting equipment. Harrowing or disking should be done to break up large clods, but a finely pulverized seedbed is neither essential nor desirable. The bean planter pulverizes and compacts the soil sufficiently for good germination if there are no large clods.

Fertilizers. Beans are a legume, and for many years only phosphorus and potash were used in the fertilizer. It is not an efficient legume and makes such rapid growth that nitrogen fertilizers give a good response in most areas. This is especially true in the intensively cropped areas where snap beans are grown. In the Northeastern states, amounts of fertilizer equivalent to 300 to 500 pounds of 8-16-16 per acre are used. On light soils extra nitrogen as a side-dressing is a common practice. Less fertilizer is needed when beans are grown in rotation with field crops or where manure is used. Only phosphorus and potash fertilizers are needed on the organic soils in Florida, but the beans grown on sandy soils usually receive about 1,000 pounds of 5-6-8 or its equivalent per acre. In wet seasons a side-dressing of nitrogen and potash is also used. The fertilizers used in Florida also supply magnesium, manganese, copper, and zinc. On the Pacific Coast where pole beans are grown under irrigation, the common fertilizer is 300 to 500 pounds of ammonium phosphate (16-20-0) per acre. Additional nitrogen is supplied in the irrigation water. Pole beans require more fertilizer than bush beans because the growing season is longer and yield greater than that of most bush varieties.

Dry beans, such as the pea, medium, marrow, and kidney types, are generally grown as a farm crop, and little or no fertilizer is used. In New York and Michigan, they are fertilized in much the same manner as snap beans on many farms. In the dry-land farming areas of the West, no fertilizer is used, and usually none is used in the irrigated areas.

Many experiments have shown that it is unsafe to apply fertilizer in the row in contact with the seed. Most experiment stations recommend placing the fertilizer in bands about 3 inches to the side of the seed and slightly deeper than the seed. The high concentration of soluble salts resulting from fertilizer placed in contact with the seed delays germination and may kill some of the seedlings. The slower germination usually results in poor stands owing to greater damage from soil insects and disease organisms. Fertilizer injury is likely to be troublesome when the soil is dry and on light soils, while high soil moisture and heavier soil types tend to reduce the amount of injury. Banding the fertilizer is more efficient than broadcasting since the bean plant does not produce a large root system.

The bean plant does not have a high requirement for minor elements, and deficiencies are seldom reported. In Florida responses to copper, manganese, zinc, and magnesium have been reported on light sands and organic soils. Magnesium deficiency is common where beans are grown on very acid soils in rotation with potatoes, especially on sandy soils. The requirement for zinc is higher than many other vegetables, according to Viets, Brown, and Crawford (1954). They reported that zinc deficiency of beans occurred in the Yakima and Columbia Valleys in Washington where leveling the land for irrigation had exposed the calcareous subsoil. Applications of zinc sulfate in the fertilizer or as a foliage spray corrected the deficiency.

Beans are sensitive to high concentrations of aluminum and manganese, and toxicity symptoms frequently are present on very acid soils. Many workers have noted that a small application of boron may be toxic to beans. Page and Paden (1949) reported that 10 pounds of fertilizer borate (rasorite) per acre injured beans, but they were not damaged by 40 pounds per acre of colemanite (calcium borate), which is slowly soluble. Beans may be injured by boron when they follow canning beets in rotation since large amounts of borax are commonly used on the beet crop.

Planting. Common beans are tender to frost and usually are planted after that danger is over. The seed germinate slowly at a soil temperature of 60°F., and at lower temperatures they may rot in the ground. Cold, wet soil invariably results in a poor stand. Home gardeners and market gardeners growing for the early market often take chances on frost and make small plantings before the danger is over. The main crop of snap beans, especially those grown for processing, and all types of dry beans are planted after danger of frost is over and the soil has become warm. Two, three, or more plantings of snap beans are made in most areas to have a continuous harvest during the growing season. In areas where frost does not occur, plantings are made at intervals throughout the year, although commercial production may be limited to the cooler parts of the year. Fewer plantings of pole beans are necessary for a continuous supply since they have a longer bearing season than bush types.

The rate of planting of beans varies considerably depending on the kind and variety grown and the region in which grown. In dry-land farming areas, less seed is planted than in humid regions or where irrigation is practiced. The number of seed per pound varies greatly depending on the variety, but the same variety may vary from year to year owing to growing conditions. Bush snap beans are planted at rates of 50 to 150 pounds per acre, but 70 pounds is probably most common. Pole snap beans require only 20 to 30 pounds of seed per acre since the rows are usually spaced farther apart than with bush types. In the Northeastern states, pea beans are sown at rates of 30 to 40 pounds of seed per acre, while Red Kidney may require as much as 100 pounds per acre. In irrigated areas in the West the common rate of seeding Pinto and similar types is 50 to 60 pounds per acre, but only 15 to 25 pounds of seed is planted where the crop is not irrigated. The spacing between the rows varies from 24 to 48 inches. In the main producing areas of snap beans the row spacing is about 30 inches. In dry areas without irrigation the rows may be as much as 48 inches apart.

In the Southeastern states pole beans are sometimes planted in hills 3 by 3, 3 by 4, or 4 by 4 feet apart, with 4 to 6 seeds in each hill, and are thinned to 3 or 4 plants. The poles are usually set before the seeds are planted. On the Pacific Coast and in some other areas pole beans are planted 3 to 5 inches apart in rows 4 to 7 feet apart in much the same manner as bush types are planted. A trellis of some sort to support the plants is erected over the rows after the seedlings emerge. Moore and Allmendinger (1954) found that increasing the distance between the rows of Blue Lake pole beans in Washington decreased the yield about 1 ton per acre for each additional foot between the rows. Where mildew was a problem 5 feet was the closest spacing that could be used to avoid excessive damage from mildew. Some types of pole beans (cornfield beans) are planted with corn, and the cornstalks serve as supports for the vines.

The depth of planting varies, but beans should be planted no deeper than necessary to get the seed in the moist soil. The depth should be less on heavy than on light soils. In humid regions, 1 to 2 inches deep on heavy soils and 2 to 3 inches on light soils are usual.

Supporting Pole Beans. Poles 8 to 9 feet in length are employed in some areas for supporting the climbing varieties of beans. The bark and stubs of small branches are left on the poles as a rough surface is an advantage to the plant. The poles are usually set in the ground to a depth of 18 to 24 inches before the beans are planted. Where the pole beans are planted in hills the poles are set into the ground at an angle and are set several inches deep. The tops of four poles are usually tied together, forming a tepee-like arrangement of poles. The poles are removed after the crop has been harvested and last for several years if stored under cover. In Florida a cultivated weed, sesbania, is grown for use as poles for supporting beans. The poles are light but are sufficiently strong for one season. They are usually tied together at the top, and after the crop has been harvested the sesbania poles can be disked into the soil.

Various sorts of trellis supports are used in the main pole bean–producing areas and are constructed after the beans have been planted. Heavy posts are set at the end of the rows; lighter posts or stakes are set at intervals of about 20 feet; then 2 strands of No. 10 wire are fastened to the posts, one at the top and one near the ground. Light twine is used to connect the two wires. The twine is fastened to the lower wire, then is passed over the upper wire and back under the lower one, and continued in a zigzag fashion to the end of the row. The bean plants twine around the string until they reach the upper wire. This method of supporting vines makes picking easy but requires a lot of labor in construction. In most areas the poles are set with a hydraulic attachment on tractors. Another tractor-mounted machine follows which strings out the strands of wire with the twine wrapped around them. The wire is stapled to the poles by workmen following the machine. These machines greatly reduce the expense of building trellises and the time required to do so.

Cultivation. Clean, shallow cultivation should be practiced. Deep cultivation is likely to cause injury by destroying the roots near the surface. Experiments carried on for 3 years at Ithaca, N.Y., show no benefits for the soil mulch. Good shallow cultivation was compared with merely scraping the surface to keep down weeds. There were three plots in each treatment, and the results were consistent and showed no benefit from the cultivation other than weed control.

A study of the root system showed that most of the roots were in the surface 6 to 8 inches of soil, with some 1½ to 2 inches deep. The main root zone was between the depths of 3 and 8 inches from the surface. The roots were fairly plentiful 24 inches below the surface, especially immediately under the row, and some reached the depth of 30 inches.

When the plants reach full size, cultivation is likely to do more harm than good unless there is considerable weed growth. Cultivation should not be given when the vines are wet, since the spores of the fungus causing anthracnose are easily carried from diseased to healthy plants at such times.

Chemical Weed Control. Many bean growers use chemical herbicides to control the weeds in the row and eliminate the hand hoeing that is sometimes necessary. Dinitro materials are sprayed on the soil at rates of from 3 to 6 pounds per acre before the beans emerge. In warm weather the spray can be applied immediately after planting the beans, but in cooler weather it is best to delay the spraying until just before the beans emerge. The usual practice is to spray a band about 1 foot wide directly over the row, since the weeds between the rows can be controlled with the tractor cultivators. This spray kills all annual weeds that emerge within 2 or 3 weeks after application and, unless the soil is stirred up, eliminates weeds for the rest of the season. Where perennial or late-germinating weeds are a problem, the dinitro sprays are not successful. The amount of dinitro materials used varies with the area and soil type. On light soils in hot weather, the beans may be damaged if excessive amounts are used. The amount of material to apply can be learned from local agricultural authorities.

Varieties. Bean varieties are listed under hundreds of names, many of which are synonyms. Many of the listed varieties are of little importance now but were important in the past. Each year new varieties are introduced which replace presently popular varieties. Bean varieties have been classified on the basis of seed, pod, blossom, and plant characteristics by different workers.

Varieties of beans may be classed according to their uses as: (1) snap beans, those grown for the edible pod, (2) green-shell beans, those used in the green-shelled condition, and (3) dry-shell beans, or ripe seed, those used in the dry state. Beans are also classed according to the color of the pods as green-podded and yellow- or wax-podded. For convenience in grouping, they are divided into dwarf or bush varieties and climbing or pole varieties and as field and garden beans. The term *field beans* is usually applied to those grown for use in the dry state and includes four types: kidney, marrow, medium, and pea.

The medium-type field bean is the most important in terms of quantity produced. The Pinto bean is pinkish buff with small dark-brown blotches and is grown in the Southwestern states, mainly Colorado and New Mexico. Great Northern is a white bean grown mainly in Nebraska, Wyoming, Montana, and Idaho, but the production has decreased while Pinto has increased. Sutter, Pink, Bayo, and Small Red, or Red Mexican, are also important in the Western states. There are many improved strains of these varieties which have more desirable characteristics than the older types.

Pea, or navy beans are second to the medium types in total production. The most important varieties are Michelite, Robust, and Monroe, which are all resistant to mosaic. They are grown mainly in Michigan and New York. The Small White is grown in California.

Red Kidney beans are grown mainly in New York, Michigan, and California. There are many strains which have certain improved characteristics. Much of the California production is for seed purposes. Of minor importance are Mahogany Red Kidney, grown in Michigan, and White Kidney, grown in New York.

The marrow types are not widely grown. Yellow Eye is grown in New York and New England, Perry Marrow in New York, and Cranberry in California.

Green-shell beans are of little importance but are popular in certain areas, especially New England. Low's Champion, French Horticultural, Dwarf Horticultural, Brilliant, and Flash are popular bush varieties, and London Horticultural and Red Cranberry are pole types.

There are many varieties of snap beans grown commercially, and new varieties appear each year. The variety to grow depends on the location where grown and the use for which they are intended. A good fresh-market variety may be unacceptable to a processor, and vice versa. The flat- and oval-podded varieties are used mostly for fresh market. Canners favor round-podded varieties with long straight pods and white seeds since dark seed coats discolor the liquid in the can and detract from the appearance of the product. Small quantities of flat-podded varieties are processed as sliced, or "French-style," beans.

Wax- or yellow-podded bush types are grown for market and, to some extent, for processing. Cherokee Wax, Pencil Pod Black Wax, and Brittle Wax are popular market varieties, and Kinghorn Special is the leading variety for processing. The latter is almost identical with Brittle Wax except that it has white seeds.

Green-podded bush types are the most widely grown snap beans. They are grown for market and processing in all sections where beans are grown. Bountiful and Plentiful are flat-podded early varieties for market and are used by processors for sliced, or French-style, beans. Stringless Black Valentine has long oval pods and is a popular market variety since it holds its quality well after picking. Dixie Belle, Florida Belle, and Contender are similar varieties with resistance to some of the important bean diseases. They are popular in Southern areas where bean diseases are most troublesome. The most popular round-podded types for processing are Stringless Green Pod, or Tendergreen, and related varieties, such as Supergreen, Tenderlong, Tenderpod, King Green, and Slendergreen. Similar varieties with outstanding resistance to certain diseases include Rival, Logan, Ranger, Seminole, Top Crop, and Tenderlong 15. The Refugee types were popular processing varieties at one time, but they mature later than the above-mentioned varieties and have a dense foliage which makes picking difficult. They are still grown in some areas to extend the canning season.

Pole, or climbing, types are grown in areas where the season is long enough to obtain enough pickings to justify the expense of supporting the vines. Most of the processing beans in Washington and Oregon are the Blue Lake variety which has round pods with white seeds and are an excellent processing type. Many strains of Blue Lake have been developed which have resistance to some diseases. Kentucky Wonder is an old standard home-garden pole bean, and White Seed Kentucky Wonder 191 is grown in California for the fresh market. McCaslan, an early white-seeded pole bean, is grown in Florida for the fresh market. White Creaseback (Blue Lake) is popular in Southern areas as a home-garden and market bean.

Harvesting Snap Beans. Snap beans are usually harvested before the pods are full-grown and while the seeds are small. Most varieties become tough and stringy if left on the plants until the seed develops to considerable size. All varieties should be harvested before the seeds are large enough to cause the pod to bulge around the seeds since the market price is much lower when seed development is visible externally. Snap beans are usually ready for harvest 12 to 14 days after the first blossoms have opened, but the time required varies with weather conditions. Since all of the blossoms do not open on the same day, there is considerable variation in the size of the beans at the time of harvest. As harvest is delayed the total yield increases, but the quality decreases rapidly after seed development is visible. The time of harvest is a compromise between total yield and high quality and should be made at such time that the grower will obtain the maximum yield of high-quality beans. Picking is usually done by hand, and amount of labor required restricts large-scale production to localities which can obtain a sufficient supply of labor at the right time. Transient labor housed in labor camps is used in many regions. In large commercial plantings of the bush-type snap bean two pickings are made, but in some instances there is only one picking. Mechanical pickers have been developed for use with bush types of snap beans and do a satisfactory job of picking, but some varieties are better adapted to mechanical harvesting than others. The machine destroys most of the foliage on the plant, and only one picking is possible. Most growers make the first picking by hand and use the machine for the second picking. Pole beans blossom over a long period of time, and harvests are made at intervals of two to five days, depending upon the quality desired and weather conditions.

In large-scale operations, snap beans grown for market are hauled to packing sheds in field containers and are run through a machine that blows out leaves and other debris. The beans then are carried over movable belts where workers pick out trash and pods that are not suitable for market. The beans are packed in baskets or wire-bound boxes for marketing. In some areas consumer packages are put up in transparent-film bags. When grown for processing the beans are usually hauled direct from the field to the processing plant where they are cleaned and sorted into sizes by machinery.

There has been some interest in spraying beans with various chemicals to delay the development of seed and provide a higher-quality product without numerous pickings. Mitchell and Marth (1950) reported that beans sprayed four days before harvest with 4-chlorophenoxyacetic acid were delayed in maturity. The spray reduced water loss from the pods and slowed down undesirable color changes of the pods while in storage. Guyer and Kramer (1951) sprayed beans with para-chlorophenoxyacetic acid when they had reached the 4 per cent seed stage of maturity. The final yield was not affected by the spray, and development of seed and fiber was retarded. However, the quality of the processed product was reduced because of undesirable changes in color, flavor, and shape of pods. Many pods were blistered and spongy as a result of the spray. Spraying the plants at the 4 per cent seed stage with maleic hydrazide retarded development of seed and fiber, but greatly reduced yield and grade of the beans.

Snap beans can be kept in storage for several days at about 40°F. and at humidities above 90 per cent. Results of experiments by Platenius, *et al.* (1934) show that beans kept better at 40°F. than at either 32 or 50°F. When beans are transported long distances during warm weather they are shipped in refrigerated cars. Hydrocooling the beans immediately after harvest has given good results provided the beans are kept refrigerated after hydrocooling.

Harvesting Dry Beans. Dry beans are harvested as soon as a large percentage of the pods is fully matured and has turned yellow. As most varieties do not ripen evenly, it is desirable to watch the field and to begin harvesting before the lower pods get dry enough to shatter. Some varieties shatter more than others. In dry areas, where irrigation is practiced, it is possible to mature the beans rapidly by withholding water. In humid regions, rains cause much damage owing to the rotting of pods and discoloration of white varieties of beans. The drying process can be speeded by applying chemical defoliants or desiccants when the beans are almost mature. The most common chemicals used are potassium cyanate and borate-chlorate mixtures. Potassium cyanate is a desiccant and causes the leaves to dry quickly without dropping. It is useful when the beans are nearly mature and where the fields are very weedy. Low concentrations of borate-chlorate mixtures are good defoliants and cause the leaves to drop gradually. They can be applied before the beans are mature with good success. The beans are allowed to dry standing until they are ready for harvest and the danger of discoloration due to rainfall is minimized. When the beans are sufficiently dry they are pulled in the morning when wet with dew and combined later in the day.

The bean plants are pulled with bean harvesters which are equipped with cutting bars to cut off the plants below the surface of the ground. Guard rods attached above the cutting bars move the bean plants into a single row after they have been cut. Two to four rows are cut at one time, and the vines are left in the windrow until they are dry enough for threshing. Formerly, beans were stacked in small stacks in the field, but this practice has become obsolete because of the large amount of hand labor involved.

Threshing Dry Beans. Beans are commonly threshed with machines similar to grain threshers. The common type of thresher used for beans has two cylinders which will run at lower speeds than is common in threshing wheat and rye, etc. Grain threshers are sometimes used, but they are unsatisfactory even when the speed is reduced. In some areas, the beans are left in the windrow until thoroughly cured, and then they are picked up by a mobile threshing machine either self-propelled or pulled by a tractor. In other areas, the beans are loaded on wagons and hauled into a stationary thresher. Thresher injury is severe on certain varieties of garden beans and Lima beans. According to Harter (1930), the epicotyl is fractured just below the plumule, and this results in a condition known as *baldhead,* in which the growing point and part or all of the primary leaves are absent in the seedling plant. Baldhead plants produce few or no pods. When beans are grown for seed purposes, extreme care must be taken during the harvest and threshing operations to prevent seed injury.

Diseases. Beans are subject to several serious diseases such as anthracnose, bacterial blight, mosaic, dry root rot, and rust and also to a few of minor importance.

ANTHRACNOSE. This disease is caused by the fungus *Colletotrichum lindemuthianum,* which attacks the stems, leaves, pods, and seeds. On the stems and leaf veins it causes elongated, sunken, dark-red cankers. On the pods the disease causes rounded or irregular sunken spots with pink centers surrounded by a darker-reddish border. In severe cases the pod may be entirely covered by the spots and produce no seed. In other cases the fungus penetrates the pods and enters the seed, causing dark spots. Diseased seeds carry the fungus from season to season.

Prior to 1920 anthracnose was the most destructive bean disease. No satisfactory control measures have been discovered to stop the spread of the disease once it is started. Only a few varieties of beans are resistant to the disease. The use of seed grown in areas where the disease does not occur is the only practical means of control. The widespread use of seed grown in California, Idaho, and Wyoming has been so successful in eliminating the disease that there is little interest in developing resistant varieties.

BACTERIAL BLIGHTS. These are bacterial diseases caused by any one of several species and varieties of bacteria, whose life histories are much the same. The disease appears on the leaves as large brown blotches, often bordered by a yellow or reddish halo. The stem may be girdled at one of the lower nodes, in which case the entire plant dies. On the pod, cankers develop as water-soaked spots usually with reddish margins. Infected seed may or may not be discolored.

Bacterial blights are controlled in the same way as anthracnose by obtaining seed from regions that are free from the diseases, as parts of California and Idaho. Only a few bean varieties are resistant to any of the bacterial blights, but better varieties are being introduced from time to time. Among the snap beans Fullgreen has good resistance, while Dixie Belle and Logan have some degree of tolerance to halo blight (*Pseudomonas phaseolicola*). Several varieties of dry beans, Pinto, Great Northern, Red Mexican, and Michelite, have good resistance to halo blight, but no variety of beans has resistance to common blight (*Xanthomonas phaseoli*) or to fuscous blight (*X. phaseoli* var. *fuscous*).

MOSAICS. There are three important bean mosaic diseases, each caused by a different strain of virus. The leaves are ruffled and crinkled and have mottled yellow areas between normal green areas in various patterns. The pods from infected plants may be rough, curved, or deformed. Common bean mosaic and its variant, New York 15, are carried in seed from diseased plants and may be transmitted from diseased to healthy plants by aphids. One or more of these diseases occur wherever beans are grown. The yellow bean mosaic is mainly a disease of sweet clover, red clover, crimson clover, and gladiolus and is spread from these crops to beans by aphids.

The only means of control is to control the aphids which transmit the virus and to grow resistant varieties. No variety of beans is resistant to the yellow bean mosaic, but many are resistant to the common and New York 15 virus. Some of these are Rival, Top Crop, Contender, Logan, Supergreen, Tenderlong 15, Florida Belle, Stringless Blue Lake, and Kentucky Wonder among the snap beans; Robust, Michelite, Monroe, and various strains of Pinto, Red Mexican, and Great Northern among the dry beans.

ROOT ROTS. Root rots occur wherever beans are grown but cause more damage in the older bean-growing areas of the Eastern United States than in the West. At least four different organisms cause root rots, and all are fungi which live in the soil for long periods of time. Damage to the plant is greatest in cool weather when the soil is cold and wet. The plants are stunted, sometimes yellowed, and usually wilt during warm weather. The plant may not die, but it does not produce a full crop.

The only effective control is long rotations, 4 or 5 years of crops that are not damaged by the organisms, such as small grains, clover, and alfalfa. Improving drainage and soil structure helps prevent damage. Strict attention should be paid to fertilizer applications. A high level of fertility helps the plant recover from a mild attack, but fertilizer in contact with the seed delays come-up and accentuates the effects of the disease.

RUST. This is a serious disease of dry beans in irrigated areas of Colorado, Wyoming, Nebraska, and Montana and causes serious losses in pole beans in Oregon, Washington, Florida, and California. The organism (*Uromyces phaseoli typica*) usually attacks the leaves and is favored by high relative humidity. The leaves are covered with small reddish-brown spore masses. Within a few days after the rust pustules appear, the leaf begins to turn yellow, then brown, and dries up and drops off. The organism lives over winter in old bean straw, and the spores are spread in the spring by wind.

Dusting the plants with sulfur gives some measure of control, but several applications may be needed. Most varieties of bush snap beans are tolerant of rust, especially Florida Belle, Dixie Belle, Plentiful, and Fullgreen. The most widely grown pole bean varieties are susceptible to rust, but Kentucky Wonder No. 4 and No. 191 are tolerant. All of the commercial varieties of dry beans are susceptible to most races of rust.

Bean Insects. Many insects attack the bean, the most important being the Mexican bean beetle, the bean weevil, bean leaf beetle, bean thrips, bean aphis, and the bean fly, or seed-corn maggot.

MEXICAN BEAN BEETLE (*Epilachna varivestis*). This is the most serious insect pest attacking growing beans in regions where it is abundant. It is a serious pest in most of the important bean-growing sections of the United States.

The Mexican bean beetle feeds mainly on the common bean and the Lima bean, but if these are not present the insect will feed on cowpeas, soybeans, alfalfa, sweet clover, and beggarweed. Both the adult and the larva are injurious, and when present in abundance, they feed on all parts of the plant. The larva feeds entirely on the underside of the leaf and eats the epidermis of the blade, leaving the midribs and veins and usually the upper epidermis. The adult also feeds from the underside but frequently eats through the upper surface.

The adult beetle is nearly hemispherical in shape, about $\frac{1}{4}$ inch long and $\frac{1}{5}$ inch wide. The color of the adult ranges from orange to copper. Each of the two wing covers bears eight black spots. The larva is orange-colored, varies in length from about $\frac{1}{20}$ inch when young to about $\frac{1}{3}$ inch when full-grown, and is covered with long branched spines.

The insect can be controlled by spraying or dusting the undersides of the leaves with an insecticide as soon as the beetles are noticed. The materials commonly used are rotenone, parathion, malathion, and cryolite.

BEAN WEEVIL (*Bruchus obtectus*). This insect is a small dull-colored beetle found in stored beans. The eggs are laid in the pods in the field, and the larvae or grubs develop in the seeds and transform into beetles in cavities just under the seed coat. The beetle cuts a circular opening through the seed coat in emerging. Several beetles may develop in a single seed. In the South there may be six or more generations in a year, but in the North there is usually only one. Where there is more than one generation, the breeding may be continuous in storage. The number of generations depends on the temperature.

Beans infested with weevils should not be planted since the germination is likely to be poor. The weevils in the beans can be killed by fumigating with carbon disulfide at the rate of 3 to 8 pounds to each 1,000 cubic feet of space to be fumigated, the amount to be used varying with the tightness of the container and the temperature. The liquid should be poured over the top of the seeds to be fumigated. It quickly vaporizes, and the gas, being heavier than air, sinks to the bottom of the container, filling the air spaces. For best results, the temperature should be 75°F. or above. It is not effective at 60°F. or below. For fumigating small quantities, place the beans in a tight receptacle and use 1 ounce to each bushel to be fumigated. Heating the beans to 130°F. for 30 minutes also destroys the weevil. At low temperatures the insects do not feed and cause damage; hence cold storage prevents injury. A 3 per cent DDT dust mixed at the rate of ½ ounce to each bushel of beans is also effective in preventing weevil injury, but should be used only on seed beans. It should not be used on beans to be eaten by human beings.

In addition to the common bean weevil there are several other species that attack beans, but the same control measures are effective for all of them.

BEAN LEAF BEETLE (*Cerotoma trifurcata*). This insect is a small beetle, about ⅓ inch long, yellowish to reddish, and has six black dots on the wing covers. The beetles eat large holes in the leaves, feeding from the underside. The eggs are laid on the ground at the base of the plant, and the grubs feed on the roots and the main stem just below the surface. From one to three broods occur each year, depending on the length of the growing season.

Dusting or spraying, as recommended for the Mexican bean beetle, is effective in controlling this insect.

BEAN THRIPS (*Heliothrips fasciatus*). In the Far West this insect sometimes injures the bean crop seriously. The adult insect is about 1/25 inch long, grayish in color. Infested leaves of the bean plant turn pale and drop off. The pod takes on a silvery-white appearance.

Thorough coverage of the plant with DDT or parathion results in good control if the insecticide is applied before the number of insects is very large.

BEAN APHID (*Aphis rumicis*) is a small black plant louse, widely distributed, but is especially injurious in California. The insect passes the winter in the egg stage on various cultivated shrubs. It feeds on many vegetables and on many common weeds.

The aphids may be controlled by spraying with parathion, malathion, TEPP, or nicotine.

SEED-CORN MAGGOT (*Hylemyia cilicrura*). The adult fly is somewhat smaller than the housefly and is greenish gray in color. The larva is a small white maggot, about ¼ inch in length. It feeds on the sprouting seeds and on the plumule. Later it burrows into the cotyledons and sometimes through the radicle.

This insect can be controlled by coating the seed with an insecticide, such as chlordane, lindane, dieldrin, or aldrin, applied as a methocel slurry. The insecticide coating is applied by most seed companies, and a fungicide is usually included. This treatment gives good results in most cases, but some maggot damage may occur if come-up is delayed by placing fertilizer in contact with the seed or by planting the seed too deep.

LIMA BEAN

Green Lima beans (*Phaseolus lunatus*) are grown for home use, for fresh markets, and for canning and freezing in various parts of the United States, southern Canada, and Latin America. The acreage for fresh market in the United States has been decreasing steadily since about 1940. In 1953, 1,433,000 bushels valued at $4,045,000 was marketed from 18,500 acres. The leading states were Georgia, Florida, New Jersey, and South Carolina. The increased popularity of frozen Lima beans and the high cost of picking for fresh market have caused the decline in acreage. The frozen pack (138,595,000 pounds) in 1953 was second to peas in quantity frozen. The acreage of Lima beans for processing more than doubled from 1940 to 1953. The estimated acreage in 1953 was 109,190 acres, producing 105,900 tons of shelled beans valued at $16,206,000. The states leading in acreage for processing in 1953 were California, with 27,600 acres, Delaware with 21,500 acres, and Wisconsin with 8,200 acres.

Lima beans for use in the dry-shelled state are grown mainly in California. According to figures published by the U.S. Department of Agriculture[1] the average annual production for the 3 years 1951–1953 was 1,844,000 bags of 100 pounds each. About two-thirds of the production was the large-seeded, or standard, Lima, and the remainder the small-seeded, or baby, type.

History and Taxonomy. Linnaeus believed that the Lima bean was of African origin, but it is now known to be of tropical American origin. The fact that seeds of Lima beans have been found in Peruvian tombs and that the plant has been found growing wild in Brazil led some authorities to believe in South American origin. Mackie (1943) presents evidence suggesting Guatamalan origin, and distribution from there in three directions in pre-Columbian times. The three lines of distribution follow the trade routes, and according to Mackie, one of the routes was northwestward through Mexico into the Southwestern part of the United States. A second route was along western slopes of the mountains to the lowlands of the Isthmus of Tehuantepec, across to the coast of the Gulf of Mexico, and easterly across Yucatàn, thence to the islands of the West Indies. The third route was southward through Central America, Colombia, and Ecuador to its final termination in Peru.

Some authorities consider the large-seeded and the small-seeded Lima beans as belonging to two species, while others consider them as belonging to a single species. Both the small-seeded and the large-seeded types of Lima beans have climbing and bush, or dwarf, forms. Many other characters which were once considered distinctive are found in both types. Mackie (1943) presented considerable evidence in favor of the one-species concept, and this concept is followed here.

Climatic Requirement. The Lima bean is a tender plant that will not stand frost, and the seed will not germinate if the soil temperature is much below 60°F. It requires a longer growing season than the common varieties of snap beans, but this is due, in part, to the fact that it is grown for seed whereas snap beans are grown for the pods. Pole varieties require a longer season than do the bush varieties. In fact, the pole varieties of the large-seeded types do not produce a satisfactory crop in regions having less than 4 months frost-free period with warm weather a considerable part of this period. On the other hand, one of the serious problems in growing Lima beans is the failure of the blossoms to set seed during hot weather. Atmospheric humidity and soil moisture are also important during the pod-setting period. The main production areas of the Fordhook and other large-seeded types are the coastal regions of southern California and on Long Island. The small-seeded types, such as Henderson, can be grown successfully over a much wider range of climatic conditions.

[1] *Agricultural Statistics,* 1953.

Marth and Wester (1954) reported that spraying Fordhook 242 Lima beans with 1½ or 3 parts per million of 2,4,5-T resulted in blossom drop and cessation of vegetative growth for a period of 20 to 30 days. When growth resumed, the plants were very bushy and blossomed profusely and produced larger yields than the unsprayed plants. The increase in yield resulted from the plants flowering during favorable weather for pod set and high yields. The same yield was obtained when the flowering was delayed by manual defloration. This type of spray offers some possibility for use when weather conditions are unfavorable and only a few of the pods set. Spraying the plants with 2,4 5-T would cause drop of the young pods and remaining flowers and delay further flowering until weather conditions might be more favorable.

Soils and Fertilizers. In general, the soils suitable for snap beans are satisfactory for Lima beans, but in regions having a short growing season, light soils are preferable to heavy ones provided that other conditions are favorable. Where the growing season is long, loams and silt loams are preferred to the sands and sandy loams because of greater water retention. Lima beans are more sensitive to excessive soil acidity than are snap beans and should be grown on soils where the pH is maintained between 6.0 and 6.5. Poorly drained and poorly aerated soils seldom produce profitable crops of Lima beans. The fertilizer requirement for Lima beans is similar to that of snap beans, but it is probable that the former can use more nitrogen to advantage than the latter. Tiedjens and Schermerhorn (1939) published results of experiments in New Jersey which indicated that the Fordhook variety has a higher requirement for nitrogen than the small-seeded varieties. In California, nitrogen is the only fertilizer used on Lima beans. Manure is applied in the fall at rates of 300 to 1,000 cubic feet per acre, and the beans are fertilized with as much as 250 pounds of actual nitrogen per acre after planting. Lima bean seeds are very sensitive to injury from excessive soluble salts resulting from too much fertilizer or fertilizer placed too close to the seed. Best responses are obtained with the fertilizer banded near the seed, but it should be about 3 inches from the seed so that danger from injury is minimized.

Planting. Since the Lima bean seed will not germinate but will rot in cold soils, it should not be planted until the soil is warmed up. In cool soils the emergence is slow and uneven and there is the danger of damage by diseases and insects. Toole, Wester, and Toole (1951) studied the germination of Lima beans at various soil temperatures. Poor stands due to attack by rhizoctonia resulted when the seed was planted in unsterilized soil at 59°F. and the stand was improved by soil sterilization. At higher soil temperatures, 68 and 86°F., the effect of rhizoctonia was less noticable since the beans emerged more rapidly than at 59°F.

There was some improvement in come-up in the sterilized soil at the high temperatures, but the effect was not as great as at the low temperatures. At soil temperatures of 59°F. the hard seeds had not germinated 21 days after planting.

Another common cause for poor stands is mechanical damage during threshing and milling operations in the seed house. This type of mechanical damage is not visible to the naked eye, but parts of the embryo may be broken or the cotyledons may be broken from the embryo. Further mechanical damage occurs in the planter if it is not properly designed to handle Lima bean seed. High-speed operation of planters causes considerable mechanical damage and reduces the stand in the field. In California the Ventura-type indent-cup planter is used for all Lima beans. This planter has small cups which lift up single Lima bean seeds and drop them into the furrow and causes less mechanical damage than other types of planters. With other types of planters special seed plates for Lima beans should be used to obtain the desired spacing and the tractor should be driven at low speed to prevent excessive mechanical damage. The seed should be planted only 1 or 2 inches deep in heavy soils and slightly deeper in light soils. Warren (1950) found no difference between planting 1 or 2 inches deep, but planting 4 inches deep reduced the stand and the yield.

Planting distances between rows and in the row vary widely. Pole varieties grown for harvesting in the green-shell stage frequently are planted in hills 3 by 3 or 4 by 4 feet apart with three to four seeds per hill for training on poles. Another method is to plant the seed from 6 to 12 inches apart in the row and support the vines on string or wire, as mentioned for climbing varieties of snap beans. In California, where the climbing or running varieties are grown for dry beans, the plants are allowed to grow on the ground. Since they are grown during the dry season in California, there is little or no injury to the pods from contact with the soil. Bush varieties of Lima beans are planted in rows 28 to 36 inches apart in most regions, with the plants 2 to 8 inches apart in the row. Most experiments indicate that the small-seeded varieties can be planted closer together than the large-seeded ones. Usually, large-seeded types, such as Fordhook, are planted 4 to 6 inches apart in the row, while the Henderson or other small-seeded types are planted from 3 to 5 inches apart in the row. The amount of seed required to plant an acre is about 120 to 150 pounds for the large-seeded types and 50 to 70 pounds for the small-seeded types.

Varieties. All of the Lima beans grown for processing and most of those grown for market are the dwarf, or bush, types. The climbing, or pole, varieties are grown mostly for home-garden use or limited fresh-market sales. There are two distinct seed types among Lima beans, known to the trade as baby Limas (the small, thin-seeded types), best represented by Henderson, and the potato types (the large, thick-seeded types), represented by Fordhook.

Most of the bush Lima bean acreage is made up of two varieties and selections from these varieties: Henderson Bush Lima and Fordhook. Henderson is fairly resistant to unfavorable environmental conditions and is grown in areas where other types are not likely to succeed. Cangreen and Thorogreen are similar to Henderson in all respects except that these two types have green cotyledons rather than white.

Fordhook has been largely replaced by Fordhook 242 and Concentrated Fordhook. Fordhook 242 is more vigorous and more resistant to hot weather than is Fordhook. The pod set of Concentrated Fordhook is concentrated both in time and position on the plant and is widely grown for freezing in California. Evergreen, Triumph, and Peerless have small thick seeds and usually are classed as "baby potato" types. The seed is similar to Fordhook except that it is much smaller.

Challenger is a Fordhook-type pole Lima bean. King of the Garden is a popular climbing variety in home gardens and has large but thin seeds. The most important climbing variety is the Carolina, or Sieva, the butter bean of the South, which is quite resistant to drought and hot weather.

The varieties grown for production of dry Lima beans in California are Ventura, Wilbur, and Weston, all of which are climbing types but are allowed to run on the ground. The dry beans of the Ventura variety are known as standard Limas and are large thin beans. The dry baby limas, which are small thin seeds, are produced from Weston and Wilbur. Weston is resistant to nematodes and is gradually replacing Wilbur in some areas.

Harvesting. Green Lima beans for the market are picked by hand when the seeds have become nearly full grown but before the pods begin to turn yellow. Usually several pickings are made, and the high cost of hand picking limits the acreage of green Limas for market. Those grown for processing are cut with mowing machines, and the vines are hauled to the vining station or to the cannery where the beans are shelled by machinery. In some areas, self-propelled viners are used, so that only the shelled beans are hauled to the cannery or freezing plant.

Since Lima beans flower over a fairly long period of time, there are beans in all stages of maturity on the vines when harvested for processing. The greatest weight of beans per acre could be obtained if harvest was delayed until the youngest pods were mature. This is not practical since the oldest pods will be far past the stage desired for processing. Harvesting is a compromise of yield and quality, with the highest yield of top-quality beans being obtained when the beans show 3 to 5 per cent white seeds. The seeds are not satisfactory for canning or freezing after they turn white. As the seeds mature, the starch content increases and the sugar content decreases and the color of the seed changes from a dark to pale green, then to white.

Dry Lima beans are harvested in much the same way as common field beans. In California, a cutter is used which cuts four rows at a time about 2 or 3 inches under the soil. The vines are brought together in windrows which consist of eight field rows. The cutting and windrowing are done when the pods are toughened by dew, usually at night or in the early-morning hours. The vines are allowed to dry about 10 days in the windrow and are threshed with self-propelled threshers. The threshed beans are bulk-handled in large boxes with fork-lift tractors.

Preparation of Green Lima Beans for Market. Lima beans to be sold in a fresh condition should be picked as soon as the beans have attained full size and before they turn white. The high cost of hand picking limits the acreage that is grown. Although the beans keep better in the pods, some markets demand them as shelled beans. There are small machines on the market which will shell beans in the pod, but the mechanical shelling usually results in considerable bruising and splitting of the seed coat so that appearance suffers and storage life is reduced. Shelled green Lima beans are subject to spotting and stickiness, which could be avoided by marketing in the pods. Brooks and McCulloch (1938) have shown that the spotting is caused by fungus and the stickiness by bacteria, both of which are spread to the beans in the process of shelling. Lowering the humidity of the storage atmosphere resulted in a decrease of both stickiness and spotting, but did not give satisfactory control. Washing the beans in a 30 per cent solution of ethyl alcohol or in a 4 per cent solution of chlorinated lime gave complete control of spotting and good commercial control of the stickiness. Recently there has been interest in marketing shelled Lima beans in consumer packages. Scott and Mahoney (1946) have shown that packaged beans stayed in acceptable condition for 11 days at 28 and 32°F. At higher temperatures the quality deteriorated more rapidly than at the temperatures mentioned. They found that there was a loss in ascorbic acid in storage, and the greatest loss was during the first part of the storage period. At low temperatures the beans retained about two-thirds of the ascorbic acid for 11 days.

Diseases. Lima beans are not seriously affected by disease in most regions. In some sections downy mildew, bacterial spot, pod spot, and leaf blight cause considerable losses in some years.

DOWNY MILDEW. This disease is caused by *Phytophthora phaseoli* Thaxt. It is primarily injurious to the pods, attacking them in all stages of growth from flower to maturity. The older, diseased pods show the thick white growth of mycelium that is characteristic of downy mildew. This is the most destructive disease of Lima beans on the Atlantic Coast.

Long rotations, destruction of the diseased vines at the end of the season, and selection of seed free from the disease are important control measures. Spraying with Bordeaux mixture or dusting with copper-lime dust (20-80) is suggested as a supplement to the other control measures. The insoluble, or fixed, coppers may be used instead of the Bordeaux mixture.

Organic fungicides of the nabam, zineb, and maneb groups are satisfactory also if applied at frequent intervals. These materials cause less foliage injury than copper fungicides. The fungus grows rapidly in cool damp weather and is difficult to control under such conditions.

BACTERIAL SPOT. This disease is caused by *Pseudomonas syringae*. It attacks all the aboveground portions of the plant, causing the development of lesions of a reddish-brown color. The most serious phases of the disease on Long Island are on the pods. The young diseased pods often drop off the plant, resulting in a reduction in yield.

The bacterium causes blight of lilac, wild cherry, and several other plants. Lilac and wild cherry are the main source of inoculum in most regions, and it spreads rapidly from these sources during warm, rainy periods. The materials used for control of downy mildew will control bacterial spot also. Lilac and wild cherry should be eliminated from hedgerows around the fields.

POD SPOT OR LEAF BLIGHT. This disease, caused by *Diaporthe phaseolorum*, produces brown patches on the leaves and on the older pods. The fungus lives on the seed and on the old refuse in the soil. Control measures suggested for the other diseases of Lima beans are recommended for this disease where it is important enough to justify them.

Insects. The same insects that attack snap beans also attack Lima beans. The same control measures are recommended.

PEAS

Peas are grown for home use by home gardeners and for market by market gardeners in many areas. The pea crop for processing is exceeded in value only by tomatoes. It is the leading vegetable in frozen foods, constituting about one-fifth of the total pack of frozen vegetables in 1953.

Statistics of Production. The acreage and production of peas for fresh market increased from 1918 until 1939, as shown in Table 23.3. Since 1939 the acreage and production have steadily declined. In 1953, the acreage was only 12,570 acres and the production was 1,345,000 bushels of peas in the shell. California grew about one-half of the fresh-market pea acreage, and the other important areas were Colorado, Texas, and New York. The decline in fresh-market pea production has been due to the high cost of hand picking and the increase in use of frozen peas. The consumer will not pay high prices for peas in the pod when comparable quality can be obtained in the frozen product.

Table 23.3. Estimated Average Annual Acreage, Production, and Value of Green Peas Grown for Market, 1918–1953

Years	Acres	Yield per acre, bushels	Production, bushels (000 omitted)	Price per bushel	Value (000 omitted)
1918–1927	24,279	73	1,793	$2.04	$ 3,631
1928–1937	97,197	76	7,373	1.31	9,442
1938–1947	76,784	88	6,743	1.73	11,002
1948–1953	23,933	103	2,614	2.58	5,225

The acreage of peas grown for processing fluctuates widely from year to year, but the trend has been markedly upward since 1918, as is shown in Table 23.4. In 1953, 430,640 acres of peas for processing was grown and the value of the crop was $43,473,000. Wisconsin was the leading state with 130,600 acres, followed by Washington, 58,900 acres; Minnesota, 56,500 acres; and Oregon, 46,400 acres. Illinois, New York, and Pennsylvania were also important producing areas. Most of the peas grown in the Western states are frozen, while the majority of the peas grown in other areas are canned. The frozen pack of peas in 1953 was 222,543,000 pounds, with 70 per cent of the pack coming from the Western states.

Table 23.4. Estimated Average Annual Acreage, Production, and Value of Peas Grown for Processing, 1918–1953

Year	Acreage	Yield, tons per acre	Production, tons	Price per ton	Value (000 omitted)
1918–1927	170,505	1.00	168,334	$59.83	$10,035
1928–1937	252,762	0.77	193,372	52.86	10,193
1938–1947	394,972	0.95	383,252	68.62	27,365
1948–1953	414,618	1.01	422,690	89.12	37,698

History and Taxonomy. The garden pea is of very ancient origin, and its wild prototype has never been found. The pea was grown by the ancient Romans and Greeks, and some historical writers believe that it was an ancient Egyptian plant. The plant was grown at the time of

Cato (149 B.C.). Hedrick (1928) states that the ancients did not distinguish carefully between peas, beans, vetches, chick-peas, and lentils. This makes it difficult to determine from the written accounts what plants were being discussed.

From the evidence available it seems fairly certain that the pea *Pisum sativum* has its origin in Europe and western Asia. The garden pea was grown in midddle and northern Europe in the Dark and Middle Ages. In England it was an important crop in the eleventh century.

In "Peas of New York," Hedrick divides *Pisum sativum* into six subspecies, the garden pea being listed as *P. sativum* subsp. *hortense* Asch and Graebn and the field pea as *P. sativum* subsp. *arvense* Poir. Edible-podded peas are found in both of these subspecies, but these are not of much importance in the United States.

Climatic Requirements. The garden pea thrives best in relatively cool weather and is grown in the South and in the warmer parts of California during the fall, winter, and early spring. The only regions where peas are grown successfully during midsummer and late summer are those having relatively low temperatures and a good rainfall or where irrigation is practiced. The most important regions from which peas are marketed during the hottest part of the summer are the cool coastal sections of California, Washington, and Oregon; regions of high elevation in Colorado and other Western states; and in parts of New York and New England.

The seed will germinate at relatively low temperatures. The minimum temperature for germination is about 40°F., but the process proceeds slowly at this temperature and the time required for emergence decreases rapidly as the temperature increases. The optimum temperature for germination in about 75°F. At higher temperatures, while germination is rapid, loss of stand may result from various decay organisms present in the soil.

Boswell (1929) has shown that as temperature during the growing season rises the yield drops off rapidly. This fact explains the reasons for low yield of late-planted peas in regions where they are planted in the spring. Vittum and Hamson (1954) found that the highest yield of peas in New York was obtained when the peas were planted during the first 2 weeks of April. For each 2 weeks delay in planting after that date, the yield decreased about 400 pounds of shelled peas per acre. Walker (1929) has shown that the yield of peas per acre in Erie County, N.Y., was closely correlated with the rainfall during the month of June. The correlation coefficient was $+0.89 \pm 0.01$. These data are based on average yield per acre on an Erie County farm growing a large acreage of peas from 1914 to 1925. For each tenth of an inch variation in rainfall, there was an average variation in the yield of 4.4 bushels. All of the effect attributed to rainfall may not have been due to water alone since lower temperatures usually accompany rain during this period of the year.

Soils and Soil Preparation. Peas are grown on a great many kinds of soils, from the light sandy loams to the heavy clays. For a very early crop, a sandy loam is preferred. For large yields where earliness is not as important, a well-drained clay loam or silt loam is preferred. Good drainage is essential, for the pea plant will not thrive on soggy or water-soaked land. In regions where irrigation can be practiced, the texture of the soil is of little importance so long as the soil is well drained. Differences in the water-supplying power of various soil types are not so important where irrigation is available.

The pea plant does not thrive on highly acid soils. When the soil is more acid than pH 5.5 it is desirable to apply lime for the crop. The range of desirable reaction is between pH 5.5 and about 6.7. In Maine, peas are frequently grown on potato soils where the pH ranges from pH 5.0 to 5.3. It is impractical to lime the soils up to the desired pH for peas because this would result in scab on the succeeding crop of potatoes. Terman and Murphy (1952) reported that drilling 300 to 400 pounds of dolomitic limestone per acre with the seed gave increases in yield of about 600 pounds of shelled peas per acre when harvested at a tenderometer reading of 100 or less. This small amount of limestone applied in contact with the seed resulted in good early growth of the peas and increased the yield, but did not affect the soil reaction unfavorably for the following potato crop.

Thorough preparation is necessary for peas as for other vegetables. It is especially important where the seed is broadcast or planted with a grain drill since under these methods no cultivation is given the crop. Fall plowing is desirable for the early crop since planting often is delayed greatly when the land is plowed in the spring. The surface should be smooth and free from clods so that the drill plants all the seed at the same depth. Uneven come-up of the seed results in wide variations in maturity of the peas at harvest time. This increases the difficulty of timing the harvest and may result in a decrease in grade and price. When the crop is grown for the cannery, effort is made to leave the surface smooth by rolling either before or after planting or both, as a rough uneven surface interferes with the use of the harvesting machinery.

Fertilizers. In some of the important growing regions, peas are grown without fertilizer or with very small amounts. Talbot and Tavernetti (1934) reported that 200 to 300 pounds of superphosphate per acre resulted in increased yield in the Imperial Valley. Nitrogen and potash did not give any response. They state, also, that in the Salinas Valley some nitrogen should be applied in the fertilizer if manure is not used, and suggest 200 to 400 pounds of nitrate of soda or sulfate of ammonia per acre. Baur and Tremblay (1948) reported that the standard fertilizer for processing peas in Washington was 60 pounds of P_2O_5 and 60 pounds of K_2O per acre, banded or drilled before planting. There was no response to nitrogen fertilizers. In humid regions, a complete fertilizer is usually recommended. In the Northeastern states, the usual fertilizer application is 500 pounds of a 10-10-10, but on soils that are low in available phosphorus, a 1-2-1 ratio is used. Barnes and Clayton (1945) recommended 600 to 800 pounds of a 5-10-5 or 4-12-4 fertilizer per acre for peas grown on the coastal plain soils in South Carolina. Side-dressing with additional nitrogen did not give increases in yield.

Sayre (1946) has shown that nitrogen has a marked effect on yield and quality. Peas from plots well fertilized with nitrogenous fertilizers remained in good canning condition, as indicated by the tenderometer, longer than those in similar plots not fertilized or from those receiving only phosphorus and potash. Younkin *et al.* (1950) reported that increasing nitrogen fertilization increased the yield and the size of peas regardless of the rate of seeding. Increasing the rate of seeding reduced the size of the peas at low nitrogen levels but generally resulted in increases in yield. Fertilization with nitrogen may decrease the yield of small peas, even though the total yield increases.

Peas for processing are grown largely in rotation with general farm crops, and manure is used in the rotation or sod is turned under so that less fertilizer is needed than where cultivated crops only are grown. Since fertilizer represents only a minor part of the total production cost, it does not seem wise to reduce rates of fertilization unless there is good evidence that the high rates of fertilization do not pay.

The method of application of fertilizer is of great importance because severe injury results when the fertilizer is applied in contact with the seed. Sayre and Cummings (1936) suggest that it is better not to use fertilizer at all than to apply it in contact with the seed, as is a common practice when old grain drills are used. They recommend placing fertilizer in bands 2½ inches to the side and 1 inch deeper than the seed. When machinery is not available for side placement, it is suggested that the fertilizer be drilled as a separate operation before planting.

Inoculation. Considerable difference of opinion exists regarding the importance of inoculating pea seed with nitrogen-fixing bacteria. Experiments have given inconclusive results, although there has been response, generally, when inoculated peas were planted on new land. It seems advisable to inoculate the seed unless it is known that inoculation does not pay. There is evidence that it is profitable to inoculate seed to be planted on highly acid soil even though peas were grown on the area the previous year. The inoculating material is relatively inexpensive, and it seems desirable to use it when there is any doubt about the soil's containing the bacteria in abundance. Most growers do not inoculate their seed because it involves more labor in handling the seed. Many feel that it is simpler to provide the nitrogen for peas in the fertilizer rather than treat the seed.

Planting. The pea is relatively hardy and does not produce well in hot weather, especially if it is hot during blossoming and pod set. For these reasons, early planting is important in regions where the crop is grown in summer. While the smooth-seeded type, as Alaska, will stand more cold than the wrinkle-seeded type, early planting is of greater importance for late-maturing varieties than it is for quick-maturing varieties. Since late-planted peas produce low yields in most regions, the best method of obtaining a succession of peas is to plant early, medium, and late varieties at about the same time. Late planting is seldom profitable except in a few favorable localities where the summer temperature is relatively low.

Most pea seed is planted too deep; this results in slow come-up and poor stands. A depth of 1 inch is sufficient in moist heavy soil and $1\frac{1}{2}$ inches on a dry heavy soil. A covering of $1\frac{1}{2}$ to 2 inches might be given on a dry sandy loam, but a depth greater than 2 inches is seldom if ever justified in humid regions.

Peas in the home garden and some of the peas for fresh market are planted in rows 2 to 3 feet apart. The tall-growing varieties are supported on trellises of wire or heavy string. Another method used in home gardens is to stick brush into the ground along the row. Most of the peas grown for processing and many of them grown for fresh market are planted with a grain drill in the same manner as oats or other small grain. The rows are usually about 7 inches apart. The quantity of seed to be planted varies from $3\frac{1}{2}$ to 5 bushels per acre, depending upon the size of the seed planted. Enough seed should be planted so that for single-stem varieties, such as Alaska and Surprise, there will be 18 to 20 plants per yard of row. Varieties which branch, such as Perfection, should be sown so as to attain 14 to 16 plants per yard of row. To make most efficient use of the seed, the seeds should be treated with Spergon or some other seed treatment to reduce the loss of plants due to diseases present in the soil.

Chemical Weed Control. Since most of the pea acreage is planted in rows 7 inches apart, it is not possible to cultivate to control weeds. Spraying the pea field immediately after planting with about 3 pounds of dinitro materials per acre usually gives excellent control of annual weeds, both broad-leaved and grasses. In some areas, peas are used as a nurse crop for legumes and a preemergence application of dinitro materials cannot be used since it would kill the seeding of legumes. Peas seeded with legumes can be sprayed with dinitro after the peas and weeds have formed a protective canopy over the legume seedlings or when the peas are from 3 to 6 inches tall. The dinitro does not injure the peas since it runs off the waxy leaves, but it sticks on the leaves of the weeds. Some damage to peas may be encountered if sprayed with dinitro during hot weather. The amount of dinitro to use after the peas have emerged varies from ¾ to 1½ pounds per acre, depending upon the temperature; the lower amounts are used at high temperatures. Usually it does not pay to spray peas when the temperature is less than 60°F. because the weed control will be poor, and at temperatures above 80°F. the peas may be injured by the dinitro even though applied in very small amounts. In many areas of the Eastern United States, wild mustard (*Brassica arvensis*) is the major pest in peas, and excellent control of this weed can be obtained by using the dinitro sprays either as a pre-emergence spray or after the peas come up.

Varieties. There are two types of garden peas based on the seed, smooth-seeded and wrinkle-seeded. The Alaska is the most important variety of the smooth-seeded type. It was once the standard canning pea grown in the United States. It is early and very hardy, but the quality is now considered too poor to be generally acceptable as a pea for processing. It has been replaced by other varieties. Alaska has a medium vine height and is easy to handle with machinery. The peas have a tough skin which is not greatly affected by the heat of canning and remains firm when reheated for the table. Other varieties similar to Alaska are Super Alaska, Supergreen, and Alaska Wilt Resistant. The canning peas are divided into two classes, the Alaska and the sweet or sugary cotyledon group. There is a wide range of maturity in the sweet types. The most important early canning variety of the sweet type is Surprise, but Resistant Surprise is gaining in popularity because of its disease resistance. Among the midseason varieties which ripen about a week later than the early varieties Pride, Early Perfection, Wasatch, and Ace are fairly widely grown. The late sweet varieties mature about 14 days later than Alaska, and the important varieties are Perfection and its various strains, such as Darkgreen Perfection, Bridger, Superior, New Era, and Shoshone, all late-maturing canning varieties. Most of the late-maturing canning varieties have larger seed than canners usually desire. The canning industry prefers the small peas because the consumer associates small size with high quality. Canning varieties usually have a tough skin that holds its shape during the canning process. The varieties grown for freezing must have a dark-green color and tender skins. The size is not so important since the large sizes seem to be acceptable as frozen peas. The most widely grown freezing variety is Thomas Laxton. It is the earliest of all the freezing varieties. It has good color and excellent flavor but is not always high-yielding. Similar varieties which have more vigor are Laxton 7, Freezonian, and Shasta. The season can be extended with later-maturing varieties, such as Freezonian, Victory Freezer, Wyola, Perfection Freezer, and Darkgreen Perfection. For home-garden use, varieties like Little Marvel, Laxton's Progress, World's Record, and Alderman, or Dark Colored Telephone, are useful. Wando has found a place in many home gardens since it holds its quality well during hot weather.

Harvesting. Peas grown for home use and for the fresh market are picked by hand. This is the most expensive operation connected with the production of the crop. Some growers make two or three pickings, while others make only one. In the latter case, the vines are pulled and all the pods are picked off. It costs less to pick an acre of peas by this method, but the quality of the product is better and the yield higher when two or more pickings are made. Peas for the processor are harvested with machines of various types. In some areas the vines are cut with a mowing machine, windrowed, and loaded on trucks with a hay loader. Pea harvesters which mow the peas and load directly into a truck or wagon are in most common use in the main growing areas. The pea vines are hauled to a vining station where the peas are removed from the vines and pods by machinery. In a few localities self-propelled pea viners are used. The peas are mowed and windrowed, and the self-propelled viner shells the peas from the vines as it moves down the field.

The time to harvest is determined largely by the appearance of the pods. These should be well filled with tender young peas and changing in color from dark to light green. The harvest should be made when the peas are still in prime condition, but without sacrificing yield. Many workers have shown that there is an inverse relationship between yield and quality after the peas reach a certain maturity. The work of Pollard *et al.* (1947) shows this relationship clearly in Table 23.5. As harvest was delayed the yield increased, as did the tenderometer value and starch content of the peas, but the proportion of small peas (No. 2 and No. 3) decreased steadily. A delay of a day or two results in greater yield, but the quality may be reduced enough so that the total value of the crop might decrease.

Quality of peas is determined by many factors, but high quality is generally associated with tenderness and high sugar content. During maturity the sugar content decreases rapidly and there is a rapid increase in the content of starch and other polysaccharides and insoluble nitrogen compounds, mainly proteins. These latter compounds which increase with maturity are designated collectively as "alcohol-insoluble solids."

Sayre, Willaman, and Kertesz (1931) have shown that migration of

Table 23.5. Influence of Time of Harvest on Yield and Certain Measures
of Quality of Early Perfection Peas Grown in Utah in 1944 and 1945
(Data from Pollard *et al.*, 1947)

Days after initial harvest	Yield, tons per acre	Tenderometer value	Per cent small peas No. 2 and No. 3	Per cent starch
0	1.58	90	32.0	2.44
2	2.02	96	28.2	2.73
4	2.36	102	22.5	2.99
6	2.62	109	16.8	3.22
8	2.89	118	13.6	3.50
10	3.18	135	5.5	4.44
12	3.64	160	2.1	5.82

calcium to the seed coat as the peas ripen increases the toughness of the skin. Toughness of the seed coat and firmness of the pulp are measures of maturity and can be determined by mechanical means such as the tenderometer and other similar instruments. Lee (1941) correlated several objective methods of measuring quality with organoleptic tests. The tenderometer value, texturemeter value, specific gravity, and per cent alcohol-insoluble solids all increased with maturity and were negatively correlated with the organoleptic ratings of quality. The tenderometer is used by most canners to assess quality, and a high value indicates low quality. The highest price is paid for peas with a low tenderometer reading, and the price drops rapidly as the reading increases. In some areas the emphasis is on size, and the price paid the grower is based on the sieve size of the peas.

Boswell (1929) has shown that temperature has a marked effect on the rate of ripening of peas, and for this reason when the temperature is high at harvest time, it is important that there be no delay in harvesting when the peas reach the right stage. His results indicate that there is no appreciable difference in quality or in chemical composition of peas ripened under different temperatures if the crop is harvested at the proper stage. The lower quality often obtained during very hot weather is probably a result of rapid rate of maturing, so that the peas were not harvested at the best stage.

Many processors use a system of accumulated degree-hours, or "heat units," to determine dates of planting of peas. All the acreage the processor contracts cannot be planted at the same time since this would bring all the peas into harvest at about the same time and the great volume could not be handled efficiently. The number of degree-hours above 40°F. required to bring a certain variety to maturity is calculated each season. This accumulated information is used to determine the interval between plantings. The number of degree-hours between plantings is equivalent to the number that is expected to accumulate during the desired interval of harvest. By planting on the basis of degree-hours rather than actual calendar days it has been possible for some processors to handle a fairly uniform volume of peas over a long season. Many scientists have criticized the degree-hour, or heat-unit method, of predicting harvest, on the basis that temperature is not the only factor influencing growth of the crop. Reath and Wittwer (1952) reported that taking the photoperiod into account gave better results than degree-hours alone. They grew peas in the greenhouse at different temperatures and under different photoperiods and found more uniformity in predicting maturity when the degree-day was multiplied by hours of photoperiod. Similar results were obtained in the field, but the differences in photoperiod were not so great. This type of work obviously precludes the possibility of using the same value for degree-hours to maturity in every locality, but the fact remains that this method is used successfully by many processors. The information should be obtained in each locality and on several soil types to be of greatest usefulness.

Grading and Packing. When peas are prepared for market the over-matured yellow pods, the flat pods, the diseased and insect-injured pods, and the trash should be removed before the peas are packed. In many cases, careful picking would eliminate the trash and defective pods. Peas are packed for shipment in baskets, hampers, and boxes of various types. It is important to have the container well filled so that it will not be slack when it reaches market.. The U.S. Department of Agriculture has promulgated standards for fresh peas, and these should be used where feasible. Peas for processing are graded into four grades based on the size of shelled peas, and the smaller sizes are considered to be the best quality and bring the highest prices from canners. The sieves used for separating the sizes have mesh ranging from $1\frac{8}{64}$ to $2\frac{4}{64}$ inch in diameter. While size is important in determining maturity of peas, many processors buy peas on the basis of tenderometer grade rather than sieve size. The tenderometer reading or some similar measure of quality is much better than size alone. Small peas may be overmature and of poor quality, while large peas may be tender and not yet mature.

Precooling and Refrigeration. Peas that are shipped to distant markets should be kept cool if they are to reach the market in edible condition. If the peas are warm when harvested, it is desirable to precool them. This can be done by immersing in cold water or by other means; if they are washed, it is important to keep them under refrigeration until they reach the destination. By placing crushed ice in the package or over the top of the load, or both, and shipping in refrigerator cars or refrigerated trucks, the load can be kept cool, provided the bunkers are kept loaded with ice.

Fresh peas can be kept for 2 weeks or more in cold storage at a temperature of about 32°F. Jamison (1934) reported results of storage experiments showing that peas stored at 32 and 40°F. were in good condition at the end of 15 and 18 days. Those stored at 32°F. were kept for another week and were in good edible condition at that time. Similar peas held at 70°F. were unfit for sale at the end of 5 days.

Diseases. Several diseases attack the pea plant, including powdery mildew, root rots caused by several organisms, ascochyta blight, bacterial blight, fusarium wilt, anthracnose, septoria leaf spot, mosaic, and others of minor importance. Only a few of the more important ones are discussed here.

POWDERY MILDEW. This disease, caused by *Erysiphe polygoni,* is widely distributed and is particularly serious during warm weather. On the host plant, the fungus forms a dense mycelium which frequently covers the leaves, stems, and pods. It is recognized by the white or grayish covering on all parts of the plant.

As this disease is most destructive in warm weather, it is best to plant early or to use quick-maturing varieties. The vines and refuse should be turned under as soon as possible after harvest to prevent the production of the overwintering stage. Dusting with sulfur has given good results in the control of this disease, but sometimes as many as six or seven applications are necessary to ensure a crop.

ROOT ROTS. Root rots are caused by several parasites that produce symptoms so much alike that it is not easy to distinguish them by a casual examination. They occur on the roots or on all the underground portions of the plants and sometimes a short distance above the surface of the soil. Root decay often begins at the tips of the feedroots and progresses upward to the main root. Sometimes the main root is the first to be affected.

Early planting on well-drained soils; a long rotation, including only crops that are not attacked by the organisms; thorough soil preparation and seed treatment with Spergon or Arasan are control measures recommended.

ASCOCHYTA BLIGHT. This disease is characterized by the formation of black or purplish streaks on the stem. The leaves and pods may show spots of various sizes, either irregular in shape or more or less circular. The blight might be caused by any of three different parasites: *Ascochyta pisi* Lib., *Mycosphaerella pinodes* (Berk. and Blox.) Stone, and *A. pinodella* Jones. The disease may occur in all states east of the

Mississippi River but is rarely if ever found in the semiarid, seed-producing regions of the Northwest.

Since the causal organisms are carried on the seed, it is recommended that only clean seed be used. The organisms may also live from season to season on refuse in the field; as it is not feasible to destroy all refuse, plowing it under as soon as the crop is harvested is suggested.

WILT AND NEAR WILT. These two diseases are similar in many respects and are caused by two distinct races of *Fusarium oxysporum* f. *pisi*. Near wilt has a higher optimum temperature for development in the soil than does wilt and therefore is more damaging in warm seasons, on late plantings, and on late varieties. The symptoms of the two diseases are alike in most respects. The lower leaves become yellow and the plants stunted. Affected leaves show a downward curling of the margins. When infection occurs while the plants are small, they may die without producing any peas; if plants are of considerable size, they may produce a few, poorly filled pods. Infection takes place from the soil through the roots, and the organism follows the water-conducting canals up the stem, often into the branches, thus obstructing the movement of water.

The only means of control is growing resistant varieties. There are many pea varieties of all types resistant to wilt, but Delwich Commando is the only variety resistant to near wilt. New resistant varieties appear from time to time.

Insects. Several species of insects attack peas, but only two are considered of sufficient importance to be discussed here. These are the pea aphid and the pea weevil.

PEA APHID (*Macrosiphum pisi*). The pea aphid is the only insect pest that seriously affects peas. This is one of the larger species of plant lice, pale green in color. It attacks the young vines, sucking the juices first from the growing tips but eventually covering the entire plant. During midsummer the lice are nearly exterminated by predaceous insects and disease, but as cool weather approaches they increase in numbers again.

The pea aphid can be controlled by spraying or dusting the plants with DDT, parathion, malathion, TEPP, or nicotine sulfate. The type of material to use depends on the nearness of harvest and whether the vines are to be fed to livestock. The insecticide should be applied as soon as the insects are noticed.

PEA WEEVIL (*Bruchus pisorum*). The pea weevil is a serious enemy of the field and garden pea. It is now found in nearly all parts of the world but does comparatively little damage in the colder portions of Europe and North America. The eggs are deposited on the surface of the pods. In the vicinity of Washington, D.C., a considerable number of the weevils mature and leave the seeds in the latter part of the summer, but farther north and in high altitudes the adult remains in the seed until the following spring. The weevil passes the winter in the adult stage, either in secluded spots in fields and buildings or in the pea itself. The weevil has only one generation a year and does not reproduce in dry seed.

The same insecticides used for the pea aphid give satisfactory control. A rotenone dust containing lubricating oil is sometimes used for weevil control. They should be applied when the pods are quite small. Since peas mature rapidly, there is some danger of excessive insecticide residues at harvest. The manufacturer's instructions should be strictly followed for both concentration and time of application.

CHAPTER 24

Solanaceous Fruits

Tomato   Pepper
Eggplant   Husk tomato (Physalis)

The solanaceous fruits, tomato, eggplant, pepper, and husk tomato, all belong to the same botanical family, Solanaceae. All are tender plants grown as annuals and produced for their fruits. The methods of culture for all are similar. From the standpoint of both relationship and cultural requirements they are here grouped together for discussion.

TOMATO

The tomato is one of the most popular vegetables as well as one of the most important. It is grown in nearly all home gardens and by a large percentage of market gardeners and truck growers. It is produced as a forcing crop in greenhouses in the Northern part of the United States and in other countries, especially in Europe. As a processing crop it takes first rank among the vegetables.

Few products lend themselves to so great a variety of uses as does the tomato. It is one of the most popular salad vegetables in the raw state and is made into soups, conserves, pickles, catchups, sauces, and other products. It is served raw, baked, stewed, fried, and as a sauce with various other foods.

Statistics of Production. The tomato ranks next to the potato in total farm value in the United States and heads the list in value among the perishable vegetables. The estimated annual acreage and production of tomatoes grown for the fresh market in the period 1948–1952 were more than double that for the years 1918–1927. The farm value increased nearly fourfold, as shown in Table 24.1.

The leading states in production of tomatoes for market were California with 8,318,000 bushels; Florida, 8,280,000; Texas, 3,628,000; New York, 1,960,000; New Jersey, 1,472,000; Michigan, 1,348,000; and Virginia 1,080,000 bushels. These 7 states produced about 77 per cent of the total

Table 24.1. Estimated Average Annual Acreage, Production, and Value of
Tomatoes Grown for Fresh Market in the United States, 1918–1952

Years	Acres	Production, bushels (000 omitted)	Farm value (000 omitted)
1918–1927	114,555	15,809	$ 29,857
1928–1937	119,215	18,657	24,657
1938–1947	235,165	28,468	67,045
1948–1952	233,744	33,322	113,893

of the 29 states for which statistics are given. Other important states
are Georgia, Ohio, Pennsylvania, Maryland, Massachusetts, and Washington, each of which produced over 500,000 bushels in 1952. There is
considerable variation in yields in the various states from year to year.

The acreage and production of tomatoes grown for processing are
much greater than those grown for market in the fresh condition, as can
be seen by comparing Tables 24.1 and 24.2.

Table 24.2. Estimated Average Annual Acreage, Production, and
Farm Value of Tomatoes Grown for Processing in the
United States, 1918–1952

Years	Acres	Production, tons	Farm value (000 omitted)
1918–1927	259,023	1,147,660	$18,424
1928–1937	356,116	1,455,830	18,607
1938–1947	480,267	2,657,820	58,947
1948–1952	372,826	3,144,700	88,398

The average annual production of tomatoes for processing in the
period 1948–1952 was more than twice that of the 10 years 1918–1927 or
1928–1937. Production increased much more than acreage, and total
farm value increased more than production. The leading states in
production in 1952 were California with 1,758,400 tons, or about one-
half of the total for the states for which figures are published. Other important states in 1952 were Indiana, New York, Ohio, New Jersey,
Pennsylvania, Maryland, Illinois, Michigan, and Utah. Marked fluctuations in total production in the United States are shown by the statistics
for the 3 years 1950–1952. In 1950 the production was 2,643,000 tons;
1951, 4,267,070; and 1952, 3,452,000 tons. The production in some of the
states fluctuates more than that for the United States.

The tomato is an important vegetable in practically all countries and is found on the market in most cities of the world. It is grown commercially in parts of Mexico and Cuba for shipment to the United States. In 1951 the shipment of tomatoes from Mexico to the United States reached about 171 million pounds and from Cuba 17 million pounds.

History. The native home of the tomato is Central America and South America where it was well known and highly prized prior to the discovery of America. Its use is very ancient. According to Sturtevant (1919) and McCue (1952), the earliest mention of its use was by Matthiolus in Italy in 1544. It was known in Germany, France, and other European countries prior to 1600. It is probable that it was used as food in parts of Europe, Africa, Central and South America, and the West Indies long before it was so used in the United States. The first reference to the use of the tomato for culinary purposes in the United States was by Jefferson in 1781, although mention had been made of its presence in the Carolinas, Georgia, and Florida earlier in the eighteenth century. It was not until about 1835 that the tomato became generally cultivated in the United States, and even at that time, there was considerable prejudice against its use as food. The tomato-growing industry made rapid strides in the latter half of the nineteenth century and still greater in the first half of the twentieth century. McCue has published a good bibliography on the history of the use of the tomato in various parts of the world.

Taxonomy. The tomato belongs to the nightshade, or Solanaceae, family and to the genus *Lycopersicon*. The genus comprises a few species of annual or short-lived perennial herbaceous plants. The many branches are procumbent or partly erect. The stems are round, soft, brittle, and hairy when young, but become angular, hard, and almost woody when old. The leaves are alternate, 5 to 15 inches long, odd-pinnate, with seven to nine short-stemmed leaflets. The flowers are borne in clusters, located on the stem between the nodes. The flowers are small; corolla deeply five-cleft, yellow, the petals recurving and broadly lanceolate; calyx with five long linear or lanceolate sepals, which are shorter than the petals at first, but increase in size as the fruits mature. The stamens are five in number and are borne in the throat of the corolla; anthers large, borne on short filaments. The fruit is a two- to many-celled berry with fleshy placentae and many small kidney-shaped seeds covered with short stiff hairs.

Most authorities recognize two distinct species, *L. esculentum* and *L. pimpinellifolium*, with four or five botanical varieties under the former. Others believe that the pear and cherry tomatoes represent true species rather than botanical varieties belonging to the species, *L. esculentum*. Bailey (1949) classified tomatoes into two species, *L. pimpinellifolium* and *L. esculentum*, with the following botanical varieties under the latter:

Var. *commune:* Common tomato
Var. *grandifolium:* Large-leaved tomato
Var. *validum:* Upright tomato
Var. *cerasiforme:* Cherry tomato
Var. *pyriforme:* Pear tomato

Muller (1940), after an elaborate study, recognized six species of *Lycopersicon,* including the two mentioned and the following four additional ones: *L. cheesmanii, L. peruvianum, L. hirsutum,* and *L. glandulosum.* He gives a key to the species and a description of each.

Climatic Requirements. The tomato is a warm-season plant and requires a relatively long season to produce profitable yields. It is tender and will not withstand a hard freeze. In regions having less than $3\frac{1}{2}$ months frost-free period the tomato is not likely to be profitable. High humidity with high temperature favors the development of foliage diseases. On the other hand, hot drying winds often result in the dropping of the blossoms. The tomato plant produces large yields under irrigation in semiarid and arid regions.

Hamner, Bernstein, and Maynard (1945) and others have shown that light intensity is a very important factor in ascorbic acid content of tomato fruits. Under low light intensities the ascorbic acid content is much lower than under high intensities. Increases in ripe fruit of 66 per cent ascorbic acid resulted when plants were transferred from shade to sunshine at the time the fruit was mature green, in the experiments by Hamner *et al.* (1945). This explains the difference in ascorbic content of the same variety of tomatoes grown in different regions. Soil type, fertilizer applications, and other factors have been found to have little direct effect on the ascorbic acid content of tomato fruits. Ellis and Hamner (1943) have shown that carotene content of tomato fruits was less when produced in the greenhouse, whether in summer or winter, than fruit produced outside during the summer. Results similar to those reported above have been obtained by other workers, and, in addition, both high and low temperatures have been shown to exert a marked effect on market quality, especially color of the fruit.

Soils and Soil Preparation. The tomato is grown on many kinds of soils from the sands to heavy clays. Where earliness is of great importance, as for an early crop in the Northern part of the United States and Canada, sandy or sandy-loam soils are preferred. Such soils are preferred also where the growing season is too short for a good yield on heavy soils. Where large yields are most important, as in the production of the crop for processing, loams, clay loams, and silt loams are preferred to the lighter soils, provided the growing season is long. Authorities are agreed that a well-drained soil is essential for high production.

The tomato plant has been considered as tolerant to rather high acidity, and liming has not been recommended unless the soil pH was 5.0 or lower. However, on some soils of pH 5.0 to 5.5 yields can be increased markedly by liming. Sayre (1947) reported an increase of 4.2 tons of fruit from an application of 3 tons of dolomitic limestone to the acre on Fulton loam soil testing pH 4.8 (Fig. 24.1).

The soil used for growing tomatoes should be prepared as described in Chap. 3. If manure is used or a soil-improving crop precedes the

Fig. 24.1. Effect of lime on growth of tomato plants on Fulton loam soil of pH 4.8 before liming. Left, no lime; right, 3 tons dolomitic limestone to the acre. (*Courtesy of C. B. Sayre, N.Y. State Agricultural Experiment Station.*)

tomatoes, it is important that the material be plowed under completely considerably in advance of setting the plants. Unless the material is well turned under it will interfere with the setting of the plants by machine planters.

Fertilizers. Commercial fertilizer is the main source of nutrients applied to the soil for tomatoes, although animal manures are used to some extent, especially where available on the farm. In most tomato-growing areas of the United States the cost of manure has become prohibitive and growers are depending more and more on soil-improving crops and chemical fertilizers. Where manure is available on the farm, it can be used to advantage at the rate of 8 to 10 tons to the acre supplemented with some chemical fertilizer, especially phosphorus. Where manure can be purchased at a moderate price near the farm, some market gardeners find it profitable to use it for an early crop of tomatoes to be sold on local markets. Manure is used with profit in growing tomatoes in the greenhouse. Under most conditions in the United States, however, chemical fertilizers and soil-improving crops are the main materials used to maintain soil fertility.

A complete fertilizer, or one containing nitrogen, phosphorus, and potash, is used for the tomato crop in most areas. The analysis and quantity of nutrients applied vary through wide limits because of difference in natural fertility of the soil, the previous treatment, and the cropping system followed. On infertile sandy and sandy-loam soils the fertilizer applied supplies 50 to 100 pounds of nitrogen, 80 to 160 pounds of P_2O_5, and 60 to 120 pounds of K_2O to the acre. In some areas, as on the sandy soils in parts of Florida, larger quantities are applied than the highest figures mentioned above. On fairly fertile loam, silt-loam, and clay-loam soils smaller quantities are required than on the lighter soils. In fact, in some areas there has been little response to applied fertilizers.

Nitrogen is the element most likely to be deficient because it leaches out of the soil. An adequate supply of available nitrogen is essential for high yields of good-quality fruit through its effect on growth of foliage. Good growth of foliage is necessary for food manufacture and protection of the fruit from sunscald. Phosphorus is likely to be next in importance to nitrogen. It is important in root development and tends to hasten maturity of the fruit. On most soils potash is likely to be third in importance, but on some sandy soils this element may be of equal importance to the other two nutrients. On the other hand, some soils are so well supplied with potash that application of potash salts has no effect on yield. It should be borne in mind, however, that application of any essential element would have a marked effect on yield if the soil were deficient in that element. In some areas, there are deficiencies of other elements such as calcium, magnesium, manganese, boron, zinc, and copper. Calcium, magnesium, and sulfur are usually added in sufficient quantity where superphosphate is used in a mixed fertilizer and dolomitic limestone is used to correct acidity. The other elements should be added where deficiency is known to exist. Any one of these elements may be added to the fertilizer mixture.

The fertilizer ratios generally used are 1-2-1, 1-2-2, 1-3-1, and 1-4-1. The 1-2-1 and 1-2-2 are used mainly on the lighter soils where tomatoes are grown in rotation with other cultivated crops. For sandy soils the 1-2-2 ratio is preferable to the 1-2-1 ratio. The 1-3-1 and 1-4-1 ratios are recommended mainly for tomatoes grown on loam, silt-loam, and clay-loam soils where the crop is grown in rotation with field crops, including a sod crop with manure in the rotation. The 1-2-1 ratio is preferable to the wider ratios where the tomatoes are grown in rotation with cultivated crops without manure on the heavier soils.

TIME AND METHOD OF APPLICATION. The time and method of application are very important, especially where large quantities are used. Results of many experiments have shown that application of fertilizer in bands by the side of the row at planting time is better than broadcast application when only a relatively small quantity is used. When large quantities are applied (1,000 pounds or more to the acre of such analyses as 5-10-5, 5-10-10, 4-12-4), it is desirable to apply part before or after plowing and part at planting time or soon thereafter, as discussed in Chap. 5. Where nitrogen is needed in large quantities, it is best to apply part of it immediately before or at planting time and the remainder later when the fruit is developing. Under most conditions, there is no advantage in making more than one application of phosphorus and potash. On very light sandy soils dividing the application of potash may be advantageous, but there are no conditions under which phosphorus needs to be applied more than once. In an experiment in Indiana, Jones and Warren (1954) compared various methods of placement of phosphorus and found that deep placement under the row was more efficient than banding beside the plants or broadcast. Differences in yield due to fertilizer placement were not so pronounced where a complete starter solution was used at planting.

Starter solutions are rather generally used at the time of setting the tomatoes in the field, and results of many experiments indicate that it is a good practice. Results obtained by Hornby (1949) indicated that application of a starter solution to the plants a few days before they were taken from the flat significantly increased the early yield but had little effect on the total yield for the season. Starter solutions are made by dissolving fertilizer chemicals in the water used at the time of setting the plants in the field.

Plant Growing. Tomato plants are started usually in specially prepared beds a few weeks in advance of planting in the field or garden. In regions of short-growing seasons, seed is sown in greenhouses or hotbeds, while in areas where the growing season is long, cold frames and open beds are used for starting the plants. Greenhouses and hotbeds are used also to some extent for growing the plants where earliness is important, even though the season is long enough to produce a crop from outdoor-grown plants. Where greenhouse or hotbeds are used for starting the plants it is common practice to transplant them to cold frames. The various methods of growing plants are described in Chap. 7.

In some areas seed is sown in place in the field and the plants are thinned before they become crowded. This method is feasible only in regions where the growing season is long. It has the advantage of saving labor of transplanting and often reduces loss from damping-off. More seed is required to grow a given acreage by this method than by the other methods followed. Sowing seed in place is a common practice in California, parts of Florida, and other Southern states and for the processing crop in some of the Northern states. The only advantage in starting plants in prepared beds where the growing season is long is the ease with which the plants can be cared for in the seedling stage. Allowing 4 square inches per plant, a plant bed 100 square feet in size will produce enough plants for an acre of land at the average space given plants in the field. It is obvious that much less labor would be required in caring for the plants (watering, control of diseases and insects, etc.) grown in a seedbed 100 square feet in size than the same number growing on an acre of land in the field.

The time of sowing seed is determined by the methods followed in growing the seedlings, the climatic conditions, and the purpose for which the crop is grown. If the plants are not to be transplanted prior to setting in the field, 6 weeks is sufficient time from seed sowing to field planting. If they are to be transplanted once before field setting, 8 to 10 weeks should be allowed, but the length of time should vary with the spacing. Casseres (1947) reported results obtained at Ithaca, N.Y., in which plants 7 weeks from seed sowing to field planting produced significantly higher early and total yield than plants 11 weeks old. These plants were grown at 60 to 70°F. most of the time from seed sowing to field planting, and the spacing of plants in the flats was 2 by 2 and 4 by 4 inches. Similar results were obtained by Hornby (1949) at Ithaca in 1947 and 1948. In both of these studies plants spaced 4 by 4 inches apart in the flats produced highly significant increases in early yield over those spaced 2 by 2 inches apart. In Casseres' experiments the total yield was significantly larger from the 4- by 4- than the 2- by 2-inch spacing. Romshe (1954) reported results obtained in Oklahoma in which both early and total yield increased with increase in space. Plant bands 2 by 2, 3 by 3, and 4 by 4 inches, all 3 inches deep, made of wood veneer, manila paper, and heavy asphalt paper, were compared by Romshe, and he obtained significant increase in yield as size of container increased. There was no significant difference in yield for the three kinds of materials used.

Many growers start their plants too early because they believe that slow growth is desirable, but experimental results indicate that this might be overdone. Plants kept too long in the plant bed either get too leggy or become too woody if growth is checked to hold them back. In either case the plants do not make a quick start when set in the field,

Tomato seed is usually planted in rows about 2 inches apart in flats or in rows 4 to 6 inches apart in a hotbed, cold frame, or greenhouse. If the plants are not to be transplanted prior to setting in the field, they should be thinned to stand 1 or 2 inches apart, preferably the latter distance, or even more when they are to remain in the seedbed for several weeks. Most market gardeners and other commercial growers in the North transplant the seedlings when they reach a height of about 2 inches, spacing them about 2 inches apart each way. The plants are often transplanted a second time when they begin to crowd; at this transplanting, they are spaced 3 by 3 or 4 by 4 inches apart each way, or else are put in pots, paper bands, veneer bands, or tin cans. Experimental results indicate that transplanting is of no particular value if the plants are given the same space without transplanting. However, transplanting once is usually necessary to economize on greenhouse or hotbed space, but very often the second transplanting may be eliminated to the benefit of the plant and result in a saving of labor as well.

Experimental results reported by Loomis (1925) indicate that transplanting once while the plants are small may be of some advantage but that a second transplanting prior to setting the plants in the field is more likely to be injurious than beneficial. In other words, the extra expense of the second transplanting is not justified, provided sufficient space is allowed at the first transplanting. The advantages that have been claimed for transplanting have been due to increase in spacing and other factors rather than to transplanting.

Tomato plants usually are hardened before setting them in the field. This is done by subjecting them to temperatures too low for rapid growth, or by allowing the soil to become dry, or by a combination of the two. Any treatment that results in checking growth results in hardening. It is not possible to harden tomato plants sufficiently to enable them to withstand ice formation in the tissues, and it is questionable if hardening is desirable under average growing conditions. Certainly the hardening treatment should not be severe or of long duration.

Setting Plants in the Field. Since the tomato is tender it should not be set in the field until the danger of hard frosts is past. In the areas of the United States where frosts seldom occur, it is a common practice to grow the crop for market during winter and spring, in which case the plants are set out in the fall or winter. In nearly all other sections of the United States the plants are planted in the spring or early summer. In many tropical and subtropical regions tomatoes may be grown any time of the year.

The spacing given plants in the field varies greatly, depending on the fertility of the soil, the variety grown, the method and equipment used for disease and insect control, and whether the plants are pruned and trained or allowed to grow naturally without pruning and training. Large-growing, spreading varieties are given more space than small-growing ones. Where large equipment is used for spraying or dusting the tendency is to have the rows 4 to 5 or more feet apart and to set the plants close together in the row. When the plants are to be pruned to a single stem and tied to stakes or trellises they are set closer in the row than when they are allowed to grow naturally. However, in one area in Florida, unpruned plants are spaced 12 to 18 inches apart in rows about 7 feet apart, while in one section of California, pruned trained plants are spaced 12 to 18 inches apart in rows 3 to 4 feet apart. Most of the tomatoes grown in the United States are not pruned and trained, and the most common spacing allows 12 to 16 square feet per plant.

Many experiments on field spacing of tomato plants have been conducted, and most of them have shown that close spacing results in larger yields than wide spacing. Reeve and Schmidt (1952) reported results of four tests in Illinois and Indiana in which higher total yields generally were obtained from plants given 7 square feet of space than those given greater space. In these tests spacings varied from 7 to 21 square feet. In three of these tests the rows were 3½ feet apart, and in one test they were 4 feet apart, with the plants spaced 2, 3, 4, 5, and 6 feet in the row. In all tests the difference in yields between the intermediate spacings (10½ to 16 square feet per plant) was negligible. Ine one test the difference in yield between 7 square feet and 10½ and 14 square feet was not statistically significant. Results of experiments reported by Vittum and Tapley (1953) at Geneva, N.Y., were similar to those of Reeve and Schmidt. In the New York experiment the Gem, a determinate-type variety, was used and the plants were spaced 2, 2½, and 3 feet apart in rows 5 feet apart grown under two fertility levels— high and low. These experiments were conducted for 4 years and indicate that the close spacing produced a higher yield than the other two spacings. The highest yield was obtained from close spacing and high fertility.

Considering the results of the experiments mentioned above and those obtained by other investigators previously, it is evident that under most conditions the wide spacing formerly used by many growers was too great for highest yields. Spacing the plants to give each one up to 10 or 12 square feet is likely to result in larger yields than those given more space.

Cultivation. Frequent shallow cultivation should be given as often as is necessary to control weeds. With untrained plants, cultivation should cease after the vines cover the ground, as it is likely to do more harm than good when the plants have to be moved around. Experiments carried on at Ithaca, N.Y., for 6 years and on Long Island for the same number of years show that cultivation merely for the purpose of maintaining a soil mulch was of little value. It may be of value under some conditions and of no value, or even actually detrimental, under others, as explained in Chap. 9. Deep cultivation is nearly always injurious because of the destruction of roots by the cultivator and the bringing of moist soil to the surface. All the roots shown in Fig. 24.2 would have been destroyed by cultivating over 2 inches deep.

Irrigation. Irrigation is essential for tomato production in regions where there is little or no rain during the growing season. It is becoming

FIG. 24.2. Roots of tomato plant uncovered by washing off soil to the depth of 2 inches.

of increasing importance in so-called humid regions because there is seldom a growing season when water is not a limiting factor at some time during growth of the crop. Any of the methods of irrigation discussed in Chap. 10 may be used for tomatoes. It is desirable to have the soil well supplied with water before ripening begins so that subsequent irrigations may be kept to the minimum. Experimental results have shown that water on the surface of ripening fruits increases cracking.

Tomato plants are deep-rooted when grown in deep soils that are free from an impervious layer of subsoil. In irrigating it is desirable to apply enough water each time to thoroughly moisten the soil to the depth reached by the roots. The types of irrigation and the principles that should govern the frequency of application and quantity of water to apply are discussed in Chap. 10.

Pruning and Training. Pruning and training tomato plants are common practice in certain sections of the United States, especially in some areas in the Southern states and in a few other regions. Various methods of pruning and training are followed, but pruning to a single stem and tying the plant to a stake is the most common (Fig. 24.3). In this system all the shoots that grow in the axils of the leaves are removed while they are small. The plants are tied to stakes with soft twine looped around the stake and tied under a leaf stem on the side of the plant opposite the stake. The twine should not be tied around the plant in such a way that it restricts growth or cuts into the stem. Usually the plants are

Fig. 24.3. Tomato plants pruned to single stems and tied to stakes.

trimmed about once every week or 10 days. Some growers pinch out the top of the plant when it reaches the top of the stake. With two- and three-stem training, the desired number of shoots is selected and all others are kept pinched out. Each stem must be tied as in the single-stem system.

The advantages claimed for pruning and training as compared with plants allowed to grow naturally are: (1) earlier ripening, (2) larger early and total yield, (3) less disease injury, (4) cleaner fruit, (5) easier harvesting, and (6) more convenient spraying or dusting. The disadvantages usually mentioned are: (1) increase in labor and expense, (2) less total yield per acre, (3) greater loss from blossom-end rot, (4) more sunburn injury to the fruit, and (5) greater loss from cracking of the fruit.

Experimental results on pruning and training of tomato plants are conflicting. This might have been expected because the experiments were conducted under many different conditions. There was a great variation in the spacings; in some cases the experiments were of too short duration and insufficient replications to give reliable results. From the results of a large number of experiments, it seems safe to conclude that the total yield per acre is likely to be less from pruned plants than from unpruned plants, unless the pruned ones are set considerably closer than the unpruned. In nearly all the experiments, plants pruned to a single stem produced a lower yield per plant than unpruned plants. In experiments covering a period of 6 years at Ithaca, N.Y., reported by Thompson (1934), the average yield per plant was 3.77 pounds for those planted 2 by 3 feet and pruned to one stem; 7.15 pounds for unpruned plants set 3 by 4 feet; and 8.64 pounds for unpruned plants set 4 by 4 feet apart. Results of experiments conducted at three locations in Mississippi and reported by Deonier *et al.* (1944) indicate an advantage for pruning and staking. The pruned plants were set 2 feet apart in rows 4 feet apart, and the unpruned plants were set 4 by 4 feet. One treatment consisted of tying the plants to stakes without pruning, with the spacing 4 by 4 feet. This treatment had no advantage over the unpruned, unstaked plants in early or total yield and had the disadvantage of cost of stakes, labor, and twine.

Pruning tomato plants has little effect on hastening ripening, but the larger number of pruned plants usually set to the acre generally results in a larger yield per acre for the first 2 or 3 weeks. In general, the larger the number of plants, the greater the number of first clusters of fruit, and hence the greater the early yield. In most of the experiments there was little or no increase in early yield per acre from pruning and training, unless the pruned plants were set closer together than the unpruned ones.

Blossom-end rot is usually more severe on pruned, trained plants than on the unpruned, untrained ones. The fact that blossom-end rot is nearly always severe during dry weather and is worse on pruned, trained plants than on unpruned ones indicates that the pruning and training allow more moisture to escape from the surface of the soil, or else the pruned plants cannot get the moisture so well as the unpruned plants. Results of studies by Thompson (1927) indicate that both these factors probably are involved. Moisture determinations show greater loss of water from the soil growing pruned plants than from the soil growing unpruned ones, and root studies show a smaller and more restricted root system on the pruned plants. The transpiration rate is probably much higher from the pruned plants. The unpruned, untrained plants act as a mulch on the soil, restricting the movement of the air and shading the surface so that less moisture is lost by evaporation.

Training tomatoes on stakes or on other supports has a decided advantage in harvesting and in keeping the fruit clean and in some cases results in less rotting, particularly by soft rots. On the other hand, tomatoes grown on pruned, trained plants are more subject to cracking around the stem end and to sunscald on the side exposed to the midday sun.

The main disadvantage of the pruning and training is the increase in cost of production. With any practicable system of single-stem training, at least twice as many plants are required as in the ordinary method of growing unpruned plants. At 2 by 4 feet, 5,440 plants are required per acre; at 4 by 4 feet, only 2,720 are needed. The extra expense in growing the plants and setting them in the field, the cost of stakes and twine, and the cost of labor required to prune and tie the plants every week or 10 days for several weeks must be offset by the increase in returns for pruning and training to be profitable. The cost of pruning and training varies widely because of differences in plant-growing methods and of cost of stakes and labor.

Fruit Setting. The formation of the flower bud takes place under a wide range of conditions, but fruit setting is limited to a somewhat narrower range. Abscission may take place at any time during or after the opening of the flower. This dropping of the flowers may result from faulty nutrition, from unfavorable weather conditions, or from injury by disease or insects. Kraus and Kraybill (1918) have shown that the internal condition, as affected by environmental factors, has a marked effect on fruit setting. They showed that when nitrogen is deficient in the soil the plants are stunted and do not set fruit. Such plants have a high carbohydrate and low nitrogen content. When the soil contains a fairly abundant supply of nitrogen and other conditions are favorable, the plants make good growth, have a moderate content of both carbohydrates and nitrogen, and set fruit freely. When nitrogen is abundant and other conditions are favorable for growth, vegetation is vigorous and the plants are high in nitrogen and low in carbohydrates and unfruitful.

Fruit setting is associated with moderate vegetative growth and with a balance between the nitrogen and carbohydrate supplies in the plant. When conditions are such that vegetative growth is rapid, carbohydrates are used in new-tissue formation and in respiration so that the concentration of carbohydrates remains low and no fruit is set, although blossoms are produced abundantly. Bud formation may not take place under extreme conditions of high nitrogen and low carbohydrates. If the conditions are such that little growth takes place, the carbohydrates are not used in growth but accumulate in the plant, resulting in high concentration of the products of photosynthesis and the dropping of the blossom. The results of studies made by Kraus and Kraybill, by Work (1924), Nightingale (1927), and Nightingale, Schermerhorn, and Robbins

(1928) indicate that fruit setting depends on the accumulation of a considerable surplus of carbohydrates above the current needs of the plant for vegetative extension. The concentration of carbohydrates in the plant is a resultant of the balance between synthesis and utilization in new-tissue formation and in respiration.

Nightingale and Nightingale, Schermerhorn, and Robbins have shown that the length of daily illumination, along with varying nitrate supply, markedly affects the reproductive activity. Plants grown under a 7-hour day with nitrate in the nutrient solution were highly vegetative and unfruitful, while those grown with the same nutrient solution under a 14-hour day set fruit abundantly. With a short day and no nitrate, flowers set abundantly but no fruit; while with the long day and no nitrate, neither flowers nor fruit set. Watts (1931) showed that temperature has an effect somewhat similar to that of length of photoperiod. Increasing the temperature from 60 to 75°F. produced results similar to those obtained by increasing the length of photoperiod.

It is fairly well known that temperature has a marked effect on the setting of fruit in the tomato. Fruit set is usually poor when the temperature is either relatively low or relatively high. Watts (1931) found that the set of fruit was greater at 75 than at 60°F. Went (1945) and Went and Cosper (1945) concluded that the critical factor in the setting of fruit of the tomato is the night temperature, the optimum range being 59 to 68°F. (15 to 20°C.). Fruit fails to set at 55°F. or below. Moore and Thomas (1952) found that when the average maximum day temperature was above 90°F. and the average minimum night temperature was above 70°F. fruit set was low. They found also that high light intensity accompanied by high temperature was harmful to fruit set. Reducing the light intensity by shading increased fruit set significantly at high temperature, but when the temperature was satisfactory reducing the light intensity had no beneficial effect. Light intensity would affect the internal temperature of the fruit.

REGULATORS ON FRUIT SET. Plant regulators, chemicals used to regulate growth and reproduction, have been used successfully to increase fruit set in the tomato both in the greenhouse and in the field. When the days are short and the light intensity is low, fruit set of greenhouse tomatoes is low unless some regulator is used at the time of flowering. Tomato plants in the field or garden often fail to set fruit when the weather is unfavorable at the time of blossoming. Results of many experiments, including those reported by Hemphill (1949), Singletary and Warren (1951), Wittwer and Schmidt (1950), Parsons and Davis (1953), Wittwer (1954), and others have shown significant increases in fruit set and yield by the use of regulators under the conditions mentioned above. Many different materials have been and are being used, including para-chlorophenoxyacetic acid (CLPA), beta-naphthoxyacetic acid (NOA), and ortho-chlorophenoxypropionic acid (CLPP). While other materials have been used, the three mentioned seem to be the ones most generally recommended. Many methods of applying the regulators have been tested, and the results indicate that a water solution sprayed on the flower cluster is the safest and most practical method of application. The recommended concentration of the materials varies considerably. CLPA, for example, has been recommended at 15 parts per million to 50 parts per million, although 30 parts per million seems to be the most common concentration for field-grown tomatoes. Good results have been obtained with 75 to 100 parts per million of CLPP and 50 to 100 parts per million of NOA. The application is made at intervals of a week or 10 days when the conditions are unfavorable for fruit setting. When conditions are favorable for natural fruit setting, application of regulators is not recommended.

Effect of Fruit on Vegetative Growth. Murneek (1926) has shown that vegetative growth is regulated or controlled by the fruit. In his experiments this control was determined by: (1) the number of fruits on the plant and their proximity to the growing points and (2) the relative quantity of the available nitrogen supply. He found that restriction of nitrogen in the soil or of the stored nitrogen in the plant tends to retard development and that this retardation is in direct proportion to the quantity of fruit present. The fruit seems to be able to monopolize practically all of the elaborated nitrogen, thus causing a shortage in the strictly vegetative parts of the plant. The plane of nutrition of the plant determines the number of fruits a tomato plant can develop, but regardless of the nutrient and moisture supply the fruit eventually checks or stops vegetative growth. One fruit may stop growth of a plant in a very low plane of nutrition. Removal of the fruit usually results in renewal of vegetative growth and the setting of more fruit; thus we have what may be called waves of fruit setting.

Although the developing fruits retard vegetative growth, fertilization, or the union of the gametes, stimulates vegetative growth, according to Murneek (1926). This stimulation seems to affect the whole plant as well as the tissues surrounding the embryos. In Murneek's studies, plants from which the flowers were removed prior to fertilization made less growth than did those whose fruits were removed soon after they were set.

Varieties. Many varieties of tomatoes are in existence, but not so many as is indicated by the names listed in seed catalogues. Only a small percentage of the varieties grown is of much commercial importance. Probably 15 to 20 varieties constitute a large part of the crop grown for home use, for the fresh market, and for processing.

In choosing varieties the following factors should be considered: (1) the purpose for which grown, whether for home use, for market, or for processing, (2) length of the growing season, (3) yield, (4) desired quality, and (5) the susceptibility to disease, cracking, and other undesirable characteristics. When grown for home use only, the preference of the family should be considered with reference to quality, type, and color of the fruit. When grown for market in the fresh condition, the preferences of the buyers should be considered, but the grower must grow varieties that are adapted to the region. Earliness is important in regions having short growing seasons, as in parts of the United States, Canada, and other areas of similar climate, and also where early fruit brings a high price on the market. In such regions early or relatively quick maturing varieties should be grown. For processing the important characteristics are: (1) high yield, (2) good bright-red color, (3) smooth surface, (4) small core, (5) fairly solid flesh, and (6) resistance to cracking and the serious diseases. Most of these characteristics are important also for tomatoes grown for home use and for market.

Varieties frequently are classified as early, medium, and late, referring to the length of time required from planting to maturity. There are no sharply defined differences between the variety groups with reference to length of time required from planting to maturity. The variations within a varietal class may overlap in the adjoining class. Varieties that are considered early in one area may be main-crop varieties and used generally for processing in another. Those considered as main-crop varieties in some areas may take too long to mature to be of value in other areas. Boswell (1952) lists the important varieties as first-early, second-early, and main-crop varieties. Among the first-early he lists Earliana, Early Market, Morse's Special 498, First Early, Pennheart, Victor, and Bounty. Earliana is an old well-known variety of somewhat poorer quality than many of the later varieties. Early Market, Morse's Special 498, and First Early are similar to Earliana, but usually produce fruit of more uniform shape. Pennheart is somewhat similar to Earliana in fruit type but has a determinate habit of growth. Victor and Bounty are early varieties, developed for regions having a very short growing season. They are of bush type with scant foliage and small to medium-sized fruit. The second-early class contains the Bonny Best, John Baer, Chalk's Jewel, Clark's Early Coburg, Redhead, Longred, Gem, Redcap, Landreth, Pritchard, Stokesdale, Valiant, Queens, and several other newer varieties that are likely to replace some of the old ones. In some regions the Marglobe, Gulf State Market, Rutgers, and a few others in the same maturity class are considered as second-early, but more generally they are thought of as main-crop varieties, requiring a little longer to mature than the others mentioned above. Another class requiring longer to reach maturity than the second-early class includes Indiana Baltimore, Greater Baltimore, Pearson, Stone, San Marzano, and a few relatively new varieties that have not become well established. The varieties in the last-mentioned class together with Marglobe and Rutgers account for a large part of the production in the United States. Other varieties are more important in some regions. For example, Red Jacket and Longred are the only varieties grown on any considerable scale for processing in New York State. Rutgers is the most important variety grown for processing in New Jersey, Delaware, and Maryland and is an important market variety in several regions, including some of the Southern states. Pearson and San Marzano are grown mainly in California, and both are important for processing. The Pearson is grown for market also. San Marzano is an Italian variety that is used for solid pack, for tomato paste, and for mixing with other varieties to improve the color and increase the total solids of the canned product.

Since new varieties are being developed that are likely to replace many of those grown in 1955, it does not seem worthwhile to describe, or characterize the varieties listed above. Boswell (1952) gave brief descriptions of many of these varieties.

F_1 hybrid tomatoes are coming into use on a small scale in many areas, and it is expected that they will increase in importance as their value becomes better known. The main drawback to the use of hybrids is the cost of seed resulting from the large amount of work required in artificial pollination. Many plant breeders are experimenting in the development of hybrids and in methods of pollination to reduce cost. The tomato flower is largely self-pollinated. To obtain F_1 hybrids it is necessary to prevent self-pollination by removing the stamens, by making use of male sterility, or by some other method. It is also necessary to apply pollen to the stigmas of the flowers of plants selected as the female parent, and since neither wind nor insects are important in the transfer of pollen, artificial pollination, by some means, seems to be required.

Until some method is developed to reduce the amount of labor of pollination it is probable that the use of F_1 hybrids will continue on a small scale.

Diseases. The tomato is subject to the attacks of many diseases affecting all parts of the plants—roots, leaves, stems, and fruits. Doolittle (1948) listed 19 diseases caused by fungi and bacteria and, in addition, several minor fruit rots, 6 caused by virus, 3 by insects and nematodes, 7 nonparasitic, and 2 of undetermined origin. Fortunately, not all of the diseases are found in any one region, and it is seldom that those found in a given region are serious at the same time. Probably the most important diseases are fusarium wilt, bacterial wilt, bacterial canker, early blight, late blight, septoria leaf spot, anthracnose, virus diseases (tomato mosaic, cucumber mosaic, curly top), and root knot caused by nematodes.

FUSARIUM WILT. This disease, caused by *F. oxysporum* f. *lycopersici*, is very widespread and causes severe losses in many areas of the United States and elsewhere. It is characterized in its early stage by a wilting of the plant and an upward and inward rolling of the leaves. The leaves turn yellow and slowly die, the lower ones first, but finally the upper ones also. A cross section of an infected stem shows a dark-brown discoloration between the pith and bark. This discoloration of the woody layer distinguishes this disease from bacterial wilt.

Since the fungus causing wilt can live in the soil for several years, control measures must consist of soil treatment or the use of wilt-resistant strains or varieties. Soil treatment is not practicable except in the greenhouse where thorough sterilization will control the disease. Several wilt-resistant varieties, or strains, are available, some of which should be used where this disease is serious. Some of the well-known varieties that are resistant include Rutgers, Marglobe, Indiana Baltimore, Pan America, and Pritchard. Doolittle (1953) listed 15 other varieties (including 3 greenhouse varieties) that have high resistance to the disease. Several other new varieties are known to be resistant and may replace some of the old ones in certain regions. One of the newer varieties is Manalucie, developed by the Florida Experiment Station.

BACTERIAL WILT. This wilt is caused by *Pseudomonas solanacearum* and is serious in the Southern part of the United States and many other areas. It is present in the cooler regions, but usually is not very destructive. Plants affected by this disease wilt more rapidly than those attacked by fusarium wilt. Affected plants remain green for a while after they are infected, then wilt suddenly. When the stem is cut it exudes a dirty milky slime and the pith shows a dark, water-soaked appearance. The bacteria causing the disease live in the soil and infect the plant through the roots and stem. The disease may be spread to uninfected fields through infected plants, and the bacteria may be carried by drainage water from adjacent fields.

Doolittle (1948) suggested the following control measures:

When the disease occurs, tomatoes should not be planted again for 4 or 5 years; such crops as tobacco, potatoes, eggplant, or peppers should not be grown during this interval. Care should be taken that seedlings are not grown on infested soil, or on land in the immediate vicinity of infested fields. If a few wilted plants are noted in the field, they should be removed at once and destroyed to prevent further spread of the disease. If this is done, no replanting should be made at the point from which they were removed. All tomato varieties appear to be susceptible to bacterial wilt.

BACTERIAL CANKER. This is a destructive disease caused by *Corynebacterium michiganense,* a bacterium that may be carried by the seed. Seedlings frequently are infected, and they may be destroyed or may produce stunted plants that are of no value. The plants may show no evidence of the disease until some time after they have been set in the field. On older plants the first symptom is wilting of the margins of the leaflets of the older leaves. As the margins dry the leaflets curl upward. Later these leaves become brown, wither, and die, but the petiole remains attached to the stem. Open cankers are formed on the stem in advanced stages of the disease. On the fruits small, raised white spots ⅛ to ¼ inch in diameter develop. The centers of these spots break open and become brown and roughened. The white color persists about the margins of the spots, producing the bird's-eye spot typical of the disease. The measures recommended for control are: (1) use seed from canker-free fields, (2) treat seed with corrosive sublimate solution 1:2,000, or other method suggested in Chap. 12, (3) rotate crops so that tomatoes are grown on the same area only once in 4 or 5 years, (4) replace infested soil of hotbeds or cold frames with soil that has not grown tomatoes, (5) disinfect frames, covers, flats, and subsoil before new soil is put in, using 1:30 solution of 40 per cent formaldehyde, and (6) sterilize soil with steam, formaldehyde, or chloropicrin.

EARLY BLIGHT. This disease, caused by *Alternaria solani,* is found in most tomato-growing areas and is one of the most common and serious of the leaf spot diseases in the Atlantic Coast states and Central states. The fungus causes a canker and collar rot on the stem of seedlings and young plants in the field. On the leaves the fungus develops spots that may partly defoliate the plants and greatly reduce the yield and quality of the fruit. These spots develop on the older leaves and are small at first but gradually enlarge until they are ¼ to ½ inch in diameter. On the stem the disease appears as dark, slightly sunken areas that enlarge to form circular or elongated spots with light centers. The fungus attacks the fruit stems and may cause the dropping of the blossoms or the young fruits. On older fruits dark, leathery, sunken spots develop at the point of attachment to the stem.

The fungus that causes early blight of tomatoes also causes early blight of potatoes and attacks eggplant and certain wild plants of the nightshade family.

One of the important control measures is the prevention of seedling infection. The seed should be treated with corrosive sublimate, or other of the recommended chemicals, and planted in soil known to be free of the organism. The seedlings can be protected by spraying every 7 to 10 days with one of the neutral copper compounds or other recommended material. In the field, spraying or dusting often enough to keep the foliage covered is recommended. The fungicides most commonly used for control of this and other fungus diseases of tomatoes are copper compounds and organic compounds of the dithiocarbamate group. The neutral copper compounds have replaced Bordeaux mixture to a large extent because they are less injurious to tomato plants.

The development of new fungicides takes place so rapidly that it is not feasible to make specific recommendation.

LATE BLIGHT. This disease, caused by *Phytophthora infestans,* is one of the most destructive of all plant diseases, often destroying entire crops of tomatoes and potatoes in a week of cool, rainy weather. The fungus causes severe defoliation of tomatoes and a very destructive rot of the fruit. According to Doolittle (1948), the spores germinate readily at temperatures between 40 and 70°F. in the presence of moisture but are killed at 75 to 80°F. in dry weather. After infection occurs, the disease develops rapidly at temperatures between 70 and 80°F. This disease causes serious losses in all tomato-growing regions where climatic conditions are favorable for its development.

The first symptoms of late blight are irregular, greenish-black, water-soaked spots on the leaves. These spots enlarge rapidly in moist weather and sometimes show white, downy growth on the lower surfaces. The stems often show spots similar to those on the leaves. Fruit infection occurs near the stem end and may take place at any stage of growth. Small, grayish-green, water-soaked areas develop which enlarge rapidly and may cover half of the fruit. The spots take on a dark-green color, blotched with brown, as the fruits become older. The surface is firm and has a wrinkled appearance.

Control measures for late blight are similar to those used for other foliage diseases caused by fungi.

SEPTORIA LEAF SPOT. This disease, also known as blight, is caused by *Septoria lycopersici* and is widely distributed in the United States. It is of minor importance in the lower Southern states and in the mountain and Pacific Coast regions, but often causes heavy losses in the Atlantic and Central states.

The disease may occur on plants of any age and appears as water-soaked spots, the centers of which later turn gray surrounded by darker margins. The spots are smaller and more numerous than those of early blight. If the spots are very numerous the leaflet dies and drops off. Usually infection takes place first on the older leaves near the ground and progresses rapidly under favorable conditions until only a few leaves are left at the end of the stems. When defoliation is heavy sunscald of the fruit is serious. The fungus will not live over on the remains of the plants if they are buried deeply in the soil; therefore deep plowing after harvest is completed is recommended. Clean cultivation, long rotations, and spraying or dusting with copper compounds are other control measures.

ANTHRACNOSE. This disease is caused by *Colletotrichum phomoides* and is very serious in many tomato-growing sections of the United States and elsewhere. It is especially serious on tomatoes grown for processing because of loss resulting from rotting of the ripe fruit and from the very high mold count in the processed product when only a very small percentage of the fruits is diseased. Where fruit is harvested green for shipment to distant markets anthracnose is not of much importance. In the early stages infected fruits show small, sunken, water-soaked, circular spots. Later the spots become darker and more depressed with concentric-ring markings. As the spots increase in size, the center becomes dark, owing to the presence of black fungus structures beneath the skin.

The fungus lives in the soil on old dead tomato plants. It also lives in the seed. In the seedbed and in the field, spots occur on the foliage and stems, and in these infected areas the fungus remains alive until ripe fruit is available. The fungus can penetrate uninjured fruits, but infection is more prevalent where there are breaks in the skin. Development of the disease is most rapid in warm, damp weather with optimum temperature of about 80°F.

The control measures recommended for anthracnose are the same as for early blight. Zinc dimethyl dithiocarbamate is said to give better control than do the copper fungicides.

VIRUS DISEASES. There are several diseases of tomatoes caused by viruses, including tomato (tobacco) mosaic, cucumber mosaic, double virus streak, single virus streak, spotted wilt, and curly top.

Tomato mosaic is a serious trouble in most of the old tomato-producing regions. The virus causing this disease is the same as the one that is found on tobacco, pepper, eggplant, petunia, and other solanaceous plants and some of other families. The leaves affected are mottled with green and yellow. The yellow areas may die and turn brown. Affected plants are dwarfed and bear little fruit. The disease is highly infectious and spreads rapidly by handling the plants in transplanting and pruning and brushing against the plants in other operations. It may be spread also by certain species of aphids. The virus may remain active in dried tobacco leaves, and to some extent in cigar, cigarette, and pipe tobaccos.

Cucumber mosaic virus also affects the tomato, resulting in extremely malformed leaves. In some cases the leaves consist mainly of midribs and present a "shoestring" appearance, and thus the disease is known as *shoestring*, or *filiform*, leaf. The virus has many weed hosts including catnip, milkweed, pokeweed, ground cherry, and many others.

Tomato plants infected with tobacco mosaic virus also may become infected with the virus X of potatoes. Tomatoes that are infected with both of these viruses develop what is known as double-virus streak. This is another form of mosaic in which dead areas develop in the leaves, especially along the veins, and brown streaks appear on the petioles and stems giving rise to the name. Infected plants are stunted, and they set comparatively few fruits. These fruits are often rough, and on the surface there are small sunken spots which render the fruit unfit for sale.

There is also a single-virus streak that is serious in the greenhouse occasionally but is rare in the field. It is caused by a single virus similar to that of tomato mosaic. It is spread in much the same way as the tomato mosaic virus.

Spotted wilt is another virus disease that has caused serious losses in some sections of California and in Oregon, where a strain of the virus causes what is known as tip blight. The disease occurs occasionally in the field in other parts of the United States and has caused serious losses in greenhouse crops. The first symptoms in young plants are small, dark, circular, dead spots on the leaves. Badly spotted leaves may turn dark and wither. On older plants there is usually some damage to the growing tips, and the leaves may be yellowed. The fruits on infected plants have numerous spots ½ inch in diameter with circular markings which show as bands of red and yellow on ripe fruits. These fruit symptoms are the most characteristic of the disease. The spotted wilt virus also affects lettuce, celery, spinach, potatoes, peppers, and many weeds, and ornamental plants such as dahlias, calla lilies, petunias, and zinnias.

Curly top, or Western yellow blight, of tomatoes is caused by the same virus that causes curly top of sugar beets. The disease is important on tomatoes and other vegetables in irrigated and dry-farming sections of California and some of the Northwestern states and has been reported to occur in some of the other Western and Southwestern states . Curly top causes serious losses to other vegetable crops, especially to beans, table beets, spinach, squashes, and peppers. Tomato plants are susceptible to infection by the virus at any stage of growth, but susceptibility decreases with age of the plant. Infected seedlings show a yellowing of the foliage and may be accompanied by some curling of the leaves. On older, well-established plants the first symptom is a pronounced upward rolling and twisting of the leaflets, a general stiffening of the foliage, and a dull yellowing of the whole plant. The stems become abnormally erect, and the petioles curl downward.

The virus is thought to be transmitted by only a single species of insect, the beet leaf hopper, a migratory insect that breeds in weedy and sagebrush areas west of the Rocky Mountains. The leaf hoppers become carriers by feeding on wild or cultivated host plants that are affected with curly top.

Control of virus diseases consists to a large extent of sanitation to prevent infection. Destruction of weed hosts near the plant beds and tomato fields is an important control measure for all of these diseases. Destruction of infected seedlings in the seedbed will aid in preventing spread of tomato mosaic and double streak. In removing infected seedlings from the seedbed, care should be taken not to brush them against healthy plants. Control of insect vectors by use of insecticides should aid in control of those diseases in which the virus is carried by insects. Workers should not use tobacco in any form while working with tomato plants since it is known that tobacco mosaic virus may remain active in dry tobacco leaves and in other forms of tobacco. Every effort should be made to prevent the spread from infected to healthy plants in transplanting, cultivating, pruning, and other cultural practices. Development of strains resistant to the various virus diseases is the most promising method of control, and while much effort is being put forth in this direction, no resistant commercial varieties are available.

ROOT KNOT. Several species of nematodes attack tomato plants, but the root knot nematode (*Heterodera marioni*) is the most common. It is serious in the milder regions of the United States and elsewhere on field-grown tomatoes and may cause considerable losses in greenhouses in any region. The root knot nematode induces the development of irregular swellings, or knots, on the roots. It attacks all kinds of vegetables and many other plants.

Control consists of rotations in which root-knot–resistant crops are grown and the use of resistant strains or varieties. According to Walter and Kelbert (1953) the variety Manalucie, developed in Florida, is resistant to one of the five or six races of root knot nematode. Other strains and varieties are being developed. Oats, rye, beggarweed (*Desmodium molle* and *D. tortuosum*), and *Crotalaria spectabilis* are among the kinds of crops resistant to root knot nematode.

Nonparasitic Troubles. There are several troubles that generally are classed as diseases but which are not caused by a fungus, a bacterium, or a virus. These troubles include blossom-end rot, growth cracks, sunscald, and pockets, or puffiness. All of these seem to result mainly from unfavorable conditions during growth.

BLOSSOM-END ROT. This trouble affects only the fruit and, as its name indicates, occurs at the blossom end. The first evidence of injury is a brown discoloration on the blossom end of the fruit. The spots enlarge and darken until they may cover one-third or one-half of the fruit, but regardless of size, a fruit that is affected is unmarketable. The tissues shrink, and the skin becomes black and leathery, but no soft rot develops unless the spots are invaded by a soft rot organism. Blossom-end rot is a physiological disorder brought on by unfavorable conditions. It occurs most commonly during a dry period following growth under favorable conditions earlier in the season. Under such conditions a water deficit develops inside the plant, the cells at the blossom end of the fruit fail to receive sufficient water for their growth, and breakdown of the tissues occurs. The trouble can occur under periods of abundant rainfall if the soil remains nearly saturated for a considerable period. In such a case many rootlets are killed by lack of air or destroyed by certain fungi that thrive in moist soils. Root systems may be so damaged that insufficient water is taken into the plant.

Any cultural practice that conserves soil moisture and maintains a fairly uniform moisture supply aids in the control of blossom-end rot. Irrigation properly used will give good control under most conditions. Several investigators, including Evans and Troxler (1953), have presented evidence to indicate that calcium deficiency may be involved in blossom-end rot. Some varieties are reported to be somewhat resistant to this trouble.

GROWTH CRACKS. Cracking of the surface of the fruit at the stem end is a common occurrence and often results in large losses. The cracks are of two kinds, one of which radiates from the stem and the other develops concentrically around the shoulder of the fruit. Both kinds detract from the appearance of the fruit and provide points of entrance of organisms that cause decay. Radial cracking usually is more common and causes greater loss than concentric cracking.

Several environmental factors seem to be involved in the cracking of tomato fruits. It is common during rainy periods when the temperature is relatively high, especially when the rains follow a long dry period. Results of studies by Thomas (1948) indicate that water on the surface of the fruit is more conducive to cracking than high soil moisture. Both Thomas and Johannessen (1950) found that soaking the fruits in water is a good method of determining susceptibility to the development of growth cracks. According to Reynard (1951) the severity of radial cracking of susceptible strains is more closely associated with the number of days that rain fell just preceding picking than with the amount of rain in the same period. Radial cracking is more likely to develop in full-ripe fruits than on mature-green and turning stages of maturity. On the other hand, concentric cracking is relatively low on ripe fruits when it may be high on mature-green fruits. Fruits exposed to the sun develop more concentric cracking than those that are well covered with foliage, hence pruned, staked plants are more susceptible to this type of cracking than those allowed to grow without pruning and staking.

Picking fruits before they become fully ripe will reduce the incidence of radial cracking. Use of resistant varieties and strains is the best method of controlling both types of cracking. Many investigators, including those mentioned above and Frazier (1934, 1935) and Frazier and Bowers (1947), have shown that there are significant differences between strains and varieties in susceptibility to cracking. Several varieties resistant to cracking have been developed, including Sioux, Chesapeake, Manalucie, Crack-Proof, and others. According to Reynard (1951) resistance has been obtained in crosses between Crack-Proof and susceptible varieties. He states that resistance appears to be recessive to susceptibility.

SUNSCALD. This trouble occurs whenever green tomatoes are exposed to the sun and is common on plants that have lost considerable foliage from diseases and on plants with sparse foliage. Sunscald first appears as yellow or white patches on the part of the fruit exposed to the sun. The patches affected remain yellow when the fruit ripens, but frequently the tissues are so severely damaged that the patches shrink and the surface dries out. Later the patches may be invaded by fungi that cause decay.

Protecting plants from defoliation by diseases and insects, use of varieties with ample foliage, and following good cultural practices are the methods recommended to reduce sunscald injury.

POCKETS OR PUFFINESS. This trouble is most common when tomatoes are grown during winter and early spring in the United States. It causes considerable loss in fields in Florida, Texas, Mississippi, and California and in the greenhouse in most regions where the crop is grown during winter. The affected fruits are light in weight and feel soft. The fruits may be somewhat flattened over the surface between the inner walls, and the locules are only partially filled with pulp and seed. Cross section of affected fruits show empty spaces, or pockets (Fig. 24.4). Puffiness seems to be due to environmental and nutritional factors that affect pollination, fertilization, or the later development of internal tissues of the fruit. Results of experiments by Yarnell, Friend, and Wood (1937) indicate that temperature above 100°F. increased puffing in Texas and that there was a general relationship between rainfall and the percentage of puffy fruits. Corns (1937) also found that maintaining high soil moisture resulted in a greater percentage of puffy fruit than medium or low moisture. Globular fruits seem to be more subject to the trouble than the more flattened or oblate fruit. There is some evidence that fruits harvested in the mature-green stage develop a higher percentage of puffy fruits than those picked in the turning or ripe stage.

Where tomatoes are grown under irrigation it is suggested that overwatering be avoided. Less nitrogen should be used on the crop grown during short days and low light intensity than when grown under long days and high light intensity. Since there are strain and variety difference in susceptibility to puffiness, growing the less susceptible ones is suggested for regions where the trouble is likely to be serious.

Insects. The tomato is attacked by several kinds of insects, including the tomato fruitworm, hornworms, Colorado potato beetle, flea beetle, aphids, and cutworms. Only the first two are discussed here since the others are discussed elsewhere. The Colorado potato beetle, flea beetle, and potato aphid are discussed in Chap. 21, and cutworms in Chap. 12.

TOMATO FRUITWORM. This insect is a serious pest in most areas in the Southern part of the United States, in California, and in other regions where the climate is mild. The adult is a moth. The larva eats into the

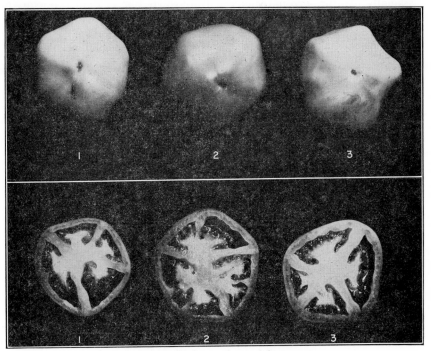

FIG. 24.4. Puffy fruits of Marglobe tomato.

green fruit, usually rendering it worthless because rots develop in the injured portion. The fruitworm is the same as the cotton bollworm and the corn earworm. Dusting with 10 per cent DDT or TDE is one of the recommended control measures. The first treatment should be made about the time the fruits begin to set, with second and third applications at 2-week intervals. The foliage should be well covered with the insecticide.

TOMATO HORNWORMS. There are two species of hornworm that feed on the foliage and fruit of the tomato. They are the larvae of large sphinx moths of two species similar in habits. The larvae are large green caterpillars that are able to eat a great quantity of foliage in a short time. The name hornworm is given because the larva has a prominent horn on the rear end. Hand picking is the usual method of control and generally is the most economical. Spraying or dusting with DDT or TDE are other control measures recommended.

Harvesting. The stage of maturity at which tomatoes are picked depends upon the purpose for which they are grown and the distance they are to be transported. Several stages are recognized, including immature-green, mature-green, turning, half-ripe, or pink, and ripe, or red-ripe. Fruits picked in the immature-green stage may not have reached full size and are usually tough, leathery, and of poor color when ripened artificially. Mature-green fruits are full-grown but have not begun to turn pink; the seed cavities are filled with a jellylike material; the color has begun to change to a whitish green, especially at the blossom end. Fruits picked at this stage of maturity will develop good color when ripened under favorable conditions. Fruits classed as "turning" show some pink, especially on the blossom end, but most of the surface is still green. Half-ripe, or pink, fruits show some pink color over most or all of the surface, varying from light pink to nearly red in color. Ripe, or red-ripe, fruits are those that have developed full color for the variety but are usually firm.

Tomatoes intended for use as ripe fruit should never be picked in a less mature stage than mature-green and, where feasible, they should be allowed to reach the turning stage, since it is difficult for the pickers to determine the mature-green stage. Most tomatoes picked before they reach the turning stage are selected on the basis of size alone. Sando (1920) has shown that size is no criterion of maturity. Lutz (1944) reported results of 5 years study of handling green-wrap tomatoes grown at Crystal Springs, Miss., which show that fruits picked in the immature-green stage do not develop good color or good quality. He found that such fruits do not develop so high ascorbic acid content as those picked as mature-green or more fully mature fruits. Similar results were reported by Hamner, Bernstein, and Maynard (1945). Fryer *et al.* (1954) found that fruits harvested in the yellow-red stage and ripened at approximately 75°F. out of direct sunlight developed normal concentration of ascorbic acid for red-ripe greenhouse tomatoes. Mature-green fruits ripened under the same conditions did not develop so high ascorbic acid content as fruits picked at more mature state.

Artificial Ripening. A large part of the tomato crop grown for distant markets is picked in what is called the mature-green stage of maturity and ripened artificially in ripening rooms held at 55 to 70°F. The temperature maintained in the ripening room is determined by the speed desired in ripening, and this is governed by the market demand. Where maximum speed is desired, the temperature is maintained at 70 to 72°F. At temperatures of 70°F. or above more decay is likely to develop than at lower temperatures. Results of experiments reported by Sayre, Robinson, and Wishnetsky (1953) indicate that at 85°F. or above tomato fruits are likely to ripen without developing a good red color. They found that it required 9 days for the fruit picked at the turning stage to become fully red-ripe when held at 80°F. daytime and 65°F. night temperature. It is important to have high humidity (90 to 95 per cent) in the ripening room in order to prevent wilting or withering of the fruit. Ethylene gas is used to some extent to hasten the ripening of tomato fruits that are picked in mature-green stage of maturity. Results of experiments on the use of ethylene have been rather conflicting, owing probably to difference in tightness of the room or container in which the experiments were conducted. Heinze and Craft (1953) found that the rate of ripening of mature-green tomatoes in small tightly closed containers was not affected to any appreciable extent by the addition of ethylene. On the other hand, ethylene hastened ripening of ventilated lots of tomatoes, and the rate was comparable with that of fruit in tightly closed containers. Tomato fruits evolve ethylene during the ripening process, and this explains why additional ethylene has little effect when ripening takes place in tight rooms.

Grading. The grading of tomatoes for market has been practiced to some extent for a long time, but prior to 1917 no concerted effort had been made to formulate grade standards. The U.S. Department of Agriculture developed tentative grade standards at that time, and since then the specifications have been revised several times. Official grade standards are available for tomatoes for fresh market and for processing. Buying of tomatoes for processing on the basis of grade is a common practice and is very important to both the processor and the good growers. When tomatoes are bought on the flat-rate basis, all growers get the same price; when bought on the graded basis, the careful grower gets the benefit of producing a high-quality product as a result of care in harvesting. The processor gains from buying on the basis of grade because he gets fewer green, overripe, rotten, and defective tomatoes and a larger percentage of red-ripe, sound fruits than when he buys on a flat-rate basis.

Tomatoes grown for the fresh market, especially those produced for local markets, are not graded as well as they should be, but the grading is improving. When the fruits are to be shipped, it is desirable to separate the fruits according to size, as well as to meet the general requirements of the grades.

Packing and Packages. Various methods of packing tomatoes are in use. For local markets little attention is given to method of packing or to the kind of package used. The top layer of fruit is often placed by hand, and too often this layer of fruit is much better than the remainder in the package.

When packed for long-distance shipment, the fruits usually are placed by hand in layers with the top layer in rows; in some packages all layers are arranged in rows. The most popular package used is the lug box. This box has been used by California and Texas shippers for many years and is now used as a shipping container in nearly all regions. Other containers used for shipment, and also to some extent for local markets, are the 8- and 12-quart handled, squarebraid basket and paperboard basket. Tomatoes for local markets are put up in all kinds of containers, including hampers, round stave, and other kinds of baskets holding 3 or 4 pecks, and boxes and crates of various kinds. Consumer packages have come into use to a large extent. These containers are mainly pasteboard cartons holding four or five fruits and having a window of transparent film in the top. These small cartons are packed for shipment in carriers holding 10, 20, or 30 units. In most cases the packaging in consumer packages is done in or near the consuming centers.

The practice of wrapping tomatoes in paper before packing is a common one in some regions where the crop is grown for shipment. Wrapped fruits may stand shipment better than unwrapped ones, but wrapping adds to the expense. There is some evidence that wrapped fruit does not develop as good quality as unwrapped fruit because of exclusion of the air.

Storage. Tomatoes can be kept in storage either in mature-green or in a more mature stage of maturity. For mature-green fruits, the best storage temperature is from 50 to 60°F., especially if they are to be held for a considerable period. Wright *et al.* (1931) state that 55°F. was the lowest temperature at which the tomatoes ripened with good color and good flavor. They found that holding tomatoes at temperatures as low as 32°F. for 5 days did not prevent subsequent ripening, but the rate of ripening was slower than fruits not so exposed. Craft and Heinze (1954) found that mature-green fruits stored at 32°F. for 9 and 14 days failed to ripen properly and showed low-temperature injury when transferred to 65°F. The ascorbic acid content showed no pronounced change with storage temperature. Platenius, Jamison, and Thompson (1934) found that if tomatoes were kept at temperatures below 49°F. for longer that 2 weeks, they decayed rapidly when allowed to ripen subsequently at 70°F. Mature-green tomatoes can be kept as long as 30 days at 50 to 60°F. Ripe tomatoes can be kept for 10 days at 40°F.

EGGPLANT

The eggplant is of minor importance in the United States although it is grown on a small scale by market gardeners in many areas. The estimated average annual acreage grown commercially in Florida, Texas,

Louisiana, and New Jersey for the period 1948–1953 was 5,285 acres, with production of 1,458,000 bushels valued at $2,168,000. Production in the four states mentioned averaged about 50 per cent greater during the period 1948–1953 than the average in the period 1938–1942. The eggplant is of great importance in the warm areas of the Far East, being grown more extensively in India, China, and the Philippines than is the tomato.

History and Taxonomy. The eggplant is probably a native of India and has been in cultivation for a long time. Some authorities claim that it can be recognized from descriptions published as early as the fifth century. It probably was not known in Europe at the time of the ancients.

It belongs to the Solanaceae, or nightshade, family and is known under the botanical name *Solanum melongena*. Almost all the cultivated varieties belong to botanical varieties of the species mentioned. The common eggplant, to which the large-fruited forms, such as New York Improved, belong, is known under the name *S. melongena* var. *esculentum*. The plant is bushy and grows to a height of 2 to 4 feet; the leaves are large and alternate on the stems; the flowers are large, violet-colored, and solitary, or in clusters of two or more. The serpentine, or snake, eggplants are placed under the variety *serpentinum*. The fruits of this group are long and slender, 1 inch or less in diameter and 12 to 15 inches long. The dwarf eggplants are known under the variety name *depressum*. These produce small, weak, spreading plants, nearly smooth. The leaves are small and thin, and the flowers are much smaller than those of the common eggplant. The fruits are small, pear-shaped, and purple in color. The dwarf forms do not require so long to mature as the common form and are better adapted to regions having a short growing season.

Climatic and Soil Requirements. The eggplant is a very tender plant that requires a long, warm growing season for successful production. The plant is killed by a light frost and is injured by long periods of chilly frostless weather. A frost-free period of about 5 months is necessary for satisfactory production of most varieties. The plants should not be set in the field or garden until the daily mean temperature reaches 65 to 70°F.

Fertile, well-drained soils are desirable for the production of eggplant. If the soil is not naturally fertile, it should be well fertilized, preferably with manure and commercial fertilizer. If manure is not available, soil-improving crops may be grown and used to supply organic matter. Where the growing season is short, a sandy or sandy-loam soil is preferable to a heavier one because the lighter soils warm up early in the spring. Soil preparation is the same for eggplant as for other vegetable crops.

Fertilizers. Where manure is available on the farm or can be purchased at a moderate price, its use is recommended. Ordinary stable manure applied at the rate of 10 to 15 tons to the acre, supplemented with a fertilizer to supply about 50 pounds of N, 100 pounds of P_2O_5, and 50 pounds of K_2O, should give good results. Where no manure is used, the application of complete fertilizer should supply about 100 pounds of N and 100 to 150 pounds each of P_2O_5 and K_2O to the acre. Since the crop occupies the land for a long period it may be desirable to apply additional nitrogen once or twice during growth. Nitrate of soda, sulfate of ammonia, ammonium nitrate, or other readily available form may be used at the rate to supply 20 to 25 pounds of actual nitrogen at each application.

Plant Growing. The plants usually are started in greenhouses, hotbeds, cold frames, or in prepared beds in the open. In regions of short growing seasons, greenhouses, or hotbeds are used and the plants are started 8 to 10 weeks before time for planting them in the field. The methods of growing the plants are the same as for tomatoes. Special care should be taken to prevent chilling the plants and in protecting them against insects, diseases, and other unfavorable conditions.

Planting and Care. Since the eggplant is very tender, it should be set in the field or garden after all danger of frost is past and the weather has become warm. If the plants are to be covered with "hotcaps" or other protective covering, they may be set out 10 days to 2 weeks earlier than if no protection is to be given. The plants usually are set 2 to 3 feet apart in rows 3 to 4 feet apart. For small-growing varieties, such as New Hampshire, setting the plants 1½ to 2 feet apart in rows 2½ to 3 feet apart is preferable to wider spacing.

Shallow cultivation should be given often enough to control the weeds. Irrigation is essential in arid regions and is important in many others.

Varieties. Relatively few varieties of eggplants are listed by American seedsmen. Black Beauty and Fort Myers Market are the varieties grown most extensively in the United States. Florida High Bush, New York Spineless, Florida Market, Florida Beauty, and New Hampshire are other varieties listed by seedsmen. Florida Market and Florida Beauty are relatively new varieties developed by the Florida Experiment Station and are said to be resistant to phomopsis fruit rot. New Hampshire is a relatively new variety developed by the New Hampshire Experiment Station. It is a small-fruited early variety adapted to regions having short growing seasons. The plants are small and should be planted closer than the other varieties mentioned.

Diseases. Fruit rot and wilt are the most important diseases of the eggplant. Fruit rot is caused by the fungus *Phomopsis vexans* and is a serious disease which attacks all parts of the plant aboveground. The spots on the leaves are brown, circular, or oblong, becoming irregular with age. The centers of the spots become grayish or light brown and the margins black. The disease on the stem is most common on seedlings, causing a damping-off. Spots on the fruits start with light-brown blotches which develop into a soft rot, frequently covering the entire fruit. Control of fruit rot consists of crop rotation, use of disease-free seed, and growing resistant varieties such as Florida Market and Florida Beauty.

Wilt, caused by *Verticilium albo-atrum*, is characterized by a yellowing of the foliage and gradual defoliation. Affected plants become stunted, and many die prematurely. Crop rotation in which crops other than potatoes and tomatoes are grown is recommended as a control measure.

Insects. Flea beetles, Colorado potato beetle, eggplant lacebug, and aphids are the most important insects that attack eggplant. The eggplant flea beetle (*Epitrix fuscula*) is a small black beetle that is a serious pest to plants in the seedbed, where it punctures the leaves and stunts the plants so that the flowers often drop. Control is the same as for the potato flea beetle.

Eggplant lacebug (*Gargraphia solani*) is a bug about $\frac{1}{6}$ inch long, which injures the plant by sucking the juices. The adult is grayish to light brown in color with lacelike wings. The nymph is yellowish and louselike up to $\frac{1}{10}$ inch long. This insect can be controlled by spraying or dusting with 4 to 5 per cent malathion. The insecticide should not be used within a week of harvest.

Harvesting. The fruits of the eggplant are edible from the time they are one-third-grown until they are ripe. They remain in an edible condition for some time after they become fully grown and colored. A heavier crop will be produced if the fruits are removed before they reach full size, but they should be well colored and of good size in order to sell well.

The fruits are usually cut from the vines since the stems are hard and woody. The large calyx and a short piece of the stem are left on the fruit, but care should be taken to prevent the stem from injuring other fruits in the package. They are heavy and should be handled with care even though they are not as perishable as the tomato. The fruits are sometimes put in paper bags, one fruit to each bag, or wrapped in paper before being packed for shipping. They are packed in various kinds of containers, including special crates, bushel baskets, and, to some extent, in berry crates. Before packing they are usually graded somewhat to separate the size and to cull out inferior fruits, but no definite grades are recognized.

PEPPER

The pepper belongs to the genus Capsicum and is very distinct from the pepper of commerce, which is the fruit of *Piper nigrum*, belonging to another family. Peppers are used in a great variety of ways. Cayenne pepper or red pepper of commerce consists of fruit of small pungent varieties ground to a fine powder. Pepper sauce of various kinds consists of the fruit of pungent varieties preserved in brine or strong vinegar. Paprika, a Hungarian condiment, is made from fruit ground after the seeds have been removed. Peppers are used in pickles of various kinds. The sweet varieties are sliced and eaten as salad. They are used in stuffing pitted olives, and the large sweet varieties are stuffed and baked. A small-fruited variety of peppers is used for decorative purposes. Pimiento, or Spanish pepper, is a mild, thick-fleshed type that is grown on a fairly large scale in Georgia and a few other areas of the United States.

Peppers have much the same cultural requirements as the tomato but perhaps are a little more subject to injury by unfavorable conditions.

Statistics of Production. The average annual acreage of peppers grown for market in the 11 important producing states increased about 2½ times from the average of the 10-year period 1923–1932 to the 1943–1953 period (Table 24.3). The average farm value increased slightly over 4

Table 24.3. Estimated Average Annual Acreage Production and Farm Value of Peppers Grown for Market, 1923–1953

Years	Acres	Production, bushels (000 omitted)	Farm value (000 omitted)
1923–1932	13,827	3,473	$ 3,855
1933–1942	20,052	4,640	3,715
1943–1953	34,706	7,908	15,545

times during the same period. The leading states in production in 1953 were Florida with 3,545,000 bushels; California, 1,566,000; New Jersey, 1,551,000; Texas, 818,000; and North Carolina, 656,000 bushels.

In addition to the peppers grown for market, an average of 23,138 acres of pimiento peppers was grown for processing during the period 1949–1953. The average annual production was 25,664 tons, and the farm value was $2,031,600 for the same period. From 1939 to 1953 the acreage and production have fluctuated widely from a low of 6,460 acres and 8,600 tons in 1944 to 32,000 acres and 44,800 tons in 1950.

History and Taxonomy. The cultivated peppers are undoubtedly of American origin. They are known from prehistoric remains in Peru, were widely cultivated in Central and South America in early times, and were unknown in Europe prior to the discovery of America. Columbus carried seed to Spain in 1493, and from there the cultivation of peppers spread rapidly in Europe. It seems probable that the first peppers grown in the United States came directly from Europe rather than from Central or South America. Linnaeus recorded two species of Capsicum in the first edition of "Species Plantarium" in 1753, and three additional species were added in 1797.

Capsicum, a genus of the Solanaceae family, is closely related to Solanum. All species of the genus except *C. anomalum* of Japan are native to tropical America. There has been considerable confusion in regard to the taxonomy of the cultivated peppers. Some early botanists recognized many species, whereas Bailey (1924, 1949) recognized only one with six botanical varieties or subspecies. Irish (1898), in a comprehensive study, recognized two species, *C. annuum* and *C. frutescens,* the former with seven botanical varieties. His classification was widely adopted and is still followed by most European and Asiatic botanists. On the other hand, most horticulturists and plant breeders in the United States have followed Bailey's treatment, which was accepted by Erwin (1932) in connection with his elaborate study of the cultivated peppers. Smith and Heiser (1951) and Heiser and Smith (1953) recognized four species of cultivated peppers, only two of which are grown in the United States, *C. annuum* and *C. frutescens.* The other two species, *C. pubescens* and *C. pendulum,* are cultivated in Latin America. According to Heiser and Smith, all of the principal varieties grown in the United States, with the exception of Tabasco, belong to *C. annuum.* The four cultivated species have been keyed by Heiser and Smith (1953) as follows:

Corolla lobes purple; seeds black; leaves rugose; stem and
    leaves rather densely pubescent.................... *C. pubescens*
Corolla lobes white or greenish-white, rarely purple; seeds
    light in color; leaves smooth; plants glabrous, or
    pubescent
        Corollas white with yellow or tan markings on throat;
            anthers yellow............................... *C. pendulum*
        Corollas without yellow markings on throat; anthers
            light blue to purple
            Corollas greenish-white (or yellowish-white); pedi-
              cels solitary or more frequently paired, or several
              at a node............................... *C. frutescens*
            Corollas clear white or dingy white, rarely purple;
              pedicels solitary, rarely two at a node.......... *C. annuum*

The following brief discussion of the four species is adapted from Heiser and Smith (1953).

Capsicum pubescens was originally described from Peru in 1790 and more recently from Colombia, Mexico, Guatemala, and Honduras. The greatest diversity of forms appears to occur in the Andes, and it is probable that this species is limited to relatively high altitudes. The fruits are variable in size and form and are mildly to strongly pungent.

Capsicum pendulum Willd. is rather widely distributed in South America but seems to be unknown in Central America. It is one of the most popular of the cultivated peppers in coastal Peru. Fruit size and shape are quite variable. Immature fruit colors vary from almost ivory white to yellow or green; colors of mature fruit vary from orange to red. *C. pendulum* is not known in cultivation in the United States, but it may prove to be of some value here in a breeding program since preliminary tests indicate that it is early and a heavy bearer.

Capsicum frutescens L. is widely cultivated in tropical and subtropical regions of the world. It is found in native agriculture of Mexico, Central America, and South America. Only one variety of this species, Tabasco, is grown to any considerable extent in the United States. Fruit size and shape are variable, "but no fruits have been seen which exceed 10 centimeters in length, and therefore they do not reach the size of *C. annuum.*" The very small fruited peppers, frequently called "bird peppers," which are considered a variety of *C. frutescens* by some and *C. baccatum* by others, are naturalized in many regions.

Capsicum annuum L. includes a large number of horticultural varieties and is by far the most important economically. Fruit size, shape, and color are extremely variable, more so than in any other species. The fruit varies in size from 1 to 30 centimeters in length, from small conical to thick-fleshed, blocky, or flattened. Both yellow and green immature and red, yellow, and brown mature fruits are common. Virtually all of the larger-fruited varieties grown in the temperate zones of the world belong to *C. annuum.* With the exception of Tabasco, all of the principal varieties in the United States belong to this species. It includes both pungent and nonpungent varieties.

Climatic and Soil Requirements. The climatic and soil requirements of peppers are similar to those for tomatoes. Climatic conditions at the time of blossom development and fruit set have a marked effect on yield of peppers. Results of studies by Cochran (1936) indicate that unfavorable temperature and unfavorable water supply are the basic factors in the dropping of buds, blossoms, and very small fruits. Low humidity and high temperature result in excessive transpiration and a water deficit in the plant. Under such conditions, abscission of buds, flowers, and small fruits usually takes place (Fig. 24.5). Low moisture supply in the soil also is an important factor in blossom drop, but under conditions of excessive transpiration a water deficit develops even when the soil is well supplied with water. In Cochran's studies, plants held at 50 to 60°F. for about 6 months made no appreciable growth, and from 40 plants only one flower developed, and this dropped without setting fruit. When plants that had developed blossoms at higher temperatures were transferred to a greenhouse held at 50 to 60°F. at the time of anthesis

Fig. 24.5. Effect of temperature on fruit set in peppers. Plants grown at 70 to 80°F. until flower buds formed, then (1) and (2) shifted to 50 to 60°F., (3) and (4) kept at 70 to 80°F.

99.3 per cent of the flowers set fruit, but all fruits developed parthenocarpically, as shown in Fig. 24.6.

Peppers are grown on many classes of soils from light sands to clays. Where growing seasons are short, sandy and sandy-loam soils are preferred. Silt soils and good clay loams are satisfactory where other conditions are favorable. The soil should be well drained and given good preparation for the crop. The pepper plant is not very sensitive to soil acidity, but a strongly acid soil should be limed to bring it to moderate or slight acidity.

Fertilizers. The fertilizer practice suggested for the eggplant should be satisfactory for peppers.

Plant Growing. Pepper plants generally are started in well-prepared beds in open fields, in cold frames, hotbeds, or greenhouses. Open-field

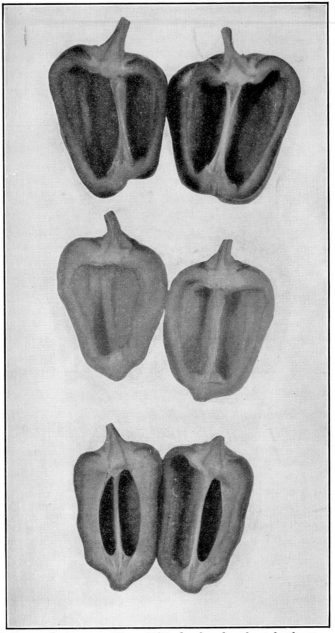

Fig. 24.6. Pepper fruits set at 50 to 60°F. developed without fertilization—no seed produced.

beds are used only where the climate is mild. In regions of short growing seasons, plants are started in hotbeds or greenhouses or purchased from growers in areas where they are grown in field beds. The latter practice is not so common with pepper plants as with tomato plants. Seed is sown usually 7 to 8 or 10 weeks before time for planting in the open. When started in hotbeds or greenhouses the plants usually are transplanted once before they are set in the field, as described for tomato plants. General methods of growing plants are discussed in Chap. 7.

Planting and Care. The pepper plant is injured by a light frost and makes practically no growth at 50°F. or below and therefore should not be planted in the open until all danger of frost is past and the weather has become warm. Most varieties of peppers are planted about 2 feet apart in rows 3 feet apart. Small-growing varieties may be planted as close as 18 inches apart in the row. Very large growing varieties sometimes are planted 2½ by 3 feet. Plants in bands, pots, or with a block of soil about the roots are planted by hand. Plants pulled from the plant bed may be planted by hand, or with a machine planter, the latter method being more economical where considerable acreage is grown.

Shallow cultivation to control weeds is recommended.

Irrigation is essential in arid and semiarid regions and is important in many so-called humid regions.

Varieties. There are two distinct classes of peppers with reference to pungency: those that are hot, or pungent, and those that are mild, or nonpungent, known as "sweet peppers." The mild, or sweet, varieties are of greater importance in the United States than the hot varieties. In general, the sweet varieties grown are larger and have thicker flesh than the pungent varieties. Some of the important sweet varieties are California Wonder, Chinese Giant, Harris Early Giant, Neapolitan, Winsor A, Ruby King, and World Beater. There are many other varieties, and more than one strain of most. Pimiento, or Spanish pepper, is a mild, thick-fleshed type that is produced on a fairly large scale in some areas, especially in Georgia, and is grown almost exclusively for canning. This type usually is more pointed and has thicker flesh than the type known as Bell peppers. Perfection is the principal variety of pimiento peppers.

The most important varieties of hot peppers are Tabasco, Anaheim, Chili, Mexican, or Native Chili, Long Thick Cayenne, Long Thin Cayenne, College No. 9 Chili, and Sport. Hungarian Paprika and Spanish Paprika are grown to some extent in the United States for drying and grinding into powder for use as a condiment in foods. These peppers are practically nonpungent.

Diseases. Doolittle (1953) listed the following diseases of peppers and gives brief descriptions and control measures. Damping-off (mainly *Rhizoctonia solani*), bacterial spot (*Xanthomonas vesicatoria*), cercospora leaf spot (*Cercospora capsici*), phytophthora blight (*Phytophthora capsici*), Southern blight (*Sclerotium rolfsii*), fusarium wilt (*Fusarium annuum*), anthracnose (*Gloesporium piperatum*), ripe rot (*Vermicularia capsici*), a fruit rot caused by *Colletotrichum nigrum*, tobacco mosaic, cucumber mosaic, tobacco etch virus, and curly top. The last four mentioned are diseases caused by viruses. Blossom-end rot and sunscald are nonparasitic troubles of peppers that sometimes cause considerable loss.

Most of the diseases of peppers are the same as or similar to those of the tomato, and the control measures are essentially the same.

Insects. Several kinds of insects attack peppers, including aphids, cutworms, flea beetles, hornworms, the pepper weevil, and the pepper maggot. All of these except the pepper weevil and pepper maggot feed on several different kinds of crops and are discussed elsewhere.

PEPPER WEEVIL. The adult is a black snout beetle about $\frac{1}{8}$ inch long with gray or yellow markings. The larva, or grub, is grayish white with a pale-brown head. Both the adult and larva feed on the pepper plant, with the larva causing the greater damage. The adult feeds on the foliage, blossom buds, and tender pods. The larva may be found in the wall of the pepper fruit, but more likely in the seed or seed core. The eggs are laid in holes which the female punctures in the blossom buds or immature fruits. The eggs hatch in 3 or 4 days, and the grub feeds on the inside of the buds or among the seeds of the immature fruits, causing dropping of the buds or the small fruits. Large fruits are likely to be misshapen and discolored. Complete development from egg to adult takes place within the blossom buds or immature fruits and may require only 15 to 20 days under favorable conditions. There may be from five to eight generations in a year, depending on the weather conditions.

The pepper weevil (*Anthonomus eugenii*) is found in California, Arizona, New Mexico, Texas, Georgia, and Florida. This species, or some other species of Anthonomus, is also a serious pest in Hawaii and other tropical areas.

Control measures include dusting with 5 per cent DDT or 50 per cent cryolite every week to 10 days or spraying with the same materials, using the concentration recommended by the manufacturers.

PEPPER MAGGOT. The larva, or maggot, is about $\frac{1}{2}$ inch long when full-grown, and the adult is a two-winged, yellow-striped fly about $\frac{3}{10}$ inch long. The larva infests the pods of peppers and sometimes causes serious losses in some areas.

This insect can be controlled by dusting with 1 per cent parathion,

1 per cent rotenone, or 5 per cent chlordane. The first application should be made as soon as the first flies appear. Subsequent applications should be made at 5-day intervals as long as any flies are present in the field.

Harvesting and Handling. The stage of maturity at which peppers are picked depends on the type and the purpose for which they are grown. The large sweet peppers usually are picked while they are still green in color but full-grown when sold on the general market, although there is some demand for red ones. For brining and canning, both mature-green and red-ripe stages are used. Pimiento and paprika varieties are harvested when dark-red ripe. Most hot peppers are harvested ripe for drying. Some are harvested either green or ripe, depending on the product to be prepared from them. The Tabasco type is picked fully red-ripe.

The fruits are picked by snapping off the brittle stems with the hands. When grown for market the fruits generally are carried to a central point where they are graded and packed. Grades for sweet peppers have been formulated by the U.S. Department of Agriculture and should be used where feasible. Peppers for market are shipped largely in 1-bushel tub baskets, but other containers, such as ½- and 1-bushel hampers, are used, especially on local markets.

Storage. While sweet peppers grown for market are not stored for any considerable period, experiments by Platenius, Jamison, and Thompson (1934) indicate that they can be kept in good condition for at least 40 days at 32°F. and at humidity of 95 to 98 per cent. Shrinkage of the fruits stored under these conditions was only 4 per cent in 40 days, which is less than for most vegetables. At 40°F. pepper fruits kept well for about 4 weeks, and at 50°F. they remained in good condition for 16 days. Dried peppers can be kept for long periods in dry storage, if protected from insects.

HUSK TOMATO

The husk tomato (*Physalis pubescens*) is cultivated to some extent in the gardens of the United States, but it is not grown commercially. The plants are decumbent and produce a small, round fruit of a yellow color inside a thin husk. There are several native species of Physalis, known as "ground cherries," found in the United States. A husk tomato found in Guatemala has been introduced and improved by workers of Iowa State College. Melhus and Smith (1953) described the plant as vigorous, semiprostrate, branching 4 to 6 inches above the ground, forming a low-spreading plant. The fruit is yellow, round, and ranges in size from 1 inch to 2½ inches in diameter; the flesh is yellow when ripe, firm and mildly acid in flavor. Plant growing and general culture are much the same as for the tomato. According to Melhus and Smith, plants transplanted outside on May 5 at Ames, Iowa, began to blossom June 15, and fruit started to ripen in late July. The vines grew 18 to 24 inches tall, had a spread of 30 to 45 inches, and produced an average yield of 2½ pounds per plant, or about 9 tons per acre.

The husk tomato can be used as food in many forms. Melhus and Smith published recipes for preparing husk tomatoes in the following forms: fried, baked, stewed, cooked with meat, and made into soup, dessert sauce, marmalade, and salad. It is not, however, an important food plant and is of no commercial importance in the United States.

CHAPTER 25

The Cucurbits, or Vine Crops

Cucumber	Watermelon
Muskmelon	Pumpkin and squash

The cucurbits, or vine crops, are tender annuals grown for their fruits. They thrive only in hot weather and will not withstand frost. All these crops belong to the same family, Cucurbitaceae, and all have similar cultural requirements as well as many of the same diseases and insect pests. From every point of view they should be grouped together for discussion. While most of the plants in this family are monoecious, some are andromonoecious and some are dioecious.

CUCUMBER

The cucumber is an important vegetable crop in the United States, being grown in the home garden, in market gardens, and truck farms, as a forcing crop in greenhouses, and as a special crop for pickles. In the United States the cucumber is consumed mostly as pickles and as a salad, whereas in some countries it is consumed also as a cooked vegetable.

Statistics of Production. The production of cucumbers in the United States for use in the fresh state increased markedly from 1918 to 1953, as is shown in Table 25.1.

Table 25.1. Estimated Average Annual Acreage, Production, and Farm Value of Cucumbers Grown for Market in the United States, 1918–1953

Years	Acres	Production, bushels (000 omitted)	Farm value (000 omitted)
1918–1927	25,698	3,449	$ 5,612
1928–1937	44,980	4,145	4,050
1938–1947	44,816	5,090	9,049
1948–1953	49,025	7,026	16,857

The figures in Table 25.1 include only the crop grown for market in the 16 most important states. Other states also produce cucumbers for market, and production in home gardens is important. The leading states in production for market, 1951–1953, were Florida, California, New York, South Carolina, Maryland, North Carolina, New Jersey, and Pennsylvania. Florida was by far the leading state, and California was second.

The production of cucumbers for processing increased fairly consistently from 1918 to 1953, as is shown in Table 25.2.

The leading states in production of cucumbers for processing in the three years 1951–1953 were Michigan, Wisconsin, California, and North Carolina, with Michigan producing nearly one-fourth of the total for the United States. The figures in Table 25.2 include production in 22 states. Several other states produce appreciable quantities.

Table 25.2. Estimated Average Annual Acreage, Production and Farm Value of Cucumbers Grown for Processing in the United States, 1918–1953

Years	Acres	Production, bushels (000 omitted)	Farm value (000 omitted)
1918–1927	67,530	3,705	$ 3,748
1928–1937	82,015	5,232	3,367
1938–1947	99,630	7,528	8,270
1948–1953	135,685	11,357	10,451

Climatic Requirements. The cucumber plant thrives best at relatively high temperatures and is killed by a light freeze, but because it matures a crop in a short growing period it can be grown in regions of short summers. Kotowski (1926) showed that cucumber seed does not germinate at a temperature as low as 11°C. (51.8°F.) but that it may remain in cold soil for a considerable time and then germinate when the temperature becomes favorable. The lower limit of germination appears to be somewhere between 11 and 18°C., since in Kotowski's experiments there was no germination at 11°, and 68 per cent germination at 18°C. The speed and percentage of germination were greater at 25 and 30°C. than at 18°C.

High atmospheric humidity is conducive to the development of some of the diseases, especially those affecting the foliage.

History and Taxonomy. The cucumber is probably a native of Asia and Africa and has been in cultivation for thousands of years. There is evidence that its culture in western Asia dates back at least 3,000 years, and it is said that the cucumber was introduced into China from the West about 140 to 86 B.C. It was known to the ancient Greeks and

Romans, and Pliny even mentions their forced culture (Sturtevant). The cucumber was known in France in the ninth century and was common in England in 1327. It was grown by the early colonists in America and is said to have been grown by the Indians in Florida in 1539.

The cucumber belongs to the genus Cucumis, of which there are about 30 species found mostly in Asia and Africa, only two, *C. sativus* and *C. melo,* being of much importance in the United States. A third species, *C. anguria,* West Indian gherkin, is found in the South and in tropical America. The cucumber is a trailing or climbing plant with hairy, angular stems and large leaves with long petioles. The flowers are axillary, the staminate being more numerous than the pistillate.

Soils and Soil Preparation. Cucumbers are grown successfully on many kinds and classes of soil from sands to heavy clays. Where earliness is of prime consideration, a sandy or sandy-loam soil is preferred; where heavy yields are most important loam, silt loam, or clay loam is preferred. The cucumber plant grows well at soil reactions between pH 5.5 and 6.7 provided other factors are satisfactory. The soil should be well drained.

Soil preparation is essentially the same as for other cultivated crops. Where drainage is poor, cucumbers often are planted on ridges.

Fertilizers. Both animal manures and commercial fertilizers are used in cucumber growing, but in most of the large producing areas commercial fertilizer and soil-improving crops are depended upon for nutrients and organic matter. Some growers follow the practice of applying a small quantity (4 or 5 tons per acre) of manure in furrows over which the rows are made. The manure is covered with soil, and the seed is planted over the manure. If large applications of manure are made, broadcasting is better than applying in the furrow. Where manure is not used the nutrient requirement is met by applications of commercial fertilizer, the kind and quantity depending on the richness of the soil in available essential elements and on the cropping system. When the crop is grown on sandy or sandy-loam soil, 50 to 75 pounds of nitrogen and 100 to 150 pounds each of phosphorus and potash should give very good results. On silt loams and clay loams less fertilizer is applied than on the light soils and the quantity of potash may be cut in half. Where the crop is grown in a general farm-crop rotation, including a legume, and some manure is applied in the rotation, usually a smaller quantity of fertilizer is used than in a vegetable-crop rotation. McCollum (1934) and Dearborn (1936) showed that nitrogen is very important in fruit development and continued vegetative growth. When plants were grown under a low plane of nitrogen nutrition, one fruit on a plant checked vegetative growth and further fruiting until the seeds were developed. The seeds draw heavily on the nitrogen supply.

Planting. Since the plant is tender and the seeds will not germinate in a cold soil, planting should be delayed until all danger of frost is over. Market gardeners often take chances on an early planting since earliness is an important factor. Some growers plant seed at two different depths at the same time, the shallow planting coming on first; if these plants are killed by frost, the deeper planting coming up later will be likely to escape. Other growers make two or three plantings side by side at intervals of a few days, and after the danger of injury is over, they select the planting which gives the greatest promise. The other plantings are destroyed.

In subtropical and tropical climates planting may be done almost any time during the year and the time selected is determined by periods of greatest demand for the product.

Planting in hills formerly was the common practice and is still followed to some extent, but a large part of the commercial crop is planted in drills. (The term *hill* as used here means planting several seeds close together in a group with intervals of 4, 5, or 6 feet between groups. The term has no reference to elevation, but probably originated from the former practice of making mounds a few inches high for planting many kinds of crops.) When the hill system is used several seeds are planted in each hill, and when the plants are well established all but two or three are removed. The hills are spaced 4 by 5, 5 by 5, or farther apart, the distance depending on the richness of the soil and the vigor of the variety or strain. In the drill method the seed is planted with machine planters, or by hand in small-scale plantings, in a continuous row using 2 to 3 pounds of seed to the acre. The rows are spaced 4, 5, or 6 feet apart, and the plants thinned to stand 1½ to 3 feet apart in the row. This method gives a better distribution of plants than the hill system, and less labor is required in planting.

Cucumber plants are sometimes started in greenhouses or hotbeds 3 or 4 weeks before it is safe to plant in the open. The seeds are usually planted in plant bands, flowerpots, or tin cans, since the plants do not withstand transplanting well if the roots are injured when removed for planting in the field. With individual containers the roots are not disturbed when the plants are set out. This method of growing plants is not likely to be profitable except where the early crop brings a high price.

Cultivation. Shallow cultivation should be given as often as is necessary to control weeds. Care should be taken to prevent injury to the vines in cultivating. After the vines cover the ground, large weeds should be pulled by hand. Chemical weed control may eliminate most of the cultivation.

Irrigation. In arid and semiarid regions the cucumber is grown under irrigation. Where the crop is grown intensively, irrigation is fairly common in many humid areas of the United States.

Varieties. There are only a few varieties of cucumbers grown in the United States and in other parts of the world. Some varieties are grown mainly for use as slicing cucumbers, a few are produced for slicing and for pickling, and others are grown only for pickling. A few slicing varieties are grown only as a forcing crop in greenhouses. The important slicing varieties grown in the United States are Marketer, Straight 8, Colorado, Burpee Hybrid, Surecrop Hybrid, Sensation Hybrid, Santee, Palmetto, and Niagara. Santee and Palmetto are resistant to downy mildew, and Niagara is resistant to mosaic. For forcing, White Spine and crosses between it and some of the English forcing varieties are grown in the United States. English forcing varieties are grown in other countries but are not popular in this country. The important varieties grown only for pickling are National Pickling, Chicago Pickling, Model, M.R. 17, and York State Pickling, the last two being recommended where mosaic is serious.

Diseases. Cucumbers are attacked by several diseases, any one of which may cause serious losses under favorable conditions for the development of the disease. In many regions disease is the main limiting factor in profitable production of the crop. The most important diseases are bacterial wilt, anthracnose, angular leaf spot, downy mildew, powdery mildew, scab, and mosaic. Some other diseases that attack the cucumber are more serious on muskmelons and are therefore discussed under the latter.

BACTERIAL WILT. This is a bacterial disease, caused by *Erwinia tracheiphilus*, that attacks cucumbers, muskmelons, watermelons, squashes, and pumpkins, but is seldom serious on the last three. Infected plants show first the wilting of a single leaf, but eventually all the leaves wilt and the plant dies. A freshly cut, wilted stem shows a sticky ooze that may be drawn out into threads.

The bacteria live over winter in the bodies of striped and spotted cucumber beetles. The plants become infected through the feeding of the adult beetles, and the bacteria multiply rapidly and become distributed throughout the vascular system. The main control measure is the eradication of the cucumber beetles. While there are varietal differences in susceptibility to this wilt, there are no highly resistant varieties available for commercial use.

ANTHRACNOSE. The causal organism is a fungus, *Colletotrichum lagenaria*, that is very destructive to cucurbits, including the cucumber. It is usually more severe on watermelons than on other cucurbits, although it may be serious on cucumbers and muskmelons. The organism overwinters on diseased vines and may be carried on seed taken from infected fruits. It is disseminated by means of rain, irrigation water, and surface water. On cucumber and muskmelon, spots formed on the leaves are light brown at first and more or less circular in outline. Later the spots turn dark brown to red. On watermelon the spots on the leaves become dark brown or black. The petioles and stems are affected by the organism causing the development of elongated cracks and streaks. These lesions are water-soaked in appearance at first, but may later turn yellow or brown. On infected fruits circular to oval sunken lesions develop which may result in breakdown on the market. Control measures consist of crop rotation with noncucurbit crops, use of disease-free seed, seed treatment, and use of fungicidal sprays and dusts.

ANGULAR LEAF SPOT. This disease, caused by the bacterium *Pseudomonas lachrymans,* is serious only on the cucumber. Angular, straw-colored spots develop on the leaves. Many of the spots dry and fall out. Infected fruits show a brown, firm rot that extends into the flesh. The organism overwinters in infected vine refuse, is seed-borne, and is spread by rain and surface water, by cultivating equipment, and by harvesters. Crop rotation, seed treatment, and dusting or spraying with copper compounds are the control measures recommended.

DOWNY MILDEW. This disease is caused by the fungus *Pseudoperonospora cubensis* and is a major disease of cucumber, muskmelon, and watermelon. It is of less importance on pumpkins and squashes. The disease develops rapidly in moist, warm weather and is especially destructive in the Eastern and Southern coastal states of the United States. It first appears as gray-tinged spore masses on the older leaves, causing small angular yellow spots, which increase in number and size. As the older leaves die, the disease begins to appear on young leaves. Loss of foliage results in a low set of fruit and poor quality. It is believed that the organism overwinters on living cucurbit plants in subtropical areas and moves northward in the United States along the Atlantic seaboard. The spores can be spread by wind, by insects such as the cucumber beetles, and by splashing rain. The fungus attacks wild cucurbits. Eradication of these wild plants may lessen losses from the disease. Long rotations and plowing under diseased vines immediately after harvest are recommended practices, but the principal control measure is thorough application of fungicide sprays or dusts once a week, and more often in rainy weather. Planting of resistant varieties, where available, is the best means of control. Palmetto and Santee varieties of cucumber, developed in South Carolina, are resistant. Resistant varieties of muskmelons have been developed by the Texas and Georgia Agricultural Experiment Stations.

POWDERY MILDEW. This disease affects the leaves and stems of cucumber, muskmelon, and other cucurbits. The causal fungus is *Erysiphe chicoracearum,* which grows on many kinds of plants besides the cucurbits. Powdery mildew appears first as round white spots on the underside of the older leaves. The spots enlarge, increase in number, and

eventually cover both surfaces of the leaf with a powdery growth. Severely diseased leaves lose the normal green color and become pale
yellow, then brown and shriveled. When the stems and young leaves
are attacked, the leaves become chlorotic and make poor growth, and
the plant may be killed. Fruits of muskmelon on infected vines ripen
prematurely and lack good texture, flavor, and sugar content. This disease causes the greatest damage in warm, rain-free growing seasons of
the Southwestern areas of the United States. According to Middleton
and Bohn (1953), powdery mildew can be controlled by dusting with
sulfur, especially for pumpkins, squashes, and watermelons, since they
are sulfur-resistant. With some varieties of cucumbers and muskmelons
sulfur can be used safely, while other varieties are injured by its use.
Temperature affects the effectiveness of the sulfur. Above 90°F. and
below 70°F. sulfur is not satisfactory. A dust mixture of 15 per cent
sulfur and 7 per cent copper (expressed as metallic copper) such as
basic copper sulfate or cuprous oxide, controls the disease when temperatures are below 70°F. Iscothan and Ovotran have been used successfully in some areas. Resistant varieties of muskmelons have been
developed for growing in arid sections of Southwestern United States,
including Powdery Mildew Resistant cantaloupe No. 5, No. 6, No. 7,
and No. 45. Georgia 47 is said to have resistance to powdery mildew and
downy mildew.

SCAB. This disease, caused by *Cladosporium cucumerinum*, occurs on
cucumbers, muskmelons, and pumpkins. The affected leaves have water-
soaked spots and become wilted, and the stems have slight cankers, but
the main injury occurs on the fruit where there is oozing of sap at first.
Later the spots increase in size and become sunken cavities lined with a
greenish mold. The scab organism lives over winter in old refuse and
on the seed. Control measures recommended include seed treatment
with corrosive sublimate, 1 ounce of powder to 7½ gallons of water.
The temperature of the solution should not be lower than 60°F. or
higher than 80°F. After soaking for 5 minutes the seed should be rinsed
in cold water, and after drying, treated with Semesan or Spergon dust,
according to directions on the label. Crop rotation and spraying or dusting as for other diseases are recommended also. The best control is the
use of resistant varieties such as Highmoor, Maine No. 2, S.R. 6, S.R. 7,
and S.M.R. 12.

CUCUMBER MOSAIC. The cucumber mosaic is caused by a virus and is
one of the most serious diseases of cucumber, muskmelon, and squash.
Slightly affected vines show the normal green of the leaf to be mottled
or have a roughened surface. Sometimes the green color is completely
lacking in the fruit, and the disease is known as *white pickle*. In severe
cases the plants are yellow and dwarfed and bear little or no fruit. The

virus is known to overwinter in a number of perennial hosts such as milkweed, catnip, pokeberry, ground cherry, and others. It is readily transmitted from its plant host by aphids, especially the melon and green peach aphid, and probably by the cucumber beetles. Control measures consist of eradication of the wild hosts within 50 yards of the edge of the field as well as in the planting itself, destruction of infected plants, control of the insect carriers, and use of resistant varieties. Growing of varieties resistant to the disease is the only satisfactory method of control. Ohio M.R. 17 and York State Pickling are resistant pickling varieties. Niagara, Burpee Hybrid, and Sensation Hybrid are resistant slicing varieties of cucumbers.

Squash mosaic virus and muskmelon mosaic virus can infect cucumber also.

Insects. The cucumber and other cucurbits are attacked by several species of insects. While some of the insects seem to prefer a particular species of cucurbits, they will feed on others when the preferred one is not available. The squash vine borer and squash bug seem to prefer squash and pumpkin plants, although they feed on other species. The important insects that feed on the cucumber are the striped cucumber beetle, twelve-spotted cucumber beetle, melon aphid, cucumber or potato flea beetle, pickle worm, and the two squash insects mentioned above.

STRIPED CUCUMBER BEETLE. This is probably the most serious insect pest of cucumbers and melons grown in the United States. It attacks the plants as soon as they emerge, devouring the leaves and eating into the stems. The main injury is done by the overwintering adults that attack the young tender plants. The beetles also carry the bacteria of cucumber wilt, while the larvae burrow into the roots and cause the plants to wilt. The species east of the Rocky Mountains is *Acolymma vittata* (F), and a closely related *A. trivittata* (Mann) is found west of the Rockies. These insects can be controlled by dusting with 0.75 per cent rotenone dust, at least 50 per cent cryolite, or 5 per cent methoxychlor as soon as the plants come up; or the material may be used as a spray. The treatment should be repeated once or twice a week as long as the beetles are present. If cryolite is used, the residues must be removed before marketing or eating the cucumbers.

TWELVE-SPOTTED CUCUMBER BEETLE. This insect (*Diabrotica undecimpunctata howardi* Barber), feeds on a large number of kinds of food plants, including the cucurbits. It is one of the very destructive insects in tropical and subtropical areas. In such areas the insects are present practically all of the time. The adult feeds on the foliage of cucumbers and other curcurbits, beans, and other vegetable plants. The larvae feed on the roots of corn and cause great damage in many areas. In the United

States the larva is known as the Southern corn rootworm. Control measures are the same as for the striped cucumber beetle.

SQUASH BUG. This insect is a true bug with a very offensive odor, giving rise to the name "stink bug." The adult lives over winter in trash and comes out of hibernation and attacks the plants as soon as they come up. The insects puncture the tissues of the leaves and petioles and suck the juices, causing the leaves to wilt. The eggs are brownish in color and are deposited in patches on the underside of the leaf. There are five stages in the development of this insect, all of which often can be seen on a single leaf. No satisfactory control is known, but burning trash in the fall, trapping the adults under boards in the spring, hand picking of adults, and destroying the eggs will aid in keeping down injury. Dusting the plants with 10 to 20 per cent sabadilla dust, or applying 5 per cent DDT dust to the soil under the plants, or spraying the soil with DDT are recommended treatments that help to control the squash bug.

SQUASH-VINE BORER. The borer is the larva of a day-flying moth (*Melittia satyriniformis*). It is one of the most troublesome pests of pumpkins and squashes and often is injurious to other cucurbits. The larva tunnels into the main stem near the ground, and usually decay follows. The first evidence of injury is the wilting of the plant, which usually is followed by death. When fully grown the larva is about an inch in length.

Cultural practices that aid in keeping the borer in check include rotation of crops, destruction of vines as soon as the crop is harvested, deep plowing in spring, and dusting or spraying with insecticides. Partial control can be obtained by applying dust containing ¾ per cent rotenone or 5 per cent methoxychlor or spraying with the same materials. Treatment should begin before the larva has bored into the vine or about the time the runners begin to develop. After the larva enters the stem nothing can be done except to cut it out with a sharp knife, or razor blade. After cutting out the larva, it is desirable to cover the injured area with soil to hasten healing and encourage the development of roots along the stem.

MELON APHID. The melon aphid (*Aphis gossypii*) is a small sucking insect that injures the plant by sucking the juice. It feeds mostly on the underside of the leaf and often escapes notice until the leaves begin to curl. It feeds on a large number of plants, including all of the cucurbits and cotton. It is less troublesome on squashes and pumpkins than on cucumbers and melons.

The melon aphid can be controlled by spraying or dusting with malathion, spraying with nicotine sulfate, or dusting with 2 or 3 per cent nicotine-lime dust. The insecticides must reach the underside of the leaf to be effective. When dust is used it is desirable to make the application on a warm quiet day and to use a canvas trailer attached to the row-crop duster so as to confine the dust for 45 to 60 seconds.

PICKLEWORM. The pickleworm (*Diaphania nitidalis*) is a serious pest of cucumbers, muskmelons, and squashes in many parts of the United States, especially in the Southern part. The larva burrows into the tissue of the blossom or bud. On the squash they may complete their growth in the blossom, but on cucumbers and muskmelons they usually migrate to the fruit. Some burrow down into the stem and complete their growth there and cause injury to the vines, but the greatest injury results from burrowing into the fruit.

Destroying waste fruits and vines by burning or composting is recommended. Other control measures are spraying or dusting as recommended for control of the striped cucumber beetle, at intervals of a week, beginning at the time of the hatching of the eggs.

Harvesting. Cucumbers are picked on the basis of size rather than age, the size being determined largely by the purpose for which they are grown. For slicing, they are picked when they are 6 to 10 inches long; for pickles, they are harvested when they are $2\frac{1}{2}$ to 6 inches long. Very small cucumbers are in demand for mixed pickles, and small to medium-sized ones are preferred for dill pickles. Frequent picking is important, as the cucumbers grow rapidly and soon get beyond the marketable stage. None of the fruits should be allowed to ripen on the vines as the development and maturing of the seeds cause a heavy drain on the plant.

Cucumbers are picked by hand, care being taken to avoid injuring the vine. The stems are left attached to the fruit.

Grading. Cucumbers for slicing are graded on the basis of size, shape, and general appearance. Usually field-grown cucumbers should be separated into two grades; in some cases three grades may be used to advantage. For pickles they are graded according to size, but shape and general appearance are taken into consideration also. When grown on contract, price differential is specified in the contract. The small sizes bring the highest price per bushel. Grade specifications for both slicing and pickling cucumbers have been developed by the U.S. Department of Agriculture and generally should be used where grading is done.

Packing and Packages. Cucumbers for market are packed for shipment in various kinds of containers, including hampers, bushel baskets, lug boxes, and climax baskets. For shipment from Florida and other producing areas the 1-bushel solid-bottom tub basket is the most important. In some other areas field-grown cucumbers are packed in 12-quart climax baskets. Greenhouse-grown cucumbers are packed in similar baskets and also in wooden and fiberboard boxes of varying sizes.

With all types of containers the cucumbers should be well placed and tightly packed so there will be no shifting in the package. Fancy grades, especially of greenhouse cucumbers, are usually placed by hand in the package, and attention is given to the attractiveness of the display when the package is opened. When shipped long distances, cucumbers are usually loaded into refrigerator cars under refrigeration.

MUSKMELON

The muskmelon is a popular crop although it is not an easy one to grow in most regions. It is grown in market gardens and as a special crop in many sections of the United States, especially in arid regions where irrigation is used.

The commercial production of the muskmelon is of recent development. Prior to 1870 it was seldom seen on American markets. It was first grown commercially in New Jersey, Delaware, and Maryland.

It was not until after the Netted Gem was introduced by Burpee in 1881 that muskmelon culture developed extensively in regions located long distances from the markets. This type of melon, which is small, round, or oval in shape and has a hard rind, is much better adapted to shipping long distances than the varieties previously grown.

The muskmelon industry at Rocky Ford, Colo., began to assume importance about 1896 with the formation of the Rocky Ford Melon Growers' Association. In 1905 the Imperial Valley of California became important as a melon-producing region.

Statistics of Production. The muskmelon is one of the important vegetable crops, ranking seventh in farm value in 1953. The estimated average annual acreage, production, and farm value of the muskmelon crop grown in 25 important states from 1918 to 1953 are shown in Table 25.3.

Table 25.3. Estimated Average Annual Acreage, Production, and
Farm Value of Muskmelons Grown in 25 States of the
United States, 1918–1953

Years	Acres	Yield, crates (000 omitted)	Farm value (000 omitted)
1918–1927	84,312	11,993	$18,805
1928–1937	116,201	14,954	15,558
1938–1947	113,860	11,561	25,967
1948–1953	130,070	14,121	44,899

The figures given in Table 25.3 do not represent all of the crop, as they do not include the crops grown commercially in the other states, the melons produced in home gardens, and Honey Dew and Honey Ball melons. The 1948–1953 average annual acreage of Honey Dew melons was 10,133 acres, with production of 3,033,000 crates and farm value of $6,077,000. The leading states in muskmelon production are California, Arizona, and Texas. In 1953 these three states produced slightly over three-fourths of the commercial crop grown in the 25 important states. Other states of importance are Michigan, Georgia, South Carolina, Indiana, North Carolina, Missouri, and Colorado.

Climatic Requirements. The muskmelon thrives best and develops the highest flavor in a hot, dry climate. In the United States a large part of the crop is grown in arid and semiarid regions under irrigation. In humid regions foliage diseases are especially serious, and if the weather is cloudy and rainy during the ripening period, the fruits do not develop the best quality. The muskmelon requires a longer growing season than does the cucumber, but otherwise the requirements are similar. High temperature and sunshine seem to result in high quality.

History and Taxonomy. Although the muskmelon has never been found growing wild, it is believed to have originated in Asia. It is not of ancient culture as no reference is found to it in the early literature. Columbus found it growing on Isabella Island in 1494, and it is mentioned as being grown in Central America in 1516, in Virginia in 1609, and along the Hudson River in 1629.

The muskmelon, *Cucumis melo* L., belongs to the family Cucurbitaceae and to the same genus as the cucumber. The fact that it is so closely related to the cucumber has led growers to attribute poor quality of the muskmelon to cross-fertilization. This, however, certainly does not normally take place.

Authorities recognize the following botanical varieties of *C. melo* as proposed by Naudin:

Var. *reticulatus,* netted melons: fruits small with ribbed and netted surface.

Var. *cantalupensis,* cantaloupe melons: fruits warty, scaly, and rough, with hard rinds, surface often warted. This type is practically unknown in the United States. The name cantaloupe is improperly applied to all varieties of muskmelons that are included in *C. melo* var. *reticulatus.* According to Parodi (1955), *C. cantalupensis* differs from the others in having twice the number of chromosomes ($2N = 48$).

Var. *inodorous,* winter melon, casaba melon: fruit with little of the musky odor, ripening late, and keeping into the winter; surface usually smooth.

Var. *flexuosus,* snake or serpent melon: fruit long and slender, 1 to 3 inches in diameter and 18 to 36 inches long, curved and crooked. Used to some extent for preserves but grown mostly as a curiosity.

Var. *Dudaim,* fruit small, about the size of an ordinary orange, surface marbled with rich brown, very fragrant; grown mostly for ornament and strong scent.

Var. *Chito,* mango melon or lemon cucumber; fruit small, the size of a lemon, used in making preserves called mango preserves. The fruits are known as orange melon, melon apple, and vegetable orange.

Soils and Soil Preparation. Muskmelons are grown on many classes of soil from the sands and sandy loams to the silt loams and clay loams.

Fig. 25.1. Muskmelon foliage showing acid yellowing.

Where earliness is important a sandy loam is considered excellent. In fact, this class of soil is considered almost ideal in most producing regions of the United States. Clay loam is the principal soil used for growing muskmelons in the Imperial Valley of California. Any friable well-drained soil is satisfactory, provided other conditions are favorable to melon growing.

Muskmelons do not thrive well in a strongly acid soil; when such soils are used lime should be applied. Most authorities recommend a range from pH 6.0 to 6.7. Melon plants grown on a strongly acid soil make very poor growth, and the leaves develop a yellowish-green color, sometimes known as "acid yellowing" (Fig. 25.1).

The soil should be well prepared as for other cultivated crops. In some areas the land is prepared for planting on ridges or beds to ensure good surface drainage. Where the crop is grown under irrigation, the land is bedded to conform to the irrigation practices.

Fertilizers. The fertilizer requirements of muskmelons are similar to those of cucumbers. While a large part of the muskmelon acreage is grown without animal manure, most authorities recommend it where it can be obtained at a moderate price. Davis, Whitaker, and Bohn (1953) state that barnyard or feed-lot manure is especially desirable in the arid interior valleys of California where the soils are low in organic matter. In most areas of the United States a complete fertilizer is recommended, but for the Imperial Valley of California only nitrogen and phosphorus are recommended because the soils used are well supplied with potash; the recommendation is 60 pounds of nitrogen in two applications and 60 to 120 pounds of phosphorus to the acre, applied at or before planting. It is suggested that one-half of the nitrogen be applied at planting and the other half when the runners start.

Analytical data indicate that the muskmelon crop, including the vines, removes considerable quantities of potassium, calcium, and nitrogen and small quantities of phosphoric acid, as shown in Table 25.4.

Table 25.4. Total Quantity of Nutrients Removed by Muskmelons,
in Pounds per Acre
(*N.J. Bull.* 310)

Part of plant	Green weight	Dry weight	Nitro-gen	Phos-phoric acid	Potas-sium oxide	Calcium oxide	Magne-sium oxide
Vines.........	3,132	939	19.8	3.8	28.2	53.5	6.8
Fruit flesh...	11,310	1,154	20.5	7.7	48.7	8.4	5.0
Seed.........	2,175	307	9.8	3.9	13.5	0.5	1.8
Total......	16,617	2,400	50.2	15.4	90.3	62.2	13.5

Most of the calcium is in the vines and is returned to the soil on decomposition. The flesh and seeds remove large quantities of potassium and nitrogen, and when the crop is grown on soils deficient in these elements, they should be supplied. Results of experiments on a gravelly sandy-loam soil in New York, reported by Carolus and Lorenz (1938), show the need of a liberal application of potash where the soil is low in available form of this element. Where manure was not used 100 pounds of K_2O to the acre seemed to be needed. Where there was marked deficiency of potash, margins of the older leaves became yellowed, followed by browning and death.

Growing Plants. A part of the muskmelon crop, grown in regions having a short season, is produced from plants started in greenhouses, hotbeds, or cold frames. The seeds are usually planted in pots, plant bands, or other receptacles, since the seedlings do not withstand the shock of transplanting well when they attain considerable size. Several seeds are planted in each receptacle, and the plants are thinned to one or two when they are well established. Some growers prefer to sow the seed in flats. Five to seven days later, when the seed leaves have developed but before the first true leaves appear, the seedlings are transplanted into pots, plant bands, or other receptacles, one plant to each. It is very important to transplant the plants while they are very small, otherwise growth will be seriously checked and many will not survive. This is one reason why planting the seed in pots or bands is generally recommended.

Romshe (1954) compared plants started in wood veneer bands in the greenhouse with plants grown from seed planted in the field in Oklahoma. In this experiment covering 3 years the average yield per year was 5,433 pounds for the direct-seeded and 8,870 pounds to the acre for the transplanted plants.

Planting in the Field. Muskmelon plants are very tender, and the seeds will not germinate at low temperatures; hence, planting in the field should be delayed until all danger of frost is over and the soil has become warm. Plants should be set before they develop more than four leaves and before they become pot-bound; for this reason the seeds should not be planted more than 5 or 6 weeks before it is safe to set them in the field.

A large part of the commercial crop is grown from seed planted in the field. While the hill method is still used, drilling the seed is more common in large plantings. The methods of planting in hills and in drills are practically the same as described for the cucumber. When planted in drills, the usual rate is 2 to 3 pounds of seed to the acre.

Plant protectors, made of various kinds of paper (Fig. 8.2), are used in the growing of muskmelons in many parts of the United States to protect them against chilling. These protectors are used in the Imperial Valley on a very large scale and to some extent in many other regions to place over hills of melon seed. In some regions they are used also to protect the melon plants when set in the field, after having been grown in greenhouses, hotbeds, or cold frames. They protect plants from wind injury, as well as against cold, and have considerable effect on earliness. Ware (1936) showed that protectors (Hotkaps) hastened germination of the seed, markedly increased the early yield, and increased the total yield over 25 per cent. These results were obtained in Arkansas over a period of 3 years.

In the use of plant protectors, care should be taken to prevent damage to the plants during hot days. After the plants are well started, it is necessary to provide ventilation under the paper during warm days. Slitting the paper on one side, usually away from the wind, is the method used. After the danger of cold weather is over, the top may be torn out of the protector, leaving a collar of paper to protect the plant against whipping in the wind. When plants begin to run, the protectors should be removed.

Cultivation. Frequent shallow cultivation should be given until the vines interfere. Some growers continue cultivation after the vines meet between the rows, but it is probable that more harm than good is done since the plants are easily injured. Moving the ends of the vine with a stick may be justified, but turning them from one row to the other may seriously injure them. Cultivation after the vines cover a considerable portion of the ground is probably of little, if any, value unless weed growth is heavy. Large weeds may be pulled by hand after cultivation ceases. Hand hoeing in the row may be desirable while the plants are small.

Experimental results with herbicides, especially Alanap (N-1-naphthylphthalmic acid), indicate that preemergence treatment may be used to advantage in weed control. It is suggested that herbicides be tested on a small scale at first and that the recommendations of specialists be followed as to methods of application and concentration of material to use.

Irrigation. A large part of the melon crop of the United States is produced in arid and semiarid regions, hence irrigation is used. In so-called humid regions irrigation is used to some extent to supplement rainfall. In regions where there is little or no rain during the growing season, the crop is dependent on water stored in the soil from winter rains and that applied as irrigation. On deep loam soils that are wet to field capacity before planting, a relatively small quantity of water needs to be applied during growth of the crop. MacGillivray (1951) suggested that 6 to 10 inches of water in properly spaced irrigations could produce maximum yields under conditions similar to those at Davis, Calif. In his experiments the soil (Yolo loam) was wet to field capacity to a depth of 6 feet before the crop was planted. On shallower soils more water would need to be supplied by irrigation than on deep soils.

Varieties. There are two general classes of muskmelons of importance in the United States, both belonging to *Cucumis melo* Naudin but of different subspecies. Most of the varieties grown in the United States are *C. melo* var. *reticulatus* Naudin, called netted melons. Davis, Whitaker, and Bohn use the term cantaloupe to designate the varieties belonging to the subspecies *reticulatus*. While this terminology conforms to commercial or market usage, it does not conform to historic or taxonomic use of the term cantaloupe. The other class of melons belongs to *C. melo* var. *inodorous* and includes Honey Ball, Honey Dew, Casaba, Crenshaw, and Persian, which have been called winter melons, probably because they are later in maturing than other types and because they can be stored for considerable periods. However, the term is not a good one.

The varieties of netted melons (subspecies *reticulatus*) grown vary from region to region. In areas where powdery mildew is very serious, as in some parts of California, varieties and strains resistant to this disease are grown. These include Powdery Mildew Resistant 45, Powdery Mildew Resistant No. 5 and No. 6, Sulfur Resistant VI, and S.R. 91. Varieties and strains of the Hale's Best group, including Hale's Best 36, Hale's Best 936, Jumbo strain, and Seed Breeders, are important in some areas where powdery mildew is not very serious. Other varieties grown in the United States, especially in the Eastern half, include Hearts of Gold, Honey Rock, Pride of Wisconsin (Queen of Colorado), Harvest Queen, a fusarium-resistant variety similar to Pride of Wisconsin, Bender, Seneca Bender, Delicious 51, and Iroquois, the last two being resistant to fusarium wilt. Many other old strains and varieties are grown to a limited extent, and new ones are introduced from time to time.

The important so-called winter melons *C. melo* var. *inodorous* are Honey Dew, Honey Ball (Melogold, Weaver Special, and Globo de Oro), Casaba (Golden Beauty), Crenshaw, and Persian, of which there are at least two strains. Honey Dew has a creamy-white or greenish-white surface, flesh moderately thick, green, firm, juicy, and very sweet. Honey Ball has skin white turning to pale tan at maturity, net fine and well distributed, flesh salmon-orange (green in original variety), moderately firm, very sweet. Golden Beauty Casaba is grown to a limited extent in California; fruits are globular with somewhat pointed stem end; surface wrinkled, green, turning to golden yellow during ripening, without net; flesh thick, white, moderately firm but juicy and sweet. Crenshaw is another type with pear-shaped fruit, smooth, dark-green skin, turning to pale yellow at maturity; flesh thick, light-salmon color. The Persian melon is popular on local markets in California; fruits globular, without sutures; skin dark green; net abundant, well distributed but fine and thin; flesh thick, bright orange, sweet with distinctive flavor.

Diseases. The muskmelon is attacked by the same diseases as the cucumber, and the same methods of control may be used. Fusarium wilt and muskmelon mosaic generally are more injurious to the muskmelon than to the cucumber.

FUSARIUM WILT. According to Middleton and Bohn (1953) the race that causes this disease is *Fusarium oxysporum* f. *melonis,* which can infect only muskmelon. The organism can survive in the soil for many years. The fungus enters the roots from the soil and grows into the water-conducting tissue. If young plants are attacked, they may rot before or after emergence or they may become seriously stunted. The first symptom on older plants is a wilting of one or more runners. The leaves of the wilted runners turn brown, and dead streaks develop on the stems near the ground line. In moist weather these streaks may show salmon-pink masses of spores. Eventually the entire plant wilts, withers, and dies.

Control measures consist of planting on uninfested land, long rotations, and use of fusarium-resistant varieties. A resistant variety, Golden Gopher, developed by the Minnesota Agricultural Experiment Station, has been recommended for use in the North Central states if the crop is to be grown on infected land. Iroquois and Delicious 51, resistant varieties developed by Cornell University Experiment Station, are grown in some areas, especially in the Northeastern states.

MUSKMELON MOSAIC. This disease is caused by a virus. The leaves of infected plants show a dark-green banding about the larger veins and later develop a yellow-and-green mottling. Some leaves may become curled and otherwise distorted. Flowers on infected plants often are deformed and fail to set fruit. The muskmelon virus infects only cucurbits and is seed-transmitted, ranging from 95 per cent in fresh seed to less than 5 per cent in seed 3 years old, according to Middleton and Bohn. It is transmitted readily by aphids. Use of virus-free seed will assure freedom from the disease in young plants, but does not ensure freedom from infection later when the plants are grown near other sources of the virus. Use of insecticides to control aphids has not been very effective in preventing loss from this disease. Work on the development of resistant varieties is in progress.

Insects. The insects discussed under Cucumber also attack the muskmelon, and the same methods of control are employed.

Harvesting. The stage of maturity at which melons should be picked depends on the length of time required to reach the market, on the variety, on the temperature at harvest time, and on the method of shipping.

For local markets, muskmelons should be left on the vines until they are fully mature but still solid; for shipment they are picked before they are fully ripe and, in many cases, so immature that they never develop good, edible quality.

It is difficult to determine the stage of maturity at which melons should be picked for long-distance shipment since there is no definite external character correlated with approaching maturity. There are certain changes that take place that may be used as an index, but these should be correlated with the internal condition. As melons approach maturity, the netting becomes fully rounded out, whereas in immature melons the netting is flattened and has a slight crease along the top. The color showing through the netting changes from a dark green or grayish green to a yellowish green as the melon nears maturity. As ripening advances, a crack develops around the peduncle at the base of the fruit, and when fully ripe, the fruit slips easily from the stem, leaving a large scar. This is known as the "full slip." In the "half-slip" stage, only a portion of the disk is removed when the fruit is pulled from the vine, and the scar on the fruit is smaller than in the full-slip stage.

Chase, Church, and Denny (1924) have shown that the soluble solids, the refractive index, and the sucrose content of the juice of muskmelons increase and the percentage of starch in the seeds decreases as the melons ripen. Edible quality depends on texture, flavor, and sweetness. The sugar content is the most important factor, and this may be estimated by determining the soluble solids in the juice of the edible portion.

In determining the stage of maturity for picking it is best to cut a number of melons and test their quality by taste and then correlate the taste with the appearance of the fruits at the time.

Careful and prompt handling after the melons are picked is very important. Rough handling causes bruises which make them more susceptible to decay. Delay in getting the melons packed and loaded into refrigerator cars may result in too rapid ripening, with consequent loss on the market. Pentzer, Wiant, and MacGillivray (1940) have shown the importance of precooling melons, especially when they are picked during very hot weather. They pointed out that melons picked in the morning precooled in much less time, and the quantity of ice used in precooling was less than for melons picked during the hottest part of the day. In their experiments it was found that to lower the temperature of carloads from 90 to 50°F. required the meltage of 9,300 pounds of ice and 11 hours operation with portable fan equipment or an operating period of 9½ hours with the mechanical refrigerating equipment tested. During the cooling period the fruits were continuing to ripen, but the rate of change decreased as the temperature became lower.

Grading. Grade specifications for muskmelons (cantaloupes) have been worked out by the U.S. Department of Agriculture; these should be used whenever feasible. The specifications are changed from time to time, and for this reason they are not given here.

The fruits should be carefully graded with reference to size, shape, color, and general appearance. Fully ripe melons should be packed separately and disposed of on nearby markets, as they will not stand long-distance shipping. Soft, green, off-type, bruised, and very small melons should be discarded, and only those that will reach the market in good condition should be packed.

Packing and Packages. Muskmelons shipped to market are usually packed in special crates made for the purpose. Carey (1950) described six sizes of crates for netted muskmelons (cantaloupes), which he called Western cantaloupe crates, and 2 sizes for Honey Dew melons that are used as shipping containers in California and other Western states. The Western cantaloupe crates vary in size from 4 by 12 by 22⅛ for the pony flat to 13 by 13 by 22⅛ for the jumbo crate. The two sizes of crates used for Honey Dew melons are 6¾ by 16 by 22⅛ and 7¾ by 16 by 22⅛ inches. In the Eastern producing sections of the United States many types and sizes of crates are in use; in most of the areas the crates are made to fit the melons.

When the crate is packed, every melon on each side should touch the slats, and the crate when covered should bulge slightly on all sides. Unless there is a slight bulge, the pack will be loose when it reaches the market and the fruits are likely to be bruised by shaking about in the crate.

Wrapping muskmelons in paper is practiced to some extent, but this is not to be recommended as the paper excludes the air, keeps the surface moist, delays refrigeration, and discourages inspection.

Storage. Melons ordinarily are not stored. Results of experiments by Platenius *et al.* (1934) and by Wiant (1938) indicate that they can be kept for a short period. Platenius *et al.* kept mature muskmelons for a month at 32°F. and at relative humidities of 80 to 90 per cent, and they were in good edible condition when removed. Wiant states that cantaloupes removed from refrigerator cars can be held for a week or longer at 32 to 34°F. Honey Dew melons, he states, can be held 2 weeks either at 32 to 34 or 36 to 38°F. Longer storage may be practicable. He found low-temperature breakdown on Honey Dew melons but not on cantaloupes. This breakdown developed more at 32 to 34 than at 36 to 38°F. It did not develop at all at 38 to 40 or at 40 to 42°F.

WATERMELON

The watermelon requires a long, relatively warm growing season for its best development. In the United States the greatest areas of production are in the Southern states. However, the crop is grown successfully in some of the Northern states by using the quicker-maturing varieties and, in some cases, starting plants in greenhouses or hotbeds.

The watermelon is grown in many countries but is more popular in the United States than elsewhere. It is used mainly as a dessert, and the rind is used to some extent in making conserves and pickles.

Statistics of Production. The estimated average annual acreage, production, and value of watermelons grown in 22 of the important producing states from 1918 to 1953 are given in Table 25.5. The farm value

Table 25.5. Estimated Average Annual Production and Farm Value
of Watermelons Grown in 22 States, 1918–1953

Years	Acres	Production, number of melons (000 omitted)	Farm value (000 omitted)
1918–1927	162,232	55,329	$ 9,986
1928–1937	248,885	67,801	7,736
1938–1947	289,928	77,066	20,977
1948–1953	375,158	98,457	35,916

increased much more in the period 1948–1953 over earlier years than either acreage or production.

The leading states in production of watermelons in the three years 1951, 1952, and 1953 were Florida, Texas, Georgia, California, and South Carolina. These five states produced about three-fourths of the total commercial watermelons in 1953. Other important states are Alabama, Arizona, Arkansas, Indiana, Oklahoma, North Carolina, Mississippi, and Maryland.

History and Taxonomy. The watermelon was unknown in Europe until the sixteenth century. Africa is considered to be its native home. It was found growing wild by Livingstone (1854) in regions not previously visited by white men. Carrier (1924) reports evidence indicating possible American origin. Early French explorers found Indians growing watermelons in the Mississippi Valley. As early as 1629 the watermelon was grown in Massachusetts, and by Indians in Florida prior to 1664.

The watermelon belongs to the genus *Citrullus,* of which there are four species, all in tropical Africa. The watermelon belongs to *C. vulgaris,* and the citron, or preserving melon, belongs to the same species, but Bailey (1949) lists the citron as *C. vulgaris* var. *citroides.*

Climatic Requirements. The watermelon, like other cucurbits, is tender to frost and requires a long growing season with relatively high temperatures. It is less affected by atmospheric humidity than is the muskmelon. The watermelon grows as well and quality is as high when produced in humid areas as in arid and semiarid regions. Foliage diseases usually are more destructive in humid than in dry regions.

Soils and Soil Preparation. Fertile, well-drained, sandy-loam soils are generally preferred for watermelons, although heavier soils are satisfactory if well drained. The lighter soils are especially desirable for watermelons grown in regions of short growing seasons. This crop is one of the few vegetables that grows well on a soil that is rather highly acid, as pH 5.0. This does not mean that a highly acid soil is required, but rather that it is not necessary to apply lime to reduce acidity if the soil tests pH 5.0 or higher.

No special soil preparation is required except where the crop is to be planted on ridges or raised beds. Ordinary plowing and fitting as for other crops are satisfactory for watermelons.

Fertilizers. The fertilizer practices suggested for muskmelons should be satisfactory for watermelons, but usually less fertilizer is used than for muskmelons. The watermelon crop is grown in a general farm-crop rotation in many of the commercial producing regions; in such rotations manure or a soil-improving crop is used to maintain organic matter. In some cases, both manure and soil-improving crops are turned under.

Commercial fertilizer is the main supplier of nutrients. Since the rows of melons are planted so far apart, some of the fertilizer should be applied in trenches near the row, or in a strip where the row is to be located.

Planting. The time and method of planting watermelons are practically the same as for muskmelons, except that they require more room and a longer growing season. In regions having less than 4 months frost-free period, watermelons cannot be grown successfully unless the plants are started under protection 3 or 4 weeks prior to the time when it is safe to plant them in the field. Under most conditions, watermelon production is not profitable where it is necessary to start the plants under cover in order to mature the fruit before frost in the fall. For home use and for special markets, starting plants in greenhouses, hotbeds, or under plant forcers may be justified. When the plants are to be grown in greenhouses or hotbeds, it is best to start the seeds in plant bands, flowerpots, or other receptacles, as the seedlings do not withstand transplanting very well. Several seeds are planted in each receptacle; when the seedlings begin to crowd, they are thinned to a single plant or two or three plants in each.

Nearly all of the commercial crop is grown from seed planted in the field. The seed is planted in hills 8 by 8, 8 by 10, 10 by 10, 10 by 12, or 12 by 12 feet apart each way, with several seeds planted in each hill. After the plants are well established they are thinned to one or two plants per hill. Some growers prefer to plant in continuous rows and thin the plants to a distance of 4, 5, 6, or more feet apart after they have become established.

Watermelon seed will not germinate at temperatures below 70°F., hence planting should be delayed until the soil becomes warm. The plants are injured by a light frost, therefore in regions where frosts occur, planting should be delayed until all danger is past.

The use of plant protectors is fairly common, especially in regions of short growing seasons and in other areas where earliness is important.

Cultivation. The cultivation and care given watermelons are essentially the same as that given muskmelons. Usually early cultivation is done with a harrow since the rows are far enough apart to permit its use until the vines obtain considerable length. After the vines meet in the centers cultivation usually ceases. Large weeds are pulled by hand after cultivation stops.

Use of herbicides, as mentioned for muskmelons, may take the place of part or all of the cultivation.

Varieties. In selecting varieties of watermelons for planting, one should consider the purpose for which the crop is grown. If for home

FIG. 25.2. Two varieties of watermelon, Klondyke and striped Klondyke.

use or for a local market, quality should be the first consideration, but size, shape, yield, and other factors must also be considered. When grown for shipment, the melons should be solid and have a relatively thick rind, or there will be serious losses in handling due to breakage. The grower, however, should not lose sight of the importance of quality, for low quality limits consumption and lowers the price. A good market melon is one that stands shipment well and is of good quality. There is more demand for small to medium-sized fruits than for very large ones.

Varieties for planting in regions having short growing seasons must be relatively quick maturing ones. Varieties in this category include Honey Cream, Dixie Cream, New Hampshire Midget, Rhode Island Red, Klondike (Fig. 25.2), Klondike R7 (fusarium-resistant), Early Kansas, Early

Arizona, Cole's Early, Kleckley Sweet, and Dixie Queen. These and similar varieties are the ones to grow in the areas of short growing seasons of the United States. They can be grown also in the milder regions of Canada. Several of the varieties in the early group are important for home-garden and local-market production, but not for long-distance shipping. The important varieties grown for shipment include Dixie Queen, Florida Giant, Tom Watson, Congo (anthracnose-resistant), Leesburg (fusarium-resistant), Blacklee (fusarium-resistant), Klondike strains, Stone Mountain, Fairfax, and Charleston Gray. The last two varieties mentioned are reported to be resistant to anthracnose and wilt. New strains and varieties that are resistant to some of the important diseases are replacing the older ones.

Where fusarium wilt is very serious, only resistant varieties should be grown. Varieties resistant to anthracnose and other serious diseases should be substituted for the nonresistant varieties if the newer ones meet the other requirements.

Preserving Melon, or Citron. This fruit resembles a small watermelon of light-green color, usually round or oval in form. The flesh is white in color and is not edible. The rind is used for making conserves and sweet pickles, and the melon is sometimes fed to hogs. It is also known as *stockmelon.* The preserving melon has about the same cultural requirements as the watermelon. It crosses readily with it and has been used in breeding to produce a wilt-resistant watermelon.

Diseases. The watermelon is subject to many of the same diseases as the cucumber and muskmelon. Bacterial wilt, anthracnose, angular leaf spot, downy mildew, powdery mildew, and cucumber mosaic are discussed under Cucumber. Fusarium wilt and muskmelon mosaic are discussed under Muskmelon. The control measures for the same diseases are similar for cucumbers, muskmelons, and watermelons. The best control measure is use of disease-resistant varieties where they are available. The varieties of watermelons that are resistant to anthracnose or wilt are mentioned in the paragraph on varieties.

STEM-END ROT. This disease, caused by the fungus *Diplodia natalensis,* is responsible for a large part of the watermelons lost in transit. The fungus gains entrance to the fruit through the stem following the removal from the vine. The fungus infects fruits only through cuts or other wounds. Infected tissue turns brown and shrivels, resulting in loss of the fruit. The disease develops most rapidly at 85 to 90°F. so that prompt removal from the field is important. Prompt coating of the freshly cut stem with Bordeaux paste containing at least 6 per cent copper sulfate will prevent the development of the disease. Care should be taken to prevent injury to the fruits in the harvesting and handling operations. Shipment of the melons at about 50°F. will deter the development of the disease in transit. The same type of decay may begin on the side of the melon where there is an injury through which the fungus may gain entrance.

Insects. The watermelon is attacked by the same insects as the cucumber and muskmelon. The melon aphid is more injurious to the watermelon than to either cucumber or muskmelon. For a discussion of insect pests, see under Cucumber.

Harvesting. It is very important that watermelons should be at the proper stage of maturity when they are harvested, but this is difficult for the inexperienced to determine. With no other common fruit or vegetable is there so little evidence of a change from immaturity to maturity. The size of the fruit gives no indication of stage of maturity. The color change that gives some indication of maturity is a change in the background color of the rind from white to light yellow on the part of the melon in contact with the ground. The sound emitted when the melon is thumped with the finger is another way of determining the stage of maturity of watermelons. Most varieties give forth a metallic ringing sound when they are immature and a more muffled or dead sound as they become more mature. The sound is not the same for all varieties, so that some should be pulled when they still give forth a somewhat metallic sound while others should be left on the vines until the sound is quite a dead one. It is only by experience that one becomes deft at selecting the ripe fruits, but with precaution and by cutting a melon occasionally the knack is readily acquired. The fruit should be cut from the vine with at least 2 inches of stem. This is very important because by applying the Bordeaux paste to the stem the stem-end rot can be prevented from developing in transit.

Grading. The U.S. Department of Agriculture has established grade standards under which a considerable part of the commercial crop is sold on the large markets. A large percentage of the shipments are inspected at shipping points and certified as to grade by licensed inspectors. The use of these grade standards by growers and shippers tends to establish confidence between buyers and sellers and provides a basis for price quotations.

Handling. After the melons are removed from the vines they are placed in rows in the field, from which they are loaded on trucks or wagons for hauling to local markets or to cars when they are to be shipped. The truck or railroad car in which watermelons are to be shipped should be cleaned thoroughly and should be lined with building paper. The paper protects the melons from bruises resulting from rubbing against the sides of the car and from possible contact with injurous chemicals left on the walls from some earlier shipment. The floor of the car is covered with about 3 inches of straw or similar material, on which the bottom tier of melons is placed. Most of the carlot shipments of watermelons are in box cars or cattle cars, but some are in refrigerator cars. The arrangement of the melons in the car depends on their size and shape. Long melons are loaded four layers high if they weigh over 20 pounds and five layers high if they weigh less. Round-type fruits are loaded three layers high if they weigh over 20 pounds and four layers high if they weigh less.

PUMPKIN AND SQUASH

These two crops are discussed together because their cultural requirements are similar and also because of the great confusion in terminology. While pumpkins and squashes are not among the most important commercial vegetables, they are grown by millions of home gardeners and many commercial producers in the United States. The Bureau of the Census 1950 reported 52,835 acres of these two crops grown commercially in the United States in 1949. They are important as food crops in many other countries. In addition to their use as fresh vegetables, they are processed in large quantities in the United States for use mainly in pies.

History and Taxonomy. There has been considerable difference of opinion as to the nativity of pumpkins and squashes. It was believed by some botanists that two of the species of Cucurbita, *C. pepo* and *C. moschata,* are of American origin and that a third, *C. maxima,* is of Asiatic origin. According to Whitaker (1947) and Whitaker and Bohn (1950), the evidence is overwhelming in favor of American origin of the three species mentioned and of the two additional species, *C. mixta* and *C. ficifolia.* Some of the varieties from Mexico and Central America that were formerly classified as *C. moschata* have been placed by Whitaker and Bohn in *C. mixta.* For a description of the five species the reader is referred to Whitaker and Bohn.

There is confusion in the literature regarding the terms pumpkin and squash. Some varieties of *C. pepo* are called pumpkin, and others are called squash. For a time there was agreement among students of this group of plants on the nomenclature. Thus Bailey (1929) and Castetter and Erwin (1927) called all types and varieties of *C. pepo* and *C. moschata* pumpkins, and all types and varieties of *C. maxima* they called squash. Under this classification the term pumpkin includes such divergent forms as White Bush Scallop, Early Yellow Bush Scallop, Yellow Crookneck, Zucchini, Connecticut Field, Small Sugar, Kentucky Field, Winter Crookneck, and Butternut. Some of these have been known for many years as summer squashes, others as winter squashes, and still others as pumpkins. The term pumpkin was not generally accepted for the varieties known as summer squashes or for such varieties as Golden Winter, Crookneck, Butternut, and others of *C. moschata.* Whitaker and Bohn define the terms pumpkin, summer squash, and winter squash as follows.

PUMPKIN. The edible fruit of any species of Cucurbita utilized when ripe as forage, as a table vegetable, or in pies; flesh somewhat coarse and/or strongly flavored, hence not generally served as a baked vegetable.

SUMMER SQUASH. The edible fruit of any species of Cucurbita, commonly *C. pepo,* utilized when immature as a table vegetable.

WINTER SQUASH. The edible fruit of any species of Cucurbita utilized when ripe as feed for livestock, as a table vegetable, or in pies; flesh usually fine-grained and of mild flavor, hence suitable for baking.

Culture. The general requirements of pumpkin and squash are similar to those of the other cucurbits. They do not require as long a growing season as the watermelon. Some varieties can be grown in nearly all parts of the United States and in many parts of Canada. The seeds of pumpkin and squash will not germinate in cold soil, and the plants are injured by light frosts, so that planting should be delayed until the danger of frost is past and the soil has become warm.

Any good type of well-drained soil will produce satisfactory yields of pumpkins and squashes if other conditions are favorable. While they are not very sensitive to soil reaction, they do better on slightly acid soil than on a strongly acid one.

The time and method of planting pumpkins and squashes are about the same as for the other cucurbits. Planting distances vary widely. Varieties of bush squashes are planted in hills 4 by 4 or 4 by 5 feet or in rows 4 to 5 feet apart. When planted in hills several seeds are planted in each and later thinned to one or two plants per hill. When planted in continuous rows the seeds are sown rather thickly, and after the plants are well established they are thinned to 3, 4, or 5 feet apart in the rows. Running varieties of pumpkins and squashes are planted in hills 8 by 8 to 12 by 12 feet or in rows 8 to 12 feet apart, depending on the vigor of the variety grown and the fertility of the soil. In the hill method the plants are thinned to one or two plants per hill, and in the drill method they are thinned to stand 4 to 6 or more feet apart in the row.

In some areas winter squashes and pumpkins are planted as a companion crop with corn. When so grown, they require no cultivation except that given corn. This method of growing is not very satisfactory where the corn is harvested with corn harvesters, as the fruits would be injured by the machine.

Home gardeners and others frequently become confused because many blossoms do not set fruit. They do not understand that the male and female parts are in separate flowers and that only the female flowers produce fruits. Under some conditions male flowers predominate, and under other conditions female flowers predominate. It has been thought that environmental conditions, especially temperature, influence the sex ratio. Nitsch *et al.* have shown that both length of day and temperature exert a profound influence on the development of the flower types of Table Queen variety. They state that high temperature and long days tend to keep the plants in the male phase, whereas low temperature and short days speed up the development of the female phase. Other types and varieties might respond differently to temperature and photoperiod. In the variety Table Queen the male and female flowers are produced in similar positions on the same stem.

Varieties. The readiness with which varieties within a species cross results in the frequent appearance of new varieties. Many varieties are listed in the seed catalogues, but only a small number of them are of much importance. Some of the important varieties of summer squash, winter squash, and pumpkin, as defined by Whitaker and Bohn, are listed below.

SUMMER SQUASH. The varieties commonly called summer squash belong to *C. pepo* and include White Bush Scallop, or Patty Pan, Yellow Bush Scallop, or Golden Custard, Yellow Crookneck, Yellow Straightneck, Caserta, Cocozelle, Zucchini, and several F_1 hybrids of the Zucchini type. There are several strains of some of the varieties listed, and these strains may have different names from those given above.

WINTER SQUASH. The varieties that are usually called winter squash belong to at least three species. Table Queen, also called Des Moines and Acorn, belong to *C. pepo;* Butternut belongs to *C. moschata;* Green Hubbard, Blue Hubbard, Golden Hubbard, Warted Hubbard, Boston Marrow, Delicious, Golden Delicious, Banana, Buttercup, Marblehead, and Turban belong to *C. maxima* (Fig. 25.3). In some areas the varieties that belong to *C. mixta* are usually called squash, but under the definition of Whitaker and Bohn they are classed as pumpkin.

PUMPKIN. The important varieties of *C. pepo* are Connecticut Field, Small Sugar, Winter Luxury, and Golden Oblong; Japanese Pie, Tennessee Sweet Potato, White Cushaw, and Green Striped Cushaw belong to *C. Mixta;* Kentucky Field, or Large Cheese (called squash in some regions), and Dickinson belong to *C. moschata;* Mammoth Chili, or King of the Mammoths, grown to some extent for stock feed and for exhibit purposes belongs to *C. maxima* and should be classed as squash.

Diseases. Pumpkins and squashes are attacked by many of the same diseases that attack other cucurbits and which have been discussed under Cucumbers. It is seldom that pumpkin and squash are seriously injured by disease, and control measures are not often applied.

Insects. The most important insect pests attacking these two crops are the squash bug and the squash vine borer. Both of these seem to prefer pumpkin and squash to the other cucurbits. These and others that are important pests of cucurbits are discussed under Cucumber.

Harvesting. Summer squashes of all types and varieties should be harvested in immature stage before the rind begins to harden. In California and in some other areas it has been the practice to harvest all of the types of summer squashes while the fruits are very small, as shown in Fig. 25.4. In other regions the tendency is to harvest earlier than was common many years ago. High quality of winter squashes and pumpkins

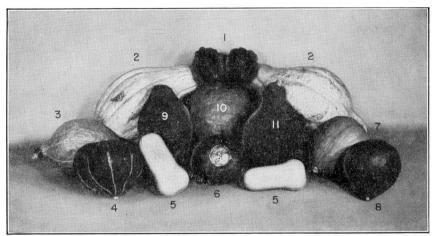

FIG. 25.3. Eleven varieties of winter squash: (1) Royal Acorn, (2) Blue Hubbard, (3) Golden Hubbard, (4) Quality, (5) Butternut, (6) Buttercup, (7) Golden Delicious, (8) Delicious, (9) Hubbard, (10) Boston Marrow, (11) Warted Hubbard. (*Courtesy of Joseph Harris Seed Co.*)

is associated with maturity, so that they should not be harvested until they are fully ripe. They should be harvested before danger of frosts since fruits that are subjected to a hard frost will not keep.

All types of pumpkins and squashes are usually pulled or cut from the vines with a portion of the stem attached. Yeager *et al.* (1945) stated that the stems should be removed from squash to be stored. In their experiments with Blue Hubbard they showed less loss from rots when the stems were removed than when they were left attached.

Careful handling, from the time of harvest until they are disposed of, is important for all varieties of pumpkins and squashes since fruits bruised or otherwise injured decay more rapidly than uninjured ones. Decay organisms usually enter through breaks in the skin. Careful handling is especially important for pumpkins and squashes that are to be stored.

Grading and Packing. Pumpkins and squashes are seldom graded to any particular specifications, but when the small summer pumpkins are packed in containers for shipment some grading is done. As a rule, fruits are selected for uniformity in size, shape, and color; those that are injured or are overmature are discarded. Even with the winter pumpkins and squashes some grading is done, especially to separate the sizes. Most markets prefer the small to medium-sized fruits, while canners and bakers prefer the large ones.

Small summer squashes are packed for market in various types of containers (Fig. 25.4). For shipment they are packed in bushel baskets, lug boxes, and crates of various kinds. Winter squashes and pumpkins

Fig. 25.4. Four varieties of summer squash in lug boxes on San Francisco market.

are usually handled in bulk, but some of the smaller varieties, such as Table Queen (Acorn), Butternut, and Buttercup, are handled in baskets, boxes, crates, and sometimes in bags.

Storage. Squashes and pumpkins can be kept for several months if they are in good condition at the time of storage and are kept at the proper temperature and humidity. The conditions necessary to keep these crops are very different from the conditions necessary to keep root crops.

After the fruits are harvested, they should undergo a ripening or curing process to harden the shell. Many growers pile the squashes in small piles in the field for curing for a week or two. Results of experiments reported by Yeager *et al.* (1945) indicate that this is not a good practice. They report much better results when the squash is taken to the storage house as soon as harvested. A curing period of about 2 weeks at 75 to 85°F. with good air circulation is desirable, and then reduction of temperature to 50 to 55°F. Artificial heat is necessary to maintain the curing temperature immediately and the storage temperature during very cold weather.

Most authorities agree that winter pumpkins and winter squashes keep best at relatively high temperatures (50 to 55°F.) and low humidity. Yeager *et al.* state that the Blue Hubbard squash does not keep well in storage at temperatures below 45°F. even with humidities as low as 20 per cent. On the other hand, Platenius, Jamison, and Thompson (1934) reported results of experiments in which squashes kept in excellent condition for 5 months at approximately 40°F. and a relative humidity below 70 per cent. At this temperature and at relative humidities between 50 and 70 per cent, shrinkage was less than 3 per cent per month, and the conversion of starch to sugar proceeded much more slowly than at higher temperature.

Under the best storage conditions loss in weight is high, owing to loss of water and of carbohydrates. Although the percentage of water may not change appreciably during storage, the actual loss by evaporation is masked by the water formed in respiration and by the loss of dry matter, mainly carbohydrates, in the same process. Phillips (1946) has reported results of chemical studies conducted over a period of 3 years with three varieties of squashes: Blue Hubbard, Buttercup, and Butternut. The following conclusions are drawn from his studies:

1. The conversion of starch to sugar is rapid and becomes practically complete on long storage.

2. The loss of carbohydrates is rapid, amounting to about one-third of the amount present at harvest time after storage for 3 months, and one-half or more after 6 months' storage.

3. The proportion of glucose to total sugars increases during storage.

4. In the Butternut, the proportion of sucrose in the total sugars is very high.

5. The results indicate slight losses in proteins and slight gains in cellulose and pectin.

CHAPTER 26

Sweet Corn, Okra, Martynia

The three crops, sweet corn, okra, and martynia, are placed together because none of them fits into the other groups, and not on account of any special similarity. They are, however, all warm-season annuals, are tender to frost, and are grown for their fruits. Only one, sweet corn, is of any great commercial importance in the United States. Sweet corn is of greatest importance in the North; okra is produced mainly in the South; and martynia is grown to a limited extent only, largely as a curiosity.

SWEET CORN

While the sweet-corn plant is tender to frost and grows best in hot weather, the main areas of commercial production are in the Northern United States and parts of Canada. Most of the acreage in the Southern states is for the fresh market and is produced during the winter and spring. California also produces some sweet corn during winter and spring. The crop is increasing in importance in the South, with large acreages in Florida and Texas. The corn earworm has limited sweet-corn production in the South, but with the proper use of insecticides and resistant varieties the production will probably continue to increase. Another important factor in production for the fresh market has been the development of marketing and handling methods which enable the grower to ship to distant markets without much loss in quality. However, the major portion of the crop produced in the United States is canned and frozen.

Since sweet corn is harvested before it begins to harden, its production is not limited by climatic conditions to the same extent as is field corn for grain. It is a very successful crop in many regions of the North where grain corn cannot be produced in most seasons.

Statistics of Production. The acreage, production, and value of sweet corn grown for processing has increased markedly since about 1940, as presented in Table 26.1. The estimated acreage in 1953 was 501,840

544

acres with a production of 1,504,700 tons valued at $35,082,000. The leading states in 1953 were Wisconsin, 113,200 acres; Minnesota, 92,200 acres; Illinois, 67,300 acres; Maryland, 34,000 acres; Indiana, 29,800 acres; Iowa, 26,800 acres; and New York, 26,300 acres. Ohio, Pennsylvania, Maine, Washington, and Oregon are the other important states. Much of the increase in acreage since 1940 has been due to the rapid development of the frozen-food industry. The estimated total pack of frozen sweet corn was 21,586,000 pounds in 1944 and 122,026,000 pounds in 1953. This increase in frozen sweet corn has not reduced the pack of the canned product, which has increased also, but not as markedly as frozen corn. The Pacific Coast states produced about 60 per cent of the frozen pack in 1953.

Table 26.1. Estimated Average Annual Acreage, Production, and Value of
Sweet Corn Grown for Manufacture, 1918–1953
(*Agricultural Statistics,* 1954)

Years	Acres	Yield, tons per acre	Production, tons	Price	Value (000 omitted)
1918–1927	261,074	2.28	593,120	$14.97	$ 8,770
1928–1937	326,108	1.98	645,190	10.85	6,983
1938–1947	425,200	2.42	1,039,560	14.99	16,030
1948–1953	465,108	2.91	1,309,530	21.98	29,071

Complete estimates of acreage, production, and value of fresh-market sweet corn by the United States Department of Agriculture were not available before 1949. Since these estimates became available, the acreage for fresh market has been about the same each year since 1949, but the production and value of the crop have increased. In 1953, the estimated acreage for market was 215,700 acres, which produced 23,963,000 units of 5 dozen ears valued at $46,422,000. The leading states in acreage were Florida, 30,800 acres; Pennsylvania, 26,000 acres; New York, 20,500 acres; California, 19,500 acres; New Jersey, 17,000 acres; and Michigan, 17,000 acres. The leading states in order of production were Florida, California, Pennsylvania, New York, Michigan, and New Jersey. Sweet corn for market was formerly considered a crop that could not be shipped long distances, but there has been an increase in production in areas some distance from large centers of population. The rail shipments to markets in 1944 were only 1,614 carloads, but shipments have increased each year, reaching a total of 5,815 carloads in 1953.

History and Taxonomy. Sweet corn is probably of very recent origin, since it was not mentioned by Jefferson in his "Notes on Virginia," 1781, nor by McMahon, 1806. A writer in the *New England Farmer,* Aug. 3, 1822, stated that sweet corn was not known in New England until a gentleman from Plymouth, who was in General Sullivan's expedition against the Indians in 1779, brought back a few ears which he found among the Indians on the border of the Susquehanna. Another writer, in September, 1822, asserted that this sweet corn was brought back by Lieutenant Richard Bagnal from General Sullivan's expedition against the Six Nations in 1779 and was called *papoon corn*. In 1832 sweet corn was mentioned by Bridgeman.[1] After 1850 it was frequently mentioned by writers. In 1851, Buist[2] mentioned two varieties; in 1854, Schenck mentioned three varieties as having been brought into notice within a few months; in 1876, Burr described 12 varieties.

The word *corn* has a special meaning in the United States and is applied only to Indian corn, or maize, while in other countries it applies to all bread grains. In Europe, the word applies to oats, wheat, rye, or barley, as well as to Indian corn. The reference to corn in the Bible probably means only the small grains since Indian corn, or maize, was not known in the Eastern Hemisphere prior to the discovery of America.

Corn, or Indian corn, was probably grown by the natives of the Americas from a very ancient date. The early explorers of this country found the Indians growing corn from Canada to Florida. The Indians taught the early settlers how to grow it. In fact, it was the leading crop among the natives of this continent at the time of the discovery of America. For many years it was believed that corn, or maize (*Zea mays*), is a native of Mexico. Thus, Harshberger (1893) stated that "all plants closely related to maize are Mexican."

In spite of many studies made to determine the origin of maize, the question as to the place of origin remains unanswered. For a discussion of this general subject the reader is referred to a monograph by Mangelsdorf and Reeves (1939) and a more recent paper by Mangelsdorf and Smith (1949), in which primitive maize, discovered in a cave in New Mexico, is described.

Sweet corn and field corn belong to the grass family and to the genus Zea. These two are considered by most authorities as belonging to the same species, *Z. mays* Linn.; sweet corn is designated by the variety name *rugosa*. It is distinguished from other corns by its high sugar content when in the milk and early dough stage, and by its wrinkled translucent kernels when dry.

Influence of Climate. Sweet corn is adapted to a wide range of climates since it is grown in every state of the United States, in Mexico, Canada, and many other parts of the world. Certain climatic factors, however, affect the yield and quality of the product and account for the concentration of acreage in certain areas. It grows best during hot

[1] *Gard. Asst.*, 1832.
[2] *Family Kitchen Garden*, 61, 1851.

weather, but most of the acreage for processing is grown in cool areas. There has been a widespread belief that sweet corn canned near the northern limit of production is sweeter and of better quality than that canned farther south. Experimental evidence shows that the product canned in Northern areas has a high quality, but this is not because Northern-grown corn develops a higher sugar content than Southern-grown corn. Straughn (1907) and Straughn and Church (1909) reported analyses of sweet corn grown in several places from South Carolina to Maine. There was no direct effect of latitude on sugar content, but in several cases that grown in South Carolina had the highest sugar content. There was no definite superiority of sweet corn grown in any area under study. Appleman and Arthur (1919) have shown that the temperature to which the corn is subjected after harvest influences the rate of sugar loss, the higher the temperature the more rapid the loss. Appleman (1923) also reported (Table 26.2) that the time required for sweet corn to pass the premilk to the best canning stage decreased markedly as the temperature rose from 60 to 85°F. The superiority of Northern canned sweet corn is a result of lower temperatures during harvest, which gives the Northern canner a better opportunity to harvest at the best stage and also slows down deterioration after it has been harvested.

Magoon and Culpepper (1926) have shown that seasonal factors have a marked effect on rate of development. For example, for several plantings of Golden Bantam the number of days from planting to silking varied from 55 to 79 days, and Stowell Evergreen from 63 to 90 days. The most important factor involved was temperature; the higher the temperature, up to a high maximum, the more rapid the development. Magoon and Culpepper (1932) calculated the total degree-hours, above various base lines, required to bring various varieties and strains of sweet corn to canning maturity. They found that the most satisfactory base line varied with variety but fell within the range of 50 to 60°F. There was much less difference in total degree-hours than in days from planting to maturity for different dates of planting and different areas.

These findings have stimulated a great amount of work on total degree-hours to maturity as a means of predicting harvest dates for processing corn. Most investigators have used the 50°F. base for their calculations. To calculate degree-hours (sometimes called *heat units*), subtract 50 from the daily mean temperature and multiply the difference by 24. Daily calculations are made and added to the previous day's total. Later plantings are not made until there has been an accumulation of degree-hours equal to that which is expected to accumulate on the desired number of days during the harvest season.

Richardson (1947) planted Golden Cross sweet corn at intervals from Dec. 15 to Apr. 14, in the Coachella Valley in California. He found that the range in time from planting to canning maturity varied from 72 to 142 days, whereas the total degree-hours varied from 43,632 to 49,444. Lana and Haber (1952) calculated the total degree-hours from planting to canning maturity for four varieties grown in Iowa over a 12-year period. The accumulated degree-hours to maturity for a variety varied from season to season. For example, the range for Ioana varied from 38,100 to 47,148 degree-hours to maturity. Also, there were variations during one season when different planting dates were compared. Golden Cross planted on seven dates beginning May 1 reached canning maturity in fewer days as planting was delayed, but the accumulated degree-hours to maturity increased. Late planting reduced the days to maturity from 94 to 76 days, but the corresponding accumulated degree-hours rose from 41,218 to 45,528 degree-hours.

The use of accumulated degree-hours has been criticized by many scientists since temperature is only one of the many factors that influence plant growth. Seaton (1955) points out that rainfall, sunlight, day length, temperature patterns, and other factors influence the number of degree-hours to harvest, but it still remains a valuable tool for the processor. Processors who used degree-hours to predict harvest dates for their sweet corn acreage were able to predict daily production of canned corn with an error of about 10 per cent.

Sweet corn requires a continuous moisture supply to produce high yields, yet it suffers from excessive water if the soil becomes waterlogged. Lack of water during any part of the growth period may reduce yields, but the most critical period seems to be at silking and during growth of the kernels. Hot dry winds and a dry soil may result in poor pollination and nearly always results in a poor "tip-fill" of the ears. This simply means that the kernels at the tip of the ear do not enlarge even though fertilization has taken place. MacGillivray (1949) reported that sweet corn needed more water to produce high yields than many other vegetables grown in California. The highest yields of Golden Cross were obtained with a total of 19 inches of irrigation water, even though the soil was initially filled with available water to a depth of 6 feet. Lack of water reduced plant size and ear size, and many ears were not marketable. Sweet-corn leaves roll laterally when the plant is water-deficient, and leaf rolling was noticed on the most heavily irrigated plots for a short time on many days. This indicates that the water loss from the plant was more rapid than the roots' water absorption even in a moist soil.

The length of day does not have a pronounced influence on growth and usually does not limit areas in which it can be grown. Sweet corn usually behaves as a short-day plant since flower production is hastened by day lengths less than 12 to 14 hours and is delayed by longer day lengths. Certain varieties may be better adapted to a specific day length than others. Some difficulty in growing sweet corn in England has been attributed to the very long summer days (17 hours) and short nights. Sharman (1947) states that most American sweet-corn varieties did not produce well unless they were planted very early. With early planting the flowers were formed before the long days occurred, while with late planting flowering was delayed through most of the summer until the days became shorter. There were pronounced differences between varieties in this day-length response.

Soils and Soil Preparation. Sweet corn is grown on almost all types of soil with good success so long as the soil is well drained. It does not thrive on wet, poorly drained soils. In Northern areas, light sandy soils are used for the early market crop since they warm up rapidly in the spring. Heavier soils, such as loams or even clay loams, are used for the processing crop since soil moisture is not so likely to be limiting as on lighter soils. In some areas shallow muck deposits that are not suited to other vegetables are used for sweet corn.

A good job of plowing is essential since plant refuse on the surface interferes with the operation of the planter. Large clods should be broken by harrowing or disking, but complete pulverization of the soil is neither desirable nor essential. The corn planter makes a good seedbed as it opens the furrow for the seed as long as there are no large clods or plant refuse on the surface. Excessive harrowing tends to compact the soil and increases the possibility of crusting after heavy rains.

Sweet corn grows well over a wide range of soil reaction from pH 5.5 to pH 7.0. It is tolerant to high acidity and is fairly resistant to aluminum toxicity, which may be a problem in highly acid soils. However, growth is better and fertilizer efficiency is greater when the soil reaction is maintained from pH 6.0 to 6.5 where practical to do so.

Fertilizers. Sweet corn grows rapidly and can utilize large amounts of nitrogen and potash, but usually it is not fertilized heavily, at least in comparison with other vegetables. On new soils and in some growing areas, phosphorus applications must be high, but in the older vegetable-growing areas the main response is to nitrogen and potash, although a complete fertilizer should generally be used.

In the Northeastern states, the usual fertilizer application is 300 to 400 pounds of 8-16-8 per acre. On light sandy soils somewhat higher amounts of 8-16-16 are used, supplemented with a nitrogen side-dressing during the early growth of the crop. In Oregon, 300 to 500 pounds of 4-12-8, or 4-16-4 per acre, supplemented with nitrogen side-dressing, is commonly used. On the east coast of Florida, sweet-corn growers apply 1,000 pounds of 4-12-6 per acre before planting and side-dress twice with 500 pounds of 12-0-6 per acre. In the irrigated regions of the West, nitrogen is the only fertilizer material used in most areas. The proper amount to apply in any locality is determined by the soil type, previous cropping, number of plants per acre, method of application, rainfall, and other factors.

Fertilizer placement influences the efficiency of fertilizer utilization by sweet corn. The almost universal recommendation is to place the fertilizer in bands 2 to 3 inches from the seed and at seed level or slightly below the seed. When broadcast applications are made, considerably more fertilizer must be used to produce high yields. Germinating seed may be damaged if the fertilizer is too near the seed or if too much is applied. This injury results from a high concentration of soluble salts due to soluble fertilizer materials. The damage is most likely to occur on light soils and in dry years when the water content of the soil is low. Good planting equipment operated at the proper speed will eliminate the danger if the fertilizer recommendations of local experiment stations are not greatly exceeded. Bushnell (1950) concluded from a long-term experiment in southeastern Ohio that the fertilizer should contain 50 pounds of N and 50 pounds of K_2O per acre, with additional nitrogen as a side-dressing on land that had been fertilized heavily in previous years. On land that had not been heavily fertilized, 120 pounds of P_2O_5 per acre should be included also. Sweet corn responded fairly well to 8-ton applications of manure if side-dressed with nitrogen, but larger manure applications were not profitable. Other crops gave a greater response, and if manure is scarce it can be used more profitably on these crops.

Clore and Viets (1949) grew sweet corn on newly irrigated land in the Yakima Valley of Washington and obtained increases in yield with both nitrogen fertilizers and organic matter. Yields of 7 tons per acre were obtained when sweet corn followed a vetch cover crop and was fertilized with 160 pounds of nitrogen per acre. The vetch cover crop was superior to winter peas or 10 tons of manure. In the older irrigated areas yields of 8 to 10 tons per acre are not uncommon.

Ware and Johnson (1950), working in Alabama, increased sweet-corn yields with manure, cover crops, fertilizer, or irrigation. The greatest yields resulted from a combination of irrigation, high-fertilizer applications, and turning under organic matter either as manure or a cover crop. Irrigating sweet corn fertilized with 1,000 pounds of 6-10-4 with 12 tons of manure plowed down gave the greatest number and weight of marketable ears.

In the main production areas of sweet corn for processing, it is generally grown in rotation with other farm crops and the organic-matter level in the soil is usually fairly high. The use of cover crops is most important in regions where sweet corn is grown for market on the same land year after year. Manure is scarce in these areas and seldom used.

Many growers sow a cover crop at the last cultivation of the corn; crimson clover in the Southern areas, rye grass in Northern states, and sometimes a mixture of the two in the intermediate states. This system has given good results in maintaining high sweet-corn yields, especially when the cover crop is fertilized after the corn is harvested and the cornstalks are chopped and not removed from the land.

Sweet corn does not have a high requirement for most of the minor elements, with the possible exception of zinc. In severe cases of zinc deficiency the leaves have pale stripes and the buds and ear shoots are almost white. Many other vegetables grow normally on soils with a zinc supply that is too low for sweet corn. On highly acid soils or sandy soils, magnesium may be in short supply. This may be remedied by adding magnesium to the fertilizer or liming the soil with dolomitic limestone. All essential minor elements are included in sweet-corn fertilizer on the sandy soils in Florida, but this is one of the few areas where it is necessary.

Planting. Sweet corn is injured by frost, hence it is not safe to plant until the danger of hard frosts is over. It is worthwhile, however, to take a chance on frost where the crop is grown for a local market in which early sweet corn brings high prices. As a general rule, it is safe to plant about the time of the last killing frost in the spring. In regions where freezing weather is not expected, planting time is determined by the time the crop is desired. When planted early in Northern areas while the soil is still cold, poor stands frequently result. Haskell (1949) studied the germination of sweet corn in cold soils and found that the percentage germination was lower as the length of time of exposure to low temperatures was increased. Seed exposed to soil temperatures of 40°F. gave better stand than when exposed to temperatures of 50°F. This was explained on the basis of better growth of pathogenic organisms at 50 than at 40°F. There were large differences in the ability of different varieties to germinate under these conditions. Torfason and Nounecke (1954) reported similar results with seed exposed to temperatures of 50°F. and below during germination. There was a reduction in come-up even though the seed was planted in a sterile medium. Greater reductions in stand, however, occurred when the seed was planted in field soil that had not been sterilized. Treating sweet-corn seed with a fungicide tended to improve the stand when the soil was cold.

In order to have sweet corn available for as long as the growing season will permit, two methods may be used. One method is to make an early planting of three or four varieties that require different lengths of time from planting to maturity and follow this with additional plantings of one of these, usually the best. The other method is to plant one variety at intervals of 2 to 3 weeks, with the last planting timed to reach maturity before unfavorable weather is expected. A combination of the two methods may be better than either method alone. Most of the crop is planted with machine planters that space the seed accurately in the row and apply the fertilizer at the same time. The planting distance varies considerably, depending on the variety grown, the fertility of the soil, and the ease of cultivation and weed control. Planting in hills spaced about 3 feet apart in each direction was popular at one time because of the ease with which weeds could be controlled by cultivating in both directions. Most of the sweet corn now is planted in drills with single plants 8 to 12 inches apart under most conditions. The spacing of the rows varies with localities and ranges from about 32 to 40 inches. Experimental results have indicated that there is not likely to be any difference in the yield between hill and drill planting so long as the number of plants per acre is the same. Pickett (1944) suggested 8 inches as the desirable spacing for Ioana in the lower Rio Grande Valley of Texas. His results indicated no significant difference in yield between hill and drill planting when the area per plant was the same. Muhr and Rost (1951) found that a maximum population of 14,000 to 15,000 plants per acre gave the greatest yield in the Middle West. The size of ear decreased as the number of plants per acre increased. When the population reached about 15,000 plants per acre the yield began to decrease because of a decrease in both size and number of ears produced. With large plant populations, there was an increase in number of barren stalks, and with small plant populations, there was an increase in plants which produced two ears. The optimum population varied with rainfall and soil fertility. Vittum and Peck (1953) obtained 5¼ tons of sweet corn per acre with plant populations of 14,000 per acre, but only 4½ tons when the plant population was 7,000 plants per acre. A field with plants spaced 12 inches apart in 3-foot rows theoretically has a population of about 14,500 plants. MacGillivray, Minges, and Clemente (1955) reported increases in yield of Golden Cross when the spacing was decreased from 26 to 8 inches at intervals of 6 inches. The maximum yield was obtained at a spacing of 8 inches only when the corn was irrigated. Spacing did not influence the size of ears in this experiment. Nettles, Jamison, and Janes (1952) reported similar results with Golden Security sweet corn in Florida. Varying the spacing of the plants from 24 to 6 inches did not affect the yield unless the crop was irrigated. Irrigation increased the yield at all spacings, and the yield of marketable ears from the 6-inch spacing was almost double the yield from the 24-inch spacing. Dolan and Christopher (1952) studied Early Golden and Golden Cross sweet corn spaced at 4, 8, and 12 inches in 3-foot rows. The greatest tonnage was obtained at the 4-inch spacing, but the ears were too small for market. The best spacing for market corn was 8 inches. The Early

Golden variety is a smaller plant than the Golden Cross and was more adapted to close spacing than Golden Cross.

In most areas 8 to 12 pounds of seed per acre is planted. The amount of seed planted is not a good guide to the plant population because seed count may vary from 1,500 to 4,000 seeds per pound, depending upon variety and growing conditions for the seed crop. Hoffman (1925) found that large kernels gave an earlier and larger yield of sweet corn than the small kernels from the same stalk. Plants from the large kernels reached canning maturity about 5 days before those from small kernels. Results obtained by Sayre (1928) in New York are similar to those reported by Hoffman in Indiana. In growing sweet corn for canning it is desirable to grade the seed and plant the same size of seed in one field. This is especially important when mechanical harvesting is done because there is less variation in maturity of the corn for processing. Most seed companies grade the seed and recommend the proper size of seed plate to use in the planter. The use of the correct seed plate ensures a uniform stand because the planter operates properly and does not damage the seed.

Cultivation. The cultivation of sweet corn is about the same as that given field corn. Many growers follow the practice of running a weeder, or a spike-tooth harrow, over the field before the corn comes up and sometimes after it is up. After the corn is up, the weeder does a good job of loosening the surface of the soil and destroying small weeds in the row as well as between the rows, eliminating some of the hand work. After the plants are 4 to 6 inches tall a cultivator is used in the space between the rows. Most effective weed control is obtained by cultivating when the weeds are small. Only shallow cultivation is required to control weeds, and deep cultivations destroy much of the root system and may result in decreased yield. There is some evidence that there may be some benefit in breaking a hard crust on the soil, but this can be done with shallow cultivation without the damaging effects of root pruning which result from deep cultivation. Fertilizer side-dressings are commonly made with an attachment on the cultivator, so that the two jobs are done at the same time.

Chemical Weed Control. Herbicides are used on much of the sweet-corn acreage to control weeds in the early stages of growth of the corn. Many formulations of 2,4-D are used to control broad-leaved weeds and are usually applied at rates of ½ to 1 pound of 2,4-D acid equivalent per acre. The heavier applications are used as a preemergence spray. The preemergence spray is not always effective because the weeds may not germinate soon enough to be killed by the herbicide. On light sandy soils there is danger of a heavy rain leaching the 2,4-D down to the germinating seed and causing injury to the young plants. Some varieties of corn may be sprayed at any time during their growth without any appreciable injury from 2,4-D, but other varieties are sensitive to the herbicide, and accurate timing of the spray is very important. The safest and most effective time to apply 2,4-D is when the corn is just pushing through the soil and is still in the spike stage. Spraying at this time has resulted in the least injury to sensitive varieties such as North Star and Seneca Dawn. When 2,4-D is used in this manner, there is no need for the careful early cultivation that would have to be made otherwise. This one application of herbicide usually controls the weeds in the row if fresh soil is not turned up. The stalk becomes brittle when sprayed with 2,4-D, and the corn should not be cultivated until the plants have recovered. The practice of spraying with 2,4-D when the plants are 8 to 10 inches high is of dubious value, because severe damage may result from high winds breaking the stalks. In market-growing areas where sensitive crops are grown near the sweet corn it is not safe to use 2,4-D since the spray drift may damage other crops. In these cases, effective weed control can be attained by using a preemergence spray of 3 to 4½ pounds of dinitro per acre. With late plantings of corn on light soils during hot weather, some damage has resulted from spraying with dinitro owing to rapid volatilization of the material. Chemical weed control properly used can eliminate hand hoeing of sweet corn and cut down the number of necessary cultivations.

Suckering. The removal of suckers from the base of the plant is a very old practice and was formerly followed to a great extent. It has been largely discontinued, and few sweet-corn growers sucker corn. The advantages claimed for the practice were increased yield, larger size, and early maturity. These advantages have never been borne out by experimental results. Thompson (1926) and Thompson, Mills, and Wessels (1930) showed that the removal of suckers tended to decrease the yield and did not appreciably hasten maturity or increase size of the ears. The plants were suckered several different times during the growth of the plant, and in no case was suckering found to be of advantage. MacGillivray *et al.* (1946) obtained results similar to those of Thompson. Neither the yield, nor number of ears per plant, nor size of the ear was improved by suckering. It was observed, however, that there was greater ease of harvesting, especially under conditions where vigorous stalk growth was promoted. Later, MacGillivray *et al.* (1955) found that suckering irrigated Golden Cross sweet corn significantly reduced the yield of marketable corn. The greater ease of harvesting did not, however, offset the cost of suckering, and no reason can be logically proposed to encourage suckering of sweet corn.

Varieties. Varieties of sweet corn are usually grouped in three classes: early, medium, and late. The terms refer to the length of time required to produce edible ears, and when varieties of these three classes are planted at the same time, early, medium, and late characterize them with reference to time of edible maturity. There is, however, some overlapping in the maturity of varieties in these various classifications. Although some open-pollinated varieties of sweet corn are grown, about 85 per cent of the 1953 crop was hybrid corn developed by crossing two or more inbred lines or crossing a true variety and an inbred line. This latter kind of hybrid is known as *top-cross* in which the inbred line is used as a pollen parent and the commercial variety as the seed parent. Many well-known hybrids, such as Marcross, Spancross, and Carmelcross, are top-cross hybrids. The most widely grown sweet-corn hybrid is Golden Cross Bantam, or Golden Cross, in which two or more inbred lines are used. The original variety has been altered so much by individual seedmen that the term Golden Cross really represents a type rather than a single variety.

Open-pollinated varieties are still grown in a few sections of the United States. Stowell Evergreen is grown to a small extent in parts of the Middle West. Country Gentleman, or Shoe Peg, is grown for processing in the Tri-state areas of Maryland, Delaware, and Virginia. Southern Shipper and Hickory King are grown to some extent in the South for their resistance to corn earworm, but they are not sweet corn at all, but merely field corn which is grown for "roasting ears."

The variety to grow depends upon local conditions, local market preferences, and the uses for which the corn is intended. The most desirable variety for processing would be one which matured uniformly, with high yield, no suckers, large ears, no ear leaves, yellow kernels of high quality, and resistance to diseases and insects. Other desirable traits are white silks, a high yield of processed product per ton of raw product, and a long period of high canning quality. On the other hand, the market grower desires a high-yielding variety, with disease and insect resistance, producing large ears with many ear, or flag, leaves and dark-green husks. The kernels should be yellow for most markets and have a high sugar content which does not deteriorate rapidly in storage.

Some of the most popular varieties in the early-maturing class are Spancross and North Star; in the medium-maturing class, Carmelcross; and in the late-maturing class, Golden Cross, Golden Security, Ioana, Iochief, and similar varieties. Calumet is popular in some regions because of its resistance to the corn earworm. Practically all of the processing corn has a maturity similar to Golden Cross since earliness is of no importance. In general, the late-maturing class of corn is of higher quality and has larger ears and better appearance than the earlier-maturing varieties. There is an extremely large number of sweet-corn hybrids on the market. Many of the experiment stations conduct corn-breeding work and maintain inbred lines for the production of hybrid seed. Some of the large seed companies and some individual growers also maintain inbred lines and produce hybrid seed from them. The sweet-corn grower should obtain his seed each year from dealers who are known to have the seed that meets his needs. New hybrids come on the market each year, and information on these new varieties can be obtained from the experiment stations or other official sources.

Insects. Several insects attack sweet corn and under some conditions do severe injury. The most destructive are the corn earworm, European corn borer, Southern corn rootworm, cutworms, white grubs, and wireworms. The last three are discussed in Chap. 12.

CORN EARWORM. This is a serious pest of sweet corn in the South, in California, and many sections of the North, but usually not present in injurious numbers in the northern part of the sweet-corn belt of the United States. This insect is the same as the bollworm of cotton and the fruitworm of tomato. It is also called the tobacco budworm, and it also attacks pumpkins, squashes, melons, peppers, and other vegetables. The worm is the larval stage of a moth (*Heliothis obsoleta*), which, when full grown, is 1½ to 2 inches long and varies in color from light green to brown. The eggs are laid on the silk, and the larvae work their way down under the husk where they feed on the silk and unripe grain. Even where the insects do not eat very much of the corn, the injury is serious because of the entrance of rain through the opening made by the worm, and this is followed by decay. While the damaged portion can be trimmed from the ear for processing corn, the housewife objects to earworms in corn on the fresh market. Satisfactory control of the corn earworm can be obtained by spraying or dusting the plants with DDT. In most cases it is only necessary to apply the insecticide directly on the silks. Three treatments are made at intervals of 2 to 3 days, commencing when the silks first appear. In cases of severe infestation, when the sprays or dusts are not effective, the insect can be controlled by injecting a small amount of mineral oil containing pyrethrins into the silk channel of the ear after pollination has been completed. This is a very laborious and expensive method since work must be done by hand. In areas where the corn earworm damages young corn as the corn budworm, mineral oil is added to the DDT spray and the spray is applied to the entire plant.

EUROPEAN CORN BORER (*Pyrausta nubilalis*). This pest was introduced from Europe and is now found in 37 states east of the Rocky Mountains. This is a serious pest of sweet corn since the ears infested with the larvae are not desirable for marketing or canning. The larvae is about ¾ inch long, yellowish gray in color, with faint reddish or brown stripes. The caterpillars bore into all parts of the plant, except the root, and cause great damage when they are present in considerable numbers. The breaking over of the tassels due to feeding of the caterpillars, the sawdustlike borings on the stalks in midsummer, and later the breaking over of the stalk just above the ear are characteristics by which the presence of the insect may be detected. The moth lays its eggs on the leaves of the corn plant. The larvae feed upon the leaves for a very short time and then migrate to the stalk and burrow in. They also burrow in the husks and feed upon the ear. Good corn borer control has resulted from spraying or dusting the entire corn plant with DDT, beginning as soon as the eggs have been laid or shortly thereafter. Three insecticide applications of 5- to 8-day intervals usually give good control.

SOUTHERN CORN ROOTWORM. This pest is the larva of the 12-spotted cucumber beetle. Great injury is often done to corn of all kinds and to many other food plants in the South and in tropical America, including peanuts, beans, and cucurbits. The injury to corn is done by the larvae when the plants are small. At this time they feed upon the roots and bud, boring through the crown at the base of the stalk to reach the bud. Injury is greatest when corn is planted in damp locations and in meadows. Spraying and dusting the soil with chlordane, dieldrin, or aldrin and thoroughly mixing the insecticide with the soil before planting have given good control of this insect. It has also been controlled by mixing one of these insecticides with the fertilizer and drilling the fertilizer in with the planter. Drilling the insecticide mixed with an inert carrier before planting has also been effective.

Diseases. Sweet corn is attacked by many foliage diseases and seedling rots in some areas, and the damage may be severe in unfavorable years. Only two are discussed here.

BACTERIAL WILT, OR STEWART'S DISEASE. This is caused by a bacterium, *Aplanobacter stewartii*. It is a very serious disease in many corn-growing regions. It makes its appearance at any stage of growth but is most noticeable when the plants attain considerable size. The plants are dwarfed; the tassel develops early, whitens, and soon dies; the leaves dry out; and the stem finally dies. A yellow slime may collect on the inner husks, and the stalk, if cut off near the base and squeezed, may show a yellow ooze at the ends of the strands. The bacterium can live over the winter in the seed and in old cornstalks left in the field. The most important source of the bacterium in the spring in Northern areas is that which overwinters in the corn flea beetle. When the flea beetles begin feeding on the young corn plants in the spring, they spread the bacterium rapidly. There is a good correlation between the incidence of Stewart's disease and the mildness of the winter. Fewer flea beetles live in severe winters and are not available to spread the disease in the field. In many states forecasts are made for severity of Stewart's wilt based on winter temperatures. The use of resistant varieties and controlling the corn flea beetle are the only control measures. The corn flea beetle is controlled by spraying or dusting the plants with DDT or similar insecticides, beginning as soon as the plants have two or three leaves. Most of the early varieties of sweet corn are susceptible to Stewart's disease, and good resistant varieties occur only among the late-maturing varieties. The cheapest method of controlling this disease is growing resistant varieties of sweet corn.

CORN SMUT (*Ustilago zeae*). This disease occurs wherever corn is grown and is easily recognized in the later stages by the black masses on the ear and tassel. The first symptom is a pale, shining, swollen area covered with a white membrane, which soon appears black because of the maturing of the spores inside. The membrane finally bursts and releases a powdery, black mass of spores. The disease is not carried on the seed.

There is no practicable control except to gather and burn the smutted ears and stalks before the spores are released. This method is usually not practiced because the disease seldom affects more than 1 to 2 per cent of the ears.

Harvesting. Most sweet corn grown for processing is harvested by machines. These machines pull the ear from the plant and convey it to a truck or wagon in which it is transported to the processor. Mechanical pickers usually are not used for market corn because the husks of the corn are damaged by the machine. Corn for market is picked by hand in a number of ways. In some areas, the corn is picked and gathered in baskets or bags which are carried out of the field to be picked up by trucks and taken to a packing house. In other areas, the corn is picked directly into the bags or crates in which it is to be sold. Some growers use trucks or wagons in the field into which the pickers throw the harvested ears. This greatly speeds up the process since the pickers do not have to carry bags. Some growers have built long conveyor belts on heavy tractors which follow the pickers, and the ears are placed on the moving belt and conveyed into a trailing wagon or cart. Others have found that much labor can be saved if the cornstalks are cut just above the ear the day before harvest. This is done with a rotary mower mounted on a high-clearance tractor, which is also used for spraying and dusting sweet corn. The pickers move down the rows faster, find the corn more easily, and do not have so much difficulty getting the corn to the conveyor or into the wagons.

It is difficult for an inexperienced person to determine when sweet corn is in the best edible condition without pulling down the husk and examining the kernels. For sweet corn to have the highest quality it should be harvested in the milk stage since the sugar decreases and the starch increases as it passes from this stage to the dough stage. The general appearance of the husk and silk and the plumpness of the ear are evidence of the stage of ripeness and are sufficient for the average grower. By observing the general characters mentioned and correlating them with the stage of ripeness as indicated by the nail test, the inexperienced person will soon learn to determine when the sweet corn should be harvested without examining the kernels. In the nail test the thumbnail is thrust into the kernel; if the exudate is milky, the corn is said to be in the milk stage; if dough is forced out of the kernel, the corn is said to be in the dough stage and is too ripe for best quality. Appleman (1921) analyzed Stowell Evergreen sweet corn at different stages of maturity. The results presented in Table 26.2 indicate that as

Table 26.2. Average Percentage Composition of Sweet Corn at Different Stages of Ripening

Crop	Stage of ripening	Number of tests	Moisture, per cent	Total sugar, per cent	Starch, per cent
Early.........	Premilk	9	85.10	6.26	3.29
Early.........	Milk	18	80.16	5.79	7.72
Early.........	Early dough	9	71.07	3.91	16.35
Early.........	Dough	18	63.92	3.17	21.62
Late..........	Premilk	14	88.75	5.76	2.71
Late..........	Milk	16	83.54	5.81	5.51
Late..........	Early dough	16	77.95	3.38	11.24

the corn matures there is a decrease in moisture and sugar and an increase in starch. As mentioned in an earlier paragraph, the temperature at the time of ripening determines the rate of change from the milk to the dough stage. The higher the temperature, the faster the corn matures, and for this reason close attention should be given to harvesting when the weather is hot. After sweet corn is harvested, it should be handled quickly and at as low a temperature as possible, for the quality deteriorates rapidly. Appleman and Arthur (1919), Stevens and Higgins (1919), and Platenius (1939) have shown that the rate of sugar loss increases with rise of temperature, at least up to 30°C.

Appleman and Arthur, working with Stowell Evergreen, analyzed sweet corn at 24-hour intervals during storage at different temperatures. The results for five temperatures are shown in Table 26.3. Appleman and Arthur found that the depletion of sugar in the corn after it is separated from the stalk does not proceed at a uniform rate, but becomes slower until finally equilibrium is reached. This takes place when the total sugar has decreased about 62 per cent and the sucrose about 70 per cent. They showed that the rate of sugar loss increased as temperature is raised, but that the raising simply hastens the attainment of the equilibrium, which seems to be about the same for all temperatures. The rate of sugar loss, until it reaches 50 per cent of the initial sugar content, is doubled for every increase of 10° up to 30°C. This follows van't Hoff's law for the rate of chemical reaction.

Table 26.3. Loss of Sugar from Green Sweet Corn during Consecutive 24-hour
Periods of Storage at Different Temperatures (Losses Expressed as
Percentages of Total Sugar Present Initially)
(Data calculated from Appleman and Arthur)

Number of hours in storage	Storage temperature				
	0°C.	10°C.	20°C.	30°C.	40°C.
24	8.1	17.1	25.6	50.4	45.8
48	11.0	13.6	26.9	13.8	26.5
72	4.0	15.0	17.9	3.3	5.0
96	5.7	17.2	12.1	6.3	

Sweet corn for processing is picked at different stages of maturity, depending on the way it is to be processed. Corn for freezing is picked at about the same stage as corn for fresh market, while corn for whole-kernel pack is picked at a slightly later stage of maturity, and cream-style corn is picked at still later maturity. Sweet corn often becomes heated after being pulled from the stalk, especially when loaded for hauling to the canning factory. The loads may stand all night, and under such conditions the quality deteriorates rapidly. Prompt handling and cooling of the corn are essential for maintaining high quality.

Grading and Packing for Market. The handling of sweet corn for fresh market has improved tremendously since about 1945, and this has been one of the main factors in the increase in production of fresh corn for market. The most effective way to maintain high-quality sweet corn is to hydrocool the ears immediately after picking. The process of hydrocooling simply involves placing the ears in circulating cold water for various lengths of time. This lowers the temperature of the ear more rapidly than placing in a refrigerator. Showalter and Schomer (1949) found that hydrocooling sweet corn for 13 minutes in water at 42°F. reduced the temperature at the center of the cob from 85 to 52°F. On the other hand, corn that was stored in wire baskets in a 40°F. refrigerator required 5 hours to reach a temperature of 52°F. in the center of the cob. Important losses in sugar can occur in a very short time immediately after harvest. Alban and Scott (1954) reported that placing crushed ice in the field containers at harvest helped maintain a high sugar content in the sweet corn. After the ears had been placed in a 40°

refrigerator for 24 hours, the corn iced in the field contained nearly twice as much sugar as corn that was not iced. Luke (1953) observed that 15 pounds of crushed ice placed in a wet-strength paper bag with 50 ears of corn lowered the temperature of the corn from 80 to 60°F. in about 4 hours. Hydrocooling and icing sweet corn are common practice in the large, market-corn-producing areas.

Corn is marketed in various types of crates and bags. The two most popular containers are flat wirebound crates, which hold 5 dozen ears, and wet-strength paper bags, which hold 50 ears of sweet corn and 10 to 20 pounds of crushed ice. Prepackaged sweet corn refers to ears that have been husked and packed in trays overwrapped with transparent films or in transparent film bags. The successful maintenance of high quality in prepackaged sweet corn depends upon immediate cooling after harvest. The ears should be hydrocooled before they are placed in packages because the packages slow down cooling in the refrigerator. After packaging, it must be kept refrigerated at all times. This method has been very successful, and its use will probably increase.

Storage. Sweet corn is not stored to any great extent. If cooled immediately after harvesting, it can be kept in fairly good condition for a week or more at 32°F. and at humidities of 90 to 98 per cent. Appleman and Arthur (1919) showed that the loss of sugar was about four times as rapid at 50°F. as at 32°F. At 32°F. more than 20 per cent of the initial sugar disappeared through respiration and conversion to starch in 4 days. Rate of sugar loss is much more rapid at the beginning than later.

OKRA

Okra, or gumbo, is an important crop in many parts of the Old World where it is used in the dry form in large quantities. In the United States it is of great economic importance only in some of the Southern states, where it is grown for market and processing. The area devoted to okra was 8,273 acres in 1939 and 16,843 acres in 1949. Practically all of this production was in the Southern states. Georgia was the leading state in acreage of okra with 4,055 acres, Florida with 3,563 acres, followed by Texas, Alabama, and Louisiana. In many areas in Louisiana, okra is the most important processing crop grown.

History and Taxonomy. Okra is thought to be of African or Asiatic origin, perhaps both. It was probably not cultivated during ancient times as it is not mentioned in early literature. It was known by the Spanish Moors and was used by the Egyptians in the twelfth or thirteenth century. Okra is mentioned as having been grown in Philadelphia in 1748 and was listed by Jefferson in 1781 as being grown in Virginia. Mc-Mahon (1806) also mentions its culture in the South.

Okra is known under the botanical name *Hibiscus esculentus* L. and belongs to the Malvaceae, or mallow family. Many other species of hibiscus are used as foods in various parts of the world. In this genus belong many species of flowering hibiscus, several of which are natives of the United States. Cotton is the most important economic plant belonging to the mallow family.

Culture. Okra is a tender plant and grows best in hot weather. In regions having a short growing season and relatively cool nights, the crop does not thrive well. In such regions a supply for home use can be grown if quick-maturing, dwarf varieties are selected and the seed is planted as soon as the soil becomes warm. Commercially, okra seed is drilled in rows $3\frac{1}{2}$ to 4 feet apart, and the plants are later thinned to stand 12 to 18 inches apart in the row, depending on the variety grown. It usually requires from 4 to 8 pounds of seed to sow an acre of okra. Seed is very slow to germinate, and good stands are obtained only when the soil is warm. Anderson, Carolus, and Watson (1953) reported that the rate and percentage of come-up of okra seed could be hastened by soaking the seed for 24 hours in water or for 30 minutes in acetone and alcohol. The accelerating effects of these seed treatments were evident only in warm soils. If the seed is soaked too long in water, it is softened too much to be planted with mechanical equipment.

Any good garden soil will produce a satisfactory crop of okra if other conditions are favorable. The usual fertilizer applications in the South are 400 to 800 pounds of a 5-10-5 or 6-8-8, broadcast and fitted in before the seed is planted. After the harvest season is begun, nitrogen side-dressings are usually made. The harvest may be delayed if excessive amounts of nitrogen are used before the plant begins to fruit. The cultivation given okra should be about the same as for any other cultivated crop.

Varieties. Okra varieties may be classified on the basis of plant size, pod shape, and pod color. The dwarf types grow 3 to 4 feet high, while the tall types may be 6 to 8 feet tall. All of the popular varieties have spineless pods in the fresh-market stage, and the range in pod color among the varieties is from creamy white to dark green. Many varieties produce pods with prominent ridges, while a few produce smooth pods.

Perkins Spineless and Dwarf Long Pod are dwarf varieties and produce green, ridged pods about 7 inches long. Clemson Spineless is intermediate height, about $4\frac{1}{2}$ feet, and produces long green pods with moderate ridging. Louisiana Green Velvet is tall and has green pods with moderate ridging. Perkins Mammoth Long Pod grows to a height of 6 to 8 feet and has green pods 7 to 8 inches long with prominent ridges. White Velvet, or Lady Finger, is 5 to 6 feet tall and produces round creamy white pods 6 to 7 inches long. Louisiana Market is moderately tall, with smooth pods 2 to 5 inches long which have a dark-green color after blanching for freezing or canning. Emerald has dark-green smooth pods 7 to 8 inches long, and the plant height is intermediate.

Harvesting. The long seed pods are the edible portion, and as these develop rapidly, they should be gathered every day. Only the younger pods are desired, as the older pods become tough and woody. The harvest starts when the first pods have developed and continues until frost if the pods are kept picked. Woodruff (1927) stated that the maximum yield is produced in September in Georgia but that the harvest is continued from the last of June until the plants are killed by frost. Perkins, Miller, and Dallyn (1952) found that harvesting the pods when they were 3 or 4 days old resulted in a continuous harvest over the entire growing season, while if pods were allowed to mature the plants stopped fruiting. The plants that were harvested frequently grew much taller with more branching than the plants with mature pods on them. According to Culpepper and Moon (1941), the eating quality of okra was rather high at the 4-day stage (from blossoming), increased to the 6-day stage, then slowly declined to the 10- to 12-day stage, after which the pods became so fibrous as to be inedible. The rate of change, however, was influenced markedly by temperature, the rate of growth of pods being doubled for each increase of 18°F. in temperature. In regions having a higher growing temperature than Arlington, Va., where Culpepper and Moon conducted their studies, the rate of growth would be more rapid, and in regions of lower temperatures the rate of growth would be slower than they found.

The tender pods are broken from the stalks and must be handled carefully because they bruise and discolor. For the fresh market, the pods are graded in various sizes and packaged in various ways, usually in a cardboard tray covered with a plastic film. They should be stored at temperatures below 50°F. with a high humidity to prevent wilting. In Louisiana the yield of okra for processing is usually 3 to 5 tons per acre.

Uses. The principal use of okra is in soups and stews in which meats form an important part, as in the so-called "gumbo" soups. The pods are also boiled or fried and eaten as a vegetable. A large part of the crop is frozen or canned, alone or as a mixture with other vegetables. A considerable amount is preserved in brine for future use in canned soups. The increased acreage of the crop indicates that more people are using okra than in previous years, before processing procedures had been developed to a high degree.

In Turkey the young pods are dried in large quantities for use in the diet. Tons of this dried product are imported by the United States for use as flavoring in preparing soups and other food products.

MARTYNIA

Martynia, or unicorn plant (*Proboscidea Jussieui* Keller), is a native of Southwestern United States. This plant has been known as *Martynia proboscidea, M. Louisiana,* and *P. Louisiana,* but according to Van Eseltine (1929), who has made a study of this group, the plant usually cultivated is *P. Jussieui.* It is grown to some extent in home gardens mainly as a curiosity, but its seed pods are used for pickling when young. The pods are green, very hairy, fleshy, 1½ inches at their greatest diameter, tapering to a long slender incurved beak or horn. The plant grows 1½ to 2 feet high and is rather wide-spreading.

In the South, martynia seed may be sown in rows 3 feet apart and the plants thinned to stand 18 to 24 inches apart in the row. In the North, the plants should be started in the greenhouse and later transplanted to the garden. A warm soil is especially desirable in the North. The general cultural requirements of this plant are about the same as for okra.

CHAPTER 27

Chayote, Yam, Dasheen, Manioc

These four crops are very important food crops for millions in tropical and subtropical areas of the world. They represent four families, and all but chayote are grown primarily for their underground parts. While the chayote is grown mainly for its fruit, the enlarged root is used as food in many tropical regions.

CHAYOTE

The chayote (*Sechium edule*) is thought to be indigenous to Mexico, Central America, and the West Indies. It is a very important food crop in tropical America, the West Indies, and in other tropical regions. In the United States it can be grown in the mild winter regions of the South Atlantic and Gulf Coast states and in parts of California.

The chayote belongs to the Cucurbitaceae family and to the genus Sechium. The plant is a perennial-rooted vine that bears large crops of edible fruits (Fig. 27.1). In subtropical and tropical regions it produces large edible tuberous roots. The fruits vary in color from dark green to ivory white and range in size from a few ounces to as much as 2 pounds; the surface is even to deeply wrinkled or corrugated; smooth to very prickly; form nearly spherical with no pronounced fissure to long flattened pear shape with a deep fissure at blossom end of fruit. In quality the fruits vary from fiberless with no pronounced seed coat surrounding the single flat seed to those having a tough, fibrous inedible seed coat with fibers radiating into the flesh.

In tropical regions without a pronounced dry period the chayote plant produces fruits continuously. One plant well cared for will produce enough fruit for a family of 4 or 5 persons.

Culture. The chayote plant grows well under a fairly wide range of conditions but seems to thrive best under moderate temperatures. However, in some areas in the Tropics it is grown under high temperatures near sea level, and under relatively cool temperatures at elevations of 4,000 to 4,500 feet. Freezing kills the entire plant.

Chayotes grow best on a rich, well-drained, loamy soil, but will produce a crop on well-drained muck or peat soil. The soil should be well prepared and well fertilized. If farm manure is available its use is recommended as suggested for the cucumber. Where no manure is used soil-improving crops and commercial fertilizers, as recommended for the cucumber, should give good results with the chayote.

FIG. 27.1. Chayote plant grown on trellis. (*Courtesy of U.S. Department of Agriculture.*)

Large mature fruits that have begun to germinate are desirable for planting. The entire fruit, containing one seed, is planted in a sloping position with the broad end down and the small or stem end slightly exposed. In regions where severe freezing occurs during winter, planting should be done as soon as the danger of frost is over and the soil has become warm.

Chayote plants require large quantities of water, so that irrigation is important when the crop is grown in regions of low rainfall or where there is a prolonged period of little or no rain.

Where the chayote is grown as a perennial in regions where freezes occur, a mulch of straw, hay, or some similar material should be applied to protect the roots from freezing. The mulch should be loose but fairly thick (3 or 4 inches). The plants may be grown with or without supports. In some areas in Central America and elsewhere the crop is grown in much the same way as squash and with about the same spacing as the running varieties of squash. The vines often are supported on trellises or other devices. A fence may be used, or the vines may be trained on large T trellises covered with heavy fencing wire of about 4-inch mesh. When such trellises are used, heavy posts are set into the ground and crossbars are nailed or bolted to them at the top. The T type of trellis should be high enough to permit workmen to work under them without having to stoop.

The chayote is attacked by some of the same diseases and insects as the other cucurbits. The root knot nematode is one of the serious diseases of chayote. This is discussed in Chap. 18. The pickleworm and the spotted and striped cucumber beetles are important insect pests of chayote. Control measures for these insects are discussed under Cucumber.

Uses of the Chayote. The fruit is the part of the plant that is most commonly used as food, especially in subtropical areas, as in parts of the United States where the plant is grown. The large tuberous roots are used as food in many tropical areas. The fruits are prepared by boiling and serving with butter or cream sauce. They are sliced, dipped in egg batter, and fried, and the boiled fruits are served cold as a salad, either alone or mixed with other salad foods. The fruits sometimes are boiled, mashed, and fried like potato cakes.

YAMS

The true yams belong to the genus Dioscorea, which contains about 250 species of climbing vines with large storage roots. Not all of the yams produce edible roots, but of the edible species a few are of great importance as food. They constitute an important source of food for millions in tropical areas of the Americas, the West Indies, the islands of the Pacific, and the tropical areas of Asia. The name yam, as used here, should not be confused with the term as applied to certain varieties of sweet potatoes. True yams and sweet potatoes belong to different botanical families, so are not even closely related. The edible species of yams produce starchy roots somewhat similar to the Irish potato in taste and food value.

The genus Dioscorea and the family Dioscoreaceae were named for Dioscorides, a Greek physician and naturalist of the early Christian Era. While most of the species are tropical or subtropical, some are native of temperate regions. Among the species cultivated for food the following are important: *Dioscorea cayenensis* Lam., yellow, or attato, yam; *D. batatas* Decne, Chinese yam; *D. bulbifera* L., air potato grown sometimes for the aerial tubers; *D. trifida* L., cush-cush, yampee, small size, but of superior quality; *D. alata* L., greater yam, which grows to very large size. Young (1923) reported that single tubers weighing 50 to 60 pounds had been produced at the Plant Introduction Garden, Miami, Fla. There are reports of still larger yams. However, small to medium-sized tubers are preferred.

There is considerable interest in certain species of Dioscorea because of their medicinal properties for use in treatment for arthritis.

Culture. The yam is adapted to a wide variety of soils, but a deep, rich, friable, well-drained soil is considered to be almost ideal. Good aeration is important for the development of the tuberous roots. According to Childers *et al.* (1950), the soil used for yams in Puerto Rico commonly is built into ridges 12 to 18 inches high to ensure good aeration and drainage. Compost, manure, or other sources of organic matter and commercial fertilizer may be incorporated with the soil in the ridge. One method is to make furrows 4 to 6 feet apart and place some of the organic material in the bottom and cover it with a few inches

of soil; then another layer of organic material, after which the ridges are built to the proper height with soil. On well-drained soil of good depth it is not desirable to build ridges 12 to 18 inches high, and it may not be necessary to use ridges at all.

The usual method of propagation is to use the crowns of the large tuberous roots or to plant whole small tubers. Any part of the tuber may be used for propagation. The tuber may be cut into pieces weighing 4 or 5 ounces to a pound, depending on the size of tuber. Some authorities recommend drying the cut surfaces in the sun for a few hours before planting to lessen the chance of decay. The pieces, or the whole tubers, are planted 2 to 3 inches deep 1 to 2 feet apart in rows 4 to 6 feet apart, or in hills about 3 by 3 feet. In regions where there is a long dry period planting usually takes place when the soil is in good condition after the rains begin.

FIG. 27.2. Yam plant (*Dioscorea* sp.) grown on trellis. (*Courtesy of U.S. Department of Agriculture.*)

Unless the soil is naturally rich or is supplied with nutrients through the use of manure or compost, commercial fertilizer should be used in considerable quantities. A complete mixture such as a 5-10-10 or some similar analyses, applied at the rate of 1,000 to 2,000 pounds to the acre in two applications, should be satisfactory. The larger quantity should be applied on infertile soils with little or no manure. It is suggested that part of the fertilizer be applied at planting time and the remainder during the growth of the crop.

It is generally recommended that the vines be supported on stakes or a trellis of some kind for highest yields (Fig. 27.2). Bamboo or wooden stakes are used in some areas, and trellises of various kinds are employed to some extent. Small plantings may be supported on the yard or garden fence. However, the crop can be grown without supports, especially on well-drained soil.

Weeds should be kept under control by cultivation and other methods that are employed with other crops.

Varieties. The varieties of yams grown for use as food represent several species. Childers *et al.* state that the Guinea, a white-flesh variety of *Dioscorea cayenensis,* is the most popular one grown in Puerto Rico. A yellow-fleshed variety of the same species, known as Congo Yellow or Guinea Yellow, is also grown to some extent. Potato and Tango (*D. aculeata*) and Agua, a variety of D. *alata,* are other white-fleshed varieties. There are purple-fleshed varieties that are grown in some areas. Purple Ceylon is perhaps the best known of the purple varieties.

Harvesting and Handling. Yams may be harvested at any time during the year in most regions. However, when grown in regions where frosts occur, they should be harvested before there is danger of a freeze. Digging should be done carefully on a bright day in order to permit the roots to dry before being stored or put on the market. Drying the freshly dug yams in the shade is thought to be preferable to drying in direct sunlight. The roots are very tender and brittle, hence must be handled carefully to prevent bruising and breaking (Fig. 27.3). Any bruised and cut surface should be dried by short exposure to the sun or in a warm, dry, well-ventilated room.

Yams may be harvested and stored after they reach maturity, or they may be dug as needed in many regions. According to Young (1923), the yams should be placed on slat shelves or in trays with slat bottoms for storage and only one layer deep. Good ventilation is essential to successful keeping. Young recommended a storage temperature of 55 to 60°F. as being the most favorable.

Preparation and Use. Yams are prepared and used in much the same ways as are Irish potatoes. They are baked, boiled, and fried. Small yams are baked whole without peeling, while large ones are cut into suitable size before baking. Some varieties should be peeled before boiling because of some color or other quality in the skin that may affect the appearance or flavor of the cooked product. The boiled product may be served without further preparation, or it may be served hot as mashed yam, or it may be served cold as a salad. The boiled product is sometimes sliced and fried or mashed and fried as yam cakes. Raw yams may be sliced and fried like French-fried potatoes.

Fig. 27.3. Tubers of yam (*Dioscorea* sp.). (*Courtesy of U.S. Department of Agriculture.*)

DASHEEN

The dasheen is a variety of taro (*Colocasia esculenta* Schott), which has been an important food crop in Oriental countries for over 2,000 years. It is now widely grown in the warmer parts of the Old World, especially in the islands of the Pacific. According to Hodge (1954), varieties of taro came into the New World from two sources. Certain coarse, acrid types were brought into the Colonies at an early date from tropical Africa along with slaves who used it as food. Later a superior variety was introduced into West Indies from China. The Oriental taro, known as dasheen, became a popular food in these islands and is common in the gardens throughout the Tropics.

The dasheen differs from most taros in that their corms and cormels (tubers) are practically free from acridity that is common in other aroids. The acridity is due to needlelike crystals of calcium oxalate. It is best not to taste any of the taros in the uncooked state because of the calcium oxalate crystals. These crystals are destroyed by cooking.

The leaf blades of the dasheen are very large and somewhat similar in appearance to caladium (Fig. 27.4). The petioles are long (3 to 7

FIG. 27.4. Field of dasheen in central Florida. (*Courtesy of U.S. Department of Agriculture.*)

feet). The underground parts consist of one or more large edible central corms and a considerable number of cormels called tubers by some writers. Both corms and cormels are ovoid in shape, but the form varies with variety and environmental conditions.

Dasheen-type taros are known under various names. In Spanish-speaking areas of the Caribbean the name *malanga* is used, and the English terms *eddo* and *coco* are used to some extent in Barbados and Jamaica. Hodge suggests that it is best to use the term taro for all varieties except those known to be of Chinese origin. Plants similar to the taro, but belonging to the genus Xanthosoma, are grown for food in some areas of the Tropics under the name of yautia, or tanier.

Culture. The dasheen grows best in a deep, rich, moist soil. Hodge states that soils similar to the hammock lands of Florida are especially well suited to the crop. The hammock soil is a rich sandy loam underlain with clay. In the United States the growing of dasheen is limited to the low lands of the coastal plain from South Carolina to Texas, although the crop can be grown in parts of California.

In parts of the United States where the dasheen is grown and in regions having similar climate, planting should be done as early as the weather will permit or about 2 weeks before the last spring frost is expected. In regions where frosts do not occur planting may be done at any time during the year, provided moisture conditions are favorable. Childers *et al.* state that the best planting period in Puerto Rico is during the cool season between December and April. The small corms weighing from 2 to 5 ounces are considered best for planting. They are planted whole 2 to 3 inches deep. Hodge reports that corms with the terminal bud living are preferred for planting unless it is desired to increase the number of corms. "If the terminal bud grows, one new corm results; if the terminal bud fails, two or more lateral buds usually start and each bud becomes a corm. Each new corm then gives rise to lateral tubers." Large-growing varieties should be planted in rows 4 feet apart and about 2 feet or more apart in the row. Small-growing varieties may be planted 1½ by 3 feet.

The dasheen draws rather heavily on nutrients in the soil, and unless the soil is rich it should be well fertilized. Where manure is available it can be used to advantage but should be supplemented with some readily available nitrogen and with phosphorus. If manure is not used a complete fertilizer should be applied in at least two applications. On sandy-loam soils an application to supply 100 pounds of nitrogen and phosphorus and 150 to 200 pounds of potash should give good results. On heavier soils less potash would be required.

Weeds should be kept under control by shallow cultivation and other means.

Harvesting and Handling. When only a small quantity is to be harvested for home use, individual tubers may be removed, leaving the small ones to continue to grow, or the entire plant may be removed when most of the tubers have matured. Harvesting is done by hand. Where a large number of plants are to be harvested, three men working together is a good arrangement. Two men with shovels loosen the plant and soil on one side, and the third man pulls the plant over. The tubers are pulled off and prepared for home use, for market, or for storage (Fig. 27.5).

In preparing the crop for market, the feeding roots, fibers, and the bases of the leaf stalks are removed. The preparation may be done in the field or in a shed or other shelter when the weather is unfavorable. First-grade tubers are fairly smooth, ovoid in shape, and weigh from 4 to 8 ounces each. A lower grade may include tubers of about 3 ounces and of irregular shape. In many cases no separation into grades is attempted.

Dasheen can be stored successfully in a well-ventilated storage kept at a temperature of about 50°F. The tubers (cormels) keep better than the corms. Hodge states that curing for several days in a well-ventilated

FIG. 27.5. A large hill of Trinidad dasheen before being broken up, showing the relative position of the larger corms and smaller lateral tubers (cormels) as they grew. This hill, which is larger than the average, contains five corms instead of the usual one or two. (*Courtesy of U.S. Department of Agriculture.*)

place is essential for successful storage. Tubers have been kept as long as 6 months in a dry basement where the temperature ranged between 40 and 50°F.

Uses of the Dasheen. The dasheen is used as food and is prepared in many ways. The tubers are boiled and baked and served about the same as the Irish potato. According to Hodge, the tubers make good chips, which have a distinctive nutty flavor; they absorb less fat than do potato chips. In Hawaii and other islands of the South Pacific a type of taro is used for making "poi," a starchy paste that is an important article of diet. The young leaves and petioles are used as food in some areas. They are prepared like kale or other greens, but it is necessary to remove the acridity, which can be done by boiling for 15 minutes in water to which a large pinch of baking soda is added; then wash with clear boiling water and again boil until tender. For a discussion of the culture and use of taro in Hawaii the reader is referred to Greenwell (1947).

MANIOC (YUCA, CASSAVA)

Manioc (*Manihot esculenta*) is a very important food crop for millions in tropical America and in many other parts of the world. It is a native of the eastern equatorial region of South America and was cultivated by the Indians in Brazil, Guiana, and Mexico before the arrival of the Europeans. The genus Manihot belongs to the Euphorbiaceae, or Spurge, family.

Manioc is known under various names including yuca, cassava, mandioc, and tapioca. The plant is a herbaceous shrub that grows to a height of from 4 to 10 feet and is cultivated for its tuberous roots 1½ to 2½ inches in diameter and may reach a length of 4 feet or more. The plant is tender to frost, and growth is checked by continued cool weather without frost. It requires a warm climate free from frost for at least 8 months. The crop has been known in Florida for about 100 years, but its culture never attained much commercial importance.

There are two general types of manioc, known as "bitter" and "sweet." According to Tracy (1903), the bitter type is more commonly grown because it produces greater yields than the sweet varieties. The tuberous roots are usually reddish or brown in color, although some are nearly white. Most, if not all, varieties contain a poisonous glucoside, which, according to Scherry (1947), is eliminated or changed to inocuous form by boiling.

Culture. Manioc is grown on many classes of soil, but a friable, fertile, well-drained sandy loam is considered better than the heavier types. A hardpan layer below the surface layer is thought to be desirable because it tends to prevent the development of the tuberous roots at too great depths.

On most soils it is desirable to apply some fertilizer, or manure, or both. The fertilizer practices suggested for the sweet potato should be satisfactory for manioc. Part of the fertilizer nitrogen should be applied during growth of the crop.

Manioc is propagated by stem cuttings 6 to 10 inches long. The cuttings should be taken from the mature parts of the plant. The stem pieces are planted in shallow trenches or furrows and covered to the depth of from 2 to 4 inches. The rows are made 3 to 4 feet apart, and the cuttings are dropped at intervals of about 3 feet. At 3 by 3 feet about 4,800 cuttings would be required to plant an acre.

The roots develop near the surface, therefore only shallow cultivation should be given. Weed control is important early in the growth of the plants. After the plants completely shade the ground there is little or no need for cultivation.

FIG. 27.6. Manioc (yuca, cassava) plant showing edible roots. (*Courtesy of D. J. Rogers, Allegheny College.*)

Harvesting and Handling. The time from planting to harvest varies considerably because of climatic and varietal differences. Rapid-growing varieties grown under good climatic conditions may be ready for harvest in 6 months from planting. Under most conditions, however, 9 to 12 months is required for good yields. For home use and for local markets the crop is harvested as needed, since there is no definite stage of maturity at which the roots must be dug. If allowed to continue growth too long, they become fibrous and low in quality. The plants are cut back to stubs 6 to 8 inches long before starting to dig out the roots. The stubs furnish a hand hold for use in pulling roots from the soil (Fig. 27.6). Harvesting usually is done by hand, using various types of hand tools for loosening the soil. The roots grow to too great a length to be plowed out or lifted with a potato digger.

While manioc roots usually are harvested as wanted, they can be kept for several weeks in a warm dry place.

Preparation and Use. Manioc roots are prepared for the table by boiling or baking and served like potatoes. Flour or meal made from the roots is used in making bread and other dishes in some areas. Starches made from manioc are used in laundering, for sizing paper, in making glue and other industrial products, and as food. The well-known tapioca of commerce is made from the starch.

The food value of the roots of manioc is similiar to that of the Irish potato.

List of Agricultural Experiment Stations

Alabama Agricultural Experiment Station, Auburn, Ala.
Alaska Agricultural Experiment Station, College, Alaska
Arizona Agricultural Experiment Station, Tucson, Ariz.
Arkansas Agricultural Experiment Station, Fayetteville, Ark.
California Agricultural Experiment Station, Berkeley 4, Calif.
Colorado Agricultural Experiment Station, Fort Collins, Colo.
Connecticut Agricultural Experiment Station, New Haven 4, Conn.
Connecticut Agricultural Experiment Station, Storrs, Conn.
Delaware Agricultural Experiment Station, Newark, Del.
Florida Agricultural Experiment Station, Gainesville, Fla.
Georgia Agricultural Experiment Station, Experiment, Ga.
Hawaii Agricultural Experiment Station, Honolulu 14, Hawaii
Idaho Agricultural Experiment Station, Moscow, Idaho
Illinois Agricultural Experiment Station, Urbana, Ill.
Indiana Agricultural Experiment Station, Lafayette, Ind.
Iowa Agricultural Experiment Station, Ames, Iowa.
Kansas Agricultural Experiment Station, Manhattan, Kans.
Kentucky Agricultural Experiment Station, Lexington 29, Ky.
Louisiana Agricultural Experiment Station, University Station, Baton Rouge 3, La.
Maine Agricultural Experiment Station, Orono, Maine
Maryland Agricultural Experiment Station, College Park, Md.
Massachusetts Agricultural Experiment Station, Amherst, Mass.
Michigan Agricultural Experiment Station, East Lansing, Mich.
Minnesota Agricultural Experiment Station, University Farm, St. Paul 1, Minn.
Mississippi Agricultural Experiment Station, State College, Miss.
Missouri Agricultural Experiment Station, Columbia, Mo.
Montana Agricultural Experiment Station, Bozeman, Mont.
Nebraska Agricultural Experiment Station, Lincoln 3, Nebr.
Nevada Agricultural Experiment Station, Reno, Nev.
New Hampshire Agricultural Experiment Station, Durham, N.H.
New Jersey Agricultural Experiment Station, New Brunswick, N.J.
New Mexico Agricultural Experiment Station, State College, N.Mex.
New York (Cornell) Agricultural Experiment Station, Ithaca, N.Y.
New York State Agricultural Experiment Station, Geneva, N.Y.
North Carolina Agricultural Experiment Station, State College Station, Raleigh, N.C.
North Dakota Agricultural Experiment Station, State College Station, Fargo, N.D.
Ohio Agricultural Experiment Station, Wooster, Ohio
Oklahoma Agricultural Experiment Station, Stillwater, Okla.

Oregon Agricultural Experiment Station, Corvallis, Ore.
Pennsylvania Agricultural Experiment Station, University Park, Pa.
Puerto Rico Agricultural Experiment Station, Rio Piedras, Puerto Rico
Rhode Island Agricultural Experiment Station, Kingston, R.I.
South Carolina Agricultural Experiment Station, Clemson, S.C.
South Dakota Agricultural Experiment Station, State College Station, S.D.
Tennessee Agricultural Experiment Station, Knoxville 16, Tenn.
Texas Agricultural Experiment Station, College Station, Tex.
Utah Agricultural Experiment Station, Logan, Utah
Vermont Agricultural Experiment Station, Burlington, Vt.
Virginia Agricultural Experiment Station, Blacksburg, Va.
Virginia Truck Experiment Station, Norfolk 1, Va.
Washington Agricultural Experiment Station, Pullman, Wash.
West Virginia Agricultural Experiment Station, Morgantown, W.Va.
Wisconsin Agricultural Experiment Station, Madison 6, Wis.
Wyoming Agricultural Experiment Station, Laramie, Wyo.

Literature Cited

No effort has been made to give an extended bibliography, but rather to list the references mentioned in the text. In citing publications of state experiment stations, the name of the state is abbreviated and the kind of publication (research bulletin, technical bulletin, bulletin, or circular) is indicated. For example, *N.J. Bull.* 353 is a bulletin published by the New Jersey Agricultural Experiment Station; *Mich. Tech. Bull.* 26 is a publication in the Technical Bulletin series of the Michigan Agricultural Experiment Station. If the publication is an extension bulletin or circular, that is indicated by the abbreviation Ext. following the name of the state (abbreviated). Citations of articles in journals and proceedings follow the usual form.

Alban, E. K., and R. C. Scott: Post harvest handling and marketing of garden fresh sweet corn, *Ohio Res. Circ.* **23**, 1954.

Allen, C. L.: "Cabbage, Cauliflower and Allied Vegetables," Orange Judd Publishing Company, Inc., New York, 1914.

Allison, F. E., and M. S. Anderson: The use of sawdust for mulches and soil improvement, *U.S. Dept. Agr. Circ.* **891**, 1951.

Anderson, E. M.: Tipburn of lettuce: effect of maturity, air and soil temperature, and soil moisture tension, *Cornell Bull.* **829**, 1946.

Anderson, M. S., S. F. Blake, and A. L. Mehring: Peat and muck in agriculture, *U.S. Dept. Agr. Circ.* **888**, 1951.

Anderson, W. H., R. L. Carolus, and D. P. Watson: The germination of okra seed as influenced by treatment with acetone and alcohol, *Amer. Soc. Hort. Sci. Proc.*, **62**:427–437, 1953.

Anderson, W. S., *et al*: Regional studies of time of planting and hill spacing of sweet potatoes, *U.S. Dept. Agr. Circ.* **725**, 1945.

Apple, S. B., and K. C. Barrons: Asparagus production in Michigan, *Mich. Circ.* **194**, 1945.

Appleman, C. O.: Study of rest period in potato tubers, *Md. Bull.* **183**, 1914.

————: Forecasting the date and duration of best canning stage for sweet corn, *Md. Bull.* **254**, 1923.

————, and J. M. Arthur: Carbohydrate metabolism in green sweet corn during storage at different temperatures, *Jour. Agr. Res.*, **17**, No. 4, 1919.

————, W. D. Kimbrough, and C. L. Smith: Physiological shrinkage of potatoes in storage, *Md. Bull.* **303**, 1928.

Artschwager, Ernst: Wound periderm formation in the potato as affected by temperature and humidity, *Jour. Agr. Res.*, **35**, No. 11, 1927.

Austin, C. F., and T. H. White: Second report on the cause of pithiness in celery, *Md. Bull.* **93**, 1904.

Babb, M. F.: Residual effect of forcing and hardening of tomato, cabbage, and cauliflower plants, *U.S. Dept. Agr. Tech. Bull.* **760**, 1940.

————, and J. E. Kraus: Orach, its culture and use as a greens crop in the Great Plains region, *U.S. Dept. Agr. Circ.* **526**, 1939.

Bailey, L. H.: "Manual of Cultivated Plants," 2d ed., The Macmillan Company, New York, 1949.

Barger, W. R., G. B. Ramsey, R. L. Perry, and J. H. MacGillivray: Handling and shipping tests with new potatoes from Kern County, California, *Calif. Bull.* **664**, 1942.

Barnes, W. C.: Effects of some environmental factors on growth and color of carrots, *Cornell Memoir* **186**, 1936.

————, and C. N. Clayton: Some factors affecting production of market or garden peas, *S.C. Bull.* **354**, 1945.

Barr, W. L., and D. W. Thomas: Irrigation on Pennsylvania farms, *Penn. Bull.* **562**, 1953.

Barrons, K. C.: The field snapping method of harvesting asparagus, *Mich. Quart. Bull.*, **28**, No. 2, 1945.

Bartholdi, W. L.: Influence of flowering and fruiting upon vegetative growth and tuber yield in the potato, *Minn. Tech. Bull.* **150**, 1942.

Barton, Lela V.: Storage of vegetable seeds, *Boyce Thompson Institute Contrib.*, **7**, No. 3:323–332, 1935.

————: A further report on the storage of vegetable seeds, *Boyce Thompson Institute Contrib.*, **10**, No. 2, 1939.

Baur, K., and F. T. Tremblay: Commercial fertilizers for canning and freezing peas in Western Washington, *Wash. Bull.* **503**, 1948.

Beattie, J. H., and V. R. Boswell: Longevity of onion seed in relation to storage conditions, *U.S. Dept. Agr. Circ.* **512**, 1939.

————, ————, and J. D. McCown: Sweet potato propagation and transplanting studies, *U.S. Dept. Agr. Circ.* **502**, 1938.

Beaumont, A. B., *et al.*: Onions in the Connecticut Valley, *Mass. Bull.* **318**, 1935.

Bell, R. S., T. E. Odland, and A. L. Owens: A half century of crop rotation experiments, *R.I. Bull.* **303**, 1949.

Bennett, H. H.: The problem of soil erosion in the United States, *First Internat. Cong. Soil Sci.* 4:748–757. Also see *U.S. Dept. Agr. Circ.* **33**, 1928.

Bernstein, Leon, K. C. Hamner, and R. Q. Parks: The influence of mineral nutrition, soil fertility, and climate on carotene and ascorbic acid content of turnip greens, *Plant Phys.*, **20**:540–572, 1945.

Bisson, C. W., H. A. Jones, and W. W. Robbins: Factors influencing the quality of fresh asparagus after it is harvested, *Calif. Bull.* **410**, 1926.

Boawn, L. C., F. G. Viets, Jr., and C. L. Crawford: Effect of phosphate fertilizers on zinc nutrition of field beans, *Soil Sci.*, **78**:1–7, 1954.

Bohn, G. W.: The important diseases of lettuce, *U.S. Dept. Agr. Yearbook* **1953**:417–425, 1953.

———— and T. W. Whitaker: Recently introduced varieties of head lettuce and methods of their development, *U.S. Dept. Agr. Circ.* **881**, 1951.

Bond, M. C.: Selling farm products through roadside markets, *Cornell Ext. Bull.* **466**, 1941.

Booth, V. H., and S. O. Dark: The influence of environment and maturity on the total carotenoids in carrots, *Jour. Agr. Sci.*, **39**:226–236, 1949.

Borthwick, H. A.: Factors influencing the rate of germination of the seed of *Asparagus officinalis*, *Calif. Tech. Paper* **18**, 1925.

Boswell, V. R.: Changes in quality and chemical composition of parsnips under various storage conditions, *Md. Bull.* **258**, 1923.

————: Influence of the time of maturity of onions on the behavior during storage and the effect of storage temperature on subsequent vegetative and reproductive development, *Amer. Soc. Hort. Sci. Proc.* 1923:234–239, 1923.

————: Factors influencing yield and quality of peas—biophysical and biochemical studies, *Md. Bull.* 306, 1929.

————: Studies of premature flower formation in wintered-over cabbage, *Md. Bull.* 313, 1929.

————: Growing the Jerusalem artichoke, *U.S. Dept. Agr. Leaf.* 116, 1936.

————: Commercial growing and harvesting sweet potatoes, *U.S. Dept. Agr. Farmers' Bull.* 2020, 1950.

————: Commercial production of tomatoes, *U.S. Dept. Agr. Farmers' Bull.* 2045, 1952.

————: Plant breeding and the vegetable industry, *Econ. Botany*, 6:315–341, 1952.

————, J. H. Beattie, and J. R. McCown: Effect of potash on grade, shape, and yield of certain varieties of sweet potatoes grown in South Carolina, *U.S. Dept. Agr. Circ.* 498, 1938.

————, S. P. Doolittle, and L. M. Pultz: Pepper production, disease and insect control, *U.S. Dept. Agr. Farmers' Bull.* 2051, 1952.

———— *et al.*: Description of types of principal American varieties of cabbage, *U.S. Dept. Agr. Misc. Pub.* 169, 1934.

———— *et al.*: A study of rapid deterioration of vegetable seeds and methods for its prevention, *U.S. Dept. Agr. Tech. Bull.* 707, 1940.

Botting, G. W.: Molybdenum deficiency in brussels sprouts, *Jour. Dept. Agr. South Australia*, 58:246–253, 1955.

Bouquet, A. G. B.: Growing snap beans, *Ore. Ext. Bull.* 705, 1950.

Bouyoucos, George J.: An investigation of soil temperature and some of the most important factors affecting it, *Mich. Tech. Bull.* 26, 1916.

————: A practical soil moisture meter as a scientific guide to irrigation practices, *Agron. Jour.*, 42:104–107, 1950.

———— and M. M. McCool: A study of frost occurrence in muck soils, *Soil Sci.*, 14, No. 5, 1922.

Boyd, J. S., and J. F. Davis: Mechanical handling and bulk storage of onions, *Mich. Quart. Bull.* 35:279–287, 1952.

Boyle, J. G.: Tomato investigations, *Ind. Bull.* 165, 1913.

Bradley, George A., and A. J. Pratt: Irrigate to make a crop—not to save it, *N.Y. State Sta. Farm Res.*, 20, No. 2, 1954.

Brasher, E. P., and K. C. Westover: The effect on yield of hardening tomato plants, *Amer. Soc. Hort. Sci. Proc.*, 35:686–689, 1937.

————, J. R. Wheatley, and W. L. Ogle: Foliar nutrition sprays on vegetable crops, *Del. Bull.* 295, 1953.

Bratley, C. O., and J. S. Wiant: Diseases of fruits and vegetables on the New York market during the months of October, November, and December 1939, *U.S. Dept. Agr. Plant Disease Reporter*, 24:154–157, 1940.

Brittingham, W. H.: A key to the horticultural groups of varieties of the Southern pea, *Vigna sinensis*, *Amer. Soc. Hort. Sci. Proc.*, 48:478–480, 1946.

Brooks, C., and L. McColloch: Stickiness and spotting of shelled green Lima beans, *U.S. Dept. Agr. Tech. Bull.* 625, 1938.

Broyer, T. C., *et al.*: Chlorine—a micronutrient element for higher plants, *Plant Phys.*, 29:526–532, 1954.

Burgess, P. S., and F. R. Pember: Active aluminum as a factor detrimental to crop production, *R.I. Bull.* **194,** 1923.

Bushnell, John: The relation of temperature to growth and respiration in the potato plant, *Minn. Tech. Bull.* **34,** 1925.

————: The normal multiple sprouting of seed potatoes, *Ohio Bull.* **430,** 1929.

————: Experiments with potatoes on muck soil, *Ohio Bull.* **570,** 1936.

————: Fertilizers for early cabbage, tomatoes, cucumbers, and sweet corn, *Ohio Res. Bull.* **697,** 1950.

————: Sensitivity of potatoes to soil porosity, *Ohio Res. Bull.* **726,** 1953.

Campbell, John A.: Irrigation for vegetable crops, *Miss. Circ.* **182,** 1953.

Carew, H. J.: A study of certain factors affecting "buttoning" of cauliflower, Cornell Univ. Thesis, 1947.

Carey, L. C.: Containers in common use for fresh fruits and vegetables, *U.S. Dept. Agr. Farmers' Bull.* **2013,** 1950.

Carlson, R. F., B. H. Grigsby, and R. L. Carolus: Weed control in established asparagus plantings with CMU (3-*p*-chlorophenyl)-1,1-dimethylurea (a preliminary report), *Mich. Quart. Bull.,* **36**:163–168, 1953.

Carolus, R. L.: Yield and quality of asparagus harvested by the field snapping method, *Mich. Quart. Bull.,* **31**:370–377, 1949.

————: Pelleted seed for precision, *Amer. Veg. Grower,* **2,** No. 5:16–17, 1954.

————, W. J. Lipton, and S. B. Apple: Effect of packaging on quality and market acceptability, *Mich. Quart. Bull.,* **35**:330–342, 1953.

———— and O. A. Lorenz: The interrelation of manure, lime and potash on the growth and maturity of the muskmelon, *Amer. Soc. Hort. Sci. Proc.,* **36**:518–522, 1938.

Carrier, Lyman: "Beginnings of Agriculture in America," McGraw-Hill Book Company, Inc., New York, 1924.

Casseres, Ernest H.: Effect of date of sowing, spacing, and foliage trimming of plants in flats on yield of tomatoes, *Amer. Soc. Hort. Sci. Proc.,* **50**: 285–289, 1947.

Castetter, E. F., and A. T. Erwin: A systematic study of squashes and pumpkins, *Iowa Bull.* **244,** 1927.

Chandler, F. B.: Boron deficiency symptoms of some plants of the cabbage family, *Me. Bull.* **402,** 1940.

————: Mineral nutrition of the genus Brassica with particular reference to boron, *Me. Bull.* **404,** 1942.

Chaney, Margaret S.: "Nutrition," 5th ed., Houghton Mifflin Company, Boston, 1954.

Chase, E. M., C. G. Church, and F. E. Denny: Relation between composition of California cantaloupes and their commercial maturity, *U.S. Dept. Agr. Bull.* **1250,** 1924.

Childers, N. F., *et al.*: Vegetable gardening in the Tropics, *Fed. Exp. Sta. in Puerto Rico Circ.* **32,** 1950.

Christierson, S. V.: Views and problems of the vegetable shipper, *Conf. on Transportation of Perishables Proc.,* **1954**:74–77, 1954.

Chroboczek, Emil: A study of some ecological factors influencing seedstalk development in beets (*Beta vulgaris* L), *Cornell Memoir* **154,** 1934.

Chucka, J. A., A. Hawkins, and B. E. Brown: Potato fertilizer rotation studies on Aroostook Farm, 1927–1941, *Me. Bull.* **414,** 1943.

Chupp, C., and R. W. Leiby: The control of diseases and insects affecting vegetable crops, *Cornell Ext. Bull.* **206,** 1953.

Clarke, A. E.; L. H. Pollard, and L. R. Hawthorn: Effect of time of seeding on the winter survival and subsequent seed stalk development of onions, *Amer. Soc. Hort. Sci. Proc.*, **59**:439–444, 1952.

Clore, W. J., and F. G. Viets, Jr.: Sweet corn fertility studies on newly irrigated lands in the Yakima Valley, *Amer. Soc. Hort. Sci. Proc.*, **54**:378–384, 1949.

Cochran, H. L.: Some factors influencing growth and fruit-setting in the pepper (*Capsicum frutescens* L.), *Cornell Memoir* **190**, 1936.

Cook, H. T.: The fungi that cause rot in sweet potatoes, *U.S. Dept. Agr. Yearbook* **1953**:444–447, 1953.

Cooley, J. S.: The sweet potato: its origin and primitive storage practices, *Econ. Bot.*, **5**:378–386, 1951.

———, L. J. Cushman, and H. F. Smart: Effect of temperature and duration of storage on quality of stored sweet potatoes, *Econ. Bot.*, **8**:21–28, 1954.

Corbett, L. W., and H. C. Thompson: Physical and chemical changes in celery during storage, *Amer. Soc. Hort. Sci. Proc.*, **1925**:346–353, 1925.

Corns, J. B.: A study of the influence of certain factors on the internal structure of the tomato fruit as related to puffing, Cornell Univ. Thesis, 1937.

Cowart, F. F., and A. H. Dempsey: Pimiento production in Georgia, *Ga. Bull.* **259**, 1949.

Craft, C. C., and P. H. Heinze: Physiological studies of mature-green tomatoes in storage, *Amer. Soc. Hort. Sci. Proc.*, **64**:343–350, 1954.

Crandall, F. K.: The response of celery to manures and fertilizers, *R.I. Bull.* **260**, 1937.

Cranefield, F.: The effect of transplanting on time of maturity, *Wis. Ann. Rept.*, 1899.

Culpepper, C. W., and C. A. Magoon: The relation of storage to the quality of sweet potatoes for canning purposes, *Jour. Agr. Res.*, 33, No. 7, 1926.

——— and H. H. Moon: Effect of temperature upon the rate of elongation of the stems of asparagus grown under field conditions, *Plant Phys.*, **14**:255–270, 1939.

Currence, T. M.: Methods of supplying electric heat to hotbeds, *Minn. Bull.* **289**, 1932.

Davis, Glen N.: Onion production in California, *Calif. Circ.* **357**, 1943.

——— and H. A. Jones: Experiments with the transplant onion crop in California, *Calif. Bull.* **682**, 1944.

———, T. W. Whitaker, and G. W. Bohn: Production of muskmelons in California, *Calif. Circ.* **429**, 1953.

Davis, J. F.: Effect of rate of application of fertilizer and spacing of plants on the performance of Cornell 19 and Utah 15 celery varieties, *Mich. Quart. Bull.*, **33**:106–110, 1950.

———, G. A. Cumings, and C. M. Hansen: The effect of fertilizer placement on the yield of onions grown on an organic soil, *Mich. Quart. Bull.*, **33**:249–256, 1950.

——— and W. W. McCall: Occurrence of magnesium deficiency in celery on the organic soils of Michigan, *Mich. Quart. Bull.*, **35**:324–329, 1953.

Dearborn, C. H.: Boron nutrition of cauliflower in relation to browning, *Cornell Bull.* **778**, 1942.

Dearborn, C. H., R. D. Sweet, and J. R. Havis: Weeding sweet corn with 2,4-D: effects of timing, rates, and varieties, *Amer. Soc. Hort. Sci. Proc.*, **51**:536–540, 1948.

Dearborn, R. B.: Nitrogen nutrition and chemical composition in relation to growth and fruiting of the cucumber plant, *Cornell Memoir* **192**, 1936.

Decker, P.: Phomopsis-blight-resistant eggplants, *Phytopath.*, **41**:9, 1951.

Denny, F. E.: Second report on the use of chemicals for hastening the sprouting of dormant potato tubers, *Amer. Jour. Bot.*, **13**:386–396, 1926.

———: Role of mother tuber in growth of potato plant, *Bot. Gaz.* **88**, No. 1, 1929.

———, J. D. Guthrie, and N. C. Thornton: The effect of the vapor of the methyl ester of naphthaleneacetic acid on the sprouting and sugar content of tubers, *Boyce Thompson Inst. Contrib.*, **12**:253–268, 1941.

Dennyl, Daniel: Windbreaks for protecting muck soils and crops, *Purdue Circ.* **287**, 1943.

Deonier, M. T., *et al.*: Pruning and training tomatoes in the South, *U.S. Dept. Agr. Circ.* **712**, 1944.

———: Cooperative studies of the delayed harvesting of sweet potatoes, *U.S. Dept. Agr. Circ.* **841**, 1950.

Dolan, D. D., and E. P. Christopher: Plant spacing of sweet corn, *R.I. Bull.* **316**, 1952.

Doolittle, S. P.: Tomato diseases, *U.S. Dept. Agr. Farmers' Bull.* **1934**, 1948.

———: Diseases of peppers, *U. S. Dept. Agr. Yearbook* **1953**:466–469, 1953.

———: Ways to combat disorders of tomatoes, *U.S. Dept. Agr. Yearbook* **1953**:454–462, 1953.

Drewes, Harm: Spinach varieties, *Mich. Spec. Bull.* **225**, 1932.

Duvel, J. W. T.: The vitality and germination of seeds, *U.S. Dept. Agr. B.P.I. Bull.* **58**, 1904.

Edmond, J. B., *et al.*: Cooperative studies of the effects of height of ridge, nitrogen supply, and time of harvest on yield and flesh color of the Porto Rico sweet potato, *U.S. Dept. Agr. Circ.* **832**, 1950.

Edson, S. N., and F. B. Smith: Soils and fertilizers for Florida vegetable and field crops, *Fla. Bull.* **514**, 1953.

Ellis, G. H., and K. C. Hamner: The carotene content of tomatoes as influenced by various factors, *Jour. Nutr.*, **25**:539–553, 1943.

Ellis, N. K., and Richard Morris: Preliminary observations on the relation of yield of crops grown on organic soil with controlled water table and the area of aeration in the soil and subsidence of the soil, *Proc. Soil Sci. Soc. of Amer.*, **10**:282–283, 1945.

Ellison, J. H., and W. C. Jacob: Further studies concerning the influence of irrigation on the nitrogen, phosphorus, and potash requirements of six potato varieties, *Amer. Potato Jour.*, **31**:141–151, 1954.

Emsweller, S. L.: An hereditary type of pithiness in celery, *Amer. Soc. Hort. Sci. Proc.*, **29**:480–485, 1932.

Erwin, A. T.: The nativity of the pumpkin, *Science*, **71**:483–484, 1930.

———: The peppers, *Iowa Bull.* **293**, 1932.

Evans, H. J., and R. V. Troxler: Relation of calcium nutrition to the incidence of blossom-end rot in tomatoes, *Amer. Soc. Hort. Sci. Proc.*, **61**:346–352, 1953.

Ezell, B. D., M. S. Wilcox, and J. N. Crowder: Pre- and post-harvest changes in carotene, total carotenoids and ascorbic acid content of sweet potatoes, *Plant Phys.*, **27**:355–369, 1952.

Flint, L. H.: Crop plant stimulation with paper mulch, *U.S. Dept. Agr. Tech. Bull.* **75**, 1928.

Forsee, W. T., Jr., and J. C. Hoffman: The phosphate and potash requirements of snap beans on the organic soils of the Florida Everglades, *Amer. Soc. Hort. Sci. Proc.*, **56**:261–265, 1950.

Foskett, R. L., and C. E. Peterson: Relation of dry matter content to storage quality in some onion varieties and hybrids, *Amer. Soc. Hort. Sci. Proc.*, **55**:314–318, 1950.

Frazier, W. A.: A study of some factors associated with occurrence of cracks in tomato fruit, *Amer. Soc. Hort. Sci. Proc.*, **32**:519–523, 1934.

————: Further studies on the occurrence of cracks in tomato fruits, *Amer. Soc. Hort. Sci. Proc.*, **33**:536–541, 1935.

————, and J. L. Bower: A final report on studies of tomato fruit cracking in Maryland, *Amer. Soc. Hort. Sci. Proc.*, **49**:241–255, 1947.

Freeman, G. F.: Southwestern beans and teparies, *Ariz. Bull.* **68**, 1912.

Friedman, B. A., M. Lieberman, and J. Kauffman: A comparison of crown-cut and clip-topped spinach prepackaged at terminal market, *Amer. Soc. Hort. Sci. Proc.*, **57**:285–287, 1951.

Fryer, H. C., *et al.*: Relation between stage of maturity and ascorbic acid content of tomatoes, *Amer. Soc. Hort. Sci. Proc.*, **64**:365–371, 1954.

Fulton, J. P.: Studies of strains of cucumber virus I from spinach, *Phytopath.*, **40**:729–736, 1950.

Gaines, J. G., and T. W. Graham: Soil fumigation to control root ills, *U.S. Dept. Agr. Yearbook* **1953**:561–567, 1953.

Garner, W. W., and H. A. Allard: Effect of the relative length of day on growth and reproduction in plants, *Jour. Agr. Res.*, **18**:533–606, 1920.

Garver, H. L., and C. L. Vincent: Manure and electric hotbeds, *Wash. Gen. Bull.* **219**, 1927.

Geise, F. W., and H. B. Farley: Variety studies of spinach, *Md. Bull.* **312**, 1929.

Ga. Agr. Exp. Sta.: The effect of variety, curing, storage, and time of planting and harvesting on the carotene, ascorbic acid and moisture content of sweet potatoes grown in six Southern States, *South. Coop. Ser. Bull.* **30**, 1953.

Geraldson, C. M.: The control of blackheart of celery, *Amer. Soc. Hort. Sci. Proc.*, **63**:353–358, 1954.

Gilbert, J. C., and D. C. McGuire: Root knot resistance in commercial type tomatoes in Hawaii, *Amer. Soc. Hort. Sci. Proc.*, **60**:401–411, 1952.

Goff, E. S.: Report of the horticulturist, *N.Y. State Sta. Ann. Rept.*, 1887.

Graham, T. O., and J. S. Shoemaker: Vegetable varieties and hybrids, *Ontario Dept. Agr. Bull.* **451**, 1952.

Greenwell, A. B. H.: Taro: with special reference to its culture and uses in Hawaii, *Econ. Bot.*, **1**:276–289, 1947.

Griffiths, A. E.: The viability of lettuce seed: a physiological and microchemical study, *Cornell Memoir* **245**, 1942.

Groth, B. H. A.: The sweet potato, *Penn. Univ. Bot. Lab. Contrib.*, **4**, No. 1, 1901.

Guyer, R. B., and A. Kramer: Objective measurements of quality of raw and processed snap beans as affected by maleic hydrazide and para-chlorophenoxyacetic acid, *Amer. Soc. Hort. Sci. Proc.*, **58**:263–273, 1951.

————, ————, and L. E. Ide: Factors affecting yield and quality measurements of raw and canned green and wax beans: a preliminary report, *Amer. Soc. Hort. Sci. Proc.*, **56**:303–314, 1950.

Haber, E. S.: The effect of various containers on the growth of vegetable plants, *Iowa Bull.* **279**, 1931.

——: Effect of harvesting, spacing and age of plants on yields of asparagus, *Iowa Bull.* **339**, 1935.

Haliburton, T. H.: The effect of soil acidity and related factors on the growth of onions on Long Island, Cornell Univ. Thesis, 1955.

Haller, M. H.: Effect of root-trimming, washing, and waxing on the storage of turnips, *Amer. Soc. Hort. Sci. Proc.*, **50**:325–329, 1947.

Hamner, K. C., Leon Bernstein, and L. A. Maynard: Effects of light intensity, day length, temperature, and other environmental factors on the ascorbic acid content of tomato fruits, *Jour. Nutr.*, **29**:85–97, 1945.

——, and R. Q. Parks: Effect of light intensity on ascorbic acid content of turnip greens, *Agron. Jour.*, **36**:269–273, 1944.

Hanna, G. C.: Asparagus production in California, *Calif. Ext. Circ.* **91**, 1947.

——: Asparagus production in California, *Calif. Ext. Circ.* **91**, 1950.

Hanson, A. A., J. G. Coulson, and L. C. Raymond: Further studies on brown heart in swedes, *Sci. Agr.*, **28**:229–243, 1948.

Hardenburg, R. E.: Further studies on moisture losses of vegetables packaged in transparent films and their effect on shelf life, *Amer. Soc. Hort. Sci. Proc.*, **57**:277–284, 1951.

——, M. Lieberman, and H. A. Schomer: Prepackaging carrots in different types of consumer bags, *Amer. Soc. Hort. Sci. Proc.*, **61**:404–412, 1953.

Harmer, Paul M.: The muck soils of Michigan and their management, *Mich. Spec. Bull.* **314**, 1941.

——: Wartime production of vegetable crops on muck land, *Mich. Ext. Bull.* **244**, 1943.

——, and Erwin J. Benne: Effects of applying common salt to a muck soil on the yield, composition, and quality of certain vegetable crops and on the composition of the soil producing them, *Agron. Jour.*, **33**:952–979, 1941.

Harter, L. L.: Thresher injury, a cause of baldhead in beans, *Jour., Agr. Res.*, **40**:371–384, 1930.

Hartman, J. D.: The relation of market quality to the price received for Long Island cauliflower, *Cornell Bull.* **716**, 1939.

Harvey, R. B.: Hardening process in plants and developments from frost injury, *Jour. Agr. Res.*, **15**:83–111, 1918.

Haskell, G.: Studies with sweet corn. I. Cold treatment and germination, *Plant and Soil*, **2**:49–58, 1949.

Hassan, H. H., and J. P. McCollum: Factors affecting the content of ascorbic acid in tomatoes, *Ill. Bull.* **573**, 1954.

Hasselbring, H.: Carbohydrate transformation in carrots during storage, *Plant Phys.*, **2**:225–243, 1927.

——, and L. A. Hawkins: Physiological changes in sweet potatoes during storage, *Jour. Agr. Res.*, **3**:331–342, 1915.

Hauck, J. F.: Roadside marketing in the Garden State, *N.J. Circ.* **560**, 1954.

Hawthorn, L. R.: Spinach under irrigation in Texas, *Tex. Circ.* **66**, 1932.

——: Cultural experiments with Yellow Bermuda onions under irrigation, *Tex. Bull.* **561**, 1938.

Heath, O. V. S.: Studies of the physiology of the onion plant. I. An investigation of factors concerned in the flowering ("bolting") of onions grown from sets and its prevention. II. Effects of length of day and temperature on onions grown from sets, *Ann. Appl. Biol.* **30**:308–319, 1943.

————: Formative effects of environmental factors as exemplified in the development of the onion plant, *Nature,* 155:623, 1945.

Hedrick, U. P., F. H. Hall, L. R. Hawthorn, and Alwin Berger: "Peas of New York," Vol. 1, Part 1, of "Vegetables of New York," *N.Y. State Sta. Rept.,* 1928.

Heinze, P. H., and C. C. Craft: Effectiveness of ethylene for ripening tomatoes, *Amer. Soc. Hort. Sci. Proc.,* 62:397–404, 1953.

Heiser, C. B., Jr., and Paul G. Smith: The cultivated Capsicum peppers, *Econ. Bot.,* 7:214–227, 1953.

Hemphill, D. D.: The effect of plant growth-regulating substances on flower-bud development and fruit set, *Mo. Bull.* 434, 1949.

Hernandez, T. P., J. C. Miller, and J. F. Fountenot: Studies in plant production of sweet potatoes including effects of chemicals, *Amer. Soc. Hort. Sci. Proc.* 55:423–426, 1950.

Hester, J. B.: Use of fertilizer solutions in leaf feeding, *Proc. Nat. Joint Comm. on Fert. Appl.,* 1951:47–48.

————, M. M. Parker, and H. H. Zimmerley: Liming Coastal Plain soils, *Va. Truck Exp. Sta. Bull.* 91, 1936.

Hibbard, R. P.: Frost protectors for early planting, *Mich. Quart. Bull.,* 7:151–153, 1925; 8:137–141, 1926.

Hills, W. A., *et al.:* Bush snap bean production on the sandy soils of Florida, *Fla. Bull.* 530, 1953.

Hodge, W. H.: The dasheen: a tropical crop for the South, *U.S. Dept. Agr. Circ.* 950, 1954.

Holland, A. H., *et al.:* Production of green Lima beans for freezing, *Calif. Ext. Circ.* 430, 1953.

Hoover, L. G.: The Chayote: its culture and uses, *U.S. Dept. Agr. Circ.* 286, 1923.

Hoover, M. W., and R. A. Dennison: The correlation of stages of maturity with certain physical measurements in the Southern pea, *Vigna sinensis, Amer. Soc. Hort. Sci. Proc.,* 62:391–396, 1953.

————, and ————: A study of certain biochemical changes occurring in the Southern pea, *Vigna sinensis,* at six stages of maturity, *Amer. Soc. Hort. Sci. Proc.,* 63:402–408, 1954.

Hornby, C. A.: Growth and fruiting responses of tomato plants to time of sowing seed, spacing of seedlings and applications of fertilizer to the flat, Cornell Univ. Thesis, 1949.

Howe, W. L., W. T. Schroeder, and K. G. Swenson: Seed treatment for control of seed-corn maggot and seed decay organisms, *N.Y. Bull.* 752, 1952.

Hruschka, H. W., and J. Kaufman: Storage tests with Long Island cauliflower to inhibit leaf abscission by using plant growth regulators, *Amer. Soc. Hort. Sci. Proc.,* 54:438–446, 1949.

Hughes, M. B., and Robert Aycock: Sweet potato clones resistant to internal cork, *Amer. Soc. Hort. Sci. Proc.,* 59:433–438, 1952.

Irish, H. C.: Revision of the genus Capsicum, *Mo. Bot. Gard. 9th Ann. Rept.,* 1898.

Isenberg, F. M.: The use of maleic hydrazide on onions, *Amer. Soc. Hort. Sci. Proc.,* 66:331–333, 1956.

Jacob, W. C., and R. H. White-Stevens: Fertilizer placement with respect to location and time in the production of cauliflower on Long Island, *Amer. Soc. Hort. Sci. Proc.* abstract, 38:162, 1941.

Jagger, I. C.: A transmissible mosaic disease of lettuce, *Jour. Agr. Res.,* **20**:737–739, 1921.

Jamison, F. S.: Studies of the effects of handling methods on the quality of market peas, *Cornell Bull.* **599,** 1934.

Janes, B. E.: Vegetable rotation studies in Connecticut, II, *Amer. Soc. Hort. Sci. Proc.,* **57**:252–258, 1951.

Jenkins, J. M., Jr.: Some effects of different day lengths and temperatures upon bulb formation in shallots, *Amer. Soc. Hort. Sci. Proc.,* **64**:311–314, 1954.

Johannessen, G. A.: Tomato fruit cracking studies, Cornell Univ. Thesis, 1950.

Jones, H. A., and S. L. Emsweller: Effect of storage, bulb size, spacing, and time of planting on production of onion seed, *Calif. Bull.* **628,** 1939.

——, F. H. Ernst, and J. R. Tavernetti: The cauliflower industry of California, *Calif. Circ.* **93,** 1935.

——, and G. C. Hanna: Crown-grading experiments with asparagus, *Calif. Bull.* **633,** 1940.

——, and W. W. Robbins: The asparagus industry in California, *Calif. Bull.* **446,** 1928.

——, and J. T. Rosa: "Truck Crop Plants," McGraw-Hill Book Company, Inc., New York, 1928.

Jones, L. G., and G. F. Warren: The efficiency of various methods of application of phosphorus for tomatoes, *Amer. Soc. Hort. Sci. Proc.,* **63**:309–319, 1954.

Jones, Limus H.: Effect of the structure and moisture of plant containers on the temperature of their soil contents, *Jour. Agr. Res.,* **42**:375–378, 1931.

Jongedyk, H. A., *et al.*: Subsidence of muck soils in Northern Indiana, *Purdue Circ.* **366,** 1950.

Kable, G. W.: Electric hotbeds, cold-frames, propagating benches and open soil heating, *National Rural Electric Project, College Park, Md., Rept.* **6,** 1932.

Kehr, A. E., Yu Chen Ting, and J. C. Miller: Induction of blooming in the Jersey type sweet potato, *Amer. Soc. Hort. Sci. Proc.,* **62**:437–440, 1953.

——, ——, and ——: The site of carotenoid and anthocyanin synthesis in sweet potatoes, *Amer. Soc. Hort. Sci. Proc.,* **65**:396–398, 1955.

Kennedy, E. J., and O. Smith: Response of the potato to field application of maleic hydrazide, *Amer. Pot. Jour.,* **28**:701–712, 1951.

Kimbrough, W. D.: Physiological shrinkage of sweet potatoes in curing, *Amer. Soc. Hort. Sci. Proc.,* **25**:59–60, 1928.

——, and M. F. Bell: Internal breakdown of sweet potatoes due to exposure to cold, *La. Bull.* **358,** 1942.

King, J. R., and R. Bamford: The chromosome number in Ipomoea and related genera, *Jour. Hered.,* **28**:279–282, 1937.

Kinney, L. F.: Spinach culture in Rhode Island, *R.I. Bull.* **41,** 1896.

Knott, J. E.: The effect of certain mineral elements on the color and thickness of onion scales, *Cornell Bull.* **552,** 1933.

——: The effect of temperature on the photoperiodic response of spinach, *Cornell Memoir* **218,** 1939.

——, and G. C. Hanna: The effect of widely divergent dates of planting on the heading behavior of seven cabbage varieties, *Amer. Soc. Hort. Sci. Proc.,* **49**:299–303, 1947.

——, and C. D. Jeffries: Containers for plant growing, *Penn. Bull.* **244,** 1929.

Kotowski, Felix: Temperature relations to germination of vegetable seed, *Amer. Soc. Hort. Sci. Proc.*, **23**:1–9, 1926.

Kramer, A.: Relation of maturity to yield and quality of raw and canned peas, corn, and Lima beans, *Amer. Soc. Hort. Sci. Proc.*, **47**:361–367, 1946.

Kraus, E. J., and H. R. Kraybill: Vegetation and reproduction with special reference to the tomato, *Ore. Bull.* **149**, 1918.

Kraus, James E.: Effects of partial defoliation at transplanting time on subsequent growth and yield of lettuce, cauliflower, celery, peppers, and onions, *U.S. Dept. Agr. Tech. Bull.* **829**, 1942.

Kuhn, R. P., *et al.*: An investigation of asparagus rust in Illinois: its causal agent and its control, *Ill. Bull.* **559**, 1952.

Kunkel, R., *et al.*: The mechanical separation of potatoes into specific gravity groups, *Colo. Ext. Bull.* **422-A**, 1952.

Lachance, R. O., P. Bertrand, and C. Perrault: Manifestation extrême de la gerçure des pétioles du céleri: maladie par carence de bore, *Sci. Agr.*, **23**:3, 1942.

Lachman, W. H.: The use of oil sprays as selective herbicides for carrots and parsnips, II, *Amer. Soc. Hort. Sci. Proc.*, **47**:423–433, 1946; **49**:343–346, 1947.

Lana, E. P., and E. S. Haber: Seasonal variability as indicated by cumulative degree-hours with sweet corn, *Amer. Soc. Hort. Sci. Proc.*, **59**:389–392, 1952.

Learner, E. N., and S. H. Wittwer: Some effects of photoperiodicity and thermoperiodicity on vegetative growth, flowering, and fruiting of the tomato, *Amer. Soc. Hort. Sci. Proc.*, **61**:373–380, 1953.

Lee, F. A.: Objective methods for determining the maturity of peas, with special reference to the frozen product, *N.Y. Tech. Bull.* **256**, 1941.

Lee, Shu-Hsien, and R. L. Carolus: Foliar abscission of stored cauliflower and cabbage, with special reference to the effects of certain growth-regulating substances, *Mich. Tech. Bull.* **216**, 1949.

Leukel, R. W.: Treating seeds to prevent disease, *U.S. Dept. Agr. Yearbook* **1953**:134–145, 1953.

Levitt, J.: The relation of cabbage hardiness to bound water, unfrozen water, and cell contraction when frozen, *Plant Phys.*, **14**:93–112, 1939.

———, and G. W. Scarth: Frost-hardening studies with living cells. I. Osmotic and bound water changes in relation to frost injury. II. Permeability in relation to frost resistance and the seasonal cycle, *Canadian Jour. Res. C.*, **14**:267–284; 283–305, 1936.

Lieberman, Morris, and R. E. Hardenburg: Effect of modified atmospheres on respiration and yellowing of broccoli at 75°F., *Amer. Soc. Hort. Sci. Proc.*, **63**:409–414, 1954.

———, and R. A. Spurr: Oxygen tension in relation to volatile production in broccoli, *Amer. Soc. Hort. Sci. Proc.*, **65**:381–386, 1955.

Ligon, L. L.: Mung beans, *Okla. Bull.* **284**, 1945.

Livingstone, David: "Travels and Research in South Africa," 54, 1858.

Loomis, W. E.: Studies in the transplanting of vegetable plants, *Cornell Memoir* **87**, 1925.

———: Temperature and other factors affecting the rest period of potato tubers, *Plant Phys.*, **2**:287–302, 1927.

Lorenz, O. A.: Internal breakdown of table beets, *Cornell Memoir* **246**, 1942.

———: The effect of certain planting and harvest dates on the quality of table beets, *Amer. Soc. Hort. Sci. Proc.*, **49**:270–274, 1947.

————, J. C. Bishop, and D. N. Wright: Liquid, dry, and gaseous fertilizers for onions on sandy-loam soils, *Amer. Soc. Hort. Sci. Proc.*, **65**:296–306, 1955.

————, and B. J. Hoyle: Effect of curing and time of topping on weight loss and chemical composition of onion bulbs, *Amer. Soc. Hort. Sci. Proc.* **47**:301–308, 1946.

————, *et al.*: Potato fertilizer experiments in California, *Calif. Bull.* **744**, 1954.

Luke, G. W.: Marketing New Jersey sweet corn, *N.J. Bull.* **768**, 1953.

Lutz, J. M.: Maturity and handling of green-wrap tomatoes in Mississippi, *U.S. Dept. Agr. Circ.* **695**, 1944.

————: Curing and storage methods in relation to quality of Porto Rico sweet potatoes, *U.S. Dept. Agr. Circ.* **699**, 1944.

————: Chilling injury of cured and noncured Porto Rico sweet potatoes, *U.S. Dept. Agr. Circ.* **729**, 1945.

————, J. K. Park, and M. T. Deonier: Influence of methods of harvesting sweet potatoes on their storage behavior, *Amer. Soc. Hort. Sci. Proc.*, **57**:297–301, 1951.

————, and J. W. Simons: Storage of sweet potatoes, *U.S. Dept Agr. Farmers' Bull.* **1442**, 1948.

MacGillivray, J. H.: Effect of irrigation on the growth and yield of sweet corn, *Amer. Soc. Hort. Sci. Proc.*, **54**:330–338, 1949.

————: Effect of irrigation on the production of cantaloupes, *Amer. Soc. Hort. Sci. Proc.*, **57**:266–272, 1951.

————, A. E. Michelbacher, and C. E. Scott: Tomato production in California, *Calif. Circ.* **167**, 1950.

————, P. A. Minges, and L. J. Clemente: Studies on sweet corn suckering and spacing, *Amer. Soc. Hort. Sci. Proc.*, **65**:331–334, 1955.

Mackie, W. W.: Origin, dispersal, and variability of the Lima bean, *Phaseolus lunatus, Hilgardia*, **15**, No. 1, 1943.

MacLeod, D. J., and J. L. Howatt: The control of brown-heart in turnips, *Sci. Agr.*, **15**:435, 1935.

Madariaga, F. J., and J. E. Knott: Temperature summations in relation to lettuce growth, *Amer. Soc. Hort. Sci. Proc.*, **58**:147–152, 1951.

Magoon, C. A., and C. W. Culpepper: The relation of seasonal factors to quality in sweet corn, *Jour. Agr. Res.*, **33**:1043–1072, 1926.

————, and ————: Response of sweet corn to varying temperatures from the time of planting to canning maturity, *U.S. Dept. Agr. Tech. Bull.* **313**, 1932.

Magruder, Roy, and H. A. Allard: Bulb formation in some American and European varieties of onions as affected by length of day, *Jour. Agr. Res.*, **54**:719–752, 1937.

————, *et al.*: Descriptions of types of principal American varieties of spinach, *U.S. Dept. Agr. Misc. Pub.* **316**, 1938.

————: Storage quality of the principal American varieties of onions, *U.S. Dept. Agr. Circ.* **618**, 1941.

Mangelsdorf, P. C. and R. G. Reeves: The origin of Indian corn and its relatives, *Tex. Bull.* **574**, 1939.

————, and C. E. Smith, Jr.: A discovery of remains of primitive maize in New Mexico, *Jour. Hered.* **40**, No. 2, 1949.

Mann, L. K.: Anatomy of the garlic bulb and factors affecting bulb development, *Hilgardia*, **21**:195–231, 1952.

————, and J. H. MacGillivray: Some factors affecting the size of carrot roots, *Amer. Soc. Hort. Sci. Proc.*, **54**:311–318, 1949.

Marth, P. C.: Effect of growth regulators on the retention of color in green sprouting broccoli, *Amer. Soc. Hort. Sci. Proc.*, **60**:367–369, 1952.

————, and E. S. Shultz: A new sprout inhibitor for potato tubers, *Amer. Pot. Jour.*, **29**:268–272, 1952.

————, and R. E. Wester: Effect of 2,4,5-trichlorophenoxyacetic acid on flowering and vegetative growth of Fordhook 242 bush Lima beans, *Amer. Soc. Hort. Sci. Proc.*, **63**:325–328, 1954.

Marvel, M. E.: Cauliflower seed bed fumigation with methyl bromide, *W.Va. Current Rept.* **2**, 1952.

McClelland, T. B.: Studies of photoperiodism of some economic plants, *Jour. Agr. Res.*, **37**:603–628, 1928.

McCollum, J. P.: Vegetative and reproductive response associated with fruit development in the cucumber, *Cornell Memoir* **163**, 1934.

McCool, M. M., and P. M. Harmer: The muck soils of Michigan: their management for the production of general crops, *Mich. Spec. Bull.* **136**, 1925.

McCubbin, E. N.: Influence of sprouts on plant emergence, growth, tuber development and yield of potatoes, *Amer. Pot. Jour.*, **18**:163–174, 1941.

————, A. H. Eddins, and E. G. Kelsheimer: Growing cabbage plants in seed beds, *Fla. Bull.* **656**, 1948.

McCue, G. A.: The history of the use of the tomato: an annotated bibliography, *Ann. Rept. Mo. Bot. Gard.*, **39**:299–348, 1952.

McGoldrick, F., and O. Smith: Killing potato vines, *Amer. Soc. Hort. Sci. Proc.*, **51**:401–405, 1948.

McGuire, D. C.: Hybrid tomatoes pay, *Hawaii Farm Sci.*, **3**:4–5, 1954.

McLean, F. F., and B. E. Gilbert: Manganese as a cure for chlorosis in spinach, *Science*, **61**:630–637, 1925.

McMahon, B.: *Amer. Gard. Calendar* **200**, 1806.

Meadows, M. W.: A study of the factors affecting vascular discoloration in potatoes, Cornell Univ. Thesis, 1950.

Melhus, I. E., and F. O. Smith: The Mayan husk tomato, a tropical fruit comes to Iowa, *Iowa Farm Sci.*, **7**:211–212, 1953.

Merkle, F. G., and C. J. Irwin: Some effects of intertillage on crops and soils, *Penn. Bull.* **272**, 1931.

Metcalf, H. N.: Effect of leaf and terminal bulb removal on yield of Brussels sprouts, *Amer. Soc. Hort. Sci. Proc.*, **64**:322–326, 1954.

Michael, Ralph, and Paul G. Smith: Stimulation of sweet potato sprout production, *Amer. Soc. Hort. Sci. Proc.*, **59**:414–420, 1952.

Middleton, J. T., and G. W. Bohn: Cucumbers, melons, squash, *U.S. Dept. Agr. Yearbook* **1953**:483–493, 1953.

Miller, J. C.: A study of some factors affecting seed-stalk development in cabbage, *Cornell Bull.* **488**, 1929.

————: Collards, a truck crop for Louisiana, *La. Bull.* **258**, 1934.

———— and W. D. Kimbrough: Sweet potato production in Louisiana, *La. Bull.* **281**, 1936.

————, *et al.*: Louisiana Allseason tomato, *La. Ann. Rept.*, **1947–1948**:89, 1949.

Miller, P. R.: The effect of weather on diseases, *U.S. Dept. Agr. Yearbook* **1953**:83–93, 1953.

Minges, P. A., and L. L. Morris: Sweet potato production and handling in California, *Calif. Circ.* **431**, 1953.

Mitchell, J. W., and P. C. Marth: Effect of growth regulating substances on the water-retaining capacities of bean plants, *Bot. Gaz.* 112:70–76, 1950.

Molenaar, A., and C. L. Vincent: Studies in sprinkler irrigation with Stokesdale tomatoes, *Amer. Soc. Hort. Sci. Proc.*, 57:259–265, 1951.

Monson, O. W.: Irrigation of seed and canning peas in the Gallatin Valley, Montana, *Mont. Bul.* 405, 1942.

Moore, E. L.: Some results with crosses of a tomato from Costa Rica with North American varieties, *Assoc. South. Agr. Workers*, 51:118–119, 1954.

—— and W. O. Thomas: Some effects of shading and para-chlorophenoxyacetic acid on fruitfulness of tomatoes, *Amer. Soc. Hort. Sci. Proc.*, 60:289–294, 1952.

Moore, G. C.: Soil and plant response to certain methods of potato culture, *Cornell Bull.* 662, 1937.

Moore, J. F., and D. R. Allmendinger: Blue Lake pole beans in Western Washington, *Wash. Bull.* 548, 1954.

Montelaro, J., and E. C. Tims: Louisiana shallots, *La. Agr. Ext. Pub.* 1051, 1950.

Morse, F. W.: A chemical study of the asparagus plant, *Mass. Bull.* 171, 1916.

Morse, W. J.: Cowpeas: culture and varieties, *U.S. Dept. Agr. Farmers' Bull.* 1148, 1920.

Moses, B. D., and J. R. Tavernetti: Electric heat for propagating and growing plants, *Calif. Circ.* 335, 1934.

Mosier, J. G., and A. F. Gustafson: Soil moisture and tillage for corn, *Ill. Bull.* 181, 1915.

Muhr, G. R., and C. O. Rost: The effect of population and fertility on yields of sweet corn and field corn, *Agron. Jour.* 43:315–319, 1951.

Muller, C. H.: A revision of the genus Lycopersicon, *U.S. Dept. Agr. Misc. Pub.* 382, 1940.

Munn, M. T.: A method for testing the germinability of large seeds, *N.Y. Bull.* 740, 1950.

Munsell, H. E.: Composition of food plants of Central America. IV. El Salvador. *Food Res.* 15:263, 1950.

Murneek, A. E.: Effects of correlation between vegetative and reproductive functions in the tomato, *Plant Phys.*, 1:3–56, 1926.

Myers, C. E.: Report of horticultural department, *Penn. Sta. Ann. Rept.*, 1915.

——, and J. S. Gardner: A variety test of cabbage, *Penn. Bull.* 154, 1919.

Neenan, N., and O. G. Goodman: Varietal susceptibility of brassicas to molybdenum deficiency, *Nature*, 174:953–954, 1954.

Nelson, Ray, G. H. Coons, and L. C. Cochran: The fusarium disease of celery (*Apium graveolens* L. var. *dulce* D.C.), *Mich. Tech. Bull.* 155, 1937.

Nettles, V. F.: Two years' results of the effect of several irrigation treatments on the yield of cabbage and snap beans, *Amer. Soc. Hort. Sci. Proc.*, 51:463–467, 1948.

——: Yield responses of beans to repeated use of soil fumigants and three sources of nitrogen, *Amer. Soc. Hort. Sci. Proc.*, 63:320–324, 1954.

——, F. S. Jamison, B. E. Janes: Irrigation and other cultural studies with cabbage, sweet corn, snap beans, onions, tomatoes, and cucumbers, *Fla. Bull.* 495, 1952.

Newhall, A. G.: Seed transmission of lettuce mosaic, *Phytopath.*, 13:104–106, 1923.

————: Studies on tipburn of head lettuce, Cornell Univ. Thesis, 1929.

————: Blights and other ills of celery, *U.S. Dept. Agr. Yearbook* **1953**:408–417, 1953.

Nightingale, G. T.: The chemical composition of plants in relation to photoperiodic changes, *Wis. Tech. Bull.* **74**, 1927.

————, L. G. Schermerhorn, and W. R. Robbins: The growth status of the tomato as correlated with organic nitrogen and carbohydrates in roots, stems and leaves, *N.J. Bull.* **461**, 1928.

Nissley, C. H.: Vegetable plants from seedbed to field, *N.J. Ext. Leaf.* **118**, 1944.

Nitsch, J. P., *et. al.*: The development of sex expression in cucurbit flowers, *Amer. Jour. Bot.*, **39**:32–43, 1952.

Norton, J. B.: Methods used in breeding asparagus for rust resistance, *U.S. Dept. Agr. B.P.I. Bull.* **263**, 1913.

Nylund, R. E.: The response of onions to soil and foliar applications of manganese and to soil applications of other trace elements, *Amer. Soc. Hort. Sci. Proc.*, **60**:283–285, 1952.

————: The relation of defoliation and nitrogen supply to yield and quality in the muskmelon, *Minn. Tech. Bull.* **210**, 1954.

O'Brien, D. G., and R. W. G. Dennis: Raan or boron deficiency in swedes, *Scottish Jour. Agr.*, **18**:326–333, 1935; **19**:40–46, 1936.

Odland, T. E., R. S. Bell, and J. B. Smith: Influence of crop plants on those which follow, V, *R.I. Bull.* **309**, 1950.

Packard, C. M., and J. H. Martin: Resistant crops the ideal way, *U.S. Dept. Agr. Yearbook* **1952**:429–436, 1952.

Page, N. R., and W. R. Paden: Differential response of snap beans, crimson clover, and turnips to varying rates of calcium and sodium borate on three soil types, *Soil Sci. Soc. Amer. Proc.*, **14**:253–257, 1949.

Parodi, L. R.: *Cucumis melo* var. *flexosus* rara hortaliza cultivada en la Argentina, *Revista Argentina de Agronomia*, **22**:5–10, 1955.

Parsons, C. S., and E. W. Davis: Hormone effect on tomatoes grown in nitrogen-rich soil, *Amer. Soc. Hort. Sci. Proc.*, **62**:371–376, 1953.

Peikert, F. W.: Portable pipe irrigation practices in Michigan, *Mich. Quart. Bull.* **29**:194–204, 1947.

Pentzer, W. T., and P. H. Heinze: Postharvest physiology of fruits and vegetables, *Ann. Review Plant Phys.*, **5**:205–224, 1954.

————, J. S. Wiant, and J. H. MacGillivray: Maturity, quality and condition of California cantaloups as influenced by maturity, handling and precooling, *U.S. Dept. Agr. Tech. Bull,* **730**, 1940.

————, *et al.*: Precooling and shipping California asparagus, *Calif. Bull.* **600**, 1936.

Perkins, D. Y., J. C. Miller, S. L. Dallyn: Influence of pod maturity on the vegetative and reproductive behavior of okra, *Amer. Soc. Hort. Sci. Proc.*, **60**:311–314, 1952.

Peto, F. H.: The cause of bolting in turnips (*Brassica napus* var. *napobrassica* (L.) Peterm.), *Canadian Jour. Res.*, **11**:733–750, 1934.

Pew, W. D.: Effects of the sodium and chlorine ions on the growth and yield of table beets, *Beta vulgaris,* Cornell Univ. Thesis, 1949.

Phillips, T. G.: Changes in the composition of squash during storage, *Plant Phys.*, **21**:533–541, 1946.

Piovano, Abelardo P., and Luis O. Melis: Variedades comerciales de pimientos, Universidad Nacional de Cuyo, Mendoza, Argentina, *Experimenta* **1**:59–87, 1954.

Piper, C. V.: The wild prototype of the cowpea, *U.S. Dept. Agr. B.P.I. Circ.* **124**, 1913.

Plant, W.: The control of "whiptail" in broccoli and cauliflower, *Jour. Hort. Sci.,* **26**:109–117, 1951.

Platenius, Hans: Physiological and chemical changes in carrots during growth and storage, *Cornell Memoir* **161**, 1934.

———, F. S. Jamison, and H. C. Thompson: Studies on cold storage of vegetables, *Cornell Bull.* **602**, 1934.

——— and J. E. Knott: Factors affecting onion pungency, *Jour. Agr. Res.,* **62**:371–379, 1941.

Pollard, L. H., E. B. Wilcox, and H. B. Peterson: Maturity studies with canning peas, *Utah Bull.* **328**, 1947.

Pope, D. T., and H. M. Munger: Heredity and nutrition in relation to magnesium deficiency chlorosis in celery, *Amer. Soc. Hort. Sci. Proc.,* **61**:472–480, 1953.

——— and ———: The inheritance of susceptibility to boron deficiency in celery, *Amer. Soc. Hort. Sci. Proc.,* **61**:481–486, 1953.

Porte, W. S.: Commercial production of tomatoes, *U.S. Dept. Agr. Farmers' Bull.* **2045**, 1952.

Porter, A. M.: Retarding effect of hardening on yield and earliness of tomatoes, *Amer. Soc. Hort. Sci. Proc.,* **33**:542–544, 1935.

Pound, G. S.: Diseases of spinach, *U.S. Dept. Agr. Yearbook* **1953**:476–478, 1953.

Powers, W. L., and A. G. B. Bouquet: Use of boron in controlling canker of table beets, *Ore. Sta. Circ. of Information* **213**, 1940.

Pratt, A. J.: Irrigation: a form of insurance, *N.Y. State Sta. Farm. Res.,* **18**, No. 2, 1952.

——— et al.: Yield, tuber set, and quality of potatoes, *Cornell Bull.* **876**, 1952.

Price, R. H.: Sweet potatoes, *Tex. Bull.* **28**:327–346, 1893.

Purvis, E. R., and W. J. Hanna: Vegetable crops affected by boron deficiency in Eastern Virginia, *Va. Truck Exp. Sta. Bull,* **105**, 1940.

——— and R. W. Ruprecht: Cracked stem of celery caused by a boron deficiency in the soil, *Fla. Bull.* **307**, 1937.

Raleigh, G. J.: The effect of manures, nitrogen compounds and growth promoting substances on the production of branched roots of carrots, *Amer. Soc. Hort. Sci. Proc.,* **41**:347–352, 1942.

———, O. A. Lorenz, and C. B. Sayre: Studies on the control of internal breakdown of table beets by the use of boron, *Cornell Bull.* **752**, 1941.

Reath, A. N., and S. H. Wittwer: The effects of temperature and photoperiod on the development of pea varieties, *Amer. Soc. Hort. Sci. Proc.,* **60**:301–314, 1952.

Reeve, E., A. L. Prince, and F. E. Bear: The boron needs of New Jersey soils, *N.J. Bull.* **709**, 1944.

——— and W. A. Schmidt: Influence of plant spacing on canning tomato yield, *Amer. Soc. Hort. Sci. Proc.,* **59**:384–388, 1952.

Reynard, George B.: Inherited resistance to radial cracks in tomato fruits, *Amer. Soc. Hort. Sci. Proc.,* **58**:231–244, 1951.

Richards, M. C.: Downy mildew of spinach and its control, *Cornell Bull.* **718**, 1939.

Richardson, H. B.: The effect of temperature on the time from planting to maturity of certain vegetables, Cornell Univ. Thesis, 1947.

Rick, C. M.: Rates of natural cross-pollination of tomatoes in various localities in California as measured by the fruits and seed set on male sterile plants, *Amer. Soc. Hort. Sci. Proc.*, **54**:237–252, 1949.

Robb, O. J.: Rhubarb, *Ont. Dept. Agr. Circ.* **120**, 1952.

Robbins, W. R., G. T. Nightingale, and L. G. Schermerhorn: Premature heading of cauliflower as associated with the chemical composition of the plant, *N.J. Bull.* **509**, 1931.

Roberts, R. A.: Sweetpotato weevil, *U.S. Dept. Agr. Yearbook* **1952**:527–530, 1952.

Romshe, F. A.: Studies of plant production methods for vegetable crops—cabbage, tomatoes, onions, melons, cucumbers, *Okla. Bull.* **B-421**, 1954.

Rosa, J. T., Jr.: Investigations on the hardening process in vegetable plants, *Mo. Res. Bull.* **48**, 1921.

――――: Sex expression in spinach, *Hilgardia*, **1**:259–274, 1925.

Rose, D. H., R. C. Wright, and T. M. Whiteman: The commercial storage of fruits, vegetables, and florists' stock, *U.S. Dept. Agr. Circ.* **278**, 1949.

Russell, E. W.: The relation between soil cultivation and crop yields, *Ann. Rept. Rothamsted Exp. Sta.*, **1949–1950**:130–147, 1950.

Sakr, el Sayed, and H. C. Thompson: Effect of temperature and photoperiod on seedstalk development in carrots, *Amer. Soc. Hort. Sci. Proc.*, **41**:343–346, 1942.

Salaman, R. N.; "The History and Social Influence of the Potato," Cambridge University Press, New York, 1949.

Sando, C. E.: The process of ripening in the tomato considered especially from the commercial standpoint, *U.S. Dept. Agr. Bull.* **859**, 1920.

Sandsten, E. P., and T. H. White: An inquiry as to the cause of pithiness in celery, *Md. Bull.* **83**, 1902.

Sawyer, R. L., and S. L. Dallyn: The effect of gamma irradiation on storage life of potatoes, *Amer. Pot. Jour.*, **32**:141–143, 1955.

Sayre, C. B.: Winter forcing of rhubarb, *Ill. Bull.* **298**, 1927.

――――: "Topping" of tomato plants sometimes advantageous, *N.Y. State Sta. Farm Res.*, **11**, No. 2, 1945.

――――: Nitrogen improves quality, increases yields of peas, *N.Y. State Sta. Farm Res.*, **12**, No. 2, 1946.

――――: Limestone increases yields of tomatoes on acid soil, *N.Y. State Sta. Farm. Res.*, **13**, No. 4, 1947.

―――― and G. A. Cummings: Fertilizer placement for cannery peas, *N.Y. Bull.* **659**, 1936.

――――, W. B. Robinson, and T. Wishnetsky: Effect of temperature on the color, lycopene, and carotene content of detached and vine-ripened tomatoes, *Amer. Soc. Hort. Sci. Proc.*, **61**:381–387, 1953.

―――― and John Shafer, Jr.: Effect of side dressings of different sodium and nitrogenous salts on yield of beets, *Amer. Soc. Hort. Sci. Proc.*, **44**:453–456, 1944.

―――― and M. T. Vittum: Effect of different sources of fertilizer nutrients and different rates of fertilizer applications on yields of vegetable canning crops, *N.Y. Bull.* **749**, 1952.

――――, J. J. Williman, and Z. I. Kertesz: Factors affecting the quality of commercial canning peas, *N.Y. Tech. Bull.* **176**, 1931.

Schermerhorn, L. G.: Sweet potato studies in New Jersey, *N.J. Bull.* **398**, 1924.

Scherry, R. W.: Manioc: a tropical staff of life, *Econ. Bot.* **1**:20–25, 1947.

Schudel, H. L.: Vegetable seed production in Oregon, *Ore. Bull.* **512**, 1952.

Schwalen, H. C., K. R. Frost, and W. H. Hinz: Sprinkler irrigation, *Ariz. Bull.* **250**, 1953.

Sciaroni, R. H., *et al.*: Brussels sprouts production in California, *Calif. Ext. Circ.* **247**, 1953.

Scott, L. E., and C. H. Mahoney: Quality changes during storage of consumer packages of sweet corn and Lima beans: progress report, *Amer. Soc. Hort. Sci. Proc.*, **47**:383–386, 1946.

Seaton, H. L.: Scheduling plantings and predicting harvest maturities for processing vegetables, *Food Tech.*, **9**:202–209, 1955.

Shafer, John Jr., and C. B. Sayre: Side dressing beets with salt gives marked returns, *N.Y. State Sta. Farm Res.*, **12**, No. 3, 1946.

Sharman, B. C.: Short nights: an unappreciated hinderance to maize cultivation in England, *Jour. Roy. Hort. Soc.*, **72**:195–202, 1947.

Shear, G. M.: Watercress growing in Virginia, *Va. Bull.* **424**, 1949.

Showalter, R. K., and H. A. Schomer: Temperature studies of commercial broccoli and sweet corn prepackaging at the shipping point, *Amer. Soc. Hort. Sci. Proc.*, **54**:325–329, 1949.

Shuck, A. L.: Some factors influencing the germination of lettuce seed in seed laboratory practice, *N.Y. Tech Bull.* **222**, 1934.

Singletary, C. C., and G. F. Warren: Influence of time and methods of application of hormones on fruit set, *Amer. Soc. Hort. Sci. Proc.*, **57**:225–230, 1951.

Smith, F. G., and J. C. Walker: Relation of environmental and hereditary factors to ascorbic acid in cabbage, *Amer. Jour. Bot.*, **33**:120–129, 1946.

Smith, M. A., and G. B. Ramsey: Brown-spot disease of celery, *Bot. Gaz.*, **112**:393–400, 1951.

Smith, O.: A study of growth and development of the potato plant, *Amer. Soc. Hort. Sci. Proc.*, **28**:279–284, 1931.

———: Studies in potato storage, *Cornell Bull.* **553**, 1933.

———: Effect of soil reaction on growth, yield, and market quality of potatoes, *Cornell Bull.* **664**, 1937.

———: Influence of storage temperature and humidity on seed value of potatoes, *Cornell Bull.* **663**, 1937.

———: Potato research at Cornell, *Amer. Pot. Jour.*, **17**:27–37, 1940.

———, M. A. Baeza, and J. H. Ellison: Response of potato plants to spray applications of certain growth-regulating substances, *Bot. Gaz.*, **108**:421–431, 1947.

——— and W. C. Kelly: Fertilizer studies with potatoes, *Amer. Pot. Jour.*, **23**:107–135, 1946.

Smith, Paul G., and C. B. Heiser, Jr.: Taxonomic and genetic studies on the cultivated peppers. *Capsicum annuum* L., and *C. frutescens* L., *Amer. Jour. Bot.*, **38**:362–368, 1951.

———, C. M. Rick, and C. B. Heiser, Jr.: *Capsicum pendulum* Willd., another cultivated pepper from South America, *Amer. Soc. Hort. Sci. Proc.*, **57**:339–342, 1951.

Somers, Lee A.: Asparagus: its planting, care, management, *Ill. Ext. Circ.* **507**, 1940.

Spencer, A. P., and C. M. Berry: Subirrigation, *Fla. Ext. Bull.* **5**, 1916.

Starring, C. C.: Premature seeding of celery, *Mont. Bull.* **168**, 1924.

Stewart, F. C., and A. J. Mix: Blackheart and the aeration of potatoes in storage, *N.Y. Bull.* **436**, 1917.

Stout, G. J., *et al.*: Methods of heating hotbeds, *Penn. Bull.* **338**, 1936.

Sturtevant, E. L.: Sturtevant's notes on edible plants (ed. by U. P. Hedrick), *N.Y. State Sta. Rept.*, Part. II, 1919.

Talbot, P., and A. A. Tavernetti: Growing and handling market peas in California, *Calif. Ext. Circ.* **85**, 1934.

Tavernetti, A. A.: Production of globe artichoke in California, *Calif. Ext. Circ.* **76**, 1947.

———: Artichokes, how to grow them in California, *Calif. Ext. Leaf.* **37,** 1954.

Terman, G. L., and H. J. Murphy: Yield and quality of peas for processing as affected by lime and fertilizer, *Proc. Soil Sci. Soc. Amer.*, **16**:182–185, 1952.

———, *et al.*: Rate, placement. and source of nitrogen for potatoes in Maine, *Me. Bull.* **490**, 1951.

Thomas, Florence: Studies of cracking of tomato fruits with emphasis on method of selecting resistant plants from segregating progenies, Cornell Univ. Thesis, 1948.

Thompson, H. C.: Experimental studies of cultivation of certain vegetable crops, *Cornell Memoir* **107**, 1927.

———: Premature seeding of celery, *Cornell Bull.* **480**, 1929.

———: Temperature as a factor affecting flowering of plants, *Amer. Soc. Hort. Sci. Proc.*, **30**:440–446, 1933.

———: Pruning and training tomatoes, *Cornell Bull.* **580**, 1934.

———: Spacing affects yield of asparagus, *Cornell Bull.* **822**, 1945.

——— and J. H. Beattie: Classification and variety descriptions of American varieties of sweet potatoes, *U.S. Dept. Agr. Bull.* **1021**, 1922.

——— and ———: Sweet potato storage studies, *U.S. Dept. Agr. Bull.* **1063**, 1922.

———, and J. E. Knott: The effect of temperature and photoperiod on the growth of lettuce, *Amer. Soc. Hort. Sci. Proc.*, **30**:507–509, 1933.

——— and H. Platenius: Results of paper mulch experiments with vegetable crops, *Amer. Soc. Hort. Sci. Proc.* **28**:305–308, 1931.

——— and Ora Smith: Seedstalk and bulb development in the onion (*Allium cepa* L), *Cornell Bull.* **708**, 1938.

———, P. H. Wessels, and H. S. Mills: Cultivation experiments with certain vegetable crops on Long Island, *Cornell Bull.* **521**, 1931.

Thompson, H. H.: Plant protectors in B. C., *Market Growers Jour.*, **45**, No. 8, 1929.

Thompson, R. C.: Dormancy in lettuce seed and some factors influencing its germination, *U.S. Dept. Agr. Tech. Bull.* **655**, 1938.

———: Lettuce varieties and culture, *U.S. Dept. Agr. Farmers' Bull.* **1953**, 1951.

Tiedjens, V. A.: Some physiological aspects of *Asparagus officinalis*, *Amer. Soc. Hort. Sci. Proc.* **1924**:129–140, 1924.

——— and L. G. Schermerhorn: Fertilizer requirements for Lima beans, *Amer. Soc. Hort. Sci. Proc.*, **37**:743–746, 1939.

Ting, Yu Chen, and A. E. Kehr: Meiotic studies in the sweet potato (*Ipomoea batatas*), *Jour. Heredity*, **44**:207–211, 1953.

Toole, Eben H.: Storage of vegetable seeds, *U.S. Dept. Agr. Leaf.* **270**, 1942.

———, V. K. Toole, and E. A. Gorman: Vegetable seed storage as effected by temperature and relative humidity, *U.S. Dept. Agr., Tech. Bull.* **972**, 1948.

Toole, V. K., R. E., Wester, and E. H. Toole: Relative germination response of some Lima bean varieties to low temperature in sterilized and unsterilized soil, *Amer. Soc. Hort. Sci. Proc.* **58**:153–159, 1951.

Torfason, W. E., and I. L. Nounecke: A study of the effects of temperature and other factors upon the germination of vegetable crops. I. Sweet corn, *Canada Jour. Agr. Sci.* **34**:137–144, 1954.

Tottingham, W. E.: A preliminary study of the influence of chlorides on the growth of certain agricultural plants, *Agron. Jour.*, **11**:1–32, 1919.

Tracy, W. W., Jr.: American varieties of lettuce, *U.S. Dept. Agr. B.P.I. Bull.* **69**, 1904.

Truscott, J. H. L., and C. L. Thomson: The waxing of rutabaga (turnip) roots for the retail market, *Rept. Dept. Hort. Ontario Agr. College,* March, 1941.

Viale, Emilio, and N. F. Thomas: Combate del gorgoja del camote (*Rhysomatus sp.* Curcurlionidae), *Turrialba*, **1**:247–251, 1951.

Viehmeyer, F. J.: Some factors affecting the irrigation requirements of deciduous orchards, *Hilgardia*, **2**:125–284, 1927.

——— and A. H. Holland: Irrigation and cultivation of lettuce, *Calif. Bull.* **711**, 1949.

Viets, F. G., Jr., L. C. Brown, and C. L. Crawford: Zinc contents and deficiency symptoms of 26 crops grown on a zinc deficient soil, *Soil Sci.*, **78**:305–316, 1954.

Vittum, M. T.: Irrigation experiments with canning crops, *N.Y. State Sta. Farm Res.*, **16**, No. 2, 1950.

——— and R. E. Foster: Effect of soil fertility level on the performance of eight strains of Danish Ballhead cabbage, *Amer. Soc. Hort. Sci. Proc.*, **56**:257–260, 1950.

——— and A. R. Hamson: Peas for canning or freezing in New York State, *Better Crops*, **38**:13–17, October, 1954.

——— and N. Peck: Are you planting enough sweet corn seed, *N.Y. State Sta. Farm Res.*, **19**, No. 2:4, 1954.

——— and ———: Proper spacing and irrigation can improve your cabbage, *N.Y. State Sta. Farm Res.*, **20**:16, 1954.

——— and W. T. Tapley: Spacing and fertility level studies with a determinate type tomato, *Amer. Soc. Hort. Sci. Proc.*, **61**:339–342, 1954.

Volk, G. M., C. E. Bell, and E. N. McCubbin: The significance and maintenance of nitrate nitrogen in Bladen fine sandy loam in the production of cabbage, *Fla. Bull.* **430**, 1947.

Walker, Dilworth: The production and marketing of New York market peas, *Cornell Bull.* **475**, 1929.

Walker, J. C.: Diseases of cabbage and related plants, *U.S. Dept. Agr. Farmers' Bull.* **1439**, 1938.

———: Internal black spot of canning beets and its control, *Canning Age*, **19**, No. 13. December, 1938.

——— and J. P. Jolivette: Yellows-resistant varieties of cabbage in the early and midseason round head groups, *U.S. Dept. Agr. Circ.* **775**, 1948.

———, ———, and W. W. Hare: Varietal susceptibility in garden beet to boron deficiency, *Soil Sci.*, **59**:461–464, 1945.

———, ———, and J. J. McLean: Boron deficiency in garden and sugar beet, *Jour. Agr. Res.*, **66**:97–123, 1943.

Walter, J. M., and D. A. Kelbert: Manalucie, a tomato with distinctive new features, *Fla. Circ.* **S-59**, 1953.

Ware, G. W.: Plant protectors and other factors influencing earliness and production of cantaloupes, *Ark. Bull.* **324**, 1936.

Ware, L. M., and W. A. Johnson: Effects of irrigation and other practices on sweet corn, *Amer. Soc. Hort. Sci. Proc.*, **55**:416–422, 1950.

———— and ————: Effect of rates and number of applications of the major fertilizer elements on yield and composition of potatoes and on recovery of major elements at harvest, *Amer. Soc. Hort. Sci. Proc.*, **65**:317–323, 1955.

Waring, E. J., R. D. Wilson, and N. S. Shirlow: Whiptail of cauliflower, *Agr. Gaz. N. South Wales*, **60**:21–26, 1949.

Warne, L. G. G.: Spacing experiments on vegetables. I. The effect of thinning distance on earliness in Globe beet and carrots in Cheshire, 1948, *Jour. Hort. Sci.* **26**:79–83, 1951.

Warren, G. F.: Effect of rate and depth of seeding on the yield and maturity of Henderson Lima beans, *Amer. Soc. Hort. Sci. Proc.* **55**:472–473, 1950.

Watts, V. M.: Some factors which influence growth and fruiting of the tomato, *Ark. Bull.* **267**, 1931.

————: Pruning and training tomatoes in Arkansas, *Ark. Bull.* **292**, 1933.

Waugh, F. V.: "Quality as a Determinant of Vegetable Prices," Columbia University Press, New York, 1929.

Welch, J. E., and T. W. Whitaker: Recent developments in California's lettuce industry, *Amer. Vegetable Grower*, **1**, No. 12, 1953.

Went, F. W.: Plant growth under controlled conditions. V. The relation between age, light, variety and thermoperiodicity of tomatoes, *Amer. Jour. Bot.*, **32**:469–479, 1945.

———— and L. Cosper: Plant growth under controlled conditions. VI. Comparison between field and air-conditioned greenhouse culture of tomatoes, *Amer. Jour. Bot.*, **32**:643–654, 1945.

Werner, H. O.: Soil management experiments with vegetables, *Neb. Bull.* **278**, 1933.

————: The effect of a controlled nitrogen supply with different temperatures and photoperiods upon the development of the potato plant, *Neb. Res. Bull.* **75**, 1934.

Wessels, P. H.: Soil acidity studies with potatoes, cauliflower and other vegetables on Long Island, *Cornell Bull.* **536**, 1932.

———— and H. C. Thompson: Asparagus fertilizer experiments on Long Island (N.Y.), *Cornell Bull.* **678**, 1937.

———— and R. H. White-Stevens: Studies on the relation of irrigation to the production of vegetables, *Cornell Sta. Ann. Rept.* **58**:163, 1945.

Westgate, P. J.: Blackheart of celery, *Fla. State Hort. Soc. Proc.* **64**:87–92, 1951.

Whitaker, T. W.: American origin of the cultivated cucurbits. I. Evidence from herbals. II. Survey of old and recent botanical evidence, *Annals Mo. Bot. Gard.*, **34**:110–111, 1947.

———— and G. W. Bohn: The taxonomy, genetics, production and uses of the cultivated species of cucurbita, *Econ. Bot.*, **4**:52–81, 1950.

Whitcomb, W. B.: Biology and control of *Lygus campestris* L. on celery, *Mass. Bull.* **473**, 1953.

White-Stevens, R. H., and Ora Smith: Studies of potato storage on Long Island, *Cornell Sta. Ann. Rept.*, **58**:164, 1945.

Wiant, J. S.: Market storage of Honey Dew melons and cantaloups, *U.S. Dept. Agr. Tech. Bull.* **613**, 1938.

Wilson, B. D.: Peat and muck: character and utilization, *Cornell Ext. Bull.* **320**, 1935.

Wilson, J. W., and N. C. Hayslip: Insects attacking celery in Florida, *Fla. Bull.* **486**, 1951.

Wilson, W. F., J. A. Cox, and J. Montelaro: Louisiana okra, *La. Ext. Pub.* **1141**, 1953.

Wittwer, S. H.: Control of flowering and fruit setting by plant regulators, in "Plant Regulators in Agriculture," (ed. by Tukey, H. B.), John Wiley & Sons, Inc., New York, 1954.

———, H. H. Jackson, and D. P. Watson: Control of seedstalk development in celery by maleic hydrazide, *Amer. Jour. Bot.*, **41**:435–439, 1954.

——— and W. A. Schmidt: Further investigations of the effect of "hormone" sprays on the fruiting response of outdoor tomatoes, *Amer. Soc. Hort. Sci. Proc.*, **55**:335–352, 1950.

———, H. Stallworth, and M. J. Howell: The value of a "hormone" spray for overcoming delayed fruit set and increasing yields of outdoor tomatoes, *Amer. Soc. Hort. Sci. Proc.*, **51**:371–380, 1948.

———, *et al.*: The effect of preharvest foliage sprays of certain growth regulators on sprout inhibition and storage quality of carrots and onions, *Plant Phys.*, **25**:539–549, 1950.

Work, Paul: Nitrate of soda in the nutrition of the tomato, *Cornell Memoir* **75**, 1923.

———: Better seed for commercial vegetable growers, *Cornell Ext. Bull.* **122**, 1925.

Working, E. B.: Physical and chemical factors in the growth of asparagus, *Ariz. Tech. Bull.* **5**, 1924.

Wright, R. C., J. L. Lauritzen, and T. M. Whiteman: Influence of storage temperature and humidity on keeping qualities of onions and onion sets, *U.S. Dept. Agr. Tech. Bull.* **475**, 1935.

——— *et al.*: Effect of various temperatures on the storage and ripening of tomatoes, *U.S. Dept. Agr. Tech. Bull.* **268**, 1931.

Wymore, F. H.: The garden centipede, *Scutigerella immaculata* (Newport), a pest of economic importance, *Jour. Econ. Ent.*, **17**:520–526, 1924.

Yamaguchi, M., F. W. Zink, and A. R. Spurr: Cracked stem of celery, *Calif. Agr. 7*, No. 5:12, 1953.

Yarnell, S. H., W. H. Friend, and J. F. Wood: Factors affecting the amount of puffing in tomatoes, *Tex. Bull.* **541**, 1937.

Yeager, A. F., *et al.*: The storage of Hubbard squash, *N.H. Bull.* **356**, 1945.

Youden, W. J., and P. W. Zimmerman: Field trial with fibre pots, *Boyce Thompson Inst. Contrib.*, **8**:317–331, 1936.

Young, R. A.: Cultivation of the true yams in the Gulf Coast region, *U.S. Dept. Agr. Bull.* **1167**, 1923.

Young, R. E.: The depth of planting asparagus and its effect on stand, yield, and position of the crown, *Amer. Soc. Hort. Sci. Proc.*, **37**:783–784, 1940.

Younkin, S. G., J. B. Hester, and A. D. Hoadley: Interaction of seeding rates and nitrogen levels on yield and sieve size of peas, *Amer. Soc. Hort. Sci. Proc.*, **55**:379–383, 1950.

Zimmerley, H. H.: Soil acidity in relation to spinach production, *Va. Truck Exp. Sta. Bull.* **57**, 1926.

Zink, F. W., and D. A. Akana: The effect of spacing on the growth of sprouting broccoli, *Amer. Soc. Hort. Sci. Proc.*, **58**:160–164, 1951.

Index

Acolymma vittata, 520
Allium ascolonicum, 370
  cepa, 348
  fistulosum, 388
  porrum, 368
  sativum, 368
  schoenoprasum, 371
Alternaria solani, 490
Anthonomus eugenii, 510
Anthriscus cerefolium, 273
Aphis brassicae, 277, 293
  gossypii, 521
  pseodobrassicae, 227, 293
  rumicis, 452
Apium graveolens, 233
  var. *rapaceum,* 346
Aplanobacter stewartii, 557
Armoracia rusticana, 344
Artichoke, 209–212
  grading, 211
  harvesting, 211
  Jerusalem, 211, 212
  marketing, 211
  planting and care, 210
  propagation, 210
Ascochyta pinodella, 468
  pisi, 468
Asparagus, 186–204
  beetles, 199
  blanching, 195, 196
  bunching, 202
  crates, 202, 203
  cultivation and care, 195, 196
  duration of plantation, 197, 198
  fertilizers, 188, 189
  grading, 202
  green versus white, 198, 199
  harvesting, 200, 201
  intercropping, 195
  male versus female, 191
  packing, 203
  planting, 192–195
  quality, changes in, 203–204
  removal of tops, 197
  rust, 198
  salt for, 189

Asparagus, soils, 188
  statistics, 186, 187
  taxonomy, 187
  varieties, 198
  wilt, fusarium, 199
Atriplex hortensis, 224
Autographa brassicae, 292

Bean, 431–452
  adzuki, 431
  anthracnose, 448
  aphid, 452
  bacterial blights, 449
  beetle, leaf, 451
    Mexican, 450
  broad, 431, 432
  classification, 451
  common, 437
  cultivation, 443
  diseases, 448–450
  English (broad, Windsor), 431, 432
  fertilizers, 440, 441
  fly, 452
  harvesting, 446–448
  history, 439
  insects, 450–452
  kidney, 437
  Lima (*see* Lima bean)
  mosaics, 449
  moth, 431
  multiflora, 431, 437
  mung, 431, 433
  pinto, 431
  planting, 441, 442
  pole, 442, 443, 445
  rice, 431
  root rots, 449
  rust, 450
  scarlet runner, 431, 437
  seed-corn maggot, 452
  soils, 439, 440
  soy-, 431, 432
  statistics, 437–439
  taxonomy, 439
  tepary, 431, 433

Bean, threshing, 448
  thrips, 451
  varieties, 444–446
  velvet, 431
  weed control, 443, 444
  weevil, 451
  Windsor (broad, English), 431, 432
Beet, 318–327
  cultivation, 322, 323
  diseases, 326
  fertilizers, 321
  harvesting, 325, 326
  insects, 326–327
  internal black spot, 324, 325
  leaf miner, 226, 327
  leaf spot, 326
  planting, 322
  premature seeding, 320
  scab, 326
  soils, 319
  taxonomy, 319
  thinning, 327
  varieties, 324
  weed control, chemical, 323
Beta vulgaris, 319
  var. *cicla*, 225
Black salsify, 337
Blister beetles, 165
Botrytis, 265
  allii, 360
Brassica chinensis, 315
  juncea, 227
  napobrassica, 340
  oleracea, var. *acephala*, 228
  pekinensis, 315
  rapa, 338
Bremia latucae, 265
Broad bean, 431, 432
Broccoli, 307–311
  harvesting, 309, 310
  packing, 310
  planting and culture, 308, 309
  sprouting, 307, 311
  varieties, 309
Bruchus obtectus, 451
  pisorum, 469
Brussels sprouts, 311–313
Bulb crops, 347–371

Cabbage, 275–295
  aphids, 293
  black rot, 291
  blackleg, 290, 291
  Chinese, 315–317
  climatic requirements, 276
  clubroot, 288, 289

Cabbage, cultivation, 281, 282
  diseases, 288–291
  fertilizers, 277–279
  grades, 294
  growing plants, 279
  harvesting, 293, 294
  history, 276
  insects, 291–293
  maggot, 291
  packing, 294
  plant growing, 279, 280
  planting, 280, 281
  premature seeding, 285, 286
  root knot, 289–291
  seeding of mature, 286, 288
  soils, 277
  statistics, 275, 276
  storing, 294, 295
  taxonomy, 276
  varieties, 282–285
  worms, 292, 293
  yellows, 290, 291
Cantaloupe (*see* Muskmelon)
Capsicum annuum, 505, 506
  frutescens, 505
  pendulum, 505, 506
  pubescens, 505, 506
Carrot, 327–334
  color, factors affecting, 330
  cultivation, 331
  fertilizers, 328
  harvesting, 334
  history, 328
  planting, 329
  rust fly, 250, 251, 333
  soils, 328
  statistics, 327, 328
  storage, 334
  taxonomy, 328
  thinning, 329
  varieties, 332
  weed control, 331, 332
    chemical, 332
Carrot rust fly, 250, 251, 333
Cassava (*see* Manioc)
Cauliflower, 295–307
  blanching, 305, 306
  boron deficiency, 301–304
  browning, 301–304
  buttoning, 304, 305
  climatic requirements, 296
  fertilizers, 298
  grading, 306
  harvesting, 306
  packing, 307
  physiological disorders, 301–305
  plant growing, 300

Cauliflower, planting, 300, 301
  seed, 299
  soils, 297, 298
  statistics, 295, 296
  storing, 307
  varieties, 299, 300
  whiptail, 301
Celeriac, 346
Celery, 230–255
  blackheart, 233, 234
  blanching, 241, 242
  blights, 247–249
  bolting, 243–247
  climatic requirements, 231
  cracked stem, 234–236
  cultivation, 240, 241
  diseases, 247–250
  fertilizers, 232–236
  fusarium yellows, 248, 249
  harvesting, 251, 252
  history, 231
  insects, 250–251
  mosaic, 249, 250
  phoma root rot, 249
  pithiness, 247
  plant growing, 236, 237
  planting, 236–238
  premature seeding, 243–247
  preparation for marketing, 252, 253
  seed sowing, 236
  seedstalk development, 243–247
  soils, 232
  statistics, 230, 231
  storage, 254, 255
  tarnished plant bug, 251
  taxonomy, 231
  varieties, 242
  yellows, 249, 250
Cephalosporium apii, 249
Ceratostomella fimbriata, 418
Cercospora apii, 247
  beticola, 326
  capsici, 510
Cerotoma trifurcata, 451
Chaerophyllum bulbosum, 348
Chard, 225, 226
Chayote, 565–567
  culture, 565, 567
  uses, 567
Chemical elements essential to growth, 54–62
  boron, 59, 60
  calcium, 58
  chlorine, 62
  copper, 62
  iron, 60
  magnesium, 59

Chemical elements essential to growth,
  manganese, 60, 61
  molybdenum, 61, 62
  nitrogen, 55, 56
  phosphorus, 56, 57
  potassium, 57, 58
  sodium, 62
  sulfur, 58, 59
  zinc, 61
Chemical weed control (*see* Weed control)
Chervil, 273
  turnip-rooted, 345
Chicory, 271, 272
Chinese cabbage, 315–317
Chive, 371
Cibol (ciboule), 368
Cichorium endivia, 269
  intybus, 271
Citron melon, 536
Cladosporium cucumerinum, 519
Classification of vegetables, 17–23
  based on hardiness, 21
  based on methods of culture, 22
  based on parts used, 21
  botanical, 17–21
  horticultural, 76
Cold frames, 93
Cole crops, 275–317
  (*See also* specific cole crops)
Collards, 228, 229
Colletotrichum lagenarium, 517
  lindemuthianum, 448
  nigrum, 510
  phomoides, 492
Colocasia esculenta, 570
Companion cropping, 150–152
Composts, 43, 44
Consumer packaging, 172–174
Corn (*see* Sweet corn)
Corynebacterium michiganense, 490
  spedonicum, 393
Cover crops, 44–51
Cowpea (Southern pea), 434–436
Crambe maritima, 212
Cress, garden, 273
  water, 274
Crioceris asparagi, 199
  duodecimpunctata, 199
Cucumber, 513–523
  angular leaf spot, 518
  anthracnose, 517
  aphid, melon, 521
  bacterial wilt, 517
  beetles, 520, 521
  climatic requirements, 514
  cultivation, 516

Cucumber, diseases, 517–520
  downy mildew, 518
  fertilizers, 515
  flea beetle, 520
  grading, 522
  harvesting, 522
  history, 514, 515
  insects, 520–522
  manures, 515
  mosaic, 519, 520
  packing, 522, 523
  pickle worm, 522
  powdery mildew, 518
  planting, 516
  scab, 519
  soils, 515
  squash bug, 521
  squash lady beetle, 523
  squash vine borer, 521
  statistics, 513, 514
  taxonomy, 514, 515
  varieties, 517
  wilt, 517
Cucumis anguria, 515
  melo, 515, 528
    var. *cantalupensis,* 524
    var. *chito,* 525
    var. *Dudaim,* 525
    var. *flexosus,* 524
    var. *inodorus,* 524, 529
  sativus, 515
Cucurbita ficifolia, 538
  maxima, 538
  mixta, 538
  moschata, 538
  pepo, 538
Cucurbits or vine crops, 513–543
Cultivating implements, 125, 126
Cultivation, 117–127
  effect of, on nitrification, 124, 125
    on soil moisture, 120–123
    on soil temperature, 123, 124
    on yield, 117–120
  experiments, 118–120
Cutworms, 165
Cylas formicaris elegantulus, 421
Cynara scolymus, 209

Dandelion, 229
Dasheen, 570–574
  culture, 572
  handling, 572, 573
  harvesting, 572, 573
  uses, 573, 574
Daucus carota, 327
Diabrotica undecimpunctata, 520

Diaphania nitidalis, 522
Diaporthe phaseolorum, 458
Dioscorea alata, 567
  batatas, 567
  bulbifera, 567
  cayenensis, 567
  trifida, 567
Diplodia natalensis, 536
  tubericola, 420
Disease control, 153–164
  equipment for, 161, 162
  importance of, 153, 154
Diseases, 153–164
  general crop, 159
  importance of, 153, 154
  methods of control, 154–161
    application of chemicals, 160, 161
    crop rotation, 145, 146
    destruction of refuse, 154
    resistant varieties, 154, 155
    seed treatment, 155–157
    soil treatment, 157–160
  (*See also* specific names of vege-
    tables)
Dolichos lablab, 431

Eddo (*see* Dasheen)
Eggplant, 500–503
  climatic requirements, 501
  fertilizers, 502
  flea beetles, 503
  fruit rot, 502, 503
  harvesting, 503
  history, 501
  lace bug, 503
  soils, 501
  taxonomy, 501
  varieties, 502
  wilt, verticillium, 503
Endive, 269, 270
Epilachna varivestis, 450
Epitrix fuscula, 503
Erosion, 31–36
Erysiphe chicoracearum, 518
  polygonia, 468
Erwinia atroseptica, 393
  tracheiphilus, 517

Fertilizers, commercial, 52–69
  analysis, 62, 63
  application, 66–69
  chemical elements, 52–63
  chemical tests, 54, 55
  formula, 63–65
  importance of, 52

Fertilizers, commercial, ratio, 65, 66
  (*See also* Manures)
Freezing of vegetables, 9–11
French endive, 271
Fungicides, 163
Fusarium annuum, 510
  apii, 249
  batatas, 418
  bulbigenum, 496
  conglutinans, 290
  hyperoxysporium, 418
  oxysporum, 290, 418, 420
    lycopersici, 489
    melonis, 529
    pisi, 469

Garden centipede, 200
Garden cress, 273
Gargraphia solani, 503
Garlic, 368–370
Gleosporium piperatum, 510
Grades, 170, 171
Grading, 170
Grasshoppers, 165
Green-manure crops, 44–51
  legumes, 46–48
  nonlegumes, 48–49
  selection of, 45, 46
  turning under, 49–51
Greenhouses, 86–88
  advantages of, 87
  sash, 87, 88

Hardening of plants, 104–106
Harrowing, 32, 33
Harvesting, 168
Helianthus tuberosus, 211
Heliothis obsoleta, 556
Herbicides, 128–135
  application, 130–132
    equipment for, 132
  crop tolerance to, 129, 130
  mode of action, 129
Heterodea marioni, 145, 494
Hibiscus esculentus, 562
Home gardening, 5–7
Horse-radish, 344–345
Hotbeds, 88–93
  covers, 90
  frame, 89
  heating of, electric, 92, 93
    flue, 91, 92
    hot-water, 92, 93
    manure, 90, 91
  location of, 89

Hotbeds, pit, 90
  sash, 89
  use of, 88, 89
Husk tomato, 511, 512
Hydrogen-ion concentration, 70
Hylemyia antiqua, 360
  brassicae, 291
  cilicrura, 452

Insect control, 153–166
  equipment for, 161, 162
  importance of, 153, 154
  (*See also* Insects, methods of control)
Insecticides, 162, 163
  application, 160–161
Insects, 153–166
  general crop, 159
  importance of, 153, 154
  methods of control, 154–166
    application of chemicals, 160, 161
    destruction of refuse, 154
    seed treatment, 155–157
    soil treatment, 157–160
Intercropping, 150–152
Ipomoea batatas, 406
  littoralis, 421
  sagittata, 421
Irrigation, 136–144
  planning of system, 143
  spray, 139
  subirrigation, 139
  surface, 137–139
  types of, 139–143

Jerusalem artichoke, 211, 212

Kale, 226, 227
Kohlrabi, 313, 314

Lactuca sativa, 256
Leek, 368
Lettuce, 255–269
  bottom rot, 264
  brown blight, 265
  climatic requirements, 256, 257
  cultivation and care, 260
  diseases, 264–267
  drop, 264
  fertilizers, 257, 258
  grading, 269
  growing plants, 258
  harvesting, 268
  history, 256

Lettuce, mildew, 265
  mosaic, 266, 267
  packing, 269
  planting, 259, 260
  premature seeding, 267
  soils, 257
  statistics, 255, 256
  storage, 269
  taxonomy, 256
  tipburn, 266
  varieties, 260–263
  yellows, 265, 266
Lima bean, 452–458
  climatic requirements, 453, 454
  diseases, 457, 458
  fertilizers, 454
  harvesting, 456, 457
  history, 453
  planting, 454, 455
  preparation for market, 457
  soils, 454
  statistics, 452, 453
  taxonomy, 453
  varieties, 455, 456
Lime, 69–74
  application, 73, 74
  effects, 72
  forms of, 72, 73
Lycopersicon cheesmanii, 474
  esculentum, 473
  glandulosum, 474
  hirsutum, 474
  peruvianum, 474
  pimpinellifolium, 473

Macrosporium pisi, 469
Malanga (*see* Dasheen)
Mandioc (*see* Manioc)
Manihot esculenta, 574
Manioc, 574–576
  culture, 574, 575
  handling, 575, 576
  harvesting, 575, 576
  preparation, 576
  uses, 576
Manures, 37–44
  application, 42, 43
    rate of, 42, 43
    time for, 42
  composition, 39, 40
  composting of, 43, 44
  green (*see* Green-manure crops)
  losses in, 41
Market gardening, 7
Marketing, 167–178
  cooperative, 176, 177

Marketing, grading for, 170, 171
  packing for, 172, 174
  preparation for, 169
Markets, 176–178
  roadside, 177, 178
Martynia, 564
  Louisiana, 564
  proboscidea, 564
Melittia satyriniformis, 521
Meloidogyne, 289
Melon (*see* Muskmelon; Watermelon)
Monilochaetes infuscans, 419
Muck soil, 27–29
Mulches, 127, 128
Murgantia histrionica, 293
Muskmelon, 523–532
  acid yellowing, 525
  analysis, 526
  climatic requirements, 524
  cultivation, 528
  diseases, 529, 530
  fertilizers, 526
  fusarium wilt, 529
  grading, 531
  growing plants, 527
  harvesting, 530, 531
  history, 524, 525
  insects, 530
  irrigation, 528
  manures, 526
  packing, 532
  planting, 527, 528
  soils, 525
  statistics, 523, 524
  storage, 532
  taxonomy, 524, 525
  varieties, 528, 529
Mustard, 227, 228
Mycosphaerella pinodes, 468
Myzus persicae, 222, 395

Nasturtium officinale, 274
New Zealand spinach, 223, 224

Okra, 561–563
  culture, 562
  harvesting, 563
  history, 561, 562
  taxonomy, 561, 562
  uses, 563
  varieties, 562, 563
Onion, 347–368
  chemical weed control, 357
  cultivation, 356, 357
  curing, 364

Onion, diseases, 358–360
    fertilizer, 351–353
    grading, 363, 364
    harvesting, 362, 363
    history, 348
    insects, 360, 361
    maggot, 360
    mildew, 359
    neck rot, 360
    packing, 364
    photoperiod, 348–351
    pink root, 359
    planting, 354, 355
    premature seeding, 348–351, 361
    propagation, 353, 354
    sets, 367
    smut, 358
    soils, 350, 351
    statistics, 347, 348
    storage, 364–367
    taxonomy, 348
    temperature and growth, 348–351
    thinning, 356
    thrips, 360
    varieties, 357, 358
    Welsh, 368
Orach, 224

Packages, 172–174
    consumer, 172
Packing of vegetables, 172–174
Parsley, 272, 273
Parsnip, 335–337
Pastinaca sativa, 335
Pea, 458–470
    aphid, 469
    blight, ascochyta, 468
    climatic requirements, 460
    diseases, 468, 469
    fertilizers, 461, 462
    grading, 467
    harvesting, 465, 466
    history, 459
    inoculation, 462
    insects, 469, 470
    mildew, powdery, 468
    packing, 467
    planting, 463
    precooling, 467
    refrigeration, 467
    root rots, 468
    soils, 461
    statistics, 458, 459
    taxonomy, 459
    varieties, 464, 465
    weed control, 463

Pea, weevil, 469
    wilt, 469
Peat soil, 27–29
Pegomyia hyoscyami, 222, 326
Pepper, 504–511
    climatic requirements, 506, 507
    diseases, 510
    harvesting, 511
    history, 505
    insects, 510, 511
    plant growing, 507–509
    planting and care, 509
    soils, 506, 507
    statistics, 504
    storage, 511
    taxonomy, 505, 506
    temperature on fruit set, 506, 507
    varieties, 509
Perennial crops, 186–213
Peronospora destructor, 359
    effusa, 221
Petroselinum hortense, 272
Phaseolus aconitifolius, 431
    acutifolius, 431, 433
    angularis, 431
    aureus, 431
    calcaratus, 431
    coccineus, 431
    lunatus, 431, 452
    Metcalfei, 431
    multiflorus, 431
    mungo, 431
    vulgaris, 431, 437
Phoma apiicola, 249
    lingam, 290
Phomopsis vexans, 502
Physalis pubescens, 511
Phytophthora capsici, 510
    infestans, 374, 392, 491
    phaseoli, 457
Pieris rapae, 292
Plant growing, 88–106
    commercial, 106
    containers for, 103
    structures, 88–93
Plant protectors, 114–116
Planting, 107–116
    depth of, 108
    machines for, 112, 113
    methods, 109
    rate of, 109, 110
    time of, 107, 108
Plasmodiophora brassicae, 288
Plowing, 31, 32
Pontia protodice, 292
Potato, 372–404
    aphids, 397, 398

Potato, beetle (Colorado), 396, 397
  black spot, 395, 396
  blackleg, 393
  botany, 374–376
  chemical weed control, 388, 389
  climate requirements, 376–378
  cultivation, 387, 388
  diseases, 392–396
    virus, 394
  fertilizers, 380–382
  flea beetle, 397
  grading, 403
  harvesting, 398–400
  history, 374–376
  insects, 396–398
  internal black spot, 395, 396
  late blight, 392
  leaf hopper, 397
  leaf roll, 394
  manure, 382
  marketing, 404
  mosaic, 394, 395
  packing, 403, 404
  photoperiod, 377
  planting, 386, 387
  ring rot, 393
  scab, 392, 393
  seed, 383–386
  soil preparation, 378–380
  soils, 378–380
  statistics, 372–374
  storage, 400–404
    sprouting in, 402
  varieties, 389–392
  verticillium wilt, 393
  wireworms, 398
  (*See also* Sweet potato)
Potherbs, 214–229
Precooling, 175
Proboscidea Jussieui, 564
  Louisiana, 564
Pruning of plants, 111
Pseudomonas apii, 248
  lachrymans, 518
  phaseolicola, 449
Psila rosae, 333
Puccinia asparagi, 198
Pumpkin and squash, 538–543
  culture, 539, 540
  diseases, 540
  grading, 542
  harvesting, 541
  history, 538, 539
  insects, 541
  packing, 542
  storage, 542, 543
  taxonomy, 538, 539

Pumpkin and squash, varieties, 540
Pyrausta nubilalis, 556
Pyrenochaeta terrestris, 359

Quick freezing, 9–11

Radish, 341–344
Raphanus sativus, 342
Red spider, 166
Rhizoctonia solani, 264, 510
Rhizopus nigricans, 419
Rhubarb, 204–208
  climatic requirements, 204, 205
  cultivation, 205
  fertilizers, 205, 206
  forcing, 207, 208
  harvesting, 207
  history, 204
  planting, 206
  soils, 205
  taxonomy, 204
  varieties, 206
Root crops, 318–346
Roripa nasturtium-aquaticum, 274
Rotation, 145–150
  effect of, on disease, 145, 146
    on insects, 145, 146
    on yields, 146–149
  experiments, 146–149
  order of, 149
Rutabaga, 340, 341

Salad crops, 230–274
Salsify, black, 337
  Spanish, 337
Sclerotinia sclerotorium, 250, 264
Sclerotium rolfsii, 510
Scolymus hispanica, 337
Scorzonera hispanica, 337
Scutigerella immaculata, 200
Sea kale, 212, 213
Sechium edule, 565
Seed, 75–85
  buying, 76–78
  certified, 78
  cost, 78, 79
  germination, 84, 85
  growing, 79–81
  longevity, 81–84
  sowing, 95, 96
  storage, 81–83
  testing, 83, 84
  vitality, 81
Seedbed, 95–98

Seedbed, care, 96
 temperature, 97
 watering, 96, 97
Selling of vegetables, 176–178
Septoria apii, 248
 bataticola, 431
 lycopersici, 491
Sewage sludge, 51
Shallot, 370, 371
Skirret, 346
Soil, 24–36
 acidity, 70–72
 class, 25
 classification, 24–30
 clay loam, 26
 drainage, 30, 31
 erosion, 31–36
 loam, 26
 muck, 27–29
 peat, 27–29
 preparation, 30–33
 reaction, 70–72
 sandy, 25, 26
 sandy loam, 26
 series, 24
 silty loam, 26
 type, 24, 25
Soil-improving crops, 44–51
 legumes, 46–48
 nonlegume, 48, 49
 selection of, 45, 46
 turning under, 49–51
Soil reaction, response of vegetables to,
 70–72
Soja Max, 431, 432
Solanaceous fruits, 471–512
Solanum andigenum, 374
 demissum, 375
 melongena, 506
 tuberosum, 374
Southern pea, 434–436
 culture of, 435, 436
Soybean, 431, 432
Spanish salsify, 337
Spinach, 214–223
 acreage and value, 214, 215
 aphid, 222
 blight, 221
 classification, 219, 220
 climatic requirements, 216, 217
 cultivation, 219, 220
 fertilizers, 218, 219
 harvesting and handling, 222, 223
 leaf miner, 222
 leaf spot, 222
 mildew, downy, 221, 222
 New Zealand, 223, 224

Spinach, planting, 219
 soil reaction, 217, 218
 thinning, 219
 varieties, 220, 221
Spinacia oleracea, 214
Spotting board, 98
Squash (*see* Pumpkin and squash)
Starter solutions, 114
Stizolobium Deeringianum, 431
Storage, 179–185
 advantages of, 179
 cellar, 182
 cold, 183
 effect on industry, 184, 185
 field, 180
 houses, 182
 requirements of, 179, 180
 temperatures, 181
Strain testing, 78, 79
Streptomyces ipomoea, 419
 scabies, 392
Succession cropping, 145, 150
Sweet corn, 544–561
 analyses, 559, 560
 borer, 556, 557
 chemical weed control, 553
 climate, 546–549
 cultivation, 553
 diseases, 557
 earworm, 556
 European corn borer, 556, 557
 fertilizers, 549–551
 grading, 560
 harvesting, 558–560
 history, 545, 546
 hybrid, 555
 insects, 556, 557
 manure, 550
 packing, 560, 561
 planting, 551–553
 smut, 558
 soils, 549
 Southern corn root worm, 557
 statistics, 544, 545
 Stewart's disease, 557, 558
 storage, 561
 suckering, 554
 taxonomy, 545, 546
 top cross, 555
 varieties, 554–566
 wilt, bacterial, 557
Sweet potato, 405–430
 black rot, 418
  Java, 420
 climatic requirements, 406
 cultivation, 415, 416
 curing, 428

Sweet potato, diseases, **418–420**
  fertilizers, 407–410
  grading, 425
  harvesting, 422–424
  history, 406
  insects, 421, 422
  internal cork, 419
  leaf spot, 418
  marketing, 424
    preparation for, 425, 426
  packing, 425, 426
  plant growing, 410–414
  planting, 414, 415
  pox or soil rot, 419
  propagation, 410–414
  scurf, 419
  soft rot, 419
  soils, 407
  statistics, 405, 406
  stem rot, 418
  storage, 426–430
    banks, 430
    changes during, 428
    houses, 441
    temperature, 427, 428
  surface rot, 420
  taxonomy, 406
  varieties, 416–418
    classification of, 416, 417
  weevil, 421, 422
  (*See also* Yams)

Tapioca (*see* Manioc)
Taraxacum officinalis, 229
Tarnished plant bug, 251
Taro (*see* Dasheen)
Tepary bean, 431, 433, 434
Tetragonia expansa, 223
Thinning, 110
Tomato, 471–500
  anthracnose, 492
  bacterial canker, 490
  blight, early, 490
    late, 491
  blossom-end rot, 483, 494
  canker, 490
  climatic requirements, 474
  cultivation, 480, 481
  curly top, 493
  diseases, 488–494
  effect of fruit on growth, 486
  fertilizers, 475–477
  fruit setting, 484–486
  fruit worm, 497
  grading, 499
  growth cracks, 495

Tomato, harvesting, 498
  history, 473
  hornworms, 497
  husk, 471, 511
  insects, 497
  irrigation, 481
  mosaic, 492
  nonparasitic troubles, 494–497
  packing, 499, 500
  plant growing, 477–479
  planting, 479, 480
  pruning, 482–484
  puffiness, 496
  ripening, artificial, 498
  root knot, 494
  soils, 474, 475
  statistics, 471–473
  storage, 500
  sunscald, 496
  taxonomy, 473
  training, 479, 480
  varieties, 486–488
  virus diseases, 492
  wilt, fusarium, 489
    spotted, 493
Tragopogon porrifolius, 337
Transplanting, 98–102
  advantages, 99–100
  difference in response to, 101, 102
  disadvantages, 100
  experiments, 100–102
  field, 110–113
  machines for, 112, 113
Transportation, 174, 175
Truck growing, 8
Turnip, 338–340

Urocystes cepulae, 358
Uromyces phaseoli typica, 450
Ustilago zeae, 558

Variety testing, 78, 79
Vegetables, 1–23
  canning, 9
  classification (*see* Classification of vegetables)
  composition, 15
  consumption, 10, 16
  farm value, 1–3
  food value, 13–16
  forcing, 11, 12
  freezing, 9–11
  growing factors, climate, 12, **13**
    soil, 13
  importance of, **1**

Vegetables, production of, for processing, 8–11
   regions of, 3–5
   selling, 176–178
   (*See also* specific names of vegetables)
Verticilium albo-atrum, 393
Vicia faba, 431, 432
Vigna sinensis, 431, 434
   var. *cylindrica,* 434, 436
   var. *sesquipedalis,* 434, 436
Vine crops, 513–543

Water cress, 274
Watermelon, 532–538
   climatic requirements, 533
   cultivation, 535
   diseases, 536
   fertilizers, 534
   grading, 537
   handling, 537, 538
   harvesting, 537
   history, 533
   insects, 537
   planting, 534
   preserving, 536
   soils, 533
   statistics, 532, 533
   stem-end rot, 536

Watermelon, taxonomy, 533
   varieties, 535, 536
Weed control, 117–135
   chemical, 128–135
   chemicals used for, 132–135
     carbamates, 134
     dinitro compounds, 133
     inorganic salts, 132
     petroleum products, 133
     substituted ureas, 133, 134
     2,4-D-type materials, 134, 135
White grubs, 165
Wireworms, 165, 398
Witloof chicory, 271

Xanthomonas campestris, 291
   phaseoli, 449
   vesicatoria, 510

Yams, 567–570
   culture, 567–569
   handling, 569
   harvesting, 569
   preparation, 569
   varieties, 569
   (*See also* Sweet potato)
Yuca (*see* Manioc)